# AGING & SOCIETY
## A Canadian Perspective

### Second Edition

MARK NOVAK
University of Manitoba

**Nelson Canada**

Published in 1993 by
Nelson Canada,
A Division of Thomson Canada Limited
1120 Birchmount Road
Scarborough, Ontario M1K 5G4

**Canadian Cataloguing in Publication Data**
Novak, Mark W.
   Aging and society

2nd ed.
Includes bibliographical references and index.
ISBN 0-17-604141-9

1. Aging - Canada. 2. Aged - Canada. 3. Aged - Canada - Social conditions. 4. Gerontology - Canada. I. Title.

HQ1064.C2N68   1992      305.26'0971    C92-094382-9

**Acquisitions Editor**  Dave Ward
**Supervising Editor**  Nicole Gnutzman
**Developmental Editor**  Bob Kohlmeier
**Art Director**  Bruce Bond
**Designer**  Janet Riopelle
**Cover Illustration**  Susan Leopold

Printed and bound in Canada
  2  3  4     WB     96  95  94

**Photographs**
Part 1  Reproduced by permission of the Baycrest Centre for Geriatric Care.
Part 2  NFB. Photo by G. Hunter, August 1952. Reproduced by permission.
Part 3  Reproduced by permission of the Baycrest Centre for Geriatric Care.
Part 4  Reproduced by permission of the Baycrest Centre for Geriatric Care.
Part 5  Canapress. Photo by Chartrand, June 1985. Reproduced by permission.

# Contents

• • • • • • • • • • • • • • • • • • • • •

## PART 4 *Institutional Change* 187

# *Preface*

Many changes have taken place in Canadian gerontology since the first edition of this text was published. More researchers have entered the field of aging and have produced many new studies. A new census gathered the latest data on Canada's population. The government has released many reports that summarize studies of health, disability, and social supports. And new consortia of researchers and research centres have begun studies that will shape social policy into the next century.

As Canada moves into the twenty-first century, the study of aging will increase in importance. Our country's population will have more older people and a greater proportion of older people than ever before. These people will make new demands on Canada's health care, retirement income, and housing resources. They will also bring to old age new interests, new skills, and a new perspective on aging. People young and old will need to understand the process of aging.

I set the same goals for the second edition of this book as I did for the first. To begin with, I wanted a readable book—one that students could read without stumbling over social science jargon and dense academic prose. I have defined most technical terms within the text so that students will not have to flip to a glossary or interrupt their reading by looking at footnotes. I also present examples, charts, or graphs to illustrate difficult points. I hope that these techniques will free students to think about what the text says.

Second, I wanted a text that presented aging in the context of Canada's history and social life. In the past I have used U.S. texts in my aging courses, and each year I have had to delete large sections of the text from the assigned readings. Canadian students don't need to know how many older people live in Arizona, the workings of the U.S. Social Security system, or the differences between aging U.S. blacks, whites, and Mexican Americans. These are interesting topics, but Canada has its own geographic regions, social policies, and mix of cultures and ethnic groups. Canadian students should first learn about aging in their own country.

Third, I wanted a text that described Canada's social institutions—its health care, income, and housing systems, as well as its family and community life. Canadian students should know that their health care system, for example, provides free health benefits to all older people and that the retirement income system provides a basic income to older Canadians. These systems create a social safety net for older people and provide the basis for a decent old age today.

Canadian students should also know that their society has problems. Many Canadians hold negative stereotypes about older people (my own children put me down by telling me I am getting old); the fast pace of modern society often pushes older people to the sidelines (imagine trying to cross a six-lane city street if you have arthritis in your legs); and some groups of older people (many of them very old women) still live in poverty. Canadian society needs improvement. Students need to know what parts of the social system work for older people and what parts work against them. *Aging and Society: A Canadian Perspective* gives students the facts about aging and helps them sort through and understand the issues surrounding aging today.

This new edition has a fourth goal: to improve on the first edition. Many instructors and students across the country have used the first edition over the past five years. They have commented on what they liked and did not like about the text. I have used their comments in revising the text.

Like the first edition, this one contains the most up-to-date information available on aging in Canada. It also has new sections that reflect users' suggestions: Chapter 2 includes new material on gerontological theory; Chapter 4 has more information on individual health and illness than was present in the first edition; Chapter 7 provides a new section on drug use and abuse in old age; and Chapter 12 contains an expanded section on sexuality in later life. In addition, each chapter has more discussion of theories as they apply to specific topics. This edition also provides new exhibits that expand and clarify points made in the text.


## ORGANIZATION

This book begins by describing large-scale (macroscopic) changes in society. It then shows how these changes affect people and social institutions and concludes by showing how individuals respond to these changes and how individuals' actions give new direction to society. The structure of the book reflects a dialectical model of social change.

Part 1, Gerontology Today (Chapters 1 and 2), introduces students to the field of aging. It shatters many of the myths people have about aging and shows the range of topics gerontologists study. It also describes the theories and methods gerontologists use when they study aging.

Part 2, Historical Change (Chapters 3 and 4), looks at the changes in Canada's history and demographic structure that led to population aging (the increased proportion of older people in the population). It also places aging in Canada in a world context.

Part 3, Maturational Change (Chapters 5, 6, and 7), looks at individual aging—the biological/physiological, psychological, and developmental changes that come with age.

Part 4, Institutional Change (Chapters 8 through 14), looks at Canada's institutions—the health care, social security, and housing systems as well as the family, the community, and the institutions responsible for death and dying.

Part 5, Societal Change (Chapters 15 and 16), looks at Canada's political structure, political action, and the effects of aging on Canadian society in the future.

Together these chapters give students a broad understanding of how aging affects the individual and society.

## SPECIAL FEATURES

A number of features will make this both a useful and an easy-to-use book. First, the chapters are organized into topics that most instructors cover in their courses. Each chapter represents a unit of study and presents the facts and issues related to one topic (e.g., housing, health care, etc.). This will allow instructors to use this text in either a one- or a two-term course. Instructors of a two-term course will be able to use the entire book, while those teaching one-term courses can assign specific chapters and know that a topic will be covered in depth. A one-term course, for example, might include those chapters that deal specifically with population aging and Canada's social institutions (i.e., Chapters 1, 3, 4, 8, 9, 10, and 11).

Second, each chapter starts with an outline of the chapter's contents and an introduction to its main themes.

Third, in each chapter the text is supplemented by exhibits, including graphs, charts, and excerpts from other publications. Some of the exhibits present controversies in the literature; others present case studies that show the human side of aging. Most graphs and charts have accompanying explanations that describe them and show their relation to the text.

Fourth, each chapter concludes with a series of main points that summarize the text, followed by an annotated list of important sources students can consult for further reading.

Fifth, the book concludes with a reference list of all the sources referred to in the text, in alphabetical order of author's names. Each listing has beside it a number (or series of numbers) that corresponds to the chapter(s) in which the reference appears. A student will find this list helpful when doing a research paper. All the references in Chapter 11 (Housing and Transportation), for example, have an "11" beside them. A student who decides to do a research paper on housing can quickly pick out all the references for housing and transportation.

## ACKNOWLEDGMENTS

David Ward, Senior Acquisitions Editor of the College Division of Nelson Canada, guided me through this project. He contacted instructors throughout the country for comments on the first edition, arranged for reviews of the revised text, and worked diligently to get the book out on time. Like all good editors, David cleared away editorial problems so that I could focus on the research and writing. I thank him for his support. I also thank Nicole Gnutzman, Supervising Editor at Nelson Canada, for her careful work and creative suggestions.

Sharon Kuropatwa worked as my research assistant helping me gather information from government documents in the early stages of revision. She patiently sifted through many reports to come up with the information I needed.

Patricia Peet, Marnie Wall, and Evelyn Pawsy worked heroically in editing and printing the final drafts of the manuscript. Maureen Forrest coordinated secretarial assistance on my behalf. I thank all of them for their hard work and attention to detail.

My son, Christopher, helped me throughout the rewriting by conducting library research, developing ingenious methods for tracking bibliographical changes, and making suggestions for improving the text. He has brought a university student's perspective to his reading of the text, and many of his suggestions led to improvements in this edition. I value the time and enthusiasm he brought to this project. He has become a colleague and a scholar whose good sense and helpful advice have made this a better book.

Many Canadian colleagues in the field of gerontology sent me their papers and research reports. I cannot thank them all here, but want to acknowledge that they helped make this a better text. A few people deserve special mention. Neena Chappell, my friend and colleague, discussed many of the ideas in the text with me. Anju Joshi (McMaster University), Hazel MacRae (Mount St. Vincent University), and Sharon McIrvin Abu-Laban (University of Alberta) reviewed and commented on the book, and I have tried to honour their efforts by incorporating their suggestions in the text whenever I could. Victor Ujimoto, C.G. Gifford, and Wayne McVey also commented on specific chapters in the first edition. Professor McVey also kindly supplied me with charts and data on demographic change. These people all took time from their busy schedules to help me with this text, and I thank them for their efforts. I alone take responsibility for the text's shortcomings.

I owe special thanks to Leroy Stone, a good friend and tireless worker, who taught me the importance and the limits of demographic research. Two close friends, John Hofley and Hans Mohr, inspire all of my work. I can never repay them, only thank them, for their support and friendship.

I dedicate this book to my family—my wife Mona and my sons, Christopher, Jonathan, Sean, and Daniel. All of them deserve credit for lightening my spirits with their good humour and love.

*Gerontology Today*

C H A P T E R 1

# *What is Gerontology?*

## INTRODUCTION

Everyone needs to know about aging. First, all of us are getting older. While some are over 65 already, most adults not yet 65 will become part of the older population between now and the year 2030.[1] We will want to make old age as good a time of life as it can be. Second, between now and when those of you who are younger students reach old age, your parents, aunts, uncles, neighbours, and older friends will have grown old. You will want to know about aging so that you can help them live the best old age possible.

Third, more people work with the elderly than ever before, and more will find themselves working with the elderly in the future. Canada now has about 2.7 million people aged 65 and over. Older Canadians make up more than one-tenth of the population today (10.7 percent in 1986), and experts predict that this proportion will grow to almost 25 percent by the year 2031 (Statistics Canada 1990e). Nurses, social workers, teachers, family counsellors, and even travel agents will have more and more older people as clients.

An older population will also put new demands on Canada's social structures. Sociologists define a social structure as a relatively stable pattern of social interactions (Abercrombie, Hill, and Turner 1984, 198–99). The family, the education system, and the health care system all fit this definition, and they will change in the following ways as Canadian society ages:

- More Canadians will live in three- and four-generation families. And many people will become grandparents while they are still active in their careers.

- Schools and universities already attract more older students than ever before. These students want flexible schedules. They also need different kinds of teaching methods and different grading schemes than younger students.

- The health care system will also change. The current system favours treatment of acute (short-term) illness, but older people tend to have chronic ailments like arthritis, hearing problems, and diabetes. An aging society needs to prevent illness before it occurs.

Gerontology is the discipline that studies aging systematically. It looks at the subject from two points of view: how aging affects the individual and how an aging population will change society. This chapter describes (1) the goals of gerontology, (2) the history and structure of the field, and (3) the methods and theories gerontologists use in their work.

## ATTITUDES TOWARD OLD AGE

People hold many stereotypes about old age. Sociologists define a **stereotype** as "a one-sided, exaggerated and normally prejudicial view of a group, tribe or class of people" (Abercrombie, Hill, and Turner 1984, 209). People who hold a stereotype do not check it to see if it is true. If they meet someone who does not fit the stereotype, they think he or she is an exception. Stereotypes often have some basis in truth, but they exaggerate and distort the truth. Often they lead to discrimination.

When it comes to old age, we hold both positive and negative stereotypes: the wise old farmer and the kindly grandmother; the dirty old man and the sex-starved spinster. Hendrick et al. (1988) asked female undergraduates to estimate how well an "average" younger and an "average" older woman would do on a group of psychological tests. The students gave the older woman a lower score than the younger woman on measures of psychomotor speed and memory. At the same time, the students were "unrealistically generous in their perceptions of cognitive abilities, particularly in the case of older women" (Hendrick et al. 1988, 197). Ryan and Heaven (1988) studied the attitudes of 120 adults toward older people in 40 situations. The people in this study assigned older people less often to situations that required competence and more often to those that called for benevolence. These adults thought of older people as kinder, but less able than younger people.

Many of our stereotypes consist of negative views of older people and old age (Bassili and Reil 1981). Knox and Gekoski (1989) asked undergraduate students in an experimental study to compare young, middle-aged, and older people. The study found that students gave older people lower ratings than those who were middle-aged on such qualities as autonomy, effectiveness, and personal acceptability.

Even older people sometimes hold negative views about old age (Harris 1975). Studies of identity show that some people try to distance themselves from aging. They call people their own age old and refer to themselves as middle-aged (Bultena and Powers 1978; Matthews 1979).

Gerontologists call prejudice against older people **ageism**. Butler (1969) says ageism comes about because the young and the middle-aged feel distaste for aging. They see old age as a time of weakness, sickness, and dying. Ageism also comes about because people know little about old age, and because what they know is based on myth and fear.

In Canadian society today, people learn to be prejudiced against the old. These negative views come from many sources. Berman and Sobkowska-Ashcroft (1986, 1987) reviewed the treatment of older people in great books from the Bible to those of the twentieth century. They found that comedies almost always make fun of older people. Overall, in philosophy, literature, and the theatre, they found that "negative traits outnumber positive traits by about two to one" (Berman and Sobkowska-Ashcroft 1986, 141). Towler (1983) analyzed five hundred of the most popular current books for children (kindergarten to grade 6 students) and fifty of the most popular TV shows. He found fewer older people in them than expected and only a shallow development of their characters. He concluded that the media gave children a biased and misleading view of old age. Meadows and Fillmer (1987) conducted a study of basal readers from the 1960s and 1980s. They found that the readers gave a generally positive view of older people, but the readers underrepresented older people. Also, when they did appear, they played only minor roles in the stories.

. . . . . . . . . . . . . . . . . . . . . . . . . . . . . . . . . . . .

## Exhibit 1.1

## What Is It Like To Be Old?

. . . . . . . . . . . . . . . . . . . . . . . . . . . . . . . . . . . .

No one can know the answer to this question until they reach old age themselves. But Professor Paul Baker of the University of Victoria set out, at age 33, to learn about aging first-hand. In the story that follows he describes his experiment with old age.

"You're too young to be a gerontologist. How can somebody who's only 33 know what it's like to be 83?" This reaction from one of the few older students in my course on the sociology of aging bothered me. My first instinct was to haul out my academic/scientific defences and claim that you don't have to be an X to study X's (be they old, female, black or handicapped).

But I was left with the uncomfortable feeling that maybe she was right, maybe I was missing some of the more subjective and emotional aspects of aging by working only with "hard," "objective" data. Then I ran across John Griffin's classic book, *Black Like Me*, written in 1961. Griffin dyed his skin black and passed as a black man in the southern United States for a month. His book showed how different the world was for a black man, and made a lot of white people realize what racism meant at the human level.

So, how could I become old? The answer was obvious: the same kind of makeup that turned Dustin Hoffman old in *Little Big Man* might work for me, and with the help of a makeup artist in Vancouver, plus some old clothes, a cane, and a grey wig, I made the transformation. The makeup took several hours to apply, and hurt like hell going on and coming off, but it worked.

My main interest was in experiencing society's reactions to an old man. I walked around in Victoria and Vancouver about a dozen times, in different places, at night and during the day. And what I found was pretty much what I expected; a few people go out of their way to help the old, a few turn their backs, and most people simply ignore them.

One "young" woman (my own age) waited patiently for me as I struggled up the stairs at the Victoria Institute of Gerontology, held the door open, and said "have a nice day." I felt very uncomfortable: I was really a young, healthy, male but was masquerading as a decrepit old man; I actually felt like I was a "burden" and almost told her I could open doors for myself, even if I was old.

On the other hand, I was shoved off the sidewalk in front of the Empress Hotel by a large, noisy bunch of tourists. It may have been accidental, but I felt angry and frustrated. On crowded streets I could no longer stride along and know that other people would move aside. I had to be on the defensive, anticipating others' moves. Crossing busy streets became a totally different experience. I hung back so that the crowds could bolt across as soon as the light changed, and then I shuffled along, keeping my eye on the cars, which seemed like racehorses just itching for the gates to open. The lights always started flashing "DON'T WALK" before I was across. What was I supposed to do, the bunny hop?

I experimented with getting in and out of cars and using buses. The basic lesson I learned was that the world gets bigger and faster for an old man, and I became acutely aware of this dramatic change because I was really young, and hadn't gradually accepted the inevitable changes of aging.

I discovered a sense of comradeship of the old, who had the time to sit and talk. I also found a subtle difference between old Victoria and big Vancouver: it seemed easier to be old here, partly because of the size and pace, but maybe also because in Victoria we have so many old people. I think we have learned to be a little more patient.

Would I do it again? Probably not ... pretending to be old hurt my back, my legs, my feet. It was hard to explain to friends and neighbours what I was doing. I think I'll wait for old age to creep up on me slowly, and in the meantime, I think I have gained a better understanding for my old friends.

**Source:** Paul M. Baker, "Old Before My Time," videotape distributed by the Centre on Aging, University of Victoria, Victoria, B.C. V8W 2Y2, 1983b. Reproduced with permission of the author.

• • • • • • • • • • • • • • • • • • • • • • • • • • • • • • • • • • • • •

Other mass media also foster prejudice against older people. Newspaper stories, for example, sometimes point to older people as the cause of rising health care costs in Canada. Harding and Neysmith (1984) say that this practice overlooks the deeper reasons for rising health care costs and creates a negative image of older people.

Jokes give a negative view of old age and older people as well (Davies 1977). Demos and Jache (1981) studied humour in birthday cards. They found that cards often focused on physical or mental decline connected with aging. The cards also focused on age concealment, and most took a negative view of aging. Palmore (1971) studied attitudes to older people in humour. He looked at 264 jokes taken from ten popular joke books. He found that one-quarter of the jokes took a positive view of aging and about one-fifth took a neutral view, but more than half of them showed a negative attitude to aging or the aged. He also found a double standard in jokes about age: jokes about women, more often than those about men, portrayed older people negatively.

These jokes project our own fears about aging onto older people. But do these fears have a basis in fact? Studies of older Canadians show that they don't. A study by Health and Welfare Canada (1988a), for example, found that only 30 percent of people aged 65 and over said that life was very or fairly stressful, compared to 52 percent of people aged 55 or younger. Also, 92 percent of people aged 65 and over said they were either pretty happy or very happy, which is about the same proportion as for the 55–64 year olds (93 percent) (Health and Welfare Canada 1988a; see also Thompson 1989). Between 90 and 95 percent of seniors in another study said they felt satisfied with their families, marital status, friends, and housing (Gauthier 1991). Northcott (1982) studied 440 Edmontonians and found that older people reported higher life-satisfaction than those who were younger. Also, more often than younger people they said they felt no pressures. Northcott concluded that "old age looks far more attractive than stereotypes suggest."

## MYTHS AND REALITIES OF AGING

Gerontology has two goals. First, scholars and researchers work to produce accurate knowledge about aging. Second, professionals who work with older people apply this knowledge to create a better life for their clients. Academic gerontologists try to decrease prejudice and stereotyping in society by writing about the facts of aging today. Consider the following myths and the facts that gerontologists have found to replace them.

***Myth***   *People feel lonely and lost in retirement. They often get sick and die shortly after they retire.*

***Reality***   Few people face sickness or loneliness due to retirement (McDonald and Wanner 1990; MacLean 1983). Given the chance to retire with a decent income, most people do so as soon as they can (Health and Welfare Canada 1979). McDonald and Wanner (1990) report that retirement has little, if any, effect on health, social activity, and life-satisfaction or happiness. Streib and Schneider (1971) found that the health of some workers improves when they retire. Many start new careers, take up volunteer work, or go back to school.

***Myth***   *People in older age groups face a higher risk of criminal victimization than people in younger age groups.*

***Reality***   Older people report more fear of crime than younger people. Podnieks and her colleagues (1989, 12) report that nearly 20 percent of a random sample of older Canadians said they felt "somewhat fearful of being out alone in their neighbourhood." Brillon (1986), in a Montreal study of 210 people aged 60 and over, found that 53 percent of men and women said they felt afraid of a burglary; 53 percent of the men and 69 percent of the women in this study reported a fear of being attacked at home; and 47 percent of men and 69 percent of women said they feared an attack away from home. The Canadian Urban Victimization Survey (Johnson 1990) found that 59 percent of people aged 65 or over (compared to 37 percent of people under age 65) said they felt unsafe walking alone at night. Older women with low incomes and fair-to-poor health, and who live alone reported the most fear (Kennedy and Silverman 1984-85; Podnieks et al. 1989). Loss of social networks due to retirement, widowhood, and staying home may lead to increased fear of crime. But this fear of crime does not fit the facts about crime against the elderly.

# Exhibit 1.2
## Profile: Breaking the Stereotype of Old Age

A senior citizen who used his youthful combat training to corner a man who broke into his neighbour's house was awarded a certificate for police service yesterday.

Although the young man threatened to shoot him, "I wasn't afraid of him at all," 65-year-old Evald Asu said.

Asu, an Estonian, said that when he faced the hoodlum, he remembered resistance tactics he learned for use against the Soviet Red Army in the 1940s.

"When it comes to a serious fight, I can fight like a devil," Asu, 5-foot-8, said.

On the afternoon of Feb. 9, [1984], Asu was trying to get his Siamese cat off the roof of his Lipton Street residence when he noticed a man attempting to enter a house next door.

When he saw the man break a sidedoor window with his fist and go into the house, Asu said he grabbed his metal ice scraper and went toward the home.

"You can just about expect anything from a character like that," he said.

He was unaware that neighbour Evelyn Tolentino and her two young children were hiding in a bedroom inside.

Asu said the hoodlum was 6-foot and half his age.

"I told him to come out with his hands up, the police are here," he said. "You can't fight in a house."

"I think he was embarrassed; instead of police, there was an old man standing there."

Asu said the man swung at him, but he hit him first with his fist.

"I told him to stay," Asu said, saying he just wanted to keep the man there until police arrived.

But the man backed away toward the fence, where he put his hand into his jacket pocket and threatened to pull out a gun and shoot Asu.

Asu said he swung his ice scraper, coming down on the man's hand several times.

"If he had a gun one of us would have been dead and I didn't want it to be me," he said.

The man jumped the fence with his arm bleeding and Asu followed him down the back lanes.

It was then he said he remembered his guerilla training.

"We went barehanded. We learned to fight," he recalled.

As he followed the man between the houses, he said: "I knew exactly what I was doing. I was watching his hands, his feet."

Asu said the man pointed something at him, so he kept his distance.

"At 30 yards (27.4 metres) that kind of creep couldn't kill me," he said.

Meanwhile, the police had arrived in response to Tolentino's call.

Asu returned to meet them and then led the officers along the man's path, shown by a trail of blood.

A 21-year-old man was arrested shortly thereafter and has since appeared in court charged with break and enter with intent to steal from the Tolentino residence …

"You can't leave it to someone else to do," [Asu] said. "If we all put in a little bit, we could fight them (hoodlums) pretty good."

**Source:** Joscelyn Proby, "Combat Skills Put to Use," *Winnipeg Free Press*, 10 April 1984, 3. Reprinted with permission of the Winnipeg Free Press.

Podnieks et al. (1989), for instance, found that only 6 percent of their sample had property or money stolen from them by a stranger since turning age 65. Studies in Britain, the U.S., and Canada show that older people run less risk of victimization than any other age group. A 1981 Canadian survey found that older people made up only 2 percent of victims of personal crimes (Solicitor General of Canada 1985). Older people had only one-sixth the rate of violent and personal victimizations compared to all adults, and one-twelfth the rate of the 16–24 age group. Brillon (1987, 10) says that "elderly people are largely under-victimized, proportionately, for all types of crime." The Canadian Urban Victimization Survey (Solicitor General of Canada 1983, 3) sums up these findings. It states that "contrary to popular belief ... elderly people are relatively unlikely to be victimized by crime ... In fact, the actual sample counts of sexual assault and robbery incidents for those over 60 were so low that estimated numbers and rates are unreliable." (See Exhibit 1.4 for details of this study.)

***Myth***   *Most old people live in institutions.*

***Reality***   Only a small percentage of older people live in nursing homes, hospitals, or asylums at any given time. Ram (1990) reports that in 1986 5.4 percent of men and 9.1 percent of women lived in hospitals and other long-term care institutions.

The likelihood of institutionalization increases with age. Only 3.3 percent of 65–74 year olds live in collective dwellings. This figure jumps to 20.2 percent for people aged 75 and over (Ram 1990). Current trends in Canada may lead to less institutionalization in the future for some age groups.

Institutionalization rates have slowed for men aged 85 and over and rates have decreased for both sexes aged 80–84 (Stone and Frenken 1988). Most institutions house the very old, sick, and frail elderly—people with few social supports, who cannot live on their own.

Research shows that stereotypes about old age decrease with increased education. Palmore (1977) devised a "Facts on Aging Quiz (FAQ)" (see Exhibit 1.3). Researchers and educators have used this quiz with people from a variety of backgrounds. Studies report that scores improve with education. People with a high school education or less, for example, average 57 percent correct. Undergraduates do somewhat better, averaging 64 percent. Gerontology students and faculty on average score 83 percent (Palmore 1988). A study in Canada by Greenslade (1986 cited in Palmore 1988) found that nurses with no gerontology training scored 61 percent correct, but a group with training in geriatrics scored 83 percent. Palmore (1988, 43) concludes that "those with more knowledge tend to have less negative and more neutral attitudes."

. . . . . . . . . . . . . . . . . . . . . . . . . . . . . . . . . . . . . .

## Exhibit 1.3

## Facts on Aging Quiz

. . . . . . . . . . . . . . . . . . . . . . . . . . . . . . . . . . . . . .

Try the following quiz to see how much you know about aging in Canada. The quiz is based on Palmore's "Facts on Aging: A Short Quiz" (1977), but it incorporates suggestions made by Canadian researchers who have revised Palmore's work (Matthews, Tindale, and Norris 1985). The correct answers are at the bottom of the next page. You will find the facts to support these answers throughout this book.

### True or False?

1. A least 15 percent of the aged are living in long-stay institutions in Canada (i.e., nursing homes, mental hospitals, homes for the aged).
2. British Columbia has a higher proportion of older people in its population than any other province.
3. Older people today have less contact with their families than older people in the past.
4. Older people stand a higher risk of criminal victimization than people in other age groups.

5. Memory declines with age.
6. A decline in sexual vigour in older men is usually due to hormone deficiencies.
7. Retirees more often feel depressed, bored, and ill than those who keep working.
8. Most older people in rural areas depend on public transportation.
9. The body's systems go into a steady decline from age 40 on.
10. The majority of older people have incomes below the poverty level (as defined by the federal government).

Turn to the bottom of page 13 for the answers.

. . . . . . . . . . . . . . . . . . . . . . . . . . . . . . . . . . . . . .

Matthews, Tindale, and Norris (1985) gave a modified version of Palmore's quiz to public health nurses and also to students and faculty at Guelph University. They found that the people with the most knowledge about aging scored best on the quiz. Undergraduate students just completing a gerontology course scored highest. Introductory students in a human development course scored lowest. Their results suggest that when people learn about aging, their concept of old age improves.

Other research supports this idea. Studies show that education in general, and knowledge about aging in particular, improves people's attitudes toward old age. Gallie and Kozak (1985) found that the more education people had, the better they did on both knowledge of aging and attitude-to-aging scales. People who had a background in gerontology scored significantly higher than those who did not.

## Exhibit 1.4

Criminal Incident Rates by Age: Seven Cities

(Rates per 1,000 Population)

| Type of Incident | 16–24 | 25–39 | 40–64 | 65 or older | All Age Groups Combined |
|---|---|---|---|---|---|
| Sexual Assault | 9 | 3 | 1* | ** | 3.5 |
| Robbery | 21 | 9 | 5 | 4 | 10 |
| Assault | 123 | 62 | 20 | 8 | 57 |
| All Violent Incidents | 154 | 74 | 25 | 12 | 70 |
| Personal Theft | 134 | 73 | 38 | 13 | 70 |
| All Personal Incidents | 288 | 147 | 63 | 25 | 141 |

*The actual count was low (11 to 20), therefore caution should be exercised when interpreting this rate.
**The actual account was too low to make statistically reliable population estimates.

This table shows a decrease in victimization for each older age group. The trend holds true for each type of crime listed here. It also shows that all people, including older people, experience a higher rate of personal incidents—violence and personal theft—than other kinds of crime. These crimes may make a greater impact on older than on younger people because an older person may have a harder time making up the loss of money or valuables.

**Source:** Adapted from Solicitor General of Canada, *The Canadian Urban Victimization Survey, Bulletin 6: Criminal Victimization of Elderly Canadians* (Ottawa: Minister of Supply and Services, 1985), 2. Reproduced with permission of the Minister of Supply and Services Canada, 1991.

Knox, Gekoski, and Johnson (1984) and Gfellner (1982) studied under-graduate students. These studies found that positive contact with older people in general leads to better attitudes. So does voluntary, frequent contact between a younger person and an older person they know well. Dooley and Frankel (1990) studied a friendly visiting program where adolescents visited a specific senior each week. They found that adolescents who had a positive perception of the person they visited made a favourable attitude change toward seniors in general. This evidence supports the idea that knowledge about aging and satisfying contact with older people can relieve fears and replace negative stereotypes with a more positive view of old age (Butler 1989).

The study of aging shows that old age has its compensations. Older people in Canada have guaranteed incomes, subsidized housing, and free medical care. They also get reduced rates on buses, hotels, and car rentals. Other bonuses are tax breaks, free tuition at many universities, and financial support for recreation programs (Palmore 1979). Atchley (1985, 6) declares that in old age the positive results "outnumber the negative by at least two to one." Zarit (1977, 11) says that life for older people is "getting better all the time."

The study of aging shows that the attitudes of others cause many of the worst problems older people face. Gerontology tries to remove these obstacles to a good old age by learning and publishing the facts on aging.

## THE HISTORY OF GERONTOLOGY

Gerontology comes from the Greek words "geron" (old man) and "logos" (reason or discourse). Writings about aging can be found in the scriptures of the Far East, Biblical sources, works by the Greek philosophers, and medical writings of the Middle Ages. One list of works on aging written before the nineteenth century came to 1,800 titles (Freeman 1979, 81). Freeman describes the earliest of these works (from the first written records to those of the seventeenth century) as the products of perceptive individuals. These writings reflect their authors' biases and fears as well as the attitudes of their time. Not until the seventeenth century, with the rise of the scientific method, did researchers look at the facts about aging. These researchers' backgrounds were usually the natural sciences and medicine.

Francis Bacon, credited as the founder of the scientific method, wrote one of the best-known early books on aging, *Historia Vitae e Mortis (The History of Life and Death*, 1623). Bacon wanted to use systematic observation to learn the causes of aging, but his own work echoed the biases of the past. The following passage, for example, could have come straight from Aristotle 2,000 years earlier: "Men of age," Bacon says, "object too much, consult too long, adventure too little, repent too soon, and seldom drive business home to the full period, but content themselves with a mediocrity of success" (cited in Freeman 1979, 38).

By the eighteenth century the scientific method began to change the way researchers studied aging. Mathematicians and scientists began to use the mathematical techniques of natural science to study aging. Astronomer Sir Edmund Halley constructed the first table of life expectancy.

In the nineteenth century Quetelet, a Belgian astronomer-mathematician, conducted studies of birth rates, death rates, and others that looked at

Answer to Exhibit 1.3: All of the statements in Exhibit 1.3 are false.

• • • • • • • • • • • • • • • • • • • • • • • • • • • • • • • • • • •

## Exhibit 1.5

## Controversy: Do We Live in an Ageist Society?

• • • • • • • • • • • • • • • • • • • • • • • • • • • • • • • • • • •

Schonfield (1982, 267) says that introductory gerontology texts often give "the impression that a negative attitude toward elderly people is rampant in the United States and presumably, also, in other western countries." He goes on to say that these texts exaggerate the amount of prejudice against older people in North America. Review articles and studies by well-known gerontologists find little evidence for this supposed prejudice. Studies show that older people maintain good relations with their families, receive many services from the government, and get preferred treatment from restaurants, banks, and airlines.

Schonfield's own research shows that people have both positive and negative attitudes toward old age and aging. He found that between 20 and 77 percent of his sample agreed with stereotypes about older people,

but many of these same people said that the statement applied to only a portion of the older population. He says that "at most one in five participants could be convicted [of stereotyping]" (Schonfield 1982, 269).

Schonfield (1982, 270) concludes that: " ... some acts portray ageist attitudes, but these are insufficient to justify the generalization that ours is an ageist society. On the other hand, there seems to be ample evidence to contradict the generalization."

Schonfield's research shows the danger of generalizing about attitudes toward older people. Still, his research shows that some proportion of people (as many as one in five) do stereotype older people. More education and information about aging might decrease this proportion.

• • • • • • • • • • • • • • • • • • • • • • • • • • • • • • • • • •

how crime and suicide varied with age. In *On the Nature of Man and the Development of His Faculties* (1835) he described how human traits like strength and weight varied with age (Birren and Clayton 1975, 18).

In the early twentieth century scientific interest in old age grew more intense. In 1903 Elie Metchnikoff at the Pasteur Institute in Paris first used the term "gerontology" (Freeman 1979, 16). He wrote one of the first modern books on aging, entitled *The Problem of Age, Growth and Death* (1908). In 1912 the Society of Geriatry was formed in New York—one of the first groups in North America to study aging.

Research and writing on aging grew quickly after 1950. A study of the literature published between 1950 and 1960, for example, found as many publications in those ten years as there had been altogether in the previous 115 years (Birren and Clayton 1975). A bibliography of sources on aging for the years 1954–1974 listed 50,000 entries (Woodruff 1975). Research in gerontology now goes on in many disciplines, including biology, psychology, and sociology. Researchers now have access to the latest gerontology research through the use of CD-ROM bibliographies and on-line data bases.

# CANADIAN DEVELOPMENTS IN GERONTOLOGY

## Historical Overview

Gerontology in Canada grew slowly from 1950 to 1980. In 1950 the government set up the first of a series of committees to study aging. This committee—the Joint Committee on Old Age Security of the Senate and House of Commons—studied the effects of aging on Canadian society and on individuals. It focused on income security, but also collected information on housing, health, and welfare services (Health and Welfare Canada 1982b, vii).

In 1963 the Senate appointed a special committee to study the services, facilities, and preventive programs available to older people. At that time Canada had no national body devoted to research on aging, so the committee had to gather its own facts. It used Dominion Bureau of Statistics (now Statistics Canada) census data, research reports published by the Department of National Health and Welfare, and submissions by scholars, researchers, and agencies across the country. The committee collected the most up-to-date information on aging, and its report gives a good overview of aging in Canada at that time.

In this report the committee refers again and again to the lack of social scientific research on aging. Gaps were found in many fields (like the study of retirement in Canada) and the quality of the research in others was judged to be poor. Response to a questionnaire sent by the committee to government departments, universities, and voluntary organizations across the country indicated a lack of coordinated gerontological study. Only 78 out of 118 organizations answered the questionnaire, and less than one-third (24) reported any research on aging from 1950 to 1963. The committee learned of only 129 research projects started in Canada from 1950 to 1963—71 by universities, 38 by voluntary organizations, and 20 by provincial and federal governments—an average of only 10 research projects per year throughout the country (Senate of Canada 1966).

The committee traced the slow rate of growth in Canadian research to a lack of research funds. Federal health grants to support aging research averaged less than $75,000 per year for the ten-year period from 1955 to 1965. Only four provinces (Quebec, Ontario, Saskatchewan, and British Columbia) received these funds, and three institutions in Quebec received more than 77 percent of the total (Senate of Canada 1966).

Other groups—the federal Departments of Labour and Veterans Affairs, and a number of volunteer agencies—supported research in the 1950s and 1960s. The Ontario Department of Public Welfare, for example, started the "Longitudinal Study of Male Workers, Ontario, 1959–78." This study focused on social, economic, and health changes in male workers and offered a rare look at changes in workers over time. It also looked at the adjustments men made to aging and the kinds of services they used as they aged (Senate of Canada 1966). A number of researchers have continued to use this data set into the late 1980s (Hirdes et al. 1986; Hirdes et al. 1987). A recent analysis (Forbes, McPherson, and Shadbolt-Forbes 1989, 65) found that it contained reliable data and that it "represents an exceptionally good longitudinal study." These researchers said that the data can be used to study how health behaviours at the start of the study affected respondents' health at the end.

Canadian research activity increased during the 1960s and 1970s. In 1971 Manitoba began a province-wide survey of the needs of the elderly. Researchers set out to measure both the needs of older people and how well present resources met these needs. They questioned 3,558 people who lived in the community and 1,247 older people who lived in long-term care facilities—a total of 4,805 people over the age of 65 (Government of Manitoba 1973). The province repeated this survey in 1976 and in 1983. The results of the three surveys make up the largest, most complete longitudinal study of aging in Canada. An annotated bibliography of results from this study lists over 100 publications written between 1971 and 1983 (Rempel 1987).

In 1973 the Canadian Council on Social Development (CCSD) sponsored a nation-wide study of elderly persons' housing. The council's report, *Beyond Shelter* (Canadian Council on Social Development 1973), shaped housing policy in Canada for at least the next decade. The government also formed the Special Senate Commission on Retirement Age Policies. The commission's report, *Retirement Without Tears* (Senate of Canada 1979), described the major issues facing retired Canadians and suggested social reforms.

In 1971 Canadian researchers and scholars formed the Canadian Association on Gerontology (CAG). The CAG presents position papers to the government on issues related to aging, keeps track of research activities across the country, and sponsors the annual "Scientific and Educational Meeting." The CAG publishes proceedings from these meetings and also publishes the *Canadian Journal on Aging*. (In the late 1970s the journal's title was *Essence: Issues in Death, Dying and the Process of Aging*.) The CAG has a computerized data base of over 2,000 resource people in Canada and publishes a "Running Bibliography" on aging research by Canadian scholars.

In 1980, recognizing the need for more stable support for gerontology research, the Social Sciences and Humanities Research Council of Canada (SSHRC) for the first time awarded over $1 million to researchers through its

Strategic Grants Division program on Population Aging. The council also set aside funds to sponsor five new gerontology centres in Canada. These centres, at the University of New Brunswick, the University of Guelph, the University of Toronto, the University of Manitoba, and Simon Fraser University, conduct and encourage research, keep local researchers informed about national and provincial research activities, and sponsor forums and seminars on aging (Hancock 1984).

By 1980 Canadian gerontology had begun to come of age. In that year Marshall (1980a) published the first collection of gerontology writings by Canadian scholars, *Aging in Canada*. This collection includes papers on various topics, from demography to health care to housing, as well as articles that take a sociohistorical view of aging and others that look at intergenerational conflict. These articles show Canadian gerontology's links to European and British traditions of critical social science. Other articles show Canadian gerontology's links to U.S. research. Marshall (1980a) noted in his introduction that in 1980 Canada still lacked basic research on aging—research on family life, biological research, and studies of mental functioning in later life. He spoke of the small number of Canadian researchers as pioneers, many of whom "have worked, of necessity, virtually alone, without the benefit of colleagues who share their research interest in gerontology" (Marshall 1980a, 6).

## Developments in Francophone Gerontology

During the late 1970s and 1980s research activity in gerontology also increased steadily in Quebec. In 1976 the Quebec Department of Health set up one of the first Canadian gerontology centres (the Laboratoires de gérontologie sociale) at the Université Laval. Two years later a group of Quebec gerontologists formed *L'Association québécoise de gérontologie* (Béland 1988), and in 1980 they set up a research committee. The association has held symposia on professional issues each year since 1979 and since 1980 has held an annual scientific meeting. Proceedings of these meetings keep members of the association up to date on francophone research.

The Association québécoise de gérontologie research committee has compiled a list of gerontologists who worked in the field from 1977 to 1982. The list includes 635 people. Of these, 122 had permanent positions that allowed them to do full- or part-time research (Zay et al. 1984 cited in Béland 1988). These researchers had conducted 128 projects, about one-third of which dealt with topics in administration, psychology, sociology, or political science. Béland (1988) reports 800 articles published from 1975 to August 1986 by francophone authors. These appeared in peer-reviewed journals, symposia proceedings, policy reports, and elsewhere.

Béland (1988) surveyed the content of this research and found that it focused on three topics: psychosocial topics, demography, and program evaluation. He also found that francophone researchers prefer to use qualitative research methods. Bernardin-Haldemann (1988) traces these themes and the use of qualitative methods to the social and political context of Quebec in the 1970s. At that time, the government of Quebec defined the growth of the older population as a social problem. This led gerontologists to study demography, older people's psychosocial conditions, and their service needs.

In the 1970s the rise of Quebec nationalism led to an interest in Québécois identity, and gerontologists took up this theme in their studies. Researchers focused on the everyday lives of older people, their world views, and the issues of "*intergenerational relationships* and *socio-cultural continuity*" (Bernardin-Haldemann 1988, 329, italics in the original).

Béland (1988) posed the question of francophone gerontology's significance in the subtitle of a literature review: "An Obscure Originality or a Deserved Obscurity?" Anglophone Canadians have often overlooked francophone research, as have other North American scholars. Béland (1988) points out that francophone researchers often publish their work in French and tend to publish in research reports rather than in refereed journals. For these reasons, their work has not reached the wider North American academic community. But, as Béland's review shows, francophone researchers have conducted community studies that could interest a wider audience. They have also conducted social-psychological studies that speak to important issues like the loneliness and isolation of the elderly. Anglophone gerontologists could benefit from wider exposure to this research.

## The Current State of Canadian Gerontology

In 1982 the CAG published the first issue of the *Canadian Journal on Aging*. That year the program of the association's 11th Annual Scientific and Educational Meeting contained 129 abstracts (these included media presentations, symposia, and discussion groups, as well as papers). By 1988 over four hundred researchers and practitioners presented papers at the annual meeting. They presented their findings in over one hundred sessions (including symposia and discussion groups). The meeting also included a series of pre-conference workshops and over fifty technical, educational, and media exhibits.

Still, more research on aging needs to be done. A review of the CAG annual meetings from 1987 to 1990 shows that researchers presented more papers on health-related issues than on any other subject. We still know too little about healthy older people, even though most older people live healthy, active lives. We also need to know more about the social conditions that lead to good aging. What do people of different ethnic backgrounds need as they age? Do the needs of people in rural areas differ from those of people in cities? Do older people have unique educational needs? How do they learn best? And what do they want to know? Researchers have begun to turn to these and other questions about aging.

## SUMMARY

1. The growth of the older population in Canada has made aging a major social issue—one that will affect all of us.

2. Gerontology has two goals: first, to increase our knowledge about old age and, second, to improve the quality of life in old age. Today in Canada these goals take the form of scholarly research and the practical application of research findings.

3. Canadians have both positive and negative images of aging and older people. Many of these stereotypes have little basis in fact. Gerontology tries to replace stereotypes with facts, information, and a clearer understanding of aging.

4. Canadian research grew rapidly in all parts of Canada during the 1970s and 1980s. This has led to more scholarly publications, new research programs, and more projects to improve the lives of older people.

## SELECTED READINGS

Binstock, R., and L. George, eds. *Handbook of Aging and the Social Sciences.* 3d ed. San Diego, California: Academic Press, 1990.

This handbook contains state-of-the-art reviews of the literature in the field. It includes articles on changes in the field, migration patterns of the elderly, family life, and social supports. A basic resource for social gerontologists.

Marshall, Victor W., ed. *Aging in Canada.* 2d ed. Toronto: Fitzhenry and Whiteside, 1986.

A collection of writings by gerontologists from across Canada. Excellent reviews of the Canadian literature on topics like population change, health care, and the family.

## NOTES

[1]The terms "old," "elderly," "aged," and "senior" in this text refer to people aged 65 and over unless another age is given.

# *Theories and Methods*

## INTRODUCTION

In 1980 the Gerontological Society of America (GSA) and the Association for Gerontology in Higher Education (AGHE) set out to define the discipline of gerontology (Foundations Project 1980). They asked 111 scholars, researchers, and professionals in the field to describe a basic education program in gerontology. These experts came from disciplines as different from one another as biomedicine and economics, and their descriptions of the exact content and boundaries of gerontology varied. But they did agree on their most significant conclusion, that three broad areas of study should make up the core of a gerontology curriculum: biomedicine, psychosocial studies, and socioeconomic-environmental studies.

The first area, **biomedicine**, looks at the changes in physiology and health that come with age. This area includes studies of the biochemical causes of aging, studies of reaction time and stress, and studies of dementia. Experts disagreed least about the curriculum content for this area; this may be due to the long tradition of biomedical research on aging.

The second area, **psychosocial studies**, examines the changes that take place within individuals and between individuals and groups. This includes psychological studies of memory, learning, and personality, as well as studies of friendship and recreation.

The third area, **socioeconomic-environmental studies**, concentrates on the effects of aging on social structures like health care and education. It also looks at the effects of social structures on the aging individual, and includes the study of income policies, health care systems, and formal social supports.

The Canadian Association on Gerontology today has six sections: general, biology, health sciences, psychology, social sciences, and social policy and practice. The way this association has organized itself reflects the increase in research activity and the greater specialization of research in biology and health sciences. It also reflects gerontologists' desire to apply their knowledge. The social policy and practice section in particular, focuses on programs and practices that can improve the lives of older people.

**Social gerontology** includes psychosocial, socioeconomic-environmental, and practice-related research. It looks at aging from the points of view of both the individual and the social system. Social gerontologists often take an interest in physical and health care changes that come with age. But the focus of the social gerontologist differs from that of the physiologist or biochemist. When social gerontologists look at biological or physical change in old age they ask how these changes affect the individual's social life or society as a whole. Social gerontologists, for example, will want to know how diseases in old age affect hospital costs or how changes in lung capacity affect a person's ability to work. They will also want to know how a social norm like retirement affects an older person's health, how changes in family life in Canada affect the psychological well-being of the elderly, or what counselling methods work best with new retirees. Social gerontology has grown in importance from the 1950s to the 1990s in Canada.

This chapter will look at: (1) the theories that gerontologists use to guide their research and to interpret their findings, (2) the methods researchers use to gather data, and (3) current developments in Canadian research on aging.

. . . . . . . . . . . . . . . . . . . . . . . . . . . . . . . . . . . . . . . .

# Exhibit 2.1

## Time–Lines

. . . . . . . . . . . . . . . . . . . . . . . . . . . . . . . . . . . . . . . .

These time-lines show three dimensions of aging. Line A refers to the biomedical changes that take place with age. Biomedical aging takes place at different rates for each person, and at different rates for each system of the body. Still, we can describe the aging process in terms of some general trends that take place in the physiology over time.

Line A

1 — 18; peak of sexual vigour
2 — 30 onward; decline of 1 percent per year on average
3 — 40; physical decline shows up as greying hair, wrinkled skin, balding, loss of stamina
4 — 47; menopause
5 — 70; high risk of heart disease and stroke
6 — 72.9; (1983–85) life expectancy at birth for males
7 — 79.8; (1983–85) life expectancy at birth for females
8 — 120; (estimated) life span

Line B

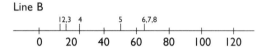

1 — 16; legal driving age
2 — 18; legal voting age
3 — 18; fluid intelligence high (e.g., ability to visualize objects in space)
4 — 25; first marriage
5 — 50; last child leaves home
6 — 65; crystallized intelligence high (e.g., ability to define words)
7 — 65; pensionable age (under rules of most pension plans)
8 — 65; person may begin a second career

Line B refers to psychosocial and socioeconomic-environmental changes that take place with age. Most psychologists and social psychologists agree that human beings develop through a series of stages (though different psychologists list different stages and different patterns of aging). Sociologists say that culture (societal values, norms, and expectations) all play a role in shaping the individual's development. This time-line lists some of the basic events in the life course in Canada today.

Only time-line A shows aging as a constant decline with age. Line B shows aging as a complex series of changes—some abilities like fluid intelligence decrease, others like crystallized intelligence may increase. Also, a person may experience declines on one dimension (e.g., physical stamina), but increases on another (e.g., more involvement in recreation in retirement). Some changes that come with age, like a second career, can only develop in later life.

Line B also reflects the social structures of society. These structures can change, and they are changing today. The Canadian government, for example, has begun to allow a choice of retirement ages for people who get benefits from the Canada Pension Plan; this will allow people to retire before or after age 65 if they choose .

. . . . . . . . . . . . . . . . . . . . . . . . . . . . . . . . . . . . . . . .

# THEORIES OF AGING

Social gerontologists use theory to guide research and to interpret the results of their studies. A good theory helps a researcher choose research methods, questions, and samples. Cockerham (1991) says that "theories specify relationships between concepts and provide a framework for explaining why certain things happen the way they do." For instance, research shows that women get more of their retirement income from public pension sources than men. Why does this difference exist? And is this an important finding or a trivial fact? Theory offers an explanation and an understanding of research findings. Feminist theory, for example, would trace this difference to gender inequalities in the workplace. Women have less opportunity to pay into private pension plans during their middle years. This forces them to draw on public pension sources in old age.

Theory gives an interpretation to the facts. But no one theory in gerontology can explain all the facts about aging (Moody 1988b). And sometimes a researcher will use several theories to explain the results of a study. Authors often select theories to fit their sense of how the world works. If you know the assumptions that underlie a theory, you know the costs and benefits of using that theory. And you know the biases that each theory brings to the facts. More than one theory can often explain a set of research findings. The theory used depends on how the researcher makes sense of the data.

Social gerontologists have generally used sociological, or social-psychological theories in their work. Sometimes they have adapted these theories to fit the study of aging. Exhibit 2.2 presents a list of the major theories discussed below.

## Two Levels of Theory

Theories describe all sorts of human activity and relationships, from individual attitudes to societal structures. The following discussion categorizes theories by placing them into a framework and it also gives examples of how gerontologists apply these theories in their work.

Gerontologists often classify theories into two categories: (1) micro-level, (2) macro-level.

### *Micro-Level Theories*

Micro-level theories focus on individuals and their interactions and are used to explain phenomena like the relationship between adult children and their parents, changes in memory with age, and the effect of negative attitudes on older people.

. . . . . . . . . . . . . . . . . . . . . . . . . . . . . . . . .

# Exhibit 2.2
## Selected Perspectives and Theories of Aging

. . . . . . . . . . . . . . . . . . . . . . . . . . . . . . . . .

**Interpretive Perspective**
Symbolic Interaction
Social Phenomenology
Exchange Theory

**Normative Perspective**
Structural-Functionalism
Activity Theory
Disengagement Theory
Age Stratification Theory
Modernization Theory

**Conflict Perspective**
Political Economy of Aging

. . . . . . . . . . . . . . . . . . . . . . . . . . . . . . . . .

**Subculture theory** (Rose 1965), for example, says that social forces in modern society lead older people to spend less time with younger people and more time with one another as they age. The existence of senior centres, senior housing blocks, and retirement villages all support this theory. Rose says that the interaction between older people in these settings leads them to develop common interests, a group consciousness, and a subculture. Some events, like the Canadian seniors' protest against proposed changes in government pensions in 1985, seem to support subculture theory. Seniors did band together for a common cause. But, in many other ways, seniors form a varied group. They come from all regions of the country, have varying ethnic backgrounds, and are members of different social classes. They do not vote as a block, and their lifelong political affiliations vary. Because it cannot account for these facts, subculture theory has gained only moderate acceptance.

**Exchange theory** (Blau 1964; Homans 1961) also takes a micro-level view of social relations. Using the model of economic, rational behaviour to study social life, exchange theory rests on the concept of reciprocity and sees social life as a series of exchanges. People try to get the most out of their exchanges at the least cost. But if the cost of a relationship outweighs the benefits, exchange theory says that people will withdraw from the relationship. Dowd (1975) used this theory to explain why some people withdraw from social life as they age. He says that older people have less power and fewer resources than younger people in social encounters. They cannot compete, and so they withdraw. Exchange theory cannot easily explain how altruism or love leads to giving and sharing. In this way exchange theory tends to oversimplify social life, but it does provide a good example of a micro-level theory.

## *Macro-Level Theories*

Macro-level theories focus on "social structure, social processes and problems, and their interrelationships" (McDaniel 1989, 51). Such theories explain phenomena like the effect of industrialization on older people's status, the history and impact of public pensions, and how gender and income affect older people's well-being. Estes (1979, 11) criticizes micro-level theories because they "focus on what old people do rather than on the social conditions and policies that cause them to act as they do." Her work looks at the effects of social policies on older people. She finds, for example, that current policies designed for older people actually work against them. These policies (like Medicare in the U.S.) segregate older people from those in other age groups, create conflicts between the old and the young for resources, and support a definition of old age as a time of decline. Worst of all these policies do not deal with the basic conditions that lead to low social and economic status for older people. This approach tends to minimize people's ability to act and overcome the limits of social structures. Still, Estes's concern for social structures and their impact on individuals provides a good example of the macro-level approach.

## Three Theoretical Perspectives

Both micro- and macro-level theories can take one of three perspectives: (1) the interpretive perspective, (2) the normative perspective, and (3) the conflict perspective.

## *The Interpretive Perspective*

The interpretive perspective focuses almost exclusively on the micro-level of social life. It looks at how people define situations, how they create social order, and how they relate to one another in daily life. Social gerontologists have made the least use of this perspective, though it can provide insights into everyday interactions. The exchange, symbolic-interactionist, and social phenomenological theories that grew out of the work of Homans (1961), George Herbert Mead (1934), and Max Weber (1978), respectively, exemplify the interpretive perspective. Mead (1934), for example, said that objects and events have no meaning in themselves. People give them meaning through everyday interaction. Grey hair, for example, can be a sign of wisdom in one society, but a sign of decline in another. People give meanings to objects and then base their actions on these meanings. Some people will refuse to wear a hearing aid because to them it symbolizes decrepitude and weakness. Weber (1978) said that to understand a social phenomenon the researcher needs to understand the meaning that people in the situation attach to their events and actions.

The interpretive perspective views the individual as a creator of social order and organization. This perspective asks the question, "How does a recognizable, predictable social order come about?" (Berger and Luckman 1967; Garfinkel 1967; Schutz 1967). The interpretive perspective can give a good understanding of how people interpret their social world, how they interact with one another, and why they do what they do. Gerontologists have used this approach in studies of the self in later life (Chappell and Ohrbach 1986), death and dying (Marshall 1986), and successful aging (Novak 1983).

Gubrium (1986) used the interpretive perspective to study Alzheimer's disease, and his findings show some of the strengths of this approach. Writers have called Alzheimer's disease "the disease of the century," and television shows have depicted the struggle spouses and children face when they have to care for a confused parent. Studies describe the signs and symptoms of the illness, but Gubrium takes all of this information and these facts as social constructions. He focuses on the way that members of the Alzheimer's community—physicians, family members, social service workers—create this disease through their discussions, writings, and interactions (Novak 1988).

Gubrium attended scientific conferences on Alzheimer's disease, meetings of the Alzheimer's Disease and Related Disorders Association (ADRDA), and caregiver support group meetings. He studied scholarly reports, monographs, the popular literature on the disease, and media reports. He studied the Alzheimer's community as an anthropologist might study a strange culture. He treated its members' speech and artefacts as the products of a unique subculture.

Gubrium shows that the members of the Alzheimer's community work together to make sense out of the disease's many contradictions. A caregiver, for example, "tries to make sense of what it is she deals with from day to day, in order to organize what, to her, seem to be reasonable courses of action in response" (Gubrium 1986, 69). Other members—neurologists, nurses, support group leaders—have their own reasons for making sense of the disease.

And each one of these actors uses different methods and bits of information to create a sensible account of the illness. Biologists see the disease as a puzzle. They use bits of tissue and slides of brain cells to make sense of it. The ADRDA sees it as an enemy and uses terms like fight, war, mission, and conquest to define members' activities and goals.

Gubrium's study shows the way that interested people create an entity, called Alzheimer's disease, that they can understand and talk about. He also shows how they form a linguistic community and a culture around the disease they have created. His study questions the meaning of common sense concepts like aging, disease, and treatment and asks gerontologists to pay attention to the social construction of reality that they often take for granted. Phenomenological studies like this one can sensitize all of us to the many meanings that aging can have. They also show that people play a vital role in creating the social world they live in.

The interpretive perspective has weaknesses as well as strengths. Like all perspectives it gives only one point of view on social life. Cockerham (1991) says that this perspective makes too little of the connections that exist among interactions, interpretations, and macro-level social phenomena like the economics of the health care system. This means that it cannot answer many of the questions gerontologists ask. The interpretive perspective, for example, cannot tell us how health care policies will have to change to serve an aging society. It also says little about power and conflict between social groups. For example, it cannot explain income inequality between men and women in old age or the effects of ethnicity on social status in later life. Fortunately, the normative and conflict perspectives do look at these questions.

### The Normative Perspective

The normative perspective holds that "social order is based on cooperation, interdependence, and shared values, adjustment by the individual to society, and societal equilibrium" (McDaniel 1989, 52). Wilson (1970) contrasts this normative perspective with that of the interpretive. While the interpretive perspective asks, "How do people create their social world through interaction with one another?" the normative asks, "What is the structure of society that people live in and how do the parts of this structure function?"

The structural-functionalist theories (Parsons 1937, 1951) that grew out of Emile Durkheim's work in nineteenth-century France best express the normative perspective. Durkheim's studies, *The Division of Labor* and *Suicide* serve as models for this approach. **Structural-functionalist theories** treat society as a system that consists of social institutions like the family, the military, and educational institutions. These systems keep society in a dynamic equilibrium. They adjust to one another as the system responds to internal and external pressures. For example, the increased number of women in the labour force has led to a decrease in the number of full-time family caregivers for frail older people. This, in turn, has led to more community care programs sponsored by government health services. The health care system has changed to meet new family demands, and this change serves the useful function of restoring society's balance.

Structural-functionalism sometimes draws the analogy between society and a living organism. Just as our bodies, for example, will adjust to an increase in our blood sugar, so will society adjust to changes in its internal condition. An increase in the number of older people, for example, may lead society to increase funding to health promotion programs. Structural-functionalism predicts that society will attempt to create an orderly transition to a new stable state.

Structural-functionalism also assumes that shared norms and values shape individual behaviour. People conform to these norms through social pressure, but also through belief in society's underlying value system. The values expressed in the commandment "Honour thy father and mother" show up in everyday behaviour and in social policies. Failure to honour a parent may lead to informal sanctions, like criticism from a sister or brother. Extreme neglect may lead to the charge of elder abuse and legal sanctions. Functionalism draws connections between large-scale (macro) social structures and individual action.

Finally, structural-functionalism assumes that society changes or evolves in a positive direction. It explains social problems as dysfunctions, and it proposes to correct these dysfunctions through the use of experts in planning and the helping professions (McDaniel and Agger 1982)

Gerontologists have used the normative perspective more than any other perspective in their study of aging. Gerontology's most influential theories, disengagement theory (Cumming and Henry 1961), activity theory (Neugarten, Havighurst, and Tobin 1968) (both discussed in Chapter 6), and **modernization theory** (a theory that describes the transition from traditional to modern society, discussed in Chapter 3) (Cowgill and Holmes 1972) all rely on structural-functionalist assumptions. Riley (1971, 1987; Riley, Johnson, and Foner 1972; Riley, Foner, and Waring 1988) also produced a dominant theory based on structural-functional principles: age stratification theory.

**Age stratification theory** focuses on the flow of age cohorts through the life cycle. Gerontologists define an **age cohort** as a group of people born in the same period of time. All of the people born between 1945 and 1954, for example, form an age cohort. According to age stratification theory, people in each cohort move or flow through society's predetermined age grades as they age. (An **age grade** is a period of life defined by society.

Childhood, adolescence, and young-adulthood, for example, are all age grades in Canada.)

People born in the same period experience the transitions from one stage to another at roughly the same time. They also experience the same historical events at the same time in their life cycle. People who are in their 40s today, for example, experienced the cultural changes of the 1960s in their teens and early 20s. These people still have an interest in the music of that period, and easy listening or soft rock radio programs cater to this large group. People in their 30s today lived through the 1960s as children. They may recall the events of that decade, but the cultural, social, and political turmoil of those years had less effect on them.

Riley (1987) says that society also changes as people age. So, the norms and roles learned by each new cohort change as society changes. The norms of adult behaviour that people learn in their childhood, for example, may no longer fit when these same people reach adulthood. Many older people today, for example, learned in their childhood that sex was immoral outside of marriage. Now, due to widowhood or the influence of the changed values of their children and grandchildren on them, many older people have had to rethink this point of view. Younger people will similarly have to make changes in their own values as they age and as society changes.

Age cohorts constantly move along as if on an escalator. As one group leaves an age grade a new group takes their place. Each age grade (youth, young adulthood, and so on) places expectations on its members and offers people new roles. Also, each cohort brings new norms and values to its age grade. This leads to a dialectic between individuals and societal structures. Changes in norms and values lead to changes in social organizations. These changes, in turn, shape the process of aging. For example, new cohorts of older people, with interests in travel and education, will bring changes to the traditional programs offered in senior centres. Some senior centres may close because they cannot meet the demands of these new seniors. Others may remain open by adapting their programs to serve newer cohorts of older people. These changes in programs will also change the way younger and middle-aged people think about later life.

Age stratification theory relies on many of the assumptions of the structural-functional approach to aging (Estes, Wallace, and Binney 1989). First, it assumes that norms and values influence individual aging. Second, it describes the relationship between the individual and society as a feedback loop. Change begins with the individual cohort or with large-scale historical or social change. These changes then lead to change in other parts of the social system. Third, it tends to see society as a homogeneous set of structures and functions that all people experience in the same way.

This perspective has its limits. For example, people of the same age do not all experience the world in the same way. The age stratification theory overlooks each person's interpretation of the world (Passuth and Bengtson 1988). The theory also makes little reference to the tensions and conflicts between social groups in society. It says little, for example, about the differences between growing old as a poor woman compared to growing old as an upper middle-class man. Streib and Bourg (1984) have criticized this theory for the latter reason. They say it overlooks inequality within age cohorts (e.g., social class differences between people aged 30–39 years old) and that such variations within cohorts may have a greater influence on people's lives than the norms and values related to their age grade. A person's race or gender will lead to different behaviours and to different responses to sociohistorical events even for people in the same age cohort. A policy change, like a decrease in government pension payments, will have differing effects on poor and wealthy seniors.

Cockerham (1991, 60) sums up this critique when he says that "a weakness of age stratification theory is that differences within, not just between, age cohorts are not given sufficient consideration. Besides socioeconomic factors, gender, race, and ethnicity may also shape the aging experience within cohorts, and age stratification theory does not account for such differences." Still, age stratification theory has made a major contribution to our understanding of aging. It orders many complex phenomena and accounts for the relationship between the individual and society.

## *The Conflict Perspective*

Few gerontologists have used the conflict perspective in their work. But a new interest has developed in social conflict and aging. Researchers have begun to study the causes of poverty in later life, women and gender discrimination, the ideology of aging as a social problem, and pensions and policies (McDaniel 1989). The conflict perspective holds that society consists of conflicts between dominant and subordinate social groups (McDaniel and Agger 1982).

The **political economy theory** that grew out of the work of Karl Marx exemplifies the conflict perspective. This theory focuses on conflict and change in social life. It traces this conflict to the struggle between social classes and to the resulting dominance of some groups and the subordination of others in society.

Marxist theory, for example, predicts that because older workers work more slowly and have less stamina, they will become less useful to industry as they get older. Companies will tend to fire or retire older workers and hire younger, faster workers at lower wages.

Work on the political economy of aging looks at aging in the modern state. Gerontologists have looked at the influence of global economics on the treatment of older people in developing nations (Hendricks 1982), the impact of retirement and pensions on aging (Myles 1984), and social policy in an aging society (Estes 1979; Guillemard 1983).

The political economy approach traces the origins of older peoples' problems to the political and economic structure of capitalist society. It also looks at how social programs and policies for older people serve the interests of middle-aged, middle-class professionals.

Myles (1984) used the political economy approach to study pensions in Canada and other liberal democracies. He traces the development of modern, state-run pension plans to the struggle between labour and the owners of the means of production. Workers today expect pensions to form part of their wage package, but employers resist paying this money. For this reason employers support government pension programs. This allows them to pay less into workers' pension programs.

Myles (citing Murphy 1982) says that for this reason Canada's Old Age Security Act of 1951 gained the support of industrialists. More recently labour unions have played an important role in deciding pension entitlements. Myles (1984) reports that increased labour union organization leads to better public pensions, as do increased political power of working class parties, and the right to strike. He also found that the electoral process itself leads to better pensions. Political parties pay attention to have-not voters when an active electoral process exists.

Myles's (1984) work shows the strengths of the political economy approach to aging. First, it places the study of aging in the context of large political, historical, economic, and social forces. Second, it views public pensions as the outcome of a struggle between competing groups. Third, it predicts that economic and political forces will shape future changes in public pensions. Myles (1984, 120) says that

> ...both the right to retire and the rights of the retired are the outcome of a political process. Thus, politics, not demography, determines the size of the elderly population. The social, legal, and political constituency we now call the elderly was created and given form by social, political, and economic forces; it can be destroyed or transformed by these same forces.

The political economy approach looks beyond the individual to understand the forces that shape individual aging today. It broadens gerontologists' understanding of aging and offers another way to interpret the origins and effects of social policies. Estes (1979), for example, shows how welfare programs lead to more middle-class jobs for service workers, but often fail to help older people.

The political economy approach emphasizes the impact of history and economics on individuals, but it sometimes overemphasizes the poverty and problems older people face. It also tends to view the individual as the product of political and economic forces and pays little attention to individuals' interpretations of social life. It says little about the ways that individuals shape their world through their interactions with others. Still, the political economy perspective presents a valuable way to understand the impact of society on the individual.

## The Future of Gerontological Theory

Baum and Baum (1980) have summed up the characteristics of gerontological theories. First, they say that in most cases gerontologists have adapted their theories from other social sciences. Social scientists, for example, have used modernization theory for many years to describe the transition from a rural, traditional society to an urban, modern society in developing nations. They have also used interactionist theory and the political economy approach to study relationships and institutions in modern society.

Second, Baum and Baum (1980) say that most gerontological theories describe relationships between age groups. **Disengagement theory**, for example, views retirement as a way to create a smooth transition from one generation to the next. Political economy theory studies the conflict between age groups over the use of economic resources.

Third, all of these theories try to make sense of the complex, multidimensional fact of aging. They show that no single explanation of aging can account for everything we know.

What theoretical ideas will emerge in social gerontology in the years ahead? Moody (1988b), Kenyon (1988), and others support the wider use of interpretive theories in gerontology. **Dialectical theory** (one type of interpretive theory), for example, says that aging has many dimensions (physical, psychological, social, and historical). Dialectical theory focuses on the asynchronies that exist between these dimensions. For example, a sudden illness (a physical change) or the death of a spouse (a social loss) can lead to a psychological crisis. Dialectical gerontology highlights the crises and tensions in individual and social life. It argues that these moments of crisis force a person to reflect critically on his or her own life and on the social environment. This reflection on life crises and our responses to them lead to growth and development. Dialectical theory and other interpretive theories (hermeneutic and critical theories) work to foster self-understanding and personal development.

Future theorists may look to the natural sciences for new theoretical insights. Some theorists, for example, have already used the general systems, catastrophe, and nonequilibrium systems theories, which are based on biological, mathematical, and thermodynamical research, respectively (Schroots 1988). Gerontological theories offer many explanations of aging. Their variety reflects the many dimensions of gerontological research. Each of these perspectives gives us a different insight into what it means to age.

## RESEARCH ISSUES AND METHODS

### Research Issues

Gerontologists use a variety of theories to direct their research and explain their findings. They also use a number of methods that help them to study the process of aging. The proper use of these methods ensures that researchers come up with reliable and valid findings. Improper use can lead to biased and confusing results. The following discussion will give a glimpse of the methodological issues that gerontologists face.

Hendricks and Hendricks (1981) say that studies done on aging in the 1960s, for example, supported many of the negative stereotypes of aging. These studies often focused on sick and institutionalized older people. There were also many conceptual and methodological problems. A whole line of research, for instance, concluded that intelligence decreases as people age. This research supported the view that people get "simple-minded" as they get older. Later studies (Schaie and Labouvie-Vief 1974) showed that this research confused **age differences** (differences between people of different ages) with **age changes** (changes due to aging). Baltes and Schaie (1982) found that younger cohorts (groups of people born at the same time) had more education than older cohorts, and more education may have led to higher intelligence scores. Educational level, they said, accounts for a large part of the intelligence difference between younger and older people.

These studies show the problems gerontologists face when they try to describe changes due to aging. Schaie (1968, 560) describes three kinds of effects that can confound findings on age changes: (1) maturational changes—changes due to aging; (2) cohort differences—the fact that younger cohorts may differ genetically from older cohorts (e.g., in strength or height); and (3) environmental (or period effects)—changes in culture like the increase in formal schooling, historical events like a war, or changes in the quality of life like cleaner water and air. Researchers have developed methods to disentangle these effects.

Much of the early research on aging used the **cross-sectional method**. This method allowed researchers to gather data in a short time at a low cost, but it caused (and still causes) problems. As the early intelligence studies show, cross-sectional studies confound environmental effects (such as lower education levels in older cohorts) with age changes (e.g., changes in intelligence due to increasing age). The findings from cross-sectional studies cannot tell us whether aging (maturation) leads to changes in intelligence, health, or any other variable that changes over time.

**Longitudinal research designs** attempt to overcome this problem. A longitudinal study looks at a single group of people at two or more points in time. For example, a longitudinal study of how aging affects intelligence might test the same group of people at ten-year intervals. These results give a truer picture of the effects of age on intelligence, because this kind of study avoids the problem of trying to compare different cohorts (e.g., people with different educational backgrounds). Gerontologists use longitudinal studies when they want to learn about age changes (Birren 1968, 549; Hultsch and Deutsch 1981, 37), but this method also creates problems. Environmental changes—historical events, changes in the economy, or changes in political values—can confound changes due to aging.

A third method, **time-lag comparison**, tries to overcome the problems raised by simple cross-sectional and simple longitudinal designs. Time-lag studies look at different groups of people of the same age at different points in time (e.g., 70-year-olds in 1960, 1970, and 1980). This type of study tries to measure differences between cohorts. Like cross-sectional and longitudinal methods, the time-lag method also presents problems. It confounds cohort effects with environmental ones. If a research study finds that 70-year-olds in 1980 visited doctors less often than 70-year-olds did in 1960, this may be due to the better health of 70-year-olds in 1980 (a cohort effect) or it may be due to some change in the health care system like higher costs to users (an environmental effect).

Each type of study creates problems when it comes to interpreting results. In addition, longitudinal and time-lag studies pose practical problems. First, they often take many years to complete—years that researchers must wait before they can show results to granting agencies or to the public. Second, they are expensive to set up and maintain. Third, subjects in longitudinal studies drop out (or die), biasing results in later rounds of the study (Birren 1968, 549).

Gerontologists have solved some of these problems by turning simple cross-sectional and simple longitudinal designs into sequential designs. Birren (1968) describes a sequential design as a series of cross-sectional studies during a longer longitudinal study. The cross-sectional studies allow for

· · · · · · · · · · · · · · · · · · · · · · · · · · · · · · · · ·

## Exhibit 2.3

Longitudinal vs. Cross-Sectional Designs

· · · · · · · · · · · · · · · · · · · · · · · · · · · · · · · · ·

The chart below shows the difference between cross-sectional and longitudinal designs. The cross-sectional study took place in 1930. It studied three age groups (10-, 20-, and 30-year-olds) in that year. The longitudinal study also began in 1930. But it measured the 1930 birth cohort three more times (in 1940, 1950, and 1960) at three different ages (10, 20, and 30 years old). The time-lag study measured 30-year-olds at four different times (1930, 1940, 1950, and 1960).

| Cohort | Time of Measurement | | | | |
|--------|------|------|------|------|------|
| 1900 | 1900 | 1910 | 1920 | 1930 | Cross-Sectional |
| 1910 | 1910 | 1920 | 1930 | 1940 | |
| 1920 | 1920 | 1930 | 1940 | 1950 | Time-Lag |
| 1930 | 1930 | 1940 | 1950 | 1960 | Longitudinal |
| | 0 | 10 | 20 | 30 | |

Age

**Source:** Adapted from P.B. Baltes, H.W. Reese, and J.R. Nesselroade, *Life-span Developmental Psychology: Introduction to Research Methods* (Monterey, California: Brooks/Cole, 1977).

· · · · · · · · · · · · · · · · · · · · · · · · · · · · · · · · ·

quick data collection. The longitudinal study provides a check on cross-sectional findings. These two methods together also provide time-lag data on the sampled members of same-aged groups at different times.

The Aging in Manitoba study (Government of Manitoba 1973) offers this kind of option to researchers by providing comparable data on health and health care needs for a random sample of older people in the province at different points in time. This type of study allows researchers to compare the needs of different age groups in a given year (e.g., 66–75-year-olds and 76–85-year-olds in 1971) (Havens 1980). It also allows researchers to study the changes in these groups' needs over time (whether the needs of the sample of 76–85-year-olds have changed in the ten years from 1971 to 1981). It also allows researchers to see whether social changes have affected all age groups (e.g., whether all groups of older people use hospitals more in 1971 than in 1981). Researchers can then separate period effects—effects due to social change (e.g., new medical care policies)—from effects due to aging (such as the need for more medical care as a person ages).

Botwinick (1984) shows that these complex designs still do not unconfound time of measurement, age, and cohort effects, though they do give researchers more information about the group under study. He concludes that unconfounding variables takes a great deal of time and effort. Without the effort, the researchers could make a fundamental error in understanding, but even with it, the researcher still has to explain, for example, what specific historical events led to changes in health care use or how these events translated themselves into different behaviours. "Separating the confounds," he says, "is not the end of the line, it is but the beginning" (1984, 400). Whatever method the researcher chooses, Botwinick's final comment on methods still holds: "Common sense and logic," he says, "must accompany the analysis separating the confounded variables" (1984, 403).

## Types of Research Methods

Gerontologists use psychological tests and surveys to study aging, but they also use other research methods. Researchers in each dimension of aging (biomedical, psychosocial, socioeconomic-environmental) have their preferred methods.

- - - - - - - - - - - - - - - - - - - - - - - - - - - - - - - - - - - - - - - -

## Exhibit 2.4

Research Methods Most Often Used in Each Dimension of Gerontology

- - - - - - - - - - - - - - - - - - - - - - - - - - - - - - - - - - - - - - - -

**Biomedical Research**
Laboratory experiments
Controlled studies
Field trials (e.g., of medications)
Clinical examinations

**Psychosocial research**
Performance tests
Paper-and-pencil tests
Questionnaires
Participant observation field work
Case studies

**Socioeconomic-environmental research**
Questionnaires
Census and other archival data
Documents
Cost-benefit analysis

- - - - - - - - - - - - - - - - - - - - - - - - - - - - - - - - - - - - - - - -

Pharmacologists, chemists, and neurophysiologists, for example, use laboratory techniques and controlled experiments to study aging; historians use libraries, archives, diaries, and even paintings (Fischer 1978; Aries 1962); literary scholars use plays, novels, and poetry (Berman and Sobkowska-Ashcroft 1985; Berman and Sobkowska-Ashcroft 1986; Berman and Sobkowska-Ashcroft 1987; de Beauvoir 1978; Manning 1989). Some studies require more than one method—a questionnaire survey of a large population, for example, may include a psychological test, and an anthropological field study may include the study of a society's literature and history as well as a measurement of the people's physical condition.

Researchers have recently expanded their interest in certain research issues. Statistics Canada publications for general use, for example, now routinely include separate information on age groups over age 65 (e.g., groups aged 65–74, and 75+) (Statistics Canada 1990e). This presentation of data recognizes that age cohorts among the 65+ group often differ from one another. It also recognizes that we need more information about the growing population of very old people. Researchers also focus more now on the differences between men and women as they age. Studies of retirement, widowhood, and social life, among other topics, all show the importance of gender differences in later life (Burwell 1984; Streib and Binstock 1990). Sociohistorical methods and critical analyses of data have developed with the growth of a political economy approach to aging. Studies of retirement policies (Myles 1984), for example, have used this approach. Gerontologists' interests continue to grow and expand. As this happens, researchers will develop and use the methods that best answer their questions.

## GERONTOLOGY TODAY

Research on aging in Canada has increased in the last ten to fifteen years, and it will continue to increase as the population ages. One series of monographs presents a detailed review of research in Canada on selected topics. The monographs include studies of demographic change (McDaniel 1986), ethnicity (Driedger and Chappell 1987), retirement (McDonald and Wanner 1990), and family ties (Connidis 1989a). The federal government in 1985 conducted a General Social Survey that focused on health and social supports. Reports from this research (Statistics Canada 1987; Stone 1988) give a detailed look at family and social supports throughout Canada.

In December 1987, Health and Welfare Canada, along with experts from various disciplines, developed the first national study of Alzheimer's disease and other dementias. Health and Welfare Canada funded a Collaborative Study Centre to conduct the study. The centre linked the University of Ottawa's Department of Epidemiology with the federal Laboratory Centre for Disease Control and with researchers from universities across the country.

The study took place in five parts of the country: British Columbia, the Prairie region, Ontario, Quebec, and the Atlantic region. Each region contains a consortium of researchers who work through a total of eighteen study centres. Each study centre will conduct the core study, but most will also focus on a single topic of interest to researchers in that region. This study will produce the first national picture of the incidence and impact of dementia in Canada. It will also produce some of the first nation-wide data of this kind in the world.

In May 1988, the Canadian Strategy for Science and Technology (Innov-Action) spent $240 million to establish Networks of Centres of Excellence across Canada. The program will sponsor between ten and twenty projects in order to "promote fundamental and long term applied research and to provide an opportunity for the nation's best researchers to work together in support of Canada's long term industrial competitiveness" (Inter-Council 1988, 1). Research in this program includes psychological research on the older worker and research into the development of new technologies for an aging society.

These studies show a trend toward large-scale, collaborative research. They also show that Canada's pool of gerontologists has grown in size and in expertise. Collaborative studies save money by pooling researchers' skills and resources. They also create interdisciplinary teams that can carry out sophisticated analyses of large data sets.

This research and the many other studies conducted by researchers throughout Canada expand our understanding of aging. They also help governments, social service agencies, and professionals to plan better programs for older people.

Chappell (1982b, 65) suggests five strategies for improving communication between researchers and practitioners: (1) researchers and practitioners should talk and listen to one another; (2) researchers should teach more research courses designed for practitioners (and practitioners should take them); (3) organizations that fund research should set up meetings between researchers and service delivery staff; (4) agencies should meet with graduate students to let them know about data sources for their research, and (5) researchers should present their findings at public forums to shape policy for the elderly.

This collaboration between researchers and practitioners will also open researchers to new research questions. Practitioners can tell researchers about their concerns and the concerns of their organizations. This can lead to co-sponsored research projects. Older people themselves should also have more input into the research process. They can serve on advisory boards to research centres, they can attend research forums, and they can encourage governments to sponsor more research to meet their needs.

Universities, colleges, and technical schools have begun to add gerontology courses to their programs. Many universities also sponsor certificate programs in gerontology. These programs allow professionals who work with the elderly—nurses, social workers, dentists, policy planners—to learn more about the latest research on aging. Nearly all provinces also have a social services division that directs programs for the elderly and a provincial gerontologist or a gerontology consultant who helps create new programs based on the latest research (Health and Welfare Canada 1982b). All of this activity makes gerontology one of the fastest-growing and most exciting fields today.


## SUMMARY

1. Three broad areas make up the field of gerontology—biomedicine, psychosocial studies, and socioeconomic-environmental studies. Social gerontology includes psychosocial and socioeconomic-environmental studies. It also includes practice-related research.

2. Gerontologists use theory to guide their research and to interpret their results. Micro- and macro-level theories exist. These include interpretive, normative, and conflict theories. Each theory gives a different and valuable insight into aging.

3. New theoretical approaches draw on current thinking in the natural sciences (general systems theory and catastrophe theory) and the social sciences (dialectical theory).

4. Gerontologists have developed methods to disentangle age effects (changes due to age) from changes in groups due to differences in cohorts, historical events, and the effects of repeated testing.

5. Gerontologists also borrow methods from traditional disciplines like biology, chemistry, history, philosophy, and anthropology. Researchers have begun to shift their interests as their knowledge grows. New statistical reports now present separate statistics for the oldest age groups. New critical methods of analysis have also emerged as gerontology has grown.

6. New research thrusts in Canada will provide national data on Alzheimer's disease, caregiver burden, and the application of research to creating products for older people.

7. Gerontology today is one of the fastest-growing fields of study. It can make old age a better time of life by increasing knowledge about aging and by modifying or creating social structures that meet the needs of older people.

## SELECTED READINGS

Birren, James E., and Vern L. Bengtson, eds., *Emergent Theories in Aging*. New York: Springer, 1988.

Reviews of social scientific theories as they apply to gerontology, traditional gerontological theories, and new theoretical perspectives. This books shows the growing richness of theoretical work on aging today.

# *Historical Change*

# Aging Then and Now

## INTRODUCTION

In Laurel Creek, West Virginia, old men retire to the porch. They watch the traffic go by, they talk to friends and neighbours, and they arrange for part-time work. Life on the porch in the early years of retirement allows a man to keep in contact with the community. When a man gets older and his health fails, life on the porch allows him to draw on his social credit. People stop to check on him, and they make trips to the store to get his groceries. If bad health keeps him indoors, his absence from the porch alerts people that he may need extra help. When a man nears death he may come out to the porch to receive last visits from friends and neighbours. Life on the porch keeps a man part of the community until he dies (adapted from *Human Behavior Magazine* 1977).

Life on the porch matches an ideal we have of late old age. It reminds us of another time—a time when people grew up and died in the same town, when neighbours knew one another well, and when the young respected the old. Today many people feel that old age has become worse. We push old people aside in retirement, advertisers tell everyone to "think young," and even birthday cards make fun of aging. One card reads, "Roses are red, violets are blue, thank goodness I'm not older than you." It seems that in the past people enjoyed old age, but that in modern society this is less so because older people get little respect or attention.

Has old age become worse over time? Did simpler societies offer a Golden Age to the old? Or do we just like to believe things were better in the past?

Social gerontologists try to answer these questions. They take two approaches: some gerontologists study ancient societies to see how such societies viewed and treated older people; others study modern societies to see how different social structures lead to different experiences of old age. This chapter will examine both points of view. It will look at: (1) how aging differs in different types of societies, (2) how social structures affect aging, and (3) how aging today differs from aging in the past.

## THREE TYPES OF SOCIETIES

This chapter looks at aging in three distinctly different types of society: (1) hunting and gathering, (2) agricultural, and (3) industrial and post-industrial. These societies range in order from the simplest to the most complex kinds of social structures and from the most ancient societies to the most modern. They give a picture of how aging has changed over time.

### Hunting and Gathering Societies

Humans lived in hunting and gathering bands for a million years or more and only settled into agriculture between ten and twenty thousand years ago (Bronowski 1976). People in hunting and gathering societies survive by gathering wild plants and by stalking or trapping wild game. These groups (sometimes as few as twenty people) move constantly from place to place in search of food. They resemble an extended family. Their technology is simple, consisting mainly of bows, spears, and fire, and they have no permanent settlement.

Archaeologists estimate that people in hunting and gathering societies had a maximum life expectancy of 40 years and a normal life expectancy of about 18 years (Lerner 1970; Cutler and Harootyan 1975; Howells 1960). Cowgill and Holmes (1972) report that these societies defined a person as old by age 45 or 50; and Simmons (1970; 1960), in a study of seventy-one contemporary simple societies, says that people in these societies were considered old at 50 or 60 years of age. He estimates, on the basis of scarce data, that these societies rarely had more than 3 percent of their people over age 65. Therefore, when the terms "old" and "elderly" are used here in connection with simple societies, they refer to people 50 to 60 years old.

Cowgill (1972), and Press and McKool (1972) present four conditions that lead to support for an older person in simple societies. First, the person needs an important role to play in social life; second, the older person must live near and fit into their extended family; third, he or she must control some important material or informational resource; and fourth, the group must value the group rather than personal development (Sokolovsky 1990). Few simple societies fulfil all of these conditions. So, treatment of older people varies among them.

Amoss and Harrell (1981) say that one condition more than the others leads to a good old age in primitive societies. They say the old have high status when their contribution to subsistence outweighs their cost to the group. Older people do well when they still have a valued role to play in the culture. Their ability to give to the group depends on two things: first, the culture must offer alternate roles for older people to play as they lose their strength, and, second, the older person must have good health.

The Inuit (Eskimo) of Canada serve as a good example of a present-day hunting and gathering society. They live in a climate that demands physical strength to survive, but they love and respect their elders and allow their older members to take part in social life as long as they can. Men, for example, "retire" slowly from work. As a man loses his strength, younger male members of the community or household do more of the winter hunting. The older man may then take shorter hunting trips or teach the young how to hunt. Older Inuit women have an easier time moving into old age than do men (this is true of women in most nomadic societies). They pass the heavy work on to younger women and spend more time taking care of the children.

Older men and women find their own ways to adapt to decreases in their strength. Older men will start to hunt early in the spring in order to stockpile food for the winter. They may also strike a bargain with a young hunter—the older man may fix the gear while the younger man hunts. Older women sometimes adopt children. The Inuit allow their elders to play new roles in society as their health and strength decline. For example, the Inuit value their old as much for their knowledge and wisdom as for their work. A person still gives something to the group when he or she recalls and passes on the knowledge of Inuit lore. This social role makes the old person useful to the group and improves his or her status and treatment in the community.

Not all groups make these arrangements for older members. The Chipewyan, for instance, who live in Canada's northern prairies, have no roles for older men to play. The Chipewyan do not place a high value on knowledge of tribal lore or craftwork. A man has status when he succeeds at

. . . . . . . . . . . . . . . . . . . . . . . . . . . . . . . . . . . . . . . . .

## Exhibit 3.1

### Do Nomadic People Abandon Their Elders?

. . . . . . . . . . . . . . . . . . . . . . . . . . . . . . . . . . . . . . . . .

In any nomadic society, if people live too long and become decrepit or demented, the group may abandon or kill them.

Jacob Bronowski (1976) shows this in his film *The Harvest of the Seasons*. In Iran, he follows a nomadic group called the Bakhtiari on their yearly journey to their summer pastures. The tribe climbs over six mountain ranges, through high passes and snow, until it reaches the Bazuft river.

Bronowski says the test for the group comes at the river. The Bazuft, a trickle in summer, swells each year with melting snow and spring rain. The group—men, women, and animals—must swim across. For the young, crossing the Bazuft stands as a test of adulthood. For them, life begins, but for the old, Bronowski says, life ends.

The camera records in detail the struggle to cross the river. The current batters horses, donkeys, sheep, goats, and people. The young men swim for their lives and help the animals get across. But then the camera pulls back to focus on two figures among the rocks—a dog and an old man. The dog races back and forth looking from the man to the group below. The man sits silently with his back against the rocks

watching the tribe cross the river. No emotion shows on his face. He no longer has the strength to cross the river, and the tribe will go on without him. "Only the dog is puzzled to see a man abandoned," Bronowski says. "The man accepts the nomad custom; he has come to the end of his journey … " (1976, 64).

Life in many nomadic cultures demands this kind of choice. The tribe must move on to survive, and the old, who cannot keep up, get left behind. This man accepts his fate. He may have left his own parents to die in the same way. This dramatic case shows the dark side of life in primitive society. "In a vigorous community," Turnbull (1961, 35–36) says, "where mobility is essential, cripples and infirm people can be a handicap and may even endanger the safety of the group."

A study by Maxwell and Silverman (1977, 37) found that 80 percent of the societies that devalued the elderly lived as nomads for at least part of the year. The harsher the environment, the greater the chance a group will kill or abandon its aged. Killing the aged shows up most often in societies that have irregular food supplies, move often, and live in severe climates (Simmons 1970, 240).

. . . . . . . . . . . . . . . . . . . . . . . . . . . . . . . . . . . . . . . . .

hunting, but when he stops hunting he loses respect and power in the group—people label him "elderly." Men will do anything to avoid this label. Some continue to hunt even when their health fails. Sharp (1981) reports the case of a man who had just recovered from a heart attack and had emphysema, but still went into the bush alone. His wife worried that he would kill himself through overexertion, but he would rather have risked his life than be called old. The Chipewyan offer fewer options to older men than do the Inuit.

Researchers report that hunting and gathering societies distinguish between two different stages of old age. In the first, a person retires from the heavy work of middle age, but he or she still has good health. In the second stage, the older person gets sick or becomes demented or frail. Simmons (1960) calls people in this second group the "overaged."

In Inuit society, for example, older people keep their status as long as they do some useful work for the group. Their status drops if illness makes them dependent. People make fun of the frail elderly, say nasty things to them, or ignore them. The "overaged" get the worst cuts of meat, have little money, and have to do without trade goods. A stranger may take in an Inuit who outlives his or her spouse, children, and close relatives, but this person will get little respect and will have to do the worst work (Guemple 1977).

The Inuit also abandon their aged when they become liabilities to the group. They do this as a last resort, and they encourage the older person to make the decision (Guemple 1980). But sometimes the group will withdraw its support rapidly, thus hastening death (Glascock and Feinman, 1981, 27).

Glascock and Feinman found this same ambivalence to old age in fifty-seven simple societies they studied. They found that in 35 percent of the societies younger people treated older members well, and in 80 percent young people showed respect for the aged (1981). Many of these same societies abandoned and killed their elderly (Koty 1933; Maxwell and Silverman 1977). Glascock and Feinman (1981) found nonsupportive treatment (abandoning and killing the aged) in some form in 84 percent of the simple societies they studied. This, they say, contradicts the idea that all simpler societies support the aged. Research shows that simpler societies vary in how they treat the aged and that treatment of the aged often depends on how much an older person contributes to or takes from the group.

## Agricultural Society

People in agricultural societies live on food produced from farming the land. These societies have more complex technologies than hunting and gathering societies. They also have more complex social structures, including social classes and bureaucracies.

Humans settled into villages and cities for the first time—in the Middle East, China, and India—about ten thousand years ago at the end of the last Ice Age. For the first time in human history, societies gathered a surplus of food. In these societies older people often owned property, and they used property rights to get support from the young. "Property rights," Simmons (1970, 36) says, "have been lifesavers for the aged ... The person who controlled property was able to get more out of life and to get it much longer. Indeed, the importance of property for old age security can hardly be overrated."

As a general rule, in agricultural societies, those with land command the most respect, those without land the least. All over the world, property rights create a legal dependence of the young on the old (Amoss and Harrell 1981). Old people among the Gwembe Tonga of Zambia today, for example, get power by owning livestock and land (Colson and Scudder 1981). Older people among the Etal Islanders of Micronesia gain respect when they own property. The Etal look down on old people who hold on to all their land, but they think of a person as foolish if he or she gives it all away. The land serves as an inheritance bribe (Nason 1981).

Americans in the past also used property to hold power in old age. Fischer (1978) studied aging in the United States from 1607 to the present. He found that young men had to wait to inherit their fathers' land before they could start families. In the seventeenth and eighteenth centuries that meant a son might reach age 40 before he owned the farm. Fischer (1978, 52) calls the land "an instrument for generational politics"; parents used it to ensure good treatment in their old age.

Fischer (1978) also found that coercion like this bred hostility. The diaries of Colonel Landon Carter, for example, report signs of growing anger between the younger and older generations. One night in 1776, Colonel Carter reports, his son, Robert Wormeley Carter, invited friends over for gambling with cards. When the enraged Colonel ordered the game to stop, his son exploded and called his father a tyrant. The two men almost came to blows. After that the Colonel carried a pistol with him in the house. He wrote in his diary, "Surely it is happy our laws prevent parricide ... Good God! That such a monster is descended from my loins!" (Greene 1965, 250, 310, 315, 713, 763, 1004, 1102, cited in Fischer 1978, 75).

Other agricultural societies in the past also expressed their dislike for the aged, some more openly than Americans. Aristophanes mocked the old in his plays; Aristotle derided the way most people grew old (though he thought a philosopher could live a good life even in old age); and, in the Renaissance Machiavelli, portrayed the old man as a lecherous fool in his play *La Clizia*.

Tension between the generations sometimes surfaced in song. An Austrian folksong (Berkner 1972, cited in Fischer 1978, 69) says:

*Papa, when will you give me the farm?*
*Papa, when will you give me the house?*
*When will you finally move to your little room*
*And tend your potato patch?*

Studies of English Canadians in the late nineteenth century show the same tensions between the young and the old. Historical accounts indicate that parents gave a great deal of thought to how they would pass their land down to their children (Gagan 1983b; Mays 1983), and the children, who worked to improve the family farm, sometimes into their thirties, expected to get it as a reward for their work. In 1853 Susannah Moodie wrote that "death is looked upon by many Canadians more as a matter of ... a change of property into other hands, than as a real domestic calamity" (Moodie 1853, cited in Gagan 1983b, 185).

Ontario farmers kept intergenerational tension low by passing the land down before they died. Synge (1980) says that the older people stayed on the land with the inheriting child and his family. The young or the old couple built a new house nearby. "They [the parents-in-law]," one woman says, "stayed on in the house till they built a place out back for them" (Synge 1980, 138). Getting the land early in life must have reduced some tensions between the generations, but it created others. Selling the land to the young, for example, risked the older generation's old-age security. Parents, when they did sell the land to their children, often kept a few acres for themselves to maintain their independence in old age (Mays 1983).

The content of farmers' wills also suggests some worry about future security. Wills stated exactly what the inheriting son was to do for his parents. One will describes in detail the kind of food ("flour, pork and butter and milk, potatoes and other vegetables"), the kind of firewood ("plenty of good wood ready for use"), the transportation ("a horse and buggy"), and the cash ("$100 a year") that a son had to give his mother for the rest of her life (Gagan 1983b, 186).

## Inequality in Old Age in Agricultural Society
Treatment of the aged in agricultural societies differed by social class. The elderly who owned land in these societies had power until they died. For this reason, older people who owned land commanded the greatest respect in societies from Canada to traditional China (Ikels 1981). The poor and landless lived less well and got little respect.

"To be old and poor and outcast in early America," Fischer (1978, 60) says, "was certainly not to be venerated but rather to be despised ... Old age seems actually to have intensified the contempt visited upon a poor man. A rich old man was the more highly respected because he was old, but the aged poor were often scorned." A New Jersey law in 1720 ordered police to search ships for old people and to send them away. In one case the crew of a ship placed a poor, sick old man on a barren island and left him there to die (Fischer 1978).

Fischer also describes drunk, crippled old men who hid in cellars and roamed the wharves at night looking for food. Poor old widows had low status too, but their womanhood made old age and poverty worse (as it did in most countries). Without money a woman was degraded and left to depend on others for support. Neighbours sometimes forced old widows to move away to keep poor rates down. Even their children sometimes turned them away. "If the aged poor were only a small minority [in early America]," Fischer (1978, 61) says, "their misery was great."

Laslett (1976) reports that in Elizabethan England the Poor Law of 1601 made children responsible for their aged parents—but only their parents. This excluded other relatives from aid by law. The existence of a law that spells out the relations between the generations suggests that custom bound children to their parents less than we may have thought. Laslett says that in some cases a parent who lived with his or her children got listed in official records as a "lodger, receiving parish relief" (1976, 95). In other cases the children moved into the family cottage and left their widowed mothers and sisters in poorhouses.

Stearns, in a study of customs in France, says that "older women were treated horribly in the popular culture of traditional society" (1977, 119). Villages expected widows over age 45 to stay single, and literature made fun of older women. Even the grandmother role got little prestige. Other historians have also documented the suffering of the aged poor in the past and in less industrialized societies (Hufton 1975). The large numbers of poor people and their misery argue against the idea of a Golden Age in pre-industrial society.

Agricultural society, in its treatment of older people, looks like a mirror image of primitive society. In the simplest societies the old had no wealth, but they received respect as long as they gave to the group. The !Kung San, for example, roam the Kalahari desert throughout their lives and have little property. The young revere their elders as storytellers, spiritual leaders, and healers (Biesele and Howell 1981). In agricultural societies the elderly get the most respect if they own property and keep it from their children until late in life or until they die. In agricultural society "a firm hold on the strings of a fat purse," Simmons (1970, 46) says, "was one effective compensation for declining physical powers" (see also Cowgill 1986, 108). The old may be respected in this kind of society, but they are not often loved by the young (Fischer 1978).

## Modern Industrial Society

The agricultural revolution created a new form of society. Agriculture produced a surplus of food and gave rise to the first cities. It created social classes and based status on ownership of property. This kind of society dominated until the middle of the eighteenth century, when three interrelated changes began to reshape social life: (1) industrialization, (2) urbanization, and (3) the demographic transition.

These changes took place over two hundred years, and they still affect society today. They began at various times in different places, and sometimes one type of change—economic change, demographic change, a change in values—had more influence on a society than another. Scholars still argue over which change came first in which society, but taken together these three changes revolutionized social life and led to a new age older people.

### *Industrialization*

By the nineteenth century most of Europe had begun to industrialize. Industry began to use steam and water power to increase productivity; the factory system gathered workers and raw materials in cities; and transportation systems spread the production of factories to all classes and countries. Some countries industrialized before others, and some more quickly, but by 1850 industrialization had changed the shape of European society (Stearns 1967).

Industrialization both caused and resulted from the breakup of rural life. Cottage industry, in which small groups of workers in villages produce mostly for local needs, failed as the factories produced more and cheaper goods. At the same time parents could no longer keep their sons on the farm with the promise of future inheritance. As death rates declined, families had too many sons who wanted the land. The younger sons had to move to the city to find work, and the city welcomed them as a cheap source of labour. The new pace of work and life in the city freed young people from traditional ties and beliefs (Stearns 1967) and led to a decrease in the status of older people.

Industrialization decreased the status of older people in another way. In North America in the twentieth century, the establishment of retirement rules, supported by both labour and management, forced older workers out of work. Management liked retirement because it allowed them to release workers who were costly because they had seniority. Unions supported retirement because in return they won seniority rights (first hired, last fired rules) from management (Haber 1978). In short, unions traded older workers' right to work for younger workers' job security. Retirement expressed in a formal rule the decline of the older person's status in industrial society.

## Urbanization

Canadian society changed from a rural to an urban one between 1851 and 1950. During the nineteenth century both men and women migrated to the cities. Cross (1983) found that Montreal attracted large numbers of young women from the crowded countryside. Bradbury (1983) describes Montreal in 1871 as a city in transition from pre-industrial to industrial life. Accounts of this time say little about the elderly.

Katz (1975) gives one of the few reports on what life was like for older people in a Canadian town. He studied Hamilton, Ontario, between 1851 and 1861. In a report on 597 land-owning men in 1851, he counted only twenty-six men aged 60 or over out of 597, or about 4 percent of the population. (Men among the poorer classes died younger and probably made up a smaller portion of the population than the land-owners.) Men who owned land had the most security in old age, and men aged 60 and over were the largest group of landowners. However, after age 60, Katz shows, a man's power began to decrease, and men over 60 had a greater chance of having less land from one year to the next than any other group. Men 60 and over were also the least likely to have a servant (a sign of wealth). After age 60, Katz (1975, 163) says, men often "decline[d] into difficult circumstances."

Synge (1980) says that in small businesses and on farms older people could adjust their work to suit their health and strength, but in industrial cities older people had to meet the demands of the workplace or quit. No public pensions existed in the nineteenth century, and many older people in the cities had no private savings. In addition, they often had to take the lowest forms of work, move into public homes for the aged, or live in poverty, especially if they were without children.

In North America, urban life undermined traditional society in another way. The cities supported a market system in which individuals could accumulate wealth outside the family structure. Inequality in society began to grow as some individuals gathered wealth for themselves through trade. Those who were successful turned from public affairs to private concerns. This focus on the self broke the individual's communal bonds, including those that linked the older to the younger generation (Fischer 1978).

Synge (1980), who studied working-class families in Ontario in the early twentieth century, found that city life made old age an uncertain time. Young people earned their own wages and gave money to their parents while they lived at home. But when these children grew up and moved out, parents lost this income. Few social services existed for older people, and an unmarried daughter often looked after her parents as they aged. Families sometimes passed the job of care from one child to the next. Synge reports the case of one old woman who lived for periods of time with each of her children for her last 25 years.

Katz (1975) found that few older people in Hamilton lived with their married children, and the poorest households were least likely to house an older relative. Only 8 percent of households in 1851 and 10 percent in 1861 had adults of two or more generations. "Only when old age and loneliness were combined," Katz (1975, 254) says, "would a parent move in with her children."

Katz (1975) also found that 58.8 percent of women aged 60–69 were widowed, almost double the rate of men. Women of the poorest social class (Irish Catholic women) faced an eight-times greater chance of widowhood than women of the highest class (Canadian-born Protestant women). Poor widows had little or no savings and no pensions from their husbands. The poorest women, especially those without children, would finally be recipients of charity (a special charity, the Ladies' Benevolent Society, grew up to help them) or live in a "house of refuge and industry" (Katz 1975; Synge 1980).

On the surface the new freedom and equality in urban industrial Canada made all people more alike, but for the old they meant a decrease in status. "A really democratic ethic," Cowgill (1986, 51) says, "is incompatible with any system of stratification based on ascribed statuses … You cannot have gerontocracy [rule of the eldest] and democracy at the same time."

## The Demographic Transition

The demographic transition refers to the changes in population that led to a high proportion of older people among the developed nations (of Europe and North America). This transition, which took place in North America at the end of the nineteenth century along with industrialization and urbanization, was a three-stage process. The stages outline how European and North American societies shifted from a youthful to an older population structure.

*Stage 1: 1300–1750.* Before the eighteenth century, population had been relatively stable. High birth rates were balanced by high death rates. French studies of the seventeenth century estimate that there were about eight children to a normal marriage and that about 70 percent of the households had children. Children made up 45 percent of the French population at that time (compared with half that rate in industrial societies today) (Laslett 1965).

Only a small number of people lived to old age in pre-industrial society. Figures exist only for scattered populations before 1800, but they give some idea of the proportions of people 65 and over. A national census in Iceland in

Exhibit 3.2

Demographic Transition Theory

The Demographic Transition

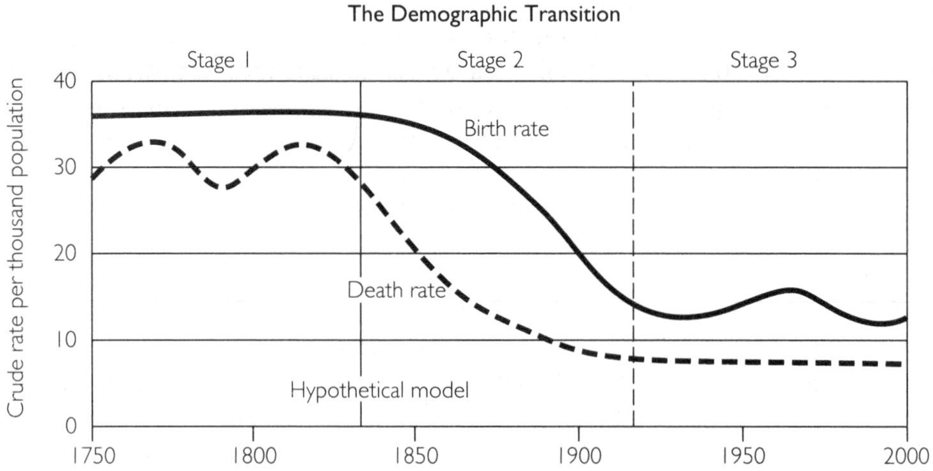

**Stage 1:** Demographic transition theory says that before industrialization, societies had high birth rates and high death rates. Population size stayed small because of the high (though variable) death rates. The proportion of old and young in society also stayed stable.

**Stage 2:** Industrialization led to a decrease in death rates. Birth rates stayed high, and the population grew in size. These societies had a growing proportion of young people.

**Stage 3:** Further into industrialization the birth rate dropped. Death rates stayed low, and population size stayed stable. The birth rate sometimes fluctuated (as with the Baby Boom of 1946–1964). Society has a growing proportion of older people.

Source: Chart based on McVey 1987, personal communication. Reprinted with permission of the author.

1703, for example, reported 4.6 percent of the population was 65 or over; Belgrade in 1733 reported 2.1 percent; and Nishinomiya, Japan, in 1713 reported 6.6 percent. A listing of counties in England from 1599 to 1796 showed people aged 65 or over made up between 1.4 percent and 6.4 percent of the population. Rarely in any of these places did the 65-or-over population top 10 percent, and Laslett (1976) cautions that past the age of 60 people tended to exaggerate their age.

*Stage 2: 1750–1850.* Three phenomena caused rapid population growth in Europe from 1750 on, and also changed the proportion of young and old people in society. First, the death rate decreased, because war fatalities decreased; the cycle of epidemics ended; improved hygiene in cities led to better health; border controls stopped the spread of disease; and food supplies increased due to better climate and more open land (Braudel 1981; Stearns 1967).

Second, the birth rate stayed high and in some cases increased. New lands opened and allowed earlier marriage in the countryside. Young people in the cities, who did not have to wait for their parents' land, married young. Better nutrition and more opportunity led people to have more children.

Third, more people lived to old age, and the proportion of older people in the population began to grow. In France, the first society in Europe to have an aged population, the proportion of the elderly rose from 7.3 percent of the population in 1776 to 10.1 percent in 1851 (Laslett 1976).

*Stage 3: 1850–Present.*     The birth rate and death rate in Western Europe had both declined by 1900. This completed the transition to an aging population. The biggest change in death rates came from improvements in the general standard of living. Diet and hygiene in the cities improved. Clean underwear, soap, coal for heat, and glass in the windows all helped people stay healthier. Improved housing and more efficient treatment of water and sewage decreased disease. As the standard of living rose, the virulence of disease—and so the death rate—declined.

These changes led all social classes to decrease the number of children per family (Stearns 1967). Middle-class families led the way. They had smaller families to ensure that their children would have the money needed to enter the middle class themselves. Rural families followed later in order to ensure that each of their children would get a good portion of land. Children had a different meaning in agricultural and industrial societies. In an agricultural society children are an economic asset: they help produce food, care for the farm, and increase a family's wealth. In an urban society children are an economic liability. They cost the individual family money to raise, and the family gets little economic benefit from them. These facts led to a decreased birth rate.

From 1850 onward the proportion of older people in the developed nations grew. Longer life expectancy meant that more people lived into old age. But more than anything else, it was the decrease in the birth rate after industrialization that led to a higher proportion of older people in society.

The three trends mentioned previously—industrialization, urbanization, and the demographic transition—put an end to almost all of the following conditions, each of which had supported the high status of older people:

1. Ownership and control of property
2. A monopoly on special knowledge
3. Ancestor worship and a high value placed on tradition (where the old provide a link to the gods)
4. Society organized around kinship and extended family
5. Small stable communities
6. High mutual dependence of group members
7. Small numbers of older people
8. Special roles for the aged (Rosow 1965; Eisdorfer 1981)

In the past two centuries the economy, the structure of family life, and the relations of the old to the young changed. Old age became more common, but it also lost its privileged status (Fischer 1978).

## MODERNIZATION THEORY

Cowgill and Holmes (1972) refer to the shift from agricultural to urban society as a process of modernization. Modernization according to Cowgill (1974, 127), is "the transformation of a total society from a relatively rural way of life based on animate power, limited technology, relatively undifferentiated institutions, parochial and traditional outlook and values, toward a predominantly urban way of life based on inanimate sources of power, highly developed scientific technology, highly differentiated institutions matched by segmented individual roles, and a cosmopolitan outlook which emphasized efficiency and progress."

Cowgill and Holmes (1972) theorized that the status of older people decreases with increases in modernization. They reviewed studies of fourteen contemporary societies from around the world. These ranged from a study of the Sidamo of Southwest Ethiopia to two studies of Israeli society (one of a kibbutz) to a study of the aged in the U.S.S.R. They found that small numbers of older people, ancestor worship, low social change, extended families, a value system that emphasized the importance of the group, stable residence, and low literacy (where the group values the old for their knowledge) all lead to high status in old age. In modern societies, where such conditions are reversed, older people have low status (Cowgill and Holmes 1972). Cowgill and Holmes (1972) concluded that these trends support modernization theory.

Other research supports this theory. Palmore and Whittington (1971) studied the change in status of the elderly in the United States between 1940 and 1969. They used a "similarity index" to compare the status of the aged (65 and over) and the non-aged (14–64 years old) and found a decrease for the aged in the weeks and hours worked as well as a decrease in income and education level compared to younger people. They found improvements only in the health status of the elderly. They conclude that even with improvements in health and health care, the elderly lost status relative to the young over the thirty years they studied.

A later study by Palmore and Manton (1974) also supports the idea that status drops in old age in modern society. Palmore and Manton compared people 65 and over to people 25–64 in thirty-one countries. They used an "Equality Index" (EI) to compare these groups. This index measured employment status (employed or not employed), occupation for those employed, and years of education completed for each group. The researchers then computed the similarity of the young and the old in each country. EI scores ranged from the 90s for underdeveloped countries like Iran to the 50s for developed nations like the United States or Canada. (A score of one hundred means perfect equality.) "This indicates," the researchers write, "that the socioeconomic status of the aged is almost equal that of younger adults in some underdeveloped countries, but has apparently declined to about one-half of equality in some of the modernized countries" (Palmore and Manton 1974, 207). Bengtson and his colleagues (1975) studied more than 5,000 men in six developing countries and found that negative views of aging increased with increased modernization.

Other writers, many of them historians, have criticized modernization theory. Laslett (1976) says that the theory compares the present with its problems to an idealized past. He shows, to the contrary, that the treatment and status of the aged varied from time to time and from place to place before modernization (as it varies today among simpler societies). O'Rand (1990) says that modernization theory cannot account for the complexities of social change. It misses the differences within the older population based on age cohort differences, socioeconomic differences, and historical conditions. Within a single society researchers often find ambivalent feelings toward the aged (Vatuk 1982; Trexler 1982).

Most people think of Japan, for example, as a country that reveres its aged. Traditional tenets urge respect and honour for the elderly, and the Japanese try to follow this rule (Plath 1972). But Plath found a second view of aging in Japanese culture—*obasute* or "discarding granny." This theme of abandoning the old, he says, runs through Japanese literature from the sixth to the twentieth century. Even within industrial societies the treatment and status of the aged has differed from class to class and between women and men (Achenbaum and Stearns 1978; Quadagno 1980).

A study by Cherry and Magnuson-Martinson (1981) also questions the simple application of modernization theory to all developing nations. They propose that researchers look at the country's political economy to understand the status of the aged. These writers studied the status of older people in modern China. They learned that China had a tradition of great respect for the elderly based on authority, power, and prestige, but that this system of age stratification had declined in recent years. They did not find, however, that industrialization, urbanization, education, demographic change accounted for the decreased status of the old. Instead, their research showed that the decline in older peoples' status came about as a result of government social and economic policies.

Communist laws, for example, ended arranged marriages, which was one way the old had maintained power over the young, and gave married couples more autonomy. Land reform also led to less control of property by the old and less leverage for fathers over sons. The Chinese government emphasized equality between the generations. Older people would now get recognition for helping their families with child care, housework, or industrial work.

Cherry and Magnuson-Martinson (1981) suggest some modifications to modernization theory be made based on their work. First, the theory needs to take into account social policies that affect age group relationships. Second, a society can alter the status of the aged directly (through political action) rather than through processes of modernization. Third, some groups in a society will experience a greater change in status than others (e.g., men compared to women).

Some research describes a middle ground between the pro- and anti-modernization camps. Cohn (1982) found that the status of the old does drop at the start of modernization. Changes in education, leading to more professional and technical jobs, cause this drop. But, as modernization increases, the educational and occupational gap between the old and the young decreases (Palmore and Manton 1974). New cohorts of people move into old age, and the status of the aged improves. Palmore and Manton (1974), after studying thirty-one countries, found a J-shaped curve: the status of the aged drops with the start of modernization but improves as time goes by. The modern welfare state Maddox (1988, 3) says, has "tended to treat older adults rather generously." Improved retirement benefits, more adult education, and job retraining will raise the status of the aged in the future.

# Exhibit 3.3

## The Dega and the Nacirema: Then and Now

About 30 years ago, an anthropologist named Horace Miner described some of the peculiar body rituals among a tribe called the Nacirema. Most of his writing concerned the repressive sexual attitudes and primitive medical practices of that culture. Very little was said about the position of older people among the Nacirema. However, an unpublished manuscript was recently discovered which describes the relationship between the Nacirema and another tribe called the Dega. This manuscript was written in 1958 by Dr. L.N. Rekab of Adanac University, and portions of it are presented…below.

I believe this material is vitally important because it gives us an eyewitness account of the abuses inflicted upon the Dega by the Nacirema culture, and because it offers a historical baseline by which we can judge the progress which has been made since that time.

For some time now, members of the Dega tribe have been migrating into the village occupied by the Nacirema. Relations between the two cultures are far from cordial. Perhaps the best way to describe the situation is that the Nacirema treat the Dega like visiting relatives who have overstayed their welcome. The Nacirema prohibit the Dega from taking any active part in the economy, except for some child-care work, or tending the sick and the lame among their own group. This work is called *gnireet-nulov* and is never rewarded with pay or goods. The Nacirema explain that the Dega refuse to accept compensation because that would take away the honor of *gnireet-nulov* and turn it into mere labour. The Dega told me they had never been offered any pay.

The Dega appear to be slaves to the Nacirema, although neither group seems aware of the relationship. The Dega are not subjected to long days of hard labour, but are kept in a state of enforced idleness. They are given a meagre allowance for food and clothing, called a *noisnep*, which gives them a standard of living not much better than the poorest Nacirema. Some of them are permitted to live in their own individual huts, but many of the Dega are forced to live in group quarters called *gnisrun* homes. They are confined to small rooms, usually shared with another Dega, all their personal possessions are taken away from them, and they are tended by apprentices of the village witch doctor.

The daily life of the Dega is occupied mainly by sedentary activities. The Nacirema encourage them to play children's games and to do some weaving, but the articles they produce are given away, not sold in the market. A favorite pastime of the Dega is a sport called *flog*. Small white rocks are hit with a stick, over a large area of long grass, sand pits, and ponds. The aim of the game is to find the rock after you hit it. Each player has to buy a dozen special rocks from the Nacirema who makes them, who is called the *orp*. The player who returns at the end of the day with the most rocks is given free drinks by the other players. Sometimes the wealthy Nacirema also play *flog*, but never on the same day as the Dega. The Nacirema complain that the Dega take too long to finish the game. One of the Dega told me that the reason they played so slowly was that they had nothing else to do anyway, so enjoyed the company and the fresh air…

The temple is the major gathering place for the Dega. They attend the religious ceremonies regularly, but conversations with the priest and the Dega revealed a curious discrepancy. While the priest was sure that they believed fervently in the religious teaching, most of the Dega said that they did not really believe, but like to see their friends and listen to the music.

The temple is also used for activities which are a major source of excitement for the Dega. The most popular activity is a game of chance called *ognib* which consists of chanting by the priest and the creation of magic geometric shapes by the Dega. At the end of each chant, one of the players shouts the name of the game and jumps up and down with great excitement. The priest inspects the magic shape to see if it has been done correctly, and if it was, presents a clay pot to the winner...

The sexual practices of the Dega are either nonexistent, or are very well-hidden. No births have ever been observed among the Dega, so it may be inferred that they are beyond their reproductive years. However, there seems to be no sexual activity at all. I asked one Nacirema warrior if he had ever heard of such activity among the Dega, but he just laughed loudly, saying 'that would be like two rocks trying to lay an egg!' When I asked if any Nacirema had sexual relations with the Dega, he turned pale, spat on the ground, and told me he would rather sleep with a wild pig. Even though some of the Dega are very good-looking, the Nacirema consider them all as sterile, sexless individuals.

What will become of the Dega? Their future looks bleak, but I observed that new members arrive almost daily from the forest outside the village. Because of this immigration, there seems to be an increase in their numbers each month. When food was scarce, there was some talk among the young Nacirema warriors of attacking the Dega, but this was discouraged by the older warriors, who seemed more sympathetic to them.

The total population in the village seems to be kept in check by the disappearance of the Nacirema warriors after the ceremony of the gold sundial. This ceremony occurs only among the oldest of the Nacirema, who are given a small sundial and sent off into the forest to rest before they battle with the great spirits. Only one warrior ever returned while I was in the village, and he had gone crazy. He came back and began embracing the Dega, crying out 'Brother! Sister!' He was put out of his deluded misery by a young warrior.

What has happened in the quarter century since Dr. Rekab wrote this account? Well, the Dega have not died out. In fact, their numbers have increased dramatically since then, and most of the abuses put upon them by the Nacirema have disappeared. The *gnisrun* homes have been improved, the *noisnep* plans are providing a better standard of living for the Dega, and the Dega themselves are taking on a more active role in Nacirema society. To be sure, there are still some problems that need solving. However, it is a sure bet that the Dega will never again be second-class citizens.

**Source:** Paul M. Baker, "The Dega and the Nacirema," in B. Hess and E. Markson, eds. *Growing Old in America,* 3d ed. (New Brunswick, New Jersey: Transaction Books, 1987). Reprinted with permission of the publisher.

• • • • • • • • • • • • • • • • • • • • • • • • • • • • • • • • • • • •

# POST-INDUSTRIAL SOCIETY

Today some people in the developed nations still live badly in old age—they have poor housing, poor nutrition, bad health, and little money. Studies also show that some people still hold negative attitudes toward the aged. Baker (1983a) studied Canadian university students' attitudes toward various ages. He found that the youngest and oldest ages received the lowest ratings. Middle-aged people received the highest ratings. He found the same pattern in attitudes regardless of the social class, gender, or age of the people making the judgment. He describes the findings as an inverted U with status low early in life, rising to mid-life, and falling in old age.

Graham and Baker (1989) replicated this study with a sample of older people (mean age 67). Their results showed that the older people gave less negative ratings to all age groups, and they rated the young and old less negatively compared to the middle-aged. Still, the researchers discovered the same inverted U-curve in the older sample's ratings as was found in the earlier university student sample. The researchers say that these similar findings from two diverse samples support the idea that Canadians see old age as a time of low status.

Knox and Gekoski (1989) studied fourteen hundred undergraduates' judgments and attitudes toward age. They studied two different approaches to making judgments. The researchers found that regardless of their rating method students gave older people the lowest rating on two of three scales—effectiveness and personal acceptability.

A study of selected Canadian literature for children (de Vries 1987) found some loving portrayals of older people. "Older characters always have their annoying side," de Vries (1987, 43) says, "but attempts are made to appreciate their point of view." A study of novels over four decades found both positive and negative views of old age. Matthews and Thompson (1985) studied forty novels—half of them winners of the Governor General's Award for Fiction. They found that most older characters had high self-esteem and high life-satisfaction, but they also concluded that more recent novels treated the aged as comic figures and saw this as a possible sign of growing negative attitudes to the old.

These studies show that in Western society people feel ambivalent toward old age. Kastenbaum and Ross (1975) call this an "approach–avoidance dilemma." They say that limited resources and the physical decline that comes with old age make it unattractive in all societies. On the other hand, most people know and like older individuals, and at all times in history younger people have cared for and loved their aged relatives and friends.

In spite of some negative attitudes toward old age, older people as a group in North America live materially better lives than older people at any time in history. Schulz (1980) reports "major breakthroughs" in private and public programs that deal with economic problems in old age.

He cites as proof the increase of private pensions, property tax relief, and a rise of almost 100 percent in U.S. Social Security benefits from 1970 to 1980 (Schulz 1980). He could also have included in his list improvements in Canadian Old Age Security benefits, the Canada Pension Plan, and Canada's free nationwide health care coverage for the elderly. All these programs increase older people's independence and freedom.

Some writers predict an age-irrelevant society in the future (Fischer 1978; Neugarten 1980). This kind of society will react toward individuals on the basis of what they can do, rather than on the basis of sex, race, or age. This fits with the trend in North America to eliminate racism and sexism today. Fischer (1978) points to the end of mandatory retirement as a sign of this trend, and Atchley (1980) cites better treatment of old age on television as a sign of improved attitudes toward and treatment of the elderly in industrial nations.

## AGING IN THE WORLD TODAY

In the year 2000 about 18 percent of the population of the developed nations (like the U.S. and Canada) will be over age 60 (Salas 1982). Cockerham (1991, 35) says that "Australia and the world's entire northern tier of countries, including Canada and the United States, all of Western Europe (less Turkey), Eastern Europe and the Soviet Union, and Japan, will have at least 13 percent of their populations age 65 or older." This will be caused mostly by a decrease in birth rates and to a lesser extent by increased longevity.

The developing nations (such as the Latin American, African, and Middle Eastern countries) make up three-quarters of the world's population, and they too will see changes in their population structures. These countries have relatively young populations, with large numbers of children and proportionately few older people—some with as few as 2 percent of the population aged 65 and over (e.g., Ivory Coast and Afghanistan) (Araba 1988). But, the death rates in these countries have begun to fall and many more people now live into old age.

The low proportion of people aged 65 and over in the developing nations, compared to that in the developed nations, tells only part of the story of aging in these countries. These countries will also have the greatest percentage increase of older people. And many of these countries will face a crisis due to these future large numbers (Cockerham 1991). Africa, for example, will see a large increase in its population aged 60 and over between 1980 and 2025. The United Nations (UN) projects an increase in this age group by a factor of 4.4, which means moving from 22.9 million in 1980 to 101.9 million in 2025 (Araba 1988). The UN projects an even greater rate of increase in older people in Latin America and also projects an increase in Latin Americans aged 70 and over from 9.4 million in 1980 to 80 million in 2025 (DeLehr 1988).

In South Asia the older population will grow 174 percent from the year 1980 to 2000. In Japan it is expected to grow from 15 million people in 1980 to 33 million by 2025—from 12.7 percent to over 25 percent of the total population in forty-five years (Salas 1982). Also, the less-developed nations make up nearly 75 percent of the world's population (Population Reference Bureau 1980). The greater number of people surviving to old age in developing nations, added to the already large number of older people already in the developed nations, will swell the world's aged population.

In 1950 about 200 million people in the world were aged 60 or over. By 1975 that population had grown to 350 million, and projections estimate that there will be 1 billion people aged 60 and over by 2025. This population will have grown by 224 percent in about fifty years, while the total world population will have grown by only about 102 percent. By 2025 the world population of the elderly (60+) will be about 14 percent of the total world population (Salas 1982).

Sixty percent of the world's elderly (60+) will live in the developing nations by the year 2000, and by 2025 that figure will climb to almost 75 percent. China alone in the year 2025 will have as many people aged sixty or over as the entire population of the United States (Sokolovsky 1990 citing Nusberg 1982). For poorer nations, with few of the resources and with little of the social machinery needed to meet older people's needs, these changes will create problems never seen before (Salas 1982).

When nations develop, the young often move to the cities. This leaves the aged in rural villages with little family or social support. These villages lack communications, transportation, supplies, and services that the elderly need. Older workers sometimes return to their home countries after years of working in another country. They have no work, no skills, and no pensions, and will grow old in poverty (DeLehr 1988). In rural settings, DeLehr (1988, 7) reports, old people must work as long as they have the strength. In larger centres a growing number of older people survive by "scratching out a living from rubbish dumps or peddling goods on the streets." She predicts things will get worse unless these countries develop basic services to help older people.

Solutions that fit Western industrialized countries do not necessarily fit the developing nations (Gillin 1986). These countries have neither the social services nor the economic resources to help the elderly poor. Nor can these countries afford the housing, health, or welfare services for the old that Western nations have set up. China, for example, had 65.2 million seniors in

• • • • • • • • • • • • • • • • • • • • • • • • • • • • • • • • •

## Exhibit 3.4

### Controversy: Modernization vs. Dependency Theory

• • • • • • • • • • • • • • • • • • • • • • • • • • • • • • • • •

Modernization theory views developed industrial societies as the model for less-developed nations and proposes that less-developed nations set up policies for older people like those used in developed countries (Neysmith and Edwardh 1983). But developed nations' solutions often do not fit the needs of developing societies.

Some theorists propose an alternative theory of aging—dependency theory. Dependency theory uses a critical Marxist approach to study aging. It says that the social and economic structures in a society create the status of the old and that to understand the developing world gerontologists have to understand aging in the economic relations between nations. Dependency theory looks at "the dynamic process involved in societal transformation" and at the societal and world-wide forces that decide the fate of older people (Hendricks 1982).

Dependency theory begins with the fact that structured inequality exists between developed and less-developed societies. Less-developed or peripheral nations now depend on the developed or core nations for their economic well-being. The peripheral nations of Latin America, Africa, and Asia produce raw materials, crops, and manufactured goods for the core nations. The core nations decide what a peripheral country should grow or make for its markets. This keeps the peripheral country dependent and poor, and it disrupts the country's economic, familial, and political life.

Younger people move off the land to work in the cities. Also, the gap between rich and poor people in the peripheral country grows. Families, for example, grow less food for their own use. They begin to grow cash crops for export. This makes it harder for them to support large families that include older members (Gillin 1986). Older people also lose status in these societies because their knowledge does not serve the core nation's needs (Hendricks 1982). "Old people do not simply become out of date," Hendricks (1982, 343) says, "they are made obsolete. If one goal of gerontology is to upgrade the quality of life for older people in any given society, then it must first understand the structural imperatives that have shaped their control over potential resources." Dependency theory adds this understanding to the study of aging and society.

• • • • • • • • • • • • • • • • • • • • • • • • • • • • • • • • •

1988—more than double the population of Canada. India had 32.7 million seniors (4% of its population). Krishnan (1990) says that even a basic pension of 100 Indian rupees would cost $3 billion Canadian and "the Indian States do not have money even to meet this rock bottom" pension.

Sokolovsky (1990) reports that some of the world's poorest countries have public pension systems. But only one-third of the working population can get benefits. Often these benefits come to only small amounts. And few rural people can expect much from public pensions. One case that shows the kinds of problems people face in these countries was described in the *Globe and Mail* (1983, B8): "After 35 years as a farm labourer, Feliciano Rodriguez has retired. The Peruvian Social Security system is giving him a pension equivalent to 10 cents (U.S.) a month. All is not lost, however … He gets an extra 2 cents a month because he is married."

Gerontologists need new theories of aging to explain the changes taking place in these countries (see Exhibit 3.4) and new plans for social change that fit the needs of an aging world.

## CONCLUSION

Did older people live better lives in the past than they do today? Can we learn something about aging from past societies? Will aging in the future differ from aging today?

Older people's status in the past differed from time to time, from place to place, and from class to class. Some societies treated their aged badly, some treated them well, but all of these societies had fewer older people than societies today. We cannot look to the past for ways to create a good old age today. The large number of older people in the world today "remains irreducibly novel," Laslett (1976, 96) says, and "it calls for invention rather than imitation."

In the future, as in the past, aging will differ from society to society. The wealthier nations will have the best chance of creating a materially satisfying old age for their people. The poorer societies will struggle under the burden of more people—old and young. One thing, however, seems certain: aging populations will challenge all countries in the world. The economy, the political system, the culture, the level of development, and the age structure of a society will all affect how a society responds to this challenge.

Canada, like other countries, cannot copy past societies in its treatment of older people, but it can learn something from the past and from simpler societies. The !Kung San elders heal the sick through dance and music. In Chinese culture the older woman works as a matchmaker. Among the Coast Salish tribe of British Columbia the old serve as ritual leaders. Wherever older people have had valued roles to play in their societies they have lived respected and purposeful lives. Canada can make this a goal of its policies for older people.

## SUMMARY

1. Culture, custom, and the economic life of the group all influence how a society treats its older members. A study of three types of societies—hunt-

ing and gathering, agricultural, and industrial—shows that treatment of the aged differed in the past from time to time and from place to place. None of these societies created a Golden Age for older people.

2. Like most societies, past and present, modern Western societies show an ambivalence toward the aged. Negative stereotypes exist, and some discrimination against the aged takes place. Modern societies also offer older people independence, a high standard of living, and many opportunities for life satisfaction.

3. The developed nations have a high percentage of older people. They will have to shift resources to serve the changing needs of their populations. Post-industrial societies show an ambivalence toward older people. They provide pensions and services, but they also show prejudice toward older people. Some writers predict that this prejudice will end and that post-industrial societies will be "age-irrelevant" societies in the future.

4. Modernization theory predicts a decline in the status and treatment of the aged in modern society from those of societies in the past. Some studies that compare developed and developing nations today support modernization theory, but critics of the theory argue that it oversimplifies life in the past, ignores differences in treatment of the elderly within a society, and undervalues the opportunities for a good old age today.

5. The developing nations have large numbers of older people, even though older people make up a small percentage of their populations. This increase in the numbers of older people poses service delivery, economic, and health care support problems for developing nations. Dependency theory says that the economic exploitation of these nations by the developed nations of the West deepens the misery of older people in these societies.

6. Population aging has become a worldwide challenge. The response a nation makes to the challenge of aging will depend on its traditions, culture, level of development, and economic strength.

## SELECTED READINGS

Amoss, P.T., and S. Harrell, eds. *Other Ways of Growing Old: Anthropological Perspectives.* Stanford, California: Stanford University Press, 1981.

This book of readings shows the varied ways people grow old around the world. It removes some of the romantic ideas we have about aging in simpler societies and also shows how social and economic conditions shape old age.

Cowgill, Donald O., and Lowell D. Holmes, eds. *Aging and Modernization.* New York: Appleton-Century-Crofts, 1972.

This book of readings set off a major controversy about aging today and in the past. The articles themselves, studies of various societies, make good reading, showing how aging differs from culture to culture.

Laslett, P. "Societal Development and Aging." In R.H. Binstock and E. Shanas, eds., *Handbook of Aging and the Social Sciences.* New York: Van Nostrand Reinhold, 1976.

A fascinating look at aging in Europe in the past. Laslett challenges the myth that past society offered older people a Golden Age. Instead, he shows that treatment of the aged varied from time to time and from place to place.

Synge, Jane. "Work and Family Support Patterns of the Aged in the Early Twentieth Century." In Victor W. Marshall, ed., *Aging in Canada: Social Perspectives.* Toronto: Fitzhenry and Whiteside, 1980.

A close look at intergenerational relations in Ontario in the early 1900s. One of the few studies of aging in Canada in the past.

# Aging in Canada

## INTRODUCTION

When people think about aging, they think of wrinkled skin, grey hair, and false teeth. But societies age too. From 1901 to 1986 Canada's population grew about four and a half times. During this same period the older population grew by almost *ten* times—more than twice the rate of the general population. From 1976 to 1986 the total population grew by 10 percent; in this period, while the population aged 0–14 decreased by about 2 percent, the older population grew by 35 percent. The proportion of people aged 65 and over rose from 5 percent of the total population in 1901 to 10.7 percent of Canada's population in 1986. This makes Canada's population one of the oldest in the world, and demographers expect Canadian society to age even more in the next fifty years (Statistics Canada, 1984b; Statistics Canada 1989a; Stone and Frenken 1988).

This chapter will look at: (1) why Canadian society has aged, (2) the population structure of Canada today, and (3) the impact of population aging on health care and pension programs.

## AGING AROUND THE WORLD

The United Nations groups the ages of societies by the proportion of their populations aged 60 years and over. It defines a country as "young" if less than 4 percent of its population is aged 60 and over; "youthful" if between 4 and 6 percent of its population is in this age group; "mature" if 7 to 9 percent of the population is in this age group; and "aged" if 10 percent or more of the population is aged 60 and over. Exhibit 4.1 presents proportions of older people for a sample of countries.

European countries that went through demographic transitions first have the largest proportions of older people. Almost a century ago more than 7 percent of the populations of France and Sweden were aged 65 or over (France had 8.2 percent in 1900; Sweden had 8.4 percent in 1900). England and Wales, along with Germany, became mature societies around 1930; both had 7.4 percent of their population aged 65 or over in 1930 (Laslett 1976). The high death rates for young men and the low birth rates during World War II speeded up societal aging in these countries. By 1985 12.4 percent of France's population was over age 65; that of England and Wales was 15.1 percent; and Sweden had a 16.9-percent rate—the highest percentage in the world (U.S. Census Bureau 1987).

Canada is a relatively young nation compared with these European countries. Until 1900 less than 5 percent of its population was aged 65 and over.

## Exhibit 4.1

Percentages of Population Aged 60 Years and Over,
Canada and Selected Regions and Countries, 1980

| Country | 1980 | Projected 2020 |
|---|---|---|
| World | 8.3 | 12.6 |
| Developed Nations | 15.2 | 22.4 |
| Developing Nations | 6.0 | 10.6 |
| Sweden | 21.9 | 28.4 |
| France | 17.0 | 24.6 |
| United States | 15.7 | 22.0 |
| Union of Soviet Social Republics | 13.1 | 19.4 |
| Japan | 12.9 | 26.5 |
| *Canada* | *12.8* | *23.0* |
| Israel | 11.5 | 15.6 |
| Jamaica | 8.5 | 11.4 |
| China | 7.3 | 16.4 |
| Egypt | 6.8 | 9.5 |
| Turkey | 6.4 | 10.7 |
| Mexico | 5.2 | 10.0 |
| Nicaragua | 3.9 | 6.9 |
| Kenya | 3.0 | 3.7 |
| Kuwait | 2.3 | 10.3 |

**Source:** Adapted from United Nations, *Periodical on Aging.* 1(1):Tables 3, 10, 17, 24, 31, 38. (New York: Department of International Economic and Social Affairs, 1984)

The country aged gradually through the first part of this century and became a mature nation by UN standards in 1951 (with 7.8 percent aged 65+) (Statistics Canada 1984b). In 1986 Canada qualified as an aged nation, since 2,697,600 people or 10.7 percent of its population was 65 and over. By the year 2031 the portion of Canada's population aged 65 and over could be almost one-quarter (24 percent) of the total population—almost five times the proportion of older people in 1900 (Statistics Canada 1990). (See Exhibit 4.2).

## Exhibit 4.2

Growth of Percentage of Canada's Population
Aged 65 and Over, 1901–2001

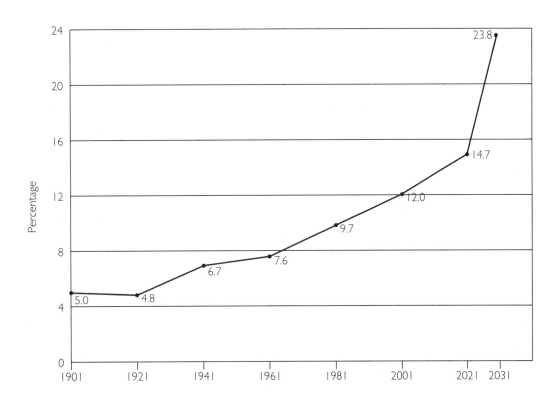

**Source:** Statistics Canada, *The Elderly in Canada*, 1984b, Table 1; Health and Welfare Canada, *Factbook on Aging in Canada*, 1983, 17, Figure 3.1; Stone and Frenken, *Canada's Seniors*, 1988, Chart 2; Statistics Canada, *A Portrait of Seniors in Canada*, 1990. The Figures for 1991–2021 are estimates. Adapted with the permission of the Minister of Supply and Services Canada, 1991.

What caused Canada to age in the twentieth century? What will keep it aging in the years ahead? And what effect will population aging have on Canadian society? A look at Canada's population—past and present—will answer these questions.

## CANADA COMES OF AGE

Demographers study three conditions that affect a population's size and structure—immigration, death rates, and birth rates. Each of these demographic forces caused the Canadian population to age from the mid-1800s to the present (Beaujot and McQuillan 1982).

## Immigration

Of the three demographic forces—immigration, birth rates, and death rates—immigration played the smallest part in the aging of Canada's population. It also affected different parts of Canada in different ways. Waves of immigration in the early twentieth century brought new groups of young adults to Canada. Between 1901 and 1911 1.5 million people arrived in Canada—as many as in the previous forty years combined. Immigration in the first decade of this century accounted for 44 percent of Canada's total population increase (Statistics Canada 1981a). Most of these immigrants came to Canada as children or young adults (20–34 years old) (Northcott 1988). These young people (and the families they raised) helped keep Canada's population young at the start of this century (see Exhibit 4.2).

Immigration continued to add to Canada's population until the start of the Great Depression. From 1901 to 1931 successive waves of immigration brought from 3.5 to 4.5 million people to Canada. These immigrants did more than simply increase the number of people in Canada; they also changed the face of Canadian society. Immigrants before 1900 came mostly from the British Isles, but Leacy (1983) reports that Canadians of "other European" origin rose from 37 percent of the European-born population in 1881 to 43 percent of the same population in 1911. Germans, Norwegians, Mennonites, Doukhobors, Chinese, and Southern and Eastern Europeans arrived in large numbers. Most of these immigrants were young males.

Many of the Eastern Europeans, along with Icelanders and Mennonites, settled on the Prairies. Provinces like Manitoba in the 1880s and Saskatchewan around 1911 had high birth rates due to the large number of young immigrants in their populations (Henripin 1972). This large wave of immigration partly explains the drop in the proportion of people over age 65 in Canada from 5 percent in 1901 to 4.7 percent in 1911 and 4.8 percent in 1921. This same group added to Canada's older population as they aged. Statistics Canada (1981a) estimated that more than half of the country's older immigrant population had come to Canada before 1929. Older immigrants made up 16 percent of Canada's older population in 1981 (Statistics Canada 1984b).

Population projections show that the proportion of immigrants in the older population will grow in the years to come. A major wave of immigration in the early 1950s accounts for about 6 percent of Canada's growth from 1946 to 1978. The mainly young immigrants lowered the median age of Canadians and added children to the Baby Boom of the 1950s and 1960s. They will add to the size of the older population in the next century (McDaniel 1986).

Recent immigration will also change the character of the older population in the future. In the period 1956-60 most of Canada's immigrants came from the United Kingdom, Central Europe, and Southern Europe. Immigrants from these areas made up more than 60 percent of Canada's total immigrant population. By 1989 this pattern had changed. In 1989 the largest portion of immigrants came from the developing nations of Asia, the Caribbean, South America, and Central America—46 percent from Asia and 15 percent from the Caribbean, and from South and Central America (Logan 1991). Many of these people (32 percent of all immigrants) came as family members of Canadian residents (Logan 1991).

Compared to other demographic forces, immigration has little effect on the aging of Canada's population (Dumas 1990). Fertility, not immigration causes population aging or rejuvenation. But immigration does alter the make up of Canadian society, and it creates new challenges for organizations and groups that serve older people.

## Death Rates

By the late nineteenth and early twentieth centuries, death rates began to drop across the country. The best figures for this period come from Quebec. Henripin and Peron (1972, cited in Beaujot and McQuillan 1982) say that the crude death rate in Quebec dropped by half from 24 per 1,000 in 1871–75 to 12.9 by 1921–25. These figures probably overestimate the drop in death rates for Canada as a whole. Historians say that Canada's large cities still suffered from high death rates (Gagan 1983a; Cross 1983; Torrance 1981; Artibise 1977), but a steady, if not dramatic, decline did take place. Life expectancy at birth rose from 41.9 years for men and 44.2 years for women born in 1851 to 60.0 years for men and 62.1 years for women in 1931. Life expectancy at age 65 had increased to 78 years for men and 78.7 years for women in the same eighty years. This meant that more people lived longer and that more lived into late old age (Legare and Desjardins 1976, cited in Beaujot and McQuillan 1982; Nagnur 1986).

Life expectancy increased steadily for men and women at all ages between 1951 and 1981, but infants gained the most (see Exhibit 4.3). Infant

## Exhibit 4.3

Evolution of Life Expectancy by Age and Sex, Canada, 1931–1987

| Year | At Birth | | At Age 60 | | At Age 80 | |
| --- | --- | --- | --- | --- | --- | --- |
| | Males | Females | Males | Females | Males | Females |
| 1931 | 60.0 | 62.1 | 16.3 | 17.2 | 5.6 | 5.9 |
| 1941 | 63.0 | 66.3 | 16.1 | 17.6 | 5.5 | 6.0 |
| 1951 | 66.4 | 70.9 | 16.5 | 18.7 | 5.8 | 6.4 |
| 1961 | 68.4 | 74.3 | 16.8 | 19.9 | 6.2 | 7.0 |
| 1971 | 69.4 | 76.5 | 17.0 | 21.5 | 6.5 | 8.0 |
| 1981 | 71.9 | 79.0 | 18.0 | 22.9 | 6.9 | 9.0 |
| 1985–1987 | 73.0 | 79.7 | 18.4 | 23.2 | 6.9 | 8.9 |

This table shows a steady increase in life expectancy at birth and at age 60 from 1941 to 1985–87 for both sexes (life expectancy at age 80 has remained almost stable). Note that until 1985–87 women gained more in life expectancy than men at birth and at age 60 in each time period. This may be due to differences in lifestyles, habits, or environmental conditions (e.g., working conditions). The most recent figures show a change in this trend. Men in all age groups gained more years in life expectancy than women between 1981 and 1985–87. The oldest women (age 80) showed a slight decrease in life expectancy. Changes in lifestyle for men and women may account for this reversal.

**Sources:** Dhruva Nagnur, *Longevity and Historical Life Tables 1921-1981 (Abridged) Canada and the Provinces*, Statistics Canada, Cat. No. 89-506 (Ottawa: Minister of Supply and Services Canada, 1986); Statistics Canada, *Canada Year Book 1990*, Cat. No. 11-402E/1990 (Ottawa: Minister of Supply and Services Canada, 1989); Statistics Canada, *Health Reports, Supplement No.13*, Vol. 2, No. 4, "Life Tables, Canada and Provinces 1985–1987," Cat. No. 82-0038 (Ottawa: Minister of Supply and Services Canada, 1991). Adapted with the permission of the Minister of Supply and Services Canada, 1991.

mortality rates (the death rates of children less than a year old) decreased by about 78 percent for both males and females from 1953 to 1986 (Statistics Canada 1990). By 1986 less than 1 percent of children died before their first birthday (compared with about 10 percent in 1921) (Parliament 1987).

Control of childhood disease, better prenatal care, and improved nutrition account for most of this change. Between 1931 and 1981 the death rate for children under 5 decreased by 90 percent (Parliament 1987). Nagnur and Nagrodski (1988, 26) report that "infectious and parasitic diseases, including tuberculosis, accounted for almost 15% of deaths in 1921; in 1986, however, only about half of one percent of all deaths were the result of these diseases."

Life expectancy at birth increased from 1931 to 1986 by 13 years (from 60.0 to 73.0) for men and by almost 18 years (from 62.1 to 79.7) for women (Perrault 1990; Dumas 1990).

Canada since 1951 has also seen a drop in the most common causes of death in adulthood—cardiovascular disease (including ischemic heart disease, strokes, arterial disease, hypertension, and rheumatic heart disease) (Parliament 1989). Due to these changes men aged 65–69 showed a 19-percent decrease in mortality rate between 1951 and 1986. Women in this age group showed a 43-percent decrease during this same period.

People in the oldest cohorts, aged 80 and over, show some of the greatest improvements in life expectancy (Beaujot and McQuillan 1982). Dumas (1990, 64), for example, says that, "the most spectacular progress [in the extension of life expectancy has been] realized at very advanced ages: the probability of living 10 years beyond one's 80th birthday rose from 28% in 1966 to 41% in 1986, or nearly 50 per cent in 15 years" (Dumas 1990, 64).

Better medical care, a safer environment, and a higher standard of living mean that today 98 percent of all children born in Canada can expect to live through infancy; 90 percent can expect to live to age 50; 66 percent to age 70; and 40 percent to age 80 (Statistics Canada 1981a). This gives Canada—along with Sweden, Denmark, Norway, and the United States—one of the highest life expectancies in the world and means that more people than ever will enter old age in this country.

## Birth Rates

A population ages when its proportion of younger people declines. Quebec in the 1700s, for example, had a young population and one of the highest birth rates ever recorded. From 1700–1730 women averaged births of one child every two years until they reached age 30. Women who reached the age of 50 averaged eight or nine children. In the middle of the eighteenth century the average was thirteen children apiece (Henripin 1972). During this time the birth rate ran two to six times higher than the death rate, and Quebec's population grew twenty times from 1608 to 1765, and by one and a half times again by 1851 (Kalbach and McVey 1979). Death rates in Quebec began to decline after 1780, but despite this the province's birth rate was still high and the population stayed young (Kalbach and McVey 1979; Henripin 1972).

Frontier regions in Ontario also had high birth rates. McInnis (1977) and Henripin (1972) report rates similar to Quebec's in rural Ontario in the mid-nineteenth century. A writer of the time reported that children "in Canada [are a man's] greatest blessing, and happy is that man who has a quiver full of them" (Philpot 1871, cited in Gagan 1983b). McInnis says that Upper Canada at the time "had one of the highest birth rates in the world" (1977, 202). Gagan (1983b) estimates that settled Ontario families in Peel County had eight to nine children. New immigrants to Canada before 1830 often had more.

Around 1850 Canada began its demographic transition when the birth rate decreased. Henripin (1972) shows that the birth rate in Canada as a whole dropped by about 30 percent from 1851 to 1951 (with a sharp drop during the 1930s). Though the provinces all showed the same declining trend, individual rates varied: the Quebec birth rate dropped least, at about 20 percent from 1851 to 1921; Ontario showed a sharp drop of about 50 percent during this same time; Manitoba between 1881 and 1921 showed a drop of more than 60 percent; and Saskatchewan showed a similar drop between 1901 and 1921 (Henripin 1972). This drop in the birth rate, more than any other demographic change, led to the aging of Canadian society.

## Baby Boom and Baby Bust

Two phenomena affecting the birth rate—the Baby Boom and the Baby Bust—account for the greatest changes in Canadian population from 1951 to the present.

From 1946 until about the early 1960s Canada went through a Baby Boom. Between 1941 and 1961 the **total fertility rate,** defined by Beaujot and McQuillan (1982, 220–21) as "the average number of children that would be born alive to a woman during her lifetime if she were to pass through all her childbearing years conforming to the age-specific fertility rates of a given year," rose from 2.83 to 3.84. The age-specific birth rate (the number of births in a given age group per one thousand women in that age group) nearly doubled for 15- to 19-year-olds from 30.7 to 58.2 (Statistics Canada 1978c, cited in Beaujot and McQuillan 1982). Total births soared from 264,000 in 1941 to almost 476,000 in 1961 (Statistics Canada 1978c, cited in Beaujot and McQuillan 1982). The Baby Boom reversed a general trend of decreased fertility rates that had begun in the nineteenth century (Henripin 1972). It also reversed a century-long trend in population aging (excluding the years 1911 to 1931) that began in the late nineteenth century.

After 1961, Canada went into a Baby Bust cycle. The total fertility rate dropped from 3.84 (children per woman) in 1961 to 2.81 in 1966—a rate below that of 1941, to 1.67 in 1989 (Beaujot and McQuillan 1982; Lachepelle 1988; McVey 1987; Statistics Canada 1989a; Perreault 1990). The crude birth rate (the number of live births per thousand population in a given year) dropped from 26.1 in 1961 to 22.2 in 1981 to 14.7 in 1986 (below the rate of the 1930s) (Beaujot and McQuillan 1982; McVey 1987; Statistics Canada 1975; Statistics Canada 1989a).

# Exhibit 4.4

Median Age* of the Population, Canada, 1881–1986
(Excluding Newfoundland)

| Year | Median Age | Year | Median Age |
|---|---|---|---|
| 1881 | 20.1 | 1951 | 27.8 |
| 1891 | 21.4 | 1961 | 26.5 |
| 1901 | 22.7 | 1966 | 25.6 |
| 1911 | 23.8 | 1971 | 26.4 |
| 1921 | 23.9 | 1976 | 27.8 |
| 1931 | 24.7 | 1981 | 29.6 |
| 1941 | 27.0 | 1986 | 31.6 |

*Half the population is older and half is younger than the median age.

Canada's median age, according to the table, rose 11.5 years from 1881 to 1986. The table also shows a jump in the median age of 3.7 years between 1931 and 1941. This reflects the sharp drop in the birth rate during the Depression years. The table also shows a steady rise in the median age throughout this century until 1961, followed by a drop from 1951 to 1966. During these years the rise in the birth rate (the Baby Boom) led to a decrease in the median age by 2.2 years to 25.6 years. In 1976 the median age rose again to its 1951 high of 27.8. By 1981 about half the population was over the age of 30. Demographers project a continued increase in the median age for the rest of this century.

**Sources:** Dominion Bureau of Statistics *Census of Canada* (1961 Census), Bulletin 7:1–4 (Ottawa: Queen's Printer, 1964); Statistics Canada, *1966 Census of Canada*, Vol.1(1–11) (Ottawa: Queen's Printer, 1968); Statistics Canada, *Census of Canada (1971 Census)*, Bulletin 1:2–3 (Ottawa: Information Canada, 1973); Statistics Canada 1978b, cited in Warren E. Kalbach and Wayne W. McVey, *The Demographic Bases of Canadian Society*, 2d ed. (Toronto: McGraw-Hill Ryerson, 1979), 161, Table 6:3; Mary Sue Devereaux, "Aging of the Canadian Population," *Canadian Social Trends*, Winter, 1987, 37–38. Adapted with the permission of the Minister of Supply and Services Canada, 1991.

This led to a sharp drop in the number of young people in Canada. Between 1976 and 1986, for example, the population of young people 0–14 years old decreased from 5.9 million to 5.4 million, which was a 4-percent decrease, from 25.6 percent to 21.4 percent of the population (Statistics Canada 1989a). Statistics Canada projects a continuing decline in the proportion of the population made up of younger people as we move into the next century. If these projections are right, the younger population (under age 20) will fall to less than 20 percent of the population, while the older population will grow to 25 percent of the population (Romaniuc 1984; Statistics Canada 1990).

This decrease in the birth rate, especially the sharp drop since the 1960s, speeded up the rate of population aging in Canada. Between 1961 and 1986 the population aged 65 and over rose by more than three percentage points, moving from 7.6 to 10.7 percent of Canada's population (Statistics Canada 1984b; Stone and Frenken 1988). The older population will increase sharply again in the first decade of the twenty-first century when the Baby Boom generation moves into old age.

## Summary of Population Aging in Canada

Canada's demographic transition took place from before 1850 to the present in three stages. In the first stage, before 1850, Canada had both high death

· · · · · · · · · · · · · · · · · · · · · · · · · · · · · · · · · · · · · · ·

## Exhibit 4.5

### How to Read a Population Pyramid

· · · · · · · · · · · · · · · · · · · · · · · · · · · · · · · · · · · · · · ·

Population pyramids graphically portray a society's population structure at a certain point in time and allow researchers to compare societies at a glance. Most pyramids have the same design:

**The title:** The title contains the name of the country and the year this "snapshot" was taken. The title answers the questions: What? Where? When?

**The centre line:** The centre line divides the pyramid by sex—males on the left, females on the right.

**The base:** The horizontal axis can represent absolute numbers or percentages. The pyramids for Canada, 1986–2036 (See Exhibit 4.6), use absolute numbers. The centre line marks 0, and each point on the baseline marks two hundred thousand people (males to the left of the centre, females to the right).

**The tiers:** Each tier or level of the pyramid stands for an age cohort (conventionally a five-year group). The lowest tier stands for the youngest age cohort (0–4 years old), and as one moves up the pyramid the cohorts get older. The top cohort (90+ in the Canadian pyramids) contains everyone over a certain age. (Note that this large top tier takes in a larger age span than the other tiers. It includes people from age 90 to over 100.)

Pyramids allow a viewer to compare age cohorts within a country (e.g., the size of young cohorts can be compared to the size of older cohorts), to compare sex differences within cohorts (by comparing the size of a tier to the right and left of the centre line), and to see unusually large or small cohorts at a glance. Gerontologists also use population pyramids to study population change over time and to compare one country with another.

· · · · · · · · · · · · · · · · · · · · · · · · · · · · · · · · · · · · · · ·

## Exhibit 4.6

Population Pyramids by Age Group and Sex, Canada, 1986
(Census), 2011 and 2036 (Projection 1)
(Projection 1 [1986 Census], Low Growth Scenario,
Total Fertility Rate = 1.20, Net Immigration = 140,000 per year

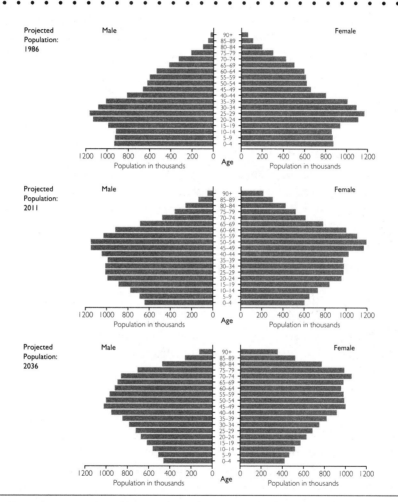

These pyramids show at least three important trends: first, the dramatic growth in size of the older age cohorts (aged 40+); second, a growing proportion of women compared to men in the oldest cohorts; and third, the movement of the Baby Boom cohorts into old age. The 2036 pyramid is top-heavy, with small younger age groups below a large older population.

**Source:** Adapted from J. Perreault, *Population Projections for Canada, Provinces and Territories, 1990–2011*, Statistics Canada, Cat. No. 91-520 (Ottawa: Minister of Supply and Services Canada, 1990), Figure 5. Reproduced with permission of the Minister of Supply and Services Canada, 1991.

and high birth rates, and, in Ontario and the Maritimes, a high rate of immigration. These forces kept the average age of Canadians low. Gagan (1983a) says that in Ontario in the mid-nineteenth century half the population over the age of 15 was made up of men under the age of 30. Kalbach and McVey (1979) put the average age of Canadians in the mid-nineteenth century at around 20 (compared to a median age of almost 32 in 1986) (Devereaux 1987).

The second stage of the transition began after 1850 as major declines in birth and death rates took place (Kalbach and McVey 1979). This stage differed from the second stage in Europe's demographic transition, where death rates declined and birth rates stayed high for some time before they dropped to complete the transition. In Canada both birth and death rates dropped (with some important fluctuations in birth rates) until the present. These changes transformed Canada from a young nation (under 4 percent aged 65+) in the late 1800s to a mature nation (with about 7 percent of the population aged 65+) by 1950.

Today, in the third stage of the transition, Canada has low death rates, low birth rates, and an aging population. Into the next century Canada's population pyramid will change from that of a wide-based, triangular shape to a more rectangular one (see Exhibit 4.6).

## AGING IN CANADA TODAY

Older people differ by age, sex, marital status, and health. They come from different ethnic backgrounds, have lived through varying historical events, and live in diverse parts of the country. These differences make older people one of the most heterogeneous age groups in the country.

### The Aging of the Older Population

The older population itself has aged in the past eighty years. In 1901 people aged 80 and over made up about 15 percent of the older population, by 1986 they made up almost 20 percent of the older population (Stone and Frenken 1988). In the 1980s Canada's oldest age groups grew at a faster rate than did corresponding age groups in the other developed nations. The number of males aged 90 and over, for example, doubled in size from 1966 to 1986, and the number of females aged 90 and over tripled in size (Statistics Canada 1990). Stone and Frenken (1988) project a sharp future increase in the oldest age groups (aged 85+) compared with the total population aged 65 and over. They say that this trend will lead to "a veritable population explosion among seniors of advanced age" (Stone and Frenken 1988, 35).

An Ontario White Paper says that, "the increase in the number of elderly citizens, and particularly the older elderly, is creating a new generation of issues" (cited in Stone and Frenken, 35). These issues will influence social policy and the use of resources in the future. For example, the group aged 75 and over, compared to people aged 65–74, shows more health impairment, greater activity limitation, and greater need for daily support (Statistics Canada 1987b). This group will, therefore, need more institutional supports, medical care, household maintenance, and community health care supports in the future.

At the same time that the oldest cohorts grow in size, the younger cohorts 65 and over will also get larger. Projections show approximately a doubling in the population aged 65–74 from 1986 to 2021 (McVey 1987). This large number of older Canadians will make new demands on society. The younger elderly will change retirement patterns by retiring early or by staying at work past age 65. This group will want more recreational and educational opportunities. Services like job bureaus, schools, and counselling programs will also be needed to serve these people.

Programs for all types of older people will cost taxpayers more money. In 1986–87, for example, Canada spent $54 billion on its social security system (compared with $42.9 billion in 1982–83). More of this money went to older people than to any other age group. The single largest amount of this money went to the Old Age Security program (including the Guaranteed Income Supplement and the Spouse's Allowance). These programs cost about one quarter of the total spent on social security programs (Statistics Canada 1989a). During this same time (1986–87), the retirement payments for the Canada/Quebec Pension Plans increased 97 percent (Statistics Canada 1989a). If the proportion of older people more than doubles in the next fifty years as expected, will the public be willing to pay out even more of the country's income for older people? Or will the costs lead to resentment and a crisis in Canadian society? We will discuss these issues in more detail later in this chapter under the topic of dependency ratios.

## Ethnicity

In 1986 people of British background made up almost half (45.9 percent) of Canada's older population; people of French background made up a quarter (22.5 percent); and the rest came from a wide variety of backgrounds including non-French and non-British European, African, and Chinese cultures (Statistics Canada 1986a). Compared to younger people, a higher proportion of older people spoke a language other than English or French at home (11 percent of people aged 65 and over compared with just over 6 percent of people under age 50) (Health and Welfare Canada 1983).

These figures reflect the high immigration rates of the early 1900s and the recent immigration of older family members who join their families in Canada. In the mid-1980s, more than half of immigrants aged 65 and over come from non-British and non-French background (Statistics Canada 1986a). In the past these non-charter-group immigrants came mostly from Eastern Europe. But newer immigrants tend to come from Asia, South America and the Caribbean (Dumas 1990).

In 1987 slightly more than 20 percent of all immigrant seniors came from India (10.5 percent) and the Philippines (10 percent) (Government of Canada 1989b). As these people age, they will create a new mix of ethnicities among the older population. These people, who learned a language other than English in their native countries, continue to use this language at home. Having now reached old age, they make the older population today a more ethnically diverse group. Exhibit 4.7 shows the proportion of older people from Canada's largest ethnic groups.

Some ethnic groups have a higher proportion of older people than others. Exhibit 4.8 shows the proportion of people aged 65 or over *within each ethnic group*. Note that more than 16 percent of people claiming Jewish ethnicity and almost 15 percent of people claiming Polish ethnicity are aged 65 or older. These are two of the "oldest" ethnic groups in the country. At the other extreme, only about 7 percent of people who claim Chinese or Italian ethnicity are aged 65 or over. Native peoples have a very "young" population with less than 4 percent of their population aged 65 and over. The high proportion of Jewish older people shows the effect of low fertility rates on the aging of the Jewish population. The small proportion of older Natives shows the effect of high fertility rates on their population (Statistics Canada 1984b).

Gerber (1983) reports that both the size of an ethnic group and the proportion of older people in the group determine the institutional supports that older people can expect from their group. A large group with a moderate proportion of its population aged 65 and over can provide a more complete community life for its elderly. A small group with a high proportion of older people may be able to offer little support. Also, the concentration of the group (how near to one another members live), their location (urban or rural), the proportion of old-old to young-old, family size, and cultural values all affect the number of supports older people can draw on.

People of Finnish background, for example, tend to live in rural areas and have small families. This can lead to hardship in late old age if a person needs health care services or informal (family) supports. As these people age, spouses and friends die, and their social networks get smaller. This can lead

## Exhibit 4.7

The Elderly and Non-Elderly Populations by Ethnicity, Canada, 1981

| | Per 100 of Age Group | |
| Ethnicity | 0–64 | 65+ |
| --- | --- | --- |
| Total | 100.0 | 100.0 |
| British | 39.3 | 49.3 |
| French | 27.1 | 23.0 |
| British/French* | 1.9 | 0.8 |
| Jewish | 1.0 | 2.0 |
| Polish | 1.0 | 1.7 |
| Ukrainian | 2.1 | 3.3 |
| German | 4.7 | 5.4 |
| Dutch | 1.7 | 1.4 |
| Chinese | 1.2 | 0.9 |
| Italian | 3.2 | 2.3 |
| Native peoples | 2.2 | 0.8 |
| All other | 14.7 | 9.2 |

*Multiple response.

Note: This table includes British, French, and British/French, plus the eight ethnic origins (single response) with the largest counts for the total population.

**Source:** Statistics Canada, *The Elderly in Canada* (Ottawa: Minister of Supply and Services Canada, 1984b), Table 8. Adapted with the permission of the Minister of Supply and Services Canada, 1991.

to a lack of care and support in late old age. People of Italian background, on the other hand, have large families, tend to live in cities, and tend to live with their children. Older Italians have more access than members of smaller groups to community resources and family support in old age.

This brief look at ethnicity and aging shows that ethnic groups vary in their size, their location, their proportion of older people, and their **institutional completeness,** a term that refers to the amount of community support they offer their older members. For this reason Driedger and Chappell (1987, 75) say that "ethnicity can have significant implications for care and

## Exhibit 4.8

Population 65 Years and Over as a Percentage of the
Total Population for Selected Ethnic Groups, 1981

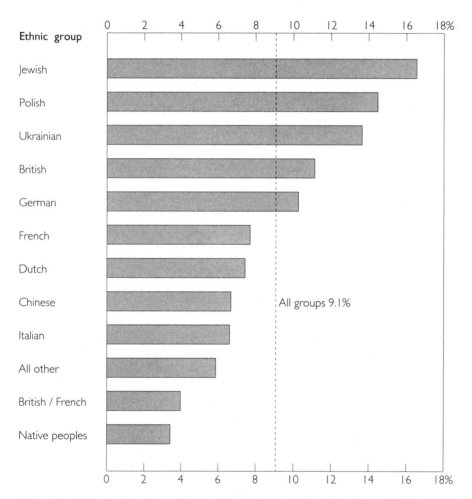

**Source:** Statistics Canada, *The Elderly in Canada* (Ottawa: Minister of Supply and Services Canada, 1984b), Chart 6. Adapted with the permission of the Minister of Supply and Services Canada, 1991.

supportiveness in old age," and so policies for older people from different types of groups (large, small, rural, or urban) will have to vary. Driedger and

Chappell (1987) advise planners and policy makers to take ethnicity into account, along with socioeconomic status and physical mobility, when designing programs for older people.

## Regional Distribution

Seventy-four percent of Canada's older people lived in Ontario, Quebec, and British Columbia in 1986, but Saskatchewan, Prince Edward Island, and Manitoba had the three highest *proportions* of older people in their total populations—12.7 percent in Saskatchewan and Prince Edward Island, and 12.6 percent in Manitoba. Prince Edward Island had the highest proportion of people aged 80 and over in its population—3.0 percent. Saskatchewan came next with 2.4 percent (Statistics Canada 1990).

These figures tell only part of the story of where older people live in Canada. Some regions within the provinces have much higher proportions of older people than the overall figures indicate. Northcott (1984) shows that migration patterns influence the proportion of older people in a province's population, especially migration of the young. "Where non-elderly net out-migration is heavy," he says, "as in Saskatchewan and Manitoba, such provinces tend to have a high and an increasing proportion of aged residents."

Manitoba towns with between 2,500 and 4,999 people, for example, had an average of 26 percent of their populations aged 65 and over. In Saskatchewan towns between 2,500 and 4,999 people had on average 19 percent of their populations aged 65 and over (Stone and Frenken 1988). Canada as a whole may show this proportion of older people in its population only in the next century. These shifts in small-town population structures due to migration (largely the effect of non-elderly outmigration) have important policy implications. As younger people leave an area to find jobs or get training and education, the older people who remain may need more formal social supports.

Cape (1987) says that rural areas in Ontario, for example, often lack housing for seniors. They also have few chronic health care supports and poor quality supports where they exist. Cape (1987) also found a lack of support for routine care. The absence of supports often forces older women (especially widows) into institutions.

In large Canadian urban centres (500,000+) in 1986 older people made up about 10.2 percent of the population. They make up a larger percentage (14.7 percent) of the population in small urban centres that have populations of between 1,000 and 2,500. Areas with some of the highest proportions of older people include Vancouver (12 percent), Winnipeg (12.4 percent), and Victoria (18 percent) (Stone and Frenken 1988). People aged 65 and over

. . . . . . . . . . . . . . . . . . . . . . . . . . . . . .

## Exhibit 4.9

### Victoria: Preview of Aging in Canada?

. . . . . . . . . . . . . . . . . . . . . . . . . . . . . .

The elderly currently are outnumbered nationally by more than four to one by those 24 and under, but because of a falling birth rate, the declining immigration of young adults and longer life expectancy the over-65s are catching up. In Victoria they already have—with consequences that make the B.C. capital like no other city in Canada. Said [Mayor Gretchen] Brewin: "We have to respond to kids who want to skateboard on the sidewalks and to seniors with frail bones who would just as soon the kids didn't." But the city administration, she concedes, faces far more complex problems that one day will test every major centre in the country ...

**Youth employment.** As more and more of the city's resources are diverted to serving the elderly, said Brewin, the number of jobs outside the service industries steadily decreases. She added, "We somehow have to find enough exciting opportunities to keep our young people here." ...

**Nursing homes.** Victoria already has about eight times as many nursing homes and homes for the aged per capita as Toronto, five times as many as Montreal and nine times as many as Halifax. But it needs more to shelter the 10 per cent of those 65 and over who need some form of institutional care. Brewin said that it is becoming harder and harder to find locations for nursing homes that do not arouse opposition from other age groups in the neighbourhood but are, at the same time, within walking distance of stores and bus stops ...

**Political power.** ... Said Brewin: "Grey power is growing. People retiring today are in better health and have a lot of political smarts. They know what they want, and they lose no time in telling you what it is. If you ignore them in this town, you are absolutely in trouble, and politicians across the country had better realize that they are facing the same situation." ...

Mayor Brewin added: "A lot of people entertain this image of Grandma sitting on the front porch in a rocking chair with a blanket wrapped around her knees. Well, let me tell you: Grandma doesn't do that any more. Today she's downtown shopping for a trip to Hawaii."

**Source:** Rae Corelli, "A Matter of Care," *Maclean's*, 6 October 1986, 51. Reprinted with permission of the publisher.

. . . . . . . . . . . . . . . . . . . . . . . . . . . . . .

make up only 6.2 percent of the population in rural farm areas, and people aged 75 and over make up less than 2 percent in these areas.

## Geographic Mobility

Older people follow internal migration patterns similar to those of younger people, but they are less mobile than the non-aged (Northcott 1984; Statistics Canada 1990). Between 1981 and 1986 half of all Canadians aged 5–54 moved, but less than one-quarter of those aged 55 and over did so (Statistics Canada 1990). The older the age group, the less likely the chance of moving.

Litwak and Longino (1987) describe three stages of later life when people may choose to move. The first is the retirement stage, when freedom from the need to live near work allows people to move to a more pleasant climate and for a more relaxed lifestyle. In the second, or disability stage, some limitation may lead the older person to move closer to children or others who can give them help. The severe disability stage is the third phase, and it requires the older person to move to a nursing home or other institution.

Northcott (1988) reports a peak in migration among older age groups around retirement age (60–69 years). This corresponds to Litwak and Longino's (1987) retirement stage. Many of these people moved out of their locality, and they most often relocated to improve their quality of life (Northcott 1988). British Columbia and Prince Edward Island showed the greatest rates of gain in older migrants, according to the 1981 census. The Northwest Territories and the Yukon, Quebec, Manitoba, and Saskatchewan showed the greatest rates of loss (Northcott 1988). A larger than average group of older people in the Atlantic provinces have moved there from another province (Health and Welfare Canada 1983; Northcott 1988; Statistics Canada 1984b). These people may have migrated because they sought a certain lifestyle in the Atlantic provinces. Overall mobility trends in Canada show a higher concentration of older people in certain places (e.g., older people tend to move westward and tend to concentrate in Ontario and British Columbia) (Northcott 1985).

Migration patterns also show a multi-directional flow. But some trends do appear. Litwak and Longino's (1987) second and third stages of migration help explain these trends. Older people, for example, tend to move from farms to towns or cities, and most older movers (60 percent) relocated within their local area. People probably move in order to live closer to their children or to the services that towns and cities offer. Provinces and towns with increased numbers of older people, will face new challenges in the future (See Exhibit 4.9.)

## Increased Numbers and Proportions of Older Women

The death rates for older women have decreased faster than they have for older men through most of this century. Between 1921 and 1976 the death rate of Canadian women aged 70-74 decreased by 50 percent, while men in this age group showed only a 10-percent decrease (Statistics Canada 1979a). In 1931 the life expectancy for a 60-year-old woman was 17.15 years; in 1961 it was 19.90 years; and in 1983-85 it was 23.36 years. (For a 60-year-old man

• • • • • • • • • • • • • • • • • • • • • • • • • • • • • •

## Exhibit 4.10

## Canadian Snowbirds: Are They a Grey Peril?

• • • • • • • • • • • • • • • • • • • • • • • • • • • • • •

Some older Canadians stay in place, others move within Canada. But, some choose a third option. They migrate south for the winter. These "snowbirds" settle in Florida, Arizona, Texas, and other southern states in the U.S. Most of them stay in the U.S. for less than six months of the year because the Canadian health system requires at least six months residence in Canada. These seniors move to their winter homes when the snow falls and return to Canada again in the spring.

Longino (1988b) found that Florida attracts more older Canadians (60+) than any other non-border state. He also reports that many Floridians along with other Sunbelt natives have a "gray peril mentality" (Longino 1988a). They fear that older seasonal migrants will place a burden on local social and health care services.

To test this idea, Longino and a group of Canadian and U.S. researchers conducted a survey of Canadian seasonal migrants in Florida. They asked about Canadians' background, health, social life, and migration patterns. This survey included the responses of 2,731 (mostly English-speaking) Canadians who lived in Florida in 1986 (Tucker and Marshall 1988; Tucker et al. 1988). The people who answered the survey had a median age of 69.2 years; more than half (57 percent) were between 65 and 74 years old; and about a fifth (21 percent) were aged 75 or older. Nearly all of them (89.6

percent) were married. More than half had graduated from high school and most reported former middle- to upper-middle class occupations (Tucker and Marshall 1988).

Marshall and Longino (1988) reviewed the health status of these people. More than 80 percent of them reported excellent or good health. Only about 10 percent of any age and gender group reported any sick days. Less than 10 percent of the sample had recently consulted a family doctor or other health professional. And few of these people used any health or social services in Florida.

Most of the snowbirds in this study reported good physical and psychological health, good social supports and high life satisfaction (Mullins et al. 1989). A third of them said that they had better health when they visited Florida. One respondent said, "My wife finds that her bronchitis is ... considerably better in Florida, as a result of the sun and warmth" (Tucker et al. 1988, 227).

This study shows that Canadian seasonal migrants make few demands on Florida's health care or social service system. The large majority of these people live healthy active lives. Most of them (89 percent) moved to Florida for the climate or for the lifestyle (67 percent). Longino (1988a, 451) says that "the search for [an] ... impact on specialized services for the aging by seasonal migrants has turned up disappointingly little evidence for the gray peril."

• • • • • • • • • • • • • • • • • • • • • • • • • • • • • •

# Exhibit 4.11

Ratio of Females to Males in Selected Age Groups,
Canada, 1951 to 2001

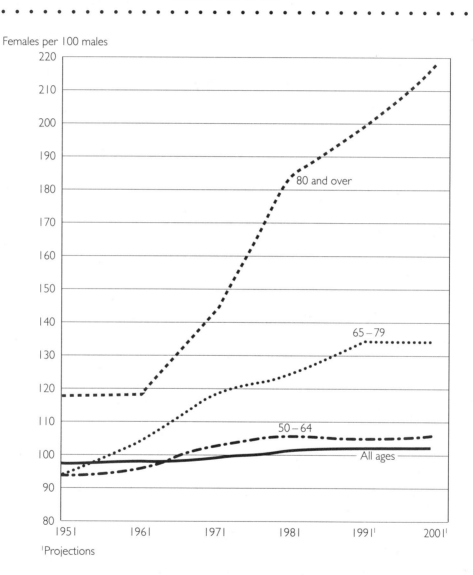

Females per 100 males

¹Projections

**Source:** Health and Welfare Canada, *Fact Book on Aging in Canada* (Ottawa: Minister of Supply and Services, 1983), Figure 3.3. Reproduced with permission of the Minister of Supply and Services Canada, 1991.

it was only 16.29 years in 1931, 16.73 years in 1961, and 18.39 years in 1983-85) (Statistics Canada 1989a).

As a result of these changes, the proportion of older women in the population has grown. At the turn of the century there were 105 men for every 100 women aged 65 and over, and in the mid-1950s older men still outnumbered older women, but by the 1960s the pattern reversed itself. By 1986 there were 138 women for every 100 men aged 65 and over (Statistics Canada 1987a; Health and Welfare Canada 1983; Stone and Fletcher 1980).

Projections show that the gap between the number of men and the number of women in the older population will level off at about 134 women to 100 men aged 65–79, but the gap will get wider for the group aged 80 and over. Projections show that by 2001 women aged 80 and over will outnumber men at the rate of 218 to 100—or better than two to one (Statistics Canada 1987c; Health and Welfare Canada 1983). (See Exhibit 4.11.)

This means that policies and programs for older people will have a greater impact on women than on men, simply because more women will live longer and so, be affected by them for more years. This is especially true of health care, housing, and income support programs. We will study these programs in detail in the chapters ahead. For now, we will look at the overall impact of population aging on Canada's economy.

## THE IMPACT OF POPULATION AGING

### The Dependency Ratio and the Cost of an Aging Population

Concern about the increasing numbers of older people typically pits the old against the young. The Science Council of Canada (Auerbach and Gerber 1976, 3) calls an older population of between 13 percent and 15 percent "a significant social burden." Statistics Canada (1979a, Introduction) reports that old age creates problems that "are the nation's concern," and some writers say that an older population could lead to intergenerational conflict (Tindale and Marshall 1980). These sources assume a high dependence of older people on the young, and they suggest that the young will rebel or resent the burden of a large older population.

Gerontologists use a figure called the **overall dependency ratio** to gauge the burden that the old and the young place on people in middle age. Experts arrive at this ratio by adding the number of people under age 18 to the number of people aged 65 and over. They then compare this figure to the population aged 18–64:

$$\frac{\text{(Population aged 0–17) + (Population aged 65+)}}{\text{(Population aged 18–64)}}$$

(Some writers use ages 0–14 or 0–20 as the age span for the younger group.)

Denton and Spencer (1980) used the dependency ratio to look at dependency in Canada. They found that while the ratio of people aged 65 and over to those aged 20–64 will nearly double from 1976 to 2031, the proportion of young people will decline. When they combined these projected changes in the young and old populations, they found that this led to "a somewhat lower overall dependency ratio for the remainder of this century and throughout the first decade of the next, as compared with 1976, and then a pronounced increase in the following two decades or so" (Denton and Spencer 1980, 24–25; see also Perrault 1990). In spite of this increase, in 2031 (when the Baby Boom will have created large increases in the over-65 population) the overall dependency ratio may not be much higher than in 1976 (Chawla 1991). Exhibit 4.12 shows Statistics Canada dependency projections based on two sets of population assumptions.

*Assumptions A* lead to a relatively modest increase in the overall dependency ratio in 2031. *Assumptions B* lead to a more dramatic increase in the overall dependency ratio in 2031, but still a rate lower than 1961. Chawla (1991) also projects a rate close to the 1976 figures. Denton, Feaver, and Spencer (1986, 86) say that figures like these should reassure "those who are concerned about the possible inability of the economy to support its dependent population—young and old—in the decades ahead."

The Ontario Ministry of Treasury and Economics says that the "crude dependency rates" presented in Exhibit 4.13 tell only part of the story. These rates tell us little about the economic burden of an older population (Stone and Fletcher 1980). Chawla (1991), for example, projects roughly the same dependency ratio in 2030 as in 1965. But in 1965 people aged 65 and over made up only 19 percent of the dependent population. Chawla (1991) projects that in 2030 people aged 65 and over will make up 55 percent of the dependent population. This will give Canada a dependency ratio with one of the largest proportions of older people of any country in the world (Chawla 1991).

A study by Canada's Treasury Board Secretariat (1977) estimated that in 1976 government expenditures for people aged 65 and over came to two and a half times the amount for people aged 0–17. Burke (1991) reports roughly the same figure for 1980. The secretariat found that education costs for the young came to about the same amount as Old Age Security costs for the old. But medical care costs for people aged 65 and over came to twice the costs for people aged 0–14; Canada Assistance Plan costs for the old were triple the

## Exhibit 4.12

Dependency Rates for Canada, Selected Years 1901 to 1986;
Two Projections for Selected Years 1991 to 2031

| Year | 65+/18–64 | | 0–17/18–64 | | Overall Dependency | |
|------|-----------|---|------------|---|--------------------|---|
| 1901 | 9.3 | | 74.9 | | 84.2 | |
| 1921 | 8.7 | | 72.6 | | 81.3 | |
| 1941 | 11.2 | | 56.5 | | 67.7 | |
| 1961 | 14.3 | | 72.8 | | 87.1 | |
| 1976 | 14.4 | | 52.8 | | 67.2 | |
| 1981 | 15.6 | | 45.2 | | 59.8 | |
| 1986[1] | 16.8 | | 40.8 | | 57.6 | |
| | A | B | A | B | A | B |
| 1991[2] | 18.7 | 18.6 | 38.0 | 39.9 | 56.7 | 58.5 |
| 2001 | 21.4 | 20.7 | 31.6 | 41.6 | 53.0 | 62.3 |
| 2021 | 33.4 | 27.6 | 25.7 | 40.7 | 59.1 | 68.3 |
| 2031 | 45.3 | 33.5 | 25.5 | 43.5 | 70.8 | 77.0 |

[1]Census data 1986. Cat. No. 91-101.

[2]Assumptions of Projections A and B: Projection A is the "most plausible course of events in the short term." It is a low-growth scenario. It assumes a fertility rate (the number of children per woman by 1996) of 1.4. Projection B assumes "a complete reversal in fertility ... trends." This is a high-growth scenario. It assumes a fertility rate (the number of children per woman by 1996) of 2.2. Both projections assume that life expectancy at birth will increase to 74.9 years for men and 81.6 years for women by 1996.

**Source:** Figures for 1991 to 2001: Statistics Canada, *Population Projections for Canada, Provinces and Territories*. 1984-2006, Cat. No. 91-520 (Ottawa: Minister of Supply and Services, 1985, 41); Figures for 2021 and 2031: Statistics Canada Demography Division, unpublished data provided to Statistics Canada, Health Division, Social Security Section, September 1987. Reproduced with permission of the Minister of Supply and Services Canada, 1991.

costs for the young; and hospital costs for older people came to more than ten times the costs for the young (Treasury Board Secretariat 1977).

The Ontario Ministry of Treasury and Economics (1979) calculated "effective dependency rates" based on these differences in the costs for older and younger age groups. It concludes that with a crude total dependency ratio in 2031 that is about the same as the crude rate in 1976, but with more

## Exhibit 4.13

Projected Dependency Rates Relative to 1976

| | 1976 | 1981 | 1991 | 2001 | 2011 | 2021 | 2031 |
|---|---|---|---|---|---|---|---|
| **1.** Relative Crude Dependency Rates | | | | | | | |
| Total | 1.00 | 0.89 | 0.86 | 0.82 | 0.78 | 0.89 | 0.99 |
| Aged | 1.00 | 1.03 | 1.16 | 1.22 | 1.30 | 1.74 | 2.20 |
| **2.** Relative Effective[1] Dependency Rates | | | | | | | |
| **(a)** Equal Growth | | | | | | | |
| Total | 1.00 | 0.98 | 1.02 | 1.01 | 1.02 | 1.20 | 1.43 |
| Aged | 1.00 | 1.14 | 1.40 | 1.48 | 1.59 | 2.11 | 2.72 |
| **(b)** 1% Growth Differential | | | | | | | |
| Total | 1.00 | 0.94 | 0.89 | 0.82 | 0.78 | 0.86 | 0.96 |
| Aged | 1.00 | 1.08 | 1.23 | 1.23 | 1.24 | 1.56 | 1.85 |

[1]Assuming 1.8 fertility rate and net immigration of 100,000.

**Source:** Ontario Ministry of Treasury and Economics, *Issues in Pension Policy: Demographic and Economic Aspects of Canada's Ageing Population* (Toronto: Ontario Ministry of Treasury and Economics, 1979), 15, Table 4.

older people and fewer younger people in the population, the effective total dependency rate in 2031 exceeds the 1976 rate by 43 percent (see Exhibit 4.13) (Ontario Ministry of Treasury and Economics 1979).

A study by Denton, Feaver, and Spencer (1986) also concludes that service costs may rise as the population ages. They projected dependency ratios from 1980 to 2030, and then estimated the changes in government program and service costs in the future. They report two trends: first, a shrinking labour force in the years ahead looks likely. This could lead to a decline in the Gross National Product (GNP) from 2010 to 2030 and an increase in service costs above growth in the GNP for these two decades.

Second, they predict a shift in government service costs. They also project a decrease in education expenses of about 15 percent between 1980 and 2030, but forecast a tripling in social security payments and almost a doubling of health expenditures for this period. They also note that, given present arrangements, the federal government will bear most of the cost of social security and health care increases. This, they believe, could lead to tensions between the provincial and federal governments and to a shifting of responsibilities for health care services to the provinces. Some recent changes in funding arrangements suggest that this may already have begun (Canadian Council on Social Development 1990).

Burke (1991) says that in the years between 1980 and 2040 pension costs will rise more than any other expense and projects a 204-percent increase over this time. If this comes to pass, pensions will "account for 38% of social spending, up from just 24% in 1980" (Burke 1991, 7). At the same time health care costs will increase by 118 percent and account for 33 percent of social spending (compared with 29 percent in 1980). These trends would lead to an increase in social spending of 87 percent in Canada, which is quite high compared with predictions of 65 percent for the U.S. and 40 percent for Japan.

Researchers may disagree about the specific impact of an aging population on health and income resources. But nearly all of them agree that more health care and income resources will go to serve older people and that this will cost more money. This shift in resources to the older population will force Canadians to make some hard choices. Burke (1991, 8), for example, says that "Canadians will most likely have to choose between increasing tax rates and social security contributions or lower levels of social benefits." The next fifty years will see increased debate over the allocation of health and income resources.

Reports on the future look gloomy, but dependency ratios tell only part of the story. Myles and Boyd (1982, 259) say that "alarmist exercises in futurology ... have produced more oversight than insight" when it comes to the issue of dependency in the future. Even small changes in Canada's economy and social norms, for example, could lead to large decreases in the effective dependency rate (Chen 1987). Denton, Feaver, and Spencer (1986, 90) say that "non-demographic forces [e.g., changes in the demand for services, increases in per capita worker output, or changes in the federal government's commitment to fund programs] could easily be more important quantitatively than demographic ones in their effects on government expenditures."

Most projections, for example, assume a traditional retirement age of 65 (when people become entitled to Old Age Security payments). But government policy could change and this age could be raised, or Old Age Security payments could be taxed back, which the present government has begun to do. Also, because more middle-aged workers today have private pension plans and savings, they may rely less on government pension supplements when they reach old age than pensioners do today. More flexible retirement plans will allow some people to work full- or part-time after age 65. The Canada Pension Plan has changed its rules to make both early and late retirement more attractive. All of these trends will change current dependency patterns and alter future projections (Chen 1987).

A stronger economy would also ease the dependency burden. Even a small improvement in the income of middle-aged people, compared to costs for services to the old, would significantly decrease the effective dependency rate. The Ontario Ministry of Treasury and Economics (1979) found that if income for working people increased even 1 percent faster than dependency costs, the effective dependency rates would be less than in 1976. In a strong economy higher costs for services to the elderly may not create a burden for the middle-aged.

Weller and Bouvier (1981) point to one of the greatest weaknesses of using dependency rates to project into the future. They say that dependency rates focus too narrowly on the costs of having more older people in society. They remind us that an older population will also bring benefits, such as a lower crime rate, a lower auto accident rate, and increased concern for fitness, diet, and disease prevention. Higher numbers of older people may also improve the economy: they will likely spend their savings to consume the services of travel agencies, restaurants, and professionals (McDaniel 1986). These trends may reduce some waste of social resources and create a higher quality of life for people of all ages.

McDaniel (1986) says that demographic trends do not determine social change. But demography does shape individual experience and social life. The Baby Boom generation, for example, had to fight harder for schooling, jobs, and housing because of their large numbers. They have also gotten used to society meeting their needs (for housing, child care, etc.). Will this generation demand an unreasonable level of social support as it ages? Or will the Baby Boomers develop a broader view of their relationship to society and moderate their expectations?

Demographers need to study the connections between demographic facts, political realities, and social change. How much choice do countries have in how they will respond to demographic change? What determines the choices a country makes? Are there models of preferred adaptation to an aging population?

Countries like Sweden and Norway could serve as models for Canadian policy. Already, more than 14 percent of the populations of these countries are over age 65, and they have not faced crises as a result. Progressive programs have been put in place to serve older people, and citizens pay more in taxes to support them. These countries show that the transition to an older society can come about without social conflict and distress (Myles 1982).

Canadian society has its own history, its own mix of ethnicity, age/sex ratios, economic institutions, and values. Canada will face still unknown political, economic, and social challenges. So, Canada will have to discover its own responses to population aging. The Science Council of Canada says that the adjustments necessary to an older society "can be done"—and done without social upheaval (Auerbach and Gerber 1976, 3). These changes will take planning, thought, and creative social action, and all of us will play a part in this societal transformation.

## SUMMARY

1. Canada has a younger population than most of the other developed nations. It had about 11 percent of the population aged 65 and over in 1986. Demographers project that this population will more than double by 2031 and will equal almost 24 percent of the total population.

2. Canada went through a demographic transition between 1850 and 1950. During this time immigration increased, the death rate decreased, and, most important of all, the birth rate decreased. Between 1850 and 1950 the older population grew from about 4 percent of the population to over 7 percent.

3. Canada today has a diverse older population. Older people differ by ethnicity, sex, income, education, and marital status. They also differ by age. Longer life expectancy in old age has given rise a wide range of age groups within the older population. Large increases in the very old population will place new demands on health care and social service resources.

4. The growth of the older population (and the decrease in the younger population) has led some people to predict an economic crisis due to the large numbers of dependent older people. Gerontologists measure the dependence of young and old people on middle-aged people and call this measure the overall dependency ratio (or rate).

5. Experts look at dependency rates to project the future costs of an aging society. Future dependency rates will depend on a number of social conditions. A weak economy, low birth rates, low immigration rates, and a rise in costs of services for the old (compared to per capita income for the middle-aged) will increase the burden on middle-aged people. A strong economy, higher birth rates, more immigration, and a rise in per capita income for middle-aged people (compared to costs in services for the old) will mean less burden on middle-aged workers. Changes in social values and retirement ages as well as better preparation for old age by middle-aged people today could also decrease effective dependency rates.

6. Dependency rates focus on the costs of an aging society. But an aging society may have a lower crime rate, a lower accident rate, and more concern for lifelong health and fitness. These changes would decrease the waste of social and economic resources and improve the quality of life in Canada.

7. Canada can grow old without upheaval and conflict; most of the developed nations have done so. But the transition to an aging society will take planning, thought, and creative social action.

## SELECTED READINGS

McDaniel, Susan A. *Canada's Aging Population.* Toronto: Butterworths, 1986.

A good overview of aging and demography in Canada. This book covers basic demographic concepts like dependency ratios, population pyramids, and population age/sex structure. It also examines current issues in population aging, including aging in a world context, policy implications of population aging, and the future of aging in Canada. Well written, with up-to-date sources throughout the text.

Northcott, Herbert C. *Changing Residence: The Geographic Mobility of Elderly Canadians.* Toronto: Butterworths, 1988.

A detailed analysis of older peoples' geographic mobility. The book presents concepts related to mobility, facts about moving within Canada, and a discussion of mobility patterns across the life span. It also compares Canadian mobility to mobility in other developed countries.

Statistics Canada. *Canadian Social Trends.* Cat. No. 11-008E. Ottawa: Minister of Supply and Services, Annual.

Statistics Canada publishes this journal four times a year. Articles report on data from recent government studies in a readable magazine format and are accompanied by charts and graphs that help to interpret the statistics. Each issue contains useful and up-to-date information on topics like demography, living arrangements, and aging in Canada. A good resource for professionals and students of aging.

# Maturational Change

# Personal Health and Illness

## INTRODUCTION

Mr. Shigechiyo Izumi died at the age of 120 on the island of Tokunoshima, Japan, in February 1986. At the time he died, he was the world's oldest man of those whose ages could be verified. He attributed his long life to "the daily cup of *shochu* [sugar-cane liquor] and keeping a simple diet" (*Time* 1986b). Other centenarians attribute their long life to regular sex, walking five miles a day, or drinking a shot of whiskey before bed. One 100-year-old man claimed that eating a pound of peanuts a day led to his long life.

Scientific research supports some of these methods for longer life: moderate drinkers live longer than teetotallers (though no one knows why) (Woodruff 1982); a simple diet low in fats, salt, and sugar can decrease disease; and exercise leads to good health and possibly a longer life (Ausman and Russell 1990). But even with good habits, a good diet, and a good environment, physiological aging takes place. Older people on the covers of health and nutrition

. . . . . . . . . . . . . . . . . . . . . . . . . . . . . . . . . . . . . . .

## Exhibit 5.1

### Controversy: The Long-Lived People of Abkhazia

. . . . . . . . . . . . . . . . . . . . . . . . . . . . . . . . . . . . . . .

"Work hard and never worry," say the Hunza people of Pakistan. The Hunza claim to produce some of the longest-living people in the world. They say they live such long lives because they have good water and a good climate, and they stay happy. The Vilcabambans of Ecuador also claim long lives (Mazess and Forman 1979). About 1 percent of them claim to live past the age of 100 (compared to about 1 in 10,000 in North America). The Abkhazians, one of the best-known and most-studied of the long-lived peoples, live in the Caucasus mountains of the Soviet Union. The Soviet census reports that 70 percent of Soviet citizens 110 years old or over live in this region (Benet 1976, 7).

Some Abkhazians (like the Hunzas and Vilcabambans) claim to be 120, 130, and even 160 years old. Pitskhelauri, a Soviet researcher, reports that the oldest man in one district of Abkhazia is 139 years old. This man, he says, works as a farmer and has "150 children, grandchildren, great-grandchildren, great-great-grandchildren" (1982, 53).

Stories like this have led journalists, television crews, and researchers from all over the world to study and visit the Abkhazians, but few scientists outside the Soviet Union believe their claims. Hayflick (1974, 43) says that researchers have "reported these claims without sufficiently emphasizing the meager evidence for the allegations. ... Claims of super-longevity should be taken with as much skepticism as any claim unsupported by proof."

Careful studies of the Abkhazians' ages reveal that "only 38 percent of the 115 [people] thought to be over 90 were actually verified as being over 90 ... Furthermore, none of those reevaluated were found to be actually over age 110" (Palmore 1984, 95; see also Medvedev 1974). A study of the Soviet census by Bennett and Garson (1986) found that only a small fraction of the number of people who claim to be over 100 years old have actually reached that age. These studies have put an end to the myth that a long-lived people exists, but the latest research leaves open two important biological questions. First, why do so few humans in any society live past 100 years of age, if humans have a potential life span of 110 to 120 years? Second, what are the causes of biological aging?

. . . . . . . . . . . . . . . . . . . . . . . . . . . . . . . . . . . . . . .

magazines beam good health—but they still have white hair, brown spots on their skin, and wrinkles, like older people all over the world.

Gerontologists distinguish between the maximum life span (the maximum number of years a member of a species can live) and life expectancy (the number of years at birth an average member of a society can expect to live).

Scientists think that the maximum human life span of somewhere between 110 and 120 years has stayed the same for the past 100,000 years. Kraus (1987), for example, reports 114 years as the oldest authenticated age ever recorded in Canada. Human life expectancy at birth, on the other hand, has increased in the past 2,000 years from an average of 22 years in ancient Rome to around 70 years today. Technology and biomedical science continue to extend life expectancy (Stone and Fletcher 1986; Parliament 1987), and if this trend continues, more and more people will live close to the maximum human life span (Botwinick 1984). This means that more people will live to old age and more will live longer in old age than ever before.

The study of biological aging has two goals: to understand the biology of aging and to apply this knowledge to extend and improve human life. This chapter will look at (1) why people age; (2) what effects aging has on health, behaviour, and everyday life; and (3) how older people cope with physical change.

## THE CAUSES OF AGING

Strehler (1977) divides aging processes into two categories: determinate (or intrinsic) processes of aging and ancillary (or extrinsic) processes of aging. **Intrinsic aging** includes the loss of lung elasticity, the accumulation of debris in aging cells, and the slowing of a person's reaction time. It includes genetic predispositions toward illnesses like heart disease and diabetes, and physical changes such as baldness and wrinkling. **Extrinsic aging** includes the effects on a person's physiology of smoking, air pollution, and a calcium-poor diet. Scientists try to separate intrinsic from extrinsic processes in order to understand the causes of aging (Manton 1990).

Strehler (1977; see also Thompson and Forbes 1990; Pfeiffer 1990) lists the following four criteria as defining intrinsic aging:

1. True (intrinsic) aging occurs universally. All members of a species will show age changes if they live long enough, though the rate of change will vary from culture to culture. People exposed to the sun, for example, will show signs of aging skin—wrinkles and stiffness—early in life, while people who stay covered from the sun may wrinkle at a later age. Still, all people will show some decreased elasticity in the skin, if they live long enough.

2. True aging is basic to the organism. A person cannot change or manipulate the rate of this process. Until recently scientists considered atherosclerosis (thickening of the interior of the artery due to fatty deposits) to be a sign of intrinsic aging, but today scientists view it as a disease that may or may not occur as underlying processes of aging take place. Smoking, a fatty diet, and high blood pressure can all increase the risk of atherosclerosis. Decreased lung elasticity, on the other hand, seems like a true sign of aging.

3. True aging is progressive. It takes place gradually and leads to a cumulative decline in function. Strokes, heart attacks, and tumours—major killers in old age—come on quickly, and therefore they probably do not represent unchangeable parts of the aging process. These diseases may develop as a result of many gradual changes in molecular and cell function. Biological research will have to look to the molecular level of the body, at the aging cell, to understand many of the diseases of old age.

4. True aging is deleterious; it leads to functional decline that makes death more likely. True aging or senescence leads to a gradual decline in a person's ability to cope with environmental demands.

Disease, accidents, or social conditions do not cause intrinsic aging. Eating yogurt, jogging, or massaging the skin will not stop it. Scientists trace intrinsic aging to changes within the human cell over time. All animal cells, for example, have built-in limits on the number of times they can divide (Hayflick and Moorehead 1961). Hayflick and Moorehead (1961) found that human embryo cells can divide 40 to 60 times before they die. Cells in adults can divide only 20 times. Older cells also produce less energy, make enzymes more slowly, and allow waste to fill up inside them (Hayflick 1970). Biologists call this the "Phase III" phenomenon or "Hayflick limit."

Some theories of biological aging trace aging to chemical changes in the cell. Free radical theory, for example, traces biological aging to a class of highly active molecules, called "free radicals," that tend to bond with other molecules in the cell (Gordon, Ronsen, and Brown 1974). Free radicals create large fatty deposits in cells that show up as "liver spots" on the skin. They also interfere with the cell's ability to get rid of waste. Free radicals can also cause links across the strands of the DNA spiral. These "cross-links" inhibit cell division and lead to plaque build-up on the walls of arteries and clouding of the eye lens (Cerami, Vlassara, and Brownlee 1987).

Other theories suggest that as the cell ages genetic programs switch off the cell's ability to divide (Strehler 1977). Harley (1988) says that gene activity in the cell may serve a positive function early in life, but may damage the system later. Walford (1969) proposed an autoimmune theory of aging. This theory says that white blood cells called T cells attack the body's healthy cells. This could explain the rise in cancer, rheumatoid arthritis, and diabetes in older adults.

None of these theories give a complete explanation for why people age. But researchers will continue to look at the structure and function of the cell for a single explanation of aging.


# THE EFFECTS OF AGING ON BODY SYSTEMS

Current models of aging propose that intrinsic changes in the cells cause aging and that over time these changes lead to changes in the body's systems. Strehler (1982) says that from age 30 onward the body shows an average decline in function of about 1 percent per year, though different functions decline at different rates in any one person, and some people show more decline in functions than other people. Shock (1977) says that the more a function requires the integrated work of many body systems the greater the decline in that function over time.

This section will describe some of the changes that take place in the body's systems as a person ages, including changes in bone structure, hormone production, system integration, and the senses. Many changes take place in other body systems as well, but these examples will give some idea of what happens to the body with age.


## Changes in Bone Structure

The body loses bone mass with age as mineral salts take the place of solid bone. Bones get more porous and brittle, and this leads to a higher risk of fracture, to stooped posture, and to loss of height. These changes take place in both men and women from age 35–40 on, but women more often than men suffer from an extreme loss of bone mass called **osteoporosis**. This shows up as widow's or dowager's hump, stooped posture, and compressed or collapsed vertebrae. In some cases the spine bows so much that the lower ribs sit on top of the pelvis. Loss of bone mass can make bones so weak that they cannot support a person's weight. Research shows that in some cases when an older person fractures a hip during a fall, the femoral neck (near the hip bone's ball joint) fractures first and then a person falls, rather than the other way around. Kart, Metress, and Metress (1978) report that 75 percent of people with a broken hip show some osteoporosis of the femoral neck.

Causes of osteoporosis can include decreases in the creation of new bone, hormone and vitamin deficiencies, and poor nutrition. Research suggests that lack of calcium in the diet during the growing years (McCulloch 1990), poor absorption of calcium as a person ages, or hormone loss may each play a role in the onset of the disease. A decrease in activity with age may also bring on or accelerate loss of bone mass.

Some research points to a decrease in estrogen production as a cause of bone mass loss in older women. Levels of estrogen, the hormone responsible for menstruation, decrease gradually in women from age 40 on (Glass and Kase 1970). While estrogen replacement therapy may halt or slow the process, this treatment may increase the risk of cancer.

Recent research has looked at ways to prevent or reverse osteoporosis. McCulloch (1990) reviewed the results of six controlled calcium supplementation studies. Only one study found that calcium supplements had a positive effect on women with osteoporosis. McCulloch (1990, 170, 172) says that, "dietary calcium during youth may influence peak bone density at maturity ... [but] at best, calcium supplements given to postmenopausal women for a sufficiently long period of time may be effective in reducing the rate of bone loss." McCulloch (1990) adds that moderate regular exercise like walking provides the best way to maintain bone health.

## Changes in Hormone Production—Menopause

Menopause takes place between the ages of 45 and 50 for most women. It marks the end of a woman's reproductive activity. As menopause approaches, a woman's ovaries no longer produce an egg as part of her monthly cycle. Also, production of estrogen (as has been mentioned) and progesterone, diminishes.

Menopause has two common symptoms—hot flashes and vaginal dryness. These symptoms can cause physical discomfort and psychological distress. Women describe hot flashes as "a feeling of heat and sweat flooding one's head without warning" (Boston Women's Health 1982, 77). The decrease in estrogen may cause these feelings. As the woman's body adjusts to new hormone levels the feelings tend to decrease and stop. Vaginal dryness can lead to irritation and infections. Using a lubricant during intercourse can help relieve some of the discomfort.

Some physicians recommend estrogen replacement therapy (ERT). The hormone is taken orally or applied in the form of a vaginal cream. This treatment can help relieve hot flashes and vaginal dryness. Some evidence suggests that ERT leads to some risks and side effects.

Research has found that about 20 percent of women experience either no or few menopausal symptoms (Boston Women's Health 1982). Most women cope well with the physical symptoms that do occur. Popular belief in the past linked menopause to depression and psychological distress. More recent research has found that few women report psychological distress. And the majority of women either have no feelings about menopause at all or feel relief (Tavris 1991).

## Changes in the Central Nervous System

Studies of bone structure (or any of the other body systems) focus on change in one part of the body at a time. Research on reaction time suggests that the relationships among the body's systems also cause functional decline. **Reaction time** refers to how fast a person responds to a demand from the environment. Typical tests to determine reaction time measure how fast a driver responds to a red light; how quickly an airline pilot responds to an emergency signal; or how fast a person reacts to a visual test in a laboratory. Laboratory studies of reaction time show that people respond more slowly as they age (Cerella, Poon, and Williams 1980; Goggin and Stelmach 1990; Welford 1977). Birren (1974) says that aging leads to an "electrical brownout" in the nervous system. Albert and Kaplan (1980) call this slowing the "classic aging pattern."

Researchers have studied several reasons for the decline in reaction time. Among them are decline in the senses (the older person perceives the stimulus less clearly), decline in neuromuscular action (the muscles respond more slowly), and changes in the central nervous system (the brain processes the need for a response more slowly) (Salthouse 1985). Welford (1984) suggests that more "noise" in the system (poor circulation to the brain) leads to a decreased "signal" in the system. This then leads to slower reaction time.

Botwinick (1984) suggests that a decrease in reaction time comes about when the central nervous system and the autonomic nervous system, the system that regulates body activities like heart rate, lose their integrated style of functioning (see also Thompson and Marsh 1973). This research suggests that the disintegration in the relationships between physical systems, rather than a decline in any one physical system, causes a decline in physical function.

## Sensory Changes

All five senses—smell, taste, touch, hearing, and sight change with age, but the most dramatic changes take place in the senses of sight and hearing.

Naeyaert (1990) says that a gradual change in vision begins at about age 40 for most people. Another study found that noticeable changes take place by age 50 (Johnson and Choy 1987 cited in Fozard 1990). Kosnik et al. (1988)

## Exhibit 5.2

### Aging Body Functions

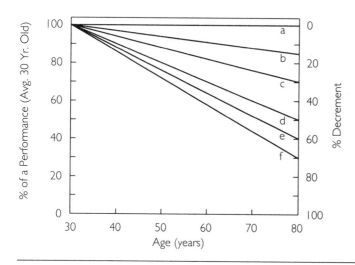

a : Fasting Blood Glucose

b : { Nerve Conduction Velocity, Cellular Enzymes }

c : Cardiac Index (resting)

d : { Vital Capacity, Renal Blood Flow }

e : Max. Breathing Capacity

f : { Max. Work Rate, Max. O₂ Uptake }

Age decrements in physiological functions in males. Mean values for 20- to 35-year-old subjects are taken as 100%. Decrements shown are schematic linear projections: (a) fasting blood glucose, (b) nerve conduction velocity and cellular enzymes, (c) resting cardiac index, (d) vital capacity and renal blood flow, (e) maximum breathing capacity, and (f) maximum work rate and maximum oxygen uptake.

**Source:** Diagram from N.W. Shock, "Systems Integration," in C.E. Finch and L. Hayflick, eds., *Handbook of the Biology of Aging* (New York: Van Nostrand Reinhold, 1977), 640. Orig. N.W. Shock, "Energy Metabolism, Calorie Intake and Physical Activity of the Aging," in L.A. Carlson, ed. (Uppsala: Aluiquist and Wiksell, 1972). © Swedish Nutrition Foundation. Reproduced with permission of the publisher.

studied changes in vision in adults in their natural environment. They report a decline in these visual abilities of between two and six times across the adult life span. They found that older people had problems with glare, dim lighting, and in doing visual work. Older people also had problems following moving objects and picking an object out of a complex background (Kosnik et al. 1988).

A number of illnesses can cause loss of sight in later life. These include macular degeneration, the loss of central vision, caused by infection or hypertension; cataract, clouding of the eye's lens, caused by a chemical change in the lens; and glaucoma, a disturbance of the optic nerve, caused by the build-up of fluid in the eye.

The loss of sight can lead to the loss of basic skills, a decrease in life satisfaction, and changes in personality. Some people can compensate for loss of sight with low-vision aids like large print books and even TV readers. Also, they can adapt by using more lighting, by using contrasting colours to give them cues about shapes of things, adopting techniques to organize objects for ease of use in their homes.

Fozard and Popkin (1978) say that older people in institutional settings should have control of the lighting, so that they can set the lights at the level they find comfortable. Older drivers will benefit from brighter signs at night (Fozard 1990).

Naeyaert (1990) reports that about 10 percent of people aged 65 and over have a visual impairment that restricts daily activity. The Canadian National Institute for the Blind (CNIB) (1988) reports that 65.9 percent of its clients are aged 60 and over. The group aged 60 and over made up 75.5 percent of new CNIB clients in 1988. The growth of the senior population will lead to more people with visual impairment in the future.

Lai (1990) reports that at least 50 percent of people aged 60 and over suffer from hearing loss. People aged 80 and over show a failure rate of over 80%. People can lose their hearing because of something simple like a wax build-up in the ear or because of incurable inner ear damage to nerve fibres. Hearing loss decreases a person's ability to communicate. The impaired person may seem confused, difficult to work with, or withdrawn.

Captioning, improved lighting, good signage, aural rehabilitation, and hearing aids (to name only a few supports) can help many seniors. Studies show that simple techniques for talking with older people who have a hearing problem can make up for their hearing loss. Speaking louder, however, may make things worse. It raises the pitch of the speaker's voice (making it harder for the older person to understand) and puts the older person on the defensive. Instead, speak "low and slow." Speak in a lower tone with distinct enunciation, speak slowly, and find other words to say the same thing if you have to repeat yourself. Someone with a hearing loss often gets meaning from the context. Barrett (1972) found that people with a hearing loss fill in the gaps when they listen to familiar music. People also do this when they listen to someone speak. Take your time when you talk to someone with a hearing loss.

A speaker should also keep in mind that a person's vision can help compensate for hearing loss. Face the older person who has a hearing problem and, when speaking, let the light in a room fall on your face (not behind you and in the older person's eyes). Older people with a hearing loss often read your lips without knowing they do it. Get a person's attention by touch or gesture first, so they hear what you say from the start.

Only 28 percent of people with a hearing disorder use a hearing aid. And 13 percent of people who need a hearing aid say they cannot afford one (Secretary of State 1986). People with hearing disabilities have a higher unmet need for help than people with any other disability.

## Changes in Health

Decreases in bone strength, menopause, slower reaction time, and a decline in the senses all point to a general decline in physical and central nervous system functioning with age (Fozard 1990). Thompson and Forbes (1990) say that functional decline moves a person into a higher risk group for health or adverse physical problems. But how much do these declines affect the older person's health and social life? Does physical decline lead to a decline in the older person's well-being?

Researchers have asked two questions about the effects of physiological aging on the older person's well-being. First, do health problems increase with age? Second, does physiological aging limit the older person's activities?

### Changes in Health Status

The 1985 General Social Survey asked a sample of 11,200 community-dwelling Canadians aged 15 and over about their health (Statistics Canada 1987). The study asked about limits to activity, well-being, and chronic health problems.

Older people in this study reported more chronic illness than the younger population. They reported high rates of arthritis, rheumatism, hypertension, diabetes, and heart disease (Statistics Canada 1987). (See Exhibit 5.3).

The General Social Survey (Statistics Canada 1987) also found that specific groups among the older population report high rates of chronic conditions. Women, for example, reported higher rates of hypertension, arthritis, and rheumatism than did men. Also, Chappell, Strain, and Blandford (1986, 44) report that women "have more days per year of restricted activity, more days of bed disability, more doctor's visits, higher expenditures for health care and higher rates of institutionalization than men." These figures may reflect the continuation of a pattern of health care use by women during their middle years. They may reflect a denial of health problems by men, or they may reflect the fact that a greater proportion of men are married and have someone to care for them outside of an institutional setting.

. . . . . . . . . . . . . . . . . . . . . . . . . . . . . . . . . . . . . . . . .

## Exhibit 5.3

Percentages of Population in Each Age Group, by Sex,
Self-Reporting Selected Health Problems, Canada, 1985

. . . . . . . . . . . . . . . . . . . . . . . . . . . . . . . . . . . . . . . . .

| Health Problem | 15+ | 65+ | |
| --- | --- | --- | --- |
| | Both Sexes | Males | Females |
| Arthritis/Rheumatism | 22 | 46 | 63 |
| Hypertension | 16 | 33 | 43 |
| Heart Trouble | 7 | 28 | 24 |
| Respiratory Problems | 11 | 26 | 23 |
| Diabetes | 2 | 9 | 9 |

These findings show that males aged 65 and over were twice as likely as the rest of population to report respiratory problems, hypertension and arthritis, or rheumatism. Males aged 65 and over were four times more likely than the rest of the population to report heart trouble. Females aged 65 and over were more than 2 1/2 times as likely as the rest of the population to report hypertension and almost three times as likely to report arthritis and rheumatism. Both men and women aged 65 and over were more than four times as likely as the rest of the population to report diabetes.

**Source:** Statistics Canada, *Health and Social Support, 1985*. General Social Survey Analysis Series. Cat. No. 11-612 E, No. 1 (Ottawa: Minister of Supply and Services, 1987), 153, Table 51. Adapted with the permission of the Minister of Supply and Services Canada, 1991.

. . . . . . . . . . . . . . . . . . . . . . . . . . . . . . . . . . . . . . . . .

Studies show that the oldest age groups among people aged 65 and over have more health problems than the younger groups. Some researchers (Chappell and Havens 1980) divide the older population according to differences in their health status. For women they describe three groups: young-old (aged less than 75), middle-old (aged 75–84), and old-old (aged 85 and over); for men they describe two groups: the young-old (aged less than 80) and the old-old (aged 80 and over). The Canada Health Survey (Health and Welfare Canada and Statistics Canada 1981) divides the older population into two age groups, (65–69), and (70 and over). The survey reports that chronic conditions increase with age.

Slightly more than 20 percent of the group aged 65–69 reported no chronic conditions, but this dropped to only 16.5 percent for the group aged 70 and over. Almost 35 percent of the 70 and over group reported three or more chronic conditions compared to only 29 percent of the group aged 65–69 (Health and Welfare Canada and Statistics Canada 1981). Chronic illness may lead to functional decline. And this may decrease an older person's quality of life.

### Limits on Activity Due to Physical Decline

Chappell, Strain, and Blandford (1986, 36) define **functional disability** as a "functional limitation on the *performance of normal daily role activities* as a result of illness or injury" (emphasis added). This measure looks at the effects of illness on a person's everyday life.

Statistics Canada (Dunn 1990) asked about the activity limitations faced by a sample of Canadians chosen from the 1986 census. All of the people in the sample said that they had a disability. The sample included only people who had problems managing their daily living activities due to their disability and people who had had a disability for at least six months.

The study found that people aged 65 and over made up about 40 percent of the disabled population aged 15 and over. Also the disability rate increased with age (Statistics Canada 1990b). The group aged 0–14 years had a 5.2-percent disability rate; people aged 35–64 had a 15.7-percent rate; the group aged 65–74 had a 37-percent rate; and people aged 85 and over had a rate of 82 percent (Nessner 1990). The study found that 45.5 percent of people aged 65 and over had some disability. Women made up more than half (60 percent) of this group (Statistics Canada 1990b). Older disabled people tended to have more than one disability and they usually had a severe disability (Nessner 1990).

Disabilities impaired some functions more than others. Disabled seniors most often said they had trouble walking from room to room or standing for a long time. They also had trouble with agility (e.g., bending, dressing, or grasping things) and hearing (Statistics Canada 1988). Fifty-nine percent of them needed help with heavy chores; 55 percent needed it for housework; and 49 percent needed help with meal preparation. Community services sometimes helped them, but these disabled seniors reported that they could have used more help (Dunn 1990).

Chappell, Strain, and Blandford (1986, 37) compared the rate of chronic illness with the influence of illness on daily activity. They found that

> both the number of chronic conditions and the extent of functional disability tend to increase with age. However, chronic conditions do not necessarily translate into functional disability ... That is, while over three-quarters of elderly persons have at least one chronic condition, only about half experience some functional disability. Even fewer, about one-fifth, require assistance with basic activities.

Most older people cope with declines in their health. They accept the health changes that come with age, adjust their expectations about their activities, and gradually make changes in their lives to cope with physical decline (Chappell, Strain, and Blandford 1986, 43). Even among the most disabled seniors, those in institutions, 21 percent report that they go shopping, and 18 percent manage their own finances.

## COPING WITH PHYSICAL CHANGE

The research on physical functioning, reaction time, and health makes old age seem like a time of loss and suffering. But older people vary on these measures. Studies show that 80 percent of old people live without functional handicaps on certain activities (like toileting and bathing) (Branch and Jette 1981). And in one Canadian study 65 percent of people aged 65–74 years old and 57 percent of people aged 75 and over reported good or excellent health. The survey also found that 80 percent of people aged 65–74 years old and 76 percent of people aged 75 and over said they felt very satisfied or somewhat satisfied with their health (Statistics Canada 1987).

These reports suggest that older people adapt to changing physical problems, by adapting their expectations and activities. Cape and Henschke (1980, 299) report that "only beyond the age of 80 does this picture begin to change significantly."

Studies of reaction time, for example, show that groups of older people make more varied responses than groups of younger people (Botwinick and Thompson 1968), and some older subjects do just as well as younger subjects on these tests. A study by Surwillo (1963) found that age accounted for only about 4 percent of the variance in reaction time. In studies of real-life performance based on many years of practice (like typing), older people did as well as younger people (Salthouse, 1984 cited in Spirduso and MacRae 1990). Studies show that exercise (Botwinick and Thompson 1968), practice (Murrell 1970), and motivation (Botwinick, Brinley, and Robbin 1958, 1959) all decrease the differences in reaction time between young and old people (though they do not entirely eliminate age group differences) (Spirduso and MacRae 1990). Welford suggests that exercise, for example, may increase cardiovascular fitness, which leads to better blood flow to the brain and to better mental functioning (Welford 1984). And Spirduso (1980, 1982) suggests that muscle activity in exercise may directly improve the structures of the central nervous system.

Older people can also make up for declines in the senses, muscles, and organs as they age. More than one-third of seniors with a hearing disability, for example, use a hearing aid. Eighty-two percent of seniors with a seeing disability wear glasses. And 31 percent of seniors with a mobility disability use a mobility aid (most often a cane, wheelchair, or walker) (Statistics Canada

1990b). Older people can hire homemakers to help with heavy housework, and they can change their diet to make up for slow digestion and poor food absorption. Three responses to aging can decrease the effects of physiological decline: changes in environment, changes in lifestyle, and improvements in technology.

## Changes in Environment

Sense thresholds, the points at which a person can begin to perceive a stimulus, begin to increase as early as age 30, and by age 60 most people notice changes in their senses. Hearing aids and glasses can help correct some of these problems, but hearing aids amplify all sounds, even background noises. In one case an elderly man with a hearing aid in a university class showed up to take the course a second time. Surprised, the professor asked him why. The man said that students talking behind him, a bus depot across the street, and a noisy heating system all made his hearing aid useless. Some days he left it at home or shut it off and tried to read the professor's lips. "I only got half of what you said last time," he told the professor. "So I've come back to get the rest." This man needed a quieter classroom setting.

Fozard (1990, 165) says that "the elderly appear to benefit as much as or more than younger adults from good context ... " Older people need to make educated guesses at the meaning of sensory inputs due to a decline in the senses. A beneficial environment can help the older person live a fuller life.

Charness and Bosman (1990, 446) say that the motto for good design should be "know the user." Designers, architects, and planners need to use knowledge about older people when they design environments for them. A number of manuals exist to guide planners and designers today. These guides give advice based on research and experience with older people.

Charness and Bosman (1990) say that researchers need to conduct more research on the anthropometry (the measurement of the shape, size, and movement capability) of older adults. They also suggest that designers use low technology solutions, where they can. These often cost less than high technology solutions, and older people have less trouble adapting to them.

Changes in the environment—including changes in the way other people speak to or treat an older person—can help that person cope with physical decline.

## Changes in Technology

Benjamin Franklin invented bifocals in the eighteenth century by cutting his glasses in half when he found he needed to watch the speakers' expressions at the French court. Today technology helps older people cope with aging in

. . . . . . . . . . . . . . . . . . . . . . . . . . . . . . . . . .

# Exhibit 5.4

## Good Settings to Live In

. . . . . . . . . . . . . . . . . . . . . . . . . . . . . . . . . .

The Manitoba Health Services Commission published the *Planning Guide for Personal Care Homes in Manitoba* in 1980. The guide suggests environmental changes that help older people cope with sensory loss. The commission based the guide on years of informal research in more than one hundred rural and urban personal care homes in the province. It gives an example of the kinds of things that designers need to keep in mind when they design environments for older people.

### Lighting

The commission recognized that older people on average see less well than younger people and in the guide warns against pockets of light that create an uneven effect on walls and floors of hallways. This can lead a person to misjudge the floor's height or the distance to a wall. It can also increase a person's fear of falling and thereby decrease the older person's movement in the home. The guide also suggests soft indirect lighting at entrances, since direct lighting can create too great a contrast between the outside and the entry of the home.

### Sound

Sounds from TVs, radios, and intercoms can blend into an audio mush that can distract and tire residents. In the guide, the commission warns against "a constant source of meaningless sound in social areas." Designers can use fabric textures, pile carpets, and soft drapes to dampen background noise, making it easier for people to hear one another. Also, small lounges or quiet areas allow people to communicate.

### Decoration

Designers should avoid rough surfaces on walls, as they can cause skin abrasions. Patterned carpets or vinyl blocks can lead to optical illusions. Zigzags or stripes, for example, give the illusion of movement, and sharp contrasts in colours suggest a change in depth. People may try to step up or down and lose their balance. This can lead to frustration and cause people to avoid public space and withdraw to their rooms.

Personal care homes house only a small percentage of older people, but acknowledging these principles of design can improve the quality of their lives.

. . . . . . . . . . . . . . . . . . . . . . . . . . . . . . . . . .

dozens more ways. Some people wear electronic pacemakers to regulate their hearts; people with severe arthritis can have joint replacement surgery; and in some cases a person can have a childhood problem corrected in old age. One woman lived her first sixty years with her hip bones outside their sockets. Her muscles and ligaments allowed her to walk, but she limped and tired quickly. Her muscles weakened as she aged, and her doctor said she would have to spend the rest of her life in a wheelchair. She searched for and found a doctor who agreed to operate on both of her hips. He told her it would endanger her life, but she decided to try the operation. She now has both hips in place in their sockets and she stands two inches taller than in her youth.

Technological aids to older people range from the simple (e.g., a thick piece of rubber tubing that fits over a wooden spoon handle to help a person with arthritis or a weak grip) to the complex (e.g., a Century tub with a crane-like lift and a swing-like seat that lifts an immobilized or frail older person into a stainless steel tub. Water and pre-measured amounts of soap come out of jets at the sides of the tub. The person sits up to their chest in the water, while it swirls them clean). Technological aids range from the common (e.g., rubber strips for the bottom of the bathtub to prevent slipping) to the unusual (e.g., a chair with a seat that lifts a person to a standing position when they press a button). In the future, computers may also allow housebound older people to order groceries, get their mail, or play Scrabble with a grand-child across town.

Haber (1986) says that in the future robots may help older people with their daily chores. They might also be used to help bathe and feed people in nursing homes. Voice-activated robots will pick things up or move them around. Robots may also help patients do passive exercises, help them walk, or bring them something they need. Haber argues that robots could free nursing home staff from unpleasant work and allow them more enjoyable time with patients. He says that voice-activated robots would give aware, but immobilized, older people a feeling of control over their environment, thereby increasing their life-satisfaction. Research will have to be done to see whether robots further dehumanize institutional settings; whether older peo-ple (or institutions) can afford complex machines; and whether people will use high-tech equipment if they have the chance.

LaBuda (1990) cautions that designers will have to make complicated technology easy to use. Computer manufacturers may need to adjust their products to serve an older market. Charness and Bosman (1989) found, for example, that middle-aged and older adults showed the best performance on computers with black on white screens. They also found that older people could learn a software package as well as younger adults, but that older peo-ple took longer to complete the test on their knowledge and needed more help from the experimenter. The older people also learned well in pairs (Zan-dri and Charness 1989).

Lowe (1990) reports that only 6 percent of people aged 65 and over could use a computer, compared to 82 percent of 15–19 year olds. And only 3 percent of seniors had computers at home, compared to 35 percent of 15–19 year olds. When compared with non-owners in their age group, computer owners aged 65 and over tended to have higher incomes and higher levels of education. These figures suggest that future generations of older people may feel comfortable with computerized solutions to everyday needs. But the current generation of older people needs aids that use simpler technologies.

Present transportation technology helps solve many disabled seniors' problems. But sometimes the technology does not meet seniors' needs. The Health and Activity Limitation Survey (Dunn 1990), for example, found that 92 percent of disabled seniors engage in leisure activities outside their homes. But these seniors report problems with boarding and leaving planes, long distance buses, and trains. They also have problems with local transportation, finding it difficult to get to and wait at bus stops.

The study also found that 8 percent of people who need mobility aids do not have them; 31 percent who need a hearing aid do not have one; and 10 percent of people who need a visual aid do not have one. Seniors often report that they cannot afford the aids they need.

The National Advisory Council on Aging (NACA) (1988) says that for technological aids to be useful: (1) people have to know about them; (2) people have to understand their usefulness; and (3) products have to be affordable and physically accessible. NACA also says that manufacturers should set up norms and standards of safety and suitability for new products. The Manitoba and federal governments have set up a new organization for this purpose. The Canadian Aging and Rehabilitation Product Development Centre (ARCOR) will contract with private firms to develop, produce, market, and test new products for seniors. ARCOR will also develop training packages for seniors, their families, and professionals on product availability and use.

## Changes in Lifestyle

People can also change their habits to cope with biological aging. Heavy smoking and drinking put wear and tear on the body; overeating can increase a person's risk of heart disease and diabetes; and long exposure to the sun increases the risk of skin cancer. People can cut back on such activities and habits that speed the process of aging.

Some recent figures show that people have already begun to change their habits. McKie (1987) compared the findings on cigarette smoking from the 1978–79 Canada Health Survey and the 1985 General Social Survey. The data show that in 1985, compared with 1978–79, every age group of men and women (except women aged 65+) showed a decline in the proportion of people who reported regular cigarette smoking. Men aged 65 and over showed the greatest proportion of any age or gender group (49 percent) who had given up smoking, while less than 20 percent of older women reported having given up smoking.

People can also begin activities that improve their physical condition. O'Brien and Vertinsky (1991) say that much of what people accept as aging falls into the category of **hypokinesia,** or disuse, which causes decline in muscle and bone mass, and a loss of function.

A study by Smith, Reddan, and Smith (1981), for example, found increased mineral content in the bones of older women who exercised. The researchers studied thirty women whose average age was 84. Twelve of these women took part in an exercise program; eighteen did not. The researchers matched the two groups for age, weight, and walking ability. The experimental group exercised for thirty minutes a day, three times a week, for three years, while the control group did no exercise. The researchers found that the control group had a more than 3-percent loss in bone mineral in three years, while the group that exercised showed a gain of more than 2 percent over the same time. The researchers say that the exercise program accounted for more than 96 percent of the difference between these two groups. A study at Stanford University supports these findings. Lane et al. (1986) reported that runners had 40-percent higher bone density than non-runners (*Time* 1986a, 68). Goldberg and Hagberg (1990) in a review of the literature on exercise and bone mass, say that weight-bearing exercise (e.g. walking or jogging with light weights) leads to the greatest improvement in bone mass, but they also called for more research on the effect of different types of exercise on bone mass.

Men can also benefit from regular exercise as they age. A study of 17,000 male Harvard alumni showed that men who exercise regularly can expect to live a year longer than those who do not (Paffenbarger et al. 1986). Paffenbarger, chief researcher for the study, says that "for each hour of physical activity, you can expect to live that hour over—and live one or two more hours to boot" (*Time* 1986a, 68).

The study also found that exercise could lessen the risk of illness for smokers and for people with high blood pressure. The study found that "men who walked nine or more miles a week (thereby burning off at least 900 calories), for example, had a risk of death 21 percent lower than those who walked less than three miles a week" (*Time* 1986a, 68). The researchers say that exercise could extend the lives of some men by ten to twenty years. This study looked only at white upper-middle-class men. Future studies will have to see whether the same conclusions apply to women, minorities, or people with low incomes.

These studies point the way to a new view of aging. Science cannot stop or reverse the process of aging, but individuals can improve their environment and can delay chronic problems through lifestyle changes and exercise. O'Brien and Vertinsky (1991) say that physically active women, for example, have a physical condition ten to twenty years younger than women who do not exercise. Older athletes, who take part in special national and international competitions into their 70s, can match the ability of sedentary people in their 20s. Leo and Blonarz (1981) report on one medical expert who says that "the body is now felt to rust out rather than wear out." Over time organs lose their **reserve capacity**, the amount of work they can do under conditions of great demand. But "if loss of reserve function represents aging in some sense, then exercising an organ presents a strategy for modifying the aging process" (Leo and Blonarz 1981).

## THE COMPRESSION OF MORBIDITY HYPOTHESIS

Will a longer life for Canadians mean more years of health and activity with a short period of illness at the end? Or will it mean a slow decline in health with more years of disability? Will we wear out quickly like Oliver Wendell Holmes's "one hoss shay" that fell apart all at once? Or will we rust out over many years like an old Chevrolet? How many people will want to live 120 years, if they know that they will spend their last 30 in a nursing home with dementia or a stroke.

Fries (1980) gave an optimistic answer to the question of what a longer life would mean. He predicted three things: first, that more people would live a life that approached the hypothetically fixed life span of 110–120 years; second, that longer life would come about primarily through the reduction of chronic illnesses like heart disease, cancer, and stroke; and third (Fries and Crapo 1981), that severe chronic illness would occur for a short time near the end of life (the "compression of morbidity hypothesis"). In other words, if Exhibit 5.5 had a line that described the decline in function in the older population, this line would look similar to the most recent survival curve in this chart. Researchers have challenged all three of these predictions. A closer look at Canadian figures will show the reasons for researchers' doubts.

*Challenge 1:*   Canadians' life expectancy has increased over the past half century. This trend gives the impression of rectangularization of the survival curve. Exhibit 5.5 illustrates this trend, using the example of Canadian women at three time periods.

Note that according to Exhibit 5.5 cohorts born more recently die off at a slower rate than those born earlier. Also, note the drop off in numbers at later ages for the most recent cohorts. This begins to make almost a right angle on the chart and gives the name "rectangularization" or "squaring" to the survival curve. Fries and Crapo (1981) conclude from these curves that a finite life span exists and that modern populations have begun to approach this limit.

. . . . . . . . . . . . . . . . . . . . . . . . . . . . . . .

## Exhibit 5.5

Survivors Out of 100,000 Born Alive at Selected Ages,
Females, Canada, 1921, 1951, and 1981

. . . . . . . . . . . . . . . . . . . . . . . . . . . . . . .

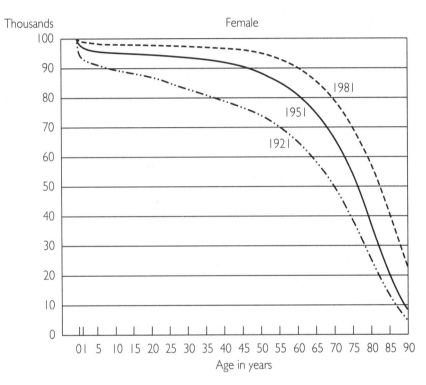

**Source:** Dhruva Nagnur, *Longevity and Historical Life Tables, 1921–1981, Canada and the Provinces*, Statistics Canada, Cat. No. 89-506 (Ottawa: Minister of Supply and Services Canada, 1987), 77, Chart C4. Adapted with permission of the Minister of Supply and Services Canada, 1991.

. . . . . . . . . . . . . . . . . . . . . . . . . . . . . . .

Note something else in Exhibit 5.5. The tail of the most recent cohort does not come as close to the zero point as the tail for earlier cohorts. This means that the oldest older women show a decreasing mortality rate. This suggests that the life span may have a flexible rather than a finite limit. It also creates a "derectangularizing" of the curve as the tail moves further to the right (Myers and Manton 1984). Simmons-Tropea and Osborn (1987, 410) conclude from this type of evidence that "although natural limits to the life span may exist, these limits are as yet unknown."

Researchers report similar findings in the U.S. (Schneider and Brody 1983) and in England and Wales (Grundy 1984). A model developed by Manton (1982) in the U.S. shows that a lower rate of chronic illness leads to lower mortality, but also to longer life expectancy. This finding goes against Fries's notion of a fixed life span. Canadian research by Kraus (1987, 59) reports a 2-year increase in the "usual life span" ("the age to which only 1 percent of a birth cohort lives")—more than 100 times Fries's prediction. "Age-sex specific mortality rates in Canada in the 65–69, 70–74 ... 85+ age groups," he says, "declined from 11 percent to 18 percent in males and from 11 percent to 21 percent in females between 1974 to 1984" (Kraus 1988, 62). This trend runs counter to the rectangularization prediction.

***Challenge 2:*** Fries (1990) says that longer life expectancy has come about through the decrease in chronic illnesses like smallpox, whooping cough, and diphtheria. In the future, he says, decreased rates of chronic illness in old age—lung cancer, stroke, and heart disease—will lead to longer life. Fries (1986) says that this indicates the possibility of a postponement of illness until late old age ("the compression of morbidity") and implies a longer and healthier life.

But some writers challenge this optimistic view of the future. Simmons-Tropea and Osborn (1987, 411) say that "the major causes of morbidity are *not* necessarily related to the major causes of mortality." Manton (1986) found that in the U.S. chronic conditions that cause death (like heart disease) produce only small amounts of disability. Manton (1986) goes on to say that chronic degenerative (but not necessarily fatal) conditions cause the most disability. These conditions include the most common illnesses reported by older people—diabetes, respiratory problems, and arthritis/rheumatism. People live with these last few diseases for many years (Statistics Canada 1987). Manton (1986, 680) concludes that "the numbers of disabled elderly adults can be expected to increase as the number of survivors to later ages increases due to mortality reduction."

Colvez and Blanchet (1981) report on U.S. statistics from 1966 to 1974 that show increases in the proportion of people 45 years and older who report "main activity [occupational activity, housework, etc.] impossible." As these people enter old age they will add to the proportion of older people with disabilities. Canadian data show a similar trend. In Canada from 1951–1978 life expectancy increased 4.5 years for men and 7.5 years for women. For this same time period, disabled years increased by 3.2 years for men and 6.1 years for women. This means that as life expectancy increased, so did the years of disability. Canadians made only small gains in disability-free years (Simmons-Tropea and Osborn 1987). This fact runs contrary to Fries's predictions.

*Challenge 3:* Trends show an increase in survivorship after the onset of chronic disease. New treatments for chronic illness explain part of this increase. Kraus reports knowing of no case where survivorship has decreased for chronic disease where treatment has taken place. Kraus (1988) studied a representative sample of 500 death certificates of people aged 65 and over in Ontario from 1975 to 1985. He looked at causes of death and the date of death to test Fries's compression of morbidity hypothesis. Not only did he find no statistically significant findings to support compression of morbidity, he also found some findings that were inconsistent with the hypothesis.

Simmons-Tropea and Osborn (1987) sum up recent findings on the compression of morbidity hypothesis. The data, they say, "strongly suggest that the years gained in life expectancy will be largely spent suffering long-term activity limitation. Less than 30 percent of the increased years of life expectancy from 1951 to 1978 can be expected to be free from limitations" (Simmons-Tropea and Osborn 1987, 419). This leads to a pessimistic conclusion. If current trends continue, Canada will have larger numbers of older people with disabilities than ever before. These people will place more demand on health and social services.

Has this debate settled the issue of morbidity compression? Fries (1990) says that healthier habits, training, and health policies can compress morbidity. He also says that the variation in ability among seniors shows room for further compression of morbidity. In other words, if some people live morbidity-free lives into late old age, other people can follow this pattern. The potential for further improvement in well-being among older people has led some authors to study the phenomenon of successful aging.

## SUCCESSFUL AGING

The biologists' focus on intrinsic processes has led to a more precise description of normal aging. But this research does not explain (nor does it try to explain) the differences in function among older people. It does not deal with the influence of the environment, life styles, and habits on physical functioning.

Rowe and Kahn (1991, 21) say that current research has produced a "gerontology of the usual." In addition to the biological focus on normal aging, they recommend the study of successful aging. This approach would look at "people who demonstrate little or no loss in a constellation of physiologic functions ... [these people] would be regarded as more broadly successful in physiologic terms" (Rowe and Kahn 1991, 22). This research would work to understand the reasons for these people's success.

Thompson and Forbes (1990) see a contradiction in the concept of successful aging. If a person can avoid decline through lifestyle or environmental change, this decline must not be intrinsic or true aging. For this reason, the concept of successful aging may have little use to the biologist. But, for the physiologist, the clinician, and others who work at improving life in old age, the focus on successful aging has some value.

Rowe and Kahn (1991) show that in a variety of studies, including research on metabolism, osteoporosis, cognitive functioning, mortality, and well-being, extrinsic influences like diet, exercise, and social relations can inhibit and sometimes reverse functional decline (see also Molloy et al. 1988; Vandervoort et al. 1986).

Roos and Havens (1991) used the concept of successful aging in a longitudinal study of elderly Manitobans. Their definition of successful aging included the following criteria: the person had survived from 1971 to 1983; the person lived in the community in 1983; and the person received fewer than fifty-nine days of home care services in 1983. The definition also included signs of well-being in measures of health, mobility, and mental ability. They found that 20 percent of the sample aged 65 to 84 fit the criteria for successful aging in 1983. They also found that people with the following characteristics tended to age successfully: spouse maintained his or her well-being; good self-reported health in 1971; did not retire due to poor health; no cancer or diabetes; and good mental status. Successful agers also reported more life satisfaction. These findings show that successful aging depends on good self-reported health and the absence of disease. But it also depends on psychosocial influences like a spouse's well-being and good mental status.

These findings suggest that researchers should use an interdisciplinary approach to the study of aging. Studies should include psychosocial as well as physiological measures of functioning and researchers should look for links between the psychosocial and the physiological findings. Also, attention needs to be paid to the people who function best in each age group, because these people may hold the key to a longer life and a better age for everyone in the future.

## SCIENTIFIC PROSPECTS FOR LONGER LIFE

People have tried to reverse or stop the process of aging at least since Ponce de Leon set out to find the fountain of youth. Drug companies have looked into the effects of animal glands, sex hormones, and chemical therapy on aging. One company that sells skin cream includes in its formula "proteins from the placentas of black sheep (because they are so resistant to disease)"

(Toufexis 1986, 51). These methods can make the skin softer or add water below the skin to temporarily smooth out wrinkles, but they do nothing to increase life expectancy or reverse aging.

Still, the search goes on. Scientists have explored many methods for increasing life span and extending youth. They have found that certain drugs, calorie-restricted diets, and lowered body temperatures (during hibernation) extend the lives of some animals in the laboratory (Schneider and Reed 1985; Ausman and Russell 1990). Will any of these methods lead to a longer, healthier life for humans in the near future?

Neugarten and Havighurst (1979) asked leading biological researchers whether their work would lead to an extension in human life span in the near future. All but two of the researchers they spoke with predicted only small changes in life expectancy. Most predicted a slow increase in life expectancy in the next few years due to better health care, healthier lifestyles, and new medical technology. An end to cardiovascular disease and cancer in Canada, for instance, would add a total of 16.6 years to the life expectancy of women born in 1981" (Nagnur and Nagrodski 1988, 27). The estimated gain in male life expectancy would be 11.9 years. The elimination of the most common causes of death would raise life expectancy at birth in 1981 to about 90 years for men and about 101 years for women (Statistics Canada 1989).

These figures still do not approach the currently estimated human life span of 110 to 120 years. And these estimates may prove too low. Humans may be able to extend human life indefinitely in the future. This will depend on whether science can alter intrinsic processes of aging—decreases in cell metabolism, increases in collagen due to cross-linkages, and gene activity. It may also depend on other physiological processes as yet unknown to science. At the moment, it seems, humans will have to make the best of the century or so that they live.

## SUMMARY

1. Human aging is universal, intrinsic, progressive, and deleterious. Heredity, culture, habits, and the environment all influence the rate of aging.

2. No single theory explains all the facts about aging. Most biological theories today focus on changes in the cell. Research shows that cell metabolism declines with age, and this allows waste to accumulate in the cells. Researchers call this the "Phase III Phenomenon." Studies also show that cross-links can damage DNA, leading to faulty cell reproduction. Also, free radicals attack DNA and the cell walls. This too leads to cell breakdown.

3. Breakdown in the cells leads to a decline in physical functions. The body's systems break down or decline in efficiency. Reaction time slows, and the risk of chronic illness increases.

4. Technology can help people cope with declines in health. Simple objects like spoons can be adapted for people with arthritis, computers can increase a person's contact with others, and in the future robots may help people bathe, exercise, and do daily tasks. Eyeglasses, hearing aids, and a supportive environment can make up for losses in the senses.

5. Research shows that changes in diet and exercise can slow the aging process. People can even improve their lung capacity and bone density through exercise. This can lead to a longer and healthier life.

6. The compression of morbidity hypothesis says that people will live longer and have more disability-free years in the future. But recent research questions this view, suggesting instead that a longer life may lead to more years of disability.

7. Many older people stay healthy and active as they age. They live without physical handicap and without special help. Studies of successful aging show that people can extend the number years they live in good health. In the future, science may find a way for people to live past the current limits of the human life span.

## SELECTED READINGS

Schneider, Edward L., and John W. Rowe, eds. *Handbook of the Biology of Aging*. 3d ed. San Diego: Academic Press, 1990.

A review of the latest findings in the field of biology and aging by senior researchers. Topics range from studies of cells to studies of physiological change in later life. Readers with little scientific background may find the chapters difficult to understand, but this is an excellent resource for the latest findings in the biology of aging.

Statistics Canada. *Health and Social Support, 1985*. General Social Survey Analysis Series. Catalogue Number 11-612E, Number 1. Ottawa: Minister of Supply and Services, 1987.

Good summary statistics and discussions about the health habits, illnesses, and support networks of Canadians.

# The Psychology of Aging

## INTRODUCTION

A few years ago, one of Canada's leading geriatric specialists gave a talk on memory to a group of seniors. He told the group that, in the absence of disease, memory stays about the same in old age as in youth. Young people and old people both forget things, he said, but older people notice it more, because they expect memory loss to come with age. A man stood up at the end of the talk and said, "I respect your views, Doctor. But I know my memory has gotten worse with age. What I want to know is what I can do about it." This response fits with two things research has found out about older people and memory: first, older people believe their memories are getting worse (Dixon and Hultsch 1983; Dobbs and Rule 1987; Hultsch, Hertzog and Dixon 1987), and, second, memory failure upsets them, even if they forget something unimportant (Cavanaugh, Grady, and Perlmutter 1983).

Many people, older people included, accept the stereotype that cognitive decline is a normal part of aging. But recent research on memory, intelligence, and creativity questions this belief (Perlmutter 1988). Studies show that people can learn and grow intellectually in old age as well as in youth. On some measures mental ability may even improve with age. Dramatic declines in mental functioning are due to physiological disorders or distress, not to normal aging.

This chapter will look at: (1) memory and intelligence in later life, (2) creativity, and (3) the psychological problems some older people face.

## NORMAL CHANGES IN PSYCHOLOGICAL FUNCTIONING

### Learning and Memory

Memory is the recall of information after learning has taken place. Most measurement of memory takes place in psychology laboratories. Psychologists in the field of aging have spent more time on the study of memory than on any other topic. Poon (1985) reports that between 1964 and 1974, 72 percent of the papers in the psychology sections of gerontology journals dealt with memory. In 1979 and 1980, 58 percent of all papers dealt with memory. Psychologists show a strong interest in memory and aging for a number of reasons. First, popular stereotypes about aging and early psychological research on memory predict a decline in memory with age. If this is true, studies of memory can trace the causes of this decline. Second, psychologists can study memory in the laboratory under controlled conditions. This makes research on memory relatively easy to do. Third, studies of memory have produced testable models of how the mind works. These models attempt to explain complex processes like learning, forgetting, and the storage and retrieval of information. For all of these reasons the study of memory has dominated the study of psychological aging.

Much of the research on memory and aging points to some decline in memory with age (Waugh and Barr 1982; Arenberg 1977). Welford (1958), for example, referred to the decline in learning ability in old age (the decline in retention of information) as an established fact. Many studies show that older people take longer to learn new information, longer to search for it in memory, and longer to use it when they need it. Cerella (1990) says that **latency** (the length of time a person takes to process information or make a response to a question) increases with age. He says that this occurs regardless of the content of the task. He calls this process "generalized slowing" and considers this a classical and well-accepted finding in the field of cognitive psychology.

Research shows that some types of memory decline more than others. **Explicit memory**, where the person intends to remember, decreases more with age than **implicit memory** where memory occurs without intention (Hultsch and Dixon 1990). Also, external conditions influence an older person's actual ability to remember. Studies show, for example, that the design of memory tests, their content, and the use of cross-sectional designs (which compare older and younger people at one point in time) may all lead to exaggerated estimates of memory decline in older people. Hundreds of studies have tried to sort out the effects of age on memory.

In particular, the research has focused on differences in learning (acquisition) between younger and older subjects. Psychologists believe that retrieval and acquisition are closely related. How someone retrieves information (how they search for and find information in memory) depends on how they acquired it (the methods they used to organize and store the information).

### Laboratory Studies

Some studies have found deficits in memory in older people due to the way they learn and store information. Ska and Nespoulous (1988), for example, studied **encoding**, the process whereby a person takes new bits of information and puts them together with already stored information, and retrieval in a sample of 150 people aged 20 to 84. They found that "elderly subjects reproduced less during the encoding phase and retrieved fewer elements during the recall phase" (1988, 408). Speeded trials appear to increase the learning deficit. More than the young, older subjects miss verbal and pictorial items presented at a rapid rate. They miss late items in a list more than earlier ones, and they encode some items at the expense of others. Waugh and Barr (1982, 190) say that "the older the subject, the less efficiently and the more selectively he encodes—perhaps because ... he simply lacks the time to encode efficiently and comprehensively."

Other studies (Kausler 1982) report that older people do not automatically use **mediators**, the process of picturing a word or finding a rhyme for a word, to help with remembering (Kausler 1982). Sanders et al. (1980) found that older learners take an inactive and nonstrategic approach to memorizing their lists, while younger ones actively organized and categorized their lists as they memorized them (Sanders et al. 1980; see also Howard, McAndrews, and Lasagna 1981).

This research suggests that memory decline in older adults may be due in part to the use of inefficient processing techniques. More recent research on memory in old age questions these conclusions. Light (1990) reviewed the literature on the effects of encoding on older people's memories. She weighed the evidence on inefficient mental processing as the reason for memory decline and reported that, in total, "the literature offers no support for the claim that deficits in semantic processing underlie memory problems in old age." She goes on to say that "the organization of knowledge is quite stable across the adult years" (Light 1990, 281).

Light (1990) traces memory differences between older and younger people to deficits in older people's working memory. **Working memory** stores recent information and also attends to, selects, and manipulates this information. In addition, it processes new information, while temporarily storing other information (Hultsch and Dixon 1990).

A number of studies point to a decrease in working memory as a source of memory deficits in older people. First, older adults remember less well when irrelevant information comes between two things to be remembered. Light and Capps (1986) found that older adults did less well when they added irrelevant sentences between two things to be remembered. Second, older adults have more difficulty remembering when the material they have to remember comes in a scrambled order (Light et al. 1982). If sentences are presented in a scrambled order, the older person will have more trouble holding all the information in working memory and making sense of the information. Third, topic changes place a greater load on working memory and lead to poorer memory in older people. When a topic changes, older people appear to forget relevant information (Light and Albertson 1988).

Other factors, besides age, may account for the differences in memory between older and younger people found in laboratory studies. Differences in educational background and verbal ability, for example, may influence results in memory studies. Cavanaugh (1983) studied the recall of TV-show content and found that when subjects had low verbal ability older people recalled less than younger people. But when younger subjects and older subjects both had high verbal ability, the study showed no difference between the two age groups' scores. Taub (1979) found that the better a person's vocabulary, the greater their ability to retain pieces of prose in memory. Bowles and Poon (1982) found significant age differences in memory between young and old samples with a low vocabulary, but no age differences in high-vocabulary samples.

Test conditions can also influence older subjects' performance on memory tests. Ross (1968), for example, found that a supportive context improved older subjects' ability to learn paired words. A challenging setting, where the instructor said that she would test the students' intelligence, led to the least efficient learning. Poon (1985) found that when older people could control the pace of their learning they showed less decrement in memory.

Finally, most studies show that older people learn familiar and relevant material better than new and irrelevant material. Barrett and Wright (1981), for example, found that older people did less well than younger people on a list of words unfamiliar to them, but they showed a better rate of recall than younger people on a list of familiar words. These studies show that laboratory tests and experiments put the older learner at a disadvantage.

Laboratory studies raise an important question: how well do the results of memory research predict an older person's ability to remember details in everyday life? The answer: not very well. Memory studies done under laboratory conditions have poor ecological validity (the transferability of knowledge from lab to life). Older people rarely learn or recall well under pressure, and research shows that they remember best when they learn information relevant and useful to them.

## The Contextual Approach

The contextual view begins with the insight that many conditions influence memory, including "the physical, psychological, and social context in which the event was experienced, the knowledge, abilities, and characteristics the individual brings to the context, [and] the situation in which we ask for evidence of remembering" (Hultsch and Deutsch 1981, 153).

Charness (1981, 1985), for example, reports on a study of younger and older chess players' problem-solving abilities. He found that older players had more difficulty than younger players at the same skill level in recalling positions accurately (see also McIntyre and Craik 1987). He attributes this difficulty to older players' poorer retrieval ability. But when Charness (1981) evaluated game-playing *performance*, he found that skill level, not age, determined a player's ability. Older players did as well as younger players of the same skill level. "Given the retrieval deficits associated with aging," Charness asks, "why is there no deficit in molar [overall] problem-solving performance?" (1981, 34–35). Charness tentatively concludes that the components of chess playing may vary among people in different age groups. Also, older players may use a more efficient search for alternative solutions.

In a study of the effects of age and skill on bridge players, Charness (1985, 1987) also found that skill compensated for decreases in information processing speed. He found that older subjects reacted more slowly than younger subjects on a novel task (unrelated to bridge). But accuracy in bidding depended only on skill level (not age). Charness (1987, 241) concluded that older players may use "preassembled (and highly efficient) programs to maintain effective performance."

This study and the previous review of the literature supports the idea that factors other than biological decline can influence mental performance in older people. Research shows that different types of older people (with more or less education or skill), under a variety of conditions (supportive or nonsupportive), and exposed to varying types of materials to learn (relevant

· · · · · · · · · · · · · · · · · · · · · · · · · · · · · · · · · · · · ·

## Exhibit 6.1

### Teaching Methods for Use with Senior Students

· · · · · · · · · · · · · · · · · · · · · · · · · · · · · · · · · · · · ·

Hultsch and Deutsch (1981) suggest the following methods to help older people learn better in the classroom. Some of these methods should be used no matter what the student's age (taking breaks, giving immediate feedback on tests), while others apply more to seniors than to other age groups (giving visual and aural cues to help memory, speaking slowly and distinctly).

| TECHNIQUE | DESCRIPTION OF THE TECHNIQUE |
|---|---|
| 1. Pacing | Remove time pressures. Let people set their own pace. |
| 2. Anxiety Arousal | Decrease anxiety. Decrease competition and testing. Let people get used to new ideas or techniques. |
| 3. Fatigue | Give older students rest breaks or cut down the length of time for each lesson. |
| 4. Difficulty | Build people up by starting with simple and moving on to more complex work. Break the work into segments. |
| 5. Practice | Give people a chance to use what they know in different ways. |
| 6. Feedback | Let people know how they did as soon as possible so they can fix mistakes. |
| 7. Cues | Give older people visual and aural cues to help them with their work. Use clear diagrams, speak clearly, and repeat questions from the class so that everyone follows the discussion. |
| 8. Organization | Group information for students. Use memory aids like pictures, mental images, or verbal cues. |
| 9. Relevance/Experience | Find out what the older student wants to know. Build on students' past experiences. Show them how to apply what they learn. |

**Source:** Adapted from David F. Hultsch and Francine Deutsch, *Adult Development and Aging: A Life-Span Perspective* (New York: McGraw-Hill, 1981), 152. Reproduced with permission of the publisher.

· · · · · · · · · · · · · · · · · · · · · · · · · · · · · · · · · · · · ·

or irrelevant) differ in their ability to perform mental tasks or to remember specific information.

Only a few studies have looked directly at what older people remember about the world around them. These studies have found little of the memory deficit reported in laboratory studies. A study of memory of recent public events, for example, found no difference between younger and older subjects (between ages 20 and 80) (Poon et al. 1979). When the researchers asked about events that occurred from the 1920s to the 1970s, they found that older subjects scored better than younger subjects.

McIntyre and Craik (1987) tested older and younger subjects about their knowledge of Canadian facts. They found that older people had less ability than younger people to recall the source of their facts. But the two groups had about the same ability to recall facts after a week, and the older group had a greater knowledge of facts about Canada at the start of the experiment. The researchers note that this study of knowledge about the world, compared to typical laboratory studies, led to smaller differences in recall between older and younger subjects.

Hultsch and Dixon (1990) reviewed the literature on memory for meaningful events and materials. They found that in some studies younger adults outperformed older people. But in others older adults performed as well as younger people. One study (Hultsch and Dixon 1983), for example, looked at the ability of older and younger people to remember biographical sketches. The study found that younger adults remembered better when the sketch referred to a person known best to the younger adults. The researchers found equivalent recall rates for entertainment figures known to both the younger and older adults. Another study (Bäckman 1985) found that older people remember as well as younger people when they perform an activity related to the item they have to remember. Poon (1985, 435) concludes a review of the research on memory by saying that "in general, evidence to date shows minimal differences in memory for familiar discourse materials that may be found in the everyday environment."

The research reported to date should end the stereotyping of older people as forgetful. The current literature shows that memory depends on the external environment and the material to be remembered as well as on intrinsic changes in the brain due to aging. Older people may have different learning styles, a different attitude toward laboratory tests than younger people, and different abilities on different memory tasks. On some types of tasks they remember less well than younger adults. But, on many everyday tasks and meaningful information, older people remember as well as younger people.

. . . . . . . . . . . . . . . . . . . . . . . . . . . . . . . . . . . . . . . . . .

## Exhibit 6.2

### Controversy: Physical Change as the Source of Mental Decline

. . . . . . . . . . . . . . . . . . . . . . . . . . . . . . . . . . . . . . . . . .

Cerella (1990, 201) proposes that deficits in cognitive functioning (like memory) "could be interpreted as being distributed throughout the information-processing system rather than being localized in particular stages." He proposes that breakdowns in the neural network of the older person or slower transit time lead to slower processing of information. Each breakdown requires the input to travel a greater distance. The older the person, the greater the neural decay and the slower the processing time. This not only explains the general slowing phenomenon, but also indicates why older people do less well on tests that emphasize speed. Or why they may do as well as younger people on skilled tasks that have well-established neural networks.

This model, Cerella (1990) says, offers a simple explanation that replaces the many explanations related to specific tasks (like storage and retrieval). Cerella (1990, 217) also says that through this new theoretical development "cognitive aging reemerges as a subfield of neurophysiology rather than cognitive psychology." This work challenges current models of cognitive psychology. It needs further development, but, in the meantime, it will stimulate further refinement of our thinking about cognitive ability in later life.

. . . . . . . . . . . . . . . . . . . . . . . . . . . . . . . . . . . . . . . . . .

## Intelligence

The research on intelligence in old age parallels the research on memory: early studies assumed that intelligence also decreases in old age as the body declines. More recent research questions this simple connection between senescence and intelligence.

Psychologists use at least two definitions of intelligence. First, taking a global view, they refer to it as the "ability to negotiate environmental demands successfully" (Labouvie-Vief 1985, 506). Second, they take a pragmatic view, referring to it as "that which intelligence tests measure" (Labouvie-Vief 1985, 506) or "what the testtaker can do now" (Botwinick 1984, 250). Psychologists most often use this second (more limited) definition when they conduct research on intelligence and aging.

Early research done in the 1930s reported a decline in intellectual ability after age 20 (Miles and Miles 1932; Jones and Conrad 1933; Wechsler 1939). These findings supported the idea that mental ability declines along with the body, and all IQ tests build this expectation of decline into their design. They assume that older people will score less well than younger people, and they correct for supposed age declines in their formulas for calculating IQ. The

Wechsler Adult Intelligence Scale (WAIS–R) Manual uses this approach. It puts the peak of intelligence at between 20 and 34 years (Wechsler 1981) and assumes that each later age group will show a decline in scores.

The actual scores on WAIS–R scales support this assumption of decline with age, but they also show that decline does not take place uniformly. Scores on the WAIS–R Verbal Scale, for example, decrease steadily from a mean score of 61.42 at ages 25–34 to a mean of 51.50 at ages 70–74 (84 percent of the younger group's score). Scores on the performance scale drop earlier and more sharply from 51.14 at ages 20–24 to a mean score of 30.62 at ages 70–74 (60 percent of the younger group's score) (Wechsler 1981, 26).

Other cross-sectional studies of intelligence show a similar pattern of decline in some abilities and less decline in others (Schaie and Labouvie-Vief 1974). Researchers generally agree that a significant decline in intelligence scores takes place past age 60 (Schaie 1990a). But researchers argue over the meaning of these findings, disagreeing on at least three issues: (1) the concept of intelligence as a single structure; (2) the methods used to produce these findings; and (3) the potential of cognitive functioning in later life.

### *Intelligence as Multidimensional*

Current research on intelligence supports a multidimensional view of intelligence. The WAIS–R scales themselves point to this multidimensionality. They show what Botwinick (1984) calls the "classic aging pattern." The Performance Scale scores show a much greater decrease with age than the Verbal Scale scores (40 percent vs. 16 percent). "This classic aging pattern, relative maintenance of function in verbal skills as compared to performance skills, has been seen many times with a variety of different populations" (Botwinick 1984, 254). These findings give support to the idea that "both decrement and stability—or even growth—over the adult period [are] the rule" (Labouvie-Vief 1985, 502).

Horn and Cattell have developed a model of intelligence that explains these results. They describe two types of intelligence—fluid and crystallized intelligence (Horn and Cattell 1966; 1967; Cattell 1963). **Fluid intelligence** refers to reasoning, abstracting, concept formation, and problem solving. It makes little use of knowledge gained through reading, schooling, or work. According to Horn and Cattell, fluid intelligence relies on how well the physical and nervous systems function. Performance tests that demand the use of fluid intelligence ask subjects to manipulate unfamiliar material in new ways mentally, and they sometimes require skill at manipulating objects physically. Verbal tests that demand the use of **crystallized intelligence** depend more on stored information, acculturation, and learning (Horn 1978).

This two-part model helps explain the empirical results on intelligence. Number and verbal skill problems measure crystallized intelligence; spatial and reasoning questions measure fluid intelligence. Fluid intelligence may follow the decline of the biological system from the teen years on, while studies of crystallized intelligence show stable intelligence scores and even increases in scores with age.

Schwartzman et al. (1987) conducted a longitudinal study of Canadian World War II male army veterans. The study found declines in spatial problem solving, or fluid intelligence. But the study found that scores on crystallized intelligence, measured by vocabulary and mechanical knowledge, increased over time. Overall the study found that on both spatial problems and vocabulary problems individual scores changed only slightly (a 16.1-percent loss in spatial problem solving and a 10.5-percent gain in vocabulary) over forty years.

Charness (1982) also found multidirectional changes in older people's mental ability as measured by problem-solving tasks. He reviewed the literature on mental ability and found that older people do less well than younger people on novel problem-solving tasks, but perform about as well as younger subjects on familiar tasks that older subjects know well, like chess or bridge. Botwinick (1984) reports that chronological age accounts for only about one-quarter of the variance in IQ scores. This means that age alone is not a very sound predictor of a person's intelligence score (Schaie 1989). Baltes and Willis sum up the current research: "The striking feature of descriptive aging research, is one of much variability, both between persons and within persons for distinct abilities" (1982, 355).

### *Longitudinal vs. Cross-Sectional Methods*

Like studies of memory, most studies of intelligence use a cross-sectional method to draw conclusions about age changes. These studies ignore the fact that older and younger cohorts differ on more variables than just age. Few studies of intelligence have looked at the variability among *individuals* (differences like educational level, social class, personal experience) in their samples. Age cohorts differ in education, test-taking ability, and vocabulary. These characteristics depend on when a person was born and what they have done in their lifetime (Schaie 1990a). When intelligence tests are used to compare age groups at one point in time, they confound cohort differences with age changes.

Longitudinal and sequential studies of intelligence try to overcome this problem by measuring the same groups of people at more than one point in time. Most longitudinal studies find less decline in intelligence with age than do cross-sectional studies. Schaie (1990b, 114), for example, studied one group over time and found that "virtually none of the individuals ... showed universal decline on all abilities monitored, even by the eighties." By age 60, he reports, three-quarters of the people in the study maintained their ability over a seven-year period on four of five measures. Even at age 81 more than half the sample maintained its ability over a seven-year period (Schaie 1990b).

Schaie and Labouvie-Vief (1974) gave intelligence tests in 1970 to 301 people who had been tested in 1956 and 1963. They added new people to their study to make up for those who had dropped out since the first sample. They found that younger people scored better than older people. But they also found that older people got roughly the same scores as they had seven years before. The researchers concluded that cohort differences accounted for most of the variations in test scores between younger and older subjects.

Botwinick (1984) takes a less optimistic view of intellectual functioning in old age. He reviewed the Schaie and Labouvie-Vief (1974) longitudinal study and found that decline set in at about age 53. Earlier cross-sectional research by Schaie (1959) showed declines around age 55. "Thus, the longitudinal sequences and the cross-sectional data are not very different" (Botwinick 1984, 262). Declines in intelligence occur regardless of the method used.

Botwinick (1984, 262) also says that longitudinal studies play down the effects of age on intelligence because people with low intelligence scores drop out of the studies. This leaves more intelligent people at older ages. The longer the study and the greater the number of tests on the subjects who remain, the more the dropout factor affects the results.

A study by Botwinick and Siegler (1980) controlled for dropouts and found that both longitudinal and cross-sectional analyses showed declines in intelligence with age. Labouvie-Vief (1985) responded to Botwinick and Siegler (1980) by noting that they studied people aged 60 and over. She says that cohort differences showed up in Schaie and Labouvie-Vief (1974) mostly for groups aged 60 and under. For subjects past age 70, Schaie and Labouvie-Vief (1974) also found steady declines in intelligence with age. Labouvie-Vief (1985, 505) concludes that decline in intelligence does occur late in life, but that current research at least calls "attention to the fact that significant decrements are considerably delayed into the far end of the 60- to 70-year-old spectrum."

The debate over the effects of age on intelligence continues in the literature. Future research will focus on the causes of differences in intelligence within different age groups and between different cohorts.

## Improvements in Cognitive Functioning in Later Life

Some of the latest research on intelligence explores ways to improve older people's intellectual functioning. Charness and Campbell (1988) tested young, middle-aged, and older people's mental calculation skills. They found that older adults gained skill in calculation in the same way that younger adults did. The older group showed "marked improvement" in their ability with practice (Charness and Campbell 1988, 127). And they equalled the starting level of the youngest group before the end of the study. The researchers (Charness and Campbell 1988, 128) conclude that the older group's improvement "is testimony to the malleability of the human information processing system, even in old age."

This research shows that older people can improve their performance on intelligence tests. Instruction in test-taking methods and in problem-solving strategies can improve the cognitive performance of older subjects (Labouvie-Vief 1977; Baltes and Willis 1981; Denney and Palmer 1981; Willis and Schaie 1988; Schaie 1990a).

Some of these studies show long-term effects. After one year Sanders and Sanders (1978) found that trained subjects performed better than untrained subjects or subjects who simply practiced similar problems. These studies show that "the old, like the young, have more potential than is typically measured by the tests" (Botwinick 1984, 271).

Jackson et al. (1990) sum up the research on intellectual ability in later life. "As has been suggested by an impressive body of empirical work," they say, "some abilities decline, some remain the same, and some improve with chronological age" (Jackson et al. 1990, 115). The change that takes place depends on the ability studied and on background factors like education and health (Baltes 1987).

Studies show that people who have good health and who live in a challenging environment score better on intelligence tests than those who do not (Schaie 1975; Schooler 1990). People who read books and newspapers and who travel and talk with friends keep their minds fresh. Researchers now think of the individual as modifiable. Baltes and Willis (1982, 120–21) conclude that "people can learn to make better use of their minds at any age. The logical approach [to observed decrements in mental functioning in later life] might be the development of compensatory education programs at about the time of retirement … " The section in Chapter 12 on education discusses some of these programs in detail.

## Creativity

The bulk of research on psychology and aging has focused on changes in memory and intelligence with age. Comparatively few studies have looked at creativity in later life. At least three different measures of creativity exist in the literature (Botwinick 1984). First, some studies measure creative achievement by evaluating the greatness of a work or by counting the number of creative works by an individual. Second, some studies use psychological tests to measure creativity. These tests take place in the laboratory and allow for comparisons of old and young people in a number of dimensions. Third, some studies use a more global definition of creativity. They define creative activity as activity that brings fulfilment to the individual and possibly even to others (though it might not reach worldwide or historical importance). Studies done from each point of view have looked at whether creativity declines with age.

### Creativity as Measured by Great Works

Lehman (1953) studied the ages at which scientists, philosophers, mathematicians, painters, inventors, and other creative people produced their greatest works. He selected for his sample people who had already died (because someone still alive could still produce a great work). Lehman found that past and present scientists produced their greatest creative work between the ages of 30 and 40. Most great writers produced their foremost work before the age of 45, and most poets produced theirs in their late 20s and early 30s. Painters peaked between ages 30 and 45. In most fields Lehman found that achievement steadily decreased after age 45.

· · · · · · · · · · · · · · · · · · · · · · · · · · · · · · · · ·

## Exhibit 6.3

### Can Older People Be Creative?

· · · · · · · · · · · · · · · · · · · · · · · · · · · · · · · · ·

Henry Wadsworth Longfellow's poem "Morituri Salutamus" is a salute to creative older people and shows that people can create into late old age.

> Cato learned Greek at eighty; Sophocles
> Wrote his grand *Oedipus*, and Simonides
> Bore off the prize of verse from his compeers,
> When each had numbered more than four score years.
> And Theophrastus, at four score and ten,
> Had just begun his *Characters of Men*.
> Chaucer, at Woodstock with the nightingales,
> At sixty wrote the *Canterbury Tales*;
> Goethe at Weimar, toiling to the last,
> Completed *Faust* when eighty years were past.

**Source:** Henry Wadsworth Longfellow, *The Poetical Works of Longfellow.* (London: Oxford University Press, 1928).

· · · · · · · · · · · · · · · · · · · · · · · · · · · · · · · · ·

Lehman (1968) went on to study athletes, chess champions, orators, politicians, businessmen, and atomic scientists. He found that still-living atomic scientists, for example, showed a peak in achievement between ages 25 to 29 and a sharp drop in achievement from age 35 on. He also found that older atomic scientists (aged 60 to 64) made only one-tenth the number of contributions as the younger (25- to 29-year-old) scientists. Lehman found the same pattern for still-living astronomers, mathematicians, and botanists.

Lehman's research set off a wave of controversy. Dennis (1968), for example, challenged Lehman's conclusions about the decline in creativity with age. First, he said, Lehman's research combined people with different lengths of life. Fewer people live to old age, so there will be fewer people to create great works in later life. Lehman's findings, therefore, might reflect a demographic fact rather than a decline in creativity. Second, Dennis questioned Lehman's approach to the study of creativity. Lehman used the works of critics, historians, and experts to decide on the quality of his subjects' work. Dennis argued that experts may favour the early, groundbreaking work of great people and could find it harder to judge more recent work by a great master.

Dennis (1968) conducted his own research on creativity. He used a measure different from Lehman's to compensate for these errors. First, while Lehman studied the age when creators produced their greatest work, Dennis studied the creative output (the number of works produced) of 738 people. Second, he selected long-lived subjects, all of whom had lived past age 78, to control for the effects of mixed longevities.

Dennis measured the output of a variety of creative people: artists, scientists, scholars, and dancers. He found that each group produced the least amount of work in their 20s. In almost all fields, creativity (measured by output) peaked between ages 40 and 49, about ten years later than Lehman's finding. Dennis, like Lehman, found that people in different fields peaked at different ages. Artists (dramatists, librettists, architects) peaked earliest and showed the sharpest decline in their 70s. Dennis found that scientists also experienced declines in middle age, but they showed a sharp decline only after age 60. Scholars showed little decline with age. They produced as much in their 70s as in their 40s, and they added to their former number of books by 25 percent between ages 70 and 79.

Dennis's work expands on Lehman's, rather than contradicting it. Dennis shows that differences in the peak age of creativity may depend as much on the social structure of a discipline as it does on a creative person's age. Scholars, for example, reach a peak later than artists and stay productive longer. Dennis explains that the arts, such as painting or composing, depend more on individual creativity. An artist's output declines if he or she loses

. . . . . . . . . . . . . . . . . . . . . . . . . . . . . . . . . . . . . . . .

## Exhibit 6.4

### Portraits of Three Creative Older Canadians

. . . . . . . . . . . . . . . . . . . . . . . . . . . . . . . . . . . . . . . .

### Barker Fairley

Barker Fairley began teaching German at the University of Toronto in 1915. He wrote a book of poems and five books on Goethe during his academic career. When he retired, he turned to painting for creative fulfilment. Six years before his death in 1986 at the age of 99, Fairley was profiled by Hubert de Santana in *Today Magazine:*

> He remembers vividly the day he took up painting. "I was in my 45th year and had never made a drawing in my life. My friend, the painter and poet Robert Finch, said that I ought to paint and arranged for us to go on a field trip the following day. I was reluctant and said to my wife, 'I hope it rains tomorrow.' It didn't rain, and we went out and painted, and I did a little watercolor which has the characteristics of my later work. It was all there immediately.
>
> For lack of encouragement Fairley stopped painting for 10 years. He began again in his 60s and has painted ever since. His shows now sell out and the cost of his paintings rose from a few hundred to a few thousand dollars in the three years since he turned 90 (he was 93 in 1980). How does he sum up his long and extraordinary life? ... "Like Goethe, I never toed the line professionally or in any way. I followed my nose, I remained a lover, a Liebhaber, in that sense an amateur. I just did what I chose and liked from first to last."

### Hubert Evans

Edith Iglauer, Hubert Evan's friend and neighbour, wrote a short biographical sketch about him in 1980. He was 88 at the time. Hubert Evans wrote more than 200 published short stories, 60 serials, 12 radio plays for the CBC

and seven books of fiction from the 1920s to 1954. When his wife died he stopped writing from 1960 to 1976. Then, says Iglauer,

> he broke the long silence ... to produce two new volumes of poetry—*Whittlings* and *Endings.* The poems were so well received—Margaret Laurence, the writer, has called them 'sheer wisdom in a lunatic age'—that Evans, regaining confidence, completed a novel that had been simmering on what he refers to as 'the back burner' for almost 50 years. *O Time in Your Flight,* published [in 1979], was acclaimed across the country ...
>
> 'People are going back to what they can read and enjoy,' [he says], 'but I am writing to please myself and nobody else. I love my subject, and I like writing. I've got this thing about writers being creative people, that creativity came in a package the night I was conceived. Maybe it was something my mother had for supper. If writers don't write, they'll be like the adipose fin on the salmon. At one time it was quite a big thing, but the salmon didn't use it, and now it's no bloody good to him.'

### Elisabeth Hopkins

Elisabeth Hopkins held her first painting exhibition at the age of 80. Ann Rhodes described Ms Hopkins's career and life in a feature for *Chatelaine:*

> Today her paintings sell for up to $1,150. She still lives alone, as she always has. She [was] 89 in April [1983] ... Painting had been a purely private pleasure until, in her mid-70s, she suggested to a Galiano [B.C.] gift-shop owner that her greeting cards might sell for a nickel a piece. For a full-size painting her price was $5, the sum paid for one that came to the attention of the Bau-Xi Gallery in Vancouver, which has shown her work ever since. ...

"Sometimes," [she says], "I've no idea what I'm going to do. The animals and the flowers just appear. I think you might say it is a joy to me." There's joy too in the letters and visits from admirers of her work …

Pinned up in Elisabeth Hopkins's home is a cartoon clipped from *The New Yorker*. It shows two older women, one clearly weighed down by her years, the other sprightly. The line reads: "Well, I tried old age, but it wasn't my cup of tea."

**Sources:** Edith Iglauer, "The Unsinkable Hubert Evans," *Today Magazine*, 20 December 1980; Hubert de Santana, "Portrait of the Artist as an Old Man," *Today Magazine*, 29 November 1980; Ann Rhodes, "Five Women Who Defy the Stereotypes of Aging," *Chatelaine*, February 1983. By permission of the authors.

• • • • • • • • • • • • • • • • • • • • • • • • • • • • • • • • • • • • • • •

strength or becomes ill. Scholars and scientists can get younger colleagues (like graduate students) to help them with their work. They can stay productive even if their strength declines (Dennis 1968).

Later studies by Simonton (1977) on great composers partly supported the idea that creativity declines with age. Simonton found that total productivity peaked between ages 45 and 49 and then declined. Total themes (musical ideas) in composers' works also decreased after ages 30 to 34, though they did not decrease to a point below the totals of the composer's younger years. Studies of Nobel Prize winners (Zuckerman 1977) and high-level chess players (Elo 1965) also report peaks in creativity for people in their mid-30s.

Simonton (1990, 1988a) recently reviewed the research on creativity and aging. He concluded that in the last decade of a creative person's career, their productivity equals about half their peak output (given a normal life span). In general, he says, "if one plots creative output as a function of age, productivity tends to rise fairly rapidly to a definite peak and thereafter tends to decline gradually" (Simonton 1990, 322).

Does the quality of the work also decline with age? In other words, do the creative works of a person's later career decline in quality? Simonton (1990) says that creative people can produce great works at every age. But across an entire career he proposes a "constant-probability-of-success model" (Simonton 1990, 323). This model states that within a career, the larger the number of creative works a person produces in a given time period, the more great works they produce during this period (Simonton 1988b).

Why does creativity decline with age? A decline in health, a decrease in energy, changes in a profession, and different goals and motivations later in life all explain the decline in creative output (Simonton 1988b). But even with this general decline, creativity can continue into late old age. Sophocles, Michelangelo, Goethe, Picasso, Winston Churchill, Grandma Moses, and Georgia O'Keeffe, for example, all remained creative past the age of 80. Lehman reported many cases of creativity in old age. He found that 20 percent of atomic physicists made contributions to their field after age 65 (1968, 100).

Lehman might have argued that most of these people had created their greatest works at younger ages. Still, they continued to contribute to society and culture as they aged. And some types of creativity, like comprehensive historical studies, may be possible only in old age. It may take a historian a lifetime to amass the knowledge and gain the perspective needed to make a great contribution. Pressey and Pressey (1967) say that people in their later years bring experience, wisdom, and a concern for humanity to their work. These virtues get overlooked in discussions of quantity and quality of creative works.

Pressey and Pressey (1967) proposed the idea that wisdom may differ from creative productivity. The study of wisdom has just begun, and few studies exist on the topic. Baltes and his colleagues have conducted most of this work (Dittmann-Kohli, and Baltes 1989; Smith, Dixon, and Baltes 1989). Simonton (1990) reports that as creativity declines with age, wisdom may increase. This would parallel the shift, as a person ages, from strength in fluid intelligence (problem solving) to strength in crystallized intelligence (expertise) (Baltes, Dittmann-Kohli, and Dixon 1984). Simonton (1988b) says that people may shift their cognitive patterns to a more analytical, organized, efficient way of thinking. This shows up as a decrease in the intuitive thinking needed for creativity and an increase in broader understanding needed for wisdom. Some types of work—those requiring leadership, for instance,—require both kinds of thinking and can peak very late in life. The leader may help others produce works by showing enthusiasm, and giving encouragement and advice (Simonton 1988a).

## *Creativity as Measured by Psychological Tests*
Lehman (1953, 1968), Dennis (1968), and Pressey and Pressey (1967) studied unique groups of people—people famous enough to have their work noted in history. But what about "average" people—those who carry out most of the work in society? Does creativity change with age? Creativity studies of the general population often rely on psychological tests. Like memory and intelligence studies, most creativity studies show a decline in test scores with age with a peak around age 30 (McCrae, Arenberg, and Costa 1987; Simonton 1990). None of these studies show an increase in creativity in later life (Cornelius and Caspi 1987).

A study by Jacquish and Ripple (1981) found a complex pattern of change in creativity with age. They studied 218 men and women 18–84 years old. They found that the oldest group (61–84) had lower fluency and flexibility scores, but scored as well as the youngest group (18–25) on originality. The middle group (40–60) scored best on all measures. This study suggests that some measures of creativity may decline more than others with age.

A study by Crosson and Robertson-Tchabo (1983) suggests that a person's background and experience may also influence creativity in later life. This study compared two groups of women. One group included 271 women artists and writers aged 23–87. A second group included 76 women aged 26–74 who had not had careers in the creative arts. The study found that the noncreative career subjects over 60 scored significantly lower than the noncreative career people under age 50. But the study found no significant correlation between age and creativity in the creative group. Crosson and Robertson-Tchabo suggest that continued creative work may help a person stay creative longer.

Studies that use creativity tests suffer from a number of problems. First, they often use cross-sectional designs that confound cohort differences with age changes. These studies may measure differences in educational background and test-taking ability as much as creativity. Second, the measures used in these studies have low validity, which means that results on these tests may bear little relation to real-life creativity (Simonton 1990). Creativity can take forms other than great works and scores on tests.

### Creativity as Personal Expression

Creativity can refer to a great achievement, a test score, or a form of personal expression. This last perspective treats creativity as a source of individual satisfaction regardless of how other people judge the works produced.

Kenneth Koch, a professional poet and teacher, reported on the value of creative expression for personal well-being. Koch agreed to teach poetry writing to twenty-five people in a nursing home in New York City. He said that on the first day the people looked "old, sick, tired, uncomfortable. Some seemed to be asleep or almost so" (1982, 210). Other people in the class gazed around the room or showed signs of pain. Koch began with a collaborative poem. In this case he asked each person for a line about their childhood. Some people refused to contribute, but most did, and Koch put their lines together in a poem. He reported that the group members became "excited at the unaccustomed pleasure of hearing what they said read aloud, and excited at hearing it admired by me and by other students" (1982, 211). Koch (1977) eventually collected these poems in a book titled *I Never Told Anybody*. These poems represent the first formal creative works produced by these people. But it only hints at the joy writing poetry brought to their lives. Koch's (1977) report shows that older people often lack an opportunity to express themselves creatively.

Crosson and Robertson-Tchabo (1983) say that if older people had more opportunity to express their creativity they would show more creative behaviour. Butler (1974) says that today older people have to become autodidacts—

self-teachers. These kinds of people take charge of their own learning, they transform their world in response to their own concerns, and, in the process, create something new. This view of creativity makes later life a time of potential discovery and self-renewal rather than a time of decline.

## PSYCHOLOGICAL DISORDERS: ABNORMAL AGING

Studies of memory, intelligence, and creativity describe the normal changes that come with aging, but some people show abnormal changes as they age. They may suffer from psychological problems such as paranoia, anxiety neuroses, and schizophrenia. Experts call these **functional disorders** because they interfere with how a person functions. These problems have no clear organic cause, and some older people have suffered with them throughout their lives. Other people suffer from **organic disorders**, diseases of the brain such as Alzheimer's disease, Parkinson's disease, or stroke. All of these illnesses arise from a deterioration of the brain.

### Organic Brain Disorders

Organic brain syndrome, senile dementia, or dementia are general terms used to describe a variety of organic brain disorders. Organic disorders lead to confusion, forgetfulness, and sometimes antisocial behaviour. Some individuals with these disorders wander, strike out, or resist help from their caregivers. Dementia cases create stress for both professional care providers and family caregivers.

Hendricks and Hendricks (1986, 238) report that 4 to 6 percent of those aged 65–84 suffer from organic brain disorder, but that 20 percent of people aged 85 and over suffer from these illnesses. Canadian researchers say that dementing illnesses will show up in greater numbers as more people live into late old age. "Those managing to stay on till well beyond 85 will form a group with very much higher than average risk of severe dementia (i.e., a prevalence rate in the neighborhood of 25 percent)" (Stone 1986, 31). A study by Robertson, Rockwood, and Stolee (1982) in Saskatchewan supports this estimate. They found moderate to severe dementia in 2.4 percent of people aged 65 to 69, but 29.9 percent dementia in the 85 and over group. Nursing homes and hospitals in the future will have to care for more and more demented patients.

One estimate says that 50 to 70 percent of nursing home patients have some degree of Alzheimer's (Peppard 1985). These figures only estimate the prevalence of Alzheimer's disease (Watson and Seiden 1984). More precise figures require better reporting and reliable diagnosis.

Canada began its first nationwide study of dementia in 1990, the largest study of its kind. The study includes over 10,000 older people in five Canadian regions and includes institutionalized seniors as well as people who live in the community. The study has four objectives: (1) to report on the prevalence of dementias among older Canadians; (2) to assess the risk of someone's getting Alzheimer-type dementia; (3) to describe patterns of care for dementia patients and to measure caregiver burden; and (4) to create a uniform database (Gauthier, McDowell, and Hill 1990). The study also includes a number of add-on projects that will focus on topics like the genetic origins of Alzheimer's disease. This study will give a better understanding of the prevalence of Alzheimer's disease. This, in turn, should lead to better treatment of the illness in the future.

None of the research so far has produced a method to treat Alzheimer's disease. Physicians cannot even make a certain diagnosis of the disease's presence; they can only rule out other causes of confusion and personality decline like brain tumours, blood pressure problems, or hyperthyroidism. Dozens of other illnesses must be ruled out before an illness can be diagnosed as Alzheimer's. Caution prevents doctors from doing so; a patient might have a treatable illness or a problem like overmedication or infection. The inability to diagnose Alzheimer's quickly leaves families in limbo and forces patients to go through dozens of tests.

Organic disorders pose problems for the diseased individuals and their families. Family caregivers often feel despair because their care receiver does not recognize them any more. This can add to their burden. A better understanding of memory loss might help these caregivers cope with their care receivers' illnesses.

Sainsbury and Coristine (1986, 99) studied patients whose memories were cognitively impaired. They found that patients often could not recognize a relative's picture, but these same patients could choose the relative's picture from a set of four pictures. The researchers said that even though a person loses "recognition memory," "affective memory" remains intact. This finding suggests that cognitively impaired patients may have good feelings toward their relatives, even if they do not seem to recognize them. The researchers added that "the subject may be aware that he knows the visitor but not recall the relationship. Awareness of this fact in conjunction with the knowledge that severely memory impaired people can yet possess strong affective associations can be of considerable comfort to concerned relatives" (Sainsbury and Coristine 1986, 103).

Kraus and McGeer (1983) studied the care system for people with dysfunctional brain syndrome in Kingston, Ontario. They found that people who suffered from this condition needed more appropriate housing, more

- - - - - - - - - - - - - - - - - - - - - - - - - - - - - - - - - - - - - - - - -

# Exhibit 6.5

## The Stages of Decline Due to Alzheimer's Disease

- - - - - - - - - - - - - - - - - - - - - - - - - - - - - - - - - - - - - - - - -

Health and Welfare Canada (1984a) described the three stages that an Alzheimer's patient goes through. Some people may go through these stages in a few months; others may take years. The changes that come with Alzheimer's disease begin slowly. Often family members recognize the first signs only when they look back over a year or two of caregiving.

Stage I: A person first shows changes in memory. They forget their keys or their wallet. They may also forget recent events or forget that they did a job around a house. This gets worse in time. The person forgets more often, takes longer to do simple jobs, or begins to recheck work already done.

One woman recalls that her husband, an engineering professor, would spend three or four hours writing a fifty-minute lecture that used to take him an hour to write. Another woman recalls that she first became worried when her husband, a physician, lost his way home from work one night. He planned to stop at a patient's house for a short house call around 5:00 P.M. The patient lived only a few blocks away from their house, so his wife expected him home around six. She began to worry at eight o'clock when she still hadn't heard from him. An hour later he came in exhausted. He had spent the last three hours driving around their neighbourhood looking for their house.

Stage II: The second stage of the disease includes more memory decline, loss of speaking ability, and an end to normal daily activity. The ill person may wander at night, lose control of his or her bowel and bladder, and threaten others. One woman left a knife in her garden after she used it to weed the flower bed. Her husband picked it up and stalked through the bushes into a neighbour's yard, saying to the neighbour, "I'm going to kill you." The neighbour ran inside and called the police. When the sick man's wife came outside to finish weeding, she found the police wrestling her husband into a squad car.

In another case a man walked into a new car dealer and signed a contract for a $20,000 car. His wife found out only after the salesman called her to check on the financing. The owner of the dealership agreed to void the contract, but only after she pleaded and explained about her husband's illness.

This stage of the disease can put stress on the family. Caregivers—most often spouses or children of the ill person—can feel tense, trapped, and exhausted. Members have to take on new roles: wives become chauffeurs or nurses; children become parents or police; and husbands become homemakers (Novak and Guest 1985). Mace and Rabins (1981, 63) report one case of a burdened husband who had to bathe his wife. "She screams for help the whole time I am bathing her. She'll open the windows and yell, 'Help, I'm being robbed!'" One man confessed to Mace and Rabins (1981, 179), "There was a time when I considered getting a gun, killing my wife, and then killing myself ..."

Stage III: The person in the last stage of Alzheimer's disease needs institutionalization and often twenty-four-hour nursing care. The person can no longer speak or communicate. He or she may wander or move constantly unless restrained. Seizures may occur. Death occurs between two and nineteen years after the disease starts (Health and Welfare Canada

1984a). Death often comes from an illness like pneumonia or heart disease, but death certificates rarely mention Alzheimer's disease as a cause of death. This makes it impossible to know the exact number of deaths caused by Alzheimer's.

Not all Alzheimer's patients show all the above-mentioned symptoms. Some show other symptoms of confusion like depression and crying. But these stages give a general picture of the disease. They also give only a faint idea of the stress that Alzheimer's disease puts on the primary caregiver.

• • • • • • • • • • • • • • • • • • • • • • • • • • • • • • • • • • • • • • •

complete assessment, and more services to support families. MacFadgen (1987), in a study of Toronto and Peel Region dementia patients, found that families felt they needed more respite beds, more home support, special assessment and treatment services, adult day care, and special units for long-term care in their area. Families identified the need for more respite/relief resources as their most pressing need. Kraus (1984) said that some families felt committed to keeping their care receiver at home. But when a care receiver's behaviour became too difficult to handle, even the best family supports and community care could not relieve caregiver burden. Then families felt they had to institutionalize their relative.

MacFadgen (1987) also found that cognitively impaired patients posed problems for health care workers, social service workers, and public housing managers. Sixty-two percent of the institutional sample in this study needed heavy nursing care. Forty-four percent of clients in the community showed disturbing or disruptive behaviour. Dawson and Reid (1987) found that cognitive deficits predicted wandering behaviour in institutional patients. Professional caregivers often feel burdened by the demands of these patients. A study by Novak, Chappell, and Miles-Tapping (1990) found that nursing assistants who were distressed by patient behaviour felt most burdened. Service workers will care for more and more clients with these illnesses in the coming years and will need to understand the basis of the illness and how to treat these clients.

## Functional Disorders

Functional disorders disrupt normal life. They include emotional upset, depression, and anxiety. Hendricks and Hendricks (1986) say that 25 to 60 percent of older people in and out of institutions in the U.S. report mental distress and that 10 to 15 percent have emotional problems that need mental health attention.

The Canada Health Survey (Health and Welfare Canada and Statistics Canada 1981) asked a sample of more than 23,000 people from all over Canada to report their health problems. The study found that compared to the population aged 15 to 64, people 65 and over had more than two and a half times the rate of self-reported mental disorder (12.3 percent of 65 and over compared with 4.5 percent of people from 15 to 64), and that older women reported mental disorders at almost twice the rate of older men (15.4 percent of women 65 and over compared with 8.5 percent of men). Statistics Canada (1990e) reports that the hospitalization rate for functional psychoses (schizophrenia, paranoid states, and other nonorganic psychoses) increased between 1971 and 1985/86, going up by 47.4 percent for those from 65 to 74 years old and 184.9 percent for people aged 75 and over.

The Canada Health Survey found that the proportion of an age group reporting frequent symptoms of anxiety and depression goes up slightly throughout adulthood. More than 4 percent of males aged 65 and over and nearly 8 percent of females aged 65 and over (7.7 percent) report frequent symptoms of anxiety and depression. This comes to slightly more than the proportion of males and females aged 45 to 64 who report these problems (3.8 percent for males and 6.9 percent for females). But more than 9 percent of the older group did not respond to this question, two to three times higher a proportion of "unknowns" than the 45 to 64 age group. Health and Welfare Canada and Statistics Canada (1981) estimate that these unknowns would probably add to the proportion of older people feeling distress. Including the unknowns, the distressed group would represent 14 to 17 percent of people 65 and over.

Cappliez (1988) reviewed the literature on depression and found that between 0.8 and 8 percent of people aged 65 and over meet the *Diagnostic and Statistical Manual of Mental Disorders* (third edition) (American Psychiatric Association 1980) criteria for major depression. Other studies use criteria based on the Depression Scale of the Center for Epidemiological Studies. These studies report a depression rate of 9 to 18 percent in the older population. One well-known study on depression (Gurland et al., 1983) reported rates of depression among older people of 12.4 percent for London, England, and 13 percent for New York. The higher rates include moderate as well as severely depressed cases (see also Gurland and Toner 1983; Murrell, Himmelfarb, and Wright 1983; Cohen 1990).

Cohen (1990) notes that controversy over prevalence rates exists for most mental disorders in later life. He reports that depression can appear as vague physical decline or complaints about more than one physical symptom. These cases would increase the estimated proportion of depressed older people. Studies that include people who have **dysphoria**, a depression having symptoms of pessimism and dissatisfaction with life, as well as people with clinical depression report rates of 20 to 25 percent.

Cappliez (1988) says that the proportion of older people with depression differs little from the proportion of people with depression in the adult population. In general, studies have found that the risk of depression decreases in later life (Chappell and Barnes 1982). People aged 65 and over have a lower risk than 17-year-olds of first experiencing depression. And those under 10 and over 60 have the least chance of suffering from depression (Gurland 1976). Cappliez cautions that only a few studies have looked at people aged 75 and over as a separate group. This group may face more risk than people aged 65 to 74. Also, current studies compare different cohorts of people. Older people today may reflect less on their feelings than younger people; they may think of their depression as a part of a physical illness; or death and institutionalization may take severely depressed people out of the general population. These conditions may explain the low rates of depression among older people.

People with resources such as social skills, problem-solving ability, and emotional support from family and friends will have less tendency toward depression. A person who appraises a situation as non-threatening or who copes actively to improve situations will show less depression (Cappliez 1988). This perspective shows that social as well as psychological conditions influence depression. Phifer and Murell (1986), for example, conclude that physical health and social support affect depression.

The "unhappy" Canadian, the Canada Health Survey reports, is likely to be old, female, widowed, low-income, in poor health, and without much education (Health and Welfare Canada and Statistics Canada 1981). The inability to get out and the loss of social supports can also lead to unhappiness or depression. This puts the mental health of many infirm older Canadians at risk.

Social support buffers the effect of poor health and protects a person from feeling depressed. We will look in more detail at the influence of social conditions on psychological well-being in Chapter 7.

## Treatment and Intervention

Butler (1975) says that often mental health experts ignore the needs of older people. Most psychiatrists, he says, like to treat young, well-educated, successful people. A study by Gibson (1970) found that many psychiatrists believe that older people will not improve as a result of therapy. Eaton, Stones, and Rockwood (1986) found that physicians often failed to detect cognitive impairment in older patients. They suggest that doctors receive more training in "geriatric assessment, treatment, and management" during medical school and as part of their continuing medical education (Eaton, Stones, and Rockwood 1986).

A whole range of treatments can help older people cope with psychological problems. Smyer, Zarit, and Qualls (1990) say that the individual's characteristics (including age), the diagnosis criteria used, the older person's adaptation patterns, and the intervention setting (community or institution) all influence the choice of treatment. Chemical therapies exist to treat some reversible organic brain syndromes. Physicians can treat alcoholics in the early stages of Wernicke-Korsakoffs dementia (a neurological disease) with large doses of thiamine. Many more therapies exist for older people with functional problems—problems related to a person's personality or social life. Drug therapy can help older people cope with functional problems like depression; behaviour therapy can help with insomnia; and psychotherapy can help the person who has a personality disorder. Life review (Butler and Lewis 1982) can help with adaptation to loss, and milieu therapy can help a person to change his or her environment.

Some clinicians suggest the use of pets to help relieve loneliness (see Exhibit 6.6). Goldmeier (1986) found that older people who had pets reported less loneliness, and that older people who lived with other people, even without pets, showed the least loneliness. Goldmeier says that pets cannot fully substitute for human companionship, but pets can create nonthreatening relationships for people who might otherwise reject therapy or other human contact.

New programs for older people with psychological disorders (LeBlanc 1985) will offer older people more options for treatment in the future. Some of these alternatives will need to take forms—such as day centres or hospital adult day care programs—that older people already feel comfortable using.

A Canadian government report (Mental Health Division 1988) recognizes the unmet needs of older people for psychiatric help. The report describes a comprehensive response to older people with psychiatric problems. It focuses on four approaches that would improve psychiatric care for older people: assessment, management and treatment, coordination of services, and the use of volunteers.

This approach fits with the current thinking about health care service in general for an aging population. Chapter 8 will discuss in more detail this general shift toward a comprehensive health care model.

## CONCLUSION

Psychological well-being means more than coping with problems, stress, and loss. It means growth, learning, and a sense of purpose. The research on the

. . . . . . . . . . . . . . . . . . . . . . . . . . . . . . . . . . . . . . . . . . . .

## Exhibit 6.6

### Pet Therapy

. . . . . . . . . . . . . . . . . . . . . . . . . . . . . . . . . . . . . . . . . . . .

One of the newest forms of therapy—pet therapy—offers older people companionship and relief from loneliness. Some experts say it can lead to better health and longer life.

A year ago Dolores Kohler, 36, an Edmonton housewife and long-time SPCA volunteer, pioneered the city's first "visitation program" by loading her part-Husky, Max, and her two cats, Snow Prince and Cricket, into her station wagon and driving them over to the Venta Nursing Home. That visit, and each of her subsequent monthly visits to the home, were a resounding success. The old folks, says Venta recreation director June Berrisford, "Brighten up the minute Dolores walks in the room. They look forward to her coming—it's a big day." Last month, Elva McCartney, the SPCA's education director, decided to expand the program, taking on six more pet owners and scheduling three more homes for regular visits.

Such success, however, is hardly news to Calgary's Humane Society (SPCA), which started a similar program two years ago and now has about 170 volunteers leading more than 200 cats and dogs through nine institutions for the elderly on a regular basis. Pet therapy is booming, according to Calgary program chairman Wendy Betts, 43, for one simple reason: "Animals give patients something to live for."

**Source:** Gail Herchak and Brian Wilford, "The Therapy of Pets," *Alberta Report*, 28 November 1983. Reprinted with permission of the publisher.

. . . . . . . . . . . . . . . . . . . . . . . . . . . . . . . . . . . . . . . . . . . .

psychology of aging shows that older people in good health stay alert, intelligent, and able to learn. They face stresses unique to later life, but they can get through these crises themselves or with the help of others. Sometimes the biggest block to older people's well-being comes from the prejudices and stereotypes other people have about old age. The research on the psychology of aging has begun to remove the basis for these stereotypes. More research and knowledge about old age and new cohorts of older people will teach us more about mental potential in later life.

## SUMMARY

1. Early research supported the myth that intellectual ability declines with age, but recent studies show more complex findings, for example, younger people do perform better than older people on some memory and intelligence tests, but the pace of testing, the types of questions asked, and the way older people learn can all decrease their performance.

2. In general, laboratory studies show that memory declines with age, though different types of memory show different amounts of decline. Recent research suggests that a decrease in working memory accounts for poorer memory in older people. Education and background differences between older and younger people may account for differences in performance in memory studies.

3. Test conditions may decrease older people's ability to remember in laboratory studies. Studies of memory in real (not laboratory) contexts shows that older people can compensate for memory declines. Studies also show that when compared, younger and older people's recall of historical and social events showed little or no deficit for older people.

4. Early studies used cross-sectional methods to study the effects of aging on intelligence. The results confused cohort differences with age changes. Longitudinal methods show declines in fluid intelligence (problem-solving skills). But they show little change and possibly some increase in crystallized intelligence (skills based on acquired knowledge). Research also shows that older people can improve their scores on intelligence tests through training.

5. Studies of both the quality and quantity of creative production show a decline in creativity with age. Comparisons of older and younger people on psychological tests also find greater creativity among younger subjects. Both of these approaches to the study of creativity emphasize the products of creative work. Reports of subjective creative development show that people can create and learn to do so at any age. Education, opportunity, and an interest in a subject can all lead to creativity in later life.

6. The number of cases of organic brain disorders like Alzheimer's disease will increase as more people live to late old age. These disorders place a heavy burden on families, and the people with these diseases often need professional health care at the end of their lives.

7. Functional mental disorders (e.g., anxiety and depression) show up less often in old age than people commonly believe. Older people with these problems can benefit from drug therapies, psychotherapy, or milieu therapy.

8. The research on the psychology of aging presents a balanced view of aging. Some mental faculties may decline, but others remain stable as long as a person is in good health. More research and knowledge about the process of aging will teach us more about mental potential in later life.

## SELECTED READINGS

Lissy F. Jarvik "Aging of the Brain: How Can We Prevent It?" *The Gerontologist* 28: 739–46, 1988.

A readable article that summarizes research on changes in intellectual function as people age. The author links the research on intellectual change with studies of Alzheimer's disease and normal aging.

Health and Welfare Canada. *Alzheimer's Disease: A Family Information Handbook.* Ottawa: Minister of Supply and Services, 1984a.

A good basic review of Alzheimer's disease—what it is, how it affects victims and their families, and what families can do to get help.

Hultsch, David F. and Roger A. Dixon. "Learning and Memory in Aging." In James E. Birren and K. Warner Schaie, eds. *Handbook of the Psychology of Aging.* 3d ed. San Diego: Academic Press, 1990.

A good, up-to-date review of the literature. Covers the literature from the mid-1980s onward. Contains references to the newest topics in the field: working memory, implicit and explicit memory, and methods to improve memory.

# The Social Psychology of Aging

# INTRODUCTION

What is a good old age? This question has guided research in the social psychology of aging for more than fifty years. Researchers have found that many patterns of good aging exist. What follows are three cases that show the variety of forms a good old age can take.

Joe Willis, 70, worked as an engineer for an oil company until he retired in 1975. Now he spends January and February playing golf in Florida and spends the summer at his cottage in the Muskokas. His company calls him back two or three times a year as a consultant; he serves on the board of directors of a seniors' centre; and he volunteers as a nursing home visitor. "I visit the old folks once a week," he says. "At Christmas I take them to a show or out shopping." Joe does not see himself as old. He works less now and has more leisure time, but he feels the same as before he retired. He stays active and involved, and has found new ways to give meaning to his life.

Birdie Caldwell's husband died fifteen years ago. She moved out of their house and into a two-bedroom apartment a year after his death. She also went back to work as a secretary—work she had not done since her teens. Now, at age 65, she still lives on her own. She has two daughters who live less than an hour away by car. She visits them a few times a month and sometimes stays for the weekend. She travels, belongs to a bridge group, and enjoys her freedom.

Rose Reitman, 73, also lives by herself in her own apartment. Her husband died three years ago. She has a bad case of arthritis in her legs which keeps her indoors most of the year. On warm days she walks a few blocks to the local shopping centre. Most of the time she watches TV, knits, or talks to friends on the phone. Rose feels content in her old age. She sometimes talks to ten or fifteen friends and relatives in a week. Nieces and nephews call her from all over the country on her birthday or on holidays. Her daughter lives two and a half hours away by car, and her son lives across the country. She has six grandchildren; their pictures cover her walls and table tops.

Three different portraits of old age. Birdie stays active; Rose lives a quiet life without social demands; Joe has found new roles to replace ones that he had lost. Each of these people show a different response to the challenges of aging, but they all report high life-satisfaction. These cases show only a few of the patterns of successful aging today.

This chapter will look at: (1) theories of human development in later life; (2) the social structural conditions (like membership in an ethnic community) that influence the experience aging; and (3) some social-psychological problems that older people face in society today.

## WHAT IS A GOOD OLD AGE?

Three social-psychological theories of aging—disengagement theory, activity theory, and continuity theory—each claim to describe the ideal way to grow old. Researchers have debated the merits of these theories since the 1960s, and references to them still show up in the literature today.

### Disengagement Theory

Rosow (1976, 458) defines a social role as a "pattern of activity intrinsic" to a social position. Cumming and Henry (1961) describe old age as a time of disengagement—a time to withdraw from social roles and to decrease activity. They base their theory on a study of 279 people aged 50 to 70 in Kansas City. The study focused on people in good health and with enough money to live comfortably. They found that in this sample social roles and emotional ties decreased with age.

Cumming and Henry (1961) describe disengagement as inevitable, universal, and satisfying to both the person and society. Disengagement, they say, serves an important psychological function: it allows older people to reduce their activity naturally as their strength declines. Disengagement also serves a useful social function. It allows older people to leave social roles before the final disengagement—death. This creates a smooth transfer of power and responsibility from one generation to the next.

Critics attacked disengagement theory on three fronts almost as soon as it appeared. First, disengagement theory supports the stereotype of old age as a time of weakness and decline. Second, the theory assumes that the old perform less well than the young and, therefore, supports the existence of mandatory retirement based on age, rather than on a person's ability to do the job. Third, the theory assumes that all older people respond to the world in the same way—that they all disengage from social roles. More recent research shows that many older people, especially those who have good health and a good income, stay active in later life (Markides and Mindel 1987).

### Activity Theory

Neugarten, Havighurst, and Tobin (1968) put forward a second major theory of aging: activity theory. This theory is just the reverse of disengagement theory. It holds that, as people lose social roles in old age, they stay happiest when they replace these roles with new ones. This theory, moreover, blames society for the process of disengagement. Modern society, it says, pushes older people out of social roles. This theory fits the North American view that happiness comes from work and activity.

Neugarten, Havighurst, and Tobin (1968) found three types of active people who reported high life-satisfaction. One group started new activities to fill in for lost social roles. The researchers called them "re-organizers." Another group held on to their mid-life roles and stayed active. The researchers said these people were "holding-on." A third group stayed active but narrowed the range of their activities, and this group the researchers called "focused." Most recent studies also find that high activity correlates with high life-satisfaction.

## Continuity Theory

A third theory of aging says that people feel most satisfied if they continue the roles and activities of their middle years (Atchley 1982). This theory says that old age is a continuation of a person's past (rather than a break with it or a change in direction from it) and that people will choose the lifestyle in old age that is most like the pattern of life they lived in middle age. Mildly active people in their younger years will prefer a mild level of activity in later life and will feel satisfied with this lifestyle. But active people will want to keep up their activity—though activity might take new forms in old age.

Research supports each of these theories. Some studies have found that older people tend to be more passive, more introverted, and less committed to achievement in old age (Riley and Foner 1968; Neugarten 1969). Neugarten, Havighurst, and Tobin (1968, 175) found support for both activity and disengagement theories. They found that many disengaged people report high life-satisfaction and have integrated personalities. These people want to live a "rocking-chair" style of aging, and they leave their social roles by choice, living contented lives with few social contacts. Other people, who also report high life-satisfaction, either stay active in their middle-life roles or replace these with new roles in old age.

Research by MacLean (1982) supports both activity and continuity theories. He found that men who could continue their activities and interests into later life showed the highest life-satisfaction. These findings support the idea that people enjoy old age if they continue the activities and relationships they enjoyed in the past.

These three theories tell part of the truth about life-satisfaction in later life, but all of them give too simple a picture of old age. People can disengage from some roles and still have high life-satisfaction (Maddox 1970; Palmore 1970; Atchley 1971a); life-satisfaction depends on what kind of activity declines. Lemon, Bengtson, and Peterson (1972) found that while a decline in group activities did not lead to lower life-satisfaction, a decline in social activity with

. . . . . . . . . . . . . . . . . . . . . . . . . . . . . . . . . . . . . . .

## Exhibit 7.1

### Men, Women, and Life-Satisfaction

. . . . . . . . . . . . . . . . . . . . . . . . . . . . . . . . . . . . . . .

Many studies have found differences in life-satisfaction and personality when they compared men and women (Lowenthal 1975; Lowenthal, Thurner, and Chiriboga 1975). Connidis (1983b) asked a sample of four hundred older Canadians how they felt about aging. She found that most people had a positive view of later life, though they had a realistic view of the problems that come with aging. She also found that men and women differed in how much they liked, disliked, and worried about old age. For example, 71 percent of men, compared with 56 percent of women, reported no worries about growing older. When the older people in Connidis's sample did complain about old age, men complained more often about physical restrictions while women complained more often about poor health.

Men and women also liked different things about aging. Men more often mentioned good health and freedom from work as things they liked about old age. Women more often mentioned contentment and freedom from family responsibility. These findings probably reflect the different social roles played by this generation of older men and women in their early and middle years. Most of these women had worked at home raising families, while the men had worked in the labour force. In later life they each feel a different kind of freedom—women feel the freedom from child rearing, and men feel the freedom from work. These kinds of responses may change in the future as women today spend time on careers as well as child rearing.

. . . . . . . . . . . . . . . . . . . . . . . . . . . . . . . . . . . . . . .

friends did. Kozma and Stones (1978, 248) conclude that activity or disengagement alone do not lead to happiness, but that "people appear to be happy if most of their experiences are pleasant and their perceived needs are met."

## PERSONALITY DEVELOPMENT

### Stage Theories

Some psychologists who study the individual in society focus on personality development. A number of researchers describe this development as a series of stages. Erik Erikson (1963), for instance, has created one of the best-known stage models of the life cycle. His model describes eight stages of ego development. At each stage, he says, the person faces a crisis with two possible outcomes. If a person gets through the crisis successfully, growth occurs.

As a result, the person reaches a new stage of development. If not, the person experiences some psychopathology that inhibits further development.

Erikson (1959) describes five stages that occur during childhood and youth, and three that occur in adulthood (see Exhibit 7.2). The adult stages correspond roughly to early, middle, and late adulthood. Each stage offers the person a specific challenge. The sixth stage, "Intimacy vs. Isolation," requires a specific task: "to lose and find oneself in another" (Erikson 1959, Appendix). Love is the virtue of this stage: the young adult will marry or make some other permanent or semi-permanent bond with another person. The crisis of this stage focuses on the experience of "intimacy." If the person fails to achieve intimacy, he or she will face "isolation."

The task of the middle adult years, Erikson says, is "to make be, to take care of" (1959, Appendix). Here the person's concern turns to what he calls "generativity" versus its opposite, "stagnation." This includes the generation of products and ideas as well as having children (Erikson 1976, 7). This stage has its unique virtue: care for oneself, but also care for others and for the world as a whole. In mid-life the person becomes concerned with the "main-

• • • • • • • • • • • • • • • • • • • • • • • • • • • • • • • • • • • • • • • • • • • • • •

## Exhibit 7.2

### Erikson's Stages of Ego Development

• • • • • • • • • • • • • • • • • • • • • • • • • • • • • • • • • • • • • • • • • • • • • •

### Childhood Stages

**Stage 1:** Basic Trust vs. Mistrust
**Stage 2:** Autonomy vs. Shame, Doubt
**Stage 3:** Initiative vs. Guilt
**Stage 4:** Industry vs. Inferiority

### Adolescence

**Stage 5:** Identity vs. Role Confusion

### Adulthood

**Stage 6:** Intimacy vs. Isolation
**Stage 7:** Generativity vs. Stagnation
**Stage 8:** Ego Integrity vs. Despair

**Source:** Adapted from Erik Erikson, *Childhood and Society*, 2d ed. (New York: W.W. Norton, 1963).

• • • • • • • • • • • • • • • • • • • • • • • • • • • • • • • • • • • • • • • • • • • • • •

tenance of the world" and with passing the culture on to the coming generations (Erikson 1976, 15, 27).

The task of late adulthood, Erikson says, is "to be, through having been, to face not being (1959, Appendix). Wisdom is the virtue of this last stage; it comes when the person achieves "integrity" and overcomes the threat of "despair and disgust" (1959, 98). Like other psychoanalytic thinkers (Buhler 1951; Jung 1976), Erikson describes old age as a time of inwardness, a time when a person reflects on the past and brings closure to life. At this point, he says, a person with a healthy personality accepts their life as the product of their own actions within a particular culture. This last stage sums up the seven earlier stages, and when a person achieves integrity, Erikson says, it brings a wholeness to life. A person who displays integrity inspires the young to trust in the culture and to follow its prescriptions for action (Erikson 1982, 63; Erikson 1963, 269).

A number of studies support Erikson's model of adult stages. They find the same order of stages he describes, and they find that the stages follow one another as he predicts (Constantinople 1969; Boyd and Koskela 1970; Ciaccio 1971).

Some writers have expanded on Erikson's outline of middle and later life. Erikson began as a child psychologist, and his life cycle model reflects his interest in children. In his classic paper "Growth and Crises of the Healthy Personality" (1950), for example, he spends forty-five pages on the first twenty years of life and devotes only five pages to the next fifty to sixty years. Peck ([1955] 1968) modified Erikson's model five years later, adding more stages to it.

Erikson's last stage, Peck said, "seems to be intended to represent in a global, nonspecific way all the psychological crises and crisis-solutions of the last forty or fifty years of life" ([1955] 1968, 88). Peck divided this last stage of life into two periods—middle and old age. He found seven crises a person had to overcome within these periods. At each stage the person gives up the narrow commitments—to the body, to people, to concepts, and finally to the self—that dominated earlier stages of life. Peck's work shows that middle and later life are complex and active periods of development.

Levinson (1978) and his co-workers at Yale also found more stages in mid-life than Erikson described. Levinson based his conclusion on the study of forty American men between the ages of 35 and 45. Ten of the men worked as executives, ten as hourly wage workers, ten as academic biologists, and ten as novelists. Levinson and his team conducted in-depth interviews over many weeks with each man.

Levinson (1978) found that a series of age-linked "shifts" took place for all these men in mid-life. He found that men alternate between stable,

· · · · · · · · · · · · · · · · · · · · · · · · · · · · · · ·

## Exhibit 7.3

### Peck's Stages of Psycho-Social Development

· · · · · · · · · · · · · · · · · · · · · · · · · · · · · · ·

### Middle Age

1. Valuing Wisdom vs. Valuing Physical Powers. After the late twenties a person needs to shift from dependence on physical power to the use of good judgment to get things done.
2. Socializing vs. Sexualizing in Human Relationships. With the climacteric (menopause), people learn to value one another for their personalities rather than their sexuality.
3. Cathectic Flexibility vs. Cathectic Impoverishment. Cathexis refers to emotional investment. When children grow up and move away, or when a spouse dies, a person has to build new relationships.
4. Mental Flexibility vs. Mental Rigidity. A person can get closed-minded and rigid when they reach middle age. They have achieved some success, and they may feel they have the answers to life. A person needs to find new answers and to ask new questions at this time of life.

### Old Age

5. Ego Differentiation vs. Work-Role Preoccupation. A person's career often defines their identity in middle life. Retirement forces a person to redefine who they are. This is a time for the expansion of activities and self-definition.
6. Body Transcendence vs. Body Preoccupation. Physical decline can lead to a preoccupation with the body and a sense of despair. Peck says that people can occupy themselves with pleasing relationships and activities.
7. Ego Transcendence vs. Ego Preoccupation. Death can threaten the meaning of a person's life as well as their physical existence. Death loses some of its sting when a person sees that their culture will go on and that future generations will benefit from what they have done.

**Source:** Adapted from Robert Peck, "Psychological Developments in the Second Half of Life," in Bernice L. Neugarten, ed., *Middle Age and Aging* (Chicago: University of Chicago Press, 1968).

· · · · · · · · · · · · · · · · · · · · · · · · · · · · · · ·

structure-building periods, and transitional, structure-changing periods. Structure-building periods last six to eight years. During a structure-building period, a man makes important choices and works to achieve specific goals. Transition periods last four to five years. During transition periods, he evaluates his present life structure, explores new possibilities, and makes choices that will move him toward a new structure. The move from home to university or from university to a first job, for example, takes place in the "early adult transition." A young man builds his first life structure as he enters

. . . . . . . . . . . . . . . . . . . . . . . . . . . . . . . . .

## Exhibit 7.4

### Levinson's Developmental Model

. . . . . . . . . . . . . . . . . . . . . . . . . . . . . . . . .

| Age | Period |
|-----|--------|
| 17–22 | EARLY ADULT TRANSITION |
| 22–28 | Entering the Adult World |
| 28–33 | Age 30 Transition |
| 33–40 | Settling Down |
| 40–45 | MID-LIFE TRANSITION |
| 45–50 | Entering Middle Adulthood |
| 50–55 | Age 50 Transition |
| 55–60 | Culmination of Middle Adulthood |
| 60–65 | LATE ADULT TRANSITION |

Levinson based these findings on a study of forty, white, middle-class, male subjects in the U.S. in the early 1970s. The stages in capital letters refer to periods where a person ends a life structure and starts a new one. A person in one of these transitions appraises their present life, explores possible changes, and makes choices that lead to a new structure.

**Source:** Adapted from D.J. Levinson, *The Seasons of a Man's Life* (New York: Knopf, 1978).

. . . . . . . . . . . . . . . . . . . . . . . . . . . . . . . . .

the work world, gets married, and has children. Levinson described nine periods that men pass through between the ages of 17 and 65.

Levinson could study only the stages up to the "Entering Middle Adulthood" period, because of his subjects' ages. He proposes that between ages 50 and 55 a man can modify the life structure set down in his forties. Then, between ages 55 and 60, he settles into middle adulthood, and from age 60 to 65 he begins the transition into late adulthood. These later stages follow a pattern of breakdown and structure-building characteristic of early stages in life.

Levinson's (1978) study has some obvious drawbacks. First, he studied only a small, homogeneous group of people (forty middle-class, white, male subjects) in a specific society (the United States) at a specific time in history (the 1970s). Only future work can say how well Levinson's model and his specific stages will apply to women, the poor, non-Anglo ethnic groups, other cultures, and other times in history.

Gould (1978) clinically observed and gave a questionnaire to 524 men and women between the ages of 16 and 50 years. He found, like Erikson, Peck, and Levinson, that people faced a series of predictable crises in adulthood. He also found that in order to grow to a new stage of development a person had to shed a "network" of false assumptions that they carried with them from childhood. "Adulthood *is not a plateau*," Gould (1978, 14) says, summing up his findings, "rather it is a dynamic and changing time for all of us."

These studies all propose that a stage model of development best describes middle and later life. Each also proposes an ideal pattern of aging and development, implying, therefore, that those who follow it live a successful old age, while anyone who deviates from it faces problems and frustrations as they age.

A number of studies question whether a set of universal stages exists. Surveys of large numbers of people, for example, have not found the stages these models predict. Lacy and Hendricks (1980), for example, looked for attitude changes predicted by Gould's work. They used data from a survey of over 9,000 people, but could not find attitude shifts to support Gould's stages.

Braun and Sweet (1983–84) reviewed data from four large surveys to see if passages from one stage of life to another existed. They compared personality differences within and between age groups. While they did find personality differences between age groups, they also found that in studies done at different times and in different countries (the U.S. and Canada) the characteristics of each age-stage differed. In addition, they found that after a passage around age 19, little developmental change took place in people's attitudes as they aged. These findings, therefore, don't support the stage model of adult development.

Butler (1975) has criticized the stage model of development for another reason. He challenges the idea that a person in old age can only accept who they are and what they have been. "People are locked in by such a theory," he says. They may look healthy from Erikson's point of view, but they suffer because they are trapped by their work, marriage, or lifestyle. "Excessive or exaggerated identity," according to Butler, "seems clearly to be an obstacle to continued growth and development through life and to appreciation of the future ... Human beings need the freedom to live with change, to invent and reinvent themselves a number of times throughout their lives" (Butler 1975, 400–401). Blau (1973, 185) warns that adults can "become too well adjusted to society's expectation and insufficiently attuned to their own nature and needs" in old age.

## Life-Span Developmental Perspective

One of the newer perspectives in the social psychology of aging—the life-span developmental perspective—sees the individual as continually changing from birth to death (Baltes and Goulet 1970). Unlike stage models, it does not describe an end point or goal of development (like integrity or ego tran-scendence). Instead, the life-span developmental model treats crisis and change as a constant part of life. "At the very moment when completion seems to be achieved," Riegel (1976, 697) says, "new questions and doubts arise in the individual and in society."

The life-span developmental model sees development as a dialectical process in which the individual changes in response to societal demands and society changes in response to individual action and adaptation (Riegel 1975). Life-span developmental theorists find many patterns and stages of aging. They say that people's personalities differ, as do their coping styles and the resources they use in coping with the world. People live in different social classes and come from different cohorts. All of this creates varied patterns of aging. The life-span developmental model also turns the researchers' atten-tion to the social context to explain the differences in the time of onset, direc-tion, and duration of developmental stages (Novak 1985–86).

## PERSONALITY AND SOCIAL CONTEXT

Life-span development researchers study three types of environmental effects: (1) non-normative events (unexpected events such as illnesses, lay-offs, and accidents); (2) normative, history-graded events (historical events that shape a person's life, such as the Great Depression of the 1930s or World War II); and (3) normative age-graded events (socially sanctioned events that occur most often at a certain age like marriage or retirement) (Riegel 1975; Baltes, Cornelius, and Nesselroade 1979).

### Non-Normative Events

Sociologists define **norms** as "shared rules or guidelines" that prescribe right behaviour under certain conditions (Robertson 1981, 60). Every society has age norms that prescribe how a person of a certain age should act. University students, for example, can hitchhike across the country with backpacks each summer, travel to Europe with Eurail passes, and sleep in railway stations or open fields. People accept this behaviour from the young, and they even expect students to take time off to travel. Social gerontologists call this a **nor-mative life event**.

People can also go through non-normative events, including accidents, sudden changes in health, or divorce. Social psychologists call them nonnor-mative because society does not prescribe that everyone go through these events and because people cannot plan for them.

. . . . . . . . . . . . . . . . . . . . . . . . . . . . . . . . . . . .

# Exhibit 7.5

The Social Readjustment Rating Scale

. . . . . . . . . . . . . . . . . . . . . . . . . . . . . . . . . . . .

Holmes and Rahe (1967) published one of the best-known measures of life events—the Social Readjustment Rating Scale (SRRS). Their scale includes normative and non-normative life events. The scale gives the highest score (100) for "death of a spouse" and the lowest score (11) for "minor violations of the law." A high total score of events predicts a decrease in life-satisfaction and higher risk of illness (Chiriboga 1984). Researchers have used the scale with many age groups, including older people.

Here is the Holmes and Rahe scale with each item ranked and given its average Life Change Unit score:

| Rank | Life Event | Mean Value |
|------|------------|------------|
| 1 | Death of spouse | 100 |
| 2 | Divorce | 73 |
| 3 | Marital separation | 65 |
| 4 | Jail term | 63 |
| 5 | Death of close family member | 63 |
| 6 | Personal injury or illness | 53 |
| 7 | Marriage | 50 |
| 8 | Fired from work | 47 |
| 9 | Marital reconciliation | 45 |
| 10 | Retirement | 45 |
| 11 | Change in health of family member | 44 |
| 12 | Pregnancy | 40 |
| 13 | Sex difficulties | 39 |
| 14 | Gain of new family member | 39 |
| 15 | Business readjustment | 39 |
| 16 | Change in financial state | 38 |
| 17 | Death of close friend | 37 |
| 18 | Change to different line of work | 36 |
| 19 | Change in number of arguments with spouse | 35 |
| 20 | Mortgage over $10,000 | 31 |
| 21 | Foreclosure of mortgage or loan | 30 |
| 22 | Change in responsibilities at work | 29 |
| 23 | Son or daughter leaving home | 29 |

| Rank | Life Event | Mean Value |
|------|------------|------------|
| 24 | Trouble with in-laws | 29 |
| 25 | Outstanding personal achievement | 28 |
| 26 | Wife beginning or stopping work | 26 |
| 27 | Beginning or end of school | 26 |
| 28 | Change in living condition | 25 |
| 29 | Revision of personal habits | 24 |
| 30 | Trouble with boss | 23 |
| 31 | Change in work hours or conditions | 20 |
| 32 | Change in residence | 20 |
| 33 | Change in schools | 20 |
| 34 | Change in recreation | 19 |
| 35 | Change in church activities | 19 |
| 36 | Change in social activities | 18 |
| 37 | Mortgage or loan less than $10,000 | 17 |
| 38 | Change in sleeping habits | 16 |
| 39 | Change in number of family get-togethers | 15 |
| 40 | Change in eating habits | 15 |
| 41 | Vacation | 13 |
| 42 | Christmas | 12 |
| 43 | Minor violations of the law | 11 |

Source: T.H. Holmes and R.H. Rahe, "The Social Readjustment Rating Scale," *Journal of Psychosomatic Research* 11: 213–18. Reprinted with permission of the authors.

• • • • • • • • • • • • • • • • • • • • • • • • • • • • • • • • • • • •

**Non-normative life events** or **life crises**—such as the death of a close friend, widowhood, or illness—can lead to shock and fear. Novak (1985) studied the response to life events in a sample of twenty-five healthy, middle-class, community-dwelling, older people in Winnipeg. These people all scored high on a standard test of self-actualization (a measure of personality development). Most of them had gone through at least one major non-normative life event—early retirement, loss of a spouse, or an illness.

Sometimes these events came about because a person felt an inner urge to change (one subject retired early so that he could devote himself to writing and to reading philosophy). Sometimes change came from outside: widowhood or illness forced a person to rethink their mid-life roles. Many of these subjects found the process of change painful and frightening.

Novak (1985) reports that these non-normative events had a common pattern. First, a person faced a problem or moment of crisis—a "challenge." These challenges included widowhood, early retirement, and illness. Second, they "accepted" the challenge and interpreted it as a demand for some response. Third, they responded to or "affirmed" their lives in spite of the challenge. This allowed them to enter a new phase of life beyond the roles and responsibilities of middle age.

These people were studied after they had passed through this life event. Did they succeed in affirming their lives because of their self-actualizing, integrated personalities, or did the life events they faced lead these people to a new integrated stage of adulthood? Studies of coping styles suggest that people bring their coping methods with them into later life (Lawton and Nahemow 1973; Lieberman 1975).

## History-Graded Events

Non-normative events describe sudden changes in a person's personal life, but history-graded events change the lives of many age cohorts. The term cohort, as stated earlier, describes a group of people born at the same point or within the same period (usually five or ten years) of time (Schaie 1968, 559; Marshall 1983, 52).

Older people who were between the ages of 75 and 85 in 1985, for example, were born between 1900 and 1910. These people share the experiences of two world wars and the Great Depression. If you talk to one of them about their past, you will almost always hear stories about the Depression and the world wars. These historic events left their mark on this cohort, shaping their family lives, their work lives, and their values (Hagestad 1990).

Tindale (1980) studied a group of poor old men in a large Canadian city. Most of them lived through the Depression as teenagers, rode the rails as hobos, and picked tobacco or fruit for twenty-five cents an hour. They have little education and few family ties.

Their lives today show the effects of their past. "They were poor before the depression," Tindale says, "poorer still during it, and only a little less poor after it" (1980, 91). These men now live alone on government pensions. They eat and sleep in the downtown missions and Salvation Army shelters. They never had much, and they do not expect much now.

The cohort born between 1945 and 1955 (30- to 40-year-olds in 1985) expect different things from life and from society, based on their experiences. These people belong to one of the largest cohorts in Canadian history. Canada built elementary schools for these people when they were children in the 1950s and 1960s, universities for them in the 1960s and 1970s, and housing for them in the 1980s. They have lived through a relatively peaceful, affluent time in Canada's history, and they expect more from society than do older age groups.

As cohorts age (and members die), cohorts replace one another in society's age structure. Riley, Johnson, and Foner (1972) call this **cohort flow**. As cohorts flow through the age structure they change the size of particular age groups (e.g., the size of the group 20–30 years old will differ in 1940 and 1970). New cohorts also bring new experiences with them as they age. Older people today, for example, have less education than younger cohorts. The 1981 Canada Census reports that almost 60 percent of the cohort born between 1897 and 1906 had less than a Grade 9 education (Statistics Canada 1984b). Younger Canadians have more schooling: 80 percent of the population under 65 had more than Grade 9, and almost 40 percent had between nine and thirteen years of school (Statistics Canada 1984b). Younger, more educated groups will probably demand more educational opportunities when they reach old age.

Riley, Johnson, and Foner's (1972) model of aging omits a few important concepts about aging and age grading. Historical events, for example, also get filtered through the **age stratification system**, the system of age grades a society uses (e.g., child, adolescent, young adult). The 1900–1910 cohort went through the Great Depression of the 1930s in young adulthood, and the Depression affected their decision to marry as it did the early years of their careers. The Depression also affected the cohort born between 1920 and 1930, but it had a different effect on these people. They lived through the Depression as children. Some of them may not remember the Depression at all; others may simply have accepted the hard times as "the way things are."

Gerontologists use the term **generation** to describe people who share an awareness of their common historical or cultural experiences, but who may come from different cohorts. The Baby Boom cohorts born between 1945 and the early 1960s form a generation; they have all lived under the threat of nuclear war, and they have lived in a relatively affluent time in Canadian history. This generation of Yuppies (Young Urban Professionals) will in the 1980s become the Gruppies (Greying Urban Professionals) of the 1990s, and the Ruppies (Retired Urban Professionals) of the 2020s.

Braun and Sweet (1983–84) found that a "generational event" theory of personality better explained the differences between age groups than did a theory of life stages. **Generational event theory** says that attitudes form for a generation in their teens. People who grow up at the same time in the same society share the same attitudes. These attitudes stay fairly stable throughout life because of what Neugarten (1964, 198) calls the "institutionalization of personality." People respond in the same ways to life's demands; others expect the same responses of them; and people choose their friends and contacts to support a stable sense of self.

These studies all show the effect of social and historical events on individual personality. Like non-normative events, history-graded events happen without warning, and sometimes the changes they bring about do not show up until years later. Society also shapes personality growth more directly through normative age grading.

## Normative Age-Graded Events

Anthropologists report that all societies move people through a series of age grades (Linton 1936). **Age grades** define certain rights and responsibilities for their members. They give order to the life course and help people judge their own development (Cain 1964).

Males of the Nandi tribe in Kenya, for example, belong to one of seven age groups—two for boys, one for warriors, and four for elders. These groups give males their status and allow them to play certain roles at given times in their lives. Likewise, pre-industrial societies recognized three stages of life—infancy-childhood, mature adulthood, and old age.

Industrialized society today includes the stages of infancy, childhood, adolescence, young adulthood, middle age, and old age. Some writers have now added a new stage, the young-old, after middle age and before late old age. This last stage makes sense in a society where people can expect to live in good health for ten or fifteen years after age 65.

Neugarten, Moore, and Lowe (1968) say that people internalize the age-grade system and know the proper time for a life event to occur. A Canadian middle-class girl who falls in love today at the age of 14 will feel it is too early to marry. A woman graduate student in her early twenties may also feel it is too early to settle down. A single career woman of 40 who wants to get married may feel it is late.

Someone for whom major life events come early or late—a teenaged mother or a newlywed octogenarian—may feel out of sync with the age-status system. Gerontologists call this **age-status asynchronization.**

Neugarten and Moore (1968) say that a person can be on time in certain ways and late or early in others. They can feel on time when they choose to marry, but late in advancing in their profession. Research shows that occupation, ethnic background, and social class affect the timing of life events.

The lower a woman's social class, for example, the earlier she tends to go through life events like marriage or having her first child (Neugarten and

Moore 1968). Neugarten and Moore found that female professionals had their first child an average of six years later than unskilled working-class women. The researchers also report that women go through different life events than men. They found, for instance, that women enter a new phase of life in their late forties. The last child leaves home, menopause occurs, and many women enter the labour market. This produces "an increasingly accentuated transition period in the lives of women, one that men do not face" (1968, 13).

Neugarten and Moore (1968) conclude that the social groups we belong to regulate our life cycle. Groups expect certain behaviours from their members, and members rely on these expectations to guide their actions. Members also observe the transition times of others and get a sense for when changes should occur (Hagestad 1990). Hagestad (1990) reviewed the literature on the life course, and found that researchers have recently increased their interest in life events, life transitions, and life trajectories.

The life-span developmental model accepts the idea that maturation and psychological change affect human development, but it says that a more complete picture of human development requires knowledge of a person's life events and social context. It shows that society and history play important parts in shaping individual development.

## ETHNICITY AND SOCIAL SUPPORTS

A person's cultural background, language, and country of origin also affect how he or she will adjust to aging. Immigrants to Canada, especially people who come to Canada in later life, face unique challenges as they age.

Sociologists define an **ethnic group** as a group of people who see themselves as being alike because of their common ancestry and who are seen as being alike by others (Hughes and Hughes 1952, cited in Driedger and Chappell 1987). Culture and ethnicity form a backdrop for psychological development in old age. Ethnic culture gives meaning to life events and can buffer life crises. The size and age composition of an ethnic community also determine the number of social supports a person has available in old age.

Gerontologists in Canada have done a relatively small amount of research on ethnicity, aging, and social supports (Wong and Reker 1985; Ujimoto 1983; Driedger and Chappell 1987), but studies done so far show that older people from different ethnic groups (including those British and French backgrounds) experience old age differently. These studies also show the importance of studying ethnicity and aging (Bengtson 1979). Most of the

Canadian research so far has explored three theories that attempt to explain these differences: levelling theory, buffer theory, and multiple jeopardy theory.

## Levelling Theory

According to levelling theory, age levels ethnic differences. A decline in health or loss of a spouse will lead all older people (regardless of their ethnicity) to depend more on their families and on social services for help. These changes outweigh cultural differences in family structure or differences in cultural values of parent-child relations.

Rosenthal (1983) found support for the levelling theory of aging and ethnicity. She studied Anglo- and non-Anglo-Canadian older people in Ontario (Anglo-Canadians here are people who report British background). Modernization theory predicts that Anglo-Canadian families will show weaker family ties compared with non-Anglo-Canadians and that non-Anglos will show more traditional family structures and more support for older people. Rosenthal (1983, 1986a) did not find support for this theory. Instead, she found that older Anglo-Canadians and non-Anglo-Canadians in her study reported similar family structures, similar views of family life, and similar family relations. She did find that slightly more non-Anglo-Canadians lived with their middle-aged children, but this difference disappeared in older age groups. Rosenthal (1983, 14) says "there is a strong suggestion that age levels these differences [between groups]."

## Buffer Theory

Buffer Theory says that ethnic identity buffers a person from role loss as they age (Holzberg 1981). A number of studies have found support for the buffer theory of aging and ethnicity. Strain and Chappell (1984; see also Chappell and Strain 1984) compared the social supports of older native people with those of non-native people in Winnipeg. They found that native people had larger numbers of friends and relatives than non-native people. Native people also reported having two and a half times as many relatives outside their household and six times as many friends as did non-native people. (Strain and Chappell (1984) say that native people may have a broader definition of friends, however, than non-native people.) Native people also have more weekly contact with their friends and relatives than do non-native people.

A third of the native people studied, but only 6.4 percent of those who were non-native, lived with their grandchildren. Strain and Chappell trace this difference to native culture. For example, "one native person explained that it was the duty of her grandparents to raise her. She lived with them and was taught the native way of life, thereby freeing her own parents for other responsibilities" (1984, 12).

Gold (1980) supports this finding. She describes the start of a small senior recreation program that was meant to serve a dozen or so native seniors. But the planners found that they also had to include the rest of the senior's family. "The culture demanded that the young serve the old," she says, but it also required that the old look after the very young. "So the food was prepared and served to the old, while the old tended youngsters" (Gold 1980, 3). This program for twelve native elders became a program for fifty to one hundred people of all ages. These elders had a role to play in their culture, even if they had low status in white society.

Vanderburgh (1988) reports that in Ontario the Ojibwe Cultural Foundation (OCF) began an Elders' Program to revive the native elders' role as mentors. This program arranges for elders to teach language skills, crafts, and healing methods to the young. This and other programs encourage elders to speak with authority at public gatherings about their experience. This mandate to speak with authority and play a guiding role in community life, rather than chronological age, is what defines elderhood. A native person who achieves this status has a buffer against the stress of aging.

Holzberg (1982) also found support for the buffer theory. She started an ethnic history program for Eastern European Jews at the Baycrest Centre in Toronto. These older people believed that they had to preserve their memories of the past for their children and grandchildren and so they decided to write and publish a book of their memoirs. This gave them a purpose in life and increased their self-worth. Holzberg (1982, 253) says that "it was the value of ethnic history to the group rather than the value of life history to the individual as a reaffirmation of self that was the rallying point of collective effort." Working for a higher cultural purpose can buffer people from the threat of meaninglessness that sometimes comes with old age and death.

## Multiple Jeopardy Theory

Multiple jeopardy theory says that aging makes life worse for members of an ethnic group. Minority members have low status to begin with, and they often have low incomes too (Markides and Mindel 1987). Aging may add to their troubles (Havens and Chappell 1983).

Wong and Reker (1985) found support for the multiple jeopardy theory. They compared a sample of forty Chinese-Canadians and forty Anglo-Canadians in Ontario. The average age of the members of both groups was 68. Wong and Reker asked each group about the kinds of problems they faced and the methods they used to cope with these problems. They found that both groups had about the same number of problems, but the Chinese-Canadians viewed their problems as being more serious than those of the Anglo-Canadians. The Chinese-Canadians also felt that they coped less well than the Anglo-Canadians, and they had lower well-being scores. Wong and Reker say that these findings support the multiple jeopardy theory. They say that stress due to living in a foreign culture and minority status add to the problems of physical aging.

Havens and Chappell (1983) also found support for the theory. They studied the cumulative effects of being old, female, and a member of a minority group. They found that on a standard psychological measure of mental function "old-elderly women of Polish, Russian, and Ukrainian descent are significantly more disadvantaged ... than any of the other groups" (1983, 129). Havens and Chappell found less support for multiple jeopardy when they asked this group whether they felt personally disadvantaged. It seems that older ethnic people do not feel (or do not report feeling) worse off than nonethnic elders.

Statistics Canada also reports multiple jeopardy for ethnic elders. Statistics Canada (1984a), in measuring economic well-being, found that older immigrants have a greater chance than non-immigrants of living in low-income families (see also Penning 1983). Specifically, the study found that 10 percent of non-immigrants aged 65 and over lived in low-income families, compared with 11 percent of immigrants who had come to Canada before 1961, 14 percent of immigrants who arrived between 1961 and 1970, and 22.5 percent of the most recent immigrants. This study also found that immigrants get more of their income from the OAS and CPP than do non-immigrants (Statistics Canada 1984a). Older members of Asian, African, and Latin American ethnic groups show some of the lowest economic well-being on measures of labour force activity, retirement income, and investment income (Wanner and McDonald 1986). These studies show that being old and an immigrant, especially a recent immigrant from a Third World nation, increases the chance that a person will have a low income.

## Limitations of Ethnicity and Aging Theories

Each of these theories gives some clues about how ethnicity affects social and psychological well-being as a person ages. But each theory has its limits. Levelling theory, for example, may hold true only for people in late old age. At that point almost everyone turns to government-run services like home care or institutions for help. Buffer theory describes aging in a culture that holds the old in high esteem, but an ethnic group with a different belief system, or a group with few members in Canada, may find that ethnicity does not buffer the effects of aging. Many Estonian men, for example, came to Canada alone and never married. A study of this group in Toronto found that 68 percent of them had no families and that, because they form only a small group, they had no community resources to draw on. Groups such as this may need more social services than other groups (Kneem 1963, cited in Department of Social and Family Services 1969).

The case of native people in Canada also calls into question buffer theory. Compared with non-native people, they have a lower life expectancy, less formal education, lower income, and are more likely to live in poor quality housing (Bienvenue and Havens 1986; Senior Citizens' Provincial Council 1988; Statistics Canada 1984b). Blandford and Chappell (1990) found that older native people reported lower life-satisfaction and more loneliness than non-native people. Further research revealed that poor health and lack of help accounted for native peoples' lower life-satisfaction and loneliness. This example again shows that membership in an ethnic group may not buffer aging even when a group values its elders and that social psychological well-being in later life depends at least as much on objective conditions like health and social supports.

Research on multiple jeopardy theory shows that ethnic elders rate less well on objective measures than nonethnic older people. But Gibson (1988) argues that the theory oversimplifies the effects of ethnicity on aging. It ignores the personal meaning of aging, the social context, and the availability of personal supports. It also fails to explain some of the findings from health research, such as the possibility that ethnic differences in mortality lessen in late old age. Worst of all, the multiple jeopardy theory compares ethnic group members to those in the majority group and focuses on the negative effects of ethnic membership. Gibson (1988) points out that ethnicity alone does not predict a decrease in well-being in old age.

What can we conclude about the effects of ethnicity on aging from these conflicting theories and research reports? What seems certain is that the effects of ethnicity on aging depend on many things other than membership in an ethnic group. The age distribution of the ethnic group's population (the ratio of younger to older people in the group); the geographic closeness of the group (how easily members can pool their resources); the degree of assimilation of the group into Canadian society (how well members can use available resources); and the time of immigration (recent immigrants have less access to public pension funds) all influence the experience of aging for ethnic elders. These conditions differ for each ethnic group, so that "ethnicity" or membership in an ethnic group can mean many things.

Rosenthal (1986b) points out that many studies of ethnicity fail to take into account the differences between ethnic groups. Eastern and Southern

European ethnic groups can differ as much from one another as they do from the British ethnic group. Studies of ethnicity need to specify the social and economic conditions of the groups under study.

The next section discusses a model for understanding the social causes of individual problems in later life. It also describes some of the ways that social breakdown can be avoided or reversed in the case of immigrant seniors.

## SOCIAL BREAKDOWN

Kuypers and Bengtson (1973) say that older people often suffer from psychological breakdown due to inadequacies in the social environment. They call this a social breakdown syndrome, and they describe it as having the following seven steps (see also Exhibit 7.6):

1. Role loss, lack of norms to guide behaviour, and the loss of friends and relatives as reference groups (i.e., groups that support one's values and behaviour) all make a person susceptible to breakdown.
2. The person begins to depend on external labels for a sense of self. In Canada these labels sometimes have negative connotations (e.g., widow and retiree).
3. Society may view the older person as incompetent. Middle-aged children may begin to take responsibility away from an aging parent. Institutions often leave nothing for older residents to do for themselves.
4. The older person may assume a dependent role in response to this treatment.
5. The older person develops skills that fit the dependent role. People learn to live down to the expectations others have of them.
6. The person loses previous skills. People in nursing homes may lose the ability to make their bed or chop vegetables because they never get the chance.
7. People label themselves as sick and inadequate. This fits the social definition of older people as incompetent and creates a further turn in the cycle of breakdown. It also makes the older person more susceptible to negative labelling.

The case of Carl Teicherow will show how this syndrome can lead to breakdown. Teicherow, 71, worked for Canada Manpower until 1979. He took early retirement at age 63. He says he retired because in the mid-1970s his department began to hire college graduates to fill new jobs. Carl had only

## Exhibit 7.6

### Social Breakdown Syndrome

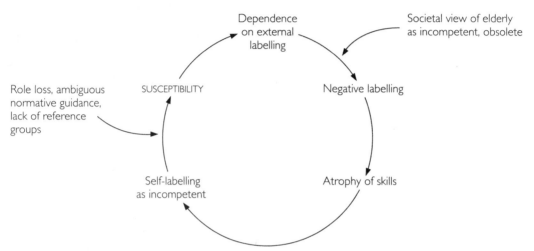

A systems representation of SBS as applied to old age with negative inputs from the external social system.

**Source:** J.A. Kuypers and V.L. Bengtson, "Social Breakdown and Competence: A Model of Normal Aging," *Human Development* 16 (1973): 181–201. Reprinted with permission of S. Karger AG, Basel.

a high-school diploma and felt that his new co-workers looked down on him. As his older co-workers retired and more young people joined his division, he felt increasingly isolated. He began to feel that the young workers got all the credit and the promotions. "Those young people they hired didn't know as much as they thought," he says. "Sure they had university degrees, but they had no common sense. They didn't know anything about people. I said, 'the hell with it, if the government doesn't care about this department why should I.' So I quit as soon as I had the chance."

Carl still feels bitter about work and the young people who joined his department. He doesn't work now, or do much of anything else. He had leadership skills during his working years: his wife says he got elected president of any group he joined. But he quit most of those groups after he retired. Now he watches TV or reads, but these activities give him little pleasure. He had a bad bout of depression a year ago and threatened suicide. His doctor gave him some pills and told him to find something to keep busy. His wife worries about his depression, but she does not know how to help him.

## Exhibit 7.7

### A Possible Social Reconstruction Syndrome

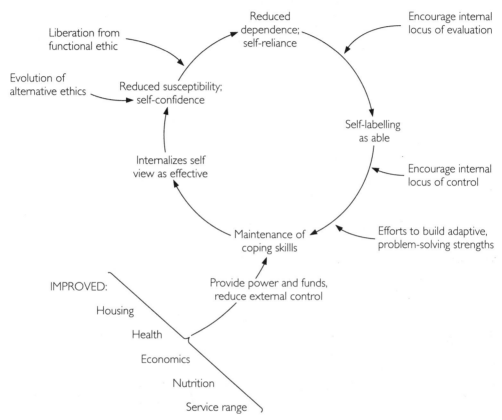

**Source:** J.A. Kuypers and V.L. Bengtson, "Social Breakdown and Competence: A Model of Normal Aging," *Human Development* 16 (1973): 181–201. Reprinted with permission of S. Karger AG, Basel.

Kuypers and Bengtson (1973) suggest a way to reverse the social breakdown syndrome. They propose a reorganization of the social system to provide older people with new ways to feel worthwhile. This approach includes: (1) a new value system that bases social worth on a person's basic humanity, not on what he or she produces; (2) greater self-reliance; (3) a strong internal sense of control; (4) learning new problem-solving strategies; (5) better-quality services such as housing and transportation, and better income; (6) maintaining coping skills; and (7) a reduced susceptibility to external judgments. An improvement in any of these areas would increase the older person's quality of life.

## Cultural Differences and Aging: An Application of the Social Breakdown and Reconstruction Model

According to Kuypers and Bengtson (1973) social breakdown begins with role loss, a lack of norms, and the loss of friends and family as reference groups. Older people whose language is neither French nor English, especially those who have come to Canada in later life, face a high risk of social breakdown. They pose special challenges to the social service system now and in the future.

The first source of breakdown for ethnic older people comes from the structure of Canadian society itself. Canada supports two ideals that conflict with one another. The first is the ideal of individual achievement, the second is that of multiculturalism. The concept of achievement says that individuals can and should achieve a higher social status than their parents, while the concept of multiculturalism says that people can and should maintain their ethnic identity. But "structural assimilation [an increase in social status from one generation to the next] is incompatible with continued ethnic pluralism" (Porter 1965, 72).

This conflict between ethnic pluralism and personal achievement often shows up as conflict in immigrant families. As young people move up in social class, they leave behind the norms and values of their traditional culture and adopt those of Canadian society. This creates a gap between what older parents expect from their children and what their children feel they can give.

Sugiman and Nishio (1983) studied family relations among Japanese-Canadians, focusing on second-generation Japanese-Canadians, the *Nisei*. The latter grew up with the value of respect for their elders, and many of them expected to care for their parents in their own homes. The children of the *Nisei*, the *Sansei*, hold less to the traditional values—deference to elders, nurturing, and belonging to the group. Instead they hold more to the North American values of dominance, achievement, and success (Sugiman and Nishio 1983). The *Sansei* want to live apart from their aging parents. The *Nisei* know this, and they expect less respect and support from their children than they gave their parents.

One woman told Sugiman and Nishio (1983, 28) that "even if I wanted to live with them [her children], I'm not sure I could. I think there would be a lot of conflict—a lot of hidden resentments which wouldn't be good. In such a case, I'd rather be left to die in an old age home." This last comment shows how this woman feels about the Western treatment of older people, but it also shows that she plans to fall back on Canadian services if she has to (see also Gerber 1983).

A second source of breakdown comes from the demographic and social structure of the older person's cultural group. Cultural groups with few older members may have developed fewer formal resources, such as senior centres or nursing homes, for older members to use. This can lead to a heavy burden on family caregivers, a lack of social support for the older person, and social breakdown.

A third source of breakdown comes from the treatment that a specific ethnic group receives from the wider society. Negative labelling and discrimination against a group can lead to social breakdown in old age. MacLean et al. (1987) studied access to three community health service centres in Montreal. The researchers found that English, French, and Portuguese older people perceived no problems with access to health service centres. However, they found that Chinese older people perceived serious problems with access to the centres. The researchers concluded that the services available to the three European groups of older people were not as available to the Chinese older people and that institutional racism may exist against older Chinese.

Supports and services can decrease the risk, and in some cases reverse the effects, of social breakdown (Kuypers and Bengtson 1973). Formal services may make the difference between a discontented or good old age for ethnic elders. Service providers need to ensure the availability and accessibility of their services to older members of ethnic groups. This requires a knowledge of ethnic differences, a sensitivity to the needs of varied groups, and a willingness to adapt programs to serve various groups.

Services, for example, will have to fit the unique religious, language, and cultural needs of ethnic elders. Differences may exist even within an ethnic group. Native people in Canada, for example, have at least eleven different language groups. One of them, Algonquian, has nine languages, including Cree and Ojibway (Statistics Canada 1985a). The Chinese community also has more than one language group. Some Chinese immigrants speak Mandarin; others speak Cantonese; and still others a local dialect. The Chinese community also has many religious and cultural organizations within it. A study of the Chinese in Ontario, for instance, found that most Chinese belong to the Presbyterian or United Church, but 31 percent claimed no religion (Gerber 1983). Many Chinese immigrants and the groups they belong to have little contact with one another (Gold 1980, 4).

Gold (1980) says that because of this diversity, programmers and planners should consult an ethnic group before planning a program. "The fact that people of different cultural backgrounds put their social worlds together differently means that their needs and resources as well as the ways in which they use the services available to them will vary" (Woehrer 1978, 335). Planners should not assume they know what a group wants or needs. Gold (1980) says that in one case a group of older Jewish people needed a senior centre worker. A young Israeli man applied for the job. He belonged to the same ethnic group and shared their religious and cultural background. But he spoke Hebrew, while the seniors spoke Yiddish. In another case, that of a project to build a high-rise within the Chinese community, Gold (1980) says it took months to learn that women were allowed to play only a low-key role in the project and were excluded from making public decisions. When the developers learned this, they had to change their approach to the group.

Holzberg (1981) says that health care services also need to adjust to ethnic differences among their clients. Zay (1978), for example, says that native people (Inuit and Indians) like to have their own people provide social and health care services. Other groups need advice on how to use the Canadian health care system. Auger (1980) reports that Punjabi older people go to herbalists, card readers, or astrologers when they get sick. Punjabi herbalists give only enough medicine for one day, so a Punjabi elder who gets a prescription for a two-week supply of pills from a Western doctor may take all the pills in one day. Doctors and other health care workers need to understand the ethnic older person's culture (Lam 1985). Ujimoto (1987) says that people from different ethnic groups have varying pain thresholds. Some ethnic groups define suffering as strength. Health care workers need to understand these different views of health and illness.

A single type of program will not meet the needs of all ethnic elders. Bienvenue and Havens (1986), for example, report that native elders in Manitoba receive very little assistance with daily living from the formal service system, much less, in any case, than non-native older people. These native elders may prefer to use informal supports, but they may also face cultural barriers that keep them from using formal supports. Program providers need to ensure that members of all ethnic groups have equal access to health care and social services.

Ethnic group members often have unique needs. Most Jews in nursing homes today want to celebrate Jewish holidays and eat kosher-style food. Italians may want a Catholic mass. Asian residents may have little interest in the organized activities offered by the staff (Ujimoto 1987). Lam offers the following suggestions for improving the present system: (1) that a cultural advisor or consultant plan nursing homes and advise on health care; (2) that students in the health sciences learn more about minority group needs; and (3) that nursing home design and food standards take into account the cultural needs of the residents.

Reports on ethnicity and aging show that members of different groups use different social, economic, and health care services. They also have different expectations about old age and diverse attitudes toward the aging process. Policy planners need to take these differences among ethnic cultures into account when they design programs for seniors (Driedger and Chappell 1987). Future research will need to study the availability and use of formal and informal supports by elders in different ethnic groups. A greater sensitivity to ethnic differences may help avoid or reverse social breakdown for many ethnic elders.

Government policies can ensure that ethnic seniors receive the support they need to live a good old age. A report from a National Workshop on Ethnicity and Aging (Canadian Public Health 1988) describes a number of problems related to government policies. First, many immigrants to Canada sponsor their parents' immigration. These seniors often do not speak English or French, and policies do not allow them to get subsidized second language training. Many of these seniors will never learn to communicate in either of Canada's official languages. If they do not meet people who can speak their language, they face isolation and risk loneliness.

Second, children who sponsor their parents may have small incomes, but they must take responsibility for the financial well-being of their parents. This can place a strain on the family. Most immigrant seniors have either small pensions or no pensions from their homeland. These seniors cannot receive Old Age Security and other Canadian pension benefits until ten years after they become landed immigrants.

Third, immigrant seniors' problems can lead to a poor quality of life in Canada. "As a result [of immigrant seniors' varied problems], they may be unhappy in Canada, unable to return home, ineligible for financial assistance, unable to speak English or French, and ashamed to ask friends or ethnocultural associations for help" (Canadian Public Health 1988, 25).

Canada's immigration policy encourages family unification, leading many middle-aged immigrants to send for their aging parents. Canada must put policies in place to support these seniors once they arrive. Social and economic supports can ease the strain on immigrant families and can decrease the risk of social breakdown among immigrant seniors in Canadian society.

## THE SOCIAL ROOTS OF PROBLEMS IN OLD AGE

Studies of how history and culture influence aging show that successful aging as well as maladjustment and psychopathology can have social roots. Some maladjustment in later life comes about because society gives older people fewer guides to define correct behaviour than it gives the young. In the case of seniors who have just arrived from another country, for example, the norms and values of Canadian culture may not fit their understanding of old age.

Rosow (1976) says that older people in modern societies occupy a tenuous status—a status or position in the social structure that does not have a role associated with it. A retiree, for example, occupies a status—that of a retired person—but does not have a role to play in society, since retirees are expected not to work, and nothing else is expected of them. The loss of roles in later life, through retirement, children growing up, or arrival in a new culture, excludes older people from taking part in society. It also signals a problem older people have today: finding meaning in later life.

## Loneliness

The absence of social roles for older people creates new social-psychological problems in old age. Some studies link loneliness to social isolation (Wood and Guest 1978). Wood (1978) describes loneliness as the loss of social identity—the identity people get from interaction with others and from holding social positions. Loneliness comes about when a person feels a "relational deficit" or gap between the number of relationships desired and the number they have (Weiss 1973; Sermat 1978).

Delisle (1988) found that most older people, though they may live alone, do not feel lonely. But others face a greater risk of loneliness. Delisle concludes that single older people, those without children, people in poor health or bedridden, people with poor education, introverts, neurotics, timid people, or those with low self-esteem face the greatest risk of feeling lonely. Wood (1978) found greater loneliness among older women than older men, among unmarried than married older people, and among older people with no university education. Other studies have found that older people feel they can do little about their loneliness (Lopata 1969; Abrahams 1972; Gordon 1976).

Perlman, Gerson, and Spinner (1978) suggest two ways to combat loneliness. First, older people should maintain their social contacts with friends and neighbours. Second, since social resources can help older people make these contacts, better transportation, well-designed housing, and more recreational facilities give older people more choice and a stronger sense of control over their lives. Most studies agree that a good old age means more than just the adaptation of older people to what, in some cases, is an inhospitable environment. Older people also need a more supportive social setting to grow old in.

## Suicide

The suicide rate in Canada for all age groups (measured in suicides per 100,000 people) increased from the 1960s through to the 1980s. The rate during the 1980s (14.6 per 100,000 in 1986) was about double the rate during the years from 1921 to 1961 (around 7.5 per 100,000). The 1980s rate was the highest ever recorded in Canada (almost one and a half times the rate of the previous high in the 1930s). A greater proportion of men than women commit suicide. Men had a rate of 22.8 per 100,000 in 1986, women had a rate of only 6.4 per 100,000. Men made up 80 percent of suicide victims in 1986 (Beneteau 1988).

But what do current findings tell us about older people and suicide? Men aged 50–54 had a rate of 30.0 per 100,000, while men aged 65–69 had a rate 24.6 per 100,000. The age group 65-69 had the lowest rate of all men aged 45 and over. But the suicide rate for very old men shows a different pattern. The oldest group of men (aged 70 and over) had the highest suicide rates in Canada (34.9 per 100,000) in 1986 (Benetau 1988).

Women's rates are much lower than men's at all ages. Women aged 50–54 had the highest rate for women in 1986 (12.9 per 100,000), while those aged 55–59 had a rate of only 7.9 per 100,000. Women aged 70 and over had a rate of less than 7 per 100,000 in 1986—about a fifth of the men's rate in this age group (Beneteau 1988).

Why do people commit suicide in old age? Reker, Peacock, and Wong (1987) found that older people, compared with middle-aged people, reported stronger feelings of lack of purpose and meaning in life. The researchers say that loss of social roles and social relations may lead people to feel suicidal. A report by Health and Welfare Canada (1977c) supports this view. The report says that loneliness and isolation, widowhood or divorce, retirement, and serious illness all increase the risk of suicide (see also Trovato 1988).

Connidis (1989a) reports that being married lowers the risk of suicide, especially for men. Jarvis and Boldt (1980) did one of the first studies of suicide among older Canadians. They studied the social backgrounds of the 154 people aged 60 and over who committed suicide in Alberta from 1968 to 1973. Their findings support the Health and Welfare (1977c) report. They found that poor health leads many older people to suicide. A large number of the older suicide cases had chronic diseases, such as heart or lung disease, and diabetes. These people also saw doctors more often, took drugs for health problems more frequently, and spent more time in hospitals than did younger suicides. Illness, Jarvis and Boldt (1980) found, leads to suicide more often in men than in women. Older women who commit suicide tend to have a mental rather than a physical disorder.

Men also choose different means to kill themselves than do women. Sixty-four percent of older men used firearms to kill themselves, but 46 percent of older women hanged themselves. Both older men and older women tend to use lethal methods, which means that when they try, they intend to succeed.

Studies (Miller 1979; Jarvis and Boldt 1980) also show that older suicide victims often have poor social lives. Jarvis and Boldt (1980) found that older suicides tended to live alone and to have little communication with others. As the population ages, the rate of suicide in old age may increase, especially among certain groups—lonely people, people with chronic illness, and widows (Manton, Blazer, and Woodbury 1987).

Miller (1979) suggests some direct ways to prevent suicide among older people. He says that family doctors should know what the cues to suicide are in older patients and what to do to help an older person at risk. Older people should have better access to psychiatric services, should they need them. The media should make people more aware of the signs of potential suicide in older people. Prevention should also include broader changes in society—such as those that would help older people stay involved in social life.

## CONCLUSION

Older Canadians face a number of threats to their social-psychological well-being. But, in general, they report high life-satisfaction. They know about the problems of old age, such as widowhood, illness, and physical decline, but they also see many good things about old age. Connidis (1983b) found that older people enjoyed their personal freedom and the chance to do the things they want to do. These advantages, she found, outweigh the problems that come with age. Northcott (1982) found similar results in a study of 440 people in Edmonton. "The elderly," he says,

> are more likely than the nonelderly to report no area of life as a major source of pressure and the older the respondent the less pressure reported from all areas of life except health. As pressure falls, satisfaction tends to rise ... In short, the picture one gets of old age is that it is a period of relatively low pressure and relatively high satisfaction, though not without its problems.

Each stage of life has its good and bad points, but "old age," Northcott (1982, 77) concludes, "looks far more attractive than stereotypes suggest."

## SUMMARY

1. Social psychologists describe at least three models of good aging—disengagement, activity, and continuity. Research shows that each of these patterns can lead to high life-satisfaction.

2. Men and women adapt to aging differently, but most older Canadians of both sexes report high life-satisfaction. They report that they feel less pressure and enjoy more personal freedom in old age than they did in their middle years.

3. Theories of personality development state that people go through a series of predictable stages as they age. Erikson described eight stages—five for youth and three for middle and old age. Other theorists have found more stages, showing that people go through many changes in adulthood. Some studies question the universality of these stages.

4. The life-span developmental perspective sees crisis and change as an essential part of life from birth to death. This view states that as people age, they make choices in response to social demands. This perspective allows for many patterns of aging.

5. Life events shape human development. These include non-normative events, history-graded events, and normative age-graded events. Studies of history-graded and normative age-graded events show the effects of social structures on personal development.

6. An ethnic group's culture and structure both shape the experience of aging. The group's values, beliefs, and degree of assimilation in part determine how young people treat older members. The group's structure, the size of a group, its geographic closeness, and its age structure also determine the treatment of older members.

7. Kuypers and Bengtson (1973) say that if society views older people negatively, older people can lose confidence in themselves. This can ultimately lead to dependence and psychological distress. They call this process a social breakdown syndrome and conclude that society should judge people by more than their productivity. A change in society's value system, they say, can reverse this syndrome, as can adequate social supports.

8. Members of different ethnic groups will need different forms of social support. Proper support can reverse or avoid social breakdown and lead to a high quality of life. Policy makers need to keep ethnic differences in mind when they plan programs for older people.

**9.** The way society treats older people can lead to personal problems like loneliness, suicide, and the breakdown of competence. Social psychologists trace these problems to the lack of social supports for older people today.

## SELECTED READINGS

Erikson, Erik. *Childhood and Society.* 2d ed. New York: W.W. Norton, 1963.

A classic. Erikson applies his psychoanalytic insights to other cultures and to the life cycle. For a follow-up try his later work, *The Life Cycle Completed* (New York: W.W. Norton, 1982). These two books show the continuities and changes in Erikson's thinking over twenty years.

Kuypers, J.A., and V.L. Bengtson. "Social Breakdown and Competence: A Model of Normal Aging." *Human Development* 16: 181–201, 1973.

A thought-provoking paper that presents the social, psychological, and environmental conditions that lead to a good old age.

Novak, Mark. *Successful Aging: The Myths, Realities and Future of Aging in Canada.* Markham, Ontario: Penguin, 1985.

This book takes an upbeat look at aging in Canada. It reviews the health care, income, retirement, and housing systems. It also looks at recreation, education, and what it takes to live a good old age. Examples of programs and case studies of older people across the country are also included.

# 4

# Institutional Change

# Health Care

## INTRODUCTION

Mrs. Granovetter, 72, lives by herself in a three-room apartment. Until six years ago, she worked as a supervisor in a nursing home, but poor health forced her to quit. She says she has an aortic aneurism that "looks like a bicycle tire with a bubble in it." She also has arthritis, and her joints get so stiff during the night that, she says, it sometimes takes her until noon to get out of bed. Still, she manages to live on her own. Her daughter, who lives on the other side of town, calls her every day, she talks to or visits with her next-door neighbour daily, and she can still drive. A few times a week she drives to a nearby shopping centre to sit and watch the people go by. She knows just where to park and how far she has to walk to the nearest bench. Last year her children took her on a trip to England. She says they didn't get to walk through the castles, but they toured around in the car and she saw the countryside. With help from family and friends Mrs. Granovetter stays active and enjoys life.

Like Mrs. Granovetter, a majority of older women suffer from arthritis and almost a quarter of them have heart trouble. But, like her, most of them cope well with some help, and they say they have good health (Statistics Canada 1987). A Canadian policy statement (Epp 1986, 3) defines health as "a resource which gives people the ability to manage and even to change their surroundings." By this definition, over 90 percent of people aged 65 and over have enough good health that they can live on their own in the community.

Health care refers to the support needed for people to maintain optimum health. The health care needs of Canada's older population range from health promotion and maintenance to long-term chronic care for people with terminal illnesses. This chapter looks at: (1) the structure and function of the health care system today; (2) how the present system fits the needs of older people; and (3) how the system is changing to meet the needs of an aging society.

## THREE MODELS OF HEALTH CARE

Social scientists use models to simplify and describe complex social systems. A model does not perfectly represent the system, but it describes the system's basic structures, functions, and values. Three models of health care have shaped the development of the health care system in Canada—the medical model, the social model, and the health promotion model.

### The Medical Model

The medical model focuses on the treatment of diseases and injuries. Treatment most often takes place in the physician's office, in a hospital, or in other health care institutions. The medical model favours surgery, drug therapy, and rehabilitation through physical therapies. Within this model, according to Chappell and her colleagues, "medical care and treatment are defined primarily as technical problems, and the goals of medicine are viewed in terms of technical criteria, such as validity, diagnosis, precision of disease-related treatment, symptom relief and termination of disease process" (Chappell, Strain, and Blandford 1986, 101). Physicians control both the organization of health care and the work of other health care professionals (Torrance 1987). They learn this approach to medicine in medical school and often get little training in other forms of health care such as counselling or long-term community care.

## The Social Model

The social model sees medical care as only one part of a complete health care system. This model sees personal and family counselling, home care, and adult day care programs as part of the health care system. This model of health care tries to keep older people in their own homes. Care within the social model often takes place in the community—in a person's home, at a drop-in centre, or in a counsellor's office. The doctor, in this model, works as part of a health care team that includes nurses, physiotherapists, counsellors, social workers, and other professionals.

## The Health Promotion Model

The health promotion model focuses on prevention and self-care. It aims to prevent disease through lifestyle change, increased knowledge about healthy behaviour, and environmental improvement. The Canadian health care system has only begun to use this model. Programs that promote fitness and those that warn about the dangers of smoking or excessive drinking follow this model. This model also includes actions that most people do not associate directly with health care, such as workplace safety regulations, seatbelt legislation, and pollution control for factories.

Each of these models plays a part in the Canadian health care system today. The social model has gained acceptance as a possible alternative to institutionalization. The health promotion model may save the health care system money in the long run by keeping people healthier longer. Recent decreases in heart disease, for example, may have come about through health promotion programs that encourage low-fat diets and discourage smoking. Still, the medical model dominates the system today. Canadians spend more money (much of it through taxes and health insurance programs) on physicians and hospital care than on any other kind of health care (Shapiro and Roos 1986).

## THE COST OF CARE TODAY

In 1957 the Canadian government put in place a hospital insurance system that covered the entire population (Chappell 1988). In 1968 the government insured physician services, and by 1972 all provinces belonged to a national medical insurance program. The provincial and federal governments shared the costs for this system of health care. The system had the following characteristics: universal coverage; access to services, including portability (a person could get the benefits in their new location when they moved); comprehensive services; and administration of the system by a non-profit public agency (Chappell 1988). The system emphasized medical and institutional care, the two most expensive types of services (Schwenger and Gross 1980).

In 1986 Canada had more than 1,000 hospitals, over 5,000 special care facilities (nursing homes), more than 55,000 physicians (including interns and residents), and 350,000 other health care workers (Statistics Canada 1990a). The country had one physician to serve every 467 people (Statistics Canada 1990a). In 1988–89 Canadians spent over $54 billion on health care or $2,091 for every person in the country. Hospital and other institution costs came to $20.6 billion in 1985, up from $12 billion in 1980 and $6.6 billion in 1975 (Federal/Provincial/Territorial Working Group 1990). In 1986–87 Canada spent about $8.4 million *per day* or $3.08 billion per year on residential care for the elderly (Strike 1989).

A government report on the health care system (Lalonde 1974) found that Canada had more physicians per capita than five of the world leaders in health care (Australia, Denmark, Sweden, the United Kingdom, and the United States). Canada also had more nurses per capita than any of these countries except Australia and ranked fourth in the number of hospital beds per capita. Canadian medical and hospital insurance matched the most complete coverage in the world, with almost 100 percent of Canadians covered (Statistics Canada 1990a).

These facts show both the strengths and weaknesses of the health care system today. Canada has created one of the most complete health care systems in the world. Older people, for example, receive free hospital and surgical care as well as free access to a range of programs that include chiropractic and optometric services (Health and Welfare Canada 1982b). But Canada also spends more on health care than other countries with comparable systems. Britain—one of the few countries with broader health care coverage than Canada—spent only 5.7 percent of its gross national product (GNP) on health care in 1983 compared with Canada's 8.4 percent (Organization for Economic Co-operation and Development 1985, cited in Economic Council of Canada 1987).

# Exhibit 8.1

## Funding Canada's Health Care System: Danger Ahead

The provincial and federal governments pay most of Canada's medical care bills ($39 billion of the $54 billion dollar total in 1988–89). About $8 billion of the payments come in the form of federal cash outlays to the provinces and territories. The federal funds help poorer provinces to offer a full range of health care programs. These funds also give the federal government some say over provincial health care policies. For example, the threat of removal of federal funds keeps provinces from allowing extra billing by doctors and hospital user fees.

Before 1977 the federal government shared the cost of health care and education on a 50/50 basis with the provinces. In 1977 the federal government began a program of Established Programs Financing (EPF). This program gave "block funding" to the provinces based on a province's population and the gross national product (GNP). Block funding has two parts: one part the federal government pays in cash, the other part the provinces raise through taxes (Canadian Council on Social Development 1990).

In 1986 the government reduced the rate of its share of block funds. It agreed to set the rate of increase in block funding at 2 percent below the GNP (instead of equal to the growth in the GNP). In its 1990 budget the federal government announced a freeze in the growth of EPF entitlements. In 1991 it extended this freeze to the end of the 1994–95 fiscal year.

Critics of this policy say that this change in funding will damage the Canadian medical care system. The National Council of Welfare (1991), for example, estimates that by 1994–95 federal EPF support per capita will have dropped below the support level of 1977–78. "In effect," the council says, "a five-year freeze on EPF entitlements would wipe out all the increases in funding made by successive federal governments since 1977" (National Council of Welfare 1991, 15). The new cuts in EPF entitlements will lead to decreasing federal payments for health care. And by the early years of the next century Ottawa will make no EPF payments to the provinces.

This will have a political as well as an economic effect on the health care system in Canada. Ottawa will have no financial leverage to use in shaping a national health care system. And this could compromise every principle of Canadian medicare—universality, accessibility, comprehensiveness, portability, and public administration. For example, poorer provinces with less money to spend on health care might have to cut back on medical services (an end to comprehensiveness). Some provinces may choose not to recognize the health care plans of other provinces (an end to portability). A two-tiered system may develop where wealthier people will pay for extra services, but poorer people will have to use a reduced basic system (an end to universality).

The National Council of Welfare (1991, 19–20) says that, if current policies continue as planned, by the year 2005–06 "the federal government will have no further stake in medicare ... and no say either. Medicare will be effectively dead as a *national* health insurance system."

The cost of Canada's medical care system grows each year. And the aging of the population may add further to these costs. Barer and Evans (1989) report that expenditures for special care homes (including nursing homes) rose by nearly 20 percent per year between 1971 and 1982. Hospital expenditures rose by nearly 12 percent per year for that same period (Chappell 1988). Auer (1987) reports that hospital costs accounted for 40 percent of the rise in health care costs between 1961 and 1980. Other sources show that older people as a group use hospitals more often than younger people and that they use them for longer periods (Health and Welfare Canada 1983). Some people fear that an aging population will cause a breakdown in the health care system.

A closer look at the health care system shows that older people account for only a small part of past increases in health care costs. Auer (1987) says, for instance, that population change accounts for only about 10 percent of the increases in costs from 1961 to 1980. Instead, Canada's commitment to the medical model of care explains most of the increase in costs. Increasing numbers of doctors, rising costs for complex treatments, unionization of hospital workers, and more tests to diagnose disease have led to increases in the cost of health care (Evans 1976; Evans 1984; Auer 1987).

Some critics of the system today question whether the medical model fits the needs of an aging society (Chappell 1988). They argue that for the same cost Canadians could buy care that more closely fits their needs (Evans 1984). "As a society," Chappel, Strain, and Blandford (1986, 112) say, "we have not yet dealt with the issue—especially during old age—'When is health care servicing inappropriate or too much?'"

## THE HEALTH CARE SYSTEM AND OLDER PEOPLE'S HEALTH CARE NEEDS

By any standards older people have more health problems than younger people and use more health care services. A study by the Alberta Senior Citizens' Bureau (1984), for example, reports that people 65 and over make up 7.3 percent of the province's population, but they accounted for 18.4 percent of hospital discharges in 1981 and used 36.7 percent of patient days. Both measures show an increase from 1976. The study also shows that people aged 75 and over used most of the patient days and accounted for most of the discharges by seniors in 1980–81.

Statistics Canada (1990e) reports that the hospitalization rate for seniors increased from 1980–81 to 1985–86. People aged 75 and over showed the greatest increases. Men aged 75 and over now have a rate four to five times the rate of all men. Women aged 75 and over have a rate two to three times the rate for all women. Statistics Canada (Maclean and Oderkirk 1991) also reports that older people have higher surgery rates than younger people. Between 1975 and 1987 the surgery rate for older people increased at more than triple the rate for people under age 65. Older surgery patients also stay in the hospital more than ten days longer on average than younger surgery patients (Maclean and Oderkirk 1991). The Alberta Department of Social Services and Community Health (Alberta Senior Citizens' Bureau 1984) spent $16.5 million for hearing aids, medical equipment, and surgical supplies for 40,400 older clients in 1982–83, and this doubled the $8 million spent in 1980–81 (though the number of clients increased only by about 10 percent).

Barer and his colleagues (1986) studied the reasons older people use more health care services today than in the past. They wanted to find out whether this increase in costs reflects changes in the diseases older people have today, or whether it reflects the way the system cares for older patients. If the costs reflect older people's increased need for treatment, population aging could lead to a sharp increase in health care costs. But if changes reflect the way the system operates, new approaches to treatment could contain costs. While Barer and his colleagues conclude that little data exist to test the first possibility (that older people have different diseases or more diseases today than in the past), they do suggest that the way the system responds to older people's needs leads them to make heavier use of the medical care system today than in the past.

First, doctors, not patients, have the biggest say in how much and what kind of medical care a person uses. Studies show that treatment rates vary by province, by county, and even by physician. For one surgical procedure (transurethral prostactectomy), for example, Saskatchewan had a rate ten times that of Prince Edward Island (Statistics Canada 1980c, 1981c). A study in Ontario (Stockwell and Vayda 1979, cited in Roos, Shapiro, and Roos 1984) found that surgery rates varied widely even within one county. Battista, Spasoff, and Spitzer (1989) say that a physician's practice setting (i.e., whether a physician practices alone or in a group), the availability of new technologies (like CAT scanners), and societal trends (like health promotion) also influence a physician's choice of treatments. These findings suggest that how doctors diagnose disease and the type of treatment they choose, if any, play a major part in determining use patterns by older patients.

Chappell, Strain, and Blandford (1986, 100) report that physicians "control approximately 80 percent of health care costs." Only a quarter of this percentage goes directly to physicians, the rest goes to hospital use (half of all health care costs), drugs, tests, and other medical expenses. Doctors control these expenses through the decisions they make about treatment and through their reliance on high technology in hospital settings.

Second, Shapiro and Roos (1986, 165) say that hospital-based care uses "about 60 percent of all health care dollars," but they determined that individual need cannot explain older people's pattern of hospital use. Looking at physicians' "hospitalization style," Shapiro and Roos (1986) found that patients of hospital-prone doctors spent, on average, twice as much time in the hospital as patients of non-hospital-prone doctors. These doctors also accounted for 73 percent of high users who had repeated hospital stays.

Data from the Manitoba Longitudinal Study on Aging also found that hospital use differs by region (Roos, Shapiro, and Roos 1984). The study found that older rural Manitobans used more hospital days and had more admissions than urban Manitobans. This difference showed up even when the researchers looked at people with the same health status. The researchers suggest that the higher number of hospital beds per capita in rural areas compared with that of cities explains this difference. Rural settings in Manitoba have 2.3 more hospital beds per 1,000 population than urban settings, and doctors in rural areas, knowing there are beds available, tend to use them (see also Shapiro and Roos 1986).

Government policy created this difference in use patterns. From 1948 into the 1960s the federal government shared the cost of building more hospitals with the provinces, and rural areas took this opportunity to increase their medical facilities. Hospitals gave people in rural communities a medical safety net; increased profits to business due to construction, equipment, and drugs; and increased employment (Crichton 1980). More hospitals also allowed small towns to compete for and attract doctors (Shapiro and Roos 1984).

These incentives led rural communities to open more hospitals than were being opened in cities. And, once open, they tended to stay open. Hospitals provide jobs for people in the community and they allow doctors to carry out complex surgical and diagnostic procedures. Shapiro and Roos (1984) see high hospital use by rural older people continuing into the future as long as the present system benefits from this approach to treatment.

Third, the federal government began to insure hospital care in 1957, ten years before it insured the cost of visits to doctors' offices. This encouraged doctors to admit patients to hospitals for treatment, since doing so saved patients money. Gross and Schwenger (1981, 129) blame the high cost of the health care system on "a heavy reliance on institutional care." They compared health care costs in Ontario with those in the U.S. and found that, when it came to institutional care, Ontario spent $323 more per year per person aged 65 and over on institutional care. "This amounts to a difference of

31 per cent, some of which can be attributed to inflation and variation in currency. However, the primary reason for Ontario's higher per capita institutional costs is that the province has more of its elderly in institutions" (Gross and Schwenger 1981, 129). Lower the rate of institutionalization, they say, and the costs of health care will come down.

## INSTITUTIONAL CARE

In 1986, 17.2 percent of women and 11.8 percent of men aged 80 to 84 lived in institutions. These rates jump to 40.5 percent for women and 28.4 percent for men aged 85 and over (Stone and Frenken 1988). Women made up 70 percent of the residents in these institutions (Strike 1989).

Rates vary from province to province. In Alberta in 1986, for example, 50.5 percent of people aged 85 and over lived in institutions. Manitoba, Ontario, and Quebec report that around 40 percent of people aged 85 and over live in institutions, close to the national average of 41.4 percent. These are some of the highest rates in the world (Stone and Frenken 1988).

Most of these people live in nursing homes. These homes go by a variety of names: special care facilities, homes for special care, and personal care homes. The term nursing home, as it is used here, refers to any institution that offers medical care for chronically ill older people but is not a hospital.

Each province has its own system for classifying patients. Most provinces define four levels of nursing home care. In Manitoba, for example: people in Levels 3 and 4 need 3.5 hours of nursing care per day and need help with two to four or more basic activities of daily living such as bathing, dressing, and eating; people in Level 2 need 2 to 3.5 hours of nursing care per day and need moderate care and help with at least one basic activity of daily living; people in Level 1 need 0.5 to 2 hours of nursing care per day and need personal help only to wash or attend activities (Forbes, Jackson, and Kraus 1987; Shapiro and Tate 1988b).

Shapiro and Tate (1985) report that in a longitudinal study of more than 3,000 older Manitobans, 11.7 percent entered a long-term care setting between 1971 and the end of 1977. They also found that people over age 85 had almost a seven times greater chance of using a long-term care bed than people between 65 and 74 (see also Shapiro and Roos 1987; Shapiro and Webster 1984). Shapiro, Tate, and Roos (1987) say that age, mental impairment, and lack of support play a major role in the decision to enter an institution.

A more detailed analysis of institution admission calculated the odds of entering an institution given certain conditions in a person's life. Shapiro and Tate (1988b, 238) found that people with the following characteristics (i.e., being 85 or over), living without a spouse, "recent hospital admission, living in retirement housing, having one or more [problems with activities of daily living] ... and having a mental impairment" had more than a 3-in-5 chance of entering an institution within two and a half years. Montgomery, Kirshen, and Roos (1988) say that the chance of residence in a nursing home increases dramatically over the four years before a person's death. These studies show that as the population ages, the numbers and percentages of older people who spend some time in an institution will increase.

Such increases would be unfortunate: institutionalization can lead to decreased well-being and even death for older residents. Gutman and her colleagues in British Columbia (1986) found a high percentage of deaths among patients within the first six months of admission to a personal care home. They concluded that admission to a long-term care institution in itself causes severe stress to older people (Gutman et al. 1986; Gutman and Herbert 1976; Wershow 1976). Shapiro and Tate (1988a) also found high mortality rates right after admission to a nursing home. They suggest that clinical instability or relocation may account for this high rate (see also Shapiro and Webster 1984). Chappell and Penning (1979) studied the well-being of over 4,000 older people and found that, given matching levels of health, people in institutionalized settings showed lower well-being than those in the community.

Most people, including government leaders, doctors, nursing home staff, and older people themselves, agree that we should keep older people out of institutions when we can. Still, institutions play a useful role in the continuum of health care services. For example, long-term care institutions reduce the use of hospitalization for residents (Shapiro, Tate, and Roos 1987; Montgomery, Kirshen, and Roos 1988). This can reduce the cost to the health care system, if hospitals close some of their beds. Shapiro and Webster (1984) also report that 15 to 20 percent of people admitted at the two highest levels of care in Manitoba showed improved health even after six years.

Nursing homes can provide special needs to patients. Tourigny-Rivard and Drury (1987), for example, report on a program that sensitizes staff to the needs of emotionally disturbed patients. The researchers found that consultations with a visiting geriatric psychiatrist improved staff understanding of patients' emotional problems. Consultations also led to more frequent therapeutic programs for patients.

Sometimes a person needs to live in a nursing home. Canada's long winters, the great distances between older people and hospitals, the need for constant care, few informal supports, and poverty sometimes make institutional life the only way for people to get the care they need (Forbes, Jackson, and Kraus 1987).

Nursing homes can do some things to decrease the adverse effects of institutionalization (Harbison and Melanson 1987). MacLean and Bonar (1983), for example, say that institutions can and should make life in the institution as much like life outside as possible. They call this the **normalization principle**.

First, people should feel the normal rhythm of the day, week, and year. They should get dressed each day, have a weekly routine, and celebrate holidays, birthdays, and anniversaries. Institutions should also include programs that keep residents active. Activity can increase the quality and length of patients' lives (Stones, Dornan, and Kozma 1989).

Second, people should get a normal amount of respect. Sometimes staff forget that patients have a right to decide things for themselves. Buzzell (1981) reports that in one home the staff decided that Edna, a 74-year-old patient, should begin walking again after a hip fracture. Buzzell calls the attempt a "nightmare." First, the staff took her wheelchair away so she would have no choice but to walk. Then, when she tried to walk, the nurses on staff called her "lazy" and threatened her if she moved too slowly. Edna suffered dizzy spells, but an aide tried to force her to walk "non-stop to the end of the corridor, sixty feet." "Edna pleaded for rest," Buzzell (1981) says. But the aide refused to let her rest in her wheelchair and threatened to take her off the active treatment program.

MacLean and Bonar (1983) say that staff should treat the older patient as an adult. They should avoid baby talk, talking down to the person, or making decisions without consulting the patient. Penning and Chappell (1982) found that older residents who felt they had freedom and the ability to make choices showed improved mental health (see also Penning and Chappell 1980). Spiers (1988) says that staff members can and should empower patients to make choices on their own behalf or as partners with other patients, the staff, and family members. This requires both a commitment by the senior staff and administration to the concept of patient choice and an organizational structure that includes patient and family councils. It also entails the practice of encouraging the patient to make choices in everyday institutional life.

Third, people should lead as normal a social life as possible. This should include sexual contact and sexual intimacy if a person has a willing partner. People should also have access to their money, and they should have their own pictures, small pieces of furniture, or pets to make the institution more like their home. MacLennan (1983) says that the institution should also expect patients to socialize and to do as much for themselves as they can. Rattenbury and Stones (1989) found, for example, that reminiscence and current-topic discussion groups increased residents' psychological well-being. Forbes, Jackson, and Kraus (1987, 92) say that older people in institutions

. . . . . . . . . . . . . . . . . . . . . . . . . . . . . . . . . . . . .

# Exhibit 8.2

## Controversy:
## The Use of Restraints in Nursing Homes

. . . . . . . . . . . . . . . . . . . . . . . . . . . . . . . . . . . . .

Many institutions use restraints to cope with residents' behavioural problems (Eaton, Stones, and Rockwood 1986). Restraints include bed rails, belts, geriatric chairs, jackets, and medications. A nursing practice conference in 1980 compared Canadian and British use of restraints. In one Canadian study of 136 patients aged 70 and over, almost 85 percent of patients had a restraint. A similar study of 172 patients in England found that only about 20 percent of patients had restraints (cited in Health Care 1980). The conference members concluded that Canada uses restraints more often than necessary.

Roberge and Beausejour (1988) studied the use of restraints in a sample of thirty-five Quebec nursing homes and chronic care settings. They found that both types of institutions used restraints on 47 percent of all residents. Institutions that used restraints used bed rails 56 percent of the time; belts and geriatric chairs 16 percent of the time; and jackets 8 percent of the time. Physicians had prescribed some of these restraints (63 percent for the nursing homes and 46 percent for chronic care institutions). In some cases (18 percent) the institutions had policies that required restraints.

But many health professionals disagree with the use of restraints. Mitchell-Pedersen and her colleagues (1985) removed 97 percent of the physical restraints in a hospital setting in one year. They found no significant increase in accidents; they also that staff attitudes toward their work improved. "Staff became highly creative in looking after patients without the use of restraints and a feeling of pride developed as they were able to provide care that honoured the autonomy of their patients" (Mitchell-Pedersen et al. 1985, cited in Forbes, Jackson, and Kraus 1987, 73).

The use of restraints raises ethical issues. Many institutions say that patients need restraints for their own safety. But patients pay the price for this supposed safety. Forbes, Jackson, and Kraus (1987, 72), for instance, say that physical and chemical restraints disturb older patients and rob them of their comfort and autonomy. Healey (cited in Health Care 1980, 22) asks, "Do we ... have a right to act against their will because we think it's in their best interests? Could it be we are more often than not selfishly protecting our own interests?"

Roberge and Beausejour (1988) say that institutions should use noncoercive methods to care for patients. They suggest that methods like occupational therapy, music therapy, and more family contacts would help staff reduce behaviour problems.

. . . . . . . . . . . . . . . . . . . . . . . . . . . . . . . . . . . . .

"have the right to make decisions about issues which affect them, and to maintain contact with their past life."

Sinclair (1984) says that a normalized environment should also include a weekly staff meeting. Meetings allow staff members to talk about problem patients and help them to rechannel frustration into methods for helping patients function better. Devine (1980) found that normalizing encourages nursing staff "to become leaders and teachers of the residents" instead of just caretakers. She found that staff stopped stereotyping older people as senile and useless because it worked against the goals of the program.

Nursing homes and other institutions will never take the place of a person's own home or apartment, but the changes suggested here can make a nursing home more comfortable for older people who have to live there.

## The Need for Change

Canada's commitment to the medical model accounts for much of the increase in health care costs today (see Exhibit 8.3). Health and Welfare Canada (1984b, cited in Auer 1987) reports that from 1960 to 1982 hospitals and homes for special care accounted for 55 percent of the increase in health care costs; physicians and dentists accounted for 20 percent of increases in health care costs; 11 percent of the increase went to pay for drugs and appliances; and 14 percent went to all other costs. Continued reliance on doctors, hospitals, drugs, and expensive treatments will drive up the costs of medical care in the future. Reliance on the medical model also sometimes leads to inappropriate care for the older patient.

The current system, Chappell, Strain, and Blandford (1986, 108) say, focuses on "institutional care rather than community care, on acute care rather than chronic care and on medical care rather than health care broadly defined." An aging population, Myles and Boyd (1982, 274–75) say, "requires a qualitative as well as a quantitative change in the health care system. An aging population requires a fundamental restructuring of health care and a redefinition of what constitutes health care" (see also Bayne 1978).

## PRESCRIPTION DRUG USE: A CASE STUDY OF THE LIMITS OF THE MEDICAL MODEL

Older people use more prescription drugs than do younger people. Though they make up only 11 percent of the population, older people receive about 25 percent of prescriptions (Health and Welfare 1989). The 1985 Health Promotion Survey found that the proportion of people who use tranquilizers increases from 5 percent for the under-55 age group to 12 percent for the 65-plus group. The proportion of people who report sleeping pill use increases from 6 percent for the under-55 age group to 21 percent for the 65-plus group (Health and Welfare Canada 1988a; Health and Welfare Canada 1988b).

• • • • • • • • • • • • • • • • • • • • • • • • • • • • • • • • • • • • • •

## Exhibit 8.3

### Myths and Realities: Older People and the Use of Health Care Services

• • • • • • • • • • • • • • • • • • • • • • • • • • • • • • • • • • • • • •

Different groups of older people use differing amounts of health care services. Studies that report aggregate data, such as those that use per-1,000-population or average-length-of-hospital-stay bases, miss these differences within the older population. "The aggregate statistics," Roos and Shapiro (1981, 656) say, "may reinforce the negative attitudes of health professionals and planners toward the elderly and add fuel to growing feelings that a so-called 'crisis' is looming as the population ages." Roos and Shapiro (1981) and a number of other researchers (Mossey et al. 1981) have used data from the Manitoba Longitudinal Study on Aging (MLSA) to shatter the myth that an older population will inevitably lead to a crisis in health care.

First, the MLSA provides detailed information about individual use of the health care system. The study shows that older people do not form a single group. Some seniors use the system more than others. Residents in senior citizen housing (self-contained apartments built by the government, religious groups, or service clubs for seniors), for example, saw the doctor more often and used more hospital days than people in other kinds of housing. Most older people use a small amount of formal health care service or none at all, and these differences in use patterns stay stable from year to year (Mossey et al. 1981, 557).

Second, the study found that less than one-quarter of Manitoba's older population stays in a hospital in any given year (Roos and Shapiro 1981), and only 5 percent of the older population uses almost three-fifths (59 percent) of the hospital days used by older people

in the year (Roos and Shapiro 1981). A small group—2 percent—of older people admitted to hospitals used 20 percent of hospital days in a five-year period. Further work showed that 5 percent of older people who died between 1971 and 1981 used 20 percent of all the hospital days used by older people (Shapiro 1983). Also, only 4 percent of people 85 and over accounted for 32 percent of acute hospital days used by people in this age group, and 9 percent of the 85-and-over group accounted for 57 percent of the acute and chronic hospital days used by people in this age group (Roos and Shapiro 1981).

The study found, too, that the average length of hospital stays for all older people rose between 1972 and 1976 by 15 percent for people 75 years old and over. But closer analysis showed that there were large differences within the older population. The length of stay for seniors who stayed in hospital fewer than 90 days dropped by one day over these years. At the same time, the 75-and-over group who stayed for more than 90 days increased their stays from 117 to 218 days over the same 1972–76 period (Roos, Shapiro, and Roos 1984).

Third, Roos, Shapiro, and Roos (1984) found that older people as a group do not make large numbers of visits to doctors (see also Segall 1987) and do not use large numbers of hospital days. The older population makes only 1.7 more visits to doctors per year than the group aged 15 to 44 and only 0.9 more visits than the group aged 45 to 64. About 20 percent of all age groups, including older people, do not visit a doctor at all in a year (Roos and Shapiro 1981).

The same researchers also found that the very old (aged 85+) use more home care, nursing homes, and hospitals than younger groups, but make the same number of visits to doctors' offices as people aged 65 to 69. They also found that older people get referred to medical consultants at a lower rate than the rest of the population (Roos, Shapiro, and Roos 1984).

These studies show that most older people do not need or use excessive amounts of institutional or medical care. The health care they do need can often be delivered in the community.

• • • • • • • • • • • • • • • • • • • • • • • • • • • • • • • • • • • • • • • • • • • • •

McKim and Mishara (1987) say that nearly all studies also report significant percentages of multiple drug use by older people. The Canada Health Survey (Health and Welfare Canada and Statistics Canada 1981), for instance, reports that 4.2 percent of men and 8.9 percent of women of all ages take three or more drugs, but that 13 percent of men and 25 percent of women aged 65 and over do so.

A number of things may account for the greater use of medication by older people. First, the elderly take longer than younger people to get well after an acute illness. So, they may need medication for a longer time.

Second, older people have more chronic illnesses (McKim and Mishara 1987). Some of these illnesses, like diabetes, may require that a person take medication for life. A study of institutionalized and community dwelling older people in Newfoundland (McKim, Stones, and Kozma 1990) found that a person's health condition best predicted their use of drugs. In general the research shows that older people take drugs because of health problems and that compared with younger people they use fewer recreational drugs like alcohol, tobacco, and caffeine (Health and Welfare 1989).

Third, increased contact with hospitals and physicians in later life may lead to more drug use (McKim and Mishara 1987). A study conducted by the American Association of Retired Persons (AARP), for example, found that visits to physicians often resulted in prescriptions. Seventy-three percent of the people aged 65 and over in this study said "their physician never suggests any other solution for their problem than taking the drug being prescribed" (AARP 1984, cited in McKim and Mishara 1987).

Another study of U.S. data (Ferguson 1990) found that, compared with 45-to-64-year-olds, patients aged 65 and over received a larger number of prescriptions per medical encounter. The study also found that, compared to younger people, a significantly greater proportion of older people received at least one prescription per medical encounter.

This study also explored whether the high rate of prescription use had any effects on older patients' health. Ferguson (1990) reported that older patients got more potentially undesirable prescriptions in total than younger patients and more of them per encounter. A Royal College of Physicians of London study (1984, cited in McKim and Mishara 1987) reports that over-prescription often leads to adverse drug reactions in the elderly. And such reactions can lead to hospitalization (Asthana and Sood 1987). Shapiro (1988) reports on a study of older people (65+) who had been hospitalized at least once in Manitoba in 1984. This study found that "adverse effects of therapeutic regimens" ranked as the third most frequent reason for hospitalization. The use of drugs accounted for 11.2 percent of the hospitalizations. Shapiro (1988) says that "some types of medications and multiple medications also appear to increase the frequency of falls" (the most common reason for hospitalization) (Shapiro 1988, 132).

Physicians' prescribing habits account for some of the over-prescription of drugs for the elderly. Lexchin (1990), for example, says that a high proportion of Canadian physicians depend on commercial information for prescribing guidelines. He studied drug advertisements in two Canadian journals that were widely read by physicians and found that the elderly appeared in only 7.1 percent of the 958 ads examined. The elderly appeared in no ads for psychotropic drugs and in only 7.3 percent of ads for cardiovascular medications. But a large proportion of older people take these kinds of medications. Lexchin (1990) says that these ads may lead a physician to overlook the differences between older and younger patients when it comes to drug reactions.

Also, physicians do not have the time to deal with the social and psychological conditions that may lead an older person to feel ill. Tuominen (1988) found that physicians more often prescribed central nervous system drugs (tranquilizers, antidepressives, etc.) than any other type. Ferguson (1990) says that doctors sometimes prescribe such drugs to solve social problems (like loneliness). Tuominen (1988) found that, compared to community-based patients, nursing home patients received more than fifteen times the number of prescriptions of psychotherapeutic drugs. Schafer (1985) says that institutions may use medication to control residents' behaviour. The wide difference in prescription rates between community-based and institution-based patients supports this point (see also Roberge and Beausejour 1988).

But doctors' practices cannot explain all of older peoples' drug use patterns. First, patients (young and old) themselves apply the medical model when they feel ill and may expect a medication to solve their problems. A Newfoundland study (McKim, Stones, and Kozma 1990) found that for community dwellers, drug use, in part, depended on a person's self-rated health. This means that people who feel ill, whether or not they have a diagnosed illness, tend to rely on drugs to help them with their perceived physical problems.

Second, many older people use over-the-counter medications in addition to any prescriptions they take. A study by Murray (1974) found that these drugs made up 42 percent of all the drugs older people took. The older people in his study took an average of 2.4 over-the-counter medications per person. Older people need to learn more about alternatives to drug therapy (like exercise, diet, improved sleep habits, or increased social interaction).

Third, older people may know little about the dangers of multiple drug use and drug interactions. Some may not think of aspirin, eye drops, nasal spray, and other common substances, like alcohol, as drugs. Yet they can interact with prescription medications and cause adverse reactions. Alcohol, for example, can have a supra-additive effect when combined with anti-depressants and tranquilizers. This can lead to rapid intoxication and in some cases death (Garver 1984; Bosmann 1984).

McKim and Mishara (1987) report a number of other problems related to drug use. For example, many studies show that older people have low compliance rates. A study by Rantucci (1989) found that 50 percent of health professionals saw this as a problem for older people. Older people may also have trouble opening child-proof bottles, and reading the small print on labels, or they may forget to take their medications. The more drugs a person takes and the more often they have to take medications the greater the non-compliance rate. Older people may fail to understand the functions of their drugs and may not understand their doctors' instructions. The better the communication between the doctor and the patient, the better the compliance (Wandless and Davie 1977).

The research on drug use by older people shows that doctors' prescribing patterns, patients' expectations about what drugs can do, and patients' compliance with instructions all influence the effects of drugs on older people (Gordon and Preiksaitis 1988). Frisk (1986) suggests that pharmacists take greater responsibility for seniors' drug use, including helping them choose the best over-the-counter drugs, keeping records on customers' drug usage, and counselling customers on drug use. Francoeur (1990) suggests that physicians, pharmacists, and seniors all need to learn more about aging and drugs.

## COMMUNITY CARE

The social model of health care looks for ways to keep people out of institutions. A health care system based on the social model of care would "have at its core a broad definition of health and would make adequate provision for noninstitutionally based chronic care" (Chappell, Strain, and Blandford

1986). Community care programs include hospitals, nursing homes, doctors' services, and community-based services such as geriatric day hospitals, adult day care, and home care.

The programs discussed below, beginning with geriatric day hospitals, form a continuum of care—from more institutional contact to little or no institutional contact. They show how the Canadian health care system has applied some of the principles of the social model of health care to meet older people's needs.

Three points are worth keeping in mind, as you read about these programs. First, some of the evaluations of programs presented here have been done by the same people who run the programs, and this could bias their reports. Second, few evaluations use control groups to see what would have happened to a similar group if they had not used this kind of program. A program that claims to save money by keeping people out of institutions should also show that a similar group of people to those in the program had to enter an institution. If the report cannot show this, then the program may have cost more money than if nothing were done. Finally, evaluation studies often report short-term changes. This makes it hard to judge the long-term effects of a program.

Even with these shortcomings, however, evaluations and reports often provide the only available information about new programs, and give some idea of what these programs do and how well they work.

## Geriatric Day Hospitals

Geriatric day hospitals offer a full range of hospital services to people who live in the community. A day hospital will assess an older person's needs and plan a rehabilitation and care program. Services include physical checkups, drug monitoring, dental clinics, diagnosis, treatment, and rehabilitation. Day hospitals can also keep an eye on older patients at risk in the community and ease older acute care patients back into the community when they leave the hospital (Agbayewa 1990).

Eagle et al. (1987) say that day hospitals can improve patients' physical and emotional well-being. But these programs will add to the cost of the health care system. To contain costs day hospitals should not offer care to a patient for more than two days per week, or for more than six to eight weeks. The day hospital should operate at full capacity to make best use of the facility. And the day hospital must take in patients who would otherwise enter an institution. Eagle et al. (1987) say that at present the health care system should treat geriatric day hospitals as pilot projects that need to prove their benefits and effectiveness.

## Adult Day Care

Adult day care programs "provide noninstitutional support for those unable to remain in the community without it" (Chappell, Strain, and Blandford 1986, 121). These programs include hot meals, recreation programs, and a chance for the older person to socialize. The programs also give family caregivers time off to rest, shop, and maintain their own social life. Adult day care offers fewer medical services and more social and recreational services than day hospitals. Some provinces require that people pay for day care services themselves, while other provinces include the service as part of the provincial health program.

As yet, research has not been able to show a conclusive reduction in the use of other services due to adult day care (or day hospital care) alone (Chappell and Blandford 1987a). Chappell and Blandford (1987a), for example, report on a controlled study of adult day care that included day care users and non-users. They found no significant difference between these groups in the use of physician services or hospital use.

Studies do report an increase in participants' well-being (Chappell 1983b; Flathman and Larsen 1976). A study of the first day care centre for handicapped older people in Victoria, British Columbia, showed that most clients improved their social skills and their self-esteem, and some improved their physical skills. Families reported better family relationships and better health for the client's spouse (Jackson 1983).

## Home Care

In 1977 the Canadian federal government started the Extended Health Care Services program to support provincial home care programs. Home care programs differ from province to province, but all of the provinces and territories in Canada have some home care and nursing services. Some provinces have extensive home care programs that include meals-on-wheels, home repair services, laundry and cleaning help, emergency alert services, friendly visitors, nutrition counselling, and transportation.

Home care is one of the most important parts of a comprehensive health care system. A report by the National Advisory Council on Aging (1986c) defines community support or home care services as "a co-ordinated and integrated range of services designed to help people live as independently as possible in the community." A federal government report (Federal/Provincial/Territorial Working Group 1990) describes three goals of home care: (1) substitution for more costly care in institutions; (2) maintaining a person at home at a lower cost to the system; and (3) prevention of functional breakdown that could lead to institutionalization.

• • • • • • • • • • • • • • • • • • • • • • • • • • • • • • •

## Exhibit 8.4

Victoria's Quick Response Team:
A Bridge Between the Medical and Social Models

• • • • • • • • • • • • • • • • • • • • • • • • • • • • • • •

Many older people enter acute care hospitals through the emergency department (Manitoba Health Services Commission 1985). And most older people use emergency care appropriately (Parboosingh and Larsen 1987). A fall, a broken bone, or a stroke, for example, can lead to an emergency admission. After the emergency passes (the medical team sets the bone or the first phase of the stroke passes) the acute hospital can do little for the older patient (Eakin 1987). Still, the patient may not be able to return home. Some patients live alone and lose the ability to care for themselves after a stay in the hospital. Some may need more help than a family member can give. Others give up their apartment and sell their furniture because they assume they will never go home again. These people must wait in the hospital for a nursing home bed (Aronson, Marshall, and Sulman 1987), and their health may get worse while they wait.

A report of the Manitoba Health Services Commission (1985) said that acute care hospitals ought to pay more attention to discharge planning and involvement of home care professionals (see also Fisher and Zorzitto 1983). This might avoid unnecessary admissions. The Capital Regional District (Victoria) in British Columbia has instituted a special program to decrease the number of acute admissions of older people from emergency departments. The Capital Regional District calls this program the Quick Response Team (QRT).

The QRT arranges for community supports at the right time to help the older person return home. A QRT liaison nurse assesses the emergency room patient at a physician's request. Criteria for admission include: acute medical condition, but hospitalization not required; patient aged 60 years old or over; home support possible; and patient nursing needs not over three hours per day.

When a patient meets the QRT criteria, the QRT liaison nurse sets the team in motion. The QRT social worker and home care nurse call the patient's family doctor, arrange live-in homemaker services, transportation, and home nursing as needed. The social worker and nurse assess the patient's home support network and arrange follow-up support like meals-on-wheels where needed. The QRT turns the case over to the regular long-term care program after a maximum of five days.

Mrs. Olive Ross, 86, is one of the QRT's success stories. Mrs. Ross broke her leg and arm in a fall. The QRT moved in a 24-hour homemaker for a month, arranged daily physio- and occupational therapy. Services were cut back as she improved. Mrs. Ross says, "I don't know what I would have done if I had to stay in hospital … When I broke my hip a while back, I was in hospital for three weeks and ended up losing 15 pounds" (Paterson 1989).

Mrs. Marion Candy, 89, also benefited from the QRT's services. She blacked out and fell in her apartment. Eventually she came around, dragged herself to the door, and screamed for help. She had cut her scalp and needed seven stitches. She got stitched up at a hospital and returned home the same day, but kept losing her balance. "I lurched a lot and grabbed on to anything I could to keep my balance," she said. Her family doctor called the QRT, and the team arranged for an array of services and supports including a homemaker, meals-on-wheels, a walker, a bath seat, and a handrail near the toilet. These supports have allowed Mrs. Candy to stay in the community (Kelk 1989).

The QRT offers the first service of this kind in North America. Eight months after the project began only eight of the QRT patients had entered a hospital (three of them for palliative care). A report on the QRT says that "this clearly indicates the QRT is a genuine alternative to hospital admission, and is not simply delaying the inevitable" (Quick Response Team n.d., 6).

• • • • • • • • • • • • • • • • • • • • • • • • • • • • • • • • • • • • • • •

Each province has its own policies for organizing and delivering home care services. In Ontario a case manager coordinates services for clients, but a referral to the home care system must come from a physician. Home care case managers do not deal with institutional services (Chambers et al. 1990). In Manitoba, Saskatchewan, and British Columbia a case manager coordinates all community care services (including institutional care). These provinces have coordinated, provincially sponsored home care programs (Ross 1983).

A large system like British Columbia's Long Term Care Program or Manitoba's Continuing Care program can tailor a program to a person's or a family's unique needs. In one case in Manitoba an unmarried middle-aged daughter lived with and cared for her mother in their home. The Continuing Care office arranged for a sitter to stay with the elderly mother during the day while the daughter worked. During the football season another sitter came in the evening so that the daughter could go to Winnipeg Blue Bombers games. This may seem an extravagant use of resources, but the night sitter relieved enough of the stress of caregiving so that the daughter could continue to care for her mother at home.

Some home care programs will arrange for **respite care**. This kind of care places an older person in a nursing home or hospital for a few days, a month, or for a two-week stay once a year. Respite gives family members a chance to take a vacation or catch up on much-needed sleep (Dunn, Mac-Beath, and Robertson 1983; Chappell 1990). Zorzitto, Ryan, and Fisher (1986) studied fifty male veteran respite patients and their caregivers. They found that caregivers valued the break from caregiving and said they would use the program again. The researchers recommend periodic readmission of patients to ease the burden of caregivers who look after high-risk patients.

Chambers et al. (1990) report that home care can lead to improvement or stability in a patient's condition. The researchers say that future research should measure the impact of specific methods of intervention (including family care and self-care) on patient well-being. This will help decision makers plan effective and efficient home care programs for older patients.

. . . . . . . . . . . . . . . . . . . . . . . . . . . . . . . . . .

## Exhibit 8.5

## Home Care Services

. . . . . . . . . . . . . . . . . . . . . . . . . . . . . . . . . .

Sometimes simple low-cost community service programs for seniors work as well as complex costly ones. A Daily Hello Service in Ottawa asks program members to call in to a switchboard each day. If a member does not call in, someone calls them or checks on them. Members in the program said they felt more secure, less lonely, and more self-reliant. Also, of the volunteers over age 65, 25 percent said they began as daily hello receivers (Psychogeriatric Clinic n.d.).

"It makes me feel somewhat independent of my children," one person said of the program.

Another said, "Now that there is no longer a family doctor who comes to see me and who cares about me, at least I know that there is someone else who cares."

"When I wake up in the morning, I usually feel blue; this is the first phone call I make."

. . . . . . . . . . . . . . . . . . . . . . . . . . . . . . . . . .

Greater use of home care could decrease the number of people who need to enter an institution. Studies report that many older people now live in hospitals and nursing homes because they lack the supports that would allow them to live in their own homes (Brown 1981; Cape et al. 1977; Chappell 1980; Grossman Task Force 1986; Health and Welfare Canada 1982b; Shapiro and Tate 1985). Home care could help postpone the institutionalization of these people.

A move to increase home care will require a change in the priorities of the health care system. Ontario, for example, set out "A New Agenda" for health and social services (Van Horne 1986). This plan includes more emphasis on preventive assessments, expanded community programs, and more coordination of services.

Community care may offer a cost-effective alternative to institutionalization for many older people, and this makes it attractive to governments. But do these programs actually save money? A number of research studies have looked at the potential cost savings from community care.

## The Costs of Community Care

Reports on alternative health care programs like day hospitals, adult day care, or home care programs often end with a statement about how much money they save over institutional care (Harshman 1982; Government of Manitoba 1984). A Woods Gordon (1984) study says that if the health care system shifts to noninstitutional forms of care, the system could save $8.875 billion per year (in 1989 dollars) by the year 2021. And this does not include savings in capital costs for new buildings, repairs, etcetera.

But not everyone agrees that community-based health care programs save money. Kane and Kane (1985) conducted a review of community care programs across Canada. They determined that increases in community care increase health care costs in the short run, since most of these new programs start as "add-ons" to the current system. Therefore, unless governments reduce the number of institutional beds as community services grow, community care programs will add more costs to the system (Denton and Spencer 1983).

Another contentious issue concerning costs has to do with the intention of community-based programs to keep older people out of institutions: research studies disagree on whether community care decreases institutionalization (Librach, Davidson, and Peretz 1972; Flathman and Larsen 1976; Chappell 1983b; Chappell and Blandford 1983). At the moment, research leaves open the question of whether community care programs save enough money (assuming they lead to some decrease in institution use) to make up for their cost.

Finally, in some cases community care costs more than institutional care. Community care programs do not always select clients to ensure savings to the system. Some users, for example, are at no risk of institutionalization.

Community care in such cases costs the system more than it saves (Thornton, Dustan, and Kemper 1988). Ellencweig et al. (1990), for example, found that institution dwellers in the British Columbia Long Term Care Program showed a decrease in the use of physicians' services and hospitals (see also Shapiro, Tate, and Roos 1987). Home-based Long Term Care Program users, on the other hand, increased their use of medical and hospital services. Clarfield (1983) says that the cost of care (and the potential saving) depends on the patient's functional level (see Exhibit 8.6). It may, for instance, be cheaper to admit a person with a low functional level into a nursing home or hospital. The findings from British Columbia support this conclusion. Ellencweig et al. (1990) say that "the close surveillance and monitoring network available in facilities" may reduce the need for acute hospital care.

Schwenger and Gross (1980, 256) say that an

> older person may be much worse off, even more "institutionalized" in a certain sense, if bedfast or housebound and with few available home-care services. The slogan, "Keep the old folks at home," can be a cruel and onerous message to some elderly persons and their relatives. [Beyond a certain point] it is no longer fair to older people, their families, or to the community to sustain the psychological, social, or financial costs of home care.

## Exhibit 8.6

Alternative Forms of Care for the Elderly:
The Variation of Cost with Level of Disability

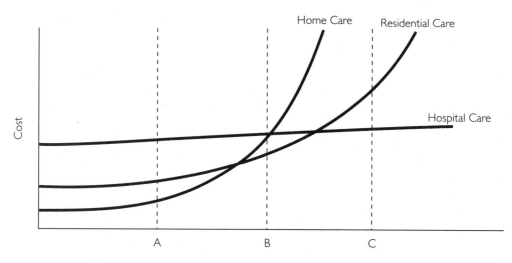

Level of Disability or Dependence

A: Person requires help with bathing, shovelling the walk, doing housework.
B: Person cannot prepare daily meals or do personal care.
C: Person requires constant medical supervision.

Consider the case of a woman who cannot care for herself (Level of Disability B). This graph shows that home care will cost as much as hospital care and more than residential care. The preferred support method for this woman (from the point of view of cost savings to the system) will be residential care. If her health gets worse and she requires constant medical care (Level of Disability C), hospital care will cost the least.

**Source:** A.M. Clarfield, "Home Care: Is It Cost Effective?" *Canadian Medical Association Journal* 129 (1983); 1182. Adapted from M.F. Drummond, *Principles of Economic Appraisal in Health Care* (Oxford University Press, 1980): 100. Reproduced with permission of the publisher.

Does this mean that Canada should abandon its commitment to community care? Hardly. Kane and Kane (1985, 253) say that community care cannot cure all the ills of the health care system, but it may be able to decrease the rate of institutionalization. Wall et al. (1991), for example, found that reduced-stay (overnight or outpatient) post-operative care for cataract surgery cost the health care system less than inpatient hospital care. But this approach makes more demands on the patient and informal caregivers. For this and other types of community care, Béland (1989) says that formal and informal caregivers need to work together. This can lead to a high quality of care and to high life satisfaction for older people in the community (Chappell and Penning 1979). "The current trend [toward community care]," Chappell and Penning (1979, 380) say, "seems to reflect one situation in which economic efficiency and humanism are not contradictory."

## HEALTH PROMOTION

So far, this chapter has focused on illness rather than health, but there is no other way to talk about the health care system. We call it a health care system, but it is actually a sickness treatment system. It serves people who are already sick, and it focuses on curing disease. This approach has its limits. Hospitals, doctors, nursing homes, or home care do not prevent disease, but only treat illness after it occurs.

The health promotion model puts health in a social context. The World Health Organization (WHO) (1984, 101) defines health promotion as "the process of enabling people to increase control over, and to improve their own health ... [it is] a mediating strategy between people and their environments, synthesizing personal choice and social responsibility in health to create a healthier future."

Canada's interest in health promotion predates this WHO definition by a decade. In 1974, Lalonde discussed this and other approaches to Canada's health care system in a report called *A New Perspective on the Health of Canadians*. There he proposed the concept of the health field. The **health field** includes the usual health services, but within it the health care system is one way—not the only way, or even the best way—to improve health. In addition to traditional medical services, the health field also includes improvements in human biology (through basic research), improvements in lifestyle, and improvements in the environment as ways to better health.

This model makes sense in Canada today. Studies show that "the majority of the aged remain functionally well until an advanced age" (Health and Welfare Canada 1982b, 43; Statistics Canada 1990e). A study of community-dwelling older people in Ontario, for example, found that only 6 percent of the 65-year-olds in the sample and 35 percent of the 85-year-olds lacked competence in five activities of daily living (Cape and Henschke 1980). Studies of seniors in both Calgary (Research and Planning Unit 1983) and Saskatchewan (Senior Citizens' Provincial Council 1983) found that 60 percent of seniors reported good or excellent health.

A study of rural older people in Alberta found that about three-quarters of the people studied reported few or no health problems and high life-satisfaction. This included older as well as younger seniors, men and women, farm and town-dwelling older people, and people who lived alone or with others. The researchers said that older people present "a picture of health not illness" (Thurston et al. 1982, 16).

Health promotion programs in general work to keep older people well. Some of these programs even take place in hospitals. Sulman and Wilkinson (1989) report on a hospital-based geriatric activity group. The staff started the group to help patients who were waiting for placement. The staff had found that the longer these patients stayed in the hospital, the worse they functioned. The program set out to decrease this decline. It involved forty-five minutes of activities at each session, including seated exercises, movies, social interaction, and gardening.

The program highlights the value of health promotion activities in an acute hospital setting. "Such programming," Sulman and Wilkinson (1989, 46) say, "also contains the possibility of moving these patients to lighter levels of care, and, in some cases, might prevent the need for placement altogether."

In 1981 Health and Welfare Canada set up a Health Promotion Directorate to "inform and motivate people to adopt and maintain healthy lifestyles" (Hansen and Ledoux 1985). The directorate runs public education and advertising campaigns, publishes health information, and funds health promotion projects (Hansen and Ledoux 1985). Programs supported by the directorate include an Alzheimer's Family Resource Centre, an education program for seniors called "Fully Alive," antismoking campaigns, and a program to help poorer older people stay healthy.

## Risk Reduction and Social-Environmental-Change Approaches

Health promotion in Canada takes two forms: risk reduction or lifestyle change, and social-environmental change. Most health promotion programs in Canada take the risk-reduction approach. These programs assume that individual actions lead to illness and that lifestyle change can prevent illness. Risk reduction includes programs that aim to decrease smoking and drug abuse, improve nutrition, and increase exercise and fitness. A number of studies have linked healthy lifestyles and habits to better mental and physical health, and to longer life (DeVries 1980; Hirdes and Forbes 1989; Hogan 1984; Manton 1989; Rechnitzer 1982).

Social-environmental improvement programs work to change the social and physical environment, and prevent illness by doing so (Hansen and Chappell 1985). Loneliness and the lack of a social network, for example, can cause mental distress. Also, the most isolated older people, who would benefit most from recreation or fitness programs, often do not use them (Biette, Matthews, and Schwenger 1983; Caloren 1980).

A program in Vancouver called the Seniors' Well-Being Activation Team and Society (SWAT) took an activist stance toward environmental change and health promotion (Wallace and Thompson 1985). The program organizers went door to door to talk to seniors about forming a health promotion program for older people in the Grandview-Woodlands section of Vancouver. The program included meal service, counselling, and the establishment of links between people in need and service agencies. This kind of program works to overcome the environmental barriers to good health (like lack of transportation, poor housing, or the lack of informal supports).

Social-environmental change can lead to even broader improvements in health care. Reduction of pollutants in food, land, and water could reduce illness. This abuse of the environment may cause as many as 75 percent of cancers (Bennett and Krasny 1981). Improved working conditions could reduce the incidence of lung diseases, cancer, silicosis, asbestosis, and hearing loss that often show up as illnesses in later life. The 1979 Canada Health Survey (Health and Welfare Canada and Statistics Canada 1981, cited in Stone and Fletcher 1986) found that among men and women aged 70 and over, the lowest socioeconomic group had the highest proportion of people with chronic hypertension (an illness that can lead to stroke and dementia). Stone and Fletcher (1986, Section 4.9) say that these findings indicate "the importance of environmental factors in physical and mental health."

Environmentally caused illnesses may be the hardest to prevent. They will require changes in the Canadian economy, in social services, and in workplace safety. A change in the public awareness of environmental causes of disease has already begun to take place. Working conditions have improved in most industries; regulations have set higher standards for pollution control; and antismoking lobbies in cities across the country have begun to change attitudes and laws about smoking in public. Changes like these may come slowly, but they must come if we want better health in old age.

## The Future of Health Promotion

Canada now recognizes the health promotion model as a model for the development of future health policy. Epp (1986), as Canada's Minister of National Health and Welfare, produced a report titled *Achieving Health for All: A*

*Framework for Health Promotion.* This report defines health as a "basic and dynamic force in our daily lives, influenced by our circumstances, our beliefs, our culture and our social, economic, and physical environments" (Epp 1986, 3). The report provides a framework for health policy in Canada and includes a description of the challenges to health in Canada, health promotion mechanisms, and implementation strategies to achieve health for all (see Exhibit 8.7).

Older people can benefit from improvements in all parts of this framework. For example, older people already engage in self-care (Segall 1987). And improvements in self-care through the proper use of medication, a good diet, and exercise can improve their quality of life. A more educated older population may also have a better understanding of how to prevent illness (Segall 1987). Likewise, mutual aid programs give people social and emotional support (Fedorak and Griffin 1986). Finally, a healthy environment will include community health services, transportation, and home care.

But will the government support changes in social structures, policies, and allocation of funds? Epp's (1986) report makes no promises. But it does recognize the need for the government to support health promotion. It also gives a good reason for this support. "We believe," the report says, " … that the health promotion approach has the potential over the long term to slow the growth in health care costs" (1986, 13).

Research at present cannot easily show the direct link between most health promotion programs and decreased health care costs. Glor (1991), for example, reports two problems that health promotion programs face. First, no agreed on quantitative measures of health exist. Second, few programs produce a measurable effect on health where scientists have tried to measure it. Some writers even question the value of helping people to live longer in good health. Evans (1984) says that these programs may lead to higher costs because they keep more people alive long enough to get chronic illnesses in later life.

Gaudette and Roberts (1988) report that, as the rates of cardiovascular disease have fallen, more people have lived into old age. This has led to a rise in the proportion of people who get cancer and die from it. This trend will lead to increased costs for cancer treatment in Canada (due to new treatments and drugs) and a heavier case load for cancer care units.

Still, disease prevention and health promotion have caught on in Canada among seniors. More than any other age group, people over age 55 say they exercise daily and more of them exercise now than in the past (Health and Welfare Canada 1988b). Also, 30 to 40 percent of older men and women reported eating less fats and less fried food in the past year than in previous years (Stone and Fletcher 1986). A report on Canada's Health Promotion

· · · · · · · · · · · · · · · · · · · · · · · · · · · · · · · ·

## Exhibit 8.7

Achieving Health for All: A Framework for Health Promotion

· · · · · · · · · · · · · · · · · · · · · · · · · · · · · · · ·

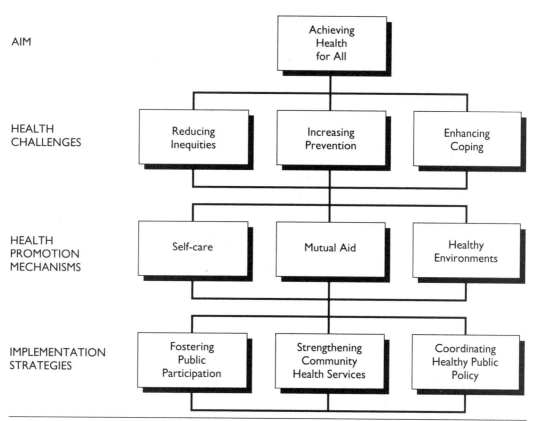

Epp's (1986) health promotion framework calls for improvements in (1) individual behaviour, (2) social structures, and (3) public policy. A useful framework must include all three types of improvement. Changes in individual behaviour, for example, may not be able to overcome health conditions due to income inequities (like poor diet due to poverty). Hirdes et al. (1986) found that a loss in income led to a perceived decrease in self-reported health. The researchers also found that decreased income may lead to decreased purchase of services, poorer nutrition, and poorer living conditions. Epp (1986, 12) says that "we cannot invite people to assume responsibility for their health and then turn around and fault them for illnesses and disabilities which are the outcome of wider social and economic circumstances."

**Source:** Jake Epp, *Achieving Health for All: A Framework for Health Promotion* (Ottawa: Minister of Supply and Services Canada, 1986), 8. Reproduced with the permission of the Minister of Supply and Services, 1991.

· · · · · · · · · · · · · · · · · · · · · · · · · · · · · · · ·

Survey found that compared with younger people seniors less often skipped breakfast, smoked cigarettes, drank alcohol, and used illicit drugs. Also, compared with younger drivers, a smaller proportion of older drivers said they drink and drive, and a larger proportion of older drivers said they used seat belts (Health and Welfare Canada 1988a). Some of these health promotion behaviours reflect the values and lifestyles (e.g., little use of illicit drugs) that seniors have brought with them into old age. But in other cases (e.g., the use of seatbelts) seniors have responded well to health promotion policies.

Researchers will continue to study the health promotion model. They will look at the effects of health practices, programs and policies on older Canadians' health. This research, if it supports recent findings, will show the usefulness of this model in an aging society.

## ISSUES FOR THE FUTURE

The health care system of the future will need to respond to older Canadians' changing needs. Three areas of the present system that will have to be revised to meet these needs are: the availability of services, access to services, and coordination of services (Sturdy and Tindale 1985).

### Availability

A program is available if it exists. Some provinces or parts of provinces have a continuum of care—from home care to acute hospital care—for older people. Other parts of the country, such as many rural areas, for example, offer only a few home care options.

One rural community care worker, for instance, described the workings of the meals-on-wheels program in her community. She arranges with a local restaurant to pick up a half-dozen to a dozen meals each day at lunch time, then delivers them during her lunch hour to people on her case load. She marvels at the good luck of city-based community workers, who can refer their clients to existing meals-on-wheels programs. Rural parts of Canada will need more community programs in the future (see, for example, Ontario Council of Health 1978).

### Accessibility

A program is accessible if an older person can get to it and make use of it. Havens (1980) studied the unmet needs of older people in Manitoba. She found that in each age cohort both men and women reported that the accessibility of services was more of a problem than their availability. In other words, even where a range of well-designed services existed, older people still found it hard to make use of them. The older the person, the more problems they had with access. Better access requires better transportation and more home-based care for very old seniors.

People with special needs may also have trouble using services. McDonald, Badry, and Mueller (1988) studied the resource use of developmentally handicapped people aged 40 to 65 in Calgary. These people show signs of aging at younger ages than the rest of the population. The researchers found that men who function well physically, but have low cognitive ability were most likely to use day care services. As a group, developmentally handicapped people tended not to use other services available to seniors. The researchers say that "the gerontological social service delivery system has not been prepared to accept these clients" (McDonald, Badry, and Mueller 1988, 145). These people have many of the same needs as seniors, but less access to the system. The researchers say that the rehabilitation and social service delivery systems need to create greater access for developmentally handicapped people.

The National Advisory Council on Aging (1989c) says that new immigrants and seniors from many ethnic groups may need special help to get services. Special dietary requirements, cultural differences, and food preferences can limit ethnic group members' use of community services. Culturally sensitive professionals can help overcome some of these barriers.

## Coordination

The health care system needs better coordination and integration (Health and Welfare Canada 1982b; National Advisory Council 1990c; Ontario Public Health Association, 1983). This need will increase with the growth of community care, because community programs decentralize care. They bring together nurses, social workers, and therapists, who often work for different agencies and whose views on how to care for a client will vary.

Sturdy and Tindale (1985) interviewed thirty health care providers in Ontario and found that only 30 percent of them felt that the system of services for older people was well coordinated. Providers saw two problems with the system: first, they said that professionals in different fields try to defend their territories, and, second, that programs in government ministries overlapped. The government lacked policies to decide who should take responsibility for a certain problem. As a result, services often "appear fragmented and the elderly person and his or her family do not know who to go to for what ... The elderly person in need of service can fall through the cracks in the system or become frustrated and give up the search" (Sturdy and Tindale 1985, 14).

Coordination avoids overlapping between services, and integration unites health and social services into one system. Changes like these will save time and may save money. They will also give older people better health care services.


## CONCLUSION

Will new programs and policies save money or add to the cost of care? Will the rising numbers of older people overload the system? Can Canada afford the rising cost of health care? Denton and Spencer (1983) studied the potential cost of health care in the future. They looked at three future population projections: a baseline rate with little change, a low fertility rate, and a high fertility rate. They found that all three demographic projections pointed to higher health care costs in the future. "Under a wide range of assumptions concerning future demographic change," they say, "the costs will rise appreciably by the early decades of the next century" (Denton and Spencer 1983, 160). By 2031, when all of the Baby Boom children have passed age 65, Denton and Spencer (1983) say that health care could take from 1.5 to 2 percent more of the Canadian GNP than in the early 1980s.

Denton, Li, and Spencer (1987) say that these projections, based on demographic data, only guess at the future costs of health care. New health care techniques, technological innovation, more efficient use of institutions, and new uses of health care workers (like nurse practitioners) will all influence future costs. And these "factors may be just as important or more important than population change" (Denton, Li, and Spencer 1987, 564).

Still, increases in health care costs seem likely in the future. Will this cause a crisis in health care? Denton, Li, and Spencer (1987) say no. They say that costs will grow slowly over time and that Canadian society can plan for this change. They also say that increases in health costs will, at worst, equal the proportion of GNP that West Germany paid for health care in the 1970s, and will come to only a little more than Sweden and the United States paid in that decade (Maxwell 1981; Denton and Spencer 1983). Changes in the system, such as an emphasis on community care and prevention, could help control costs.

The changes taking place today suggest that the health care system will look different in the future than it does today. Closer studies of older people's health care needs will allow the system to fine-tune its programs and treatments. The critique of the medical model and growing interest in social models of health care will lead to more community-based services. Also, as the population ages, more people will show an interest in disease prevention and health promotion. More comprehensive models of health care, like the social and health promotion models, will lead to better health care for older people as well as better health at all ages.

## SUMMARY

1. Health care needs for the elderly range from maintenance programs for the well elderly to long-term institutional care for those who have severe health problems.

2. Three models of health care exist in Canada today: the medical model, the social model, and the health promotion model. The medical model that dominates the health care system today is concerned with the treatment of illness.

3. Canada has one of the most comprehensive health care systems in the world, but it spends proportionately more of its gross national product on health care than do some countries with more comprehensive systems.

4. Research shows that the commitment to the medical model may account for higher than necessary health care costs. Complex medical procedures, increased salaries for medical personnel, and high institutional costs all lead to increasing health care costs.

5. Canada has one of the highest rates of institutionalization in the world. Institutions serve the needs of many older people, and programs exist that can improve the quality of life of institutionalized patients. But, sometimes people enter institutions because they cannot get the support they need to stay in the community.

6. Prescription drug use can sometimes turn into abuse. Older people use more prescription drugs than people in other age groups. They also tend to take more than one drug at a time. This can lead to side effects and illness. Physicians, nurses, pharmacists, and seniors all need to know more about the proper use of drugs by older people.

7. The social model of health care supports a continuum of services from institutional care to home care. It calls for health care programs that help older people stay in their own homes. These programs include geriatric day hospitals, adult day care programs, and home care.

8. Home care programs tailor services to fit the needs of the older person. They provide families with help to relieve caregiver burden. These programs may or may not save money, but they do achieve one goal: they allow people to stay in their homes as long as they can.

9. The health promotion model of health care supports healthy lifestyles and a better environment. It takes a broad view of health care that recognizes a need for changes in the workplace and improvements in socioeconomic status.

10. Medical costs will probably rise in the future, but economists say that an increase in the number of older people will not cause a crisis in health care costs. The system will need better coordination to limit the cost of care.

## SELECTED READINGS

Chappell, Neena L., Laurel A. Strain, and Audrey A. Blandford. *Aging and Health Care: A Social Perspective.* Toronto: Holt, Rinehart and Winston, 1986.

An excellent study of Canada's health care system. The authors put health care in a social context, and look at informal and formal types of care, community care, and the health status of older people. A readable and informative introduction to health care in Canada.

Evans, Robert G. *Strained Mercy: The Economics of Canadian Health Care.* Toronto: Butterworths, 1984.

A careful economic study of health care in Canada. The book presumes some knowledge of microeconomic theory for a full grasp of the discussion.

McKim, William A., and Brian L. Mishara. *Drugs and Aging.* Toronto: Butterworths, 1987.

A good review of the physical effects of drugs on older people. The book also discusses social issues like the prescribing practices of physicians, compliance, and the role of drugs in older peoples' lives.

# Finances and Economics

## INTRODUCTION

Jack Bruckner, aged 65, took early retirement two years ago. He gets a pension from his job and an Old Age Security cheque each month. His wife Betty, 59, never worked outside the home, so she gets no pension. They live in a small government-subsidized apartment. Last spring Jack and Betty decided to travel east. Jack knew their old car would never make the trip, so he went to the bank for a car loan. "I never thought they'd give me a loan," he says. "I went in thinking they'd just laugh at the idea. But the bank manager looked at my pension income and approved the loan. I can't believe it—I never thought, with the little we make, that we'd be able to buy a new car."

Like many older people, Jack and Betty do not have much, but they feel satisfied with what they have. Both of them lived through the Depression and through lean times when they first got married. They worry less about money now than in the past, and, Jack says, when Betty gets her pension from the federal government in a few years, their financial worries will be over.

Canada's pension system can take some of the credit for the Bruckners' financial well-being. The income of older people adjusted for inflation increased faster than that of younger people (25–64) from the early 1970s to the present. From 1971 to 1986 the income of unattached women aged 65 and over increased by 61 percent and went up by 36 percent for men in this age group. The real average income for women in the 25–64 group grew by only 28 percent and for men by only 13 percent. Family incomes of married older people rose by 35 percent compared to a 27-percent increase for the 25–64 group (Lindsay and Donald 1988). Much of this growth took place during the late 1970s and early 1980s (Statistics Canada 1990c).

The oldest older people gained the most. Families headed by men aged 75 and over had increases in income of 47 percent between 1971 and 1986 (33 percent for families headed by men between 65 and 74). Unattached men aged 75 or over gained 46 percent, while the gain for women of the same age group was 70 percent (single men and women from 65 to 74 had increases of 32 and 58 percent, respectively. The oldest older people still have incomes below that of 65-to-74-year-olds, but the gap is closing. Men 75 and over who headed families had incomes that were 79 percent of those of 65-to-74-year-olds. Unattached men who were 75 and over had incomes of 87 percent of what 65-to-74-year-olds received. And unattached women who were 75 and over had incomes of 90 percent that of those who were 65 to 74 (Lindsay and Donald 1988).

Cheal (1983; 1985a; 1985b) looked at intergenerational family trans-fers—the amount of money that passes from one generation of family members to another—to assess older people's financial well-being. He (Cheal 1985a) found that older people gave (in net value) more than they got and that there was a larger difference between what they gave and what they got than for any other age group. He concludes that older people have more money to spend than earlier studies suggested.

A number of studies and reports like these show that, as a group, older people have better incomes than many people imagine. Still, the retirement income system has its flaws, some of them serious. While income has risen in the past few years for older people in general, certain groups still have incomes below the poverty line in old age. Older people from lower-income backgrounds, people who cannot speak English or French, people without much education, and people who live in small towns tend to have lower-than-average incomes. Very old people, women, and unattached individuals (a term used by Statistics Canada to describe a "person living alone or in a household where he/she is not related to other household members") often live below the poverty line (Health and Welfare Canada 1988b, 3; National Council of Welfare 1988).

About a third of the unattached population of older people in 1988 lived in poverty (most of them women). In 1988 about one-quarter (23.3 percent) of elderly unattached men and over two-fifths (43.9 percent) of elderly unattached women lived on low incomes (Statistics Canada 1990e).

Even middle-class families can face a sharp drop in income when they retire. Statistics Canada (1990c) reports that in 1989 the average income of families headed by seniors came to 72 percent of the income of families with heads under age 65. Unattached people aged 65 and over in 1989 had an average income only 71 percent that of unattached people under age 65. For someone who earned an average wage before retirement the OAS will make up about 14 percent of their pre-retirement income. The CPP will make up another 25 percent. Therefore, the average wage earner will have to find other means to make up lost income in retirement. People who earn above the average wage will need to make up even more income in order to maintain their standard of living, and those on fixed pensions (i.e., not indexed to the cost of living) get poorer every year because of inflation. Most people, except the very rich and the very poor, will feel a drop in their standard of living when they retire.

Many individuals and groups, including the federal and provincial governments, the National Council of Women, and the Royal Canadian Legion, have suggested changes to Canada's pension system. Their concerns led to "The Great Pension Debate" in the 1980s and more recently to a debate over the universality of Canada's public pension system (Myles 1988). The results of these debates have begun to influence the retirement incomes of older Canadians. They will also influence the pensions of future retirees.

This chapter looks at (1) the structure of the Canadian pension system and how it works; (2) the flaws in the system and suggestions for pension reform; and (3) the future of Canada's retirement income system.

## HISTORICAL DEVELOPMENTS IN CANADA'S PENSION SYSTEM

Bryden (1974, 19) says that until the 1920s Canadian pension policy reflected the "market ethos." This ethos said that individuals should take responsibility for themselves in old age and that those who need help should get it from their families (Bryden 1974, 20). Bryden reports that city life and industrialization in Canada made this ethos hard to practise. The *Labour Gazette*, for example, stated in 1924 that "high rents, [and] overcrowding in houses, make it difficult for the poor to provide for their aged parents. It has been the experience of social agencies that many of the old men and women in their districts are suffering from the lack of the necessities of life" (*Labour Gazette* 1924, 665, cited in Bryden 1974, 42).

The federal government decided to act to relieve the poverty among older people. A Commons committee issued a report in 1925 that called for a $20 pension to people aged 70 or older who passed a residence requirement and a means test (a test of financial need). The committee proposed that the federal government and the provinces should each pay half the cost of pension benefits. The plan did not require pensioners to pay anything into the program. The committee saw the program as a supplement to income more than as a pension. The Old Age Pension Act became law in 1927, and all the provinces and the Northwest Territories agreed to the plan by 1936. This plan, for the first time, defined pensions as a right due to all older Canadians.

In 1951 the federal government passed the Old Age Security Act and the Old Age Assistance Act to replace the Old Age Pension Act. The Old Age Security Act set up a pension plan run solely by the federal government. The new plan paid up to $40 a month at age 70 without a means test. The federal government increased this pension to $55 a month in 1961. The Old Age Assistance Act set up a means-tested pension for people between 65 and 69 years old who could demonstrate financial need. The provinces and the federal government shared the cost for this program. The plan required no contributions and paid the same pension to all poorer pensioners, including homemakers.

These early programs supplemented the incomes of older people (they offered basic income security), but the federal government kept payments low, so people would have an incentive to provide for their own old age (National Health and Welfare 1973, cited in Chappell 1987). In the 1960s the federal government broadened the pension system by setting up the Guaranteed Income Supplement program to supplement Old Age Security. This program was designed to help the poorest older people. In 1966 the federal government and the government of Quebec started the Canada and Quebec Pension Plans. All wage earners in Canada pay a part of their incomes into these plans. By the 1970s Canada had two types of programs in place: income security programs (the Old Age Security and the Guaranteed Income Supplement) and income maintenance programs (the Canada and Quebec Pension Plans). These programs form the basis of the Canadian pension system today.

The National Council of Welfare (1984a) calls these the anti-poverty and the income-replacement goals of the system, respectively. The federal government designed the first type of program to help people meet their basic needs in retirement and the second type to help people maintain their pre-retirement income and lifestyle.

By the mid-1970s federal government **transfers** (the Old Age Security and the Guaranteed Income Supplement and other transfers paid for from tax revenues) and the Canada Pension Plan accounted for 44 percent of older Canadians' retirement incomes. By 1986 this figure had increased to 52 percent of their incomes. Occupational pensions (those from former employers) made up 16 percent of older people's total income in 1986 (up from 13 percent in 1971), and assets (investments and savings) made up more than 20 percent of retirees' income in both years (National Advisory Council on Aging 1991). Myles reports that federal government transfers make up increasingly larger portions of individuals' incomes as they age. "As each year passes," he writes, "the number of wage earners declines, savings are spent and inflation erodes the real value of both savings and private pensions" (1984, 22). This means that older people are more dependent on public policy for their well-being than ever before. And this makes the study of pensions vital to an understanding of old age today.

## THE CANADIAN RETIREMENT INCOME SYSTEM TODAY

Canada's complex system of pension plans and programs, along with earnings from work, should create a decent old age for all Canadians, but it does not. Many older people still suffer a sharp loss in income and a shocking change in lifestyle when they retire. Almost every tier and subsection of the Canadian pension system needs improvement. The following discussion will look at the structure and the limits of the Canadian pension system today.

### Tier One: Government Transfers

Canada has a three-tiered pension system shaped like a pyramid (see Exhibit 9.1). The Old Age Security (OAS), the Guaranteed Income Supplement (GIS), the Spouse's Allowance (SA) and the Widowed Spouse's Allowance (WSPA)—called federal government transfer programs—make up the first tier. Nearly all Canadians aged 65 or over, rich or poor, get the same OAS pension. The GIS goes to people with no income other than the OAS. The SA goes to spouses between ages 60 and 64 who are married to a GIS pensioner and to widows or widowers of former GIS pensioners. People do not directly contribute to these pension funds; the federal government pays them out of tax revenue. The federal government spent almost $17 billion on them in 1989 (up from $14 billion in 1984) (National Council of Welfare 1989b). These programs protect older people's incomes—especially those of the very poor—from falling below a specified level. Among seniors, more than one-third of their income on average came from federal government transfers (Lindsay and Donald 1988).

Not surprisingly, poorer people depend on transfers most. Older women, the poorest group of older people, for instance, received almost 49 percent of their income from transfer payments in 1986. Older men received only 29 percent of their income from these sources (Lindsay and Donald 1988). Men, compared with women, receive almost four times the proportion of their income from employment earnings and almost twice the proportion of income from private pensions (Lindsay and Donald 1988).

The OAS in the first quarter of 1991 came to $351.41 a month per person (or $4,217 per year) (National Advisory Council on Aging 1991). It went to about 3 million people—over 99 percent of all Canadians aged 65 and over. The federal government taxes the OAS as income, so pensioners with enough income to pay taxes will pay some or all of their OAS back to the government. The poorest older people, who pay no tax, keep all their OAS benefits.

The federal government indexes OAS payments to the Consumer Price Index or cost of living, and adjusts the rate four times a year. But in 1983 and 1984 the government capped rises in OAS payments to 6 percent and 5 percent, respectively. This policy had no effect because inflation began to fall before 1983. Full indexation began again in 1985. The high cost of this program (about $12.5 billion in 1990) makes it an obvious target for federal government cutbacks (National Advisory Council on Aging 1991). The federal government planned to de-index OAS payments in 1985, but it backed down after seniors and business groups across the country protested.

The GIS goes to the poorest seniors. In 1989 1.4 million people got the GIS (National Council of Welfare 1989b). GIS benefits in 1991 went to single older people who received less than $10,123 that year from sources other than the OAS. It went to couples with a combined (non-OAS) income of $13,187 or less (National Advisory Council on Aging 1991). The federal government does not tax the GIS, and it indexes GIS payments to the Consumer Price Index, so that they go up quarterly as the cost of living rises. A person (or a couple) get either full or partial GIS payments based on a yearly income test. In the first quarter of 1991, a single person could receive a GIS of $421.79 per month, while a married couple could get a maximum of $549.46 per month for the two of them (National Advisory Council on Aging 1991).

. . . . . . . . . . . . . . . . . . . . . . . . . . . . . . . . . . . . .

## Exhibit 9.1

Canada's Three-Tiered Pension System

. . . . . . . . . . . . . . . . . . . . . . . . . . . . . . . . . . . . .

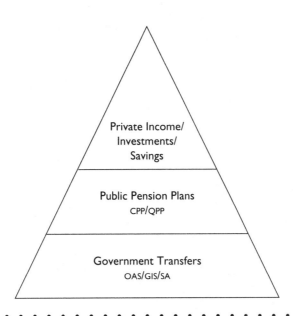

Private Income/
Investments/
Savings

Public Pension Plans
CPP/QPP

Government Transfers
OAS/GIS/SA

. . . . . . . . . . . . . . . . . . . . . . . . . . . . . . . . . . . . .

Widowers or widows could get a maximum of approximately $9,000 per year. Single pensioners, more often than married pensioners, have low enough incomes to need the GIS. Women, many of them widows, make up over 79 percent of all single people who get the GIS (National Council of Welfare 1989b).

The federal government added the SA program to Tier One of the system in 1975. The SA goes to a low-income pensioner's spouse who is aged 60 to 64 years old. It pays an amount equal to the OAS and the maximum GIS at the married rate. This couple gets the same transfer payments as a poor couple with both spouses aged 65 and over. If the GIS pensioner dies, the spouse continues to get payments. When the survivor reaches age 65, the federal government stops SA payments and the person then gets an OAS/GIS pension. The vast majority of SA payments go to women (National Council of Welfare 1989b). Without GIS and SA benefits almost half (47 percent) of all older Canadians would live below the poverty line. Eleven percent of all people who receive the GIS are so poor that they get the full amount. This program costs about $4 billion a year (National Council of Welfare 1989b).

• • • • • • • • • • • • • • • • • • • • • • • • • • • • • • • • • • • • •

# Exhibit 9.2

The Canada Pension System

• • • • • • • • • • • • • • • • • • • • • • • • • • • • • • • • • • • • •

| Pension | Maximum Benefits per Month |
|---|---|
| **Old Age Security** | $374.07 (January 1992) single |

**Requirements and Program Details:** 65 years or over; residence requirement; Canadian citizen or legal resident; noncontributory; indexed quarterly.

| | |
|---|---|
| **Guaranteed Income Supplement** | $444.54 (single, January 1992) |
| | $579.10 (couple, January 1992) |

**Requirements and Program Details:** low or no income besides OAS; noncontributory; indexed quarterly.

| | |
|---|---|
| **Spouse's Allowance** | $663.62 (January 1992) |

**Requirements and Program Details:** equal to the sum of OAS and maximum GIS at married rate; spouse married to OAS pensioner who gets GIS; spouse between 60 and 64; must satisfy other OAS requirements; noncontributory; indexed quarterly.

| | |
|---|---|
| **Widowed Spouse's Allowance** | $732.64 (January 1992) |

**Requirements and Program Details:** paid to any low-income widow or widower (60–64 years old); noncontributory; indexed quarterly.

| | |
|---|---|
| **Canada Pension Plan Retirement Pension** | $636.11 (1992) |

**Requirements and Program Details:** 4.8% of income paid into plan; half by worker; half by employer (minus a basic exemption (1992—$3,200). Up to Year's Maximum Pensionable Earnings (YMPE) 1992– $32,200; indexed quarterly.

| | |
|---|---|
| **Canada Pension Plan Survivor Benefits** | $381.67 (CPP 1992, spouse 65 and over) |
| | $358.24 (CPP 1992, spouse 55–64) |

| | |
|---|---|
| **Canada Pension Plan Death Benefit** | $3,220 (CPP, lump sum, 1992) |

**Program Details:** paid to estate of deceased contributor.

Canada Pension Plan Disability Benefit          $783.89 (CPP, 1992)

**Program Details:** paid to contributors with severe and prolonged disability.

---

Canada Pension Plan Children and                $154.70 (CPP, 1992)
Orphan Benefits

**Program Details:** paid to each orphan of contributor.

---

**Source:** Adapted from Health and Welfare Canada, *Canada Pension Plan, Family Allowance, Old Age Security, Statement on Current Benefits, 1992.* Current figures: Income Security Programs Branch, January 1992. Reproduced with permission of the Minister of Supply and Services, 1991.

• • • • • • • • • • • • • • • • • • • • • • • • • • • • • • • • •

Nova Scotia, Ontario, Manitoba, Saskatchewan, Alberta, British Columbia, Yukon, and the Northwest Territories also have provincial or territorial supplement plans to help the poorest seniors. About 15 percent of all seniors receive provincial or territorial supplements. These benefits total about $240 million per year. Most provinces and territories do not index payments to the cost of living, but they do increase the amounts from time to time (National Advisory Council on Aging 1991; National Council of Welfare 1989b).

All provinces reduce taxes for older property owners or give rent rebates to seniors. Newfoundland seniors, for example, get an exemption from local school taxes (either the poll tax or property tax). Manitoba seniors who own homes (and poorer Manitobans aged 55 to 64) get a school tax rebate of up to $175 per household (National Council of Welfare 1989b). These programs play an important part in keeping very old people and even people with occupational pensions at a decent income level.

The National Council of Welfare (1989b) reviewed the federal government transfer system and concluded that the system keeps many older people out of poverty. Still, the council says, "it is clear that the government programs that make up the first level of Canada's retirement income system are not generous enough to keep all pensioners out of poverty" (National Council of Welfare 1989b, 16). For example, in 1989 the maximum OAS/GIS pension fell $1,867 short of the low-income cut-off for a couple living in a large city. For unattached older people the gap came to $3,393 (National Council of Welfare 1990b). In 1989, 15.9 percent of people aged 65 and over lived below the low income cut-offs (Statistics Canada 1990c).

Some policies weaken the universality of the OAS pension. In 1977 the federal government introduced new residence requirements for government pensions. Until 1977, an older person who lived in Canada at least ten years qualified for an old age pension. After 1977, a person earned one-fortieth of their pension for each year in Canada after age 18. Anyone with less than ten years in Canada got no benefits. Many immigrants to Canada will now get less than a full OAS when they turn 65. This policy will erode the universality of the old age pension system (National Council of Welfare 1990b).

A new policy has further weakened the OAS's universality. The federal budget speech of April 1989 introduced a "clawback" of OAS benefits from wealthier seniors. This means that seniors who have a net income of over $50,000 per year must pay back 15 cents on every dollar of OAS benefits for every dollar of income they receive that is over $50,000. In 1989 this would have meant that a senior with an income of over $76,332 would lose all of their OAS pension (National Council of Welfare 1990b). The federal government projected that this would affect only about 4 percent of seniors in 1989 (National Council of Welfare 1989a). But unless the government raises the threshold of $50,000 to keep up with inflation, more and more people (whose retirement incomes will rise with inflation) will face a loss of their OAS payments.

## Tier Two: The Canada Pension Plan and the Quebec Pension Plan

The Canada Pension Plan (CPP) and the Quebec Pension Plan (QPP) form the pension system's second, smaller tier. Almost 12 million workers (virtually 90 percent of the labour force), their employers, and self-employed people paid about $8 billion into the plans in 1989 (National Council of Welfare 1989b). The CPP/QPP paid a maximum benefit in 1990 of $577.08 per month (or $6,925 per year) (National Advisory Council on Aging 1991) and paid out over $11 billion dollars in 1989 to more than two million beneficiaries (National Council of Welfare 1989b).

It is worth mentioning that the CPP allows a province to opt out of the plan. Quebec chose to do so and set up its own plan. The QPP differs from the CPP in a few details, but in most ways it mirrors it. This text will use the term CPP to refer to both plans.

The CPP does two things: first, it ensures that workers will have some pension beyond the OAS/GIS/SA when they retire, and, second, it will save the federal government money in GIS and SA payments in the future. The CPP combines two types of pension plans: a savings plan and a transfer plan. It works like a savings plan because each worker pays a percentage of his or her salary into it each month. In 1989, for instance, the law required workers to pay 2.1 percent of their wages into the plan (up to a maximum of $234.15 per year for 1989) (National Council of Welfare 1989b). Their employers paid a matching amount. Self-employed people paid 4.2 percent of their incomes into the plan. Because more people in the future will be eligible for CPP/QPP pensions, the CPP plans gradually to increase the contribution for all workers from 4.2 percent (the total that the employee and employer paid in 1989) to 7.45 percent in 2010 and to 11.68 percent in 2050 (National Council of Welfare 1990b). The payments are credited to individual workers, and, when they retire, their pension will depend on how much they paid into the plan.

The CPP also works like a transfer plan because the money paid in today does not go into a private account for each person. It goes to pay the pensions of retired plan members today. Today's workers will get their CPP pensions from workers' contributions in the future.

The CPP does some things well. First, it protects people from inflation. Personal savings, for example, can decrease in value over time, but the CPP promises that a person will get a pension in the future geared to the cost of living at that time. Second, the CPP covers almost all workers, so most workers will enter retirement with some CPP benefits. Third, the plan is "portable," which means it moves with workers when they change jobs. In a fluid job market, where people change jobs often, this can mean the difference between having a pension or not.

Fourth, the plan locks in both workers' and employers' contributions from the start. This is called "vesting." Workers get credit for their total payments (their own and their employer's contributions) even if they move from one employer to another. Fifth, the CPP promises to pay workers up to 25 percent of their pre-retirement earnings (to a maximum of 25 percent of the year's Average Industrial Wage) for life.

Sixth, the plan applies the same rules to men and women. Women pay in at the same rates as men, and the plan entitles them to the same benefits. Some occupational plans base benefits on different mortality tables for men and women, so women in some plans get smaller payments because on average they live longer than men. Seventh, all CPP members get survivor and disability benefits, a vital point because in Canada women often outlive their husbands and many women have no pensions of their own.

Eighth, the CPP calculates a person's pension by adjusting pensionable earnings from past years to bring them up to current wage levels. This adjusts for the fact that inflation makes earlier wage levels a poor basis for calculating a pension today and makes the CPP better than occupational plans that use lifetime earnings to calculate pension payments (National Council of Welfare 1989b).

Ninth, the CPP allows contributors to choose early or late retirement. A contributor can receive benefits as early as age 60 or as late as age 70. The

CPP decreases or increases by one-half of one percent for each month a person begins receiving benefits before or after their 65th birthday. A person who retires at age 60 would receive 30 percent of their normal CPP pension. The retiree will get this lower rate even after the age of 65 (National Council of Welfare 1989b).

Tenth, and not least, the federal government indexes the CPP to the cost of living. It goes up as the cost of living increases, so people do not fall behind each year as they do with a fixed income pension.

The CPP now pays benefits to more older people than ever before. In 1967, it paid benefits to less than one-half of one percent of older people, but in June of 1989 the CPP went to nearly three-quarters of all people 65 and over (National Council of Welfare 1989b). The number of people who get CPP pensions, the size of their pensions, and the total paid out in CPP pensions will all increase in the years ahead.

Still, the CPP has its limits. For instance, it does not help people maintain their pre-retirement income—the second goal of the Canadian pension system. For many older people today—those who retired before 1966 or those who never worked for a wage—the CPP/QPP offers no help at all, and some people who get the CPP find that it does not pay enough.

In 1989, for example, the OAS and CPP paid a maximum of $10,751 to a single person and $14,701 to married couples with one maximum CPP pensioner. The poverty lines for large Canadian cities in 1989 came to $12,037 for a single person and $15,881 for a couple. This means that the combined OAS and CPP for a single person left him or her almost $1,300 below the poverty line. A married couple did better, but still fell more than $1,000 below the poverty line (National Council of Welfare 1989b).

These low CPP payments do not replace much of the average person's income. Also, the plan pays low survivor benefits (National Council of Welfare 1990b) and the poorest older people, who get the GIS, lose $1 of their benefits for each $2 they receive from the CPP. As a result of these low rates, most people face a drop in living standards when they retire. People need private pensions or savings to maintain their pre-retirement lifestyles.

## Tier Three: Occupational Pensions, Savings, and Work

Private income makes up the third tier of the Canadian pension system. The OAS/GIS and CPP make up about 40 percent of an average wage earner's pre-retirement income (National Advisory Council on Aging 1991). For some people it makes up even less of their pre-retirement income. In 1989, for example, OAS/GIS and CPP benefits for an unattached person came to only $180 over the poverty line for a single person who lived in a city of half a million or more people (National Council of Welfare 1989b). This means that all workers need private pensions and savings to make up the difference between federal government pensions and pre-retirement income.

How many workers can count on occupational pension plans to help them in retirement? The National Council of Welfare reports that 1.2 million people aged 65 and over received over $5 billion in pension income in 1986 (National Council of Welfare 1989b).

Statistics Canada (1990d) reports that about 4.8 million Canadians belonged to an occupational pension plan in 1988. Nearly all public sector workers (such as government workers, teachers, nurses) belonged to a plan, but only about a third of private sector workers belonged (Statistics Canada 1990d). Occupational pension benefits in 1986 made up 20 percent of the income of males aged 65 and over, but only 11 percent of the income of females aged 65 and over (Lindsay and Donald 1988).

Most older people rely on savings to make up for lost pre-retirement income. Investment income makes up about 19 percent of the income of males aged 65 and over and about 24 percent of that of females aged 65 and over. These sources ranked as the third major source of income for males and the second major source of income for females (Lindsay and Donald 1988).

The federal government has encouraged more savings through Registered Retirement Savings Plans (RRSPs). In 1989, self-employed individuals, or employees with no private pension plan, could save 20 percent of their earned income up to a maximum of $7,500 a year without paying income tax on this money. Individuals who belong to a private pension plan can contribute $3,500 minus their contribution to their private pension plan or 20 percent of earned income if less than $3,500 a year. The federal government plans to increase the maximum contribution to an RRSP to $15,500 by 1995 (Department of Finance 1988; National Council of Welfare 1989b). RRSP members pay tax on the money only when they withdraw it in retirement. This defers taxes to a time when the person has a lower income—and so a lower tax rate. The number of RRSPs grew from 206,000 in 1969 (2.3 percent of tax filers) to 3.5 million in 1987 (20.4 percent of tax filers) (Statistics Canada 1990d). In 1987 contributors saved a total of over $9 billion in RRSPs (Statistics Canada 1990d). Proposed higher limits for RRSP contributions could make them even more attractive to middle- and upper-income earners in the future.

Other income in retirement includes earnings, rent subsidies, and tax exemptions. In 1987 earnings accounted for 23.8 percent of family income to households with a male head aged 65 and over, and 44 percent of income for households with a female head aged 65 and over (Statistics Canada 1990e). The federal government allows special tax credits for older people. These include a tax credit begun in 1988 of $550 per year indexed to inflation and a pension income tax credit to a maximum of $170 per year (National Council of Welfare 1989b). Also, corporations offer subsidies for goods and services, like reduced theatre ticket prices or reduced air fares for older people. Stone and MacLean (1979) say that these indirect subsidies could add at least 30 percent to older people's average total income, and this does not count other benefits such as subsidized health care costs and home care services.

How does the private pension system help most people cope with retirement? Not very well on three counts. First, coverage is low: only 37 percent of female workers and 51 percent of male workers in 1988 had private pension plans (Statistics Canada 1990d). This rate of coverage was stable for females from 1984 to 1988, but decreased for males by nearly 4 percent over this same period (Statistics Canada 1990d). These figures include workers in the public sector (government and crown corporation workers) and workers in the private sector (workers for private corporations). Only 34 percent of private sector workers in Canada in 1986 had occupational pensions (National Council of Welfare 1989b). People who work part-time, seasonal workers, and those who work for small businesses and at low-paying jobs often have no occupational pensions. Men outnumber women in private sector occupational plans by nearly 3 to 1 (National Council of Welfare 1989b).

Also, only one worker in ten with earnings either at or below the Average Industrial Wage (AIW) has an occupational pension plan. This means the poorest people have the least chance to get a private pension. In 1986 only 10 percent of people with incomes under $15,000 per year belonged to an occupational plan that they paid into. Sixty-four percent of people with incomes of $45,000 and over paid into occupational plans in that year. "[I]t seems unlikely," the National Council of Welfare (1989b, 43) says, "that occupational pension plans will ever be an important source of retirement income to people in low-wage jobs. Coverage by contributory pension plans increases sharply as incomes rise."

Second, in 1986 only 34 percent of all occupational plan members, most of whom worked in the public sector, had some automatic inflation protection. About 67 percent of public sector workers had some inflation protection, but only 7 percent of private sector members had inflation protection (National Council of Welfare 1990b). In an inflationary economy people on a fixed pension—even a good one—become poorer as they age. At 4 percent inflation a pension will lose 30 percent of its value over ten years; at 8 percent a $900 pension will be worth only $566 five years after a person retires—more than a one-third drop in their pension's value (Royal Commission on the Status of Pensions in Ontario 1980, cited in National Council of Welfare 1984a).

Statistics Canada reports that in 1987 the average annual income from occupational plans came to $9,110 for men and only $5,372 for women. "All in all," the National Council of Welfare says, "occupational pension plans play a limited role in providing retirement income for Canadians" (National Council of Welfare 1989b, 46).

Third, only a small percentage of people who belong to occupational pension plans ever collect a full pension (Senate of Canada 1979). Two things account for this. First, few plans in the past have had early vesting (vesting, as mentioned, is a person's right to their own pension contributions and their employer's contributions if they change jobs). Early vesting locks both the employer's and the employee's payments in the plan soon after employment begins. Second, most plans lack portability (portability, as previously mentioned, is the feature of plans that allows workers to transfer their pension money to another plan with a new employer). When workers leave a company today, most of them get either a deferred pension (if their money is vested and locked in) or they get their own (but not their employer's) pension contributions back—sometimes with no interest. The employer's share stays in the fund when workers get their pension contributions back, so each time a person changes jobs they lose half their fund and have to start again. This means that even if the whole labour force belongs to occupational pension plans, as long as workers change jobs often (as they do today) only workers with fully vested contributions will ever collect a full pension.

The government started the RRSP program to help people cope with gaps in the private pension system. RRSPs encourage private savings for retirement. Anyone can start an RRSP for themselves. But, in practice, the program helps people in higher income brackets the most. First, people with higher incomes can pay in the most (for a self-employed individual, 20 percent of his or her income to a maximum of $7,500). Poorer people simply do not have this much money to put aside. Also, people in higher tax brackets get more money back through the tax deductions received through this program. The higher their tax bracket, the more they get back. For instance, a person in the highest tax bracket gets a tax saving of $450 on a $1,000 RRSP deduction. A person in the lowest bracket gets a tax saving of only $264 on a $1,000 RRSP deduction (National Council of Welfare 1989b). Exhibit 9.3 shows the proportion of people from selected income levels who paid into RRSPs and the average amount they contributed.

## INEQUALITY IN LATER LIFE

Myles (1981a) uses a political economy perspective to look at the structural reasons for inequality in old age. For example, he shows that education and

• • • • • • • • • • • • • • • • • • • • • • • • • • • • • • • • • • • • • • • • •

## Exhibit 9.3

RRSP Contributors, by Income Level, 1986

• • • • • • • • • • • • • • • • • • • • • • • • • • • • • • • • • • • • • • • • •

| Income Level | Percentage of Tax Filers | Average Contribution |
| --- | --- | --- |
| Under $15,000 | 5 | $1,204 |
| $15,000–$29,999 | 28 | 1,987 |
| $30,000–$44,999 | 45 | 2,460 |
| $45,000 and Over | 61 | 4,057 |

This table shows a clear pattern. The higher the income bracket, the greater the proportion of people who paid into an RRSP. Also, the higher the income bracket, the larger the amounts of money that
people in that income bracket paid into a plan. The average contribution for people who earned
$45,000 and over was more than 3.3 times the amount on average contributed by people who
earned less than $15,000 a year. Increases in contribution limits will increase the use of RRSPs by
wealthier Canadians and will increase the gap between the contributions of the rich and the poor.
The poorest Canadians cannot afford to save in an RRSP.

**Source:** National Council of Welfare, *A Pension Primer,* (Ottawa: Minister of Supply and Services, 1989b) 49, Table 11. Reproduced with permission of the Minister of Supply and Services Canada, 1991.

• • • • • • • • • • • • • • • • • • • • • • • • • • • • • • • • • • • • • • • • •

former occupational status largely determine income in later life. A person
with a high level of education and a high status occupation stands the best
chance of a high income in retirement. These people also stand the best
chance of maintaining their status after retirement. Access to work in old age,
investments, and occupational pensions also contribute to inequality in old
age. These benefits go to people with higher levels of education and higher
job status. The National Council of Welfare (1985b) reports that the older
population has a more unequal income distribution than younger age groups.

Some groups face more financial problems than others in old age. Wanner and McDonald (1986) report that membership in a non-European ethnic
group leads to lower income in retirement. Asian, African, or Latin American
ethnic group members tend to retire later and have less chance of getting
OAS, GIS, or CPP benefits. They also have less chance of getting an occupational pension. This leads to lower income for these older men. Wanner and
McDonald (1986), using the political economy perspective, trace these trends
to public pension policies and their impact on immigrants. Recent immigrants, for example, receive only partial public pensions.

A small percentage of older people have savings and investments and live on comfortable incomes, but people who live near or below the poverty line in Canada before they retire will stay there in old age. Women, for example, face low incomes in later life and they show higher rates of poverty than men. This reflects differences in men's and women's work careers, salaries, and pension options.

## Women and Pensions

The National Council of Welfare (1984b, 24) says that "one conclusion stands out from all the facts and figures [about aging and poverty]: Poverty in old age is largely a women's problem, and is becoming more so every year." In 1987, for example, the poverty rate of elderly women was 22 percent, double the poverty rate of elderly men. In that same year, unattached women aged 65 and over (who lived alone or with non-relatives) made up 6 percent of all women, but 18 percent of poor women. The poverty rate for unattached women aged 65 and over was 44 percent in 1987, double that of elderly women as a whole (National Council of Welfare 1990a). "After a lifetime spent taking care of their spouses and children," the National Council of Welfare (1979, 48) says, "these women who had no opportunity to become financially self-sufficient are now abandoned by the generation that benefited most from their work." A government commission (Senate of Canada 1979, 65) over a decade ago concluded that "the retirement income system has failed and the failure is especially dismal with elderly women." This still applies today.

Why do women have such low incomes in old age? First, traditional expectations about women and work lead women to have different work patterns than men. Women often leave a first job to raise children; due to family responsibilities they spend three times longer than men between jobs; and they tend to work at each job for a shorter time than men (Connelly and MacDonald 1990; National Council of Welfare 1984a). When women work outside the home, they often take part-time, low-paying jobs. The traditional expectation that women will place family before career leads to this pattern and keeps women from getting high salaries and from storing up pension credits.

Second, the structure of occupational and public pensions discriminates against women—sometimes in hidden ways. Women often work for smaller, nonunionized companies with no occupational pension plans, and they also tend to work part-time. For example, 73 percent of women under age 65 worked during 1987 at some time, but 64 percent of them had part-time jobs. Women in part-time jobs often get lower hourly pay than women who work full-time, and they get no fringe benefits. These women often fail to qualify for pension coverage (Government of Canada 1982b; National Council of Welfare 1990a).

Third, women in general are paid less than men and hold lower-status jobs (Connelly and MacDonald 1990). "In 1988, women made up 44 percent of the total Canadian labour force. That same year, they received 35 percent of all incomes, while men received 65 percent" (National Council of Welfare 1990a). Armstrong and Armstrong (1981) report that women work in low wage jobs that are defined as unskilled and offer little chance for advancement. In 1988, 76 percent of women worked in "female" occupations: women make up the largest percentage of babysitters, typists, and variety store sales clerks. In 1986, 59 percent of women worked in three types of jobs. Thirty percent worked in clerical positions, 10 percent in sales, and 19 percent in services. Poorer women more than all women tended to work in these types of jobs. Women who worked in service jobs had an average income of only $15,126 per year for full-time year-round work in 1988. They had the second-lowest-paid jobs in Canada. Only female farm workers did worse (National Council of Welfare 1990a).

Women who work in service jobs often work part-time and many of the firms they work for have no pension plans. Only 37 percent of women in paid labour in 1988 belonged to an occupational pension plan (compared to 51 percent of men), and most of these women work for government or for crown corporations (National Council of Welfare 1990a). In private industry only 28 percent of women belonged to a pension plan (Statistics Canada 1990).

Even within relatively low-paying fields women find themselves in the poorest paying jobs. For instance, women tend to work as salaried clerks. Men tend to sell expensive products like cars or appliances. These jobs often pay a commission in addition to a base salary. Women work in service jobs like waitress, hairdresser, or child care worker. Men tend to work at services like police officer, security guard, or soldier. Armstrong and Armstrong (1984) found that even when women work at the same job as men they may get lower pay.

Low pay means that these women pay a smaller amount into the CPP than men, and this means a smaller CPP pension when they retire. A report on women and poverty (National Council of Welfare 1990a) says that in 1987 women on average received 31 percent of the average benefits received by men from occupational pension plans. Women received only 47 percent of the CPP benefits received by men in that year (National Council of Welfare 1990a). The gap between CPP payments to men and to women grew from 1977 to 1987. In 1987 most women got less than 60 percent and many got less than 40 percent of the maximum CPP. In that same year most men received between 80 percent and 100 percent of the maximum CPP. Low incomes and short careers at paid labour explain this gap (National Council of Welfare 1989b).

A look at newly retired workers (i.e., those aged 65–69 in June 1989) found that only 57 percent of females in that age group compared with 96 percent of males received CPP benefits. Women received only $3,120 a year on average compared with $5,340 for men. Women on average today earn only 60 to 70 percent of the earnings of men (National Council of Welfare 1990a). This means that even in the future women will have a lower proportion of the maximum CPP than men (National Council of Welfare 1989b).

The National Council of Welfare sums up these findings. Women, the Council says, "become the prime victims of the built-in injustices of our labour market, which excludes women from the best positions, pays them less than they are worth and segregates them into a narrow range of low-wage occupations with few fringe benefits and limited chances for advancement" (National Council of Welfare 1990a, 2).

## Widows

Widows make up the largest group among women 65 and over, and, of all women, they benefit least from Canada's pension system. "After fifty years or so of unpaid, faithful service," the National Council of Welfare (1979, 32) says, "a woman's only reward is likely to be poverty." In 1988, 50 percent of women aged 75 and over, most of them widows, lived in poverty. This figure does not include people who live in institutions; if it did, the poverty rate would be higher.

Why do older widows have such low incomes? First, only 51 percent of all workers belong to an occupational pension plan (National Council of Welfare 1990a), and less than half of these occupational pension plans pay survivor benefits to widows. Many of these private sector plans provided for only five years of survivor payments. "A woman who loses her husband when she is 65," the National Council of Welfare (1989b, 39) says, "and lives until age 85 could be in dire straits for the last 15 years of her life."

Only 69 percent of members of public sector plans and 27 percent of members of private sector plans provided a survivor pension if the plan member died before retirement. Even when a survivor plan exists, sometimes a woman gets nothing because her spouse has opted for higher benefits while he was alive. Many plans refund only the worker's contributions with interest if a plan member dies before retirement. Some plans return nothing to the surviving spouse (National Council of Welfare 1989b)

The public pension system also lets widows down. The CPP, for example, sets the benefits for a surviving spouse aged 65 and over at 60 percent of the deceased spouse's pension. The maximum amount payable came to $4,005 a year in 1989 (National Council of Welfare 1990a). The OAS in that year for a single person came to about $4,000. Combined, these payments came to only about two-thirds of the poverty line for a single person living in a large Canadian city (National Council of Welfare 1989b). The National Council of Welfare (1984a, 38) says that "a woman with no retirement pension of her own will suffer a drastic reduction in her living standard when her husband dies."

Women coming into old age today will do a little better. More of them work, and some of them will get CPP pensions. But even so, many women will get only small pensions. Homemakers will have no occupational pensions; they will get no CPP pension of their own; and if their husband's pension plan pays no survivor benefits, they will get no pension at all. Younger women will do better in the future because more of them work; they have begun to enter male-dominated occupations; and more of them belong to private pension plans (Connelly and MacDonald 1990; Statistics Canada 1990d). But low wages and part-time work will leave most women without occupational pensions. They too will have small CPP pensions.

The system needs reform: women and men need better occupational pension plans, and women need better survivor and homemaker benefits, and more help from the OAS/GIS/SA (Dulude 1987). The federal government has proposed some changes to the system. This sparked what some people call "The Great Pension Debate" in the early 1980s. This debate was about whether a public pension plan like the CPP or private pension plans would best serve Canadians. More recent debates have been concerned with universality of the OAS (Myles 1988).

## PENSION REFORM

Canada has stewed over pension reform since the early 1980s. A series of conferences, task forces, and white papers have all proposed changes in the pension system (Government of Canada 1982a; House of Commons Canada 1983). And some change has taken place. For example, by the late 1980s all provinces except British Columbia and Prince Edward Island had some legislation covering occupational pensions. Also, new rules have improved the public pension plan system. What follows are some of the highlights of these reforms.

First, the federal government income security system has made three important improvements over the years. (1) Improvements in GIS have led to decreased poverty rates for single older people (National Council of Welfare 1988). (2) As of 1985, all widows and widowers with low incomes would get the SA. (3) The federal government continues to index the OAS to the rate of inflation, though it has not increased the OAS to bring it closer to the Average Industrial Wage (AIW).

Second, beginning in June 1984 the CPP also allowed women and men to deduct the years they spent childrearing from their pensionable years. (Until 1984 these years counted as zero income and lowered a person's average life-time salary.) People who take time off to care for their children can now deduct from their work record the years when their children were under 7 years old. Also, the CPP now provides for credit splitting if spouses divorce. Each spouse gets an equal share of the credits accumulated during their time together. This provision, however, includes a hitch: it requires an application for credit splitting. This means that not all eligible people will apply for or arrange credit splitting. Between 1978 and June 1989, only about 4 percent of eligible couples applied and received approval for credit splitting (National Council of Welfare 1989b).

Third, in May 1985 the federal government announced changes in the Canada Pension Benefits Standards Act. These changes set minimum standards for one million federal government workers and workers in federal government industries such as crown corporations. The federal government will ask provinces to change their rules to meet these new standards. These changes will affect 3.5 million workers all told. They include:

1. Locked-in vesting mandatory after two years in an occupational plan.

2. Improved portability by transfer of vested pensions to locked-in RRSPs.

3. The right of all full-time workers to join a private plan after two years of work; all part-time workers must have the right to join if they have earned at least 35 percent of the Yearly Maximum Pensionable Earnings ($8,190 in 1985).

4. Payment of survivor benefits worth at least 60 percent of the amount the couple would have received had the contributor lived. These benefits will continue if the survivor remarries.

5. Division of pension credits and payments 50-50 if a couple divorces, unless the couple or the courts choose a different option.

These changes serve as a model for the private sector as it considers pension reform (National Council of Welfare 1985a).

Fourth, the federal government and the provinces have agreed that all occupational plans shall provide a "joint life/last survivor benefit" (National

Council of Welfare 1989b). A spouse will receive at least 60 percent of the occupational pension the couple would have received if both had lived. The pension continues even if the survivor remarries. This provision has one drawback: both spouses must agree to lower pension payments in the present. If the couple chooses a higher pension today, they forego survivor benefits in the future.

These recent changes will balance some of the inequities in the system. The poorest older people on the GIS will benefit from these changes, and so will widows and women who work part-time. But the federal government will still have to tackle some tough issues in the future. These include homemakers' pensions, the rising cost of indexed OAS pensions, and indexation of private pension plans. Women face many disadvantages in old age that current pension reform only partly addresses. Changes in the OAS will help the poorest women. But, "the whole income-security debate," Neysmith (1984, 18–19) writes, "has been defined in terms of pensions that are related to one's track record in the paid-labour force ... [And] occupationally based pensions by definition cannot meet the needs of most women" (Neysmith 1984). Canadian society will need to deal with this larger issue through broader reforms. These reforms will have to include increasing opportunities for women in the labour force.

## THE COST OF REFORM

Recent and proposed changes in private and public pension plans will mean one thing: pensions will cost more money. CPP rates, for example, will have to rise to about 9 percent of workers' earnings by the year 2030 (from 3.6 percent in 1986) just to keep CPP benefits at 25 percent of the AIW. Better occupational plans will cost more—the federal government estimates a rise in costs to about 11 percent more of a worker's pay. Better survivor benefits will cost about 0.7 percent of a worker's pay (Health and Welfare Canada 1982a). As Canadian society ages, more people will begin to draw pensions. And smaller age cohorts of younger people will have to pay for some of these costs.

How will people feel about these changes? Will younger people revolt at the high cost of pensions for the older generation? The state of Canada's economy will partly determine how younger people will feel about pension costs. A strong economy and low inflation will make it easier to pay more for pensions; increased costs and low wages will make it harder.

Myles (1982) offers two reasons why Canadians will support a stronger pension system in the future. First, he says, "the elderly are the elderly parents of the younger generation of producers." Without state support, the young would have to help care for their parents themselves, and younger people will prefer to "pool their risks" through a central pension system. Second, he says, middle-aged people, because they will be old soon themselves, have a self-interest in supporting a strong pension and social security system for the elderly.

In the end a strong pension system—given the longer life expectancy today—makes sense for everyone. As long as taxpayers see this they will continue to support improvements in Canada's retirement income system (Myles 1981b).

## SUMMARY

1. Canada's pension system has a sound structure, but the current system "is out of balance" (National Council of Welfare 1984a, 71). Some people— very old women, people from lower-income brackets, people with low levels of education, widows, and homemakers—all run a higher than average risk of poverty in old age.

2. Canada has a three-tiered system: the OAS, GIS, and SA make up Tier One; the CPP/QPP make up Tier Two; and private pensions and savings make up Tier Three.

3. The Canadian retirement system has two goals: (1) to keep all older people out of poverty; and (2) to replace pre-retirement income. At present it meets neither goal for many Canadians.

4. Poorer Canadians, the people who need private savings the most in retirement, have the least chance of having any. Private pension plans cover fewer than half of Canadian workers. The CPP at best replaces only 25 percent of a person's income up to the average industrial wage, and the OAS/ GIS/SA leave the poorest older people in poverty.

5. Women, compared with men, face a higher risk of poverty in old age, because unequal coverage by pension plans, lower-paying jobs, and different work patterns due to child-rearing often leave women with lower pensions.

6. Widows run a high risk of poverty in old age. The CPP pays a relatively small survivor pension. Private pension plans offer little help. Many of them have no survivor pension option.

7. The federal government has recently made changes to the system. Reforms include better GIS/SA payments, better CPP pensions, rules that

encourage RRSP contributions, and rules that strengthen private pension plans.

**8.** Proposed reforms to the CPP and to private plans try to ensure that more Canadians, including homemakers, get pension coverage. Better public and private pensions for these people may reduce the costs of federal government transfers in the future. This will save the government money and give more people a better income in retirement.

**9.** Canadians will pay for these reforms as long as they support the notion that everyone—young and old—gains from a strong pension system.

## SELECTED READINGS

Bryden, Kenneth. *Old Age Pensions and Policy-Making in Canada.* Montreal: McGill-Queen's University Press, 1974.

One of the few reports on the history of the pension system. Bryden is a political scientist, so he looks behind the historical events to discover trends in public policy.

National Council of Welfare. *A Pension Primer.* Ottawa: Minister of Supply and Services, 1989b.

This report on Canada's pension system presents facts and information in an interesting, readable style, and includes a glossary of terms. Like other National Council of Welfare reports (*Pension Reform* and *Sixty-Five and Older*), this report argues that the pension system needs improvement. The council will mail these and other reports on request at no cost.

Women's Bureau, Labour Canada. *Women in the Labour Force.* 1990–91 ed. Cat. No. L016-1728/90E. Ottawa: Minister of Supply and Services, Canada 1990.

Current facts on women and work. The report includes figures on labour force participation, earnings of men and women, and pensions. This source gives up-to-date information that you can interpret for yourself.

# Retirement and Work

## INTRODUCTION

Claude Rioux retired six months after his sixty-fifth birthday. He had worked as a warehouseman for an electronic supply company. Claude never thought much about retirement in his middle years, but a year or two before he retired he began to feel he had nothing in common with his fellow workers. Most of his friends had retired, and most of his new co-workers had just left high school. They talked about girls and motorcycles and listened to loud music. He had always liked work, but he began to enjoy it less each day. After he turned 65 his boss came by to ask if he had any retirement plans. Once the boss called him into his office and asked him when he planned to leave. "I said I didn't know," Claude says. "Why give him the satisfaction of thinking he could push me out. Hell, I still do a good job. Better than some of the kids who work here now. Oh, I planned to leave in January, but I wouldn't tell him. I thought, 'I'll leave when I'm good and ready.'"

No one forced Claude to retire, but he did. And he left work just about on schedule. He had little reason to keep working past age 65. He had a small pension from work as well as his CPP and OAS pensions, and he planned to open a small electronics repair shop at home. He stayed on until January only to show that no one could push him around.

Statistics Canada reports that a smaller proportion of men and women work past age 65 than ever before. In 1989 only 18 percent of men and 7 percent of women aged 65 to 69 continued to work in the labour force. After age 70 only 7 percent of men and 2 percent of women continue to work (Statistics Canada 1990e). These figures show that retirement has become a normative life event. Some people will spend a quarter or more of their adult life in retirement. Gerontologists view retirement today from two points of view: first, as a social institution and second, as a process of personal adjustment. This chapter will look at retirement from each of these perspectives. It will look at (1) the origin and role of retirement in modern society, (2) the forces that lead a person to retire, and (3) how people adjust to retirement.

## RETIREMENT AS A SOCIAL INSTITUTION

### The Origins of Retirement

Myles (1984) traces old age today to two developments. The first is the **retirement principle**—the idea that at a fixed age, regardless of mental or physical ability, a person leaves work. The second is the **retirement wage**—a pension paid by the state to support all older people. Myles (1984, 7) says that a new group of people grew out of these two developments: "a population of elders still fit for production who do not engage in economic activity."

Employers and employees both supported the retirement principle in North America. Industry supported it for two reasons: first, retirement allowed companies to retire older, skilled workers and hire younger, less skilled workers at lower wages; and, second, companies, using a philosophy of "scientific management," sought to speed up production and get more out of their workers. Unions offered to have workers work faster if companies reduced the work day, but a faster pace of work made it hard for older workers to compete with younger workers (Atchley 1985). Retirement gave older workers a graceful way to leave work.

The Canadian government supported the retirement principle for a number of reasons. Canada's first civil service commissioner, Adam Shortt, said in 1922 that retirement:

> relieves the government of the embarrassment and extravagance of retaining the services of officers who have outlived their usefulness; creates a proper flow of promotions; renders the service more mobile; deters efficient workers from leaving the public service for private employment ... [and] in general tends to promote efficiency in every way (quoted in Bolger, 1980, 8, cited in Myles 1984, 13).

Canada introduced the Old Age Pension Act in 1927 to promote the goals outlined above and to solve a social problem created by retired workers. Matthews and Tindale (1987) give three reasons for this act. First, more people lived to old age. Second, many old people lived in poverty. Third, employers needed to reduce unemployment and increase productivity. The Pension Act encouraged retirement and provided a basic income to the poorest older people.

Unions in North America supported retirement for their own reasons. Unions wanted companies to use seniority (first hired, last fired) as a method for deciding layoffs or cutbacks. Seniority gave workers a right to a job, and it gave the oldest workers the most job security. But companies resisted the seniority system because older workers cost them more and seniority rights made it hard for them to fire inefficient older workers. Retirement served both unions and employers. It limited seniority rights to people under the age of retirement and allowed companies to let older workers go. The unions traded the older worker's right to a job for job security in middle age (Haber 1978, cited in Atchley 1985, 54).

Still, few people retired in the past compared with today. First, in Canada many people worked on farms or in small businesses with no retirement age. Second, and most important, a lack of retirement income kept most people working as long as they could. Only with the increase in public pensions and social supports for older people after World War II did retirement spread (Myles 1984).

The U.S. Social Security program led the way for this change. The U.S. designed Social Security as a way to get people to retire (Myles 1984, 16). Until then governments gave social assistance to older people, but this assistance, like Canada's early old age assistance program, gave only the poorest older people a small amount of money to help them survive. The government based the program on the English poor law notion of "less eligibility." This rule held that assistance should relieve poverty, but should come to less than the lowest working wage.

Social Security, and later Canada's public pension system, set a new goal for public pensions. These programs promised to make up for a retiree's lost income. "By 1980," Myles (1984, 21) says, "the institution of retirement had been consolidated and old age had become a period in the life cycle defined and sustained by the welfare state."

Government now plays the major role in guaranteeing pensions to older retirees. Public pensions and transfer payments act as a deferred wage because people pay into the program through taxes and CPP/QPP payments while they work. In Canada, though, the amount a person gets does not depend only on how much they paid in. People today get "a share of the social product over and above any claims they may have possessed in their capacity as wage earners" (Myles 1984, 29). Myles calls this a citizen's wage. This wage makes retirement a time of economic security and freedom for many older people.

Schulz (1985) estimates that, without government support, workers would have to save 20 percent of their income each year just to get a pension equal to 60 to 65 percent of their earnings during the last five years before retirement. Few people could afford to save this much on their own. With government help, retirement has become an option for many more people than ever before. Statistics Canada reports that in January 1972, for example, 10.2 percent of men and women aged 65 and over worked. This figure dropped to 8.7 percent by January 1979 and to 6.9 percent in August 1986 (Statistics Canada 1972; Statistics Canada 1979b; Statistics Canada 1986b).

Men aged 65 to 69 showed the greatest decrease in labour force participation during the 1980s. Their participation rate fell by almost 27 percent from 1979 to 1989. Men aged 55 to 64 showed the second largest drop. Their participation rate fell by 15 percent (Statistics Canada 1990e). During this same time the dollar amount of government income security payments increased and more people received Canada Pension Plan pensions. The

# Exhibit 10.1

Proportion of Men and Women at Each Age Who
Were Retired in February 1975, and the Proportion
of Men at Each Age Who Had Left the Labour Force in June 1961

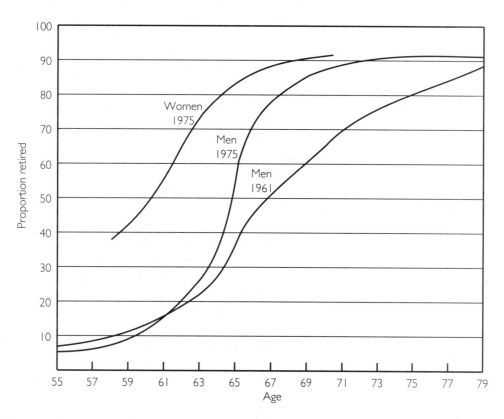

**Source:** Health and Welfare Canada, *Social Security Research Reports, Retirement in Canada: Summary Report* (Report No. 03), 5 (Ottawa: Long Range Planning Directorate, Policy Research and Long Range Planning Branch (Welfare), National Health and Welfare, 1977b). Reproduced with permission of the Minister of Supply and Services Canada, 1991.

retirement trends for the past decade support the idea that people tend to retire early if they have a good pension.

A study done by Health and Welfare Canada says that by age 60, 13 percent of men and 50 percent of women who worked sometime between age 45 and 60 had retired. By age 65, about 50 percent of men and 75 percent of

• • • • • • • • • • • • • • • • • • • • • • • • • • • • • • • • • • • •

## Exhibit 10.2

Percentage of Men and Women Aged 65 and
Over Who Were Employed, 1956–1986

• • • • • • • • • • • • • • • • • • • • • • • • • • • • • • • • • • • •

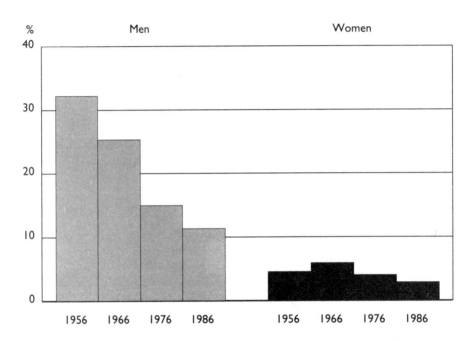

**Source:** Statistics Canada, Catalogues 71-529, *Labour Force Annual Averages*, and 71-001, *The Labour Force*, cited in Suzanne Méthot, "Employment Patterns of Elderly Canadians," *Canadian Social Trends*, Autumn 1987, 10. Reproduced with permission of the Minister of Supply and Services Canada, 1991.

• • • • • • • • • • • • • • • • • • • • • • • • • • • • • • • • • • • •

women had retired, and by age 70, about 90 percent of both groups had retired (Ciffin and Martin 1977).

Exhibit 10.1 shows that at every age after age 61, a higher proportion of men had retired in 1975 than in 1961. Ciffin and Martin (1977, 86) conclude that "there was a major shift towards earlier retirement ages between 1961 and 1975." Men shifted away from retirement at about age 70 to retirement at about age 65. Ciffin and Martin (1977, 87) predict "a further shift towards earlier retirement ages" in the future, if men have enough income. (A higher proportion of women than men had retired at all ages in 1975.)

McDonald and Wanner (1990) support this projection. They report a general trend toward lower labour force participation rates for men aged 65 and over from 1975 to 1986 (17.2 percent and 11.2 percent, respectively). Women in this age group show much lower rates of labour force participation in both 1975 and 1986 (4.4 percent and 3.6 percent, respectively) and a fairly stable rate over time. (See Exhibit 10.2.)

"In 1975," Ciffin and Martin (1977, 85) say, "age 65 clearly was 'institutionalized' with about 25 percent of men retiring at 65 and over 40 percent of the active men expecting to retire at 65. No normal retirement age existed for women." A study by Atchley (1982, 159) supports this difference in patterns of retirement for men and women. He reports that men more often than women planned to retire at a specific age and that women were more likely than men to plan to retire before age 60 or after age 70. Gee and Kimball (1987) report that pension eligibility best predicts when a woman will retire.

In Canada more women, compared to men, show a higher rate of early retirement. Many women retire because their spouse has retired. And because women often marry older men, they retire at an earlier age on average than men. They also tend to return to work after widowhood (Stryckman 1987). A Canadian study (Matthews and Tindale 1987) compared the reasons men and women retire. The researchers found that women, more often than men, retire because of the ill health of a spouse or a family member. Atchley (1982) says that these facts should "caution against relying too heavily on very general statements about women's retirement." They should also caution against using data based on male retirement patterns to draw conclusions about retirement for women.

## WHY DO PEOPLE RETIRE?

A number of personal conditions lead people to choose retirement. These include health, a spouse's decision to retire, and attitudes toward work. Social forces can also lead a person to choose retirement. These forces include: (1) mandatory retirement rules, (2) better pensions that start at age 65, and (3) a more positive societal attitude toward retirement.

### The Debate Concerning Mandatory Retirement

No federal law in Canada forces a person to retire at age 65, and no statute requires a worker to leave work at a certain age. The federal public service ended mandatory retirement in 1986 (Guppy 1989).

Still, 80 percent of pension plans, covering 72 percent of all members, used 65 as the normal retirement age (Health and Welfare Canada 1979, 119). One government report concluded that "mandatory retirement at 65 is practised by government and educational institutions, and employers in general follow this policy" (Statistics Canada 1979a, Chart 9).

The debate over mandatory retirement concerns two principles: (1) that of individual equality and justice, and (2) that of group rights (Guppy 1989). The first principle says that society should prohibit discrimination against a person on the basis of race, religion, gender, or age. The Croll Commission report, *Retirement Without Tears* (Senate of Canada 1979), used this principle in its argument against mandatory retirement, which, it said, violates the older worker's human rights. "Discriminating against people in employment because they are no longer young," the report says, "[is] clearly objectionable on social grounds. [It is] no more justifiable than discrimination because of religion" (Senate of Canada 1979, 128). The second principle says that groups have the right to a fair share of social opportunities. Affirmative action regulations are based on this principle. The debate often focuses on specific issues like the need for older workers to allow younger workers a chance to work. But beneath this and other issues lurk the conflicting principles of individual versus group rights.

The Canadian Charter of Rights and Freedoms appears to outlaw mandatory retirement based on age. The charter states in Section 15(1) that "every individual is equal before and under the law and has the right to the equal protection and equal benefit of the law without discrimination and, in particular, without discrimination based on race, national or ethnic origin, colour, religion, sex, age or mental or physical ability" (cited in Guppy 1989). But, Guppy says (1989), the charter contains other sections that make this passage unclear. For example, the charter does not regulate private conduct. So, it may not apply to private sector retirement agreements. Also, the charter protects the good of society from individual freedoms. Guppy (1989, 175) concludes that "the Charter does not ... offer a clear formula to follow in deciding the future of mandatory retirement."

On December 7, 1990, the Supreme Court of Canada ruled on a challenge to mandatory retirement brought by seven professors and a librarian in Ontario. The court ruled by a 5-2 vote in favour of mandatory retirement. The decision upheld the "constitutional viability of public service employers, including government, hospitals and universities, requiring employees to retire at age 65." The decision shows the kind of contradictions in the charter that Guppy (1989) described. The majority position written by Justice Gérard LaForest stated that mandatory retirement constitutes age discrimination and that age discrimination violates individual rights. But it allowed mandatory retirement under section one of the charter as a reasonable limitation and a "minor" infringement that will add to "the greater public good" (Canadian Association of University Teachers 1991).

• • • • • • • • • • • • • • • • • • • • • • • • • • • • • • •

## Exhibit 10.3

### Functional vs. Formal Criteria for Retirement

• • • • • • • • • • • • • • • • • • • • • • • • • • • • • • •

Mandatory retirement uses a formal criterion (a specific age) to decide when a person should retire. Critics of this approach say that people should be judged on their functional ability. People who can still do their jobs should not be forced to retire. This raises the question of how to evaluate a worker's performance. Some researchers have developed functional measures of workers' abilities that allow an employer to judge a worker's competence.

Koyl (1974) created a test called the "GULHEMP" scale (General physique, Upper extremities, Lower extremities, Hearing, Eyesight, Mentality [Intelligence], and Personality) that does this. The civil service in Canada uses this measure, and so does the de Havilland Aircraft company in Toronto. This scale, however, has its limits. Stagner (1985) says that the GULHEMP measures of intelligence and personality need to be broken down into more precise measures. Also, the GULHEMP puts too much emphasis on physical ability, given the increase in high-technology, white-collar jobs. Still, employers have used the measure with some success to place older employees in new jobs (Meier and Kerr 1976). The GULHEMP and other measures of workers' abilities could help employers find and keep the best workers for the job, regardless of the worker's age. These measures can also help older workers find work that best suits their abilities.

• • • • • • • • • • • • • • • • • • • • • • • • • • • • • • •

Employers swayed the court by claiming that an end to mandatory retirement would lead to problems in the labour force and would limit the opportunities of younger workers. The ruling did not clearly apply to the private sector, but can serve as a precedent for application to the private sector. Also, the ruling will apply in provinces like Ontario that allow mandatory retirement, but not in provinces like Manitoba, Quebec, and New Brunswick that prohibit it.

Justice Claire L'Heureux-Dubé wrote a dissenting opinion that pointed out the negative effect of mandatory retirement on women. Working women often have fewer years in the work force than men and so, have less pension coverage if they have to retire at age 65. She also pointed out that in places that have ended mandatory retirement, the new policy has had no proven negative effect: universities have kept their tenure systems; retirement plans have stayed in place; and there is no evidence of rising unemployment among young workers (Canadian Association of University Teachers 1991).

Some universities have already begun to revise their thinking on mandatory retirement at age 65. Collective agreements at York University and Carleton University, for example, have both moved retirement to age 71 (Cana-

· · · · · · · · · · · · · · · · · · · · · · · · · · · · · · · · · · · · · · ·

# Exhibit 10.4

Proportions Retiring for Various Reasons*

· · · · · · · · · · · · · · · · · · · · · · · · · · · · · · · · · · · · · · ·

| Reason for Retirement | Retired Men % | Retired Women % |
|---|---|---|
| Compulsory retirement | 29 | 11 |
| Other reasons | 29 | 39 |
| Poor health | 34 | 38 |
| Laid off | 7 | 4 |
| No answer | 2 | 8 |

*Columns do not add to 100 percent due to rounding to the nearest number.

Poor health ranks first for men and second for women as the main reason for retirement; few of these people would have kept working past age 65. Compulsory retirement affects the retirement decisions of men more often than women; women more often than men give "other reasons" for retiring. One U.S. study found that women tend to leave work when their spouse retires (Anderson, Clark, and Johnson 1980). Sometimes an older working woman will quit work to care for a sick parent or spouse.

**Source:** Health and Welfare Canada, Social Security Research Reports. *Retirement in Canada Summary Report* (report No. 03), 9 (Ottawa: Long Range Planning Directorate, Policy Research and Long Range Planning Branch (Welfare), National Health and Welfare, 1977b). Reproduced with permission of the Minister of Supply and Services.

· · · · · · · · · · · · · · · · · · · · · · · · · · · · · · · · · · · · · · ·


· · · · · · · · · · · · · · · · · · · · · · · · · · · · · · · · · · · · · · ·

# Exhibit 10.5

Summary of Major Reasons People Retire

· · · · · · · · · · · · · · · · · · · · · · · · · · · · · · · · · · · · · · ·

| Individual Reasons | Institutional Forces |
|---|---|
| Finances | Working conditions and employer policies |
| Health | Retirement age policies, pension policies, and rules |
| Attitudes to work and retirement | Societal economic conditions |
| Social supports or pressures | Historical events and social values |

**Source:** Adapted from Pauline K. Robinson, Sally Coberly, and Carolyn E. Paul, "Work and Retirement," in Robert H. Binstock and Ethel Shanas, eds., *Handbook of Aging and the Social Sciences*, 2d ed., (New York: Van Nostrand Reinhold, 1985), 513.

· · · · · · · · · · · · · · · · · · · · · · · · · · · · · · · · · · · · · · ·

dian Association of University Teachers 1991). The concern in the Supreme Court ruling about opening positions for the young through mandatory retirement, curiously comes at a time when universities face a shortage (not an overload) of young scholars. And this shortage of younger, skilled workers will appear throughout Canadian society in the years ahead. Employers may find that they have to entice older workers to stay at work (McDonald and Wanner 1990). Tindale (1991, 19) says that while "mandatory retirement will not disappear with a bang, by means of precedent-setting judicial decisions, it may well disappear with a whimper of attrition as the labour force shortage grows."

Research suggests that the continued practice of mandatory retirement will affect only a small number of workers (Dunlop 1980). The main reasons are: first, more people than ever before retire early; second, only about half of Canadian jobs have mandatory retirement regulations; and third, Gunderson and Pesando (1980) found that only 17 percent of people aged 65 and only 27 percent of those over age 65 said they retired because of mandatory retirement. The latter figures are similar to those that appeared in a Health and Welfare Canada study (1977b) (see Exhibit 10.4).

Studies in the United States and Canada (Méthot 1987; Palmore et al. 1985) report that most older workers say they do not want to work. "In March 1986," according to one report, "less than 1 percent of those 65 and over who were not in the labour force reported being available for work, compared to 6 percent of those 45 to 64 years of age" (McDonald and Wanner 1990, 69, citing Méthot 1987). Also, 85 percent of men and 79 percent of women aged 65 and over said they did not want to work full-time (McDonald and Wanner 1990, 70).

A report done by the Conference Board of Canada (Dunlop 1980, cited in McDonald and Wanner 1990) says that 70 percent of workers aged 55, who work for a company with a pension plan, will not work past age 65, and that 15 percent of these workers will die before age 65. Companies, furthermore, will lay off 6 percent of these workers, and they will not find another job. Half of the workers aged 55 will retire early either because their pension plan requires it or because of illness. A quarter of the workers will retire at age 65, and only 4 percent will work beyond age 65. A study of retirement patterns at the University of Manitoba (Flanagan 1984) (a school with no compulsory retirement) found that over 80 percent of the professional staff retired at or before age 65.

A study of 10,000 retirements in Quebec (Baillargeon 1982) found that almost 24 percent took place before age 65. Public sector employees tended to retire early because they had good financial packages, while private sector employees tended to do so due to poor health. McDonald and Wanner (1982) found a trend toward on-time or early retirement for most occupations. This trend, fuelled by improved pension plans, will lead more workers than ever before to choose retirement at or before age 65.

## Better Pensions

Studies show again and again that most workers retire as soon as they can afford to (Bixby 1976). For most Canadians this means age 65. Méthot (1987) concludes that if mandatory retirement ceased to exist, this would have little effect on the number of older workers.

At least three economic forces lead workers to retire at age 65 today. First, some workers with good pension plans may earn more money in retirement than if they keep on working. Taxes, the cost of commuting, clothes, lunches, and other work-related expenses may make work an expensive option. Second, most private pension plans begin to pay full benefits at age 65. Quinn and Burkhauser (1990) report that many occupational pension plans penalize a person for staying on past retirement age. These plans provide a strong incentive to retire. This leads many people to retire at 65 so that they can enjoy retirement while they still have good health. Third, OAS/GIS payments start at 65, as do the Canada and Quebec Pension Plan payments. A person who works past age 65 will still get these benefits, but will lose a large portion of them through higher taxes. The GIS program also discourages older people from working. In 1992 the federal government reduced the GIS by $1 for each $2 a person earned; a person who earned a provincial supplement lost the other $1 from their supplement benefits. Government policies such as these result in a 100-percent "taxbacks" on the poorest people, who get nothing for work up to the amount equal to their GIS and provincial supplements. The taxback takes money from the older person's income next year for money earned this year. This means that low-income older people, who work, risk losing next year's income supplements (as well as their salary) if they get sick or cannot find a job. These rules create a strong incentive for retirement (Burbidge and Robb 1980).

A report by Health and Welfare Canada (1979) says that most of the people who retired because of mandatory retirement felt content with when they retired. Some said they would have left work earlier if they had had the money (Pesando 1979). Only about 13 percent of retired men and 3 percent of retired women who had to retire were not satisfied with the timing of their retirement, and only 4 to 5 percent of the men would have preferred to keep on working.

Better pensions and decreased incentives to work have increased the trend toward retirement. This and increased leisure and recreational opportunities have also changed social attitudes toward retirement.

## New Attitudes Toward Retirement

Atchley (1976, 87) says that "everyone seems to know people ... who carefully planned for retirement only to become sick and die within six months after leaving their jobs." He goes on to say that, no matter what their job, he has "yet to encounter an occupational group for which retirement is related to a decline in self-reported health. It is true that many people expect retirement to adversely affect health, but very few realized their expectations."

A Canadian study by Shapiro and Roos (1982) supports this view. They studied retirees' use of health care services in Manitoba and found that retirees and workers visited the doctor for minor and serious problems at about the same rate. They conclude that "there is no evidence that retirement per se is associated with increased utilization of ambulatory physician services or admission to the hospital" (Shapiro and Roos 1982, 192).

These facts seem to have filtered down to younger workers. Atchley (1974) says that people 45 years old and over have very positive views of retirement, regardless of their age and sex. He found that only people who wanted to keep on working felt that it was unjust. In general, Canadians adjust well to retirement (Gee and Kimball 1987; MacBride 1976; McPherson and Guppy 1979). Matthews et al. (1982) found that the effect of retirement ranked 28 on a scale of 34 life events ranked from greatest effect to least effect. This study suggests that retirement has relatively little impact on most people.

Studies now show that many people prefer to retire before age 65 if they can. Stryckman (1987) reports a strong trend toward early retirement (i.e., before age 65). A Gallup poll (1984) in Canada found that 22 percent of workers said they would retire at age 65; 5 percent said they would work past age 65; and 47 percent said they intended to retire early (cited in Stryckman 1987). Stryckman (1987) reports on Quebec's attempt to encourage later retirement. Quebec in 1984 reduced QPP pensions by 6 percent per year to retirees who retired between ages 60 and 65. The plan increased QPP pensions by 6 percent per year for people who retired between ages 65 and 70. The report on the first year of this plan stated that only 2 percent of pensioners retired after age 65; 75 percent retired between aged 60 and 65; and 23 percent retired at age 60 (Stryckman 1987). Stryckman concludes that the availability of a pension, even at a reduced rate, leads to early retirement.

Statistics Canada (Lindsay 1987) reports a ten-year trend toward early retirement for workers aged 55 to 64. Labour force figures show that the number of men in this age group who had left the labour force increased by almost 200 percent from 1975 to 1985. During this same period, the total number of men in this age group increased only 23 percent.

Two types of workers tend to take early retirement: workers in poor health and those who expect a good income in retirement (McDonald and

Wanner 1990; Quinn and Burkhauser 1990). Sammartino (1987), for example, says that poor health for workers aged 60 to 67 lowers a worker's retirement age by one to three years. People also retire early because they want more leisure time and less work, and they have a positive image of retirement (Orbach 1969). Neugarten (1980) says that only a small percentage of workers (about 8 to 10 percent) fit the stereotype of the faithful worker who is forced out of work. "The evidence shows that as one gets older, the desire to continue working is clearly not as strong as it was once thought to be by many sociologists" (Schulz 1980, 199).

A survey of retirement in Canada conducted by the Canadian Pension Plan Advisory Commission (1980) found that 37 percent of men had retired early. "Of these," the report says, "58 percent had retired because of ill-health and a further 10 percent because of layoff." None of these people would have stayed at work past age 65 (1980, 17).

Some private pension plans encourage people to choose early retirement. Companies in Canada such as MacMillan Bloedel, Metropolitan Life, and General Motors sponsor early retirement plans. Early retirement allows companies to hire less costly young workers or to leave jobs empty after a retiree leaves. Imperial Oil Ltd. of Toronto says that early retirement saves as much as 30 percent of the cost of keeping an older worker on until age 65. In 1984, 68 percent of their 220 retirees retired early; on average people retired at age 58 (Finlayson 1985).

Canada's Public Service Superannuation Act allows retirement as early as age 55 with 30 years' service (Health and Welfare Canada 1979). In addition to a pension, some plans give workers a large lump sum payment to encourage early retirement, and workers tend to take these payments when companies offer them (Pesando and Rea 1977). Other pension plans in Canada allow early retirement on a reduced pension. Ninety-seven percent of pension plans covering 95 percent of their members offer this option (Health and Welfare Canada 1979). Some private plans even include a special rule allowing early retirement on an unreduced pension for a certain number of years of service or age plus service. The Canadian Pension Plan Advisory Commission (1980) reports that 12 percent of public sector plans covering well over half of their members and 3 percent of private sector plans covering 28 percent of their members offer this option.

Changes in the CPP in 1987 also encourage a more flexible retirement age. The plan now allows payments to begin as early as age 60 or as late as age 70. People who retire early get decreases in their basic pension equal to 0.5 percent for each month between the date the pension begins and the month after their sixty-fifth birthday. Retirees cannot earn more than the current maximum annual CPP pension at age 65 ($6,240 in 1987). Those who retire after age 70 receive an increase of 0.5 percent on their basic pension for every month between the date the pension begins and the month after their sixty-fifth birthdays.

Will these changes lead more people to retire early, or will they lead people to stay at work longer? No one can say yet. One thing seems certain: these changes give workers more choice in timing their retirement than ever before.

## ALTERNATIVES TO A FIXED RETIREMENT AGE

Early or delayed retirement are two options workers can choose instead of mandatory retirement at age 65. But a number of other options exist. These include flexible retirement, part-time work, and second careers.

### Flexible Retirement

Atchley (1985, 192) predicts that in the future "the small proportion [of people who do] not want to retire can expect to find it increasingly easier to stay on as long as they can still do the job." Some of these workers may choose flexible retirement. This option allows them to slowly cut back the number of hours they work each week.

A study by Health and Welfare Canada (1979) found that 38 percent of retired men and 41 percent of retired women would have preferred a part-time transition to retirement. Thirty-five percent of working men and 47 percent of working women said they preferred this option. The survey asked respondents to give their first choice for a retirement pattern with no change in pay. Forty-three percent of working men and 44 percent of working women chose a gradual shift into retirement (fewer weeks, fewer days, or fewer hours per day for the same pay). "Most of those failing to retire in the way they wanted," the report says, "were those who preferred a part-time pattern but had to work full-time until retirement" (Health and Welfare Canada 1979, 50).

Older Canadians tend to work if they have occupations that allow for choice in their retirement age and if they can work at their own pace. Two-thirds of farm workers, for example, work past age 65 and a fifth work past age 70 (Health and Welfare Canada 1982b, cited in Matthews and Tindale 1987). Snell and Brown (1987) report that people who find meaning in work and consider their work important also tend to work after retirement. This applies best to older men, who work in managerial jobs. McDonald and Wanner (1982) report that the higher a person's education level, the greater the likelihood that a person will work after age 65. Older women who work, most often work in service professions. Many older male workers worked in fishing, forestry, and mining (Matthews and Tindale 1987).

In the future more workers may be able to choose flexible retirement options. But today few workers have the option to stay on in their present jobs part-time. Paris (1989) reports that in a Canadian study 19 percent of 375 companies offered formal job sharing programs. Another 10 percent of these companies said they allowed informal job sharing.

Stryckman (1987) also proposes work sharing as an alternative to either retirement or full-time work. Work sharing spreads the available work for a position over a number of workers. This option would allow workers to work part-time in their current positions and might entice some older workers to stay at work after retirement age.

## Part-Time Work

Part-time work offers older workers an alternative to full retirement. Most people who work past age 65 choose to work part-time instead of full-time (Quinn and Burkhauser 1990). Méthot (1987, 8) reports that in 1986 "thirty percent of employed men and forty-five percent of employed women aged 65 and over worked part-time." Most of these people (85 percent of men and 79 percent of women) said they did not want full-time work. The figures for part-time older men and women have increased by about 10 percent since 1975.

A report by Health and Welfare Canada (1982b, 3) says that "opportunities to work part-time are very important to the employment of senior citizens." Some people (women without pensions, widows) want to work part-time because they need the money. Others like to work because it gives them a chance to meet new people. Sometimes a person who retired because of bad health finds that their health improves enough that they can manage a part-time job. A Canadian study (Health and Welfare Canada 1979), for example, found that 35 percent of men and 63 percent of women who retired due to ill health (about 35 percent of all retirees retire for this reason) said their health had improved. Some of these people may want to work part-time.

Older people sometimes have trouble finding work (Canadian Council on Social Development 1976b). Akyeampong (1987) reports that older unemployed workers (aged 55–64) spent an average of 31.3 weeks out of work, nine weeks longer, on average, than younger workers. The older the person, the more difficulty they will have finding work (Health and Welfare Canada 1979).

McDonald and Wanner (1990, 108) report that Canadian workers with a record of unemployment tend to get "discouraged out" of the job market.

Other workers who lose their jobs, may not find work that suits them, so they give up looking and retire. Tindale (1991) says that one recession led to 82,000 lay-offs of workers aged 55 and over. Over 40 percent of these workers stopped looking for work.

The Canadian government now sponsors Senior Citizens' Job Bureaus to help retired workers find part-time work, or other working arrangements that suit their needs. Seniors who leave Canada for the winter sometimes want seasonal work (like gardening) or short-term jobs (like office help). The Winnipeg Senior Citizens' Job Bureau, in the first eight months of 1986, for example, got requests for almost 16,000 jobs (most of them for casual work). The bureau filled over 13,000 of these requests (Senior Citizens' Job Bureau 1986).

## Second Careers

Some people retire to a "second career." Job bureaus for seniors report, for example, that teachers sometimes want to work as cabinet makers; accountants want to work as painters; and homemakers want to work in an office or a retail store. Neugarten (1980, 74) says that "many business executives become engaged in community affairs in the last years of their employment and find it relatively easy to move into those areas after they retire." These people work at second careers for more than the money. A second career allows them to develop skills they could not use when they worked full-time.

Tournier (1972, 129) calls a second career "a free career." A second career, he says, differs from leisure and from the kind of work a person does in middle age. "It has a goal, a mission, and that implies organization, loyalty, and even priority over other more selfish pleasures—not in line of duty, since professional obligations are not involved, but for the love of people. It is, therefore, not an escape, but a presence in the world" (1972, 130). A second career, Tournier says, grows out of interests that lay dormant or undeveloped in middle age. A saleswoman at The Bay, for example, spent her weekends cooking traditional Ukrainian food for her family. When she retired from work she began a career as volunteer kitchen director at her local senior centre. The work gives her a sense of purpose and allows her to use her talents in a new way.

Tournier (1972, 136) also calls a second career a "personal career" because "one has to formulate one's own aim, choose one's own method of work, set one's own daily task and assert one's identity in one's work." A bus driver began a second career as an actor when he joined a seniors' theatre group, and an electrician began a second career as a public figure when a seniors' club elected him president. These people became resources in their communities, and their second careers brought meaning and purpose to their retirement.

## ADJUSTMENT TO RETIREMENT

Social class and occupational structures determine some of the options a person will have in retirement. But retirement is also a personal choice and a social process. Atchley, for example, describes eight phases of retirement. Atchley modelled his stages of the retirement process on **continuity theory**. This approach emphasizes the continuity between the person's pre- and post-retirement life. It presents an alternative to the idea that retirement comes as a crisis in later life Atchley cautions that these phases "represent a device for making it easier to view retirement as a process, not as an inevitable sequence that everyone must go through" (1985, 196). These stages give some idea of the changes a person undergoes when they leave the labour force. They describe the changing relationship between the individual and social structures as well as the methods people use to cope with these changes.

***Phase 1: Pre-Retirement***   This phase has two stages—a near and a remote stage. The remote stage takes place many years before retirement. A person may start an RRSP in their forties or buy a piece of land in the country for a future retirement home.

In the near stage people get ready to leave their jobs. They check on pension payments, fill out the necessary forms, and train someone to take over their job. They also worry about their future income and their health. Atchley, Kunkel, and Adlon (1978) report that people create detailed fantasies of retirement and that those with unrealistic retirement plans have some of the worst problems when they retire. In one case a man bought some land for his retirement on an island off the coast of British Columbia. He fantasized about his retirement, seeing it as a return to nature and imagined himself roaming around the island bird-watching, taking pictures of animals, and collecting mushrooms. His dream turned into a nightmare when he told his wife about his plans. "I have no intention of leaving my sister and my bridge club and moving into the woods," she said. "You can go yourself if that's what you want. But count me out." This man spent the first two years of his retirement coping with his anger and disappointment.

***Phase 2: The Honeymoon***   A euphoric time for most people. They do all the things they never had time for. People with enough money often travel during this phase, taking cruises and long winter vacations.

***Phase 3: The Retirement Routine***   When they get back from their trip to Hawaii people begin to find a stable routine. This might include an exercise program a few times a week, part-time work, volunteer work, or study. People will keep this routine if they find it satisfying. Some people keep as busy a schedule as they had before they retired, often complaining about all their appointments and saying they plan to slow down. These busy people choose the amount of activity they find satisfying. Other retirees like to take things slower; they disengage from social obligations, such as volunteer board memberships, and schedule more time for socializing with friends and leisure.

***Phase 4: Rest and Relaxation***   Some people cut back their activity at first, then gradually increase it until they find a schedule that suits them. One man withdrew from all his service clubs and board memberships just after he retired. He and his wife travelled and then settled in a new city. There he started a part-time job and got involved in community service again.

***Phase 5: Disenchantment***   Matthews et al. (1982) says that in a Canadian study retirees did not report retirement as a critical life event compared with others like the death of a spouse. But, results differed for men and women. While men said that 73 percent of other events had more of an effect on them than retirement, women said that 85 percent of events were more critical. (Matthews and Brown 1987). Still, some people (almost half) said that retirement had a strong effect on them.

McDonald and Wanner (1990, 73) say that "what little research there is suggests that retirement is not a crisis for everyone, but it does affect some people negatively." Atchley (1976) found, in a cross-sectional study, that less than 10 percent of retirees feel this way. A study by Ekerdt, Bossé, and Levkoff (1985) found high life-satisfaction among retirees six months after retirement. But they found a decrease in life-satisfaction in men between thirteen and eighteen months after retirement. This drop in satisfaction passed after the first year and a half.

A crisis in a person's life at the time of retirement, like the death of a spouse or a sudden drop in income, can lead to disenchantment with retirement. In one case a man retired early so he could open a small art gallery in a resort. He found that after he moved to the resort his pension did not allow him to keep up his pre-retirement lifestyle. He was forced to get a part-time job as the manager of a small restaurant, and felt frustrated and sorry that he retired when he did.

***Phase 6: Reorientation***   People who feel disenchanted need to take stock and pull themselves together. Family and friends can help, and, in time, most people reorient themselves and adjust to retirement.

***Phase* 7: *Routine*** Many people move into this stable, enjoyable phase right after the honeymoon phase. Sociologists say these people "take up the retirement role." The **retirement role** specifies the rights and obligations a person has in retirement. A person has the right, for example, to collect a pension, but is also obliged not to work full-time. Atchley (1985, 196) says that people who adjust to this phase "know what is expected of them and they know what they have to work with—what their capabilities and limitations are. They are self-sufficient adults, going their own way, managing their own affairs."

***Phase* 8: *Termination*** A person needs independence and good health to play the retirement role. This role ends when a person returns to work or when illness or disability takes away their independence.

A number of studies have tested Atchley's stages to see how well they fit the reality of retirement. At least three studies—one in the U.S., one in Norway, and one in Canada—suggest the existence of a honeymoon phase and a disenchantment phase in retirement (Haynes, McMichael, and Tyroler 1977; Solem 1976; Adams and Lefebvre 1980). These studies all based their conclusions on mortality rates after retirement. All three report no sudden rise in mortality rates immediately after retirement, but a rise was seen about three years after retirement (the disenchantment phase). Mortality rates serve as a crude measure of response to retirement and probably reflect only the most extreme cases of disenchantment. More subtle measures are needed to determine whether most retirees follow the pattern Atchley describes.

Atchley's model, even if it proves accurate, will likely apply most to one type of worker: the middle-class, Anglo-Saxon male worker who retires at age 65. Roadburg (1985), for example, says that this model does not describe the pattern of someone who retires early. Roadburg found that many early retirees want to go back to work. He also found that, even after age 81, about half his subjects wanted to go back to work. These people missed the social contacts that work provided, and they wanted something to do.

## PRE-RETIREMENT EDUCATION (PRE)

People often retire without any help, but research shows that pre-retirement education can help people avoid problems and set goals for themselves (Bond and Bond 1980). For example, people who want a second career (or even those who want flexible retirement or part-time work) stand the best chance of success if they plan their retirement in advance. A study of retirement in Alberta found that people who planned for it had the greatest satisfaction when they retired (Perry 1980). Matthews and Brown (1987) found that people who chose the timing of their retirement reported the most satisfaction. Szinovacz (1982) found that women who planned for retirement, and especially women who carried out their plans, reported high retirement satisfaction.

PRE programs can give support to people who already have positive attitudes to retirement. These people say they are most interested in, and benefit most from, early knowledge about pensions and income. Workers also report an interest in how to stay healthy and active and how to find part-time work (Atchley, Kunkel, and Adlon 1978; Pitts 1983).

PRE programs share some basic goals. First, they educate workers about early retirement, investment options, and pension benefits. Second, they help workers and their spouses plan for changes in their relationship after retirement (Keating and Cole 1980). Third, PRE programs help people carry out their plans. They can put workers in touch with investment counsellors or help individuals sort out their goals.

Do PRE programs work? Research has shown mixed results (Health and Welfare Canada 1979; Bond and Bond 1980). Some studies have shown that they help reduce stress and decrease negative attitudes to retirement (Cox and Bhak 1978–79; Kaplan 1979). Barfield and Morgan (1974) report that PRE improved workers' sense of satisfaction with retirement (Barfield and Morgan 1974). Other authors are more critical. McDonald and Wanner (1990, 76) say that "it is not clear that they benefit participants." Atchley (1981, 82) says that most of these programs "are in a rut."

PRE programs cannot eliminate all of the challenges people will face as they enter retirement. But they can offer a modest amount of support and direction. Atchley (1981) says that PRE should be a part of long-range career planning. This makes more sense than a rush to prepare a few years (or months) before retirement.

The Croll Commission report says that "much more should be done to devise and implement effective [PRE] programs in this country" (Senate of Canada 1979, 119) and for good reason, according to Gherson (1980), who says that, "Of all employees now aged 55 and working with an employer with a pension plan, 71 percent will never work past 65 and 50 percent will retire early, either because of early retirement provisions or illness ...." Retirement has become a normal part of adult life for many Canadians.

Tindale (1991, 25) puts the issue of PRE in the broad context of "managing an aging work force." He says that workers should have PRE throughout their careers. This type of program would include information about promotions, job changes, retraining and education, family changes, and flexible retirement (Morrison 1984).

## WOMEN AND RETIREMENT

Connidis (1982) found that women follow different career paths than men. Some take up careers after raising a family; others work during their child-rearing years; some never enter the labour force; and many single women show unbroken work records (Keating and Jeffrey 1983). This variety makes it hard to describe a typical pattern of retirement for women. Few studies have looked at how women adjust to retirement or at what retirement means to them. The studies that have focused on women show diverse patterns among women subjects and large differences between women and men. Atchley (1982) says that different factors shape male and female attitudes to retirement, and different factors lead to life-satisfaction for each group. He concludes that "women's retirement is indeed a separate issue compared to men's" (1982, 165). In the past, Beeson (1975) says, researchers have treated women's retirement as a non-event. Szinovacz (1982) says that until 1975 the annual Gerontological Society of America meetings contained almost no discussion of women's retirement. This has begun to change as more women have started working outside the home (Szinovacz 1983). Researchers have begun to study women's transitions to retirement as a normative event.

Szinovacz (1983), for instance, says that changes in the work patterns of women make their retirement experience similar to that of men. Gauthier (1991) reports, for example, that more women today have occupational pensions than in the past. And he expects the proportion of women with occupational pensions to grow in the future. Szinovacz (1983) says that many women now have long, continuous work records (fifteen or more years) and a strong commitment to work, and they may feel a sense of loss when they retire. Retirement for a woman means the loss of work colleagues, the loss of contact with customers and clients, and the loss of social role.

It may also mean a big drop in income, because many women have no pension plan. Women with a strong work commitment, who have many social contacts at work, and who have low incomes, have the most negative views of retirement. They also have the strongest incentive to work (Nishio and Lank 1987). Szinovacz (1983) reports that women have different retirement needs than men. Women need programs that foster social contact and programs that offer leisure activities. McDaniel (1989) and Johnson and Williamson (1987) call for more research on women and retirement.

## NEW DIRECTIONS IN RESEARCH

Retirement research has taken some new directions. Bertaux (1981) reports on retirement for dual career couples. O'Rand (1990) reports that dual career couples fall into several categories. In most cases one spouse retires before the other, and only 20 percent of the time do they do so together. Spouses rely on pension eligibility to decide when to retire. Research has also found a return to the labour force for many of these couples. More longitudinal research on two-earner couples should study the retirement decisions couples make in response to pension eligibility, economic conditions, and marital status (e.g. widowhood).

Studies have begun to look at how life changes in other family members (sickness of a spouse or parent, marriage of children, or widowhood) affect women's careers and retirement patterns. The study of retirement will change as retirement itself changes. As more women enter the labour force, as more single women enter old age, and as better pensions make retirement an established part of adult life, social structures and individual responses to retirement will change. This will lead to new research approaches and new ideas about later life.

## CRITIQUE OF THE RETIREMENT LITERATURE

McDonald and Wanner (1990) review a wide range of theoretical perspectives on retirement. Micro-level theories like disengagement, activity, and continuity theory each prescribe a different model for a good old age: disengage from activity, stay active in new pursuits, or maintain middle-aged activities. But these theories have some common themes. All of them: (1) assume that retirement will bring a decrease in social activity; (2) focus on individual responses to retirement; and (3) assume that retirement will cause problems and that people need to adjust to live a happy life. "Most importantly," McDonald and Wanner (1990, 9) say, each of these theories view retirement "as a problem caused and solved by individual behavior."

Macro-level theories like modernization theory (Cowgill 1974) and age stratification theory (Riley, Johnson, and Foner 1972) take social structures into account. Modernization theory explains that retirement arises when a society industrializes and technology puts older people out of work. Older people then have lower incomes and lower social status. Age stratification theory describes retirement as a role that a person plays in later life. This theory assumes that members of each age cohort will enter retirement and play this role. Like the micro theories, these theories take a functionalist view of retirement. They see it as an inevitable part of modern social life. And they assume that the individual must move through this role as a normal part of the life course (McDonald and Wanner 1990).

Both micro- and macro-level theories place responsibility for coping with the retirement role on the individual. They take the social structure as given and unchangeable and expect the person to adapt. A failure to retire well amounts to a personal failure. Programs like pre-retirement education can help a person adapt, but PRE programs seldom question the social structures that create or shape retirement. And they do not criticize the social structures that allow some people to retire easily, while others struggle in old age.

**Political economy theory**, on the other hand, looks at the sociocultural conditions that shape aging. This perspective sees retirement as the outcome of "economic, political, and social structures" that existed before retirement (McDonald and Wanner 1990, 14). These include beliefs about older workers, the kinds of jobs people have, their salaries, and their opportunities to save or take part in a pension plan.

Gee and Kimball (1987) apply this perspective to a review of a study by Kaye and Monk (1984) on male and female university retirees. The study found that women did more volunteer work in retirement; men did more teaching and research. Kaye and Monk (1984) interpreted this finding to mean that men have greater opportunity or interest in continuing to work after retirement. Gee and Kimball (1987) emphasize that personal motivation explains only part of the difference in male and female retirement activities. More of the women in this sample had worked as university administrators, more of the men had been professors. Gee and Kimball (1987) say that the women in this study may have had little opportunity to continue their administrative work except as volunteers, whereas the men could carry on their research and teaching after retirement within the university structure. The difference in male and female retirement activity probably reflects the different structural opportunities open to these two groups.

This interpretation emphasizes the social forces that affect individual behaviour. The political economy perspective offers "a very useful adjunct to individual explanations ... and holds considerable promise for expanding our understanding of retirement" (McDonald and Wanner 1990, 14).


# RETIREMENT AND SOCIAL STRUCTURES

## Social Class and Retirement Options

Tournier, in his discussion of second careers, says that before some people can take up a second career they will need "sufficient resources ... for them no longer to have to earn their living" (1972, 134). Guillemard (1977) agrees, arguing that second careers and other options like volunteer work, best fit the lifestyles and backgrounds of middle-class workers (executives, technicians, or engineers). These people form a new privileged group in society. They have good pensions, good health, and higher aspirations than working class retirees. They may also have the verbal or technical skills that volunteer organizations or community groups value and need. Guillemard raises the issue of unequal opportunity in retirement.

Discussions about retirement preparation obscure the issue of pension adequacy. Studies show again and again that people will retire if they have a good pension. A study in Quebec (Baillargeon 1982), for example, found that men in both the public and private sectors with indexed pensions had a good attitude to retirement. Baillargeon (1982) and Atchley (1971a, 1971b) report that half of higher-level workers look forward to retirement.

Studies show that a person with a good income and a middle-class or upper-middle-class occupation stands a good chance of being satisfied with retirement.[1] People with money have more of a chance to take part in leisure activity, while people with poor pensions and no savings may not be able to retire at all. Middle-class and upper-middle-class workers (white-collar workers, managers, professionals) with orderly work careers (few layoffs or job changes) report high satisfaction in retirement (Simpson, Back, and McKinney 1966).

Studies also show that people with the most education and the highest incomes, married men and single women tended to find or keep work after age 65 (McDonald and Wanner 1990). Women, more than men, reported that they worked because of financial need (McDonald and Wanner 1982). Quinn (1981) studied men 58 to 63 years old. He reports that about a third of the men on salary or wages worked part-time, while 60 percent of self-employed men (many of them professionals) worked part-time. Health and Welfare Canada (1982b) reports that older men with university degrees, for example, have four times the labour force participation rate of older men with less than Grade 5 education. Older women with university degrees have five times the participation rate of older women with less than grade 5. Professionals such as doctors, lawyers, and professors can work as consultants or work part-time at their careers (Health and Welfare Canada 1982b; McDonald and Wanner 1990).

A study of fifty-eight older physicians in Quebec found that 93 percent of them still worked in their practices and 65 percent said they had no plans for retirement, even though they averaged 71.54 years of age (Grauer and Campbell 1983). A report by Statistics Canada (1986b) on husbands and wives in the top percentile of families by income showed that at every age more husbands and wives in these families work compared with all families, and that this gap between the top percentile and other families in the proportion of those working grows with age. In 1980, for example, in all families in which both husbands and wives were aged 65 and over, 25 percent of the husbands and 7 percent of the wives worked. In high-income families with both spouses aged 65 and over, 69 percent of the men and 21 percent of the women worked. Statistics Canada (1986b, 104) says that in high-income families people worked "well beyond the normal age of retirement." Even at ages 75 and over almost half of the high-income men and more than 10 percent of the high-income women still work (Statistics Canada 1986b). The fact that they work puts these people in the high-income group, but also the kinds of work they do—running their own companies or working as independent professionals—allow them to ease out of work at their own pace. In sum, good income predicts that a person can and will retire. But independent professionals, even though they have a good income, often choose to continue working.

## SOCIAL STRUCTURES AND RETIREMENT OPTIONS

Dowd (1980) says that social structures and economic conditions, more than personal preferences, explain why people retire when they do. Dowd (1980, 77) divides the economy into two sectors: "one sector is highly organized and characterized by high wages and pension systems, and the other is marked by low wages and few, if any fringe benefits." Exhibit 10.6 shows the effect of social structure on the chances of getting a private pension. It shows that workers in the core sector stand a better chance of getting a private pension than workers on the periphery (see also McDonald and Wanner 1987). Calasanti (1988) found that, due to this inequity, periphery retirees have a greater concern about satisfaction with finances. This reflects "the monetary struggles they have experienced throughout their lives" (Calasanti 1988, 22).

In Canada women more often than men work in the peripheral sector—45.8 percent of all women workers provide services; 17.9 percent are in trade occupations; and 2.9 percent work in agriculture (Labour Canada 1986). These occupations often have no mandatory retirement rules, and they allow for easy entry, flexible hours, and part-time work (Robinson, Coberly, and Paul, 1985). At the same time, these occupations pay less than core occupations, and in general they offer fewer private pensions. This gives women fewer choices than men when it comes time to retire. McDonald and Wanner (1984), for example, found that single women have one of the lowest rates of early retirement in Canada. They say this probably reflects their concentration in occupations with lower incomes and poorer pensions" (1984, 108). They go on to show (1984, 114) that poorer people of either sex tend not to retire early.

- - - - - - - - - - - - - - - - - - - - - - - - - - - - - - - - - - - - - - - - - - -

# Exhibit 10.6

Private Pension Plan Coverage of Paid Workers by
Industry and Sex, Canada, December 1987

- - - - - - - - - - - - - - - - - - - - - - - - - - - - - - - - - - - - - - - - - - -

| Industry | Pension Plan Members as % of Paid Workers | | | Women as % of all Pension Plan Members |
|---|---|---|---|---|
|  | Women | Men | Total |  |
| **Core** |  |  |  |  |
| Mines, quarries, oil wells | 51.0 | 69.6 | 67.0 | 11.0 |
| Construction | 12.9 | 35.9 | 33.3 | 4.3 |
| Manufacturing | 36.7 | 59.7 | 53.0 | 20.0 |
| Transportation and communications | 61.2 | 71.8 | 69.0 | 23.6 |
| Finance, insurance/real estate | 50.8 | 53.0 | 51.6 | 61.7 |
| Public administration | 70.9 | 83.9 | 78.9 | 34.6 |
| **Periphery** |  |  |  |  |
| Agriculture | * | 52.8 | 47.9 | * |
| Trade | 19.6 | 31.8 | 26.1 | 35.4 |
| Community, business, and personal service | 38.8 | 43.4 | 40.4 | 61.6 |

*Sample inadequate for reliable estimate.

As a percentage of paid workers, a higher percentage of men compared with women belong to a pension plan (this is true for both sectors). Except for construction and manufacturing, the core industries, compared with the peripheral industries, have higher percentages of the total labour force in pension plans. Women have less chance to get private pensions because more than two-thirds of them work in the peripheral sector. Except in real estate and personal service occupations, women make up fewer than half of all pension plan members.

**Source:** Adapted from Women's Bureau, Labour Canada, *Women in the Labour Force, 1990–91 Edition.* Labour Canada Cat. No. L016-1728/90E (Ottawa: Minister of Supply and Services Canada, 1990), Table 9. Reproduced with permission of the Minister of Supply and Services Canada, 1991.

- - - - - - - - - - - - - - - - - - - - - - - - - - - - - - - - - - - - - - - - - - -

Today, not all Canadians have an income or occupation that produces a satisfactory retirement. Greater equality in retirement opportunity will come only with a decrease in the social inequities based on class and gender.

Orbach (1981, 126) sums up the research on retirement today. "One would have to conclude," he says,

> that most persons today have a generally positive attitude toward retirement as a future status, and are more likely to strongly exhibit this attitude the higher their expected retirement income, the better their health, the greater their educational and occupational level and attainment, and the less they find work to be the major or only source of intrinsic satisfaction in life ...

The variety within the older population based on differences in gender, social class, age, and so on, leads to varied responses to work in later life. People can have full- or part-time work, full retirement, second careers, etcetera. This variety suggests that retirement needs further study and that "the term 'retirement' may well conceal more than it reveals" (Quinn and Burkhauser 1990, 320).

## SUMMARY

1. Most people want to retire, and they retire as early as they can if they have a good pension.

2. Some people want to continue working, and they have challenged compulsory retirement rules in court. The Supreme Court of Canada has supported compulsory retirement, except in provinces that prohibit it.

3. Arguments over mandatory retirement may suggest that most workers want to work past age 65, but studies show that if their health is poor or a good income awaits them most people will leave work before age 65. People now accept retirement as a reward they have earned for years of work, and they will want to collect that reward as soon as they can.

4. Canadians now have more choice about when they retire and what pattern of retirement to follow. Some people take full retirement at age 65, others work part-time, and still others start second careers. In the future, older workers may have the option of flexible retirement.

5. A good income gives retirees the most options and the best chance to plan for and enjoy retirement.

6. Some studies of retirement show that retirees adjust to retirement in stages. New theories of retirement and new research approaches may emerge as more women retire from the labour force.

**7.** Retirement research has focused in the past on how individuals cope with retirement. A sociostructural view of retirement links individual behaviour to social and economic inequities in society. More research needs to be done on the effects of gender, educational background, and socioeconomic status on retirement.

## SELECTED READINGS

McDonald, P. Lynn, and Richard A. Wanner. *Retirement in Canada.* Toronto: Butterworths, 1990.

A comprehensive review of the Canadian literature on retirement. This book discusses current theories and looks at the social history of retirement as well as how people respond to it. The book presents an excellent discussion of the way social structures influence individual experience.

Myles, John. *Old Age in the Welfare State: The Political Economy of Public Pensions.* Boston: Little, Brown and Company, 1984.

One of the few Canadian studies in the field of aging that takes a political economy perspective. The author presents a sociohistorical view of retirement. He compares retirement in a variety of industrial societies, develops a typology of pension systems, and discusses poverty and social inequality in modern society. A thought-provoking book about how society shapes the experience of aging.

Roadburg, Alan. *Aging: Retirement, Leisure and Work in Canada.* Toronto: Methuen, 1985.

This book gives an overview of the Canadian pension system. It then describes the results of a study on retirement conducted by the author. The book presents cases of how people respond to retirement and quotations from them about their experience.

## NOTES

[1]The term "social class" refers to both the market condition and work situation of a worker. The market condition refers to the pay, security, and opportunity for promotion of a job. The work situation refers to the tasks a person does, the social relations between workers and managers, and the control systems in a workplace. This definition assumes that the market rewards and the working conditions get better as a person moves from a lower to a higher social class (Abercrombie, Hill, and Turner 1984).

# Housing and Transportation

# INTRODUCTION

Lydia Wosk, 73, lives alone in her own home—a one-and-a-half-storey wood frame house just outside the downtown core. She has only a half-block walk to the bus, and she goes downtown almost every day. Three times a week she rides out to the university for classes. Lydia's husband died seven years ago of a sudden heart attack. The loss left Lydia in shock. One Sunday, about six months after the funeral, her three sons and their wives came over for dinner. "Mom," her oldest son said, "we've been thinking. You don't need a house this big. And you're all alone. Why not move in with us? You could live part of the year with each of us so you wouldn't have to worry about being a burden on anyone."

"I knew what they were planning," Lydia says. "So I was ready. This is my house,' I told them, I own it. I paid for it. And this is where I'm going to stay.' "

Lydia's house gives her more than just a place to live. It gives meaning to her life. The wall over the TV, for example, holds pictures of her children and grandchildren. The couch and chairs all have hand-crocheted covers she made herself. She says the couch reminds her of the times she and her husband used to watch hockey together on Saturday nights.

A home allows older people like Lydia to feel more independent (Rutman and Freedman 1988). Rutman and Freedman (1988, 24) studied older apartment dwellers and found that home meant "comfort, familiarity, security and independence." It also meant a place where they had control and where they could express their individuality. "I love my home," one woman said simply in a letter to the Ontario Advisory Council on Senior Citizens. "I live alone," another woman said, "but I am never lonely. I like baking, and my door is always open to visitors. I am never too busy to make them a cup of tea with a scone and black currant jelly" (Ontario Advisory Council on Senior Citizens 1978, 1980–81).

Not all older people need or want to live in a single-family house. Some older people live in apartments; others live with their children; still others live in sheltered housing (where they get help with meals and cleaning); and some live in rooming houses. The kind of housing that an older person needs depends on their health, marital status, income, and lifestyle. A single-family house, for example, demands good health, knowledge about home repairs, and enough income to pay for heat and taxes. An apartment demands less know-how and less worry about heating costs. An apartment with meals served in a common dining room helps people too frail to prepare their own meals. A nursing home cares for people too ill to care for themselves. People's housing needs change as they age. Havens (1980, 218–19) found that housing

• • • • • • • • • • • • • • • • • • • • • • • • • • • • • • • • • • • • •

# Exhibit 11.1

## Continuum of Housing by Degree of Independence

• • • • • • • • • • • • • • • • • • • • • • • • • • • • • • • • • • • • •

| Housing Type | Criteria |
|---|---|
| *Independent Household* | |
| Fully Independent (approx. 87% of Canadians aged 65 and over) | Self-contained and self-sufficient; resident does 90% of housework. Includes house, apartment, townhouse, duplex, condominium |
| Supported Independent Living (4% of Canadians aged 65 and over) | Self-contained but some help with chores (e.g., Meals-on-Wheels, Homemaker Services). Sheltered or enriched housing. Cooking and household chores may be part of community life (e.g., communal dining room). |
| *Dependent Living* | |
| Collective Dwellings (9% of Canadians aged 65 and over) | |
| Hotels and Rooming Houses (2% of Canadians aged 65 and over) | Serviced dwellings may provide meals and housekeeping services. |
| Personal care home, Home for the Aged, or Nursing Home (7% of Canadians aged 65 and over) | Not self-contained, not self-sufficient. Personal care help in health care, grooming, bathing, and household work. |

This chart shows that the need for support increases as people's ability to care for themselves decreases. A good system gives people the support they need, while allowing them to do as much for themselves as they can.

**Source:** Adapted from Satya Brink, "Housing Elderly People in Canada: Working Towards a Continuum of Housing Choices Appropriate to Their Needs," in Gloria Gutman and Norman Blackie, eds., *Innovations in Housing and Living Arrangements for Seniors* (Burnaby, B.C.: Gerontology Research Centre, Simon Fraser University, 1985), 17. Reproduced with permission of Simon Fraser University Press.

• • • • • • • • • • • • • • • • • • • • • • • • • • • • • • • • • • • • •

ranked as the second highest unmet need for women aged 65 to 79, the third-highest unmet need for women aged 80 to 84, and the fourth- or fifth-highest unmet need for women aged 85 and over. Housing declines as an unmet need with age in part because more very old people, compared to younger old people, live in institutions.

Canada's housing system today allows older people many choices about where to live. Housing options include private houses, apartments, congregate housing, homes for the elderly, and nursing homes (see Exhibit 11.1). All of these housing options have a place in the housing market.

This chapter will look at (1) the housing options available to older people, (2) the programs and policies that exist in Canada to help older people meet their housing needs, and (3) transportation systems that enable older people to keep in touch with their community and use the resources available to them.

## AN ECOLOGICAL MODEL OF HOUSING

Lawton and Nahemow (1973) created an "ecological model" that describes the relationship between the older person and his or her environment. Their model describes the interrelation of two variables: individual capability (competence) and the demands of the environment (environmental press). Lawton and Nahemow define **capability** as the aggregate of a person's abilities, including health, psychological adjustment, and intelligence. They define **environmental demand** as environmental forces that, combined with need, lead a person to make a response (1973, 659). A person feels the most comfort when their capability matches the demands of the environment and they can fulfil their needs. Too great or too little environmental demand leads to a decreased feeling of well-being and a maladaptive response (see also Schooler 1990). A healthy person in a hospital bed, for example, will feel bored and lethargic because the environment demands too little. A person recovering from a stroke may feel fatigued after a ten-minute conversation because the conversation demands too much from them. The Lawton-Nahemow model says that people try to find a comfortable fit between what they can do and what they need to do to meet their needs (see Exhibit 11.2).

Parmelee and Lawton (1990) propose an updated version of the person-environment fit model. This revised model redefines the competence dimension as "autonomy" and redefines the environmental press dimension as "security." An autonomous person (one with high competence) can pursue their own goals with their own resources. They have a freedom of choice and action. A secure environment (one with little press) can help a person to achieve their goals if they have some disability. A secure environment offers dependable physical and social resources. Autonomy and security, Parmelee and Lawton (1990, 466) say, "form a dialectic that lies at the heart of person-environment relations in late life." An increase in security, for example, a move to a nursing home, puts limits on a person's autonomy. Likewise, greater autonomy, like driving a car, entails some risk.

# Exhibit 11.2
## The Lawton-Nahemow Ecological Model

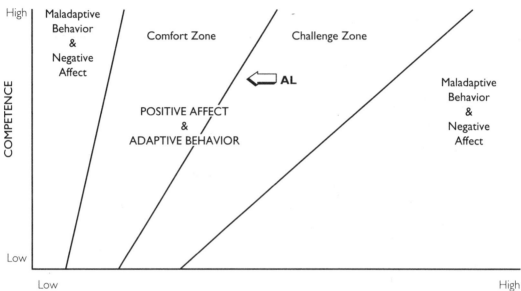

The ecological model posits that "when a person of a given level of competence behaves in an environment of a given press level" the result could be placed on a chart like the one above (Lawton 1980, 11). The chart shows the results of the fit between a person's competence and environmental press in terms of the person's behaviour and their affect (feeling). The model shows that varied combinations of competence and press can lead to adaptive behaviour and positive affect. Likewise the model shows that improvement in person-environment fit can take place on two dimensions: the person can move to or create a less demanding environment; the person can improve his or her competence; or they can do both.

The chart also illustrates the following points:

1. The mid-point of the chart (AL) represents average press at a given level of competence. To the immediate left of the mid-point is the "comfort zone" where a person feels most at ease.

2. As press increases adaptation takes place until the press goes beyond the person's ability to adapt (the right diagonal).

3. If a press decreases below the adaptation level, a person will feel bored and anxious (the left diagonal).

4. The "challenge zone" represents the points where press encourages the maximum use of a person's ability.

5. The greater the competence, the greater the adaptive ability; the lower the competence, the lower the adaptive ability.

6. No matter how high a person's competence, at some level of press they will lose the ability to adapt. No matter how low a person's competence, they still have some adaptive ability.

7. A person with low competence can be easily upset by even a small increase in press. But a person with low competence can benefit from even a small improvement in the environment (Lawton 1980).

**Source:** M.P. Lawton and L. Nahemow, "Ecology and the Aging Process," in C. Eisdorfer and M.P. Lawton eds., *Psychology of Adult Development and Aging* (Washington: American Psychological Association, 1973). Reproduced with permission.

Housing and transportation should maximize autonomy but provide enough security for a feeling of comfort. Loss of a spouse, changes in a person's informal supports, and illness may all lead to changes in a person's autonomy. And this may lead to changes in their housing needs. Some people will need help in order to feel secure. Help can include home maintenance, financial aid, and changes that adapt the environment to fit the person's level of autonomy. Housing options offer different balances between autonomy and security. The most suitable choice will depend on the older person's ability, and this will change over time.

The current approach to housing for older people in Canada focuses on "aging in place" (Blackie 1986, 5). This policy attempts to provide older people with environmental, social, and economic supports so that they can stay in their own homes. But, as Parmelee and Lawton (1990) point out, a move from one type of housing to another may offer the best autonomy-security balance.

This chapter uses the ecological model to look at the housing and transportation options that exist for older people. An ideal housing system would help people match their ability to the environment's demands. It would help them to stay where they are as long as they want to stay there, and it would allow a smooth movement from one setting to another when a change in a person's ability or needs makes a move necessary.

## LIVING ARRANGEMENTS

Living arrangements refer to the type of household a person lives in. This can include living in an institution, living with a spouse, living with grown children, living with relatives or non-relatives, or living alone. Older Canadians live in all of these types of arrangements. But the figures differ for men and for women. Statistics Canada reports that in 1986, 81.7 percent of men aged 65 to 74 lived in family households compared with 60.4 percent of women in this age group. Of the men aged 65 to 74 in 1986, 11.8 percent lived alone compared with 30.4 percent of women in this age group. About 3 percent of both men and women in this age group in 1986 lived in institutions (Statistics Canada 1990e).

One of the most dramatic changes in living arrangements over the past several decades has been the increase in the proportion of older people, particularly women, who live alone. Ram (1990) reports that the number of men aged 65 and over who lived alone increased by 142 percent from 1961 to 1986 (see also Priest 1988). Wister (1985, 127) calls this an "unprecedented rise in single person living among seniors." Béland (1987) reports a similar trend for the province of Quebec. He says that the number of older people who lived alone more than tripled in Quebec between 1956 and 1976, going from 5.6 percent to 19.1 percent. This corresponds to a drop in the proportion of older people who lived with family members. Béland says that a decrease in the number of children older people might move in with may account for this trend. He also links the increase in people living alone to the norms of independence and autonomy. People who live with their children, he says, "are mostly women, very old, widowed, ill, and suffering from some functional incapacities" (Béland 1987, 797; Béland 1984b).

Men and women aged 75 and over, compared with people aged 65 to 74, show even more dramatic differences in the tendency to live alone. Two-thirds (66.2%) of men aged 75 and over lived in families in 1986, either with their wives or with never-married children. Only a third (34.2%) of women in this age group lived in families in that year. Less than a fifth (17%) of men aged 75 and over lived alone in 1986; but more than a third (38.4%) of women in this age group lived alone in that year (up by 2.5% from 1981) (Statistics Canada 1990). A report from Statistics Canada (Stone and Frenken 1988) shows a slowdown in the trend toward living alone among elderly women for younger age groups (65–85 years) (Stone and Frenken 1988). This corresponds to a decline in widowhood rates. Still, elderly women make up 77 percent of all older people who live alone (Canadian Social Trends 1989).

Three things explain this trend toward women living alone. First, demographic changes and social norms make it more likely that a woman, rather than a man, will live alone in old age. The National Council of Welfare (1990) reports that in 1979, 74% of women could expect to live as widows at some time in their lives. By the late 1980s this figure rose to 84% of women compared with only 60% of men. In 1986 widows aged 65 and over outnumbered widowers in this age group by almost five to one. (Stone and Frenken 1988). And fewer widowed women remarry than widowed men (Connidis and Rempel 1983; Fletcher and Stone 1980). Social pressure works against remarriage for women. Also, social norms say that a woman should choose a man her own age or older when she remarries. At the same time, it is more socially acceptable that a man choose to remarry a younger than an older woman. (Abu-Laban 1978; Veevers 1987). This leaves older women with a small pool of potential mates. In Canada in 1986 there were only twenty-seven potential grooms for every one hundred unmarried women aged 65, and only thirty potential grooms for every one hundred unmarried women aged 70 to 74 (Stone and Frenken 1988).

Second, better government pension plans and subsidized housing make living alone in a private household a more viable option for more women today (Krivo and Mutchler 1989). Community-based health care supports

## Exhibit 11.3

Percentages of Population in Selected Living Arrangements,
by Sex for Selected Age Groups, Canada, 1986

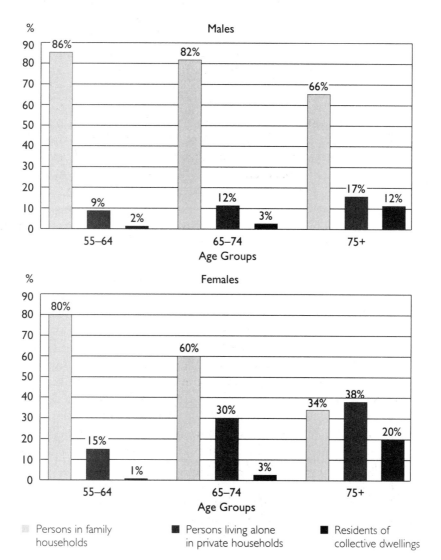

**Source:** Adapted from Health and Welfare Canada, *Fact Book on Aging in Canada* (Ottawa: Minister of Supply and Services, 1983), Figure 9.1.2, 69; Statistics Canada, *A Portrait of Seniors in Canada*, 1990, Cat. No. 89-519, Chart 7, 19. Reproduced with permission of the Minister of Supply and Services Canada, 1991.

. . . . . . . . . . . . . . . . . . . . . . . . . . . . . . . . . . . . .

# Exhibit 11.4

## Intimacy at a Distance

. . . . . . . . . . . . . . . . . . . . . . . . . . . . . . . . . . . . .

Children and their elderly parents now share what Rosenmayr and Kockeis (1963) call "intimacy at a distance." Young people keep in contact with their parents. Parents and children visit one another, help one another, and keep in touch by phone, but they rarely live with each other.

The National Advisory Council on Aging (1986a) asked seniors living in a seniors' residence why they prefer to live alone. Here are some of their comments:

ALBINA TENNIER: When my doctor advised me that I shouldn't be living alone, my daughter was willing to have me move in with her, but I prefer the independence we have here.

VIOLET SMITH: My son lives in Toronto, and he used to worry about me, but now he knows that someone looks in on me everyday. I looked after my mother-in-law for 14 years, and I decided that no one was going to go through that with me.

HILDA TICKELL: My son-in-law and grandsons are very supportive, but they respect my independence.

They're only a phonecall away if I need them, but I wouldn't want to be waiting around for them to call, nor would I ever want them to feel that they have to call. I have my own life to live.

VELMA WOULD: I lived with my granddaughter and her husband and that would have worked out except that I began to feel isolated because they were away at work all day. We didn't live close to public transportation, and I began to feel I couldn't get out, especially in winter. I decided to move here because I'm the kind of person who likes to have other people around.

These comments raise some important questions. How much of older people's desire for independence comes from their feeling that they do not want to become a burden on their children? And how much of their desire for independence reflects the fact that in modern society older people have no place in their children's busy lives? Intimacy at a distance helps to solve this cultural dilemma. It allows older people to keep in touch with their children, but without intruding on them.

Source: Excerpted from National Advisory Council on Aging, *Expression 3*, no. 1 (Ottawa: National Advisory Council on Aging, 1986a), 3.

. . . . . . . . . . . . . . . . . . . . . . . . . . . . . . . . . . . . .

also make it possible for older women with health problems to stay in their own homes, rather than move to a nursing home.

Third, a change in attitudes and values explains this trend. Connidis (1983a), for example, found that most older people say they would rather not live with their children, and Wister (1985) found that older people prefer the privacy and independence that come with living alone. They prefer what Rosenmayr and Kockeis (1963) call "intimacy at a distance." (See Exhibit 11.4.)

Wister (1985) predicts that an increasing proportion of older women will live alone in the future. Priest (1985) projects a 6 percent per year average increase of women aged 75 and over living alone over the next twenty years. He projects that by the year 2001, 45 percent of women aged 75 and over will live alone Priest 1988). Stone and Fletcher (1986a) say that this will lead to an explosion of the number of women living alone past age 75.

This trend has policy implications. Unmarried older people have smaller support networks than married people, and they rely more on formal health care services (like home care) than do married couples (Hess and Soldo 1985). They may also neglect their health. Niewind, Krondl, and Lau (1988), for example, report that people who live alone have less varied diets than people who lived with others. People with less social contact also showed less use of nutritious foods like vegetables. "The findings on dietary quality come as an additional argument for special attention to dental health and to the housing arrangements for the geriatric population" (Niewind, Krondl, and Lau 1988, 45).

More single older people living alone will increase the demand for suitable apartment housing and better public transportation. Many older women who live alone have low incomes. The Canada Mortgage and Housing Corporation estimates that "44 percent of unattached elderly women had 'core' housing need in 1985" (National Council of Welfare 1990, 104). This means that their housing "was either inadequate or cost more than 30 percent of their income" (National Council of Welfare 1990, 104). These women will need housing alternatives like supported housing and homesharing programs.

## TYPES OF HOUSING

### Single-Family Houses

Most homeowners want to stay in their own homes after they retire. In 1988, 63.5 percent of households with a head aged 65 and over owned their own home (compared to 62.5 percent of all households) (Statistics Canada 1990e). And a large majority (91%) of homeowners aged 55 and over live in detached houses (Berger, Godin, and Harvey 1986). Over 54 percent of households headed by a senior (aged 65+) own their homes and live mortgage free (compared with 31.3 percent for all households) (Statistics Canada 1990e).

Home ownership differs across the country. The Northwest Territories has the lowest proportion, among the provinces and territories, of seniors who own homes: 34 percent for those aged 65 to 74, and 42 percent for people aged 75 and over. Newfoundland, compared with the other provinces, has the highest proportion of homeowners among its seniors. Eighty-eight percent of people aged 65 to 74 and 83 percent of people aged 75 and over own their own homes.

Older homeowners tend to have older homes (Berger, Godin, and Harvey 1986) and pay less for rent (including electricity, heating, and services) than younger homeowners and renters at any age. The large proportion of people who live mortgage free in the oldest age groups probably accounts for this difference (Statistics Canada 1990e).

Most older homeowners take good care of their houses. Only 12 percent of homeowners 65 to 79 years old and 10 percent of those aged 80 and over say their houses need major repairs. More than three-quarters of people aged 65 and over say their houses need only regular maintenance (Health and Welfare Canada 1983). A study of retirees in Canada found that 71 percent of people who owned their own homes said they were satisfied with their housing, compared with two-thirds of all men and women (Health and Welfare Canada 1977b).

Older men, more often than older women, tend to live in single-family houses. Rose and Macdonald (1984) found that in southern Ontario 78 percent of men compared with 63.3 percent of women, lived in a house (rather than an apartment or collective dwelling). Four-fifths of men who lived in a single-family house, compared with a little more than three-fifths of women, owned their own homes. Connidis and Rempel (1983) say that fewer women own their own homes because a woman often has to move out of a single-family home as she ages. First, when her husband dies she may have less money to spend on housing. Increased heating costs, maintenance, and taxes can all force a woman to sell her home and move into an apartment. Second, women give up their homes because they know less about how to care for a home. "This is not to say that women are incapable of such tasks but rather that their patterns of socialization have not typically included the knowledge and practice necessary for a comfortable sense of mastery over them" (Connidis and Rempel 1983, 10). This and the cost of hiring people to do work leads many women to sell their homes. A number of programs in Canada work to help men and women stay in their own homes.

## Tax and Home Maintenance Programs

Homeowners without mortgages live rent free and have more financial assets than people who rent (Fraser 1982), so they should have the least trouble paying for housing. But many older people have trouble keeping up their homes. They own large older houses—85 percent of them are single-family, detached—that cost a high proportion of the owner's income to heat and maintain (Statistics Canada 1978a, cited in Health and Welfare Canada 1982b). A study supported by the Canada Mortgage and Housing Corporation (Fraser 1982) found that a third of older homeowners in cities had trouble paying their housing costs, and that half of the money they spent on housing went to pay for utilities. A study in Saskatchewan found that one-third of older homeowners in the province put over 30 percent of their income into housing costs (Saskatchewan Housing Corporation 1984).

The federal government and the provinces help older homeowners through grants, loans, and tax rebates. In 1988, 630,000 housing units got some financial aid (National Advisory Council on Aging 1991). British Columbia, for example, allows seniors who have lived in the province for at least one year to defer payment of property taxes until they sell their home. At that time they pay the outstanding taxes with interest (at below market rates) out of the money they get for their home. The federal government Residential Rehabilitation Assistance Program offers loans of up to $10,000 for city dwellers and $25,000 for rural homeowners to help people improve run-down housing. In 1984, for example, 41 percent of residential rehabilitation grants went to seniors. (Government of Canada 1988). The government also grants loans to improve building structures, fire safety, wiring, plumbing, or heating, or to make a house accessible to a wheelchair. By May 1981 loans for house repairs in Canada totalled $118 million. The government forgave close to 90 percent of the loans to those 3,400 older households with low incomes (Health and Welfare Canada 1982b).

Some provinces also sponsor home repair programs that offer low-interest and forgivable loans to low-income older people. Many provinces also offer older people a rebate or tax credit on school property tax.

These programs help some older people stay in their own homes. But Blackie (1986) says that they have too many restrictions. They focus on only the most needy cases and on people with health or safety needs. They also focus more on limited home repairs, rather than on maintenance or adaptation of homes to help people stay in their homes.

## Reverse Mortgages

A program known about but almost ignored in Canada that could give some older people enough income to stay in their homes is the reverse mortgage. Reverse mortgages allow older people to unfreeze the money tied up in their houses. Statistics Canada reports that between 1969 and 1976 homeowners aged 65 and over had 46 percent of their total wealth invested in their homes (Statistics Canada 1980a, 23). Some homeowners would like to use this money to live on, but as long as they stay in their homes they live asset rich but cash poor. Someone with $150,000 in equity might not have enough cash income to pay the gas or water bill.

Several types of reverse mortgages exist. The most common plan is called the Reverse Annuity Mortgage (RAM) (Bartel and Daly 1981; Canada

· · · · · · · · · · · · · · · · · · · · · · · · · · · · · · · · ·

## Exhibit 11.5

### Case Study of Reverse Mortgages

· · · · · · · · · · · · · · · · · · · · · · · · · · · · · · · · ·

Few companies offer reverse mortgages in Canada, and few people know about them. But they may become more common in the future. A company in Vancouver now offers a RAM program that gives some idea of what reverse mortgages can offer homeowners.

James Rogers, the president of a company in Vancouver that offers one of the few programs in Canada, calls it a "reverse insurance policy." People collect the policy's payment in instalments while they live and make one lump-sum payment (their house) when they die. Two examples will show how this plan worked in 1986.

A man, aged 65, who owns a $135,000 house joins the reverse mortgage plan. The plan allows him and his wife to live in the house rent free, and it also pays him $350 a month for life. If he dies before his wife, she continues to receive payments. The company gets the house after they both die.

What about younger people with less equity in their homes? A woman, aged 60, who owns a $100,000 house and joins the program is able to live in her home rent free until she dies. She also gets $260 a month for life. The house goes to the company when she dies. Lower interest rates and rising house prices today make this an attractive plan for mortgage companies.

Source: Author's notes, based on a Canadian Broadcasting Corporation production, telecast in 1986.

· · · · · · · · · · · · · · · · · · · · · · · · · · · · · · · · ·

Mortgage and Housing n.d.). In this plan an older person uses their house to secure a loan from a bank. They then buy a lifetime annuity from an insurance company with the money from the loan. The insurance company pays the bank loan and pays the older person a set amount to live on for life. The older person can stay in their home as long as they want. The bank takes over the house when the last survivor of a couple dies (Bartel and Daly 1981). This plan has at least one major limitation. The interest payments to the bank will go up if interest rates rise, thus reducing the older person's income. Some firms in the U.S. stopped offering RAMs when interest rates soared in the late 1970s and early 1980s. But, in a time of low interest rates, RAMs could solve the economic and housing problems of many older people.

Reverse mortgages will not catch on in Canada until the government decides to support their use. Revenue Canada has not ruled whether the government will tax RAM income. If RAM income were to count as taxable income, many people would lose part of it to taxes. Also, poorer people, who get the GIS, might lose some of their benefits due to their RAM income. A tax break for reverse mortgage income would attract more people to the program.

• • • • • • • • • • • • • • • • • • • • • • • • • • • • • • • • • •

## Exhibit 11.6

## The Canada Mortgage and Housing Corporation (CMHC)

• • • • • • • • • • • • • • • • • • • • • • • • • • • • • • • • • •

Since the early 1960s CMHC programs have built over 146,000 housing units and established 47,000 hostel beds for older people. Forty thousand more units in Canada, mostly for older people, receive a rent subsidy through CMHC, and since the mid-1970s more than 174,000 houses (85 percent of which are owned by seniors) have gotten forgivable loans through the Residential Rehabilitation Assistance Program (RRAP). Gross (1985) says that from 1960 to 1985 the CMHC helped renew, build, or support 16,000 housing units a year for older people. The CMHC also helps older people buy and sell homes through loan insurance programs.

The CMHC supports non-profit groups and cooperatives through Section 56.1 of the National Housing Act. These groups build low-income housing for older people. The CMHC will insure up to 100 percent of a loan to one of these groups and will lower interest costs to as low as 2 percent. People who live in these units pay as little as 16 to 25 percent of their income on housing (Nicklin 1985). CMHC policies and programs like these create new rental housing for seniors and give them more choice about where they can live.

• • • • • • • • • • • • • • • • • • • • • • • • • • • • • • • • • •

Bairstow (1985) estimates that if the program catches on, at least 400,000 older people who own homes might use reverse mortgage programs.

Reverse mortgages alone will not solve all the financial problems older homeowners face. Seniors who want to tap their home equity should consult with legal and financial experts first (Canada Mortgage and Housing 1988). But, along with tax credits and government aid for repairs, reverse mortgages can help some people stay in their own homes. Bartel and Daly say that "faced with the rising costs and consequent financial strain of home ownership, the very act of parting with an interest in their home, through a reverse mortgage, may generate the income to financially enable senior citizens to remain there for the rest of their lives" (cited in Economic Council of Canada 1981).

## Apartment Living

Statistics Canada (1990e) reports that 38.4 percent of people aged 65 to 74 who live in private households live in apartments (including semi-detached houses, row houses, and apartments in duplexes). This figure increases to 48 percent of people aged 75 and over. About 12 percent of people aged 65 to 74

. . . . . . . . . . . . . . . . . . . . . . . . . . . . . . . . . . .

## Exhibit 11.7

### Little Old Lady in a Hard Hat

. . . . . . . . . . . . . . . . . . . . . . . . . . . . . . . . . . .

Most older people adapt their lifestyles to fit the housing option they can afford, but a small number of older people adapt to environmental demands by transforming their environment. Alice Thompson in Calgary chose this approach to meet her housing needs.

Twice a month for nearly a year, 75-year-old Alice Thompson put on a hard hat and inspected a 60-suite apartment block rising in Downtown Calgary.

She was past president of the Elder Statesmen, a group of old people who organized to design, build and manage housing for the elderly. Alice and the rest of the executive of the Elder Statesmen would attend meetings in a trailer on the construction site. The four women and one man—all retired—would then don their blue hard hats and follow their architect, construction manager and the city inspectors, even climbing ladders to get from floor to floor of their six-storey building.

The knew what they wanted. They would not be deterred by workmen accustomed to doing things their own way. They endured freezing weather, strikes and construction errors, once spotting a concrete patio ceiling that had been incorrectly measured and had to be torn out. Finally, several months behind schedule and $182,000 over the $1,850,000 budget, Bow Claire was opened in June 1978, with Alice Thompson as one of its first tenants.

Bow Claire was more than home to Alice; it was a testament to the bold notion that elderly people can have a role in planning their own destiny …

**Source:** Audrey Grescoe, "Little Old Lady in a Hard Hat," *Today Magazine*, 17 January 1981.

. . . . . . . . . . . . . . . . . . . . . . . . . . . . . . . . . . .

and about 19 percent of people aged 75 and over live in high-rise (i.e., five or more storeys) apartment buildings. Older people often choose to move into an apartment when they can no longer care for a house. A study in British Columbia found that almost one older person in five who moved into a seniors' high-rise did so because they had "difficulty looking after their residence" (Gutman 1983, Table 12). A study (Hodge 1984a) of seniors in eastern Ontario who wanted assisted housing found that about one in six said they could not stay in their home due to age, and about one in ten said they were not well enough to look after their home.

People with good incomes can choose from a wide range of apartments: a high-rise or a low-rise, a two-bedroom suite with a balcony and a view, or an apartment near a bus route and shopping. Other older renters have to settle for less. A study published by the Canada Mortgage and Housing Corporation in 1982 reports that older renters had average assets of only $14,000 and had less than $8,000 in liquid assets that year (Fraser 1982). In that same year the CMHC found that "24 percent of renter households with heads aged 65-69 and 32 percent of the households with heads over 70 experienced 'core need'" (i.e., they spent more than 30 percent of their total income on housing) (Canada Mortgage and Housing 1982, cited in Brink 1985). In 1985 the CMHC estimated that 44 percent of unattached older women had "core" housing needs (cited in National Council of Welfare 1990). These figures show that many older people need rent support to ease the burden of housing costs.

The provincial governments offer several kinds of help to renters: property tax credits to renters, school tax rebates, subsidized low-income housing, and shelter allowances. Tax credits and rebates refund money to renters based on both the amount of rent a person pays and their income (Zamprelli 1986). In Quebec, for example, almost 200,000 seniors in 1983 received tax refunds totalling $36 million. This program helped more seniors than any other housing program and accounted for the greatest expenditure on seniors' housing in Quebec (Renaud and Wexler 1986).

Most provinces have built subsidized apartments for low-income seniors. Ontario spent $60 million in 1984 to build or support self-contained apartments for older people (Corke 1986b). Seniors lived in about 46 percent of all public housing apartments in 1984 (National Advisory Council on Aging 1991). Most of the other provinces, along with the federal government, also offer aid to renters in low-income housing. These programs keep a person's rent at or below 25 percent of their income.

Some provinces offer shelter allowances to older people. These allowances subsidize the person, not the housing project (Zamprelli 1985). They allow older people to choose their own apartment from those available in the marketplace. This frees people from having to move into government housing. About 46 percent of rent supplements went to seniors in 1984 (National Advisory Council on Aging 1991).

Quebec offers a housing allowance program called Logirente. The program gives rental assistance to seniors who spend more than 30 percent of their income on housing. This helps older people to age in their own place or to choose an alternative to public housing (Renaud and Wexler 1986). The Manitoba SAFER program (Shelter Allowance for Elderly Renters) also gives older renters more choice. The program pays cash rebates (up to a maximum amount) to older tenants who spend more than 25 percent of their income on rent. The rebate depends on the amount by which rental costs exceed 25 percent of the household income. An average of 3,300 households received this allowance in 1984 and Manitoba spent $3.4 million in 1984 on SAFER subsidies for people over age 60 with low incomes. This came to an average of

$1,030 per household for households that received a subsidy (Zamprelli 1986).

A study of the SAFER program by the Manitoba government found that the program increases older people's choice of housing. The study found that 96 percent of the people who get allowances said they feel satisfied or very satisfied with their current housing, and 86 percent of the people in the program said that the program allowed them to spend more money on food (Minuk and Davidson 1981).

Zamprelli (1985) compared shelter allowances and low-income housing programs in Canada. He concluded that:

1. Shelter allowances offer a simple, easy-to-use system to support older people. They give people more freedom to choose the housing they want.

2. Low-income housing offers more control of housing quality, and government-subsidized housing can offer health and social services where people live. This can help many older people live in an apartment on their own, even if their health declines.

Zamprelli (1986) reports that in Manitoba 65 to 70 percent of rental households with the head of the household aged 65 or older receive some social housing benefits or shelter allowance. Many of these households contain unattached people with low incomes. Both shelter allowances and subsidized apartments for seniors give low-income older people more opportunity to choose an apartment that meets their needs. These programs allow low-income seniors to live in affordable, high quality housing.

## Preferences in Apartment Living

Lawton (1982) cautions that no single type of housing fits all older people, but older people do prefer some types of apartments and neighbourhoods over others. Studies have looked at seniors' preferences for age-segregated vs. age-integrated housing, high-rise vs. low-rise housing, and normal vs. special design.

### *Age-Segregated vs. Age-Integrated Housing*

A survey in Ontario (Hough 1981) found that 66 percent of senior respondents wanted neighbours without children, and that more than 64 percent of senior respondents preferred to live in a building among people their own age.

A study by Lawton (1982) of 150 housing sites in the U.S. found that older people who lived in age-segregated housing showed more feelings of well-being. Hough (1981) reports that seniors accept mixed-age housing if the majority of tenants are seniors and if each age group lives in its own building. This allows the seniors to choose when and how often they want to interact with families (see also Canada Mortgage and Housing 1978).

Kaill (1980) concludes that people prefer building segregation because it gives them more control over their social contacts with other age groups. He adds that "this interpretation does not necessarily imply that older people do not wish to be in contact with younger members of the population, but simply that they wish to retain choice in the matter" (1980, 85).

## High-Rise vs. Low-Rise Housing

Studies show that older people prefer single homes and apartments in low-rise rather than high-rise buildings. Lawton (1982, 42), in the U.S., says that "the higher the building, the less satisfied were its tenants with their housing and the less mobile they were in the surrounding community ... "

Another U.S. study found that people in high-rises showed more boredom, knew fewer people by sight, and engaged in less activity than people in garden apartments. The study also found that smaller numbers of units (under 100) led to a better quality of life (Cranz and Schumacher 1975).

A study of 219 people 55 years old and over in Winnipeg with middle to low incomes (Epstein 1976) found that people in low-rise buildings and in single homes preferred the kinds of settings they already lived in. (Lawton (1982) calls this the principle of people preferring what they have.) Still, 48 percent of people in single detached houses said they preferred medium-rise or row housing to high-rises, and 40 percent of the sample made high-rises their last choice (Epstein 1976).

Other studies in Canada show that older people can and do adapt to high-rise housing. Gutman (1983) reports in one study that 52.8 percent of people living in a high-rise building preferred this type of building. She says that "where a trade-off is required between a high-rise in a 'good' location (i.e. close to public transportation and to community facilities and services) and a low-rise in a 'poor' location, the high-rise should be the structure of choice" (1983, 193).

## Normal Design vs. Special Design

Appropriate design can help a person stay in their apartment even if they lose some abilities. It also creates a safer, more secure environment. "Design," a CMHC guide says, "can be a positive factor in stimulating effective employment of leisure time, the development of new roles, and a sense of purpose for those of advancing years" (Canada Mortgage and Housing 1978, 2). Gutman (1983, 187) says that "greater compliance with such guidelines would do much to improve the quality of units built for seniors while not substantially increasing construction costs." She found, for example, that older residents liked having easy access to public transportation and downtown services.

A study done by the University of Winnipeg Institute of Urban Studies found that people wanted their own kitchen, a separate bedroom, and a caretaker for the housing block (Epstein 1976). The study also found that older people dislike bachelor apartments (apartments without a bedroom). A study by the Canadian Council on Social Development (1976a) reports this same finding.

Older people also need space for meetings, lounges, coffee shops, chapels, greenhouses, beauty parlours, and exercise rooms. Apartment housing in the past often ignored this need, but some new buildings now include extra public space. They also include recreation and entertainment programs that help people use the space.

Studies show that seniors choose the kind of housing that gives them both security and freedom. Béland (1984a, 184) says that "senior housing represents for [the] elderly a place where some protection is available, while enabling them to preserve personal autonomy."

## Enriched Housing

Enriched housing, sometimes called sheltered or congregate housing, builds extra protection for the older person into the housing design. This type of housing gives people more social and health care support than they get in a normal apartment building. Minuk and Davidson (1981, 55) describe enriched housing as "a housing facility where supportive services (meals, housekeeping, medical services) are available on-site on a regular basis for a moderate fee." Baker (1990), in a review of the literature on enriched housing, concludes that all enriched housing includes a resident warden and an alarm system, and that most also include communal facilities like a dining room and laundry rooms (citing Harper 1984). Heumann and Boldy (1982) estimate that in Great Britain between 5 and 10 percent of older people need this kind of housing.

The term "enriched housing" can apply to any type of housing (Saskatchewan n.d.). Enriched housing in Canada ranges from converted hotels which offer rooms and hot meals for single men, to campus-like settings with high- and low-rise housing and many levels of health care (Byerts 1982). The amount of enrichment differs from setting to setting. Sometimes enrichment means only a lounge with a television set in an apartment building. More elaborate enriched housing includes lounges, shops, and in some cases clinics. Some buildings employ activity workers and program planners who show films and organize exercise programs and field trips for residents

(Baumgarten et al. 1988). Half the people who got SAFER support in Manitoba said they would move to this kind of building (Minuk and Davidson 1981). Béland (1984b) found that people chose housing like this because it gave them some protection, but still allowed autonomy. A study in Ontario (United Senior Citizens of Ontario 1985) found that 47 percent of respondents chose supportive housing as a preferred future housing option.

Critics of enriched housing say that it can lead to early dependency by giving people too many services and that it attracts sick or less able people (Gutman 1978; Lawton 1985), but studies have found more benefits than drawbacks to this kind of housing. Lawton (1976) found that people in enriched housing reported high morale and high life-satisfaction. He says that proper planning can discourage dependence. In some cases enriched housing can even foster independence, because it allows individuals to live on their own rather than in institutions. An alarm system for each apartment gives people a sense of security and can save a person's life in an emergency. But something as simple as "I'm okay" signs for door knobs in apartment buildings encourages neighbourliness. Enriched housing offers an important alternative to people who need support, but who do not need the high levels of care given in a nursing home or hospital.

This type of housing can lead to unique problems, however. For example, the average age of residents increases over time as residents age. Some buildings that began with a mixture of age groups among residents ten or fifteen years ago now house a markedly older group, whose average age is 80 or older. This may compromise the self-government that exists in these buildings (Streib, Folts, and LaGreca 1985). Enriched housing complexes could become high-rise nursing homes over time.

## Multi-Level Enriched Housing

Multi-level housing bridges the gap between enriched housing and institutional care. Multi-level enriched housing refers to an enriched housing complex or building with a mix of self-contained suites, board residence (where the residents eat in a common dining room), and personal, intermediate, or extended care settings all in one building or on one site. People who approve of multi-level housing say it decreases the stress arising from relocation, allows couples to stay near one another if the health of one spouse declines, and lowers costs because developers can build one large complex (Gutman 1978).

Gutman (1978) studied satisfaction with multi-level housing in British Columbia. She compared tenants in multi-level housing with a control group in the community. She found that eighteen months after their move, multi-

• • • • • • • • • • • • • • • • • • • • • • • • • • • • • • • • • • • • •

## Exhibit 11.8

## Jack's Hotel: A Unique Enriched Housing Option

• • • • • • • • • • • • • • • • • • • • • • • • • • • • • • • • • • • • •

The term "single-occupant room" (SRO) hotel implies a "low-cost, central city" hotel that serves a "clientele likely to consist of socially marginal people" (Lawton 1985, 466; Ehrlich and Ehrlich 1976). These hotels offer privacy and tolerance for deviant lifestyles (Eckert 1980; Sokolovsky and Cohen 1981). Only a small number of older people in Canada (less than 0.7 percent of men and 0.4 percent of women 65 and over) live in these hotels. Still, Lawton (1985, 466) says, they meet the needs of a specific group of older people and "an active effort should be made to preserve this resource."

In Winnipeg, Jack's Hotel serves as a model for how a city can maintain this kind of housing. Jack's houses forty-two older men in an enriched setting. The building sits on Winnipeg's Main Street strip in the core of the city. A group of designers, social workers, and archi-tects formed a corporation that arranged to remodel the building. The designers left the foot-thick walls in the building and the old wooden doors on the rooms, but they built a game room, a TV lounge, laundry rooms on each floor, a restaurant, and dining room. They also hired a housekeeper as part of the staff. This person works at the front desk, sets up field trips and billiard tournaments, and helps the men with medical needs. She will call in a nurse if someone needs help, or arrange doctor's appointments for the men.

The men who stay at Jack's say they like it there. Most of them had drifted from hotel to hotel along Main Street before they moved to Jack's. Few of them stayed in one place more than a year. A study by Smith (1979) found that half of Jack's tenants had lived there more than three years, a sign that Jack's meets the needs of these men.

• • • • • • • • • • • • • • • • • • • • • • • • • • • • • • • • • • • • •

level housing tenants showed higher morale and had more interaction with neighbours than the control group. She also found no decrease in satisfaction with friends or in visiting friends. People "got out" and "dressed up" more often after eighteen months in multi-level housing than before their move.

Gutman (1985) studied both groups again nine years later. She found that the proportion of people in the multi-level setting, who liked living there, had risen from 75 percent to 85 percent over the nine years. She also found even more improvement in lifestyle for the multi-level tenants and found that tenants showed an increase in visiting and entertaining friends, while controls in the community showed a decrease in visiting with friends. All of the data Gutman collected on health, physical function, morale, and interaction with others, she says, "failed to support the hypothesis that resi-dence in a multi-level, multi-service housing environment fosters dependency and disengagement" (1985, 6).

She did, however, find three problems with multi-level housing. First, these settings can lead healthy residents to report decreased satisfaction if the nursing home group goes beyond 25 percent of the population. Second, low-rise structures, where the healthy people see the less healthy people all the time, lead to dissatisfaction. Gutman (1985) recommends that multi-level housing be built as high-rises to keep the groups more clearly apart. Third, these settings cannot always allow people to shift from one level of care to another as promoters of multi-level housing often promise. The high cost and demand for personal care beds means that, when a bed comes open, the staff will fill it with someone from outside the building. This means that an open bed might not be available when a resident in the building needs it.

This kind of setting will not appeal to everyone, because older people have diverse needs. But multi-level housing successfully serves people who want or need nearby support if their health declines.

Apartment housing comes in many packages. High-rise, low-rise, public, private, non-profit, age-segregated, age-integrated, without services, or enriched with services. Older people need this variety because their needs and abilities differ. They also need tax rebates, shelter allowances, and subsidized housing so that they can freely choose the housing that best suits their needs.

Rural seniors have special needs. Joseph and Fuller (1991) say that while rural communities often have programs for young and frail older people, they lack a range of options for people who have varied needs for supports. Joseph and Fuller (1991) report that rural communities often lack housing like enriched housing for semi-independent seniors. Hodge (1987) says that where senior's housing does exist, it often fails to meet design standards. He studied seniors' housing blocks in nine Ontario rural communities and found that "*only two of the projects have more than 50 percent of the physical and architectural features considered desirable* for senior citizen shelter care facilities ... " (Hodge 1987, 149, emphasis in the original). The best project he studied had only 60 percent of the desirable features studied. Projects lacked consistency in design, and many lacked safety features and aids to help people with their daily activities. Hodge (1987) also found that designers had placed many of the buildings in out-of-the-way locations, making it hard for seniors to use community resources. Some of the criticisms of design and location in this study would apply to urban housing for seniors too.

## Living Arrangement Passages

Stone and Fletcher (1987) hypothesized that people move from one housing alternative to another in a predictable pattern throughout adulthood. They

• • • • • • • • • • • • • • • • • • • • • • • • • • • • • • • • • • • • •

## Exhibit 11.9

## Homeless Older People

• • • • • • • • • • • • • • • • • • • • • • • • • • • • • • • • • • • • •

Some people fall through the cracks of the current housing and social welfare system. They move from place to place, and some of them live on the street or stay in missions or at the Salvation Army. Doolin (1986, 229) says that "the older person on the street is a multiply-disadvantaged individual," often someone who suffers from alcoholism, unemployment, and a broken family.

Men in this category can find a bed at the Salvation Army or the Harbour Light Mission, but homeless women—some of whom carry everything they own in a shopping bag—have few places to go. Almost no research exists on these women in Canada.

Schull (1981) reported on one of these women for *Today Magazine*:

Ruby, an 80 year old woman, lived for 15 years in a culvert in a Montreal park. Lucy Stofle of Auberge Transition, a shelter in Montreal, found her one day in 1976. "It started to rain," she says, "and I ran for cover under some concrete steps. I looked down and there was a dugout hole, a depression in the earth where there were some rags. The rags started to move. I just freaked! I thought, 'Oh, my god, what's that?' I saw it was an old woman. She was just wearing a couple of coats and looked like a part of the earth. She sat up, and I said hello, and she said hello, and I felt embarrassed because I was in her home. She told me she would sleep there and then she'd leave and go down to Ogilvy's department store and use their washroom and sit the rest of the day on the benches of Ste. Catherine and Crescent streets."

**Source:** Christiane Schull, "Bag Ladies," *Today Magazine*, 15 April 1981, 15-16.

• • • • • • • • • • • • • • • • • • • • • • • • • • • • • • • • • • • • •

further hypothesized that age would predict the presence of an age cohort's members in a specific living arrangement. Major life events, they say, trigger living arrangement transitions. And because many life events cluster at certain ages (e.g., retirement, widowhood, decline in mobility), age should predict living arrangements. The researchers recognize that people differ in the amount of family support they have and also in their income, gender, and ethnic background. Still, they expected to see some patterns in living arrangement transitions.

The researchers tested this hypothesis by tracking middle-aged and older age cohorts across a number of Canadian censuses. They found that the tendency for women to live alone begins in middle age. For example, women have a decreasing tendency to live in husband-wife families as early as ages 30 to 34, while men show an increasing tendency to live in husband-wife families into ages 40 to 44. This tendency among women to live alone increases until the late-70s when women show a trend toward movement into collective dwellings.

The findings from this study lend support to the idea that living arrangement transitions follow a predictable pattern. This pattern can help planners prepare for the needs for formal supports, suitable housing, and income assistance of an aging population.

# NEW IDEAS IN HOUSING

## Garden Suites

Connidis (1983a, 361) asked 400 older people in an Ontario community a simple question: "If circumstances were to change and you had to choose between living with a child or in a facility for seniors, which would you prefer?" She found an "overwhelming tendency to choose a facility for seniors rather than living with children" (1983a, 363). A study in Regina supports Connidis's findings. The Regina study found that "only 8% of the sample indicated that they would move in with a child if they needed 'someone to keep an eye on them' (no health care) suggesting that the majority of seniors 'draw the line' at placing this type of demand on a younger family member" (Senior Citizens' Provincial Council 1981, 47; see also Okraku 1987).

The design of modern houses may have influenced these findings. Most modern houses have only two or three bedrooms and no room for another kitchen, bedroom, or bathroom to house an aging parent. The Australian state, Victoria, started a new kind of housing for older people that overcomes the problems of modern house design. They call this alternative a "granny flat." A **granny flat** consists of a portable modular cottage for a parent. The government arranges to move the cottage onto a son's or daughter's property, then the government connects the flat to the electricity, sewer, water, and telephone services of the house. When the older person dies or moves to a nursing home, or if the family moves, the government takes the cottage away. This allows children to care for their parents as long as they can. The Australian government set up about 1,000 granny flats between 1975 and 1982 (Lazarowich and Haley 1982). By 1990 the program had 3,000 units in place (Lazarowich 1990). Granny flats cost little (compared with a house), and the older person and the relatives can support one another.

Lazarowich (1986) says that almost all moves to a granny flat start with an invitation from the older person's children. When a family does agree to set up a flat, the family—parents and children—need to talk about what they expect from one another. Most older people do not want to become twenty-four-hour babysitters. Neighbours will also have to accept the granny flat idea, because the flats increase the density of housing in a neighbourhood.

Granny flats may face trouble in Canada from zoning laws and neighbours' attitudes. The flats increase population density in neighbourhoods and neighbours may feel that the flats will lower property values.

A trial program in Ontario called Portable Living Units for Seniors (PLUS) has adapted the granny flat concept to Canada (Spence 1986). (Canadian literature most often refers to granny flats as "garden suites" (Canada Mortgage and Housing 1987).) The PLUS program will run for three years. It will study how well the units work and how neighbours, the host family, and the older residents feel about them. So far, Corke (1986a, 11) says, "the reception which has been given to the demonstration has been so heartwarming that we are confident some good will come of it." The Ontario program found that most neighbourhoods accepted the garden suites (Romanick 1986), and already other provinces have started to plan trial projects, some of them in rural areas where zoning laws and lot size will pose less of a problem.

Corke (1986a) reports one problem with the garden suite concept. A flat in Canada costs about $42,000 installed (almost double the cost of early estimates). She describes this finding as a "price shock." But the price could come down if the idea catches on and factories produce more units.

A program in Vancouver uses duplexes and four-plexes the way garden suites are used. This program overcomes some of the zoning and building problems in cities. In the Vancouver system, an older person sells their home and uses the money to help buy a duplex that houses them and their child's family. The older person and younger family members share the taxes, repair costs, and any mortgage costs for the new property (Evans and Purdie 1985).

These new housing arrangements will lead to new social interdependencies and new challenges to family relations. What will happen if the older person's child separates from or divorces his or her spouse? Or if the child's family moves to another city? Studies of these options will have to show that they make social as well as financial sense, and trial projects can answer only some of these questions. Only longer-term studies will show whether or not garden suites can work in Canada.

## Home Sharing

Blackie (1985) defines home sharing as two people sharing the bathroom, kitchen, and living rooms of a house, but each having their own bedrooms. Such arrangements make sense because a person with a home may need help with household chores due to poor health, or someone in good health may need companionship and a lower rent. They both gain by living in a shared home. Shared homes (unlike boarding homes) make no profit.

Many models exist for home sharing. People in a shared home can hire a housekeeper and someone to cook, or they can do the housework themselves.

One person can move into another's home, or two or more people can move into a new house together. People can decide on their own to move in together, or an agency can arrange a match, set up a trial stay, and then offer counselling after the home gets going.

A program in Ontario found that people shared their home for three reasons: they wanted to stay in their home; they needed income from a sharer; or they felt lonely. The program found that people want to move into a shared home for companionship or cheaper housing, or because they have poor health (Rapelje 1985). Turner and Mangum (1982, cited in Blackie 1985) found that 6 percent of people who own homes and 10 percent of people who rent housing said they had an interest in shared housing, and Rapelje (1985) predicts that as many as 52,000 older people in Ontario might want to share a home.

But shared housing has some problems. First, the Ontario program found more people who want to share their homes than those who want to move into a shared home. Second, Rapelje (1985) says that most matches last less than a year (see also Pritchard 1983). Sharers split up for a few reasons: one of the sharers may decide to move into their own apartment; one sharer may want to live closer to their family; or one of the pair may remarry.

Rapelje (1985) says that of sixty people in a home-sharing program only three left the program because of a bad match, and most say they would consider sharing a home again. Still, Rapelje's data show that sharers stay together only a short time, and this raises several questions. First, is home sharing worth the trouble and the cost, given the short time that matches last? Second, does the breakup of a match lead to hardship or distress for some sharers? If it does, is this a housing option worth pursuing? More research may be able to answer these questions. In the meantime, shared housing will probably appeal to some people because it will give them a housing option they can afford, the companionship they need, and an alternative to living in an institution (Blackie 1985).

# TRANSPORTATION

A home has to suit an older person's abilities and meet his or her needs, but a house or an apartment becomes a prison if the older person cannot get to services, friends, and recreation (Bernardin-Haldemann 1982).

## Public Transportation

Only a few studies have looked at the transportation needs and use patterns of older people in Canada. Most of these studies report that current systems fail to meet older people's needs (Joseph and Fuller 1991). The National Advisory Council on Aging (1989d) lists transportation and mobility as the third greatest barrier to seniors' independence. A national study of older people's needs, sponsored by the Canadian Red Cross Society (1983), found that older people need better transport for shopping, making social contacts, and getting medical care. Transportation ranked as one of the top five senior needs in all provinces. Baker and Thompson (1985) conducted a random sample study of people 55 and older in Victoria, British Columbia. Nearly 20 percent of their respondents reported that transportation was a problem for them. These studies support Havens's earlier research in Manitoba (1980). She found that for older men and women "accessibility of resources" ranked as the highest unmet need for each age cohort in the study (Havens 1980, 218–19). The National Advisory Council on Aging (1985c, 2) says that 11 percent of people aged 55 to 64 are "transportation handicapped"—either they have no public transport or they have trouble using it. This figure jumps to 34 percent for people 80 years old and over.

Rural and urban seniors have different transportation problems. Cities have services, but older people often cannot use them. A survey by the United Senior Citizens of Ontario (1985) found that 9 percent of older people had problems using public transportation. These seniors placed inconvenience first on their list of transportation problems. Rigid routes and schedules make it hard for older people in the suburbs to travel. In the winter long waits for buses, icy sidewalks, or snow mounds at bus stops keep people housebound.

Rural areas often lack public transportation (Health and Welfare Canada 1982b; Hodge 1987). Grant and Rice (1983) describe many rural seniors as "transportation disadvantaged." This group includes (1) people who feel lonely, dissatisfied, and without a confidant, (2) physically frail people over age 74 who never socialize outside their homes, and (3) low-income, widowed women without a car or someone to drive them. A study by the Senior Citizens' Provincial Council (1982) reported that 20 percent of rural seniors could not find transportation to shop in their town and 23 percent said that due to a lack of adequate transportation they had trouble getting to a larger centre once a month.

People in rural areas need more options. First, designers can place seniors housing close to the downtown in small towns (Hodge 1987). Seniors could then walk to the services and shops they need. Second, in small towns transportation programs might include volunteer-run shuttle buses or car pools for seniors.

In the cities most older people do not need special transportation services; instead they need to have existing services improved. Only 9 percent of older people in 1981 either used special transportation or said they needed such services but could not get them (National Advisory Council on Aging 1985c). Ninety percent of the transportation disadvantaged said they could use services that already existed if the services changed slightly. Suggested changes include well-lit subway stations (55 percent of seniors in Montreal say they fear using public transit at night), wider doors, easy-to-read signs, lower steps and rails, and bus stops cleared of snow and ice (National Advisory Council on Aging 1985c). These modifications would help people of all ages.

## Private Transportation

Older people, like younger people, prefer auto travel to other forms of transportation (Atkinson 1991; National Advisory Council on Aging 1986b). Sixty percent of Canadians 65 and over own and drive their own cars (Statistics Canada 1984c). Canada now has over 2.5 million drivers over age 55, and the number of older drivers has increased in the past few years. In 1966, 35 percent of older people in Ontario had driver's licences, but by 1982, 50 percent had licences (National Advisory Council on Aging 1986b). In 1986, 87 percent of senior couples said they owned a car or truck. This figure dropped to 63 percent for unattached older men and 33 percent for unattached older women (National Advisory Council on Aging 1991). Still, MacDonald (1989) reports that 70 percent of people aged 55 and over have driver's licences.

A study in Saskatchewan by Grant and Rice (1983) found that 51 percent of rural older people drive themselves, 17 percent ride with another household member, and 33 percent ride with a relative or friend outside the house. A survey by the Senior Citizens' Forum of Montreal found that 33 percent of seniors said they used a car more than any other form of transportation (National Advisory Council on Aging 1985c). More older people will use cars in the future as lifelong drivers reach retirement age (Atkinson 1991).

This increase in senior drivers raises some new transportation issues. First, older people who drive will have to include the rising cost of auto insurance in their budgets. Second, people over age 60 have more accidents and more fatalities per distance driven than middle-aged (40-to-60-year-old) drivers (Evans 1988). Also, older drivers (aged 60+), compared to younger drivers, have more multi-vehicle accidents and stand a greater chance of a serious or fatal injury (MacDonald 1989). This has led the Canada Safety Council to set up a program called 55 Alive (Health and Welfare Canada 1989–90), which helps seniors improve their driving skills and understand how aging affects driving. Some people have suggested special driver's licences for daytime-only drivers and non-highway driving. Some provinces require drivers over age 65 to take a driver's test every year. Third, older

. . . . . . . . . . . . . . . . . . . . . . . . . . . . . . . . . . . . . . . .

## Exhibit 11.10
### A Typology of Transport Lifestyle Groups

. . . . . . . . . . . . . . . . . . . . . . . . . . . . . . . . . . . . . . . .

**A** Independent, Own Auto—people with money and physical ability to drive own car and live alone; most mobile seniors. Finances and physical ability impose major limits on car use. This group may switch to other means of transportation as they age.

**B** Dependent, Access to Auto—people who live with others (mostly for financial reasons) with own car; less mobile.

**C** Independent, No Auto—have money and independence but may not be able to afford many options like car rental, taxis, or buses.

**D** Dependent, No Access to Auto—live with others; no auto; much less mobile.

**E** Sheltered or Group Housing—some physical and economic dependence; can meet transportation needs because of group setting.

**F** Disabled—all income types, but these people have some physical disability and need special transit programs like those used by disabled non-seniors.

**G** Institutionalized—poor health; others care for needs; have the least unmet mobility needs (because the institution meets their needs).

Groups vary in their physical ability, their income, and the support they get. Each lifestyle group has its own transportation needs. More transportation options will give all older people more freedom and independence.

**Source:** Adapted from Ontario Ministry of Municipal Affairs and Housing, Research and Special Projects Branch, *Towards Community Planning for an Aging Society* (Toronto: Queen's Printer for Ontario, 1983), 7.

. . . . . . . . . . . . . . . . . . . . . . . . . . . . . . . . . . . . . . . .

people in high-rises and downtown apartments will need parking spaces for their cars. These issues point to the changing transportation needs of a healthier, more affluent older population.

## New Transportation Needs and Programs

Transportation needs for older people in the future will go beyond current use patterns. New programs may rely on technological change and on "organizational and service-related innovations" (National Advisory Council on Aging 1986b, 3). Older people will run some of these programs themselves. One program in Edmonton, referred to as a "transportation brokerage," matches passengers with services that meet their needs. Another program described as a "mobility club" in Moncton and the Acadian peninsula helps people in small towns and rural areas. This club formed a non-profit, self-help transport service. People with cars call in to tell a dispatcher about trips they plan to make in the next week or so. People who need rides call a day before they have to take a trip. A dispatcher matches riders with drivers. Drivers also volunteer for up to one emergency trip per month (Grant and Rice 1983).

In Ottawa senior volunteers help run a bus service that takes 25 to 30 seniors grocery shopping each week. Volunteers help people on and off the bus, help them carry packages, and give people rides to other appointments during the week (National Advisory Council on Aging 1986b). Saskatchewan has set up a Rural Transportation Assistance Program (RTAP), which helps small rural communities form a local transit service. The provincial government subsidizes the cost of using a car or van to travel twice a week between these towns and a larger centre (Grant 1983). Grant and Rice (1983) say that rural communities may need to combine a number of options to serve their older people.

## THE FUTURE OF HOUSING AND TRANSPORTATION

Often different providers deliver housing, transportation, and social and health care services to older people. Different policies govern these systems, and they sometimes lack coordination. A number of studies suggest that seniors benefit from an integration of these systems. Blandford, Chappell, and Marshall (1989) describe a program that links seniors' housing to existing community services: in this program tenant resource coordinators (TRCs) were placed in seniors' housing. The TRC provided tenants with information about community services and also coordinated services for tenants (e.g., grocery delivery or friendly visitors). The researchers found that the TRC placements led to improvements in services for seniors and increased dissemination of information about services to tenants. This type of support can help older people get the services they need at a modest cost to owners and managers.

A report titled *Freedom to Move is Life Itself* presents a variety of proposals that would improve transportation services for older people. The proposals range from changes in technology (easier automobile entry, better bus shelters, special traffic lights) to supportive social arrangements (use of volunteer drivers, developing transportation regions with varied services in each region, conducting research on transportation needs and options) (Ontario Advisory Council on the Physically Handicapped 1987). Joseph and Fuller (1991) call for an integration of housing, service, and transportation policies to meet the needs of seniors (especially those in rural settings). This type of integration would help seniors maintain their autonomy and receive the type of support that best meets their needs.

## CONCLUSION

People can cope with environmental demands in several ways as they age. They can maintain or improve their abilities (through self-help or rehabilitation). Or they can change their environment (by modifying their homes, moving, or getting help through changes in social policy). Most older people live in a few types of housing. Younger old people, couples, and widows, tend to live in their own houses and apartments. As people age, they need more support to maintain their independence. This chapter has focused on the policies and programs in Canada that help older people live in an environment that suits their abilities. This review shows that with some help most older people can live high-quality lives in their own homes and apartments into late old age.

## SUMMARY

1. Research on housing and transportation shows that older people enjoy old age most when they feel in control of their environment. People can maintain this control by changing their environment (for example, moving to an apartment from a single-family home or getting help through social policy reform).

2. A good match between a person's ability and environmental demand leads to high life-satisfaction. An ideal housing system offers older people a range of housing choices because people's needs differ. People should be able to move from one type of housing to another—from a house, to an apartment or to enriched housing—as their needs change. Or they should be able to get support to help them stay where they are.

3. Most older people want to stay in the kind of housing they now occupy. Government policies and programs—like rent subsidies, tax rebates, and repair loans—help older people stay where they are. Other programs—like loan guarantees, new building programs, and shelter allowances—allow older people to move to the kind of housing that suits their needs.

4. Canada offers older people a wide range of housing options. These include single-family homes, apartments, enriched housing, and multi-level enriched housing. New types of housing—garden suites and share-a-home programs—will increase seniors' housing options in the future.

5. Good transportation links older people to their community—to services, recreation, and friends. But both urban and rural transportation systems need improvement. Most older people in cities could use the transporta-

tion that exists if it were modified to suit their needs. Poor lighting in subways, snow at bus routes, and rigid schedules make urban transportation systems unsuitable for many older people.

6. Rural seniors often have no available transportation, but new programs in rural settings include bus services shared by a number of small towns, volunteer bus services, and people who pool their resources to help one another get around. Older people in rural settings have begun to set up the transportation services they need.

7. Good housing and transportation lead to increased life-satisfaction for older people. An environment that fits the person's abilities helps keep older people satisfied, active, and in touch with their community.

## SELECTED READINGS

Government of Canada. *Housing and Aging Population: Guidelines for Development and Design.* Cat. No. H-71-3/6-1987E. Minister of Supply and Services Canada, 1987.

A valuable guide to housing design. This report comes out of a Task Force organized by the National Advisory Council on Aging. The report presents a detailed discussion of how to develop a housing project from conceptualization to operation. The report also includes a checklist of desirable features and a design workbook for developers, including specifications for housing features from entrances, to garbage chutes, to pools and saunas.

Gutman, Gloria, and Norman Blackie, eds. *Innovations in Housing and Living Arrangements for Seniors.* Burnaby, B.C.: Gerontology Research Centre, Simon Fraser University, 1985.

A collection of papers presented at a 1984 symposium on housing for older people in Canada. The book includes selections by scholars, private consultants, and government policy makers. It presents discussions of some of Canada's most creative housing programs for seniors.

Joseph, Alun E., and Anthony M. Fuller. "Towards an Integrative Perspective on the Housing, Services and Transportation Implications of Rural Aging." *Canadian Journal on Aging* 10:127–48, 1991.

A review of rural housing needs and options with a focus on Ontario. The researchers present a two-tier model that calls for an integration of housing, services, and transportation. The paper then discusses policy options to meet rural seniors' needs.

C  H  A  P  T  E  R  **12**

# *Leisure, Recreation, and Service*

## INTRODUCTION

Dan Kreske worked as an insurance agent until he retired six years ago. He had a good income from his investments, savings, and Canada Pension Plan. He heard about free university classes and started to attend. Now he goes to class two or three afternoons a week (depending on the courses offered). He has also renewed his interest in athletics. He played golf all through his working years, and he jogged and swam, but in retirement he found he had more time to develop his ability. In the winter of 1986 he competed at Lake Placid, New York, in the Masters Division of the North American Speed Skating Championships. He made two third- and two fourth-place finishes, and won ten points for his team. "I lost to guys twenty-five years younger than I am—it was one of the greatest thrills of my life."

Many older people like Dan Kreske continue to develop established skills and talents in retirement. Other older people discover new interests when they retire, or they discover a talent for poetry, acting, or art. Still others turn to community service, or they may start to do volunteer work in a hospital or senior centre part-time.

Seniors today have more opportunities for self-development and community service than ever before, and many of them have a great desire to develop themselves and give to others as they age. For many older people the years after retirement become a time of search, discovery, and fulfilment. This chapter will review some of the programs and activities that help seniors live a satisfying old age. This chapter will look at: (1) how seniors today spend their time, (2) new personal development programs for seniors (recreation, fitness, and education), and (3) seniors' community involvement.

## WHAT DO OLDER PEOPLE DO?

Retired men and women report more free time than any other age group (Harvey, Marshall, and Frederick 1991). Older people use this time to engage in a variety of social activities including participation in political or charitable organizations, or in neighbourhood, community, and school groups. More than two-fifths of older people (over one million seniors) say they attend church weekly (Statistics Canada 1990). But, research shows that compared with younger people, they spend more of their time on solitary activities and at home (Harvey and Singleton 1989). Statistics Canada's General Social Survey (Statistics Canada 1990e) found that people aged 65 and over spent about 16 percent more time on personal care (including sleep) than people aged 15 to 54. The 1981 Canadian Time Use Pilot Study found that, compared to 45-to-64-year-olds, older Canadians (aged 65 and over), spent 60 percent more time on housework and shopping. The older group spent 80 percent more time than the younger group on cooking and food preparation (Statistics Canada 1981b).

The General Social Survey (Statistics Canada 1990e) reports that, of people who watched television, men and women aged 65 and over watched more than any other age group (see also Harvey, Marshall, and Frederick 1991). Women watched TV an average of 3.7 hours per day (compared with 2.5 hours in 1977) and men watched an average of 4.1 hours per day (compared with somewhat more than 3 hours in 1977) (Statistics Canada 1990e). Statistics Canada also reports an increase in video cassette recorder ownership. In 1983 2.3 percent of people aged 65 and over owned video cassette recorders. This figure increased to 20.8 percent by 1988.

A study of seniors living in enriched housing in eastern Ontario found that 93 percent of them watched TV every day (Hodge 1984b). Some writers say that people who live alone use TV as a form of social contact (Werner 1976). McPherson (1983) says that TV helps structure time for people who live alone. An older person may watch a morning talk show over breakfast, eat supper with the evening news, and go to sleep after the national news. Some people schedule their days around the afternoon soap operas.

Older people also spend a lot of time reading. Statistics Canada (1989b) reports that over ninety percent of senior couples and about eighty percent of unattached seniors buy reading material. Kinsley and Graves (1983, cited in McPherson and Kozlik 1987) found that people aged 65 and over spent almost an hour and a half per day reading—compared with only 22 minutes for 15-to-17-year-olds and 45 minutes for 25-to-44-year-olds. All studies on leisure activities show the same trend: older people spend most of their time on passive, "receptive," media-related leisure (McPherson and Kozlik 1987; Searle 1987). They spend a lot of this time alone at home, or indoors with friends and relatives. When older people do take part in outdoor activity, the activities usually demand little exertion (like miniature golf and spectator sports) (Strain and Chappell 1982b).

Eight out of ten older people in one study said they had visited friends or relatives in the past week; 40 percent of retired people said they saw friends or relatives more than three times a week; and 20 percent said they saw them daily (Health and Welfare Canada 1983). Chappell (1983a) found that doing something relaxing (like playing cards, walking, or talking) with someone their own age brought older people the greatest pleasure (see also Romsa and Johnson 1983; and Statistics Canada 1987b).

Other research supports these findings. Tenants in a seniors' housing co-op, for example, ranked talking on the telephone, visiting friends, and visiting relatives, in that order, as their three most important activities (Marmel, Sawyer, and Shell 1983). People look forward to these activities in retirement. A study of working men and women asked them what activities they thought led to a good retirement. Almost three-quarters of them rated seeing relatives and family as an important activity, and more than half rated seeing friends as important. More than three-fifths of these men and women said they expected to have more time to see relatives and friends in retirement (Health and Welfare Canada 1977b).

Older people as a group show some common approaches to the use of their time. They often engage in socially satisfying, nondemanding, non-strenuous activities. This appears to support the disengagement theory of aging. The Canada Health Survey (cited in Statistics Canada 1983a, 32), for example, said that the low level of seniors' activity was "to be expected in view of the general deterioration which is part of the aging process."

Other research questions this pessimistic conclusion. Studies show different activity preferences among different types of seniors. Income, region, and social status all influence what an older person chooses to do. People with the lowest income and those with the highest show the least interest in spectator sports (McPherson and Kozlik 1980). Those with no income and little education and those with high income and a university degree show the lowest involvement in popular culture activities (like watching TV, listening to records, going to movies, engaging in crafts, and reading newspapers). People with middle incomes and either a high school diploma or some secondary education show the most involvement in popular culture activities. People with university degrees tend to read more books than other groups (McPherson and Kozlik 1987). "Even within the same age cohort," McPherson and Kozlik (1980, 115) say, "life chances and lifestyles vary because of differences in social status."

Other studies in Canada show that, compared with seniors in Eastern Canada, those in the West report more physical activity and more involvement in sports (Curtis and McPherson 1987; McPherson and Kozlik 1987; Statistics Canada 1987b). Also, higher income and more education lead to more active leisure (Milton 1975; Hobart 1975). Roadburg (1985) found that (middle-income) service workers took part in sports, exercise, and dancing, but (lower-income) clerical and sales workers mostly read.

Studies also show that gender influences activity level. Zuzanek and Box (1988) report that women, more than men, say they take part in visiting, religious activities, reading, bingo, sewing, and shopping. Men, more than women, say they take part in sports, outdoor activity, gardening, visiting pubs, do-it yourself projects, and auto repairs. In general, women spend their free time on expressive social activities, while men spend theirs on passive media consumption and competitive or repair-related activities (Harvey, Marshall, and Frederick 1991; Zuzanek and Box 1988). The researchers say that traditional male and female roles shape leisure activities in later life.

McPherson and Kozlik (1980) support this idea. They found that at all ages men are more active than women in sports. The low participation in sports by women may reflect the fact that fewer women than men have spouses with whom to share sports activity. Studies show that married people living with their spouses have more active lifestyles (Roadburg 1985). Low participation in sports by women may also point up the lack of opportunity women have had to participate in sports in the past. In either case the difference in activity level between men and women may disappear in the future. Longer life expectancy means that couples will live and stay active together longer. Also, fitness programs (more than sports) appeal to both sexes. Already, women show the same amount of participation in exercise programs as men (McPherson and Kozlik 1980).

This research shows that health, education, income, and social status all shape leisure in retirement. Also, McPherson and Kozlik (1987) say that age cohorts may develop leisure subcultures. Older cohorts today may prefer more passive leisure, while younger cohorts may live a more active old age. Each cohort will have its preferred way of spending leisure time, in part based on members' past experience. This means that future cohorts of older people will bring their own interests with them into old age. And they will probably enjoy a wide variety of leisure activities (McPherson and Kozlik 1987).

## LEISURE

What theory of aging best describes leisure activity in later life? Most of the research on aging and leisure supports the continuity theory of aging. McPherson (1985) says that often people keep the leisure preferences in retirement that they had in middle age (see also Searle 1987; Tinsley et al. 1987; Cutler and Hendricks 1990). People who enjoyed athletic activity, socializing, or travelling will continue to do these things when they retire (unless something like a sharp drop in health prevents them).

A study by McGuire, Dottavio, and O'Leary (1987), however, suggests that we need at least two theories to account for older people's leisure patterns: continuity theory and the life-span developmental perspective. These researchers looked at data from a nationwide recreation survey in the U.S. and found two patterns of leisure involvement in older adults. One pattern fits the continuity theory of aging. People who fit this pattern were called **contractors**. This group had stopped at least one outdoor activity in the past year and had not learned any new activity since age 65. A second pattern fits the life-span developmental perspective. The researchers called the people who fit this pattern **expanders.** This group had not stopped any activities in the past year and had added at least one new outdoor activity since age 65.

The study found that contractors had continued the same activities they had learned in childhood. Expanders, on the other hand, continued to add activities throughout life. The researchers could not predict group membership by the use of income, age, race, or gender, and said that leisure service providers should create many options for older adults today. At least one type of older person, the expander, will take advantage of these new opportunities.

Can people learn to make better use of their leisure time? Zuzanek and Box (1988) found that people restructure their time after retirement. They maintain some activities, but they also trade off old activities for new ones. These findings show that people can change and expand their repertoire of activities, and they can develop new interests as they age.

Searle and Mahon (1991) report on a controlled study of a leisure education program in a day hospital. The program included the development of self-awareness, leisure awareness, attitudes, decision making, social interaction, and leisure skills. The researchers found that leisure competence increased with leisure education, and that self-esteem also increased with leisure education. In addition, it was found that leisure education can play a role in rehabilitation settings like day hospitals and can also help healthy people by expanding their knowledge of leisure activity choices (Verduin and McEwen 1984).

# NEW ACTIVITIES IN OLD AGE

## Outdoor Recreation

Leisure and recreation programs for seniors exist across the country. In Saskatchewan seniors can get free fishing licences and free access to provincial parks. British Columbia gives seniors free camping privileges and reduced rates on fishing licences. Manitoba, Saskatchewan, and Quebec schedule assisted travel tours. Nova Scotia runs fitness and recreation classes. Alberta has a recreation consulting service and promotes senior involvement in theatre. Airlines, buses, theatres, restaurants, and travel agencies across the country offer senior citizens' discounts.

Most of Canada's national parks now have wheelchair facilities, and special picnic tables and parking areas. Also, parks across Canada have programs for seniors. Riding Mountain National Park in Manitoba, for example, has "grandparent hikes" for grandparents and their grandchildren. Prince Albert National Park in Saskatchewan has a yearly seniors' golf tournament and La Mauricie National Park in Quebec has three lakes reserved for seniors. Parks in Cape Breton and Nova Scotia have special films for seniors. Riding Mountain National Park also has a program that gives older people a chance to do something for others. It offers special camping privileges to seniors if they agree to give information and help to other visitors (Hayashida 1983). All of these programs and services help older people stay active.

Recreation planners need to keep seniors' special needs in mind when they plan programs. For example, older people may lack transportation to get to parks, concerts, or recreation sites. Many cultural events take place in the evening, when older people tend to stay at home. Also, poor design of recreation settings sometimes keeps older people out. One woman noticed that the restrooms at a historical site had been redesigned for wheelchair use, but that a person in a wheelchair would have had to climb twenty steps up the side of a hill to get to them. More awareness of the needs of handicapped people (young and old) will lead to improved facilities, enabling handicapped seniors to enjoy recreational activities.

## Fitness

Both the Canada Health Survey (Health and Welfare Canada and Statistics Canada 1981) and the General Social Survey (Statistics Canada 1987b) found that activity declines with age. But a closer look at the findings of the Canada Health Survey shows that decline after age 65 depends more on health than on age. Comparisons of the healthy people in each age group showed that, barring ill health, people stayed active into old age. Of the healthiest 45-to 64-year-olds, 13 percent ranked as "very active," and 18 percent as "sedentary." Of the healthiest people aged 65 and over, the same portion—13 percent—ranked as "very active." Moreover, only 15 percent ranked as "sedentary"—3 percent less than the 45-to-64-year-olds. Finally, the figures for healthy people aged 65 and over do not differ much from the total population (20 percent "very active" and 14 percent "sedentary") (Health and Welfare Canada and Statistics Canada 1981, 79–80). The Canada Health Survey (Health and Welfare Canada and Statistics Canada 1981) says that people in good health and with positive emotional well-being at all ages tend to remain very active and that this is particularly true of older people.

A study of seniors in one housing co-op found that even people with health problems try to stay active. The study found that 49 percent of the tenants had fair-to-poor health; 18 percent had heart or circulation problems; and 45 percent had arthritis and rheumatism. Twenty-eight percent of these people use wheelchairs, walkers, and canes. Still, this study found that 60 percent of these people did full or partial body exercise, and 60 percent of those who exercised did so every day (Marmel, Sawyer, and Shell 1983).

Research shows that, as a group, older people are more active today than in the past. The Canada Fitness Survey (Fitness and Amateur Sport 1982) found that the two oldest groups (55–64 years and 65+) showed the largest increases in fitness activity from 1976 to 1981. The second-oldest age group (55–64 years) doubled its participation in sports from 1976 to 1981, and the oldest group (65+) reported nearly a three-fold increase in sports activity in those years. The oldest group showed an even more rapid increase in exercise activities. On average, able-bodied people aged 65 and over reported a 13-percent increase in exercise activity between 1976 and 1981, compared with only a 3-percent increase for able-bodied people of all ages. These figures do not show whether people have become more active over time or whether newer cohorts of older people bring more active lifestyles into old age. Whatever the reason for the increase, the results are clear: able-bodied older people have a higher rate of exercise participation than all of the other groups in the study, except the 15-to-24-year-olds. (This measure excluded people with disabilities. Older people have lower rates of participation than younger groups, if the figures include people with disabilities.)

## Fitness and Health

Some decline in physical function is due to true aging (for example, the slow-down in cell metabolism or decrease in lung elasticity) (DeVries 1975). Research shows, for example, that aerobic capacity and peak performance decline with age even in trained athletes (Stones and Kozma 1980; Ericsson 1990). Researchers still do not know, however, how much of this decline is due to aging and how much is due to past health problems, past habits, and underuse of the body (Stones and Kozma 1982). Studies of fitness training show that exercise can slow and even reverse some of this decline (Cunningham et al. 1987; Goldberg and Hagberg 1990; Shephard 1986).

DeVries (1975), one of the first researchers to study the effects of exercise on older people, says that declines in physical function have more to do with decreased activity than with true aging (see also Goldberg and Hagberg 1990; Ericsson 1990). Kraus and Raab (1961) call this the "hypokinetic disease." They say that the lack of activity can lead to mental and physical problems, while increases in activity can prevent or reverse these problems.

Other studies find clear signs of improvement in physical and mental well-being as a result of exercise. Spiroduso and MacRae (in press) report that aerobic exercise can improve information-processing speed. Aerobics can also lead to improvements in memory, intelligence, and cognitive speed (O'Brien and Vertinsky 1991). Studies by Fischer (1977) and Clarke (1977) show improvements in arterial and muscle flexibility. Cunningham et al. (1987) conducted a controlled study of a clinical training program for retired men. The researchers found significant improvements in the exercise group in maximum volume of oxygen, ventilation, and grip strength. Shephard (1978)

# Exhibit 12.1
## Fitness and Aging

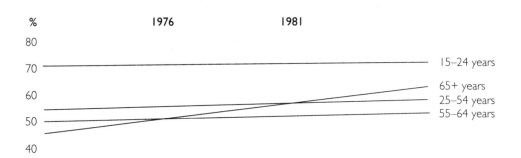

* Includes individual, dual, team, aquatic, and winter sports. Excludes exercise activity.

**Source:** Adapted from Fitness and Amateur Sport, *Fitness and Aging: Canada Fitness Survey* (Ottawa: Minister of Supply and Services, 1982), 4. Reproduced with permission of the Minister of Supply and Services Canada, 1991.

* Walking, running, jogging, cycling, calisthenics, and exercise classes.

**Source:** Adapted from Fitness and Amateur Sport, *Fitness and Aging: Canada Fitness Survey* (Ottawa: Minister of Supply and Services, 1982), 5. Reproduced with permission of the Minister of Supply and Services Canada, 1991.

studied thirty-eight people in Toronto over age 65 who took an exercise program four times a week. In seven weeks these people increased aerobic power by 30 percent. After a year they had increased muscle mass and bone density, and people in the program had lost three-quarters of their excess fat (Edwards 1983). Smith (1982), in a study of older women, found increases in bone mass due to exercise. DeVries (1975, 265) concludes from this literature that "the older organism is definitely trainable. Indeed the percentage of improvement [shown by older people who exercise] is entirely similar to that of the young."

## Fitness and Well-Being

Fitness programs can improve the psychological well-being of older people as well as their health (O'Brien and Vertinsky 1991). A controlled study by Gutman, Herbert, and Brown (1977) studied two kinds of exercise program: a standard program of walking, bending, and running in place, and a program called "Awareness Through Movement," designed by Dr. Moshe Feldenkrais. The Feldenkrais method, which is used in a number of senior programs across Canada, works to reduce pain and help older people do more for themselves. The program also increases people's awareness of how they move and teaches them to make smoother, more integrated movements.

The researchers ran these two programs for six weeks and then asked people how much they liked their program. About 85 percent of the people in each exercise class rated their programs as excellent. One hundred percent of the people in both groups said they felt satisfied with their program and said they would tell others to take it. Four-fifths or more of the people in each group said they would take another six-week class. The people in both programs claimed physical benefits, said they felt stronger and more flexible, and had better health in general.

They also said the programs gave them a "mental lift" and made them feel more relaxed. The researchers reported that the standard program led to "better contact" with new people. Other fitness programs show similar results. Perri and Templer (1984–85) report that older people in an exercise program improved their self-concept and felt more mastery over their environment.

Mittelman et al. (1989) found similar results in a study of thirty-three seniors who bicycled from Victoria, British Columbia, to St. John's, Newfoundland, in the summer of 1983. The group bicycled 6 days a week, averaging about 90 km per 7-hour day, and made the trip in 100 days. The researchers studied the seniors at three points: before they started, at the mid-point of the trip, and two days before the end of the tour. (Eleven seniors dropped out during the tour.) The seniors filled out questionnaires that asked about their background (age, marital status, etc.), health, exercise habits, expectations for the trip, their psychosocial condition, and anxiety. The researchers also gathered data on the seniors' physical condition (weight, height, etc.), strength, heart rate, blood pressure, blood chemistry, and food intake.

The study found that the seniors increased their flexibility during the tour, showed improved cardiovascular response to work, and had blood samples that suggested bone-mineral turnover (a sign of bone mass growth or maintenance). Eighty-five percent of the seniors rated the tour as enjoyable or extremely enjoyable. About a quarter of the group reported that they felt stronger and felt increased well-being. Members also reported increased self-confidence, better fitness, and a sense of accomplishment. The researchers conclude that "bicycle touring has a generally positive effect on the initially fit senior citizen" (Mittelman et al. 1989, 154).

Even in institutions, exercise programs can improve participants' sense of well-being. People in an activity program in a nursing home reported that they felt better, slept better, and did more of their own personal care (LaRocque and Campagna 1983). Studies also show that exercise leads to improved social life and increased happiness (Stacey, Kozma, and Stones 1985; Myers and Hamilton 1985). "This finding alone," Stacey, Kozma, and Stones (1985, 73) say, "provides sufficient justification for enroling in an exercise program."

## The Challenge to Fitness Programs

All fitness programs for older people face two hurdles: getting older people involved and keeping them involved (Myers and Gonda 1986). A Canadian study of physical activity found that the proportion of people who say they never exercise jumps from 19 percent of people under age 55 to 36 percent of people aged 55 and over (Statistics Canada 1987b). The Canada Fitness Survey, for example, found that people aged 65 and over, more than any other group, said they did not want to increase their present level of activity. And, more than any other group, they said that nothing would get them to increase their activity (Fitness and Amateur Sport 1982).

A report by the Red Cross confirms that most seniors today will not join fitness programs. The report also says that seniors avoid fitness classes because they have not done much of this kind of group exercise in the past (Canadian Red Cross Society 1983). The continuity theory of aging supports this view. It says that in old age people will tend to do the things they have always done or try to find substitutes for these activities. This, in part, explains the lower participation rates of women in physical activities. O'Brien and Vertinsky (1991) say that women take part in physical activity to a lesser degree than men from adolescence on. Women also avoid exercise and exertion. The stereotyping that labelled exercise and sport as male activities in the past helps explain this decrease in female physical activity with age. Other factors that lead to decreased activity for women in old age include: arthritis, chronic heart disease, caregiving demands, cost, and fears about injury.

Gutman, Herbert, and Brown (1977) found that half the people in their exercise study had dropped out by the end of the program. Cape (1983) also reported problems with attendance. She ran a fitness program in a nursing home and found that people dropped out, missed classes, or joined in the middle of the program. Mittelman et al. (1989) found that one-third of the seniors in the cross-country bicycle tour already mentioned dropped out before the end. Six of the eleven seniors who left the tour did so because of conflict with the tour leader. Only one senior left the tour because of the work load. Stacey, Kozma, and Stones (1985) report that the people who drop out may need the programs most. They say that older, less happy, and more anxious people tend to drop out of programs.

Programs have to motivate people to join and then to keep them in the program. Experts in program design report that:

1. People stay in programs when they have some say in the content of the program. Program leaders should consult with seniors when they start a program, and they should allow older people to help shape the program once they join.
2. People stay in programs when they enjoy them.
3. People stay in programs when they feel welcome.

Programs should give people a chance to socialize before and after classes (Stewart 1982; Stirling et al. 1986). Leaders of these programs need to support and encourage participation (O'Brien and Vertinsky 1991).

Leaders also need to choose programs that fit seniors' approach to exercise. Research shows that the best training program consists of high-intensity and high-frequency exercise (Sidney and Shephard 1978). But seniors tend to drop out of this type of program. Myers and Gonda (1986, 177) say that most seniors can improve their physical condition with a less strenuous exercise program. "Walking, dancing or swimming can also be used to enhance aerobic capacity," they say, "and may be more appropriate for older adults than such activities as jogging-running, skating or cross-country skiing." Less strenuous programs fit the needs of more seniors today and they encourage people to attend more often.

• • • • • • • • • • • • • • • • • • • • • • • • • • • • • • • • • • • • •

## Exhibit 12.2

### New Activity in Old Age

• • • • • • • • • • • • • • • • • • • • • • • • • • • • • • • • • • • • •

Two years ago, Hugh Clifford, 75, ran a marathon for the first time. He finished the 26-mile race in a slow four hours, 41 minutes and 46 seconds. Last May he competed in the Vancouver International Marathon and won the Canadian masters medal as the fastest marathoner over 70, with a time of 4:04:17 ...

When he retired at 64, he had a mild heart attack, a warning that set him to cycling, swimming and losing 25 pounds. He eventually gave up swimming for jogging, an activity he hated but kept at until he'd done a mile three times. Then he was addicted. Now he's replaced the hiking boots he first ran in with six pairs of good running shoes. He paid $5 for his first pair, and he still owns them; he calls them his dancing shoes. He runs every second or third day, about 50 kilometres a week, following a route along city streets and blacktopped seaside paths. In between runs, he does stretching exercises, reads magazines about running, lifts weights, keeps a daily diary of his distances in which he works out his minutes-per-kilometre rate. He trains for many annual distance races, attending a weekly marathon clinic at his local YMCA and joining "fun runs," where he gets a kick out of running with people much younger than himself.

He has a sense of physical well-being he never had before: "I am fit. Without a blush, I tell you that I am really fit."

**Source:** Excerpted from Audrey Grescoe, "Good Old," *Today Magazine*, 9 January 1982, 11–14, 16.

• • • • • • • • • • • • • • • • • • • • • • • • • • • • • • • • • • • • •

## Fitness in the Future

Shephard (1990, 189) says that most older people require an amount of energy per day at the minimum range for adults. But, he adds, "the main reason why many of the elderly—particularly the institutionalized—have a low energy requirement is that they have become even more inactive than their younger peers." Shephard (1990) says that low fitness, not having anyone to exercise with, lack of transportation, and lack of money all discourage people from exercising. This may change in the future as new groups of people enter old age.

Godin et al. (1988) studied the intention to exercise of current and retired staff at the University of Toronto. People who said they intended to exercise tended to have the following characteristics: female, clerical worker, close to a fitness centre, currently a member of the university athletic facility, had taken part in an exercise program in the past five years, and felt that they had below-average fitness for their age. These characteristics support some of the earlier findings and point to the future of exercise among older people in

Canada. First, those who have exercised will continue to exercise. Second, women have begun to show an interest in exercise. And third, people tend to exercise if they have ready access to a program or facility.

The Canada Fitness Survey found that middle-aged people (25–54 years old) had a better attitude to fitness than older people (55+) today. More of them than the older group said they took part in activity for fun and pleasure, to relax and reduce stress, to learn new things, and to challenge their abilities (Fitness and Amateur Sport 1982). This group may bring these attitudes and habits with them into old age. Canada's recreation system has already begun to change to meet their needs (Delisle 1982; Parks Canada 1973).

In 1980, for example, Alberta sponsored Canada's first games for people aged 55 and over: the Alberta Seniors' Games. Alberta also has a Senior Citizens Sport & Recreation Association (ASCSRA). The association has branches in eight Alberta Games zones in the province. Christie (1983) says that in 1982 (the second time the province held the games) 21,000 older people competed in playoffs for the games. The twenty-six events included trap shooting, tennis, handicrafts, and performing arts. Nine hundred seniors, among them retired doctors, homemakers, and homesteaders, made the playoffs. The average age of the competitors was 67. The oldest was a 92-year-old man from northern Alberta. The Alberta government has agreed to give $200,000 to support future games every two years.

Christie (1983) reports that people get more from the games than medals. Senior volunteers plan and run the games, serving as scorekeepers, referees, and administrators as well as contestants. The games, she says, inspire seniors to improve their skills. They also lead to new friendships and give seniors a chance to try new activities in a nonthreatening way.

## SENIOR CENTRES

Most cities and towns across Canada have senior centres. They form the closest thing to a nationwide recreation system for older people. People drop in to their local centre, meet other seniors, play cards, take classes, and in some cases get medical help.

The number of centres in Canada grew considerably from the early 1970s to the 1980s. In Saskatchewan, for example, the number of centres in the province grew from 3 in 1971 to 412 in 1983. Today seniors go to centres to socialize, take part in recreation, or get information. In small communities the centres sometime offer the only opportunity for social contacts. Some centres offer social and health care services as well as recreation. The Regina Native Elders Incorporated runs a centre that offers meals-on-wheels, crafts, and health checkups. Other native people's centres offer help with letter writing, filling out forms, and transportation to activities. Almost all activity centres in Saskatchewan belong to the Saskatchewan Seniors Association Incorporated (SSAI). This group promotes new programs and helps centres share information. The SSAI has over 20,000 members, making it one of the largest organizations of seniors in the country (Senior Citizens' Provincial Council 1983).

In Winnipeg, a non-profit agency called Age and Opportunity, Inc. (A & O), runs a system of full-service centres. These centres meet the strict standards set by the National Institute of Senior Centres in the United States. A & O centres offer programs like bingo, billiards, and folk dancing, but they also offer members financial and personal counselling and health care. The staff and the members of A & O centres share the work. While the staff ensure that the centres have programs like counselling, education, and health clinics, the members decide on recreation programs, fundraising, and centre maintenance (Age and Opportunity, Inc. 1983b). Each centre has a unique program that reflects members' interests and needs. At one centre classes might include English as a second language, at another conversational French. Centres also offer lunch and supper.

In 1990, A & O provided more than 183,000 units of service to older people (Age and Opportunity, Inc. 1990). These units included thousands of meals served at six centres, responses to requests for information, leadership training, and health information (Age and Opportunity, Inc. 1990). Seniors at A & O centres also give to their communities. Members plan programs and help prepare meals, sing in centre choirs, and visit local schools to perform for the students.

Ferraro and Cobb (1987) in the U.S. found support for two models of senior centre membership: the social agency model and the voluntary organization model. They found that older people in poor health use the centre as a social agency. They attend for lunches and for health maintenance services. Married seniors, with high life-satisfaction, and who live with a spouse, use the centre as a voluntary organization or social club.

This finding highlights the challenge that neighbourhood centres face from other recreational programs. In 1982 the federal government called senior centres "the most important source of recreation and cultural activity" for older people in Canada (Health and Welfare Canada 1982b). And the Canadian Red Cross Society (1983) found that seniors used senior clubs more than any other recreation service. But today, many young-old seniors see senior centres as one recreational option among many. Figures suggest that the use of senior centres may decrease in the future. Statistics Canada (1987b) reports that only about a quarter of people aged 65 and over said they had attended a senior club or meeting in the past month.

• • • • • • • • • • • • • • • • • • • • • • • • • • • • • • • •

## Exhibit 12.3

### Hanging Around the Mall

• • • • • • • • • • • • • • • • • • • • • • • • • • • • • • • •

Some older people choose not to join a senior centre or other organized group. Researchers Sijpkes, MacLean, and Brown (1983) of McGill University studied older people who spend their days at the Complexe Desjardins mall in Montreal. They found that many older people use the mall as a drop-in centre.

They describe a typical case:

An old man who lives in a twenty dollar a week room on Sherbrooke Street in Montreal leaves his room at eleven in the morning of a cold windy day. The streets are treacherously slippery. He carefully negotiates the two blocks to the Jeanne Mance entrance of the subway system. There he takes the escalator down to begin a long subterranean walk, occasionally enlightened by a glimpse of the outdoors, past the metro station, through the Place des Arts complex; he nips under Ste. Catherine Street to finally end up in the main space of Complexe Desjardins. By now he is quite warmed up from his cold outside walk, and he sits down on one of the many benches in the space, talks to some of the older people he knows, reads a newspaper which one of them has bequeathed him, and carefully smokes a cigarette.

Around noon he wanders over to the very centre of the space where he stands for a while watching the daily production of a live TV show for a French local channel. He splurges on a coffee which is available from a variety of little shops in the complex. On his way home he talks to some more people he knows and winds his way back through the underground system.

**Source:** Excerpted from Peter Sijpkes, Michael MacLean, and David Brown, "Hanging Around the Mall," *Recreation Canada,* February 1983, 44–46.

• • • • • • • • • • • • • • • • • • • • • • • • • • • • • • • •

Education programs at universities and colleges, for example, now attract many seniors who might once have been satisfied with the programs at a senior centre. Also, more mobile, younger seniors may prefer to attend an art gallery or fitness program across town that better meets their needs. This will leave less well, less mobile older people to use neighbourhood centres. These people take a less active role in leadership and tend to use the centres over a shorter time. A concentration of less healthy seniors in the neighbourhood centre of the future will move centres more toward the social agency model.

Ouellete (1986) studied the recreation preferences of French and English senior citizens' club members in New Brunswick. The findings from this study suggest that Canadian senior centres need to take into account members' sociodemographic and ethnic background. Ouellete (1986) found that marital status, gender, and ethnicity all influence leisure enjoyment and participation. The French Canadian women in this study, for example, said they enjoyed spiritual activities more than physical ones, while the English Canadian men said they enjoyed mass media activities more and spiritual activities less. Ouellete (1986) traces the difference in spiritual interest to gender, but also to traditional cultural differences between the French and English. Ouellete says that leisure education and counselling need to take gender and ethnicity into account. He concludes (1986, 226) that "there is some justification to develop and offer programs or services that would differ in orientation and/or content" for particular ethnic groups. Senior centres will need to take ethnicity into account as they alter their programs to fit the needs of a changing older population.

## EDUCATION

Most schools today serve the same basic function they did a century and a half ago, when they first began: teaching children to become adults and preparing young people for specific jobs in society (Macleod 1985). This system offers little to the older person, who is already an adult and retired from a job. Statistics Canada says that in 1981 fewer than 1 percent of men and women aged 65 and over enrolled in credit courses. A Statistics Canada (1989b) study found that 9 percent of couples aged 65 and over said they spent some money on education. The study gave no figures for unattached seniors because so few of them reported spending anything on education.

Of seniors who went to school, 70 percent went part-time (Health and Welfare Canada 1983). Devereaux reports that 4 percent of people aged 65 and over take part in formal education (not necessarily for credit). This contrasts with 10 to 29 percent in other age groups (Devereaux 1985). Devereaux (1985) says that, of the people aged 65 and over who enrolled in adult education courses, more than three-quarters of men and over 90 percent of women took hobby courses (e.g., woodworking, painting, cooking) or personal development courses (e.g., history, music appreciation).

These figures suggest that the school system, with its emphasis on testing, grading, and credentials, does not appeal to older learners. Standard theories of aging, like disengagement theory and activity theory cannot explain older adults' interest in education (Covey 1983). The growth of education programs for seniors today shows that seniors stay engaged. Some older people enrol in formal university and college classes, but many more older people engage in less formal kinds of education, like programs at senior centres and community clubs. Few seniors take up middle-aged types of education that lead to degrees and credentials as activity theory says they should (National Advisory Council on Aging 1990e).

## Exhibit 12.4
### Illiteracy Among the Older Population

Statistics Canada conducted a Survey of Literacy Skills Used in Daily Activities in October 1989. The study included a representative sample of 9,500 people aged 16 to 69. The study defined literacy as the skill needed to use print material normally found at work, at home, or in the community. Most Canadian adults, the study found, read well enough to allow them to carry on their daily activities. But nearly 2.7 million adults, or 15 percent of Canadians aged 16 to 69 had trouble reading most of the written material in their environment.

Compared to other age groups people aged 55 to 69 had the lowest proportion of people with adequate reading skills. Only 36 percent of this older group could meet everyday reading needs. But 63 percent of people aged 35 to 54 could meet these needs, as could 71 percent of people aged 16 to 24 (Statistics Canada 1989c).

These figures may reflect differences in educational background for the different age groups. The study found, for example, that people with the lowest education had the least reading skills. Other studies (Creative Research Group 1987, cited in One Voice 1989) report that poorer people, Francophones, and male seniors all have higher than average illiteracy rates. Also, illiteracy varies by region: for example, 28 percent of people 55 and over in British Columbia are illiterate while 50 percent of this

age group in the Atlantic provinces are illiterate.

The study showed that a large proportion of seniors today (and in the next few decades) will have problems with everyday reading tasks. Jean Woodsworth, President of One Voice, a seniors' advocacy association, says that people need to be able to "read the directions on a bottle of medicine or tell the difference between a can of cooking oil spray and oven cleaner at the grocery store. People who need community support services have to be able to use a telephone book, at the very least" (One Voice 1990b, 1). An older person may lose social supporters as they age. If, in the past, friends and relatives did the reading for the older person, the older person may now find themselves at risk.

A report of the first national conference on seniors' literacy (One Voice 1990a) says that literacy programs for seniors get low funding priority. The report also calls for more research on the types of literacy programs that work best with seniors. Programs for immigrant seniors, for example, require sensitivity to cultural differences. One Voice used the results of this conference to produce a *National Literacy Strategy for Older Canadians* (Aitkens 1991). The strategy focuses on public awareness, promoting literacy programs for older people, a commitment to lifelong learning, and improved support systems for older people with low literacy (Aitkens 1990).

Continuity theory gives one explanation for older people's choice of education; it says that a life time of experiences leads a person to certain choices in later life. For example, people with many years of formal schooling will

· · · · · · · · · · · · · · · · · · · · · · · · · · · · · · · · · · · ·

## Exhibit 12.5

## Modal Patterns of Education for Seniors

· · · · · · · · · · · · · · · · · · · · · · · · · · · · · · · · · · · ·

Moody (1988a) describes four modal patterns of education for older people: rejection, social services, participation, and self-actualization. These patterns, he finds, correspond to four views of later life:

1. The pattern of *rejection* sees old age as a time of obsolescence. Someone with this view of old age would see little reason to educate older people. This view fits the functionalist model of education that sees schooling as a way to prepare the young for work.

2. The pattern of *social services* sees older people as dependent and in need of services. The welfare state provides many services to older people, including education. Education fills time and gives people private satisfaction. It has a low priority.

3. The pattern of *participation* sees later life as

a time to take part in community life. Education helps people do this and helps them live more self-sufficient lives. It also creates new relationships between older people and those in other age groups.

4. The pattern of *self-actualization* sees old age as a time to develop wisdom. Education can free the older person to discover new possibilities in life and can lead to ego integrity and fulfilment. Few education programs follow the last two patterns. But these high ideals of participation and self-actualization suggest new types of educational programs (Moody 1988a).

· · · · · · · · · · · · · · · · · · · · · · · · · · · · · · · · · · · ·

tend to return to school in old age. Also, people who have enjoyed learning as a form of leisure will opt for this type of learning experience. This fits with some of the facts about aging and education today. For example, older people with higher levels of education tend to return to school. But continuity theory cannot account for the older person who attends university for the first time in retirement, or for the person who takes up a new interest in theatre, film, or music in later life.

The life-span developmental perspective offers another reason older people keep learning. This perspective says that growth and change take place at every stage of life, and that people grow and change in many dimensions. For example, a person may have severe arthritis that keeps them housebound. But they can still learn and grow intellectually. The life-span developmental perspective emphasizes the uniqueness of later adult life stages and the need for a flexible educational system to serve older people. This perspective fits with current theories of life-long learning. Adult educators (Kidd 1973) say that older learners' needs differ from younger learners. Older learners most often come back to school for personal development and to find meaning in later life. Older learners ask: Is the knowledge useful? Does it help me make better sense of my life and the world around me? Does it help me live more fully and enjoy my life more?

Schools will have to change their ideas about education and educational settings to meet the older student's needs. Myles and Boyd (1982, 271), for example, describe what an older person faces when he or she walks onto a university campus today.

> Mrs. Smith arrives ... and finds classes dispersed over a large campus with limited facilities for getting around. The principles of credentialism which lead to the organization of academic activity around exams and the accumulation of credits are of little relevance to her. When she attempts to relax in a recreation area she is subjected to loud music which she finds noxious. ... In effect, what Mrs. Smith is encountering is a social institution designed and organized for the young.

To meet the needs of older learners like Mrs. Smith, universities will have to give older students more options about class times, subject choices, and testing methods. They will also have to increase the kinds of social supports—like counselling or pre-registration assistance—that they give to older students. Some of these changes have begun, and others will take place as more older people come back to school.

Universities, for example, have begun to adapt their programs to older learners. Many offer free tuition and special classes for seniors. They give library cards to seniors and involve them in the planning and design of senior education programs. Teachers learn that they need to change their teaching style to fit older students' learning styles. Studies on learning and memory, for example, show that older people take more time to learn something new, and that anxiety, fatigue, and a lack of practice at school tasks make it harder for older people to succeed. Also, older people will drop out of a program if they cannot link what they learn to what they already know. Instructors need to take more time to present material, allow time for students to ask questions or state their views, and match the pace of their instruction to students' abilities.

The use of appropriate teaching methods along with more flexible schedules and open enrolment will encourage more older students to take secondary or post-secondary courses. A number of universities have started special programs for seniors.

The University of Moncton in New Brunswick and the Université de Sherbrooke in Quebec, for example, each support a program for francophone seniors called Université du Troisième Age (U3A). Each U3A group arranges to set up its own programs with the help of a university. Programs often include access to normal university classes, study groups, study trips, and fit-

. . . . . . . . . . . . . . . . . . . . . . . . . . . . . . . . .

# Exhibit 12.6

## Homebound Learning

. . . . . . . . . . . . . . . . . . . . . . . . . . . . . . . . .

Education programs have begun to attract more older people. Most take place in schools or in other community centres. But what about the homebound senior? Frail older people, people with disabilities, or people who must stay in because of bad weather—all of these people miss the chance to take part in community-based education programs.

A program in Winnipeg called Homebound Learning Opportunities (HLO), sponsored by Creative Retirement Manitoba, meets the needs of homebound seniors. The program serves people aged 50 and over. A facilitator visits a senior at home to offer a course once a week for four to eight weeks. The program also serves groups in hospitals and personal care homes.

In one case, for example, a woman had always wanted to learn to paint. But she had a continuous oxygen feed, and others told her that paint fumes would interfere with her breathing. A Homebound Learning consultant suggested the use of acrylic paints and then arranged for her to take a painting course (Kelly 1987). In another case, a woman said she'd always wanted to learn to tap dance. But she now had arthritis in her legs and could barely stand. Could Homebound Learning help? The program arranged for another senior, a dance instructor, to visit this woman. The instructor arranged for the woman to learn tap dancing while sitting on a kitchen stool.

The program began in 1988 with $35,000 from a local foundation. By 1989 a program review found that 232 people took part in 151 individual or group courses for a total of 1,334 class hours. In addition, 27 people subscribed to an audio-visual lending library and 70 people took part in an eight-part educational sampler series. The most popular individual courses included portable computer operation, a distinguished lecturer series, and armchair fitness exercise. The most popular group topics included armchair fitness, , Tai Chi, and acrylic painting.

Do people enjoy the program? Reports from students show that they do (Homebound 1989). A husband and wife, for example, began guitar lessons through the HLO program. "We played our first duet the other day," they say. "We hugged each other and laughed, feeling grateful for the opportunity to learn to play guitar at our age. [I have] even practised as much as 3 hours a day on my guitar since starting this course."

Another participant says that he's gained benefits from his relaxation training course. "My wife even listens in on my course and has learned from it. It's doing me good. I think it's a great thing for homebound seniors. It was a God-send for me because I can't get out much anymore. I hope this program stays around."

A guest-home owner says that "the frail residents in our facility definitely show a difference as a result of participation in armchair fitness classes ... Residents are clearly more talkative and cheerful both during and after these classes. Residents in particular appreciate being led by a facilitator who is an older adult herself. If she can do it, they feel they should be able to participate."

This program shows that people want to learn throughout life, even if they have a physical problem. It also shows that in an aging society educational programs need greater flexibility than ever before. Kelly, Steinkamp, and Kelly (1987) say that the types of leisure activities people need will change with age. They found that as people age, many social and leisure activities decline. But social and home-based activities show little decline and in some cases an increase. These activities lead to the highest subjective well-being. A homebound learning program fits the social and home-based preferences of many older people. As the older population ages, this type of program will grow in importance.

• • • • • • • • • • • • • • • • • • • • • • • • • • • • • • • • • • • • • • • • • •

ness programs. Courses most often focus on the arts, social issues, and the humanities (Radcliffe 1982). A group at Glendon College in Toronto, called Third Age Learning Associates, helps older people across the country set up third-age learning groups (National Advisory Council on Aging 1989b).

Distance education methods also open education to older people. Ryerson Polytechnical Institute offers courses by radio through its Open College. The director of the program says that people aged 65 and over make up between 10 and 20 percent of students in the courses (National Advisory Council on Aging 1989b). Other innovative delivery methods, like homebound learning, will increase educational opportunities for older people.

In the future more older people will probably return to school, and life-long learning will become a part of Canadian society. Moody (1988a) gives several reasons for this increase in life-long learning. First, schools show a greater concern for the older student today. They offer more flexible schedules, advice on courses, and in some cases special orientation programs for mature students (Thacker and Novak 1991). Second, career changes and new demands at work lead people to return to school. Almost three-quarters of men and half of women (of all ages) in the labour force take job-related or academic education programs (Devereaux 1985). Third, studies show that people with more education tend to keep taking classes (both academic and recreational) as they age (Vigoda, Crawford, and Hirdes 1985; Denton, Pineo, and Spencer 1988).

Already, more people go to school for more years than ever before. Statistics Canada says that in 1981 24 percent of people aged 65 and over had a high school education or better, but 39 percent of people aged 45 to 64 had more than a high school diploma, and 64 percent of people from 25 to 44 had at least a high school education (Health and Welfare Canada 1983; see also Mori and Burke 1986). Cyr and Schnore (1982) project a 15-percent increase between 1971 and 2011 in young-old men (65–74 years) with post-secondary education and an 8-percent increase in young-old women with post-

• • • • • • • • • • • • • • • • • • • • • • • • • • • • • • •

# Exhibit 12.7
## Elderhostel

• • • • • • • • • • • • • • • • • • • • • • • • • • • • • • •

As more older people continue their education, new educational programs will emerge to meet their needs. The Elderhostel program serves as an example of educational innovation for seniors. About two hundred and fifty universities and colleges in Canada (at least one in each province, Yukon, and the Northwest Territories) will sponsor Elderhostel programs on their campuses for about 20,000 people in 1991 (Elderhostel 1991b). Elderhostel combines university campus life with the European concept of hostelling (travelling from place to place and staying in inexpensive, safe lodgings). Elderhostel students live on a university campus while they take courses. The program also offers "homestay programs," in which students live with a host family. These programs give hostellers a chance to travel, meet new people, and learn things in a variety of settings they might not otherwise see.

The Elderhostel program accepts students over age 60 and their spouses. It does not matter how much education a person has had in the past. Most programs last one week—from Sunday afternoon until the following Saturday morning. A one-week program typically includes three courses. Elderhostel tries to keep the class size small: most programs enrol from thirty-five to forty-five students at a time. In 1991 the typical total fee for the week—including food, rooms, course fees, and fees for extracurricular tours and activities—was $295 in Canada. Fourteen percent of every course fee goes toward administration of the Elderhostel program and toward "Hostelships" (or bursaries) to assist people who cannot afford the program fee.

Elderhostel began in 1975 and now offers courses worldwide to over 300,000 people in over 70 countries at 1800 institutions, including Mexico, Bermuda, England, France, the Netherlands, the U.S., and Canada. The University of New Brunswick offered the first course in 1980, and Canadian programs have expanded quickly. From 1980 to 1981 the number of participants in Ontario more than doubled, and in the Maritimes the number of programs grew from one program in 1980 to programs in all four provinces by 1981 (Elderhostel 1981). In 1987, Elderhostel sponsored programs at twenty-one sites in the Maritime provinces (Elderhostel 1987). In addition French programs now exist in six provinces. The Canadian Elderhostel program produces a bilingual catalogue three times a year that goes to 55,000 Canadians.

Robert Williston, Executive Director of Elderhostel Canada, recalls the first courses he ran at the University of New Brunswick in 1980.

> One course was called Short Stories of Atlantic Canada. After the second day of classes I met the instructor at the photocopying machine. He said, "I can't get an undergraduate student to read one short story a class, but this group has gone through six in two days. They show up on time. They want to buy me coffee and talk about Atlantic writers who aren't even on the course. I'm learning more than they are. (O'Brien 1989, 23).

A few excerpts from the Summer 1991 Canadian Elderhostel Catalogue (Elderhostel 1991a) will give you some idea why this program has grown so fast:

- The Ulyssean Society/Niagara-on-the-Lake Chapter, Ontario, offers three courses with resource people from the Shaw Festival and Brock University: The Shaw Festival (a chance to learn about George Bernard Shaw, the Festival, and a chance to meet members of the company); Liberation Theology (the impact of this viewpoint on Christianity and a discussion of faith's role in practical life); Winemaking in Niagara (students visit a winery and learn about vine planting, wine tasting and the use of wines with food).

- Dalhousie University in Halifax, Nova Scotia, offers three courses: History of Nova Scotia (study the ethnic mix of Nova Scotia by understanding its history); Family History Research (learn to trace your roots and use a public archive as a learning laboratory); Computers: Introduction and Explanation (lectures and hands-on sessions to overcome computer-phobia).

- Bamfield Marine Station, Vancouver Island: Spineless Wonders (a study of marine invertebrates found in B.C. waters); Fishy Fun (trawl the waters in the station's research vessel, also learn Japanese fish printing); Seaweeds...Edible? Incredible (a discussion of seaweed and its future use as a food, also walk the beaches to learn about seaweed in the environment).

- Concordia University, The Loyola Campus, Montreal: The 20's: Age of the Metropolis (study the artistic richness of the modern city); The Folk Music of Quebec (learn about the reels, dances, stories and songs that make up Quebec's musical heritage); T'ai Chi (Chinese exercises to bring harmony to the mind and body).

   This selection of programs from across the country gives a glimpse of the options Elderhostellers can choose. Each institution has its own character and history, and Elderhostel students can choose the courses and the ambience to suit their interests.

**Source:** Adapted with the permission of Elderhostel Canada, 1991.

• • • • • • • • • • • • • • • • • • • • • • • • • • • • • • • • • • • • • • • • •

secondary education. Denton, Pineo, and Spencer (1988) make a similar projection. They estimate that the increase in the number of older Canadians, along with an increase in educational level for older people, will lead to over 200,000 older people enrolled in courses in the year 2010. This will mean a 141-percent increase over 1985 course enrolments. This increase in older students will reshape the philosophies and structures of our educational institutions.

## COMMUNITY SERVICE THROUGH VOLUNTEER WORK

Exercise, recreation, and education lead to increased life-satisfaction for older people. So does community service work or volunteer work—through the chance to give to others. Stone (1988) reports that seniors gave at least seven types of assistance to others: donations of money, transportation help, personal care, babysitting, housework, yardwork, and volunteer work. Rates of

# Exhibit 12.8

## Creative Retirement Philosophy

Creative Retirement Manitoba, one of the largest seniors' learning centres in Canada, describes some educational principles that present a new view of education for older people.

1. Retirement is a great creative opportunity for individuals, groups, communities and society.
2. People of all ages have the ability to learn, to grow, to change, and to be useful.
3. People of all ages have the right of access to education appropriate to their interests and needs.

4. Lifelong learning promotes not only intellectual growth, but also physical, emotional and social well-being.
5. Older people are a great source of wisdom, experience, and knowledge.

**Source:** Creative Retirement Manitoba (Brochure), September 1991. Reproduced with permission.

# Exhibit 12.9

## Profile

Older people can provide valuable resources to their community when the community finds ways to use seniors' talents. The example below shows one potential use for senior volunteers.

Every Monday and Wednesday after school, 10-year-old Kenny arrives at the apartment of Alexander Goldring, 86, for five or six cookies, a glass of milk and an hour's reading aloud followed by a spelling test. His tutor is a retired chartered accountant who speaks with a broad New York accent ... Kenny says proudly that because of Mr. Goldring's tutoring, his marks in reading have risen from mostly Cs to As and Bs.

A love of books and children and the simple conviction that "if I want to be happy I should make others happy" led Mr. Goldring to join a group of volunteers in Manhattan who worked as tutors. When he moved to Toronto with his wife seven years ago from New York, he discovered that volunteer tutoring in the public schools was virtually non-existent. Fortunately, he found Clinton Street Public School receptive to the idea, and he now holds weekly readings of poetry and stories for three classes and assigns them compositions and spelling tests. "There's always a glass of water and a nice chair waiting for me. The other day, a grade six class give me a tearful ovation after I read a very sad story about two boys raising money to support their sick sister's stay in the hospital."

**Source:** Excerpted from Penelope Jahn, "Good Old," *Today Magazine,* 9 January 1982, 11–14, 16.

giving differed for each activity. Less than 10 percent of people aged 55 and over engaged in personal care. But, more than half of people aged 55 and over donated money to an organization or to other people outside their household. And over 15 percent of people aged 55 and over reported doing volunteer work (Stone 1988).

Statistics Canada (1989a) reports that in 1987 Canada had 50,000 agencies registered as charitable organizations. Twenty-seven percent of adults in a 1987 survey reported that they do volunteer work often in health and welfare field services, administration and client supports, and transportation. Stone (1988) reports that almost one person in four between the ages of 55 and 70 gave transportation help to others. Most of this help (60 percent) went to friends and neighbours.

Statistics Canada (1990e) reports that 19 percent of men and 22 percent of women aged 65 and over work in charitable or service organizations as volunteers (see also Searle 1987). The higher a person's education level the greater the chance that they do volunteer work for an organization. In general, compared with people who live alone, those who lived with a spouse also tended to volunteer more (Stone 1988).

Some research suggests that more older people would work as volunteers if they had the opportunity. A study of people aged 60 and over in Northumberland and Newcastle, Ontario, for example, found that many older people would like to work as volunteers in schools (Hawkins 1980). Many of the subjects in this study said they would start work right away, if they had the chance. Seventeen percent said they would work in a library; 14 percent said they would listen to a child read; and 14 percent said they would teach students about seniors' hobbies and skills.

Some programs already use older people's talents in the schools. Studio Two, a seniors' drama group, presents plays and skits for students. Creative Retirement Manitoba (a learning centre for seniors; see Exhibit 12.8) arranges for older people to visit schools and speak about Manitoba history. A similar program was started in Montreal to enrich the school curriculum and to bridge the generation gap. In this program, a worker from the Centre local de services communautaires arranged for a group of seven older people in the downtown core to work with children in a local school. The seniors, who ranged from 55 to 90 years of age, worked with a class of twenty-seven students for ten weeks. Classes included attending a performance of the Montreal Symphony, a slide show on Venice organized by the seniors, and a play put on for the seniors by the students. The classes ended with a bus trip to Canadiana Village and a picnic lunch (Nahmiash 1985).

Volunteer programs can benefit seniors and their communities, but they require coordination. A program in Niagara, Ontario, called Senior Volun-

• • • • • • • • • • • • • • • • • • • • • • • • • • • • • • • • • • •

# Exhibit 12.10

## The New Horizons Program

• • • • • • • • • • • • • • • • • • • • • • • • • • • • • • • • • • •

Government programs often confine themselves to helping people meet their basic needs. Most Canadians know about the Canada Pension Plan and the health care system. But government programs can also help older people meet their higher needs—the needs for self-actualization, creative expression, and a sense of purpose in life. In 1972, the federal government sponsored a program called New Horizons to help seniors meet these higher needs.

New Horizons was designed to help groups of seniors start their own recreation and service projects. The program requires that seniors' groups have at least ten members, most of whom must be over 60 years old and retired. New Horizons will not pay a salary for full-time staff except in special cases, and it will not give money to groups or agencies that perform services for seniors. All the money goes as direct contributions to older people to use for projects they design. New Horizons allocates its funds according to the percentage of older people in each electoral district. This spreads the money across the country to urban and rural areas. On average New Horizons supports 2,000 projects a year (2,081 in 1988–89). It has assisted a total of 34,073 projects since 1972, for a total value of $212.6 million (Bourdeau 1991).

When the program began, most groups started recreation centres. But since 1982 New Horizons has encouraged seniors to start community service and mutual help projects. About 20 percent of projects in 1987 delivered services (Program Audit and Review Directorate 1989). Through these projects seniors do things for their communities. Projects range from meals-on-wheels programs to home repair services to a theatre group that tours nursing homes, schools, and hospitals. A massage class visits two nursing homes once a week to give residents treatments and to teach self-massage.

New Horizons has also funded advocacy and lobby groups across the country. It has helped start regional seniors' councils and provincial seniors' societies. These groups sponsor programs like the Alberta Seniors' Games and education programs. They also lobby the government for better policies. A 1982 report on New Horizons said that seniors had "formed seventy-eight major regional groups which are affiliated with approximately twenty-five provincial organizations. These in turn are affiliated with one of several national federations" (Health and Welfare Canada 1982d, 8).

The total New Horizons budget for 1989–90 came to a little over $16,267,300 (down from $17 million in 1985–86). About 75 percent of this money goes directly to support seniors' projects (the rest goes to staff salaries and administrative costs). Each project received an average of $7,817 in 1989–90 and served an average of 100 people (though programs ranged from small writing workshops of 25 people to large senior centres of 500 people). The program served 276,261 people in 1989–90 at a cost of $58.88 for each person in a program. The cost to the government, per capita for all Canadians over age 65, came to a little over $6 for the year (Bourdeau 1991).

The New Horizons program costs very little and serves people in all parts of the country. Each year nearly 12 percent of people aged 65 or over take part in a New Horizons project;

the portion of all older people who have taken part in projects since 1972 is much greater. An evaluation of the program in 1989 found that New Horizons participants as a group closely matched the characteristics of seniors in general (Program Audit and Review Directorate 1989).

Ninety-six percent of project leaders felt very satisfied or somewhat satisfied with the program. They said they met new friends, developed new skills, and felt less lonely because of the program. Ninety-three percent of the projects lasted for at least a year after the end of New Horizons funding. Members themselves took the initiative to find further funding and keep these programs going.

New Horizons encourages self-respect, independence, and self-sufficiency; it shows that given the opportunity, "older people will continue to be active, creative, and productive members of their communities" (Health and Welfare Canada 1982c, 8).

**Source:** Adapted from Mark Novak, "The Canadian New Horizons Programs," *The Gerontologist* 27 (1987): 353–55.

teers in Service links volunteers with community needs. The program uses the services of volunteers aged 55 or older. In 1986, 250 people volunteered for more than 3,000 hours a month as friendly visitors, meals-on-wheels helpers, and foster grandparents. Some volunteers helped older people with transportation, shopping, or household chores (Rapelje, Goodman, and Swick 1986).

Senior volunteers can have a global as well as a local impact. The federal government sponsors a program called Canadian Executive Service Overseas (CESO). The program recruits senior volunteers and assigns them to work in underdeveloped countries or with native groups in Canada. Volunteers, who are mostly retired people between the ages of 60 and 70, give technical and management advice to businesses, do feasibility studies, and help train workers and managers. The program pays travel and maintenance expenses.

From 1969 to 1982 the program sent about 3,000 volunteers to work with native groups, and it has about 750 volunteers on its active list. From 1967 to 1982 CESO had finished about 3,000 overseas projects, and it had about 2,700 people ready to take on new projects (Health and Welfare Canada 1982b).

Volunteering, whether at a local school or in a foreign country, can give an older person a sense of purpose in life. Bond (1982) studied 323 older volunteers and found that people who volunteer their services have higher life-satisfaction than people who do not. He suggests that counsellors prescribe volunteer work for clients who feel dissatisfied with their lives.

## SUMMARY

1. Older people spend a great deal of their time on passive media-related activities like reading the newspaper and watching television. Older people often spend their time alone, but they also enjoy spending time with others.

2. Income, lifestyle, gender, and health influence what people do and how active they remain in old age. Older people in good health have shown one of the highest rates of increase in sports and exercise activities in the past few years.

3. Physical functions do decline with age, but fitness training can reverse some physical decline. Fitness training can also lead to better sleep patterns, a better self-image, more social contacts, and increased happiness. Even in institutions fitness programs can improve residents' health and well-being.

4. Older people will join and stay in fitness programs if they have control over program content and feel relaxed and unthreatened by competition. More and more older people now value fitness and exercise.

5. Senior centres across the country offer education, counselling, and recreation for older people. They form the closest thing to a network of recreational programs in Canada. Centre activities will need to change in the future to meet the needs of younger, more active seniors.

6. People with many years of schooling will keep on learning as they age. Universities often sponsor special programs for seniors. Programs like Elderhostel, Creative Retirement Manitoba, and the University of the Third Age offer alternatives to traditional schooling. These programs are designed to fit the older person's interests and learning styles.

7. Many older people volunteer to help others. More older people might offer their skills and services to the community if they had the opportunity. New programs help older people find ways to use their skills. Studies show that volunteers report an increase in life-satisfaction.

8. The New Horizons Program helps older people fulfil their own aspirations. This program has helped set up thousands of self-help, community aid, and mutual aid programs, all run by seniors. New Horizons also sponsors political action groups that help create better government policies for all seniors.

## SELECTED READINGS

Fitness and Amateur Sport. *Fitness and Aging: Canada Fitness Survey.* Ottawa: Minister of Supply and Services, 1982.

A summary, with charts, of seniors' participation in fitness and athletic programs. The report shows the trend toward seniors' interest in exercise and fitness.

McPherson, Barry D., and Carol Kozlik. "Age Patterns in Leisure Participation: The Canadian Case." In Victor W. Marshall, ed. *Aging in Canada.* 2d ed. Toronto: Fitzhenry and Whiteside, 1987.

A sociological study of differences in leisure patterns by age, occupation, and income. The study shows a continuity of individual leisure patterns from mid-life to old age. It also shows that age, period, and cohort effects all influence leisure activities.

# Family Life and Social Relations

# INTRODUCTION

Rising divorce rates, the generation gap, and high residential mobility all point to major changes in the modern family (Nett 1988). Add to this the fact that more older people live alone than ever before, and it seems as though families have abandoned their aging members. Shanas (1979) calls this the "hydraheaded myth" of family breakdown. People continue to believe it, even though studies show over and over again that it is not true. Research shows that older people keep in contact with their families, that they rely on family members for help when they need it, and that middle-aged children feel responsible for their aging parents (Bond, Harvey, and Hildebrand 1987; Brody 1990; Campbell and Brody 1985). Studies also show that (not including spouses) children supply most of the help older people need (Morris and Sherwood 1983–84). Brody (1983, 597) concludes, in a study of three generations, that "values about family care of elderly adults have not eroded despite demographic and socioeconomic changes."

Today, most older people, even single older women, prefer to see their children, but not to live with them. Better incomes, government rent supports, and health services allow more people to choose this option than ever before. This chapter will look at three influences on family life and social supports: (1) normative age-graded changes (like marriage and widowhood), (2) informal social supports (like help with activities of daily living), and (3) new roles that people take on as they age (such as becoming a grandparent).

# NORMATIVE AGE-GRADED LIFE EVENTS

Normative age-graded life events are expected changes in life that correlate with chronological age. They include high school graduation, retirement, and marriage. Some gerontologists now also define widowhood as a normative life event for older women. Normative age-graded events define a person's status in society, the person's roles, and the person's relationships. When an event takes place, it signals a change in a person's social status and often also a change in their social network. The following discussion will focus on two normative events: marriage (including sexuality) and widowhood.

## Marriage

Nearly all Canadians get married. Gee (1987) reports that in Canada by ages 45 to 49, 92.5 percent of men and 94.2 percent of women have married. About 3 percent of people aged 65 to 74 report that they have divorced. This rate doubled from 1976 to 1986 and represents a shift toward greater acceptability of divorce among older people (Statistics Canada 1990e). Bengtson, Rosenthal, and Burton (1990) say that money, education, and strong social networks lead to good adjustment after divorce. But little research exists on divorced older people.

The proportion of married people drops (largely due to mortality) from about age 40 onward. For people aged 65 to 74, 80 percent of men and only 52 percent of women are married. For people aged 85 and over, 46 percent of men and only 8 percent of women are married (Statistics Canada 1990e). These figures show that women face a greater chance of widowhood than men and a greater chance of living alone in old age.

Married people have some advantages over their unmarried age mates. First, married couples tend to have more financial resources than unmarried people aged 65 and over. Couples tend to be younger than single older people, and often one or both members of the couple work. Even among people the same age, married couples have more money. This may be because they had a higher lifetime income than single people, more savings, and a family home.

Second, the large majority of older people report marital satisfaction, and they say they enjoy their marriage now more than ever (Connidis 1989a). Almost three-quarters of married couples aged 65 and over say they are "very satisfied" with their romantic relationship, and these people report higher satisfaction with their romantic relationship than any other age group (Statistics Canada 1980b; Connidis 1989a). Hess and Soldo (1985) say that older couples report high life-satisfaction because these people (and their marriages) have survived economic hard times and the stress of raising children, and have overcome any irritation with their partner's quirks and habits. Couples with children also enjoy a new freedom in old age. They live adult-centred lives that allow them to travel, visit with friends, share work at home, and do things together (Abu-Laban 1978).

Third, research shows that married people adjust better than nonmarried people to aging (Bengtson, Rosenthal, and Burton 1990). A good marriage gives the couple intimacy, mutual support, and high life-satisfaction (Connidis 1989a; Strain and Chappell 1982a). It also leads to longer life (especially for men) and better health (Connidis 1989a). Married older people, compared to non-marrieds, have fewer acute and chronic illnesses, fewer limits on their activities, and shorter hospital stays (Hess and Soldo, 1985). They also stand the best chance of staying out of nursing homes if they get sick, because they have someone to care for them. Marriage gives a person a live-in support system (Chappell and Blandford 1987b). Wister (1986), for example, found that married seniors feel less need for outside social relations. They also report a greater likelihood than nonmarried seniors of having sexual relations. Connidis (1989a) cautions that these findings apply only to good marriages. Constant bickering and dissatisfaction in a marriage can lead

# Exhibit 13.1

Percentages of Population Aged 50 and Over in Selected
Marital Status Groups, by Sex and Age, Canada, 1981

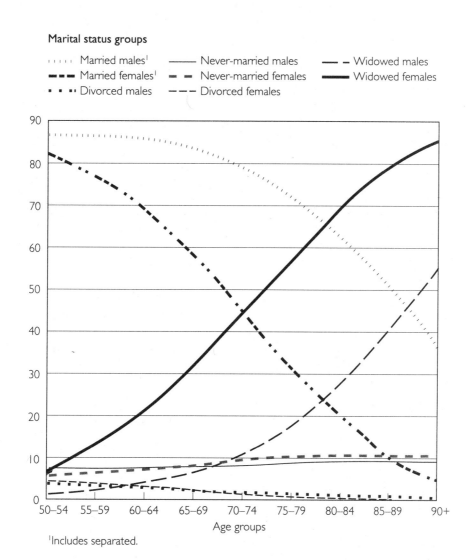

**Marital status groups**

¦¦¦¦¦ Married males[1]  ——— Never-married males  — — Widowed males
▬ ▬ Married females[1]  ▬ ▬ Never-married females  ▬▬▬ Widowed females
▪ ▪ ▪ Divorced males  ― ― Divorced females

[1] Includes separated.

**Source:** Health and Welfare Canada, *Fact Book on Aging in Canada* (Ottawa: Minister of Supply and Services, 1983), Figure 9.1.1, 67. Reproduced with permission of the Minister of Supply and Services Canada, 1991.

to depression and illness. Connidis (1989a) says that researchers need to look at the quality of a marriage as well as a person's marital status to understand the impact of marriage on well-being.

## Sexuality

Studies show that most older people have an interest in sex throughout life and that, given good health and a partner, older people can (and do) have sexual relations into late old age. Pfeiffer, Verwoerdt, and Wang (1968; also Verwoerdt, Pfeiffer, and Wang 1969) report on findings from one of the first studies of sexuality that included a large number of older people, the Duke Longitudinal Study of Aging. This study included data on 254 people between the ages of 60 and 94 years old. Cross-sectional analysis showed a drop in sexual interest and activity with age, but longitudinal data showed many patterns of sexual change. About 20 percent of the men, for example, showed an increase in sexual interest and activity with age. The researchers found that on average men stopped having intercourse at age 68, but the age when men stopped ranged from 49 to 90. Masters and Johnson (1970) report that men stop having sex because of boredom, interest in outside activities, fatigue, eating or drinking too much, illness, or fear of failure.

Women stop having sexual relations earlier than men—on average at age 60. This reflects the higher rates of widowhood for women in old age. Research shows that whether a woman maintains an active sex life or not depends on the presence of an active sexual partner. Widowhood or a husband's decision to stop having sex often put an end to a woman's sexual activity.

The Duke University research found that sexual activity in old age depends most on a person's pattern of sexual activity in the past. Men and women who have a partner and who enjoyed sex in the past will continue to enjoy it as they age (Palmore 1981). The Duke study also found that sexual activity leads to high life-satisfaction and good health for people between ages 45 and 70. Palmore sums up the Duke findings: "These statistics," he writes, "show that most older married persons are not asexual; on the contrary, substantial proportions remain sexually active until at least their 80s. They also show that impotence and sexual problems in old age are reversible, and that substantial proportions at all ages report increasing sexual activity" (1981, 89).

## Adaptations in Sexuality Due to Age

Sexually active older people have to adjust to changes in their bodies as they age. A man, as he ages, takes longer to get an erection, takes longer to feel

## Exhibit 13.2

### Seniors Show a Strong Interest in Sex

Starr and Weiner (1981) studied a convenience sample of 800 people between the ages of 60 and 91 from across the U.S. Two-thirds of the sample were women. All of them lived in the community and reported good health. Starr and Weiner found that older people report a strong interest in sex. "They think about it, desire it, and engage in it when they can, with the same average frequency that Kinsey reported for his 40-year-olds" (Starr and Weiner 1981, 35). Nearly all of these people (97 percent) said they like sex and the majority (75 percent) said they enjoy it as much or more now as in their youth. A 72-year-old woman said that now she had "no concern about pregnancy, [and] therefore an increase in pleasure" (Starr and Weiner 1981, 88). A 74-year-old widower said that lovemaking now was "Great. Now you can do things that you could not do before" (Starr and Weiner 1981, 194). Eighty percent of the sample thought sex had a good effect on an older person's health. About two-thirds (66.5 percent) of the sample considered orgasm very important to their sexual experience. Half of the sample (51.6 percent) thought that intercourse was the most important part of sex. Over seventy percent (71.7 percent) said that their sexual experiences left them satisfied.

The findings also show that people adjust their expectations and their activities to meet their needs. For example, nearly half the men (43.6 percent) and women (47.0 percent) said that they masturbate. This proportion increased among the widowed, divorced, and single people in the sample. About a fifth of the sample (19.9 percent) said that they masturbate if a sexual experience leaves them unsatisfied. Almost another fifth (17.8 percent) said they keep on trying. About two-thirds (62.2 percent) of the sample said that "sexy pictures, books, or movies" got them excited. One 72-year-old man said that he "often read sexy books as an aphrodisiac" (Starr and Weiner 1981, 50). These findings show that while their bodies change with age, people can maintain a good attitude toward sex and live active, enjoyable sex lives into their ninth decade.

This study gives an insight into sexuality in old age, but it has a built-in bias. The people who filled out the Starr and Weiner questionnaire may differ in some important ways from those who did not. People who answer questions about their sex lives, for example, may have more active sex lives than those who won't answer these questions. This makes it hard to generalize from these findings. Future studies will need to use random samples of seniors to see whether these findings fit the general population.

ready for intercourse again, and may have shorter, less intense orgasms. A woman, as she ages, may find that her vagina loses elasticity and opens less fully, and that she may have shorter orgasms. Older couples may need to use vaginal lubrication.

Weg (1983) says that people can accept many changes as they get older—changes in strength, the senses, and athletic ability. But, she says, a change in sexual function can visit "painful damage upon self-concept, motivation, and the zest for life. Culture still equates sexual performance with manliness or womanliness ... " (Weg 1983, 46; see also Turner and Adams 1983) Butler and Lewis (1976) describe a "second language of sex" that can overcome the feelings Weg describes. This language focuses on responsiveness, caring, and affection.

Sometimes a couple will need medical help or counselling to cope with changes in sexual performance (Szasz 1980). This can take the form of a medical checkup, information about changes in the body with age or sex therapy (Corby and Zarit 1983; Weg 1983). Studies show that older people can (and many do) make these adjustments as they age.

## Changing Attitudes to Sex in Old Age

Many researchers say that negative individual and societal attitudes toward sexuality may inhibit sexual activity in later life (Schlesinger 1983; Weg 1983). Schlesinger (1983), for example, says that virility in a young man gets labelled as lechery in an old man. Older people in institutions face special problems because they have less control over their lives (Kassel 1983). The views of the staff and the policies in some institutions can limit a person's sexual activity.

Mullens (1983) studied the sexual activity of older people in seniors' housing and in nursing homes. He found that people in nursing homes, compared with people in seniors' housing, had less privacy and freedom. Only 28 percent of the homes gave staff training in sexuality and aging. "With a few exceptions," Mullens (1983, 5) says, "sexual relations among residents were either not allowed or not encouraged except for married couples." Mullens found that older people themselves took a restrictive view of sex and he concludes that seniors "adhere to their Victorian upbringing" (1983, 7).

These attitudes of staff and older people toward sexuality will change for several reasons as new cohorts of people enter old age. First, gerontology courses teach younger people and professionals the facts about sex in old age. This can change the attitudes of those who work with older people (Damrosch 1984). Second, books that give advice to older people now, more than in the past, encourage sexual activity. In the past these books typically spoke to middle-aged children about caring for their aging parents, but a more recent study of these books found that they now give advice directly to older people (Arluke, Levin, and Suchwalko 1984). Third, cohorts differ in their views on sexual relations. Older cohorts have a more conservative view of sex, and most older people today do not favour sex outside of marriage. When a spouse dies, many women are left without a chance to enjoy sexual relations. Younger cohorts have more open attitudes to sex, and if they bring these attitudes with them into old age, there will be more sexual activity among older people in the future.

Weg (1983), however, warns against any new vision of sexuality in old age, saying that older people will only face a new stereotype if they feel they must have a partner and stay sexually active as they age. "There is no one way to love or to be loved;" Weg says (1983, 76), "there is no one liaison that is superior to another. No one life-style in singlehood or marriage, heterosexual or homosexual, will suit all persons. Self-pleasuring, homosexuality, bisexuality, celibacy, and heterosexuality are all in the human sexual repertoire."

## Homosexuality in Later Life

Most studies of sexuality in later life have focused on married or single heterosexuals. Few studies report on male and female homosexual seniors (Lee 1987). Do they face unique problems as they age? Do male and female homosexuals adapt better or less well than heterosexuals to sexual changes with age? Like heterosexuals, gays and lesbians decrease their sexual activity with age. Weinberg (1969) says that the gay and lesbian culture values youth more than the straight culture, and this may cause problems for male and female homosexuals as they age. But this may differ for men and women. Laner (1979) reports that, compared with men, lesbians have a less negative view of the physical changes that come with age. A collection of autobiographical writings (Adelman 1987) suggests that the women's movement has reduced the generation gap between young and old lesbians.

Lee (1987) conducted the first study of gay aging men in Canada. He studied 47 English-speaking men aged 50 to 80 years of age and interviewed them once a year for four years. Lee found that men who had partners in the past—a wife, lovers, or a combination of both—reported life-satisfaction even if they now lived alone. Lee found that homosexual men with lovers tend to report high life-satisfaction, but he also says that having a lover in later life "is not easy to achieve" (Lee 1987, 147). Only two men, out of the eight who lived with lovers, had found their lovers during the four years of his study.

Lee also found that men who preferred other gays as friends and those who knew an older gay man as a role model showed higher life-satisfaction. This supports another finding from this study. Lee found that gay men involved in gay social life reported high life-satisfaction.

Lee's findings show that older gay men get life-satisfaction from many of the same things as heterosexual men—companionship, sexual fulfilment, and friendship. They also have unique sources of satisfaction and face unique challenges as they age. Lee's study shows that gay men can adapt to the changes that come with age and that "it is possible to achieve ... happiness alone or by sharing life with a lover, even one found late in life" (Lee 1987, 151).

One theme appears in nearly all the studies of homosexuality in later life. Societal attitudes toward homosexuality have shaped and continue to shape the lives of gay and lesbian older people. Many older gay and lesbian people have had to adapt their lives in order to live in a heterosexual world. Societal homophobia led many gay and lesbian older people to hide their homosexual relationships (Kehoe 1989). They feared that exposure might cost them their jobs. Friend (1991) says that gay and lesbian adaptations to a hostile society may lead to successful aging. First, he says that gays and lesbians have experience in constructing a positive image of themselves in spite of social definitions. This may help them construct a positive image of themselves as they age. Second, gays and lesbians have experience in creating supportive relationships. This may help them create the support networks they need as they age. Third, many gays and lesbians have experience with political advocacy. These people will be better able to defend their rights as they age.

Research on homosexuality in later life has only begun. Lee (1991) proposes some research questions that need study. These include the longitudinal study of aging gay and lesbian couples, gay widowhood, and aged gays and lesbians in the homosexual community. Studies of gay and lesbian aging show that societal influences and past experiences shape a person's life in old age. They also show that sexuality plays an important part in homosexual as well as heterosexual aging.


## Widowhood

Nagnur and Adams (1989) report that, in Canada, the large majority of older couples (70 percent) remain married until widowhood. But men and women differ in their tendency to remarry after the loss of a spouse. In 1985, 5 percent of widows could expect to remarry compared with 14 percent of widowers. Nagnur and Adams (1987) report that men aged 55 and over have a marriage rate (3.3 per 1,000) twice that of women the same age (1.7 per 1,000). This meant that in 1986 almost half (48 percent) of women aged 65 and over were widowed (and remained unmarried) compared with fewer than 14 percent of men in that age group (Devereaux 1988).

Widows outnumber widowers for three reasons: (1) women live longer than men; (2) women marry older men; and (3) men, more than women, tend to remarry after widowhood. Exhibit 13.3 shows the outcome of these three trends.

## Exhibit 13.3

Life Patterns of Men and Women in Canada, 1987

• • • • • • • • • • • • • • • • • • • • • • • • • • • • • • • • • • • • • •

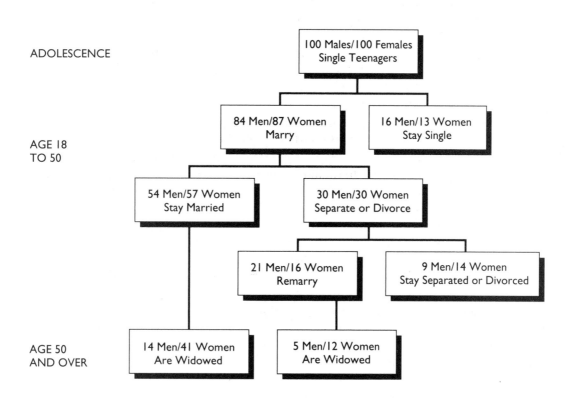

This chart compares the marital life patterns of men and women in Canada. It shows that 67 out of 100 women end up alone later in life after some period of marriage compared to only 28 out of 100 men. This makes living alone in later life a typical outcome for women today.

**Source:** Adapted from the National Council of Welfare, *Women and Poverty Revisited* (Ottawa: Minister of Supply and Services Canada, 1990) 16, 134. Reproduced with permission of the Minister of Supply and Services Canada, 1991.

• • • • • • • • • • • • • • • • • • • • • • • • • • • • • • • • • • • • • •

Today almost 70 percent of widows are over age 65. Statistics Canada says that a widow at age 65 can expect to live almost nineteen more years. A woman widowed at age 80 can expect to live almost nine years after her spouse dies (Statistics Canada 1984d, cited in Matthews 1985). Matthews

(1987) calls widowhood an "expectable life event," one that creates a great deal of stress (Holmes and Rahe 1967; Matthews 1982; Matthews et al. 1982). This means that many men and most women will go through the pain of widowhood (Gee 1986). Studies of widowhood have focused on two themes: the social supports that buffer widows' and widowers' stress and the differences between widows' and widowers' responses to widowhood.

## Widowers

Most studies of widowhood contain too few men to compare with women, but a few studies show how the loss of a spouse affects each gender. First, studies of family supports, friendship, and confidants (someone in whom one confides) show that women have more social supports than men. Most older men today have spent their lives focused on their careers, while older women today have spent their lives focused on people. This gives older women more close relationships than men in old age. It also makes men more vulnerable when illness and the death of a spouse occur. "Widowed men," Hess and Soldo (1985, 75) say, "are doubly bereft—they have lost both a helpmate and confidante ... Conversely, the widowed woman is unlikely to be entirely devoid of close friends."

Second, wives link men to wider social networks. Women more often than men say they have close relationships with family and friends besides their husband. They often name these friends, relatives, and children as their confidants, and they keep up these relationships when their husband dies (Connidis and Davies 1990; Powers and Bultena 1980; Strain and Chappell 1982a). A man whose wife dies loses a wife, a companion, and a social secretary (Antonucci 1990). This may explain why many men rush into another marriage after they lose a spouse.

Third, men find it harder to make new friends or to join groups for help. Dr. Alan Lyall, who directed a program for widowers at the Clarke Institute of Psychiatry in Toronto, says that "men are not apt to use talking as a source of support. The women come to the Clarke and the men go across the street to the Silver Dollar tavern" (Wylie 1981, 34–38). Studies show that widowers suffer from isolation and loneliness (Pihlblad, Adams, and Rosencranz 1972). Compared with women, they also run a higher risk of suicide (Resnick and Cantor 1970; Rushing 1968; Maris 1969). This literature suggests that men suffer more than women when they lose a spouse because they have fewer social contacts than women.

Wister and Strain (1986) used a large Canadian random sample to compare widows and widowers. Unlike previous studies, this study found no difference between the well-being of men and women, even though women had more friends and confidants than men (see also Matthews 1987). They say that widowers may need less social support than widows to feel satisfied. Also, men may enjoy comradeship and sharing interests with others rather than the closeness of a confidant relationships. Wister and Strain (1986) conclude that older men may not want or need the same kinds of social relations as older women:

> Overall, it is clear from the results that there is little support for the view expressed in the literature that older widowers suffer from greater social and psychological disadvantages than widows. It would appear that this myth has developed out of an inherent bias among some researchers to assume similar social-psychological needs across genders (1986, 18).

This study suggests that men and women have different friendship and confidant needs, possibly due to the kinds of relationships men and women learn to form earlier in life. More research on the social lives of widowers will show how their needs differ (if they do) from those of widows.

## *Widows*

Social supports and family roles buffer the stress of widowhood for women. Norris (1980) found that women stayed socially active in mother and grandmother roles after their husbands died, and that they also held onto their wife role. These women had lost their husbands on average ten years before, but when Norris (1980, 142) asked them if being married made their "daily activities more satisfying and easy to deal with," many of these widows agreed. She found that these widows "remained emotionally committed to being wives" even many years after their husbands died.

Studies show that a woman's age predicts how much grief she will feel when her husband dies. Younger widows, whose husbands die suddenly, feel more intense grief than older widows (Vachon et al. 1976; Vachon 1981). A woman who loses a spouse "on time" (for example, in her late sixties) tends to expect her husband's death. She has made this a part of her life plan (Matthews 1987), and, more often than a widower, she will have widowed friends, as well as siblings, to give her support.

Strain and Chappell (1982a) asked 400 older people whether they had any confidants. They found that 77 percent of the people in their sample had at least one confidant, and 51 percent had two or more. More women than men had confidants, and men more often than women named their spouse as their confidant (Chappell 1990; Keith et al. 1984).

Studies show that confidants contribute to good morale (Chappell and Badger 1989). They also buffer people from anxiety and tension. Lowenthal and Haven (1968) studied role loss in old age (not just widowhood) and found that people with no confidants felt more depressed than those who had one.

This finding held even if the person with no confidant increased their interactions and the person who had one decreased theirs. Strain and Chappell (1982a, 496) say that

> the existence of at least one confidant relationship, irrespective of the number of times one might have contact with that confidant—emerges as a significant predictor of life satisfaction. This lends support to the argument ... that it may not be the usually reported frequency of interaction that is important to the quality of life, but rather the quality of that interaction.

Strain and Chappell (1982a) found that widows often chose a sister or brother or a friend their age as a confidant. Matthews (1985) found that many widowed women get support from their sisters. She says that more than half the widows in her study saw at least one of their sisters or brothers several times a month and that more than half of them listed a sibling, often a sister, as someone who gives them social support (see also Bengtson, Rosenthal, and Burton 1990; and Connidis 1989c). Harvey (1984, cited in Matthews 1985) found that 25 percent of the widows in her sample had contact with a sibling at least once a week, and 10 percent had contact more than once a week.

McDaniel (1989) says that older women's greater life expectancy and their tendency to remain widowed leads to many of the problems that older women face. Inflation, for example, will eat away at a survivor's pension, if the widow has one. She will face a decreasing ability to look after herself in her own home. And she runs a greater risk of institutionalization than a married person because she will lack spousal supports if she gets sick (Dulude 1987; Matthews 1982). Widowhood, in spite of good social supports, may put a woman at greater risk as she ages.

## INFORMAL SUPPORTS FOR OLDER PEOPLE

Normative events and sociocultural conditions influence the quality of life in old age, but they do not determine it. Older people can and do respond actively to the changes that aging brings. Their response depends on their personality, past experience, and social resources. This section will look at the methods older people use to cope with aging.

The term formal support refers to professional caregivers such as doctors, nurses, and social workers. People pay for formal supports either from their own resources or through their taxes. The term informal supports refers to the unpaid help given by friends, neighbours, and family. Informal supports include everyday help such as rides to the doctor or to a shopping centre, help with yardwork, or just a visit from a neighbour. Informal supporters can also help an older person cope with a personal crisis, adjust to a change in health, or locate a formal service (Snider 1981). The National Advisory Council on Aging (1990d) estimates that 270,000 seniors in the community need support.

Older people who need help with daily chores or health care sometimes use both the formal and informal support systems. Béland (1989) found that in a random sample of 538 older people in Quebec, for example, high users of formal services also used informal services a great deal. Studies show that people usually turn to the formal system only after the informal system breaks down (Chappell and Havens 1985; Brody 1981; O'Brien and Wagner 1980).

Snell (1990) studied the legal history of family support in Canada in the 1920s and 1930s and found that these laws expected families to care for their older members. The federal Criminal Code still requires children to provide parents with the basic necessities of life, if the parents cannot provide for themselves. All provinces (except Saskatchewan, Manitoba, and Quebec) also have legislation that requires a child to support a needy parent, if the parent supported the child in childhood (National Advisory Council 1990a). Very few cases have gone to court to enforce these laws (Dranoff 1984, cited in National Advisory Council 1990a).

Today, most older people get voluntary informal support from their families. And people continue to get support, especially from the nuclear family, even after they face a health care crisis (Stolar, Hill, and Tomblin 1986). Informal supports can also buffer stress from life events like widowhood or illness (Rosenthal 1987a).

Stone (1988, 14) found that the availability of "primary potential support groups" changed as people aged. He defines this type of group as family and close friends who give help to the older person and who can expect help from the older person. Stone (1988) reports that about a third of people aged 65 to 79 lived with a spouse and had family and friendship ties. Men more often than women had this kind of support group structure. Past the age of 80, community-dwelling seniors tended to live alone, but they still had links outside their household to children, close friends, and other relatives (Stone 1988). Women more often than men had this kind of support group structure. Very old people in institutions probably have smaller support structures or none at all.

Stone's research describes the "potential" support group available to older people. Other studies have looked at how older people choose their informal supporters out of this potential group. Studies have also looked at what tasks informal supporters do. Two models describe the way people use informal supports: (1) the **task specificity model** says that different groups (family, friends, neighbours) have different abilities and offer different types of support (Litwak 1985). Each group plays a specific role in supporting the older person; (2) the **hierarchical compensatory model** of support states that people choose their supports first from their inner family circle. They then move outward to get support from less intimate people as they need more help (Cantor and Little 1985). This model, for example, says that a married older person will get help first from a spouse, and a widow or widower will get help from a child (most often a daughter) (Chappell 1991; Walker 1991). The older person will then turn to friends, neighbours, and formal supports in that order.

Penning (1990) compared the ability of these two models to explain older people's use of informal supports. She found only limited support for each model. Older people tended to use a variety of formal and informal supports at the same time and not in a specific hierarchical order. She also found that groups did a variety of tasks that overlapped. For example, relatives and neighbours may both help with household tasks. Penning (1990, 227) says that "it is unlikely that assistance is provided routinely and uniformly on the basis of a set order of preference ... " Penning (1990, 227; see also Corin 1987) concludes that "the issue of who provides assistance to whom, of what type, and under what conditions is complex."

Chappell (1991) adds another dimension to this complexity. Her research suggests that whether or not an older person lives with someone strongly influences the type of support they get. If an older person lives with another person, the person they live with will likely give them support for the activities necessary to daily living. Litwak (1985) found that this held true for spouses, but Chappell found that it was the case regardless of the relation of the housemate to the older person. This means that shared living arrangements (between siblings or friends) may help widowed or childless older people live in the community.

Chappell (1989a) found that men get less informal support than women from nonspousal supporters. This showed up most clearly for less serious illnesses. Chappell (1989a) concludes that women's stronger emotional bonds with friends and family lead to greater support. Chappell, Segall, and Lewis (1990) found the same trend toward greater support for women regardless of the type of illness (common ailments, health emergencies or functional disability). Compared with men, women tended to consult more family and friends regarding common ailments. Women, more often than men, said they would consult a relative outside the house for a health emergency. And women, compared with men, reported support from more helpers and more help from daughters and relatives for functional disabilities.

Rosenthal (National Advisory Council on Aging 1986a, 4), estimates that 70 to 80 percent of the health care that allows a person to stay in their home comes from informal supports—a spouse or child (though the type of support available and used may differ by gender). Chappell and Segall (1989) report that when an older person has a helping network, they feel greater subjective well-being. The researchers found that older people, who had children to help during an emergency, felt more secure and those who had spouses to help with everyday ailments felt that they had good consultation and advice.

Chappell and Havens (1985) studied 800 older people in Winnipeg. Four hundred of these people used formal home care services; the other 400 came from a random sample of the population not using these services. They found that more than half of their total sample (58 percent) received help of some kind. Ninety-four percent of those who received help got it from informal sources. Also, of the 15 percent who got formal care, 80 percent also got informal care. Chappell and Havens found that people who got help with everyday activities—dressing, shopping, telephoning—were more likely to get help from informal than formal supports. The researchers conclude that "most elderly persons cope well within the community without an inordinate amount of assistance. Further … [these findings] also support the claims that informal care to aging members is alive and well. This is true even when the elderly individuals are recipients of formal care such as that provided by [home care programs]" (Chappell and Havens 1985, 227).

## Children as a Source of Informal Support

Adult children provide much of the support needed by their adult parents. Hall (1989) found that even hospitalized older people receive informal help from their children. He studied twenty-seven adult children who care for hospitalized, chronically ill parents. The adult children reported that their parents depended on them a lot and they predicted a high future dependence. They also reported that they gave their parents a lot of psychological support, got involved in bureaucratic mediation in the hospital, and gave their parents personal care. Hall (1989) found that caregiving created stress for the children, but they continued to help their parents.

Studies show that adult children and their parents see the amount of support provided by the children differently. Many studies report that older people feel they receive less support than their children say they give (Bond and Harvey 1991). Bengtson and Kuypers (1971) refer to this as differences in the "developmental stake." Older people have a greater stake in the relationship with their children and so, tend to emphasize the existence of family harmony and solidarity. They may de-emphasize the amount of support they receive in order not to see themselves as a burden on their children. This difference in perception can create tensions in the family. Adult children may feel that their parents do not appreciate how much they do for them, even though the children may feel they do as much as they can.

Gatz, Bengtson, and Blum (1990) say that intergenerational interaction may have grown in intensity in recent years. Older people and their children live longer lives and spend more years interacting with one another. Gee (1988) reports that in Canada from the 1830s to the 1950s the number of years spent parenting declined for women. But the time spent as an adult child increased. Today, people spend more years as an adult child of living parents than as parents of young children (Bengtson, Rosenthal, and Burton 1990; Gee 1988). This trend will continue in the future. In some cases child caregivers will also need support as they grow older. Stolar, Hill, and Tomblin (1986) say that many nuclear families need more support and should get more from the formal care system.

Jutras (1988) says that changes in the family may limit informal caregiving in the future (see also Marshall 1987). She says that geographic mobility, immigration, greater numbers of 18-to-25-year-olds at home, smaller modern homes, multi-generational help needs, more pressure on fewer children, women in work force, caregiver burnout, and conflicting demands on caregivers may all put pressure on the informal care system. A lower birthrate and smaller numbers of children per family, for example, mean that middle-aged children will have fewer siblings to help support their aging parents (Gatz, Bengtson, and Blum 1990, citing Hagestad 1986).

## Friends as a Source of Informal Support

Blau (1973) says that people enjoy friends most in youth and in old age. Synge and Luxton (1984) found that 20 percent of women aged 74 and over received visits from non-relatives every day or two. Almost 30 percent said they received visits once or twice a week. Studies also show that older people get more enjoyment out of visits with friends than with family. Researchers say that people in a family may visit one another as a matter of routine or because they feel obliged to see one another. But, when older people see their friends, they do so out of choice (Antonucci 1990). Older people also may have more in common with their friends than with younger family members, and this leads to greater warmth and good feeling (Chappell 1980).

Most older people choose friends from their own age group. Chappell (1983a) studied 400 noninstitutionalized older people living in Winnipeg. Eighty-three percent of the people in this sample said that their close friends were also older people. On average these older people had less than one friend under the age of sixty. These people reported more contact with friends than with relatives (who lived outside their home) or with neighbours, and they felt more satisfied with their friendships than with other relationships outside the home.

Rempel (1985) found that childless older people create a network of supportive friends, and they report as much life-satisfaction as older people who have children. She found that compared to people with children, childless older people feel more satisfied with their health, housing, and income. Rempel concludes that "family is not necessarily the crucial element in determining high life quality in old age" (1985, 347). Still, the social networks of older childless people offer less support when the older person becomes sick. These networks also provide less support for activities of daily living (Bengtson, Rosenthal, and Burton 1990). For this reason, childless older people face a greater risk of institutionalization than do people with children.

Researchers say that friendships can help older people overcome problems caused by lost work roles and the lost spouse role in old age. Norris and her colleagues (1983) say that older people use friends and family their own age as role models and for emotional support. "Since friendship rests on mutual choice and mutual need and involves a voluntary exchange of sociability between equals, it sustains a person's sense of usefulness and self-esteem more effectively than filial relationships" (Chappell 1980, 173). Friends who are the same age often share the same physical limits, the same interests, and the same historical background. Studies of family supporters (who live outside the older person's home) and friendships show that older people often rely on friends their own age for social and emotional support. This research suggests that different people in the older person's social network (children, neighbours, friends) serve different functions in the older person's support system. A child may help a parent with activities of daily living like banking, transportation, or housekeeping. Neighbours and friends can serve as confidants and social partners. A variety of relationships creates a full and satisfying support network.

## Informal Support and Caregiver Burden

Research shows that older people often use informal supports (Chappell and Havens 1985; Thompson 1989) and that these supports succeed in keeping people out of institutions (Hess and Soldo 1985). Married people, for example, have a built-in caregiving system. Pruchno (1990) found that even old and frail people continued to give care to their cognitively impaired spouses. Hess and Soldo (1985, 78) report that "75 percent more married than unmarried elderly with functional health limitations rely exclusively on care services produced within their own households." Even in late old age, when people have serious functional disabilities, married people have half the institutionalization rate of unmarried older people (Hess and Soldo 1985).

Some caregivers report feelings of self-satisfaction and accomplishment (Colerick and George 1986). Fitting et al. (1986) found that one quarter of husbands reported improved relationships with their wives after they began caregiving. In another study, a majority of daughters, who had completed their caregiving work, said that they felt glad that they helped when they did (Lewis and Meredith 1988).

But, most families pay an emotional and psychological price when they take on informal caregiving (Bond, Harvey, and Hildebrand 1987). When policy makers talk about "shifting care to the community," this usually means shifting the job to a daughter or wife (Aronson 1985; Chappell 1982a; Hooyman 1990; Treas 1977). Caregivers often feel isolated, fatigued, and overwhelmed by the strain of care (Zarit, Reever, and Bach-Peterson 1980; Novak and Guest 1989). A respondent in one study of middle-aged children said, "I have looked after both parents for twenty-seven years and they have become very dependent on me. We are very tied down and I don't know how much more my nerves and health can stand" (Marshall, Rosenthal, and Synge 1983). In another study a woman said, "[mother] has been getting more and more forgetful and confused and can't be alone at all. I'm depressed, and I don't sleep well. How can I go to work when she needs constant supervision?" (Brody 1990, ix).

Caregiving leads to a variety of tensions for middle-aged children. They often feel both intense pressure in trying to meet the demands on their time made by work, their children, and caregiving, and emotional upset at having to deal with an ill parent (Gee and Kimball 1987; Bond et al. 1990). Gatz, Bengtson, and Blum (1990) say that caregiving brings up the inherent tension between the adult child's personal autonomy and his or her interdependence within a family. Even adult children who do not consider themselves caregivers may feel concern about their parents. A study by Marshall et al. (1983) found that about a third of adult children reported worry about the future health of their parents. The closer the feelings between children and parents and the more frequent the contact between them, the more the children worried (Marshall 1987).

Some research (Horowitz and Shindelman 1981) suggests that spouses of those receiving care suffer a greater burden from caregiving than do adult children. They may feel the strain more as they see their partner decline (especially if the person shows mental as well as physical decline). Spouses may have health problems themselves that make caregiving difficult and they may have fewer resources (financial and social) to call on than would a middle-aged child. Pruchno (1990) found that spouses got little support from others and that even task support and social support failed to reduce spouses' feelings of burden.

In the case of single (widowed or divorced) older people with children, middle-aged daughters most often take on the job of caregiving. Kaden and McDaniel (1990) found that daughters provided 87 percent of daily and weekly assistance to their parents (compared with 13 percent for sons). Mothers receive 70 percent of this care. Horowitz (1985) found that sons take on the job of caregiver only when the parents have no daughter to help. She found that sons called and visited parents less often than daughters and also that they prepared meals, cleaned house, or gave personal care to their parents less often (1985). Brody (1981) says that women often get caught in the middle—sandwiched between care for their children and care for their parents. "Such women are in middle age, in the middle from a generational standpoint, and in the middle in that the demands of their various roles compete for their time and energy" (1981, 471). Jutras and Veilleux (1991) report no difference in caregiver burden between men and women. But most studies show that females report more strain from caregiving than males (Marcus and Jaeger, 1984). These women suffer physical strain, lower morale, and greater psychological burden than men (Marcus and Jaeger 1984; Zarit, Reever, and Bach-Peterson 1980).

Gottlieb (1989) says that four conditions influence feelings of burden: past and present relationships with the care receiver, the support a caregiver can draw on, psychological coping methods, and the impact of caregiving on other spheres of life (see also Chiriboga, Weiler, and Nielsen 1990). For example, caregiving can cost a woman money, a career, and pension benefits in the future. Brody and Schoonover (1986) say that 28 percent of nonworking, middle-aged caregiving daughters in their study quit their jobs to take care of their mothers. Other women reduced their work hours, and some had thought about quitting. Brody and Schoonover found that the mothers of working women got the same number of hours of care (formal and informal) as the mothers of nonworking women, but the working women often had to pay for personal care and meal services. These paid services filled in for them while they worked.

Myles (1991, citing Canadian Advisory Council on the Status of Women 1990, 15) reports that in 1961, one-earner couples made up 65 percent of all families. This figure had dropped to 12 percent by 1986. Today, a middle-aged couple will spend 60 to 80 hours of their time at work compared to only 48 hours for a couple after World War II. The trend toward women working outside the home has created a "care-giving crunch" that places heavy burdens on women (Myles 1991, 83).

Society expects women to work as caregivers. Neal et al. (1990) found that employed caregivers, compared with employed non-caregivers, experience more stress and greater absenteeism from work. The researchers say that caregivers need family strategies to cope with stress. They also need job flexibility and community supports to help them stay at work. Aronson (1985) says that the government should pay for care given by family members. She also says that because the Canadian Pension Plan pays benefits based on average yearly earnings over a lifetime, Canadian society should allow caregivers to drop out the years they spend caregiving when they add up their pensionable years of work instead of counting them as years of zero income. Aronson admits that these reforms will cost the government more money and that the government will probably resist funding them. Unless some reform takes place, however, women will continue to absorb the cost of caregiving in the community.

Myles says that changed workplace norms and more sympathetic personnel practices can help ease this crunch. But he also calls for more radical reform, saying that "nothing short of a revolution in gender relations and in the sexual division of care-giving work is required to solve the problem" (Myles 1991, 84).

## Care for the Caregiver

A number of researchers (Chappell 1989b; Gatz, Bengtson, and Blum 1990; National Advisory Council on Aging 1990d) have proposed ways to ease caregiver burden; some of these proposals are listed below. None of them address the large-scale issues of gender inequality or the changing role of women in the labour force. Instead, they focus on ways to support care for the individual caregiver.

1. Family counselling can help ease the burden of caregiving. This works best when it takes into account the entire family system—the caregiver's spouse, children, and siblings as well as the older person. Counselling can help caregivers deal with moral conflicts about how much protection to give a care receiver. Counselling or psychotherapy can help a caregiver deal with stress and depression.

2. Support groups give caregivers information about how to cope with caregiving demands. They also give caregivers emotional support. The Alzheimer's Society, hospitals, and churches offer support groups. Some groups offer support based on a specific disease (e.g., dementia or cancer). Some of these groups have a professional leader; others work as self-help groups. People in these groups often report feelings of relief and greater ability to manage as caregivers.

3. Community services include respite services. These range from friendly visitors, who stay with the care receiver for a few hours, to full-day adult

day care, to longer institutional respite. All of these programs give care-givers a break from the demands of caregiving. Institutional respite pro-grams can last from several days to several weeks, allowing caregivers to take vacations, deal with personal needs like medical treatment, or simply rest. Burdz, Eaton, and Bond (1988) found that behaviour problems decreased after respite. But caregivers still felt some burden. Other studies have also found mixed results. Lawton, Brody, and Saperstein (1989) report little measurable benefit from respite care beyond the feeling of caregiver satisfaction.

Mohide et al. (1990) conducted a controlled study of the combined effects of a variety of intervention methods. The study offered caregivers health care for themselves, an education program on caregiving, help with problem solving, in-home respite, and a self-help support group. The control group received normal community nursing care.

The researchers found mixed results. Neither the intervention nor the control group felt less depressed or anxious after the six-month study. But the experimental group did show some improvement. Their quality of life was better; they kept their care receivers in the community longer; they found caregiving less trouble; and they felt more satisfied with nursing support. This study shows that intervention can relieve some of caregiver burden. But researchers need to use a variety of approaches to measure the benefits of support. Also, George (1990, 581) says, "given that we know little about the caregiver stress process, perhaps we should not be surprised if it is difficult to document that our interventions have strong positive effects."

Chappell (1989b) reports on a number of programs that might relieve caregiver burden. These include pay for caregivers, employers' support of caregivers through family leave programs, and a program by IBM that offers an Elder Care Referral System to help caregivers cope with the social service system. Marshall (1989) projects a rapid growth in employee assistance pro-grams for caregivers. But, little evidence suggests that payment will lead peo-ple to take on the caregiver role, or that money alone will relieve burden (Arling and McAuley 1983; Noelker and Poulshock 1982). Chappell (1989b) recommends careful research on the value of paying caregivers and on the effectiveness of corporate support programs.

Interventions cannot completely do away with all feelings of burden. Nor should they. Spouses and children will feel loss, anger, and frustration as they see a person close to them suffer through an illness. These feelings reflect a legitimate response to a parent's or spouse's suffering. But interven-tions can help caregivers understand caregiving; they can help caregivers cope with the everyday demands of care; and they can give caregivers emotional support.

• • • • • • • • • • • • • • • • • • • • • • • • • • • • • • • • • • • • • • •

## Exhibit 13.4

## Feelings of Caregiver Burden

• • • • • • • • • • • • • • • • • • • • • • • • • • • • • • • • • • • • • • •

A report published by the Canada Mortgage and Housing Corporation (Gnaedinger 1989) includes comments by caregivers about their experiences. These comments reveal the stresses that caregivers face.

• I was out of energy, out of patience … and I was afraid I was out of love, because I was starting to scream at him … and he hit me one time. Every day he is slowly dying and part of me is dying with him, and our marriage is dying with him … I am not widowed, not married … what am I?

• How many sleepless nights I had, I can't tell you. I looked like the wrath of God. Eventually my kids said to me, C'mon Dad, we're losing Mother, we don't want to lose you too!'

• He destroyed my personality … I didn't realize what an impact it had on me.

• My mother is like a baby that we care for … our life has been shattered by this disease and it continues to shape our habits, but we wish to continue this experience to the end … our mother became ill when she was 72 years old, she is now 81 years old. She continues to be our mother in spite of her soul being gone.

• I don't think I would survive if I had to go through it again today. One has to have lived it in order to understand. I am still not able to remember the whole experience unemotionally, although it has been 8 years since he passed away.

• As I am printing this I have started to cry. God help other caregivers who have to go through all the stages of this horrendous disease.

**Source:** Nancy Gnaedinger, *Housing Alzheimer's Disease at Home* (Ottawa: Canada Mortgage and Housing Corporation, 1989). Reproduced with permission.

• • • • • • • • • • • • • • • • • • • • • • • • • • • • • • • • • • • • • • •

## The Future of Informal Support

Informal supports play a vital role in the well-being of older people. But the availability of informal supports may decrease in the years ahead. At least three changes in Canadian society point to this change.

First, changes in demography may decrease the amount of informal support older people will get in the future. Family size has shrunk, so older people in the future will have fewer children to call on for help (Crimmins and Ingegneri 1990). Stolar, Hill, and Tomblin (1986) note that a decrease in the availability of nuclear family supports increases the risk of institutionalization.

Also, the number of children over the age of 65, who care for their parents, will increase in the future as more people live longer (Bengtson, Rosenthal, and Burton 1990). Abu-Laban (1980a) says about 10 percent of people aged 65 and over also have a child over age 65. Some of these children will be unable to care for their parents, and some may need health care help themselves.

Second, as people live longer, their support groups suffer from what Stone (1987) calls **cohort attrition**. Peers die off over time, leaving members of some support networks without help. This makes children a vital source of support for most older people as they age (Marshall, Rosenthal, and Synge 1981). Synge (no date), in a study of social supports, found that the older the woman the more often she turned to a child for emotional support. Thirty-one percent of women aged 40 to 54 said they turned first to a child, compared with 63 percent of women aged 70 or over.

Because women outlive men more often than men outlive women, they have to turn to children for support. Few studies have looked at how older women feel about relying on their children. Aronson (1990) found that older women feel ambivalent about depending on their children. Her qualitative study contained 14 women aged 59 to 85. Women in this study said they could depend on their daughters for help, but they wanted to be independent and self-reliant. They felt torn by the need for support and the feeling that they might burden their children. To deal with this, these older women set limits on the amount and kind of help they would accept. But they could not deal openly with the sense that they lived marginal lives in their families. Aronson (1990) says that research needs to look more closely at older women who receive care. This will give family members and policy makers a better idea of what kind of support the older person wants.

Very old people will even lose their children. Shanas and her colleagues (1968, cited in Abu-Laban 1980b) found that in Britain, Denmark, and the U.S. between 20 and 25 percent of all older people have no children. Similar trends will show up in Canada in the years ahead. Very old people (many of them women) will need more formal supports as they age.

Third, expressive ties for older people tend to decline because of widowhood and cohort attrition. This leads older people to use their remaining ties to meet expressive needs. This may cause problems for the Baby Boom generation in the future. They have had fewer children of their own than older people today. In the second or third decade of the next century, the middle-aged children of Baby Boom parents may find themselves swamped by their parents' care needs.

These trends suggest potential problems with the availability of informal supports in the future. But other trends might lead to stronger informal supports. First, longer life expectancy means that spouses will live together longer than ever before. This will give married couples more informal support as they age.

Second, current trends in health promotion (better diet, exercise, and a decrease in smoking) may lead to better health in old age (Stone and Fletcher 1986). If these trends continue, older people in the future may need less long-term health care support.

Third, new types of groups based on the mutual needs of older people may develop. Novak and Stone (1985) call these semiformal structures because they fall between the informal (voluntary) support structures of the family and the formal (professionalised) structures of the health and social service systems. Semiformal structures include car pools, groups of people in the same building who shop together, friendly visitors, or "daily hello" phone callers. These groups and relationships do not rely on informal kinship, friendship bonds, or on the fee-for-service bond of formal supports. Instead, they are based on a bond of reciprocity and on the fact that they bring mutual benefit to users. More of these groups in the future could make up for losses in older people's networks.

Both trends—the decrease in informal supports and the increase in alternative forms of support (including home care and semiformal structures)—could get stronger in the future. The well-being of older people in the future will depend on how well alternatives to traditional supports meet their needs.


## ELDER ABUSE

Most older people get support and comfort from their families, but some people face exploitation and abuse. Research shows that most elder abuse comes from family members. This leads many abused older people to suffer in silence, makes elder abuse hard to estimate and harder to eliminate.

Most Canadian research on elder abuse has used convenience samples, sometimes with low response rates. This makes generalization from these findings uncertain. Podnieks et al. (1990) conducted Canada's first random-sample survey on elder abuse. The researchers conducted telephone interviews with a sample of 2008 people aged 65 plus who lived in private households. These people present a statistically reliable picture of the 91 percent of seniors who live on their own in the community. The survey asked about abuse carried out by family members and other intimates.

The sample contained about two-thirds women; 73 percent of respondents owned their own homes; and 52 percent were married. About a third of the respondents received the Guaranteed Income Supplement (the federal government pension that goes to the poorest seniors); 63 percent reported good or excellent health; and the large majority shopped, cooked, and cleaned for themselves. Relatively few respondents reported feeling lonely, bored or downhearted. The majority by far (92 percent) said they felt fairly happy or very happy.

The researchers defined four categories of abuse—material abuse, chronic verbal aggression, physical violence, and neglect (Podnieks et al. 1990). The study counted only the most serious and obvious cases. Because of this, the researchers caution that their findings probably underestimate the number of abused older people.

The study estimates that about 4 percent of all older people in Canada (about 98,000 people) in private dwellings have recently experienced abuse. This is similar to the rate (3.2 percent) that Pillemer and Finkelhor (1988) report for a random sample study in the U.S. Most of these cases involve passive, verbal, emotional, and financial abuse, rather than physical violence or neglect. This fits with the findings of other U.S. and Canadian studies (Belanger 1981; Hickey and Douglass 1981; Stevenson 1985).

Podnieks et al. found that about 2.5 percent of seniors in the Canadian study have experienced material abuse (potentially 60,000 people nation-wide); about 1.4 percent of seniors experienced chronic verbal aggression (potentially 34,000 people nationwide); about .5 percent of seniors experienced physical violence (potentially 12,000 people nationwide); and about .4 percent of seniors experienced neglect (potentially 10,000 people nation-wide). The study also found a fifth common form of abuse—denial of access to grandchildren. About 4 percent of seniors (98,000 people) report denial of access at least once since they turned age 65. If the researchers had included this category at the start of their study, the overall prevalence rate of abuse would nearly have doubled to 7 percent of seniors (172,000 people) (Podnieks et al. 1989). Nearly .8 percent of seniors suffer from more than one form of abuse (potentially 19,000 people nationwide).

The Prairies had the lowest rate of abuse (30 per 1,000). British Columbia had the highest rate of abuse (53 per 1,000). Female victims of abuse outnumbered male victims by almost two to one. The study found that some types of people faced a higher risk for some types of abuse than for others. For example, people who reported material abuse tended to live more isolated lives and to have poor health. These people faced abuse from varied sources including spouses, friends, children, and distant relatives. People who reported neglect were most often women with poor health, low morale, and a dependence on others for functional help. These people faced abuse from spouses, children, and non-family caregivers.

People who reported chronic verbal abuse and physical violence had some things in common. They tended to be married, and they reported that most of the abuse came from their spouse. Victims of verbal abuse reported that stress and emotional problems led to abuse, while victims of physical violence reported that alcohol led to abuse and that in more than half of the cases physical violence led to injury. More than one-quarter of these cases required medical attention. "In nearly two-thirds of the cases [of physical violence]," Podnieks et al. (1989, 9) write, "victims had been slapped or hit with an object. In more than one-third of the cases, victims had been threatened with a knife or gun during the past year."

What can be done about abuse in its varying forms? The researchers suggest the following steps be taken to decrease abuse and improve intervention:

1. Older people who face victimization may need help in order to take action. Law enforcement professionals need to know how to recognize and respond to abuse. A study in the U.S. looked at the effect of training police officers to detect abuse (Thornman 1980, cited in Shell 1982). The study found that police officers who took a month-long training program made referrals to social service and health care agencies in 55 percent of all cases of family violence. Police who did not take the training program made no referrals.

2. Isolated people who face the risk of material abuse can benefit from financial and legal advice. Professionals who provide this advice need more training in how to work with older clients. Dependent older people who face the risk of neglect may benefit from caregiver support and education programs (Hess 1982).

3. People who face physical violence or verbal abuse rarely seek help. Many of them blame themselves for the abuse. Intervention programs should include emergency shelters, advocacy programs, and housing options.

4. Nearly one-third of victims (32 percent) report that they were "not very aware" of public legal services. Older people need to know more about the resources in their communities (Podnieks et al. 1990).

5. Victims suffer psychological distress from abuse, reporting depression and unhappiness. Mental health services could help these people cope with their distress. Victims said that they would benefit from individual counselling and victim self-help groups (Podnieks et al. 1990). The researchers conclude with a call for demonstration projects that will test alternative methods of intervention.

Wolf and Pillemer (1989) note that elder abuse and neglect have existed throughout history (see also Stearns 1986). What, they ask, accounts for the sudden interest in abuse and neglect? They trace this interest to four social changes: (1) the growth of the older population; (2) the increased political power of older people; (3) the women's movement and a critical analysis of the family; and (4) the state's willingness to intervene in family life. Some authors (Callahan 1986; Crystal 1986) argue that formal service agencies have adopted the cause of elder abuse in order to expand their influence and get more funding. These authors link the sudden interest in elder abuse to the expansion of the welfare state. Crystal (1986) argues that some approaches, like mandatory reporting of abuse, will do little to help abused older people. He argues that special programs aimed at reducing elder abuse reinforce negative stereotypes of older people as feeble and helpless. Wolf and Pillemer (1989) take a different view. They see health and social service professionals' intervention in child abuse and in elder abuse as parallel. In both cases professionals, on behalf of the state, set out to protect a vulnerable minority. Through this process elder abuse has become a legitimate social problem.

The research on elder abuse supports the idea that older people suffer from varied forms of mistreatment. And it supports the idea that many abused older people need help. But the research also shows that the vast majority (96 percent) of older people do not experience abuse. These figures should help us keep the issue of abuse in perspective.

## OLDER PEOPLE AS SUPPORTERS

Most of the writing on older people in families focuses on their needs and what other people do for them, but older people also give help to their families. Shanas (1967) says that "far from being the passive recipients of their adult children's bounty, reciprocal help is given in the form of home services, monetary assistance, assistance in time of illness and other crisis situations and, in addition, older parents often provide child care services."

Older people give at least three kinds of support: first, they help their spouses and children with health care and daily chores; second, they give their children financial support; and third, they give emotional support to and serve as role models for younger family members.

### Daily Help by Older People

Neysmith (1982) says that society does not see the daily help older people give to their families, because it goes on in private. She studied 200 older men and women in Ontario and found that over 80 percent of these people said they helped their family and friends. Chappell (1983a) found that spouses and peers (many of them over age 65) provide most of the social and health care support needed by their family and friends. Chappell and Havens (1985) found that, in a sample of elderly home care support users and non-users, 55 percent of users and non-users provided support to others. Most of them gave support through an informal network.

Stone (1988) reports that 21.5 percent of people aged 55 and over give transportation help to others; 15.6 percent do volunteer work; and 11.8 percent help someone with housework. Connidis (1989b) found that most people who volunteer do so for an organization and that those who help with transportation most often do so for a friend, neighbour, or relative (not living with them). Older people who help with housework or yardwork do so most often for their children, or for a friend or neighbour. And older people who help with personal care most often help a friend, neighbour, or relative (not living with them).

The types of help people provide differ by gender. More men than women give transportation help, help with yardwork, and help with home maintenance. More women than men give help as volunteers, help with housework, personal care, and babysitting. The tendency to help differs with subjective health, age, gender, education, and marital status. Connidis (1989b) found that younger old people (aged 65–69) who are in excellent health, have some post-secondary education, live with a spouse, and live on the Prairies tend to give the most help.

These findings show that most older people live interdependently with family, neighbours, and friends. They give and receive help with practical activities, finances, and advice throughout their lives (see also Antonucci 1990; Antonucci and Akiyama 1987).

## Financial Support

Older people give younger members of their families financial support. The amount and kind of support given differs by social class and ethnic group, but studies show that even middle-aged people think of their parents as givers (Baruch and Barnet 1983). Other studies show that the elderly give more money to their children than they get from them (Cheal 1983, 1989–90; 1985b; 1986; Schorr 1980).

## Emotional Supporters and Role Models

Research shows that adult children rely on their parents as role models throughout their lives and turn first to their parents for support and help if they lose a spouse (Bankoff 1983; Schwartz 1979). Older family members derive great satisfaction from the help they give to their children and to other younger family members. Neysmith (1982) asked 200 older people in

Ontario about the roles they play in their families. About half the people in the study reported the role of keeping their families together—they told family members about one another and organized family events. All of the people in this study saw this as an important job. Neysmith found that people who played this role had higher morale than people who did not.

Rosenthal, Marshall, and Synge (1980) found that older people play many roles in their families. These include the "occupational sponsor" (the person who helps others find jobs or get started in business), the "comforter" (the person people turn to for personal advice and support) (Rosenthal 1987b), the "ambassador" (the person who represents the family at ceremonies), the "head of the family" (the person who makes choices that others go along with), and the "kinkeeper" (the person who keeps people in touch with one another). Rosenthal (1985) found that women generally occupy the kinkeeper role. Families with kinkeepers tend to get together more often. Men in families with kinkeepers benefit by having stronger ties to their siblings.

Connidis (1989a) reports that older parents least enjoy helping their children with chores like cooking or shopping. But they most enjoy visiting and socializing with their children and grandchildren. Older parents bring their families together on special occasions, fostering increased contact among family members. Older women often serve as advisers and confidants to their widowed daughters.

Family roles can give meaning and purpose to an older person's life. Black (1985) found that older people had the best emotional well-being when they gave as well as received support. Reciprocity made older people feel useful, independent, and worthwhile. Black says that professionals should help older people find ways to give to their supporters, since this will create more fulfilling relationships between parents and their children.

## GRANDPARENTING

More people will enter the grandparent role today than ever before and many of them will enter this role in midlife. Connidis (1989a) says that between 75 and 80 percent of older people have at least one grandchild and most older people have four or more. Hagestad (1985, 48) calls today's grandparents "demographic pioneers." Bengtson (1985) says that grandparents differ in how they play this role. Some grandparents feel that they do enough by simply being present, others play a more active role as family arbitrators, watchdogs, or family historians. The grandparent role offers older people one of the most satisfying and enjoyable ways to give to other family members.

A study of grandmothers (Robertson 1977) found that 80 percent felt proud and happy about grandmotherhood. The younger grandmothers in the study felt they should be role models for grandchildren and teach them to work hard and be good. These younger grandmothers often had husbands and jobs, and, as a result, had less time for grandchildren than the older grandmothers. Older grandmothers—most of them widows and women without jobs—took a personal view of grandparenting. They enjoyed their role because it increased their life-satisfaction. These women spent the most time with their grandchildren, and the grandparent role meant more to them than to younger grandmothers.

Research shows that grandchildren value their grandparents. Younger grandchildren say they like grandparents for the presents they bring them, and older children like what they do with their grandparents (Kahana and Kahana 1970). Studies show that children's feelings about their grandparents depend on the relationship between the grandparents and the parents. Robertson (1977) found that only when parents approve do grandmothers get involved in activities with grandchildren.

· · · · · · · · · · · · · · · · · · · · · · · · · · · · · · · · · · · · · · ·

## Exhibit 13.5

### Volunteer Grandmother: An Answer to the Loss of Family with Age

· · · · · · · · · · · · · · · · · · · · · · · · · · · · · · · · · · · · · · ·

In a surrogate family, an older person and a younger family adopt one another. Over time they may build up the kind of feeling for one another that natural families share.

At 51, Marion is a volunteer grandmother.

Besides liking small children, Marion says she became a "granny," because her own children were taking her for granted.

"They have their own lives. I was active in the sorority for two years, but now I need to fill the void."

For Brenda Wylie [the mother of Marion's surrogate grandchildren] …Winnipeg's Grandparent-

ing Program has lessened the isolation of being in a city 2,218 km from her own parents.

"They (her parents) are in Ottawa. They're wonderful grandparents, that's why we wanted someone here. We knew what we were missing."

Brenda adds that although she was thinking of the children when she asked for a grandparent, Marion has become a friend to the entire family.

"It's nice to have someone else to spend time with. We often chat on the phone."

Marion says she is pleased with how things have turned out since being matched four months ago.

"I think I've got the best family. We fit together so beautifully. It's hard to believe we're not a natural family."

Source: "Volunteer Granny Becomes 'Friend' to All of the Family," *Winnipeg Sun*, 22 December 1985, 53. Reproduced with permission.

· · · · · · · · · · · · · · · · · · · · · · · · · · · · · · · · · · · · · · ·

What a grandparent makes of the grandparent role depends on the older person's gender, age, marital status, and relationship with his or her adult children (Bengtson 1985). Neugarten and Weinstein (1964) studied styles of grandparenting. They describe five styles: a formal style, a fun-seeker style, a surrogate-parent style, a reservoir-of-family-wisdom style, and a distant-figure style. Only a few of the grandparents (most of them grandfathers) showed a **reservoir-of-family-wisdom style**; this type of person had special skills or resources to give. Only a few of the people in this study (all of them grandmothers) showed a **surrogate-parent style**; this type of person looked after grandchildren while parents worked. About one-third of the grandfathers and one-fifth of the grandmothers showed a **distant-figure style**; this type of person had friendly feelings for their grandchildren, but they did not see them very often. About a quarter of the grandfathers and a third of the grandmothers showed a **fun-seeker style**; this type of person spent leisure time with their grandchildren and had fun with them. About a third of both grandmothers and grandfathers showed a **formal style**; this type of person left parenting to the parents and did not offer advice on childrearing. The researchers found that older grandparents (aged 65 or over) more often took on a formal style, while younger grandparents tended to take on a fun-seeker style. This research shows that the grandparent role allows room for personal expression and that older people can use it as a source of emotional satisfaction.

A more recent study by Cherlin and Furstenberg (1985) looked at the grandparenting styles of 510 U.S. grandparents with teenaged grandchildren. They report five styles of grandparenting: detached, passive, supportive, authoritative, and influential. Detached and passive grandparents were usually older than grandparents in the other groups and tended to take a more hands-off relationship to grandparenting. One woman summarized this attitude simply: "I don't think the grandparents should interfere with the parents" (Cherlin and Furstenberg 1985, 107). Detached grandparents also tended to see their grandchildren less often and to live further from them than did grandparents in other groups.

Influential grandparents tended to be younger. They were apt to get more involved in their grandchildren's lives. One grandfather said, " … if he has some problem, he'll come over to see me … And if I need some help, like getting some screens down … for the summer, I'll get him to help me bring those down … " (Cherlin and Furstenberg 1985, 108). The influential grandparents lived closer and saw their grandchildren more often than grandparents in other groups. These findings suggest that aging and decreased activity level may lead to decreases in grandparents' influence on their grandchildren. Some of the grandparents in this study used "selective investment" to focus their energy on some of their closer or more personable grandchildren.

Hagestad (1985) conducted a study of grandmothers and grandfathers in Chicago. She found that both men and women talked with their grandchildren about practical life in adult society. The grandfathers took an instrumental or practical view of their role. They gave advice on job hunting, education, and managing money. The grandmothers more often dealt with family life and relationships. Hagestad (1985) reports that grandmothers more often than grandfathers changed their own view on social issues, dress, and education due to their grandchildren's opinions on them. Hagestad (1985, 41) calls this "reversed socialization." Hagestad's work shows that grandchildren and grandparents have a mutual influence on one another.

Gladstone (1988, 1989, 1991) found that the grandparent's relationship to the grandchild relies in part on the mediation of their children and children-in-law. Gladstone (1989) studied 110 grandparents in non-intact families (in which parents have split up). He found that adult children and children-in-law act as mediators between grandchildren and grandparents. They can obstruct or arrange visits. Children-in-law, for example, could inhibit contact by keeping the former spouse from seeing children and this would, in turn, keep the grandparent from seeing the children. Contact with grandchildren of divorced or separated children depended on the grandparent's relationship to the former child-in-law, whether the child or the child-in-law had custody of the grandchild, and geographical closeness (Gladstone 1987; Johnson 1985).

Gladstone (1989) concludes that grandparents can negotiate relationships with their children and children-in-law in broken marriages to enhance contact with their grandchildren. This can present a challenge to the grandparent when emotions erupt during separations and divorces. Family practitioners can help to enhance grandparent-grandchild relationships during these times. A self-help group in Toronto called GRAND (Grandparents for Equal Right to Access and Dignity) helps grandparents who cannot get access to their grandchildren. The group provides education and support, and lobbies for changes in laws to protect grandparents' and grandchildren's relationships (National Advisory Council 1990b).

## FUTURE RESEARCH

Research on the family and social supports in later life focuses on what Abu-Laban (1980b, 196) calls the "the 'normal' (or at least the research worthy) aged … [the] gray-haired, Anglo-Celtic, heterosexual, life-long marrieds, who have produced children and grandchildren." Studies report how this ideal family copes with the normal crises of growing older. These studies then turn to "the support ties of the white-haired, Anglo-Celtic, widowed mother and grandmother" (Abu-Laban 1980b, 196).

Abu-Laban (1980b) and others (Hess and Soldo 1985) criticize this narrow view of family life. First, the literature idealizes marriage and the caregiving spouse, but it says little about the dysfunctions that marriage and the use of informal supports can create. Hess and Soldo (1985, 83) say that "under some circumstances, for some couples, there are clear drawbacks to having a spouse." Married couples, for example, make less use of formal services. The caregiver spouse may see the use of formal supports as an admission of defeat. The failure to use available supports can make life harder for both spouses. Also, when spouses rely on one another for support, they can lose contact with friends and relatives. This can lead to feelings of burden, isolation, and depression for both spouses. More research on marriage in later life should focus on both the benefits and the problems that marriage can bring.

Second, research on older people's family life has almost ignored the lives of certain types of people. Little research has been done on never-married older people (in 1986, 7.2 percent of men and 7.7 percent of women aged 65–74 had never married), divorced older people (in 1986, 2.7 percent of men and 2.8 percent of women (Statistics Canada 1990e; Abu-Laban 1978). Stull and Scarisbrick-Hauser (1989) conducted one of the few studies of never-married older people in the U.S. They found that these people have generally good health, satisfaction with their standard of living, active lives, and happiness. They appear to be similar to married, divorced or separated, and widowed older people in these dimensions. A higher proportion of the never-married people in this study, compared with the widowed and divorced or separated, live with someone else (siblings, other relatives, or non-relatives). Never-married older people also tend to rely more on siblings and friends than do married or widowed people (Connidis 1989c). These findings suggest that never-married people have good support networks and do not necessarily face a high risk of institutionalization. The researchers say that future research should look at the coping strategies that never-married people use to maintain their high quality of life.

Third, few studies have compared the family life of older people from different ethnic backgrounds. More research on ethnicity in old age should look at family relations, informal supports, and the use of social services by different ethnic groups (Driedger and Chappell 1987).

Fourth, though research during the 1970s and 1980s focused mostly on older women, making up for the absence of research on women in other parts of the social science literature, few studies have looked at gay people as they age, and few have looked at male friendships, widowers, grandfathering, or male remarriage. Studies that have described men show that they face special challenges in old age.

Fifth, current high divorce rates and remarriages in middle age will lead to new patterns of family life for older people. These trends may produce more single older people, both men and women. They may also lead to more older people with children from several marriages. The study of these family structures in the future will give a more complete picture of family life in old age.

## CONCLUSION

Older people live rich social lives. They interact with family members, friends, and neighbours as well as with their spouses. Most older people rely on these networks of family and friends for social, emotional, and health care support. Older people also give to their families and serve as role models for the young. Old age is a time of change—the death of a spouse, for example, creates one of life's greatest stresses. But research shows that most older people cope with the challenges of aging and manage to live satisfying social lives.

## SUMMARY

1. The myth persists that middle-aged children abandon their elderly parents, but studies show again and again that children maintain contact with their parents, provide them with help, and get help from them when they need it.

2. A good marriage provides support for both partners as they age. Married older people use less formal care, rely less on children and friends for support, and have a lower institutionalization rate than unmarried older people. Older women run a higher risk than older men of losing this support due to widowhood.

3. Older people have an interest in sex throughout life. Most people will need to adjust their expectations about sexual performance in later life. But, given good health and a willing partner, older people can enjoy sexual relations into late old age. New attitudes toward sexuality may encourage more sexual activity in later life. Studies of homosexuality in later life report that gay and lesbian older people can stay sexually and socially satisfied as they age.

4. Widowhood has become an expected life event for women in Canada, though it still creates stress in a woman's life. Researchers disagree about the impact of widowhood on men. Some studies show that men have fewer social supports and that they suffer from isolation, loneliness, and a high risk of suicide. More recent studies suggest that men may need less social support than women and that they adapt in different ways to widowhood.

5. More older women than ever before choose to live alone, rather than with their children. Better pensions, subsidized housing, and enriched housing will make this an option for more older women in the future.

6. Most older people keep up social contacts with relatives and friends as they age. Through visits or by using the telephone, older people (mostly women) give one another emotional support. Confidants help older people cope with anxiety and tension.

7. Older people often depend on informal support networks for emotional and health care support, but informal support can place a burden on family members (most often a wife or daughter). These burdened caregivers may lose their income from work, their pensions, and even their health due to caregiving demands. Government financial support for caregivers would make caregiving a less burdensome option for many people and would recognize their valuable service to the community.

8. Some trends, such as cohort attrition for very old people and smaller families for Baby Boomers, suggest that informal supports will decline in the future. Other trends, like longer life expectancy for spouses and the development of semi-formal structures, suggest that older people will still rely on informal supports in the years ahead. These two trends may counterbalance each other, and older people in the future may develop new types of social supports.

9. Elder abuse may affect as many as 4 percent of older Canadians (98,000 people). Most abuse takes the form of material abuse and chronic verbal aggression. A smaller proportion of older people face physical aggression and neglect. Education for police, counsellors, and seniors themselves may help reduce the incidence of abuse. Legal services, mental health services, and shelters could help older people to cope with the aftermath of abuse.

10. Older people give support as well as receive it. They help their children socially, financially, and emotionally. They help their peers by acting as confidants. Older people, like younger people, get esteem and a sense of purpose from helping others.

11. Grandparenting offers older people one of the most enjoyable roles in old age. It has few responsibilities attached to it, so older people can shape the role to suit their personality, lifestyle, and interests.

12. Many gaps still exist in the literature on family life in old age. Research on atypical groups of older people—for example, gay older people, never-married people, and widowers—will increase our understanding of family and intimate relations in later life.

## SELECTED READINGS

Matthews, Anne Martin. "Widowhood as an Expectable Life Event." In Victor Marshall, ed. *Aging in Canada*. 2d ed. Toronto: Fitzhenry and Whiteside, 1987.

An up-to-date review of the widowhood literature in Canada. The author draws on a wide range of sources, including Canadian doctoral dissertations and research papers. She also compares Canadian data with that of studies done in the U.S.

Statistics Canada. *Women in Canada: A Statistical Report.* Cat. No. 89-503E. Ottawa: Minister of Supply and Services Canada, 1985b.

A good compendium of data on women. Includes data on work, childrearing, and marital status.

# Death and Dying

## INTRODUCTION

D raw a line across a piece of paper. Put the word "birth" at the left-hand end of the line. Put the word "death" at the right-hand end of the line. Now put a dot for today's date. Put the date of your birth under the "birth" dot. Now put the date you project for your death under the dot that says "death."

How did you feel about fixing a date for your death? How did you come up with a date? Do people of different ages think the same way about death? Do you look forward to your next birthday? Or do you think about how few years you have left to do the things you want to do? How do older people think and feel about death?

This chapter will look at death in old age. It will focus on (1) attitudes toward death and on where death takes place, (2) ethical questions about death and dying, and (3) mourning and grief.

## DEATH IN OLD AGE

In the past, high infant mortality rates, childhood diseases, and high female death rates during childbearing years made death among all age groups a common event. Gee (1985, 2) says that "of 1,000 females born in Canada in 1831, approximately two-thirds would survive to age 20, less than one-half to age 44, and substantially less than one-third to age 65." Today, she says, "the vast majority of women survive to ages 20 and 45 and a large percentage (approximately 86 percent) are alive at age 65" (1985, 3). Longer life expectancy today means that death often takes place in old age (Marshall and Levy 1990). Today people aged 65 or over make up 80 percent of all dying patients (Fisher, Nadon, and Shedletsky 1983).

Only a small number of studies have looked at how older people feel about death. Marshall (1975) says that the major theories of aging avoid the subject. According to activity theory, for example, people want to stay active throughout their lives. They substitute new roles and activities for ones that they lose as they age. When people retire, activity theory says that they will have the highest life-satisfaction if they find new things to do. This theory says nothing about death (Marshall 1980b).

Disengagement theory says that people want to disengage from social roles as they age. This theory also says that retirement and withdrawal from social responsibilities leads to high life-satisfaction. According to this theory an awareness of impending death starts the process of disengagement. People know that they will die soon, so they ease their way out of social life. Disengagement produces a smooth transition of power from one generation to the next. Death has a less disruptive effect on society if older people disengage from social roles as they age. This theory focuses on the social effects of dying, but it says little about death as a personal experience or about how older people feel about death.

Erikson's (1963) theory of ego development says that the last stage of life leads to a life review. A person looks over his or her life, ties up loose

# Exhibit 14.1

## How Long Will You Live?

This is a rough guide for calculating your personal longevity. The basic life expectancy in Canada (1983–85) for males is age 73, and for females it is age 80. Write down your basic life expectancy. If you are a man aged 60, add 5 years to the basic figure. If you are a woman aged 60, add 3 years because you have already proven yourself to be quite durable. If you are over age 60 and active, add another two years.

### Basic Life Expectancy

Decide how each item below applies to you and add or subtract the appropriate number of years from your basic life expectancy.

1. **Family History**
   Add 5 years if 2 or more of your grandparents lived to 80 or beyond.
   Subtract 4 years if any parent, grandparent, sister, or brother died of heart attack or stroke before 50. Subtract 2 years if anyone died from these diseases before 60.
   Subtract 3 years for each case of diabetes, thyroid disorders, breast cancer, cancer of the digestive system, asthma, or chronic bronchitis among parents or grandparents.
2. **Marital status**
   If you are married, add 4 years.
   If you are over 25 and not married, subtract 1 year for every unwedded decade.
3. **Economic status**
   Subtract 2 years if your family income is over $40,000 per year.
   Subtract 3 years if you have been poor for a greater part of your life.
4. **Physique**
   Subtract one year for every 10 pounds you are overweight. For each inch your girth measurement exceeds your chest measurement deduct two years.
   Add 3 years if you are over 40 and not overweight.
5. **Exercise**
   Regular and moderate (jogging 3 times a week), add 3 years. Regular and vigorous (long distance running 3 times a week), add 5 years.
   Subtract 3 years if your job is sedentary.
   Add 3 years if it is active.
6. **Alcohol**
   Add 2 years if you are a light drinker (1–3 drinks a day).
   Subtract 5 to 10 years if you are a heavy drinker (more than 4 drinks per day).
   Subtract 1 year if you are a teetotaller.
7. **Smoking**
   Two or more packs of cigarettes per day, subtract 8 years.
   One or two packs per day, subtract 4 years.
   Less than one pack, subtract 2 years.
   Subtract 2 years if you regularly smoke a pipe or cigars.
8. **Disposition**
   Add 2 years if you are a reasoned, practical person.
   Subtract 2 years if you are aggressive, intense, and competitive.
   Add 1–5 years if you are basically happy and content with life.
   Subtract 1–5 years if you are often unhappy, worried, and often feel guilty.
9. **Education**
   Less than high school, subtract 2 years.
   Four years or school beyond high school, add 1 year.
   Five or more years beyond high school, add 3 years.

10. **Environment**

If you have lived most of your life in a rural environment, add 4 years.

Subtract 2 years if you have lived most of your life in an urban environment.

11. **Sleep**

More than 9 hours a day, subtract 5 years.

12. **Temperature**

Add 2 years if your home's thermostat is set at no more than 68° F.

13. **Health care**

Regular medical checkups and regular dental care, add 3 years.

Frequently ill, subtract 2 years.

Look at your projected length of life. What items most contributed to your longevity? What items reduced your life expectancy? How could you improve your longevity by improving your score on the items above? To what degree is your life expectancy determined? To what degree is it within your control?

**Source:** Adapted from Richard Schultz, *The Psychology of Death, Dying and Bereavement,* copyright © 1978 by Newbery Award Records. Reprinted by permission of Random House, Inc., 97–98.

• • • • • • • • • • • • • • • • • • • • • • • • • • • • • • • • • • • •

ends, and prepares for death. Erikson describes this as **ego integrity**. "It is the acceptance of one's one and only life cycle as something that had to be and that, by necessity, permitted of no substitutions … " (1963, 268). The integrated person accepts his or her biography and culture. And with this acceptance "death loses its sting" (1963, 268). Robert Peck ([1955] 1968) says that in the last part of this last stage a person can achieve **ego transcendence**. People in this stage feel a deep concern for others and for the culture they will leave when they die.

These theories say that older people respond to death in more than one way—some people deny it; some accept it; and some embrace it. The few studies that have tested these theories have found complex combinations of acceptance and rejection of death.

Marshall (1974) found an ambivalence toward death among older people in a retirement community and in a nursing home. All of his subjects had disengaged from the middle-aged roles of work and parenthood; most of them said they accepted death; and some of them said they desired it. But Marshall found that these people also wanted to keep on living. Many of them said they wanted to live because their lives had meaning for others. Some of them, worked for their retirement community; others said that someone depended on them, and they wanted to live to care for this person.

Chappell (1975) found that relationships with others give older people a more positive view of the future. She asked forty elderly people in a hospital how long they had to live and how they thought about the time they had left. She found that all of these people knew that they would die soon and they all said they felt ready to die. But only half the people in this study said they saw their future as a time of waiting for death. The other half saw the future as a time to keep on living. Chappell found that people looked forward to activities if they had social contacts outside the hospital. These contacts gave them continuity with the past and allowed them to extend their lives into the future.

Studies that compare older and younger people find that older people think about death more, but feel less afraid of death than the young. A Canadian study by Gesser, Wong, and Reker (1986) studied the fear of it and three kinds of death acceptance among old and young people. They found that older people showed less fear and more acceptance of death than younger people. They also found that as fear of death decreased, hopelessness decreased and happiness increased. They say that people who get over the fear of death feel satisfied with life. These people find meaning and purpose in the time they have left, and they feel in control of their lives.

People with different religious beliefs differ in their attitudes to death. Gesser, Wong, and Reker (1986) found that older people more than younger people accepted life after death. "It may be," they say (1986, 20), "that belief in the afterlife helps the elderly to find meaning and purpose in life, as well as in death … Older people overcome their fear of death because they feel that life after death goes on." Most religions teach that people get the kind of afterlife they deserve. Studies show that people with mild or uncertain religious belief fear death most, while those with strong religious beliefs or no belief at all deal with death best (Gorer 1967; Kalish 1963). People with a mild belief may accept enough of religion to believe in an afterlife, but not enough to feel they will have a good one.

## INSTITUTIONAL DEATH

Religious belief and a sense of purpose can help buffer the fear of death, but how and where a person expects to die also affects how they feel about death. In the past most people died at home, surrounded by family, friends, and neighbours. Some cultures still ensure this kind of death (see Exhibit 14.2). But in Canada almost 70 percent of all deaths (for people of all ages) take place in hospitals (Statistics Canada 1978d).

A study at the Baycrest Centre for Geriatric Care in Toronto compared the death rate in the centre's hospital, nursing home, and apartment complex. The study found that the hospital had a death rate more than 20 times greater than that of the nursing home and more than 130 times greater than that of the apartment complex. Shapiro (1983) studied hospital use by a group of more than 3,000 patients aged 68 and over and found that about two-thirds of the sample entered the hospital in the year they died.

· · · · · · · · · · · · · · · · · · · · · · · · · · · · · · · · · · · · ·

# Exhibit 14.2

## Death and Dying Among the Hutterites

· · · · · · · · · · · · · · · · · · · · · · · · · · · · · · · · · · · · ·

In an article on aging and death, Professor Joseph W. Eaton reprinted the following letter from a Hutterite farmer to his sister. The letter describes the death of their younger brother.

Dear sister, our dear brother came home on September 8, on a Wednesday morning about 5 o'clock. He said that he had a fairly nice trip. He cried a great deal because of pains. He stated that distress teaches one to pray. I went immediately the following day to visit with him. I could hardly look at him, it was so painful to me; he looked so terrible that it made my heart almost break. However, I remained with him until he died, and until the funeral was over.

Two evenings before his death, his home was full of people, approximately 25 were there. He expressed a heavenly pleasure when he saw them all and said he could not express his pleasure in seeing them. It struck me almost as a miracle when I saw this starved and weak body lying there, telling us such a strong story. We listened to him, warned him not to talk so much because it may do him harm. However, he stated, "While I am still alive, I can speak. When I will be dead, then, of course, I won't be able to tell you what I have to say." ...

He stated that dying does not cause him any difficulty; he said that he had a clear conscience and is in peace with God and all people. He asked many people in my presence whether they had something against him. However, everybody replied in the negative. They said to him that they themselves were in peace with him ...

[Just before his death] his children stood around him with a sad heart, and all realized that his departure will be soon. He called his oldest son, gave him his hand and pressed a kiss on his forehead, and advised him how he should behave in the future. Among other words he told him he should obey his preacher, the boss and the field boss, and if the community entrusted a position to him, he should execute same as well as he could, and not only superficially ...

[He then calls to his side his daughter, the colony business manager, his wife and his brother]. He said, "I am at peace with God and with all people. I have a clear and good conscience. I am ready to depart, but now everything goes so slow.

I have only one desire and that is to go to my Lord." He said quite frequently how good it is to have a clear and peaceful conscience. He advised us also that we should prepare ourselves, because the pleasure was inexpressible.

So I have described to you the events and experiences which I have seen with my own eyes, and it is my request and my wish that we all should prepare ourselves. Blessed by God.

**Source:** Joseph W. Eaton, "The Art of Aging and Dying," *The Gerontologist* 4 (1964): 94–112. Reproduced with permission of *The Gerontologist.*

• • • • • • • • • • • • • • • • • • • • • • • • • • • • • • • • • • • • •

Hospitals will take in more and more dying patients as the population ages, but studies show that many doctors and nurses in hospitals feel uncomfortable with dying patients. A study in the U.S. found that 76 percent of doctors in hospitals felt uncomfortable dealing with their dying patients. Sixty percent said they needed some kind of educational counselling (Zorza and Zorza 1979). A study of U.S. medical schools (Dickinson 1976) found that only 7 out of 107 had taken a full course on how to relate to dying patients and their families. Dickinson and Pearson (1980–81) found that physicians who had taken such courses related more easily to dying patients. Eakes (1985) found that nursing home workers who felt more comfortable with death placed a higher value on older patients.

A study at Royal Victoria Hospital in Montreal found that patients wanted to know their diagnoses and their chance of recovery, but doctors did not want to speak openly about death and had little interest in patients' emotions. Social workers also tended to play down patients' problems (Mount, Jones, and Patterson 1974). Shedletsky and Fisher (1986) replicated this study twelve years later. They found that almost all staff (97 percent) felt that patients should be told about their terminal illness, but only 80 percent said that patients on their units were told, and 70 percent of staff members said that discussions of death and dying never or infrequently took place. Nearly all staff members (97.6 percent) felt that hospitals should meet patients' emotional needs, but 41 percent felt that these needs are never or infrequently met. Skelton (1982) reports that medical staff sometimes feel guilty or angry about dying patients. Because they have spent all of their professional lives learning to keep people alive, they think of death as a failure and avoid dying patients or respond less quickly to their needs (Sudnow 1967). Health and Welfare Canada (1982d, 4) says that the dying patient does not fit the model of health care of the acute hospital. "Skills of investigating, diagnosing, curing and prolonging life [the goals of an acute care hospital where people have short-term, curable illnesses] are not relevant to the care of the dying."

# CHANGES IN THE TREATMENT OF THE DYING

The health care system has begun to change its approach to dying patients of all ages. Two doctors more than any others—Elisabeth Kübler-Ross in the United States and Dame Cicely Saunders in England—started this reform.

Kübler-Ross wrote a series of books that described death and dying from the patient's point of view. A study of death and dying courses in Canada found that 55 percent of the courses used her books and that over 20 percent of the departments that taught these courses cited her work as one of the most important reasons for the growth of interest in death and dying (Klug and Waugh 1982).

Saunders created a new institution for caring for the dying—the hospice. Her work has led to a worldwide hospice movement and to the growth of treatment centres for the dying across Canada.

## Stages of Death and Dying

Kübler-Ross (1969) described five stages that her patients went through before they died. First, she says, people deny that they are dying. They say, "Not me." They may believe that the doctor has the wrong X-rays or someone else's tests. They may go from specialist to specialist looking for a new diagnosis. They may not even hear the doctor tell them they have a fatal illness.

Second, she says, people feel angry. They begin to believe that they will die. "Why me?" they ask. At this point the person blames the doctor or a spouse or God for their illness.

Third, they begin to bargain. The person says, "Yes, me, but ..." A person may try to make deals with the hospital staff: they may promise to be a good patient and to follow doctor's orders, if only they will get better. They may bargain with God: promising to go to church or to live a more pious life. They may bargain with God for one more summer at the cottage, or for enough time to see a son married, a grandchild born, or their next birthday.

Fourth, the person feels depressed. Their illness gets worse, and they know they will die. The person says, "Yes, me," and they feel a great sadness. Kübler-Ross says that depression has two stages. In the first stage the person mourns present losses—the loss of family, career, and the things they love, like a home, car, or cottage. In the second stage the person mourns future

• • • • • • • • • • • • • • • • • • • • • • • • • • • • • • • • • • •

## Exhibit 14.3

### Can People Bargain for More Time and Win?

• • • • • • • • • • • • • • • • • • • • • • • • • • • • • • • • • • •

Some research suggests that people can put off death for some time if they have a reason to live. Phillips and Feldman (1973) first reported the hypothesis that the death rate for certain groups of people drops before important events. Likewise, the rate increases after the event passes.

They based this hypothesis on several bits of evidence. First, they looked at historical data. They studied the month of death of 1,300 famous people. They found that, statistically, more people died during their birth month and in the following three months than would be expected by chance. Fewer people than expected died before their birth month. They also found fewer deaths than expected in the U.S. before presidential elections from 1904 to 1968. Second, they studied the death rate of Jews in New York City before Yom Kippur (the day that Jews atone for their sins and receive forgiveness). They found that for 90 percent of the years they sampled, New York City (with a larger percentage of Jews than any other U.S. city) showed a greater drop in death rate before Yom Kippur than did the rest of the U.S. "It seems," Kalish (1981, 233) says, "as though some people exert their will to live until a certain important event takes place, then they permit themselves to die."

A number of researchers have attempted to replicate the Phillips and Feldman findings. Some of these studies support them; others do not. A study by Kunz and Summers (1979–80) found, as did Phillips and Feldman, that a higher proportion of deaths occur after a person's birthday than just before. Kunz and Summers say that birthdays lead to close relations between family and friends, and this may lead to delay of death.

Most other studies of whether people tend to live past their birthday (rather than die before them) have not supported the Phillips and Feldman results (Baltes 1977–78; Labovitz 1974; Harrison and Moore 1982–83). A more recent study by Harrison and Kroll (1985–86) does support the Phillips and Feldman study. These researchers found a "death dip" before Christmas and a "death surge" just after Christmas. They suggest that holidays improve people's moods and that a happy mood tends to delay death. Phillips and Feldman (1973) concluded that their research needs further support before the death dip can be considered a real phenomenon. Research over the past decade still leaves the question open. But at least some of the research so far suggests that cultural events can have an impact on the will to live and on the biological fact of death.

• • • • • • • • • • • • • • • • • • • • • • • • • • • • • • • • • • •

losses—the loss of good times to come, the chance to see children or grandchildren grow up, and other future events. The person begins to say goodbye in this stage.

Fifth, the person accepts death. He or she says, "My time is close now … it's OK." The person accepts that they will die, and they say goodbye to family and friends and die in peace.

Kübler-Ross says that at every stage a patient holds on to hope. At first a person may hope the doctor made a mistake, later they may hope for a remission if they have cancer, and later still they may hope for a painless death.

Some writers question the number of Kübler-Ross's stages or their order. Metzger (1979–80) studied two patient-spouse couples in which the patients had terminal illnesses. She interviewed each couple three times and found that in both cases patients described "hope" as their main experience along with some anger. She did not find that these subjects went through a series of stages. Shneidman (1984, 199) rejects Kübler-Ross's stage theory—"the notion that human beings, as they die, are somehow marched in lock step through a series of stages of the dying process"—on clinical grounds. He reports a wide range of emotions, needs, and coping methods that dying people use. "A few of these in some people, dozens in others—experienced in an impressive variety of ways" (1984, 199). Feigenberg (1980) criticizes Kübler-Ross's impressionistic methods and the unscientific presentation of her results. Butler (1968) says, moreover, that people have as much right to anger or denial as they do to acceptance and that they have a right to these feelings when they have them, not when a stage theory allows them. Feigenberg points out the danger of accepting these stages as a pattern that everyone must follow: "The stages of Kübler-Ross have come to be regarded as a check-list for the process of dying ... And if a patient clearly deviates from this pattern, one is now liable to hear from the hospital staff that his dying is 'wrong'" (Feigenberg 1980, cited in Shneidman 1984, 199).

Kübler-Ross (1969) herself says that patients can skip stages; stages can overlap; and people can go back over the same stage many times. Some responses, like anger, come up again and again. Also, different illnesses create different trajectories of death or different patterns of response. Kübler-Ross based her model on cancer patients in a hospital, but cancer patients who have remissions may go through these stages more than once. People with other illnesses show other trajectories. Sometimes, a person can have long plateaus between times of decline. On the other hand, someone who dies shortly after an auto accident may not go through any of these stages.

Shneidman (1984, 200) says that people respond to dying in the same way they respond to other major stresses in their lives: "One dies as one has lived in the terrible moments of one's life." However, Shneidman presents little research to support this view. He may exaggerate the individual differences among dying patients in the same way that Kübler-Ross exaggerates the commonality.

All sides of this debate share one thing: they have brought discussion and thinking about death into public life. People who have to cope with death and dying—patients, their families, and medical staff—now have a number of ways to think, and talk, about death (Novak and Axelrod 1979). This has freed many people from the fear and silence that surrounded death and dying only a few years ago.

## The Hospice Movement

The idea of a hospice dates back to at least the Middle Ages in Europe. Hospices at that time took in travellers who needed food, shelter, and care. Hospices today meet the special needs of dying patients. Dame Cecily Saunders opened the first modern hospice, St. Christopher's, in London in 1967.

St. Christopher's has sixty-two beds, in-patient and out-patient services, a home visiting program, a day care centre for the children of staff, and private rooms for older people. The hospice welcomes visitors, including children, and allows families to cook for their dying relatives if they want to. There are also rooms for relatives who want to stay overnight. St. Christopher's does not use methods to extend life; it tries to relieve symptoms and to help the patients enjoy their last days.

## Hospice Program Goals

Saunders says that a "hospice is a program, not a place" (cited in Canadian Medical Association 1987, 34). First, a hospice controls pain. People fear death for many reasons, but often people fear the pain that may accompany death more than death itself. Pain relief ensures that the person will die in comfort, and this relieves much of the patient's fear and anxiety. St. Christopher's pioneered the pain relief techniques now used by hospices around the world.

St. Christopher's created the Brompton mix—a mixture of heroin or morphine, cocaine, Stemetil syrup, and chloroform water—to relieve chronic pain. Medical staff base pain control on two techniques: first, they adjust drug dosage until it relieves a patient's pain. "The aim," Saunders (1984, 268) says, "is to titrate the level of analgesia against the patient's pain, gradually increasing the dose until the patient is pain free." Then, the nurses give the next dose before the previous one has worn off. Hospitals often wait until a person shows signs of pain before they give the next dose of pain reliever. By giving the analgesic "before the patient may think it necessary [usually every four hours] ... It is possible to erase the memory and fear of pain" (Saunders 1984, 268). Patients cared for by this method need lower dosages to maintain a pain-free state because the drug does not have to overcome the pain that has begun. Lower dosages mean that patients stay more alert. Skelton (1982), says that 90 percent of people can get complete pain relief in a hospice setting, and all but 1 to 2 percent can get some help.

Second, a hospice allows a person to die a simple death. The hospice does not use respirators or resuscitators to keep someone alive. Staff make dying a part of life in the hospice. They leave the curtains open around a dying person's bed so that patients can see that their roommates have died. Patients also know they have a say in their treatment; they can ask for medication when they feel they need it; and they can ask to die at home. Saunders (1984) reports that people who die at home often feel more pain than people who die in the hospice. And caregivers often feel burdened by the demands of care. St. Christopher's (and other hospices) agree to readmit patients whenever the patient or the family needs more support.

Third, a hospice gives people love and care. Staff members focus on the comfort of the patient, taking the time to touch patients and hold them. The hospice will serve special foods that patients like or give them soothing scented baths. The hospice also helps patients do as much for themselves as they can; this increases patients' well-being by giving them a sense of control over their treatment. The family of dying patients also receive care. A Family Service Project at St. Christopher's offers help to families who find it hard to cope with their grief (see also Levy 1987). Saunders (1984, 269) says that "staff and volunteers visit to assess the need and to offer support, and if more specialized help is indicated, this can be arranged."

Hospices spread to North America during the 1970s and early 1980s. More than 1,000 hospices opened in the U.S between 1974 and 1984. In Canada hospice organizations exist in Quebec, Ontario, British Columbia, and Manitoba (Manitoba Health Organizations n.d.). Most provinces also have palliative (terminal) care units, palliative care teams, or a palliative care expert on staff in hospitals (Health and Welfare Canada 1982d).

## Palliative Care

The palliative-care services guidelines define palliative care as "a program of active compassionate care *primarily* directed towards improving the quality of life for the dying." A complete program of palliative care includes symptom control and spiritual support as well as bereavement support and education (Subcommittee on Institutional Program Guidelines 1989, 1). Palliative care units do the same work as hospices, but they most often exist within a large acute care hospital.

The Palliative Care Foundation (Southall 1982) found 116 palliative care programs operating in Canada in 1983 (up from 2 in 1975). These programs had 266 available beds, 63 percent of them in large general or teaching hospitals and thirty-two percent in chronic and extended care hospitals (Canadian Medical Association 1987). Some provincial home care programs also offer palliative care. Ninety-five percent of the people who used these programs had terminal cancer. The Palliative Care Foundation estimates that 200 community-based palliative care programs (programs to help people stay in their homes) existed in Canada by the end of 1984 (Ley 1985).

The Canadian Medical Association (1987) estimates that people aged 65 and over make up about 70 percent of hospice patients in Canada. Older people have some special needs that hospices need to take into account. Many older people will have no one at home to provide palliative care outside the institution. Multiple pathologies may make pain control more complex. Frail older people on hospice home care may also need the use of respite beds and a day hospital (Canadian Medical Association 1987).

The Royal Victoria Hospital in Montreal opened a twelve-bed, in-patient palliative care unit in 1975 and expanded the unit to eighteen beds by 1982. The unit offers music therapy, counselling, and physiotherapy as well as care by doctors and nurses. The unit's staff works as a team and practices "whole person medicine" (Doutre, Stillwell, and Ajemian 1979). This means that they care for the spiritual, emotional, psychological, and physical needs of the patient. The program also offers a seven-day-a-week, twenty-four-hour home care service. The unit's staff keeps patients pain-free in their homes through drug therapy and gives family members advice and support in caring for the dying person. The unit ensures that a patient can come back to the hospital at any time. This allows dying patients to leave the hospital and in some cases to die at home. The unit also has a bereavement follow-up team that visits and supports families after the patient dies.

The Royal Victoria unit admits people of all ages. A five-year study of the unit from January 1975 to April 1980 found that about a third of the people admitted had lung, breast, or bowel cancer. Patients stayed on the unit an average of twenty-four days, about half stayed a week or less, and 78 percent stayed less than four weeks. The large majority of patients (86 percent) admitted to the unit died there. About 13 percent of patients in the home care program died at home; the rest came back to the hospital to die (Ajemian and Mount 1981).

One study at the Royal Victoria Hospital compared the palliative care unit with a surgical ward. Buckingham (Buckingham et al. 1976) had himself admitted as a cancer patient to both types of units. He dieted for six months and lost twenty-two pounds, exposed his skin to ultraviolet rays to make it look as if he had received radiation treatment, stuck himself with needles, and had a doctor do minor surgery to make it look as if he had had intravenous injections and a biopsy. He learned how patients with cancer of the pancreas behaved, and he imitated their behaviour. He also grew a stubbly beard and failed to bathe for several days.

Buckingham reports that he got more personal attention and kinder treatment on the palliative care ward. On the surgical ward, he found, doctors spent less than ten minutes per day with him and less than five minutes per visit. Also, doctors travelled in groups, and this discouraged patients from talking to their doctors about their feelings. Buckingham reports that staff on the surgical ward avoided eye contact with patients, called patients by their disease, not their name, dwelt on the worst things about a patient's illness, and showed little good feeling toward dying patients. His staff contacts lasted on average less than six minutes per visit.

The palliative care unit showed more interest in him as a person. The nurses looked him in the eye when they talked to him and asked him personal, friendly questions, such as what food he enjoyed eating. Buckingham reports that when families wanted to talk to their doctor the staff got the doctor on the phone as soon as possible. Families also spent a lot of time helping to care for patients: they fed patients, brought urinals, and fixed patients' pillows. The staff supported family members as they helped care for their dying relatives. Buckingham's staff contacts averaged nineteen minutes on the palliative care unit. Compared with the surgical ward, on the palliative care unit he spent almost 400 percent more time talking to staff, patients, and their families.

A study by Thompson (1985–86) supports Buckingham's findings. Thompson compared palliative care, surgical, and pediatric nurses' attitudes to death. He found that palliative care nurses "approach their work with the dying with greater ease, may enter into more personal relationships with dying patients ... and come away from their work with the feelings that the work itself is rewarding and that they have been useful" (1985–86, 240). Thompson concludes that the values of the palliative care setting (more than nurses' past experiences) explain this positive attitude to dying patients and their needs.

Buckingham also reports that patients supported and comforted one another on the palliative care unit. "The palliative care unit facilitated this powerful support system by allowing more patient-family freedom and mobility, with open visiting and encouragement of family participation in the care of the patient" (Buckingham et al. 1976, 1214). A study by Kane and others (1984) found that, compared with conventional care, palliative care created more family and patient satisfaction and less family anxiety. Buckingham concluded that palliative care units meet the dying person's special need for emotional and social support as well as physical care (see also Mount and Scott 1983).

## The Cost of Palliative Care

Some research estimates that as much as 77 percent of health care dollars go to care for people in the last six months of life (Scitovsky 1984). Most studies on palliative care and hospice programs show that they reduce health care costs (Federal/Provincial/Territorial Working Group 1990). Health and Welfare Canada (1982d) says that palliative care units create real savings—they do not just create an "add-on" service. A report on the Royal Victoria program says its home care program has saved more than $3.6 million in hospital costs in five years. This comes to a saving of more than $7,000 per patient. From July 1979 to March 1980, for example, the program saved 3,209 hospital days (a hospital day equals the cost of keeping a patient in a hospital for one day). At $276 a day (in 1980) this came to a saving of $885,684. During this time the program cost $248,900 to run, saving the health care system $636,784 (Health and Welfare Canada 1982d).

A study in Ontario also reported savings from a palliative care unit. The study (Salmon and McGee 1980) found that the cost of care for patients in the palliative care unit was only about one-third the cost of active treatment in a hospital ($107 compared with $304 per day). This unit will save about $1.5 million per year when it reaches its full twenty-two-bed size. The report says that if Canada had the same ratio of palliative care beds as the U.K., it could save at least $41 million a year in hospital costs (in 1980 dollars). Health and Welfare Canada (1982d) goes on to say that a national home care program for the terminally ill linked to a system of palliative care units could save over $700 million per year.

Most of the research on costs has been done by people who run palliative programs, and, therefore, these results could reflect a tendency to make the programs look more cost effective than they are. Still, an independent study in the U.S. supports the finding that palliative care saves money (Greer et al. 1984). Hospice care reduced in-patient days and reduced the cost of expensive services. More controlled independent research on Canadian programs needs to be done to establish the cost effectiveness of palliative care.

## Palliative Care for the Elderly

Palliative care units take in patients of all ages. Patients at Royal Victoria Hospital, for example, ranged from 20 years old to over 90. Studies show that palliative care can help most older people as well as younger people, but some older patients have unique needs. Shedletsky, Fisher, and Nadon (1982) studied the records of forty older patients (average age 80.6 years) who had died in the extended care wing of a hospital. Extended care hospital settings take in many older people with long-term illnesses who need constant medical care. These units often have a palliative care or a hospice treatment philosophy. The researchers found that older extended care patients differed from younger palliative care patients. First, older patients averaged more diagnoses than the younger patients. Second, the younger patients typically had cancer; while the older patients typically suffered from circulatory and respiratory diseases (Shedletsky, Fisher, and Nadon 1982). Third, relatively few younger patients died from respiratory failure, while respiratory failure caused about 50 percent of all deaths in the older group.

Shedletsky, Fisher, and Nadon (1982) found that drug treatment helped about 80 percent of the people with pain and skin problems. The staff reported that just before death 75 percent of the patients felt no pain or distress and 75 percent were conscious or semi-conscious. The staff found, however, that patients with respiratory problems got the least benefit from drug treatment, and this group made up the largest portion of people with discomfort before death. The researchers concluded that some groups of older extended care patients may have special palliative care needs.

Palliative care and other approaches to the treatment of dying patients raise a variety of ethical questions. Is it ethical, for example, to stop actively treating a person's illness? Does the decision not to put someone on a respirator or not to use a heroic life-saving measure contribute to the person's death? Philosophers, physicians, and legal experts have looked at these and other issues related to dying today.

## ETHICAL ISSUES

Two ethical questions come up again and again in the writing on death and dying. First, should patients be told that they have a terminal illness? Second, when should a doctor allow a person to die?

### To Tell or Not to Tell

Somerville (1989), in a discussion of informed consent in the case of surgery, says that telling patients about their condition and about the course of treatment can reduce their suffering. This information gives patients a sense of control over the process and promotes trust in the physician. She notes (1989, 130) that in some cases keeping information from the patient may lead to a "substantial benefit." But this benefit must clearly outweigh any harm that information might do to the patient. Also patients have a right to know about the choice of treatment the physician has made and about alternative treatments, including the choice of no treatment. Somerville (1989) says that physicians involved in active treatment (e.g., surgeons) should continue to communicate with dying patients. They can discuss the patient's "condition, prognosis and feelings" (Somerville 1989, 139). Failure to communicate with a terminally ill patient can lead to "a state of 'pre-mortem' loneliness" that patients can fear more than death (Somerville 1989, 139).

Glaser and Strauss (1977) describe two "awareness contexts" for dying: an open awareness context and a closed awareness context. In a **closed awareness context**, everyone (including the patient) knows the patient is dying, but no one speaks about it. Glaser and Strauss say this leads to a "ritual drama of mutual pretense" (1977, 271). Family members will talk to a patient about next summer at the cottage or Christmas in Hawaii, even though they all know the patient has only a few days to live. Glaser and Strauss say that this approach has some advantages over more open approaches. It protects the staff, family, and patient from exposing their feelings, and some patients may prefer to die this way. Glaser and Strauss go on to say that a closed awareness context can also cause problems: it can lead to loneliness and isolation for the patient.

Most dying patients today prefer an **open awareness context**, where the staff, the patient, and the family all know and share the knowledge that the patient is dying. This allows the physician to communicate clearly the degree of risk a patient faces. The physician may say, "You have a terminal illness, but you may still live several years." An open awareness context also allows the patient to speak openly about death and to share his or her feelings about dying. In addition, it gives the dying person a chance to make decisions about treatment, last-minute financial decisions, settlement of family affairs, and the opportunity to arrange the religious support he or she prefers. Some people will not want an open awareness context, and health workers should respect this right. Skelton (1982, 557) says "we should tell everyone as much as they wish to know."

A study at Royal Victoria Hospital in Montreal found that most patients want open and honest answers from their doctors (Mount, Jones, and Patterson 1974). The study also found that whether doctors felt they should tell their patients depended on whether they themselves would want to be told. Eighty-four percent of doctors who would have wanted to know their prognoses also felt their patients would want to know. But only 45 percent of doctors who would not have wanted to know their own condition felt their patients would want to know. These findings suggest that doctors may be protecting themselves from their discomfort with death when they withhold a diagnosis from a patient, and that they need more education about patients' feelings and needs. They may also need a chance to talk about and reflect on their own feelings about death and dying.

## Euthanasia

Doctors sometimes face ethical conflicts when they treat dying patients. Medical ethics says that a doctor should heal and cure patients, but the Hippocratic oath also says that a doctor should first "do no harm." What should a doctor do when machines, surgery, or drugs that extend a person's life also prolong their suffering? What should a doctor do when a patient asks to die? And what does the law in Canada say about euthanasia (helping someone achieve a painless death)?

First, when is a person dead? When they stop breathing? When their heart stops beating? Or when their brain waves stop? Harvard Medical School (1968) gives four criteria for death: the person (1) no longer makes a response; (2) no longer breathes or moves; (3) has no reflexes; and (4) has no sign of brain activity on two EEGs taken twenty-four hours apart. But what if a machine keeps someone breathing, or a heart pump keeps someone's heart beating? Are these people alive or dead? When does a family or a doctor have the right to take someone off these machines?

At present (1990) a person who lacks the mental competence to refuse treatment must rely on someone else to act for them. Family members, a friend, or a medical doctor often make this decision. Even if a person has told someone their wishes or has written a statement of their wish to end treatment at a certain point, these have no binding effect in Canada.

The Law Reform Commission of Canada (1982) reviewed the question of mercy killing in a study called *Euthanasia, Aiding Suicide and Cessation of Treatment*. The commission found that the Canadian courts have never convicted a doctor in Canada for giving a patient large doses of pain-killing drugs, for stopping useless treatment, or for deciding not to treat a secondary illness (like pneumonia in a terminal cancer patient). The courts, however, could try doctors on these grounds. This means that every doctor who decides to stop treatment risks becoming a test case in the courts. The commission feels that the Criminal Code of Canada should give doctors clearer guidance.

The commission reviewed ways to relieve doctors of criminal liability. citing the example of California, which in 1976 passed Bill 3060, called the Natural Death Act. This bill allows a person to write a **living will** that authorizes relatives or doctors to withdraw or withhold artificial methods of life support in cases of terminal illness. It also attempts to relieve doctors of responsibility for stopping treatment. Forty states in the U.S. recognize living wills.

Kelly et al. (1989) studied physicians in nine countries and found that doctors would value having specific directions on the type of care a patient wants. Using the results of the study, the researchers produced a booklet

## Exhibit 14.4

## A Living Will

The living will format below appears in the California Natural Death Act. The "Directive" below gives an idea of what such a will should contain. Read it over and consider the pros and cons of living wills. Would you fill one out? Would you witness a friend's? Do you think Canada should allow the use of living wills?

### Directive to Physician

Directive made this _____ day of _____ (month, year). I _____, being of sound mind, wilfully, and voluntarily make known my desire that my life shall not be artificially prolonged under the circumstances set forth below, do hereby declare:

**1.** If at any time I should have an incurable injury, disease, or illness certified to be a terminal condition by two physicians, and where the application of life-sustaining procedures would serve only to artificially prolong the moment of my death and where my physician determines that my death is imminent whether or not life-sustaining procedures are utilized, I direct that such procedures be withheld or withdrawn and that I be permitted to die naturally.

**2.** In the absence of my ability to give directions regarding the use of such life-sustaining procedures, it is my intention that this directive shall be honoured by my family and physician(s) as the final expression of my legal right to refuse medical or surgical treatment and accept the consequences from such refusal.

**3.** If I have been diagnosed as pregnant and that diagnosis is known to my physician, this directive shall have no force or effect during the course of my pregnancy.

**4.** I have been diagnosed and notified at least 14 days ago as having a terminal condition by _____, M.D. whose address is _____, and whose telephone number is _____. I understand that if I have not filled in the physician's name and address, it shall be presumed that I did not have a terminal condition when I made out this directive.

**5.** This directive shall have no force or effect five years from the date filled in above.

**6.** I understand the full import of this directive and I am emotionally and mentally competent to make this directive.

Signed _____

City, Country and State of Residence _____

The declarant has been personally known to me and I believe him or her to be of sound mind.

Witness _____

**Source:** Sandra G. Wilcox and Marilyn Sutton, "Directive to Physician," *Understanding Death and Dying*, 3d ed. (Palo Alto, California: Mayfield, 1985), 417. Reproduced with permission of the publisher.

called *Let Me Decide* that offers a model of a living will and of a "health care directive." The directive gives specific information to family members and doctors about the amount of treatment the person prefers under different conditions. The person also writes out a personal statement about preferences for care as part of the directive (Kelly et al. 1989).

The Manitoba Law Reform Commission (1990) reviewed two types of advance directives for the termination of health care treatment—the living will and **durable power of attorney**, which gives an attorney the right to make decisions on behalf of the ill person. None of Canada's provinces recognized the living will in 1991, and only Nova Scotia and Quebec recognized the durable power of attorney. Outside these two provinces, a doctor is not legally bound by either of these documents.

Advance directives pose problems that need public discussion. The living will, for example, raises ethical and practical questions. First, in some cases people may change their minds as they near death, but they will not get a chance to change their living will. Second, the Law Reform Commission of Canada (1982, 10) says that "a terminally ill patient has a right, not a secondary or subordinate right but a primary right, to die with dignity and not to fall victim to heroic measures."

Durable power of attorney for health care poses other problems. First, an attorney may refuse to decide or might not be available to make a decision. Second, the attorney may make an improper decision. And third, a physician may ask the attorney's permission to act too early in order to override a patient's refusal to allow treatment (Manitoba Law Reform Commission 1990). These issues and others related to limitations on and safeguards for the use of medical directives, and the role of physicians in the use of the documents need to be resolved.

The Law Reform Commission of Canada (1982) says that in Canada today doctors should not feel compelled to take heroic measures to keep someone alive and patients should not have to write advance directives to protect themselves from a doctor's fear of prosecution. The Law Reform Commission of Canada (1982) says that the law and medical ethics distinguish between killing someone and allowing someone to die. Walton and Fleming (1980, 58) say that a doctor who sets out to kill a patient—for example, by giving the patient a drug overdose—"has committed himself more firmly. He is therefore more directly accountable for the outcome." A doctor who allows death to happen—for example, by not putting a person on a respirator or by taking someone off a respirator—may or may not cause a person's death. The person may live even without the treatment. Walton and Fleming (1980) say that ethical treatment should offer the most options for the patient. "A passive course of action," they say, " … provides a sensible alternative to aggressive treatment and, at the same time, allows for unexplainable and unforeseen events which may be of great benefit to the patient" (Walton and Fleming 1980, 60).

Still, the current law leaves many questions open. Once treatment has begun, for instance, the law inhibits a doctor from discontinuing treatment. The doctor may know, through an advance directive, that after some time the patient would want treatment discontinued. But, by discontinuance the doctor risks legal action. The absence of support in the law for advance directives leaves the doctor open to civil action, criminal liability, and charges of misconduct from the medical profession (Manitoba Law Reform Commission 1990).

Both the law and medical ethics reject **active euthanasia**—killing someone either because they ask for death or to relieve their suffering. The Law Reform Commission of Canada (1982) says that a law to support active euthanasia would create more risks than benefits and might lead to new methods of euthanasia. Skelton (1982), a pioneer in palliative care in Canada, states the experts' case simply, saying that requests for active euthanasia often hide a request for better care. "I believe most sincerely," he says, "that if adequate care is given to dying patients the question of responding to requests for active euthanasia is eliminated" (1982, 558).

Henteleff (1978) puts the ethical question in the context of professional responsibility. The patient, he says, has two needs: biological and moral. The doctor can help dying patients meet both these needs: he or she can relieve a person's physical distress and avoid treatment that will keep a person from finding meaning in their last days. Weisman (1972) says that medicine can and should help people die in the way they want to die. He calls this an "appropriate death."

## The Law and Public Policy on Death and Dying

Bolton (1989, 238) says that "Canadian Courts have not yet considered in any depth issues dealing with the right to die with dignity." The courts have not ruled on any case that dealt with a guardian's right to end the treatment of a terminally ill, but incompetent person. Bolton states the arguments for and against the right of a guardian to end an incompetent, terminally ill person's life. First, she presents the **medical vitalist** argument. This view holds that no one has the right to end someone else's life, no matter how poor the quality of that life has become. Second, Bolton states the argument for a **new definition of life**. This definition rests on two premises: the capacity for consciousness of self and the ability to experience more than pain and suffering (Bolton 1989).

· · · · · · · · · · · · · · · · · · · · · · · · · · · · · · · · · · · · · · ·

## Exhibit 14.5

### Cessation of Treatment in Canada

· · · · · · · · · · · · · · · · · · · · · · · · · · · · · · · · · · · · · · ·

Section 198 of the Criminal Code of Canada says that a person who gives medical or surgical treatment should act with reasonable skill and care. Section 199 says that a person has to continue an act once they begin, if by stopping the act they endanger someone's life. These sections seem to make a doctor criminally liable for stopping useless treatment. The Law Reform Commission of Canada says that these sections do not apply to a doctor who stops treatment after careful review of a case. The Commission gives an example to show why:

> A doctor turns off a respirator, knowing, as he does so, that the patient will no longer be ventilated and thus will probably die. Let us suppose, in one instance, that before doing so he has assured himself, using standard medical procedures and tests, that the patient is already in a state of irreversible coma. Here the act of turning off the respirator, while technically constituting a positive act of cessation of treatment within the meaning of section 199, could not serve as a valid basis for criminal liability, and for two reasons. Firstly, the continuation of treatment is not reasonable in this case given the condition of the patient and, secondly, the cessation of treatment does not reflect wanton or reckless disregard for life on the part of the physician. But on the other hand, let us assume that this doctor performs the same act without first assuring himself of the patient's condition. There would probably then be grounds for applying these provisions, since by ceasing treatment without taking the precaution of assuring himself and such cessation will not endanger the patient, he would be showing wanton or reckless disregard for the patient's life or safety."

**Source:** Law Reform Commission of Canada, *Euthanasia, Aiding Suicide and Cessation of Treatment*, Working Paper 28 (Ottawa: Minister of Supply and Services, 1982), 17–18. Reproduced with permission of the Minister of Supply and Services Canada, 1991.

· · · · · · · · · · · · · · · · · · · · · · · · · · · · · · · · · · · · · · ·

Bolton reviewed Canadian legal precedents to see how a court might rule on the rights of an unconscious, terminally ill person. She found that the Canadian Charter of Rights and Freedoms guarantees the security of the person. This may mean that a person is protected from extreme medical treatment. But at present no law allows a guardian to decline medical treatment for someone else. The *parens patriae* jurisdiction of Canadian Courts of Equity could allow for guardians' refusal of treatment for the person they represent. But at the present time Bolton (1989, 242) says, "there exists a void of Canadian legal precedent in this area."

Today doctors usually decide whether to continue or stop treatment. This is a conflicting position for doctors, however, because they have both the responsibility to treat the patient and the right to decide whether to continue treatment. This also reduces the right of the patient or the patient's guardian to decide on treatment. Bolton (1989) recommends that Canada

**Source:** Law Reform Commission of Canada, *Euthanasia, Aiding Suicide and Cessation of Treatment*, Working Paper 28 (Ottawa: Minister of Supply and Services, 1982), 70–71. Reproduced with permission of the Minister of Supply and Services Canada, 1991.

**Exhibit 14.6**

Proposed Changes in Canadian Law

The Law Reform Commission proposes that the Criminal Code of Canada include the following statements.

1. Nothing in sections 14, 45, 198, 199 of the Criminal Code shall be interpreted as requiring a physician
   (a) to continue to administer or to undertake medical treatment against the clearly expressed wishes of the person for whom such treatment is intended;
   (b) to continue to administer or to undertake medical treatment, when such treatment is medically useless and is not in the best interests of the person for whom it is intended, except in accordance with the clearly expressed wishes of this person.

2. Nothing in sections 14, 45, 198, 199 of the Criminal Code shall be interpreted as preventing a physician from undertaking or ceasing to administer palliative care and measures intended to eliminate or to relieve the suffering of a person for the sole reason that such care or measures are likely to shorten the life expectancy of this person.

adopt the model used in the U.S. of judicial review by the courts. This would lead to impartial, reasoned, and public decisions about the termination of life.

## MOURNING AND GRIEF

When an older person dies they often leave behind children and sometimes a spouse. These survivors need to adjust to the loss, and society can help with this adjustment. Funeral practices and rituals structure the grieving process. They prescribe what mourners should say, what they should wear, and in some cultures how they should sit. Mourners in Christian cultures wear black; mourners in some Oriental cultures wear white. North American society values silent unemotional grieving; Chinese families hire professional mourners to make loud wailing noises at the funeral. Jewish tradition requires that the family "sit shiva" for seven days after a funeral. According to this custom, mourners tear their clothes, sit on low chairs to deny themselves physical comfort, cover the mirrors in their home, and light a candle that burns for one week. The mourning family accepts visitors throughout the week, and

• • • • • • • • • • • • • • • • • • • • • • • • • • • • • • • • •

## Exhibit 14.7
### A Family's Response to Death and Dying

• • • • • • • • • • • • • • • • • • • • • • • • • • • • • • • • •

The academic discussions of the right to decide on prolonging life often focus on medical and legal issues. But, every day in Canada people, along with their physicians and nursing staff, make decisions about their older family members. These decisions, at their best, take place within a context of openness and trust between families and health care professionals. The following case shows how one family decided against aggressive treatment:

> Mrs. Walker, 78, moved into an apartment in the Beth Sharon Senior Complex in early December. The complex offered her a supportive environment. It had a security system, access for a wheelchair, and a chance to socialize with other residents.
>
> Mrs. Walker had played an active part in her community for many years as a hospital volunteer and business woman. So, when she moved into her apartment complex, she joined the Beth Sharon Seniors Group and regularly attended their afternoon teas in a nearby centre. On January 10, as she left for the tea, she lost her balance, fell down a flight of stairs, and severely injured her head. When an ambulance arrived she was found unconscious and was taken to a nearby hospital for emergency treatment.
>
> Mrs. Walker's daughter, Phyllis, a nurse, rushed to the hospital when she was called. The neuro-

surgeon on staff had already completed a CAT scan and showed it to Phyllis. "I don't like the look of this," he said, "there appears to be severe bleeding at the base of the brain stem. She's not likely to be well again," or indeed function on her own."

> Phyllis left the ward to talk with her sister and other family members. They agreed that they would not press for an operation to remove the blood clot. Surgery would almost certainly lead to the necessity of a respirator and other artificial means of life support. Over the next few days, as the family waited for some change in their mother's condition, Phyllis would suggest various actions or ask for another test. Each time the surgeon in charge would ask a simple question, "Would your mother like us to do that?" And each time Phyllis agreed that her mother would not want aggressive treatment to prolong her life. The decision to wait became harder to sustain as Mrs. Walker's breathing faltered. But the family stayed with its decision, based on Mrs. Walker's many discussions with them. Family members and close friends supported the family's decision to follow their mother's wishes.
>
> Sixteen days after entering the hospital, and without regaining consciousness, Mrs. Walker died. She was cremated, in accordance with her request, and her family held a memorial service to celebrate her life.

• • • • • • • • • • • • • • • • • • • • • • • • • • • • • • • • •

ten men gather at the house each day for prayer. Mourning continues in less intense stages for a year until the unveiling of a commemorative stone on the grave of the deceased (Goldberg 1981–82).

Each culture has its own funeral rituals and mourning practices, but all of them have a common purpose: to help the bereaved family cope with grief and re-establish community bonds after the loss of a community member.

# Exhibit 14.8
## Controversy: Setting Limits

• • • • • • • • • • • • • • • • • • • • • • • • • • • • • • • • • • • • • • • •

Daniel Callahan, in his book *Setting Limits,* suggests one way to deal with the rising costs of health care—ration health care for the elderly. He cites three reasons for this proposal. First, compared to the health care used by children, older people as a group use a large amount of health care. Second, a large and growing portion of research and technology goes to reverse the health conditions of the elderly. Third, more than a fair share of money for health care to the elderly goes to care for dying people.

Today a person can expect to receive health care treatment if they need it and have some hope of recovery. Callahan (1987) argues against the use of medical need as a criterion for treating older people. Instead he proposes that we base the decision to treat an illness on age or on the concept of the "natural life span" (1987, 137), which Callahan defines as 70 to 80 years. He argues that society should commit itself to high quality care for people throughout this span. But, beyond this point, medicine and government support of health care should focus on the relief of suffering, not the extension of life. This policy, he says, would remove the burden of high health care costs for the very old. He presents the following three principles for the use of age as a way to decide on treatment:

1. Medical care should not resist death after patients have lived out their natural life span.
2. Medical care should only relieve suffering for those who have lived their natural life span.
3. Medical technologies that can extend life

beyond the natural life span should not have to be used for this purpose.

These policies, Callahan argues, would remove the uncertainty older people and their children face about the high cost of treatment; it would lead to a high quality of life until late old age; and it would remove the social threat posed by the rising cost of health care for the elderly.

Binstock and Kahana (1988) find that Callahan's argument lacks consistency. Callahan, for example, would make an exception for physically strong and mentally alert people who came down with a sudden illness. Also, he would apply his plan only to physically frail people or to those in need of long-term care. Binstock and Kahana (1988) say that this leaves open the question of who will decide who should get care. Will a second illness lead to the withdrawal of care? A third? And what about the mentally alert, frail person who could live a satisfying life with medical support? Why deny this person treatment? Binstock and Kahana (1988, 426) say that Callahan "does not hesitate to undertake sweeping moral judgments … [but] does not develop the moral basis for his own proposal." Why, for example, does he support the use of age as a criterion, over all others, for deciding on medical treatment?

Callahan only vaguely refers to the kinds of social, moral, and ethical changes that would have to come about for his proposal to work. And he makes little reference to how this kind of social change would occur. Still, Binstock and Kahana (1988, 426) concede that this book "is likely to be a point of reference in such discussions for some time to come."

• • • • • • • • • • • • • • • • • • • • • • • • • • • • • • • • • • • • • • • •

Regardless of the culture a person belongs to or the type of funeral they attend, each bereaved person has to work through personal feelings of grief. Some research in North America shows that mourners go through stages of grief. Lindemann (1944) describes three such stages: an initial response phase, an intermediate phase, and a recovery phase.

First, the bereaved person feels shock and disbelief. They may report feeling cold and numb, and some people say they feel dazed, empty, and confused. These feelings protect a person from feelings of sorrow. People in this phase often fear that they will break down in public. This phase can last for several weeks.

Second, the person will begin to review what has happened. This takes three forms: (a) The bereaved person obsessively reviews one or two scenes related to the death, or they may berate themselves for something they should have said or done. (b) The bereaved person searches for a meaning for the death. Religious people may find solace in knowing that God willed this death. (c) The bereaved person searches for the deceased. This may mean that a widow goes to places where she expects to see her spouse. She may also feel his presence while watching TV, eating dinner, or lying in bed. Some people even call out to their spouses and expect an answer. This phase lasts about a year.

Third, the bereaved person begins to recover. Survivors look for social contacts: they may join a club or go on a cruise. They feel that they have come through an ordeal, and say they feel stronger and more competent than before. This stage begins around the second year after the death.

Gorer (1965) says that successful grief work includes: (1) breaking bonds to the deceased, (2) readjustment to the environment without the deceased, and (3) forming new relationships. Not everyone makes a smooth trip through these stages. Sometimes a person can show a delayed emotional response to a parent's or a spouse's death. The person seems to cope well, displaying lots of zest and energy, but they may have internalized their grief. This can lead to emotional upset and physical illness later.

The case of Joanna will show the cost of morbid grieving. While her husband was in the hospital dying of brain cancer, she visited him every day. At the same time she carried on a career in real estate and worked on a Master's degree. For two years she ran herself into the ground. She went to the hospital twice a day, at noon and at supper time to feed her husband his meals; then she would jump in her car and show another house or run home to work on a paper.

When her husband died, she was determined that nothing was going to stop her. "I didn't allow myself time to grieve," she says. "After his death, I travelled. At Christmas I went to Spain, Hawaii, or wherever. At Easter I went somewhere. I went to Europe. There was never a day—I didn't allow myself any time at all. Do you get the picture? No time to breathe."

To keep going she used pills and alcohol. Then she started collecting pills and drinking more. "That was my way of coping, my way of standing the pain. I needed some kind of anaesthetic," she says. At the end of this downward spiral Joanna drove the front of her car through a restaurant window. She got out of her car, walked through the windowframe, sat down at a booth in the restaurant, and waited for the police to take her away (Novak 1985).

Only about 25 percent of bereaved people go through morbid grieving (and few people show Joanna's extreme denial) (Schulz 1978). But many people deviate from the pattern of bereavement that stage models of grieving describe (Wortman and Silver 1990). Older people, for example, tend to show a delayed and more extreme grief reaction than younger people. Sanders (1980–81) compared the scores on a "grief experience inventory" of forty-five bereaved spouses in two age groups (people over age 65 and under 63). She found that older spouses showed less grief than younger spouses at the time of a first interview (shortly after their spouse's death). At the second interview older spouses showed higher scores than younger spouses on scales of denial and physical symptoms, and increases in ten other scales compared to younger spouses. Barrett and Schneweis (1980–81, 102) also report that life after a spouse's death "persists in being stressful for years." These results show that an older person may need help long after their spouse's death.

Baker (1991) reports that spouses who have died continue to influence the living in many ways. People sometimes talk to a dead spouse, ask them for advice, or try to imagine what they would do in a situation the surviving spouse is facing. One woman said she felt her husband lie down next to her in bed some months after his funeral. Widows or widowers will sometimes decide against remarriage because of the close tie that still exists with their dead spouse. Moss and Moss (1984–85) consider this a normal response to widowhood in old age and "a nourishing link to the past" (1984–85, 204). More research on bereavement in old age will show how this experience differs from bereavement in younger people (Wortman and Silver 1990).

## CONCLUSION

This chapter has touched on some of the complex issues related to death and dying. Each religion has its own views on issues like euthanasia, funeral practices, and mourning. Each culture shapes its members' beliefs about the meaning of death, about life after death, and about care for the sick and dying. Each person will respond in a unique way to their own death and to the deaths of people they know and love. Today, changes in technology, the management of terminal illness, and the meaning of death raise new questions about death and dying. The study of death and dying can help people to understand these issues and make better choices for themselves.

## SUMMARY

1. Attitudes to death vary by age, religion, and culture. Older people generally accept death more than younger people. Like younger people, older people say they want to continue living, if they feel their life has meaning.

2. People with either no religious belief or a very strong one seem to cope with death best.

3. Death occurs more often in old age today than in the past, and it also occurs more often in an institution. These trends will increase as the population ages.

4. Elisabeth Kübler-Ross reports five stages of dying. Not everyone goes through all of these stages in the order Kübler-Ross describes, but her writings encouraged a more open discussion of death and dying when they first appeared.

5. Cecily Saunders opened the first modern hospice in England in 1967. St. Christopher's Hospice offers an alternative to hospital care for the dying. Hospices offer pain control and a home-like setting for death.

6. Palliative care units in hospitals offer the same comfort and care as a hospice. The staff of these units, as in hospices, will help patients die in their own homes. They also assure such patients that they can return to the hospital at any time.

7. Most experts and patients prefer an open awareness context for dying. A closed awareness context can lead to isolation and loneliness for the patient (though some people may prefer not to speak openly about death). Doctors today need to understand their own feelings about death and dying, so they can give their patients the kind of care that their patients prefer.

8. Doctors say that proper pain control would end the fear that leads people to ask for euthanasia. The law in Canada today does not require doctors to take heroic measures to keep a terminally ill patient alive. Canada needs clearer guidelines to help doctors decide about stopping treatment for people in comas. Canadian law does prohibit active euthanasia. Judicial

review of cases would lead to more rational decisions about termination of life.

9. Death leads to grief and mourning for survivors. Culture and religion help people cope with feelings of grief. Funerals, for example, bring the community together and give mourners support. Still, each person has to work through feelings of grief in his or her own way. Researchers say that mourners go through stages of grief and that if all goes well a person will emerge from grieving to carry on their life.

## SELECTED READINGS

Bolton, Anne M. "Who Can Let You Die?" *Canadian Journal on Aging* 8: 238–43, 1989.

A brief, informative discussion of the legal issues regarding cessation of treatment. Clearly written; understandable to non-lawyers.

Law Reform Commission of Canada. *Euthanasia, Aiding Suicide and Cessation of Treatment.* Working Paper 28. Ottawa: Minister of Supply and Services Canada, 1982.

A good, readable summary of the legal and ethical issues concerning euthanasia, suicide, and the cessation of treatment. The commission puts these issues in a Canadian context, something few other studies do.

Marshall, Victor W. *Last Chapters: A Sociology of Aging and Dying.* Monterey, California: Brooks/Cole, 1980b.

A good source of writings on death, dying, and aging. Marshall's study contains more material on death and old age than most other books on death and dying.

# 5

*Societal Change*

# *Politics and Policy*

## INTRODUCTION

Studies of aging and politics in Canada have only just begun. Pratt (1984) says that before 1980 political scientists saw little reason to study aging. First, in the 1950s and 1960s scholars concerned themselves mostly with voting behaviour and political opinions. They found that the largest changes in opinion took place as people moved from adolescence to adulthood.

The opinions of adult voters were stable, for the most part, from middle age on. As a result, political scientists tended to ignore the study of older age groups.

Second, with this focus on voting behaviour, political scientists showed little concern for policy issues such as health care, housing, or pension issues (one exception is Bryden's (1974) study of pension policy).

Third, until the 1980s gerontology sat near the bottom of the disciplinary hierarchy in Canada. Pratt (1984) says that researchers in all disciplines found it hard to get funds for aging research. Under such conditions, political scientists were not inclined to study aging.

The start of a Strategic Grants program for Population Aging in 1979 increased interest in the study of aging and politics. But this interest has grown slowly: Pratt (1984) reported fewer than ten gerontological studies by Canadian political scientists. These studies, at best, give a hint of the issues that concern gerontologists when they study politics.

Pratt's (1984) review shows that gerontologists study aging and politics from at least three points of view. First, they study political participation, including seniors' voting patterns and political attitudes, and the number of seniors who hold public office. Second, gerontologists examine senior activism and group conflict. This includes the study of senior pressure groups and public protests. Third, they look at the context of political action—the policies and structures of the government.

This chapter will look at each of these topics. It will (1) describe the range of seniors' political activity in Canada, (2) describe the government agencies that translate seniors' needs into policy, and (3) consider seniors' political participation in the future.

## POLITICAL PARTICIPATION

Sociologists define political participation as behaviour that leads to the selection of leaders and the choice of public policy. Seniors take part in politics in a number of ways. They read about political issues, and listen to and watch public affairs radio and TV shows. They also vote, hold political office, and sometimes protest government decisions.

### Voting

Studies done on voting patterns during the 1960s in the U.S. (Milbrath 1965) and in other countries supported the disengagement theory of aging. They found that young adults had lower voter turnout than middle-aged people; middle-aged people (in their forties and fifties) showed the highest voter turnout; and older people showed less voter turnout than middle-aged people, though more than young adults. Regenstreif (1965, 88) concluded from Canadian data that "there is strong evidence that people past the age of 65 suffer a diminution of interest in politics for a variety of reasons. Turn-out and general participation follow these patterns."

Later Canadian studies questioned these findings. Van Loon (1970), in a study of 1965 Canadian election figures, found only a slight peak in middle age. Laskin and Baird (1970) studied Saskatchewan local, provincial, and federal voting records in a small town and found similar voter turnout among younger and older age groups.

Other studies in the U.S. and Canada also question the conclusion that older people participate less than younger people in political activity. These studies control for socioeconomic status, health, and physical mobility. They show that given the same background, health, and mobility, younger and older people show similar levels of political activity (Hudson and Strate 1985; Jacobs 1990; Verba and Nie 1972). Yelaja (1981, 14) reports that in a study of eighty-two Canadians aged 50 and over, "in terms of political attention ... political participation and activity, the older, retired persons tended to exhibit a higher level of participation and activity than the younger and employed respondents." Kernaghan (1982) found that in the 1974 Canadian federal election the figures for voter turnout declined only after age 85.

Curtis and Lambert (1976) found similar results for the 1965 and 1968 Canadian federal elections. In one report they reviewed the voting and political interest patterns for a sample of 2,767 Canadians aged 21 years and older during the 1968 election. When they looked at their total sample, they found that, compared with younger people, older people showed less voting and election interest. This supported the findings of earlier studies that showed a decrease in voting and political interest among older age groups. Curtis and Lambert then looked at groups of people with the same income, education, occupation, region, community size, marital status, sex, and language. They found that older people with different backgrounds voted at different rates. They found that English Canadian males, for example, have a greater tendency to vote in later life than English Canadian women, but both groups show about the same interest in election issues. They also found that French-Canadian males and females show little difference in voting patterns with age, but French Canadian males show a greater political interest than French-Canadian females. They also found differences between the two language groups. They found that older (over age 50) English-Canadian males and females are more likely to vote than their French-Canadian counterparts.

When they looked at people within each group (French-Canadian male, French-Canadian female, English-Canadian female, English-Canadian male), they found no difference in voting or political interest with age. They say that "there is little or no evidence suggesting a decline in either voting or electoral interest as a function of age" (Curtis and Lambert 1976, 302). They found, instead, that even past the age of 70 people remained active in voting and their affiliations with political groups. When older people did not vote, they gave frailty or illness as a reason, not lack of interest. The researchers say they were "struck with [their] failure to detect any clear evidence for a reduction in reported organizational involvement or affiliation with age once controls are made ... So far as voting and political interest are concerned, there is either no drop-off with age or even some modest increases" (1976, 305–6).

Most of the reported Canadian research on voting patterns relies on cross-sectional data. These data allow researchers to compare the voting behaviour of different age groups at one point in time. But they do not allow researchers to draw conclusions about changes in voting behaviour with age. Researchers need to use longitudinal methods to study the effects of age on voting behaviour.

Still, the current research on voting behaviour reports that seniors take an active interest in politics. Combined with their growing numbers, this interest may give older people more political power in the future. Gifford (1982) says that the median age for voters has risen in Canada from 30 years in 1881 to 42 years in 1981. He says that the median age will rise to 48 by 2031. At that time, he says, voters aged 65 and over will make up 26 percent of the voting public, compared with only 13.3 percent in 1981 (Gifford 1983). The large numbers of future seniors and their high voter participation rate could lead them to form a voting bloc. This bloc could sway government policy through the electoral process.

Will seniors use their voting strength to shape Canadian policy and achieve specific goals? They have on one or two occasions in the past. Gifford (1982) points to "the Diefenbaker 'pension increase' landslide of 1958" as one. Kernaghan (1982) points to the National Pensioners and Senior Citizens Federation campaign to create the Canada Pension Plan between 1963 and 1965 as another (citing Bryden 1974, 194–97). But most experts do not think that seniors will form a permanent voting bloc (Binstock 1986; Heclo 1988).

First, studies in Canada show that many people keep the same political stance throughout their lives. Conservatives tend to stay that way, so do Liberals and New Democrats. Regenstreif (1965) found, in an analysis of the 1962 Canadian federal election, that the New Democratic Party got the strongest support from voters who at that time were 40 to 49 years old. These voters voted for the first time during the 1940s, when the CCF (forerunner of the NDP) led the Liberals in popular support. This historical period shaped their voting patterns, so that "the political atmosphere of the early and middle 1940s continues to cast its spell on political life" (1965, 87). Likewise, people who came of age during the Depression of the 1930s or who served in World War II will have their own view of Canadian political life and their own party affiliations.

- - - - - - - - - - - - - - - - - - - - - - - - - - - - - - - - - - - - - - - -

## Exhibit 15.1

Age Distribution of Canada's Population: % of Population
65 Years and Over, Median Age of Voters, and
Percent of Voters 65 and Over, 1881–2031

- - - - - - - - - - - - - - - - - - - - - - - - - - - - - - - - - - - - - - - -

| Year | 65+ as % of Pop. | Median Age of Voters | 65+ as % of Voters |
|------|------------------|----------------------|--------------------|
| 1881 | 4.1 | 30 | 8.5 |
| 1931 | 5.6 | 40 | 9.9 |
| 1961 | 7.6 | 41 | 12.9 |
| 1981 | 9.7 | 42 | 13.3 |
| 2001 | 12.3 | 45 | 16.2 |
| 2021 | 16.6 | 47 | 20.9 |
| 2031 | 20.9 | 48 | 26.0 |

**Source:** Adapted from C.G. Gifford, "Senior Politics," *Policy Options*, September 1983, 14. Reproduced with permission.

- - - - - - - - - - - - - - - - - - - - - - - - - - - - - - - - - - - - - - - -

Second, older people differ in social class, ethnic background, and in what part of the country they live. They have varying needs and define issues differently. Wealthy seniors, for example, may have little interest in the continued indexation of the Guaranteed Income Supplement, while a poor older widow may listen carefully to what a politician says about public pension policy. Voters in the Maritimes tend to favour the Liberal and Progressive Conservative parties, while Ontario and the Prairie provinces show the greatest support for the NDP (Clarke et al. 1980). These and other differences lead older people to vote for one party over the others and to favour certain policies and reject others. Clarke and his colleagues reviewed voting patterns by age for three federal elections (1965, 1968, 1974). They did find (for all three elections) that a larger portion of voters in older age groups (26 percent of those 21–29 voted PC, compared with 35 percent of respondents aged 60 and over) favoured the Progressive Conservative party. But they conclude that this relatively small difference provides "no evidence of pronounced differences in voting behaviour of different age groups in Canadian federal elections" (1980, 87).

Third, seniors take into account other needs than their own when they vote (Powell 1987). Most older people, for example, have children and grandchildren. A senior may vote for a politician because that person's party promises to provide jobs for the young or day care for mothers. Senior voters will vote as a bloc if a policy or party threatens to cut pensions or increase the costs of services, but most of the time senior issues play only a small part in determining seniors' voting behaviours.

Even if they do not form a voting bloc, seniors can use other methods to shape government policy. Verba, Nie, and Kim (1971, 10) say that elections set the pattern of government policy, but "the most important set of political activities may be the myriad attempts to influence governmental decisions ... between elections." A study by Kernaghan and Kuper (1983) shows that almost all provincial and federal government agencies make policies that affect seniors. Some agencies, like federal and provincial departments of health, play a central role in policy making for seniors, while others, like transportation or consumer affairs, play a smaller role. Pross (1975) says that seniors will have an impact on policy only if federal and provincial public servants recognize their right to participate in policy making.

Seniors can take an active part in Canadian policy making in at least three ways:

1. Governments have set up seniors' councils, advisory groups, and committees to shape policies for seniors. Seniors can work with these councils to create change from within the system.

2. Seniors can form advocacy groups that lobby the government for policy change. These groups would pass resolutions, write reports, and meet with government officials to discuss seniors' issues. These groups may have the greatest impact on policies for seniors. If they achieve legitimacy, advocacy groups can play an ongoing part in policy formation.

3. Seniors can form protest groups. Ongoing advocacy groups (like provincial senior societies) can protest government policies, and so can special groups that emerge to protest a specific issue. The Senate of Canada's report (Senate of Canada 1979) on retirement age policies supports this approach. It says, "the retired elderly should organize, protest and show militancy in order to improve their chances of achieving dignity, obtaining higher incomes as well as medical and other services and finding useful work" (Senate of Canada 1979, 115).

Seniors have started to work in all of these directions in the past few years. The following sections review some recent senior political activities.

## Senior Advocacy Groups

Sociologists define political power as the ability of one group to achieve its interests over those of others. A group can gain power by having its members elected to office, by violently overthrowing the government, or by putting pressure on government officials. Advocacy groups take this last approach. One of the first advocacy groups for seniors in history, the Old Age Pensioners' Organization, was formed in British Columbia in 1932 to protest the rigid use of a means test for pensioners. Later, in the 1940s and 1950s, provincial senior organizations were formed on the Prairies and in Ontario. In 1954 these provincial groups united to become the National Pensioners and Senior Citizens Federation. Senior organizations formed in the Maritime provinces during the 1960s and 1970s. These provincial organizations and national federations now meet each year to pass resolutions on seniors issues, like the cost of insurance, the quality of nursing home care, and the price of drugs. They then send these resolutions to the appropriate provincial or federal agencies. These groups also lobby government leaders between yearly meetings (Bryden 1974, 195).

Statistics Canada (1990e) found that half of all seniors report involvement in a political organization, about double the rate of their involvement in any other type of group. Many of these people belong to one or more of the 3,700 social clubs or senior centres in Canada. Few of these local clubs do direct advocacy work, but often a club belongs to a provincial or national federation.

Seven provinces have over forty special advocacy groups. These groups respond to specific issues by presenting briefs to government committees or to cabinet ministers. They include Canadian Pensioners Concerned (twenty local branches in Ontario, Nova Scotia, and Alberta), the United Senior Citizens of Ontario (with over 1,300 member clubs and between 350,000 and 400,000 members), Seniors Action Now (branches in Saskatchewan and British Columbia) and L'Association Québécoise pour la Défense des Droits des Retraites et Préretraites (fifteen branches in Quebec) (Gifford 1982; Yelaja 1989). Yelaja (1989) also reports on the rise of advocacy groups based on ethnic identity like the Association of Jewish Seniors in Toronto.

Hundreds of special needs groups also exist throughout the country. These include teachers' groups, government employee groups, and groups related to a single corporation. These groups work to protect pension plans and benefits of former employees. Other organizations like the Royal Canadian Legion have many older members and a well-developed program to help seniors.

Some national seniors advocacy associations have also emerged. One group, the Canadian Association of Retired Persons (CARP) is "a non-profit organization dedicated to improving the quality of life for Canadians 50 or over, retired or not" (Canadian Association of Retired Persons 1991, 1). CARP began in 1986 and claims it had 65,000 members nationwide in 1991. The organization produces a quarterly newsletter, provides information on hotel,

- - - - - - - - - - - - - - - - - - - - - - - - - - - - - - - - - - - - - - - - - - -

## Exhibit 15.2

### A Profile of Some Senior Groups and What They Do

- - - - - - - - - - - - - - - - - - - - - - - - - - - - - - - - - - - - - - - - - - -

### Quebec

The Fédération de l'Âge d'Or du Québec started in 1973. It is the most highly organized and financially secure of the provincial federations, and has twenty-six full-time paid staff members and maintains active contact with over a dozen departments in the Quebec government. The federation lobbies for change, publishes a newspaper, and writes briefs to the government on seniors' issues. The federation had about 200,000 individual members and 1,200 institutional members in 1991, and it has considerable influence on policy within the province of Quebec.

### Ontario

The United Senior Citizens of Ontario now has over 1,000 affiliated clubs and over 260,000 members. Members also automatically belong to the National Federation of Pensioners and Senior Citizens. The association works for pension increases, tax relief, and medicare benefits. It also presents briefs to the provincial government on health care, housing, and recreation issues, and publishes a monthly newsletter. It takes credit for better government pensions, increases in seniors' housing, and provincial tax credits for seniors.

### Alberta

The Alberta Council on Aging represents 40,000 seniors in Alberta. It has two goals: to identify seniors' needs and get senior (65+) leaders to take action. In 1979 the council conducted a study of consumer concerns; in 1980 it studied the participation of older people in the performing arts; and in 1982 it set up a community improvement program called Project Involvement. The council publishes *Foresight* a magazine for retirement planning that forty-five companies now use in their pre-retirement education programs. The council also writes briefs and letters to tell the provincial government about seniors' needs. In 1983 it opposed user fees for health care services, filed a report to the Task Force on Older Women, and expressed concern over crime and the elderly.

These groups keep the channels of communication with government open. Both seniors and the government gain from this relationship. Seniors can use these channels to stimulate policies that meet their needs, and government can learn about seniors' responses to ongoing policies and programs.

- - - - - - - - - - - - - - - - - - - - - - - - - - - - - - - - - - - - - - - - - - -

motel, and car rental savings, and makes presentations to governments on behalf of seniors.

This group seems modelled after the influential American Association of Retired Persons (AARP) in the U.S. AARP has about 25 million members and is the "largest organized interest group in America" (Jacobs 1990, 353). Its permanent headquarters are in Washington, D.C., and it employs full-time researchers and lobbyists to lobby the government on senior issues. AARP also publishes a national magazine, *Modern Maturity*, and offers services like life insurance, wholesale drugs, and travel discounts.

The U.S. has a number of other large groups that speak out on senior issues. These include the National Association of Retired Federal Employees, with more than 180,000 members; the National Council of Senior Citizens, which has about 3 million members; and the National Council on the Aging, a federation of more than 1,000 agencies that works for and with older people (Atchley 1985; Hendricks and Hendricks 1986). These groups have large budgets and bureaucratic structures that give them legitimacy in the eyes of government officials.

The U.S. also has a multi-age activist group called the Gray Panthers. This group began as a coalition of older people and students in the late 1960s, and today maintains a commitment to multi-age membership. But most new members are older people. The group's founder, Maggie Kuhn, appeared on U.S. television talk shows and was written about in the press. The Gray Panthers attract media attention because the group portrays older people as militant activists who will use street theatre or sit-ins to draw attention to their needs. The Gray Panthers have organized tenants (of all ages) in Washington, D.C., set up a multi-age living project in Boston, and helped fight for better food in school cafeterias in San Diego, California (Jacobs and Hess 1980). Jacobs and Hess say that the Panthers will probably never attract large numbers of seniors, but the group does serve a purpose. It casts older people in a new and dramatic role as social critics and activists who fight to improve life for young and old.

Canadian seniors' groups lack the national impact of either the AARP or the Gray Panthers for at least two reasons. First, in Canada, the provinces set policies for health care, housing, and social services. This gives lobbying a provincial focus and makes the provincial federations as important as the national federations as advocates of seniors' needs (Gifford 1990).

Second, pressure group activity in Canada is "more limited, more secretive and more focused on the bureaucracy than in the United States" (Kernaghan and Kuper 1983, 30). The policy system in Canada "tends to be characterized by superficial public deliberations and by the assignment of major responsibility for policy development to the political executive, the administrative arena, and recognized pressure groups" (Pross 1975). This makes it harder in Canada than in the U.S. for seniors to influence policy makers.

## Senior Activism

A social movement forms when a group (1) coalesces around a set of issues, (2) creates an image of itself in the media as concerned and important, (3) exerts pressure on government agencies, public policies, and people who make decisions, and (4) has expertise and can raise money or votes on behalf of the issues it represents (Hendricks and Hendricks 1986). Binstock (1972; see also Gifford 1985) says that age alone cannot form the basis of a cohesive social movement because seniors' groups lack the financial stability, the organizational rigour, and the large numbers of supporters needed to form a movement. Pratt (1983) disagrees. He sees a growing class consciousness among seniors in North America today and predicts that this will form the basis for a social movement. Yelaja (1981) found that a working younger group of older people (aged 50–64) reported more political activity than older groups (aged 65–74 and 75+). The youngest group reported that they took part in lobby and advocacy activities related to older people's well-being. Yelaja (1989) says that this younger group in Canada will create a more politically active senior population in the future.

Seniors in Canada have on occasion joined together in a national social movement. This has happened three times in the recent past; each time seniors felt threatened by cutbacks in government programs (Gifford 1983). Seniors acted as a movement in 1972 during the federal election campaign, when they protested low Old Age Security payments. Protests included mass meetings in Vancouver and a demonstration at Toronto's city hall (Gifford 1983). They acted as a movement again in 1980, in British Columbia, when the Social Credit government threatened to postpone a denticare program and to raise automobile insurance rates. Again, in 1985 seniors protested government policy, this time the federal government's plan to limit indexation of the Old Age Security and Guaranteed Income Supplement programs. This last case shows that seniors can wield power on specific occasions when they organize.

### De-Indexing the Old Age Security Program: A Case Study of Senior Protest and Government Response

In the winter of 1985 the Progressive Conservative government, led by Prime Minister Brian Mulroney, faced a dilemma. On the one hand, the business community demanded that the government cut spending and reduce the national debt. On the other hand, the government was obliged, in 1985, to pay out over $11 billion in OAS and GIS pensions. This amount increases each year because the government indexes the OAS and GIS programs to the Consumer Price Index (CPI) (a measure of the cost of living). The government wanted to cut these payments to appease the business community, but was unable to because the Prime Minister had committed the government to retain these universal programs.

On May 23, 1985, the then Finance Minister Michael Wilson tried to resolve the dilemma in his budget by introducing a measure by which the

. . . . . . . . . . . . . . . . . . . . . . . . . . . . . . . . . . .

## Exhibit 15.3

### Education for Action

. . . . . . . . . . . . . . . . . . . . . . . . . . . . . . . . . . .

The National Advisory Council on Aging (NACA), a federal office that gathers and disseminates information about aging, realized that older people needed to learn about political power before they could exercise it. In 1984, NACA sponsored a program to teach older people about decision making. The council called the program "Listen to Me!" (1985a). This program provided "an opportunity [for seniors] to study decision-making—who makes the decisions, how the process works, and how seniors might get involved" (National Advisory Council on Aging 1985b, 1). The program also exposed decision makers (civil servants, doctors, politicians) to older people's needs.

NACA ran "Listen to Me!" workshops in five cities—Saskatoon, Fredericton, Montreal, Toronto, and Vancouver. The workshops met in three sessions. First, the seniors in the workshop chose two or three issues to study, like housing, income, or health care. They then discussed whether decision makers consulted older people about these issues. Second, the seniors met with a decision maker to discuss

each issue. They asked decision makers how much older people have to say about decisions on the issue. Third, seniors met again by themselves to talk about the second workshop. They decided on things they could or should do to get more involved, and they summed up their findings on senior involvement in decision making.

A follow-up study (National Advisory Council on Aging 1985a) found that 89 percent of the seniors in the workshops said they understood more about decision making after the meetings. And 94 percent said that the meetings helped prepare them for future involvement in decision making. About a third of the seniors said they began to plan for increased senior involvement in decision making. Eighty-seven percent of the seniors said they now knew more about senior needs.

Programs like "Listen to Me!" play a unique role in senior politics. They give older people more information about the political system, increase their confidence, and encourage them to act.

. . . . . . . . . . . . . . . . . . . . . . . . . . . . . . . . . . .

government would only increase the pension payments if the CPI rose by more than 3 percent. Increases would only cover the difference between the first 3-percent rise and the actual CPI increase. (If the CPI rose 5 percent, pensioners would get only a 2 percent raise. If it rose 2.5 percent, pensioners would get no increase in their pensions.) The government projected that this change would save $1.6 billion by 1990–91. Wilson scheduled the change for January 1, 1986.

The plan brought a howl of protest from older people, interest groups, and politicians across the country. First, the change would cut the income of all older people, rich and poor. The poorest people, many of whom were living below the poverty line already, would fall deeper into poverty. Second, many older people had voted PC and expected the prime minister to honour his promise to leave the government pension program alone. This budget reversed his promise to treat universal programs as a "sacred trust," and many older people felt betrayed.

Seniors across the country joined together for the largest senior protest in Canadian history. They signed petitions, held news conferences, and sent letters to Parliament. Seniors also confronted politicians face to face. On June 18, 1985, seniors in Halifax confronted Finance Minister Wilson in a closed meeting and argued against de-indexation (*Globe and Mail* 1985). In the third week of June, seniors marched on Parliament Hill.

Other groups joined seniors in their protests. NDP and Liberal MPs attacked the government in Parliament daily, and some Tory MPs said that they, too, supported fully indexed pensions. The Council of Maritime Premiers united in opposition to de-indexing. Business groups and leaders also supported the seniors: The Canadian Chamber of Commerce, the Business Council on National Issues, and the Canadian Organization of Small Business stated that the government should fully protect old age pensions and find other ways to cut spending and reduce the deficit.

Interest groups like the Advisory Council on the Status of Women and the Canadian Council of Social Development (CCSD) also protested the proposed budget changes. The CCSD predicted that the government's plan would force as many as 200,000 more older people into poverty by 1990 (Cernetig 1985).

The de-indexation protest made front-page news across the country. By mid-June, after reading a post-budget poll indicating a lack of confidence in the government, the prime minister promised to re-evaluate the de-indexation plan. On June 27, after five weeks of pressure, the government gave in and agreed to continue indexing pensions to the rate of inflation. Finance Minister Wilson said the government rescinded the plan because the government "recognized the anxieties of senior citizens" (Montgomery 1985).

This nationwide protest teaches us some lessons about senior politics in Canada. First, seniors can act as a group to change federal policy, but only if they speak with a single voice. Second, seniors can use opinion polls, the media, and direct confrontation to pressure the government. Third, seniors need to ally themselves with other power blocs in society, such as political parties, and business and service groups.

Studies show that senior interest groups cannot succeed by themselves, because they lack sufficient power (Trela 1976). But they can make an issue visible and get other groups to support their cause (Neysmith 1987). Middle-aged people, for example, will often support health care and income policies for older people because middle-aged people are aware that they will be old someday themselves. Also, middle-aged children prefer to pay for services their elderly parents need through their taxes, rather than support their parents directly. Anti-poverty and women's groups will also support seniors' needs. If seniors can link their concerns with those of other groups, they will increase their political power. Gifford (1990) recommends an important future role for seniors in politics. He says that they can "set an example of global citizenship, for the survival of the planet" (Gifford 1990, 133).

## GOVERNMENT AND AGING POLICY

Political participation and power both shape public policy. But political action takes place in a social and historical context. Myles (1984) says that gerontologists need to understand the history and structure of the welfare state to understand old age (see Exhibit 15.4). "This is simply because the contemporary welfare state in the capitalist democracies is largely a welfare state for the elderly" (1984, 2). Programs for older people now make up the biggest part of the welfare state's budget, and attempts to cut this share, like the move to de-index OAS payments, will meet with protests from all parts of society (Myles 1988). "The majority of the elderly," Myles says (1984, 6), "now depend on such benefits for most of their income. The widespread reaction against benefit cuts by both young and old reflected this fact."

Myles (1984) and others (Neugarten and Havighurst 1979) predict that the state will play an even more important role in older people's lives in the future mainly for three reasons. First, the state's budget will increase as the population ages. An aging population, for example, will require a redistribution of resources from younger to older people. The state will manage this transfer through taxation and government programs. The national health care system already does this, and so does the Old Age Security and Guaranteed Income Supplement program.

Second, the state has begun to redefine its role in providing income support to older people. Recent changes to Canada's pension policies, for example, point the way to a withdrawal of support for middle-income earners through government pension plans (the OAS/GIS/SA). Instead, middle-class people have been encouraged to save for retirement by the raised limit on RRSP contributions and the concomitant increases in tax deductions. These policy changes leave income security programs to the poorest Canadians. At the same time they create a "new 'welfare state'" for middle-income seniors, who already have private pension plans (Myles 1988, 52).

• • • • • • • • • • • • • • • • • • • • • • • • • • • • • • • • •

## Exhibit 15.4

Major Federal Social Security Legislation Related to Aging

• • • • • • • • • • • • • • • • • • • • • • • • • • • • • • • •

**A**ll levels of government provide programs to help older people meet their basic needs. This chart gives a summary of the major federal government social security legislation since 1918.

| | |
|---|---|
| 1918 | Pension Act |
| 1927 | Old Age Pension Act |
| 1951 | Old Age Security Act (OAS) |
| 1951 | Old Age Assistance Act |
| 1957 | Hospital Insurance and Diagnostics Services Act |
| 1965 | Canada Pension Plan (CPP) |
| 1967 | Guaranteed Income Supplement (GIS) |
| 1968 | Medical Care Act |
| 1975 | Spouse's Allowance Act (SPA) |
| 1979 | Extended SPA |
| 1984 | Canada Health Act |

In addition to these programs, each province offers programs that include support for housing, income supplement, and health care benefits (like pharmacare).

**Source:** Adapted from Statistics Canada, *Canada Year Book*, 1990a. (Ottawa: Minister of Supply and Services Canada). Reproduced with permission of the Minister of Supply and Services Canada, 1991.

• • • • • • • • • • • • • • • • • • • • • • • • • • • • • • • • •

Third, the redistribution of wealth from young people to older people, and from the state to middle- and upper-class seniors will require more government planning. The government has already had to raise Canada Pension Plan payments to meet the needs of older people today, and it will have to plan for rate increases in the future to meet the needs of a growing older population.

A number of government agencies have been set up to develop policies for the transfer of resources to older people. These include the ministries responsible for pensions, health, and housing. In addition, some agencies advise the government on policies and programs.

- The federal Office on Aging exists within the Department of Health and Welfare. It gathers facts and information about aging in Canada and advises the government on policy issues. The office also helped produce *Fact Book on Aging in Canada* (Health and Welfare Canada 1983) and *The Seniors Boom* (Stone and Fletcher 1986)—two summaries of data on older people in Canada.

- The Minister of State for Seniors acts as spokesperson for seniors and represents their views in cabinet. The minister consults with seniors and groups throughout the country (Government of Canada 1988).

- The Seniors Secretariat exists within the Department of National Health and Welfare. The secretariat supports the work of the Minister of State for Seniors by helping to make seniors aware of the programs and services available to them through the federal government. It also consults with seniors as a part of program development and produces reports on seniors' issues (Government of Canada 1989a).

- The National Advisory Council on Aging, which began its work on May 1, 1980, has eighteen members. It meets twice a year to counsel the Minister of Health and Welfare on issues related to seniors' quality of life. It also promotes a positive image of older people and encourages seniors to take political action. Members of the council include researchers, members of national and provincial organizations, medical experts, seniors, and the general public (National Advisory Council 1989a). The council publishes an annual report and makes recommendations to the Minister of National Health and Welfare. The council also publishes a quarterly newsletter called *Expression*. Each issue presents a readable review of the latest facts on aging, comments from seniors, and reports on research. It also publishes a series of scholarly reports titled, "Writings in Gerontology" and a statistical bulletin called *Info-Age*.

- Provincial Advisory Councils present seniors' views to provincial governments. They also assess policies and work to coordinate provincial programs and services for seniors. Between 1970 and 1980 five provinces— Alberta, Saskatchewan, Manitoba, Ontario, and Nova Scotia set up advisory councils. The councils write newsletters, and produce information packages and directories of services for seniors (Long and Shelton 1982). Provincial governments also learn about seniors' needs from departments set up to coordinate seniors' programs and from senior citizens' secretariats. These agencies sometimes act as advocates for seniors in their provinces.

## THE ROLE OF GOVERNMENT IN IMPROVING LIFE FOR OLDER PEOPLE

A large government deficit and a slow economy will put limits on what older people can achieve through protest and pressure groups. A policy that cuts the federal deficit, for example, will probably also cut social support programs for seniors (Neysmith 1986).

What can seniors do to improve programs and services under these conditions? They can make some gains by lobbying for programs that meet their needs and save the government money. For example, seniors can support the coordination of government departments (Kernaghan 1982). They can also support housing programs that include recreation and health care services that work to keep older people out of institutions. Chappell and Penning (1979) say that programs like home care could save money and at the same time provide more humane treatment for older people. "The current trend [away from institutionalization]," they say, "seems to reflect one situation in which economic efficiency and humanism are not contradictory" (1979, 380). Seniors can look for and promote other programs and policies like health promotion and education programs that will improve seniors' quality of life.

Seniors who take an active part in lobbying or who write briefs and letters to the government are also helping to create better policies for the future and getting the government used to consulting with seniors on seniors' issues. The trend today points to more senior activism in the future. Agencies within the government, like the National Advisory Council on Aging, support and promote this new activist stance. Also, the trends in some countries toward proportional representation (a system that gives minority groups more influence in government) and referendums (votes on specific political issues) could give more power to older people, if these trends catch on in Canada. Gifford (1987) says that in "the four European countries in which pensioners have sought to form pensioners' political parties all have proportional representation systems."

Gifford (1987) also reports on two other trends that may affect seniors politically in the future. First, seniors may set up their own sections within the national political parties (similar to youth sections that already exist). Seniors in the Nova Scotia New Democratic Party have already done this. Second, seniors may spend more time advocating social causes. Canadian seniors have already set up groups like Veterans Against Nuclear Arms and Pensions for Peace. They also work for groups like Amnesty International, Oxfam, and groups with environmental concerns. Curtis and Lambert (1976) say that higher levels of education, better health, the existence of organizations that support activism, more free time, and the larger number of older people in the future will all lead to more political activism by seniors.

The study of aging and politics in Canada has just begun, and, as Pratt (1979, 186) says, "there would appear to be challenge enough here for several scholars." Current trends toward senior activism, for example, raise new questions for political scientists and gerontologists. Will new generations of seniors show the same consistency in voting patterns as seniors in the past? Or will they shift their votes depending on the issues? Only longitudinal studies of voting can answer these questions (Braungart and Braungart 1986). Will seniors become more vocal, organized, and effective in their lobbying efforts? Will they form a social movement? To answer these questions gerontologists need to know more about the structure of and decision-making processes in senior's political groups. Will more and more seniors turn their attention to larger social issues like environmental protection, peace, and anti-poverty campaigns? Before answering this, researchers will need to study the values and commitments of new generations of seniors.

The study of politics and aging in Canada has already moved beyond the study of voting patterns. In the future, political scientists will find many new questions to ask about the political behaviour of Canada's growing and changing senior population.

## FUTURE TRENDS IN POLITICS

Jacobs (1990) says that discussions of politics and aging often come down to the issue of the fair distribution of resources to the older and younger generations. Rosenzweig (1991) dealt with this topic in an address given at the annual meeting of the Gerontological Society of America. He said that unless older people willingly give up some of their current benefits in a time of scarcity, they will create a "disastrous'" effect on society. "Of every nondefense, noninterest dollar in the federal budget [in the U.S.]," he said, "47 cents is spent on programs for people age 65 and over." He added that this "will grow to more than 50 cents by 1995 and 57 cents by 2000" (Rosenzweig 1991, 2). He projects that these costs will lead to a conflict between retirees and the rest of society, including future retirees. And he says that leaders of interest groups ought to help their members "shape a conception of their interests that fits their own immediate needs into the needs of the larger community on whose overall well-being their own ultimately depends" (Rosenzweig 1991, 2).

These comments underscore the need for intergenerational cooperation in politics. Older people must keep in mind the needs of the young and middle-aged or they will lose support. And this support will make the difference between success and failure in seniors' political efforts. Bengtson (1991, 2) warns that "if inflation continues to rise, the elderly are more likely to be perceived as 'Greedy Geezers' in their mortgage-free houses ... " Senior groups need to show their concern for wider social and economic conditions and will have to balance their own needs with those of others and with those of future generations.


## SUMMARY

1. Recent studies of political activity by seniors show that people stay politically active as long as they have good health and mobility.

2. The increase in the median age of voters will likely continue in the near future and may give older voters more political power.

3. Long-standing commitments to political parties, as well as regional, cultural, and social class differences, will keep seniors from forming a single voting bloc.

4. Advocacy or pressure groups can have a strong effect on government policy-making, and older people have begun to organize for action.

5. Seniors' clubs throughout the country are affiliated with provincial and national associations. These groups act as advocates for older people.

6. Because the provinces take most of the responsibility for housing, health, and social service policies, senior advocacy has a provincial focus. This partly explains why seniors in Canada have never formed a powerful national lobby and why they have directed their lobbying efforts at provincial governments.

7. Seniors have joined together to protest government policy at least three times in the recent past. The most recent protest led the federal government to reverse its decision to de-index pensions. A united front, media coverage, plus the support of other influential groups helped seniors confront the government and win.

8. Seniors can influence government policies through the offices of provincial gerontologists, seniors' councils, and the National Advisory Council on Aging. They can also advocate programs that both meet seniors' needs and save the government money.

9. Seniors will probably stay politically active in the future. They will also work for social causes that help all age groups.


## SELECTED READINGS

Bryden, Kenneth. *Old Age Pensions and Policy-Making in Canada.* Montreal: McGill-Queen's University Press, 1974.

A case study of the politics of pension programs in Canada. The book gives the history of pension legislation, the ideologies that supported or opposed public pensions, and the reasons Canada's pension programs look the way they do. One of the few book-length studies of public policy and aging.

Kernaghan, Kenneth, and Olivia Kuper. *Coordination in Canadian Governments: A Case Study of Aging Policy.* Toronto: Institute of Public Administration of Canada, 1983.

A monograph that describes the federal and provincial government agencies involved in policy making for seniors. It also describes the links between agencies; the degrees of power that agencies, bureaucrats, and politicians have in the policy-making process; and the senior organizations that influence government. The authors call for co-ordination among agencies to ensure that programs for older people meet seniors' needs.

Myles, John. "Social Policy in Canada." In Eloise Rathbone-McEwan and Betty Havens, eds. *North American Elders: United States and Canadian Perspectives.* New York: Greenwood, 1988.

A review of Canada's pension policy that focuses on the pension debates of the past twenty-five years. Myles shows how tensions between social classes and interest groups shape social policy.

# The Future of Aging in Canada

## INTRODUCTION

This book began by saying that gerontology has two goals: to learn about aging and to use that knowledge to improve life for older people. Students who have read this far already know a lot more about aging than they did when they began their study of gerontology. But they may want to know about future directions in education and practice. This chapter will look at (1) issues that will challenge an aging society, (2) gerontology education in Canada, and (3) careers in gerontology.

## ISSUES THAT WILL CHALLENGE CANADIAN SOCIETY

What do all of the findings in this and the previous chapters have in common? What message can a person draw from this mass of research?

The research shows that individual and population aging will bring social change. It will even lead to changes in our concept of old age and changes in how individuals and society can respond to aging.

In 1989 the National Advisory Council on Aging published *1989 and Beyond: Challenges of an Aging Society*. This book (National Advisory Council 1989, 3) lists "the kinds of issues that will become more important or that will emerge in the years ahead as a result of the aging of the population and the changing characteristics of older people." *1989 and Beyond* covers six themes: (1) health and social care, (2) income, (3) environment, (4) information and technology, (5) activities, and (6) ethnic and native groups. Under each theme the council lists challenges that Canada will have to face in the years ahead. These include the reallocation of resources toward long-term health care, pay equity for women, the development of new ways to adapt housing, the reduction of illiteracy among seniors, an increased flexibility of timing for retirement, and greater participation by members of ethnic groups in planning services. These challenges and the other challenges outlined in the report, present a program for social reform and research in the years ahead. Social planners will need more knowledge about aging and older people to carry out these reforms.

## GERONTOLOGICAL EDUCATION

Students take gerontology courses for many reasons. The Carnegie Foundation in the United States lists three educational philosophies that guide gerontology courses: scientific, professional, and liberal. The scientific approach focuses on research and data collection using the scientific method. The professional approach focuses on improving services to older people and solving social problems. The liberal approach focuses on teaching everyone about the process of aging and about normal human development. Courses often combine one or more of these approaches. A gerontology course for nurses, for example, might teach students about human development and also involve them in a research project. A course for undergraduates might include a discussion of sociological methods and a study of normal aging. The Association for Gerontology in Higher Education (1987) found that most gerontology programs include a course on social gerontology and the psychology of aging. A large proportion of programs require courses in the biology/physiology of aging and the sociology of aging. Canadians will need all three types of gerontology education in the years ahead.

Gutman (1977) found that each province had at least one university that taught some courses related to gerontology. Most universities have undergraduate courses in the psychology of aging, the sociology of aging, or human development. These courses cover factual and theoretical knowledge about aging and social issues. Most courses include a study of attitudes toward older people, retirement, family life, and demography. Most gerontology instructors have degrees in established academic disciplines. Marcus (1980; 1978) asked thirty-seven gerontology teachers in Canada about the courses they teach. Twenty-two of her thirty respondents taught in departments of social work, psychology, or sociology. She says that this "is probably a correct indication of academic interest in gerontology. Only one instructor classified himself as a gerontologist" (1980, 8).

People who work in institutions need ongoing training. Many workers—registered nurses, licensed practical nurses, and nurse's aides—got little or no training in gerontology in the past. Other workers need to update their knowledge of older people (Matthews and Stryckman 1988). Universities and community colleges offer some of this training. Large institutions like hospitals offer practical training in aging; these programs range from lectures to in-service seminars to on-site training courses.

Skinkle and Grant (1988) report on the value of in-service training. They conducted a random sample study of eighty-six nursing home aides in Saskatchewan. The study compared aides who had taken an in-service training program and those who had not. Graduates of the program, compared with non-graduates, knew more about nursing skills, more about aging, and more about the philosophy of long-term care than aides. They also felt, more than the non-graduates, that their health team functioned effectively. Both groups showed similar positive views of older people. "[T]he results are sufficiently positive for us to recommend the further development and evaluation of such training programs across Canada" (Skinkle and Grant 1988, 56).

Certificate and diploma programs also exist in universities and community colleges to upgrade workers' knowledge. The Standards Committee of the Association for Gerontology in Higher Education (Standards Committee 1990) compiled a list of the 195 certificate programs offered in North American universities and colleges in 1987. Universities offer these programs at the graduate and undergraduate level. They generally include a series of courses as well as a practicum.

Some institutions offer continuing education certificates. These vary in both length and rigour. Some employers subsidize employees' tuition for these programs, while others offer pay raises to employees who complete certificate or diploma programs. The Department of Veterans Affairs, for example, asked its para-professional counselling staff if they wanted more training in gerontology. More than 89 percent of those who answered said they did, and the same portion wanted a diploma program. The department then

## Exhibit 16.1

### Educating the Next Generation About Older People

Universities and colleges have begun to include the study of aging in more and more programs. Professional associations and employers recognize the value of in-service training. Most of this education includes an attempt to dispel the myths about aging that people in our society have. Education programs could start earlier to give young people a more positive view of old age. A program in Calgary uses computer technology to do this.

"Bridging the Generation Gap," a program for students at Elbow Valley Elementary School in Calgary, has created a new role for seniors in the schools. The program uses computers to link twenty-seven 8- and 9-year-old students with ten seniors in Calgary and seven in Santa Cruz, California. The seniors and the students correspond regularly on the SeniorNet computer network. Students get paired with a senior and use the bulletin board to share information and ideas.

Brant Parker, the teacher at Elbow Valley Elementary School in Calgary who organized this program, says that students usually ask about "the 'olden days,' accounts of [the senior's] childhood, significant events of the past, or thoughts on the present and future" (Parker 1991). Students also tell the seniors things about their background, experiences, and achievements.

Marsha Quarter, a Grade 3 student, says, "I really look forward to the letters." Grace James, one of the Calgary seniors, says that the program, "widens your scope. [The students] ask the questions and sometimes you have to go and do some research at the library" (Ross 1990). Seniors can also use the SeniorNet network to correspond with seniors all over North America.

The students have held a tea for their computer-pals each year during Senior Citizen Awareness Week. Parker (1991) says that students have gained a new awareness of how much seniors have to offer and now have greater respect for them.

---

arranged with institutions that offered certificate and diploma programs across the country to schedule their programs at times convenient to Veterans Affairs staff (Boyce and Morgan 1982). The department offered the program for three weeks in 1981–82, and more training programs for middle and senior management, and health care workers were planned as a result.

Cohen (1990), Coordinator of the Gerontology Certificate Programme at Ryerson Polytechnical Institute in Toronto, notes the importance of training the next generation of gerontology workers (1990). She says that students should come to view themselves as advocates and facilitators who can empower older men and women. Many women who take gerontology courses do so after serving as caregivers to older family members. A survey done at

• • • • • • • • • • • • • • • • • • • • • • • • • • • • • • • • • • • • • • • • • •

# Exhibit 16.1

## An Advanced Certificate
## in Gerontology Program

• • • • • • • • • • • • • • • • • • • • • • • • • • • • • • • • • • • • • • • • • • •

Most provinces have at least one university program that offers a certificate or diploma in gerontology. "Certificate" and "diploma" can mean different things at different schools. One school may offer a certificate at the post-baccalaureate level, while another may offer a certificate to health care workers regardless of their educational background.

Hancock (1984) says that most certificate programs have a core program of courses including an overview course, psychological and sociological perspectives courses, and courses on death and dying. They all offer a multidisciplinary program and focus on normal aging and healthy older people. In most cases a centre on aging or the university division of continuing education sponsors the program.

The University of Manitoba offers an Advanced Certificate in Gerontology. This program's contents exemplify the types of courses that gerontology programs offer.

The University of Manitoba program accepts students with a bachelor's degree (or an equivalent post-secondary degree) and at least one year of experience working with older people. The program does not train people in direct-service delivery. It teaches gerontological concepts and focuses on the literature and research in the field. The program enrols about thirty students each year. Students complete the program in three to four years of part-time work.

Most students in the program work as nurses in nursing homes and hospitals. A smaller portion of students have backgrounds in social work, dentistry, recreation, or teaching. Classes allow people from many professions to learn together and to share their knowledge. The structure of this program gives some idea of what certificate programs offer and what they expect from students.

## Core Courses

**Gerontology I: The Aging Individual** (40 hours of classroom instruction). This course includes four modules: demographics and current issues; geriatrics; health; and psychology of aging.

**Gerontology II: Aging and Society** (40 hours). This course includes four modules: methodological issues; sociology of aging; social systems and aging; and social policies.

**Theories and Skills of Helping** (40 hours). This course gives students basic human relations skills. It applies these skills to issues students face in health and social service settings.

**Research Methods for the Consumer** (20 hours). This course shows practitioners how to read the gerontology literature critically.

**Independent Research Project** (50 hours of supervised research). A research project completed under the guidance of a faculty advisor.

## Electives

Four electives (20 hours each; total 80 hours). Electives change from year to year. They include: Women and Aging; Geriatric Psychiatry; Drugs and the Elderly; Death and Dying; Legal Issues; Spirituality and Aging; Philosophy and Aging; and The Family in Later Life.

Most graduates from this program report increased awareness of aging, improved relations with their clients (or patients), and a better understanding of aging in their own lives.

Some graduates report increases in pay, promotions, and new career opportunities as a result of taking this program.

**Source:** Adapted from the *Advanced Certificate in Gerontology Program Calendar* (Winnipeg: Continuing Education Division, University of Manitoba, 1992). Reproduced with permission.

• • • • • • • • • • • • • • • • • • • • • • • • • • • • • • • • • • • • •

Ryerson in the fall of 1989 found that 87 percent of respondents were women whose average age was 43. New issues raised by these women show their orientation to the field. They emphasized their need to understand aging within a broader societal context. They wanted to know about economics, law, advocacy, ethnicity, health care, and the role of women. Cohen (1990) argues for a multidisciplinary approach that would include, political science, economics, women's studies, and public administrations.

Medical doctors also need more gerontology education (Canadian Medical Association 1987). Family doctors and internists see many older people now. The Canadian Medical Association (CMA) (citing Woods Gordon 1984) says that more than 20 percent of physician services go to people aged 65 and over. Robertson (1981) projects that in the future older people will make up more than half the patients that family doctors and internists see. But, the Medical Council of Canada qualifying exams pay little attention to geriatric medicine. Less than 2 percent of the questions on the exam (between 1982 and 1987) dealt with geriatric medicine, while 20 percent of them dealt with pediatrics. A 1977 Canadian report suggested changes in this emphasis. It also suggested that medical students should study gerontology and geriatric medicine each year in school. The report suggested providing 100 hours of instruction over four years (Health and Welfare Canada 1977a). The CMA (1987) says that medical school students should spend some time working in parts of the community where older people live. Students should meet older patients in outpatient clinics, rehabilitation hospitals, and nursing homes.

The CMA also says that training in geriatrics has improved in the past few years. In 1987 fifteen of the sixteen medical schools had some geriatric medicine in their curricula. And most schools now offer students clinical rotations in geriatric medicine. Still, both Robertson (1981) and the CMA (1987) found that only one university required that medical students do clinical work in geriatric medicine in their third and fourth years. A survey of physicians who practise geriatric medicine (Skelton 1986) found that only 13 percent had had undergraduate training in geriatric medicine. Twenty percent of these physicians had only had lectures on the subject. Only 69 percent had formal post-graduate training in geriatric medicine. The CMA concludes that little post-graduate training exists for physicians outside specialist training programs.

Canada needs to train more researchers, academics, and health care workers in gerontology (Matthews and Stryckman 1988). Right now, most gerontology education takes place on the job or in post-graduate certificate and diploma programs. Rarely does gerontology education lead to more pay or to a higher-status job. Most people take these programs out of personal interest and often at their own expense. People who work as nurse's aides, orderlies, and paid homemakers receive low salaries and have the least formal gerontological education. These workers need encouragement and in some cases financial support before they will attend gerontology programs. Employers and the government should support gerontology education so that workers in the field get the knowledge they need.

## OCCUPATIONS AND CAREERS IN GERONTOLOGY

Direct service, administrative, and para-professional positions in gerontology will all increase in the future. Health and Welfare Canada (1985) reports that the number of registered nurses and orderlies in Canada increased by 50 per-cent from 1974 to 1984; the number of occupational therapists and physio-therapists increased by over 70 percent; and the number of physicians increased by 33 percent in that same time. Not all of these health care pro-fessionals work only with older people, but many of them do. Peterson (1987), for example, estimates that nurses occupy three out of every five jobs in nursing homes. And more nurses will be needed to work with older people in the future. A study in the U.S. predicts that the number of nurses who work in nursing homes will increase by two and a half times between the mid-1980s and the year 2000; the number of physical therapists will triple; and the number of occupational therapists will increase by 900 percent (National Institute on Aging 1984). Canada will need to train more of these profession-als as well as social workers, nurse's aides, physicians, and counsellors in the years ahead.

Students with a Bachelor of Arts degree and a course or two in aging will have a difficult time finding work in gerontology. However, those with grad-uate training in an established discipline like psychology, sociology, or social work will find more opportunities. Social work and the health care profes-sions (nursing, physiotherapy) offer the easiest access to working with older people. A master's degree in social work or a bachelor's degree in nursing open many jobs (Peterson 1987). A graduate degree in public health or administrative studies can lead to government work designing or administering programs for older people. Graduates with entrepreneurial drive may start businesses that serve older people. A student with a graduate degree, for example, could consult with major corporations on retirement education or staff training.

The Standards Committee of the Association for Gerontology in Higher Education (Standards Committee 1990) recommends the expansion of courses and programs in gerontology to include more courses, minors, majors, and specializations in gerontology at the graduate and undergraduate level. New developments will also include specialized programs in long-term care administration, public policy, and research. As education programs develop within professional faculties, these faculties will produce a statement of competencies for gerontology programs in their professions. All of these changes will improve the educational opportunities for students who want to work with the elderly.

## THE FUTURE OF GERONTOLOGY

Gerontologists in the future will learn more about aging, and their research will shape social policy. Their research will also help with "the most difficult challenge of all: re-connecting with aging and re-inserting seniors in all dimensions of community life" (Begin 1985, 196). Gerontology can change people's attitudes to aging and give people more knowledge about their families, their friends, and themselves. An incident in my own life made this clear to me. After my father's funeral, my mother, my sister, my father's brothers, and I got into a rented limousine and drove to the cemetery. The funeral director stopped the cars in the funeral procession at the cemetery gate. We saw the hearse pull ahead and stop a hundred yards away. I turned around to talk to one of my uncles in our car. A few minutes later the director waved all the cars on. We stopped behind the hearse and got out. It was empty. The director led us to the graveside. We stood close to the grave, but we could not see the coffin or any dirt. A blanket of fake grass covered the dirt that had come from the grave. Another blanket covered the coffin. Relatives and friends gathered to the side and behind us. The director said some prayers and a few kind words. My mother, my sister, and I stood and stared at the fake grass. I think we were supposed to leave. But I motioned to the director to pull the grass back. He looked surprised. I told him to pull the grass back. He did. We saw the corner of the coffin and the corner of the grave, and we started to cry.

I tell this story because my knowledge of aging and death and dying gave me the confidence to act. I felt I should do something, and I knew what I had to do. I find that I use my knowledge of aging in dozens of ways each day. I use it to understand my family and friends better and to understand the kinds of changes we go through as we age. Knowledge about aging allows me to plan for my own future with less fear and denial. The study of aging can make old age a better time of life for each of us and for the people we love.

## SUMMARY

1. The National Advisory Council on Aging lists a variety of themes that will challenge gerontology in the years ahead. These include health and social care, information and technology, and ethnic diversity.

2. Most universities in Canada offer one or more courses related to gerontology. Some schools offer post-graduate certificate or diploma programs. Professionals who work with older people also need ongoing training. Gerontology programs and training programs should give professionals a broad interdisciplinary view of later life.

3. Medical doctors and medical students need more knowledge of gerontology and geriatric medicine, because they will see more older patients in the coming years. Health care workers, like nurses and activity workers also need more training because they have the most contact with older patients. They often have no incentive, other than personal interest, to get training in gerontology. Pay raises linked to continuing education and tuition support for continuing education programs would encourage professionals to learn more about aging.

4. In the future, Canada will need more personnel to work with older people. People in the health care and social service professions will have the best chance to work with seniors.

5. Knowledge of aging will help you, your friends, and your family to live a good old age.

## SELECTED READINGS

Peterson, David A. *Career Paths in the Field of Aging: Professional Gerontology.* Lexington, Massachusetts: Lexington Books, 1987.

A good overview of gerontology education and job opportunities in the field of aging. A heavy U.S. orientation, but information about degree programs and proposals for continuing professional education will be of interest to Canadian students.

# REFERENCES

**1,10*** Abercrombie, Nicholas, Stephen Hill, and Bryan S. Turner. 1984. *The Penguin Dictionary of Sociology*. Harmondsworth, England: Penguin.

**7** Abrahams, R. 1972. "Mutual Help for the Widowed." *Social Work* 19:54–61.

**11,13** Abu-Laban, Sharon McIrvin. 1978. "The Family Life of Older Canadians." *Canadian Home Economics Journal* 28:16–25.

**13** Abu-Laban, Sharon McIrvin. 1980a. "The Family Life of Older Canadians." In Victor W. Marshall, ed. *Aging in Canada*. Toronto: Fitzhenry and Whiteside.

**13** Abu-Laban, Sharon McIrvin. 1980b. "Social Supports in Older Age: The Need for New Research Directions." *Essence* 4:195–209.

**3** Achenbaum, A., and P.N. Stearns. 1978. "Old Age and Modernization." *The Gerontologist* 18:307–12.

**10** Adams, O.B., and D.L.A. Lefebvre. 1980. *Retirement and Mortality: An Examination of Mortality in a Group of Retired Canadians*. Cat. No. 83-521E. Ottawa: Minister of Supply and Services.

**13** Adelman, M. 1987. *Long Time Passing: Lives of Older Lesbians*. Boston: Alyson.

**8** Agbayewa, M.O. 1990. "A Psychiatric Clinic Within a Geriatric Medical Day Hospital: Descriptive Study." *Canadian Journal on Aging* 9:5–12

**12** Age and Opportunity, Inc. 1990. *Working Arrangements Between Staff and Senior Centre Membership Organizations*. Winnipeg: Age and Opportunity, Inc.

**12** Aitkens, Andrew. 1990. "Literacy and Older Canadians: A New Imperative." Press release. Ottawa: One Voice, the Canadian Seniors Network.

**12** Aitkens, Andrew. 1991. *A National Literacy Strategy for Older Canadians*. Ottawa: One Voice, the Canadian Seniors Network.

**14** Ajemian, Ina, and Balfour M. Mount, eds. 1981. *The R.V.H. Manual on Palliative/Hospice Care*. New York: Arno Press.

**10** Akyeampong, E. 1987. "Older Workers in the Canadian Labour Market." *The Labour Force* 43:85–120.

**5** Albert, M.S., and E. Kaplan. 1980. "Organic Implications of Neuropsychological Deficits in the Elderly." In L.W. Poon, J.L Fozard, L.S. Cermak, D. Arenberg, and L.W. Thompson, eds. *New Directions in Memory and Aging: Proceedings of the George A. Talland Memorial Confer-* ence. Hillsdale, N.J.: Lawrence Erlbaum Associates.

**8** Alberta Senior Citizen's Bureau. 1984. *Older Persons in Alberta: Their Use of Programs and Services 1984*. Edmonton: Alberta Social Services and Community Health.

**6** Alpaugh, Patricia K., and J.E. Birren. 1977. "Variables Affecting Creative Contributions Across the Adult Life Span." *Human Development* 20:240–248.

**8** American Association of Retired Persons. 1984. *Prescription Drugs: A Survey of Consumer Use, Attitudes and Behavior*. Washington, D.C.: American Association of Retired Persons.

**6** American Psychiatric Association. 1980. *Diagnostic and Statistical Manual of Mental Disorders*. 3d ed. Washington, D.C.: American Psychiatric Association.

**3** Amoss, P.T., and S. Harrell. 1981. "Introduction: An Anthropological Perspective on Aging." In P.T. Amoss and S. Harrell, eds. *Other Ways of Growing Old: Anthropological Perspectives*. Stanford, California: Stanford University Press.

**10** Anderson, Kathryn, Robert L. Clark, and Thomas Johnson. 1980. "Retirement in Dual-Career Families." In Robert L. Clark, ed. *Retirement Policy in an Aging Society*. Durham N.C.: Duke University Press.

**13** Antonucci, Toni C., and Hiroko Akiyama. 1987. "Social Networks in Adult Life and a Preliminary Examination of the Convoy Model." *Journal of Gerontology* 42:519–27.

**13** Antonucci, Toni C. 1990. "Social Supports and Social Relationships." In Robert H. Binstock and Linda K. George, eds. *Handbook of Aging and the Social Sciences*. 3d ed. San Diego: Academic Press.

**3** Araba, Nana. 1988. "Social Change: Family Role and Responsibilities of the Elderly in Africa." In *Aging Around the World: A Report on the President's Symposium, "Aging in Tomorrow's World: An International Perspective."* The Gerontological Society of America.

**6** Arenberg, D. 1977. "Memory and Learning Do Decline Late in Life." Paper presented at a Conference on Aging and Social Policy. Vichy, France.

**2** Ariès, Phillipe. 1962. *Centuries of Childhood: A Social History of Family Life*. Trans. Robert Baldick, New York: Alfred A. Knopf.

**13** Arling, G., and W. McAuley. 1983. "The Feasi-

**Numbers indicate the chapter(s) in which this source is cited.**

bility of Public Payments for Family Caregivers." *The Gerontologist* 23:300–106.

13   Arluke, Arnold, Jack Levin, and John Suchwalko. 1984. "Sexuality and Romance in Advice Books for the Elderly." *The Gerontologist* 24:415–19.

9    Armstrong, Pat, and Hugh Armstrong. 1981. *Women and Jobs: The Canadian Case.* Ottawa: Canadian Centre for Policy Alternatives.

9    Armstrong, Pat, and Hugh Armstrong. 1984. *The Double Ghetto: Canadian Women and Their Segregated Work*, rev. ed. Toronto: McClelland and Stewart.

13   Aronson, Jane. 1985. "Family Care of the Elderly: Underlying Assumptions and Their Consequences." *Canadian Journal on Aging* 4:115–25.

8    Aronson, Jane, Victor W. Marshall, and Joanne Sulman. 1987. "Patients Awaiting Discharge from Hospital." In Victor W. Marshall, ed. *Aging in Canada: Social Perspectives.* Toronto: Fitzhenry and Whiteside.

13   Aronson, Jane. 1990. "Older Women's Experiences of Needing Care: Choice or Compulsion." *Canadian Journal on Aging* 9:234–47.

4    Artibise, A. 1977. *Winnipeg: An Illustrated History.* Toronto: Lorimer.

8    Asthana, S., and V.P. Sood. 1987. "Prescribing for the Elderly: One Hospital's Experience." *Geriatric Medicine (Canada)* 3:113–117.

7,10 Atchley, Robert C. 1971a. "Disengagement Among Professors." *Journal of Gerontology* 26:476–80.

10   Atchley, Robert C. 1971b. "Retirement and Work Orientation." *The Gerontologist* 11:29–32.

10   Atchley, Robert C. 1974. "The Meaning of Retirement." *Journal of Communications* 24:97–101.

10   Atchley, Robert C. 1976. *The Sociology of Retirement.* Cambridge, Mass.: Schenkman.

3    Atchley, Robert C. 1980. *The Social Forces in Later Life.* 3d ed. Belmont, California: Wadsworth.

10   Atchley, R.C. 1981. *The Process of Retirement: Comparing Women and Men.* Oxford, Ohio: Scripps Foundation Gerontology Center, Miami University.

7,10 Atchley, Robert C. 1982. "The Process of Retirement: Comparing Women and Men." In Maximiliane Szinovacz, ed. *Women's Retirement.* Beverly Hills, California: Sage.

1,10, Atchley, Robert C. 1985. *Social Forces and Aging.*
15   4th ed. Belmont, California: Wadsworth.

10   Atchley, Robert C., Suzanne R. Kunkell, and Carl Adlon. 1978. *An Evaluation of Preretirement*

*Programs: Results from an Experimental Study.* Oxford, Ohio: Scripps Foundation Gerontology Center, Miami University.

1    Atkinson, Wally. 1991. "Improving Transportation Systems for Seniors Benefits All." Paper presented at the FCM National Forum on Seniors Transportation titled, *Freedom to Move Is Life Itself,* Winnipeg.

8    Auer, Ludwig. 1987. *Canadian Hospital Costs and Productivity: A Study Prepared for the Economic Council of Canada.* Ottawa: Minister of Supply and Services.

4    Auerbach, Lewis, and A. Gerber. 1976. *Perceptions 2: Implications of the Changing Age Structure of the Canadian Population.* Ottawa: Supply and Services Canada for the Science Council of Canada.

7    Auger, Jeanette. 1980. "Cross Cultural Issues in the Aging Experience." Paper presented at the 9th Annual Scientific and Educational Meeting of the Canadian Association on Gerontology, Saskatoon.

6    Backman, L. 1985. "Further Evidence for the Lack of Adult Age Differences on Free Recall of Subject-Performed Tasks: The Importance of Motor Action." *Human Learning* 4:79–87.

10   Baillargeon, Richard. 1982. "Determinants of Early Retirement." *Canada's Mental Health* 30:20-22.

1    Bairstow, Dale. 1985. "Shared Appreciation and Home Equity Conversion: Ideas Whose Time Have Come for Canadians." In Gloria Gutman and Norman Blackie, eds. *Innovations in Housing and Living Arrangements for Seniors.* Burnaby, British Columbia: The Gerontology Research Centre, Simon Fraser University.

3    Baker, Paul M. 1983a. "Ageism, Sex, and Age: A Factorial Survey Approach." *Canadian Journal on Aging* 2:177–84.

1    Baker, Paul M. 1983b. "Old Before My Time." Videotape. Victoria, B.C.: Centre on Aging, University of Victoria.

3    Baker, Paul M. 1987. "The Dega and the Nacirema." In B. Hess and E. Markson, eds. *Growing Old in America.* 3d ed. New Brunswick, N.J.: Transaction Books.

14   Baker, Paul M. 1991. "Socialization After Death: The Might of the Living Dead." In B. Hess and E. Markson, eds. *Growing Old in America.* 4th ed. New York: Transaction Books.

11   Baker, P. M., and M. Prince. 1990. "Supportive Housing Preferences Among the Elderly." *Journal of Housing for the Elderly* 7:5–24.

11   Baker, P. M., and Victor Thompson. 1985.

"Victoria Seniors Survey 1: Needs and Utilization of Services." Paper presented at the 14th Annual Scientific and Educational Meeting of the Canadian Association on Gerontology.

14 Baltes, M.M. 1977–78. "On the Relationship of Significant Yearly Events and Time of Death: Random or Systematic Distribution." *Omega* 8:165–72.

7 Baltes, Paul B., Steven W. Cornelius, and John R. Nesselroade. 1979. "Cohort Effects in Developmental Psychology." In John R. Nesselroade and Paul B. Baltes, eds. *Longitudinal Research in the Study of Behavior and Development.* New York: Academic Press.

7 Baltes, P.B., and L.R. Goulet. 1970. "Status and Issues of a Life-span Developmental Psychology." In L.R. Goulet and Paul B. Baltes, eds. *Life-span Developmental Psychology: Research and Theory.* New York: Academic Press.

2 Baltes, P.B., H.W. Reese, and J.R. Nesselroade. 1977. *Life-span Developmental Psychology: Introduction to Research Methods.* Monterey, California: Brooks/Cole.

2 Baltes, P. B., and K.W. Schaie. 1982. "The Myth of the Twilight Years." In Steven H. Zarit, ed. *Readings in Aging and Death: Contemporary Perspectives.* 2d ed. New York: Harper and Row.

6 Baltes, P.B., and S.L. Willis. 1981. "Enhancement (Plasticity) of Intellectual Functioning: Penn State's Adult Development and Enrichment Project (ADEPT)." In F.I.M. Craik and S.E. Trehub, eds. *Aging and Cognitive Processes.* New York: Plenum.

6 Baltes, P.B., and S.L. Willis. 1982. "Toward Psychological Theories of Aging and Development." In J.E. Birren and K.W. Schaie, eds. *Handbook of the Psychology of Aging.* New York: Van Nostrand Reinhold.

13 Bankoff, Elizabeth A. 1983. "Aged Parents and Their Widowed Daughters: A Support Relationship." *Journal of Gerontology* 38:226–30.

8 Barer, Morris L., Robert B. Evans, Clyde Hertzman, and Jonathan Lomas. 1986. "Toward Efficient Aging: Rhetoric and Evidence." Paper prepared for presentation at Third Canadian Conference on Health Economics, Winnipeg.

8 Barer, Morris L., and Robert G. Evans. 1989. "Riding North on a South-bound Horse? Expenditures, Prices, Utilization and Incomes in the Canadian Health Care System." In Robert G. Evans and Greg L. Stoddart, eds. *Medicare at Maturity: Achievements, Lessons & Challenges.* Calgary: University of Calgary Press.

10 Barfield, R., and J. Morgan. 1974. *Early Retirement: The Decision and the Experience and a Second Look.* Ann Arbor, Michigan: Institute for Social Research.

12 Barrett, Carol J., and Karen M. Schneweis. 1980–81. "An Empirical Search for Stages of Widowhood." *Omega* 11:97–104.

5 Barrett, J.H. 1972. *Gerontological Psychology.* Springfield, Illinois: Charles C. Thomas.

6 Barrett, J.R., and M. Wright. 1981. "Age-Related Facilitation in Recall Following Semantic Processing." *Journal of Gerontology* 2:194–99.

11 Bartel, Henry, and Michael J. Daly. 1981. *Reverse Mortgages: A New Class of Financial Instruments for the Elderly.* Discussion Paper No. 188. Ottawa: Economic Council of Canada.

5 Bartoshuk, Linda M., and James M. Weiffenbach. 1990. "Chemical Senses and Aging." In Edward L. Schneider and John W. Rowe, eds. *Handbook of the Biology of Aging.* 3d ed. San Diego: Academic Press.

13 Baruch, G., and R.C. Barnet. 1983. "Adult Daughters' Relationships with their Mothers." *Journal of Marriage and the Family* 45:601–6.

1 Bassili, John N., and Jane E. Reil. 1981. "On the Dominance of the Old-Age Stereotype." *Journal of Gerontology* 36:682–88.

8 Battista, Renaldo N., Robert A. Spasoff, and Walter O. Spitzer. 1989. "Choice of Technique: Patterns of Medical Practices. In Robert G. Evans and Greg L. Stoddart, eds. *Medicare at Maturity: Achievements, Lessons and Challenges.* Calgary: University of Calgary Press.

2 Baum, Martha, and Rainer C. Baum. 1980. *Growing Old: A Societal Perspective.* Englewood Cliffs, New Jersey: Prentice-Hall.

11 Baumgarten, Mona, Daniel Thomas, Louise Poulin de Courval, and Claire Infante-Rivard. 1988. "Evaluation of a Mutual Help Network for the Elderly Residents of Planned Housing." *Psychology and Aging* 3:393–98.

8 Bayne, J.R.D. 1978. "Health and Care Needs of an Aging Population." A paper prepared for the National Symposium on Aging. Ottawa.

4 Beaujot, R., and K. McQuillan. 1982. *Growth and Dualism: The Demographic Development of Canadian Society.* Toronto: Gage.

10 Beeson, D. 1975. "Women in Studies of Aging: A Critique and Suggestion." *Social Problems* 23:52–59.

16 Bégin, Monique. 1985. "The New Society: On Aging and Seniors as an Enrichment to Civilization." In Ellen M. Gee and Gloria M. Gutman, eds. *Canadian Gerontological Collection V.* Winnipeg: Canadian Association on Gerontology.

11   Béland, François. 1984a. "The Decision of Elderly Persons to Leave Their Homes." *The Gerontologist* 24:179–85.

11   Béland, Francois. 1984b. "The Family and Adults 65 Years and Over: Co-Residency and Availability of Help." *Canadian Review of Sociology and Anthropology* 21:302–17.

11   Béland, François. 1987. "Living Arrangement Preferences Among Elderly People." *The Gerontologist* 27:797–803.

11   Béland, François. 1988. "Research in Social Gerontology in Québec: An Obscure Originality or a Deserved Obscurity?" *Canadian Journal on Aging* 7:293–310.

8,13  Béland, François. 1989. "Patterns of Health and Social Services Utilization." *Canadian Journal on Aging* 8:19–33.

13   Belanger, L. 1981. "The Types of Violence the Elderly are Victims of: Results of a Survey Done with Personnel Working with the Elderly." Paper presented to the Gerontological Society of America 34th Annual Scientific Meeting.

5    Benet, S. 1976. *How to Live to be 100.* New York: Dial.

7    Beneteau, R. 1988. "Trends in Suicide." *Canadian Social Trends* Winter: 22–24.

7    Bengtson, Vern L. 1979. "Ethnicity and Aging: Problems and Issues in Current Social Science Inquiry." In Donald E. Gelfand and Alfred J. Kutzik, eds. *Ethnicity and Aging: Theory, Research, and Policy.* New York: Springer.

13   Bengtson, Vern L. 1985. "Diversity and Symbolism in Grandparental Roles." In Vern L. Bengtson and Joan F. Robertson, eds. *Grandparenthood.* Beverly Hills: Sage.

15   Bengtson, V.L. 1991. "Age-Group Relations May Worsen, Says GSA President." *Gerontology News* January:2.

3    Bengtson, V. L., J.J. Dowd, D.H. Smith, and A. Inkeles. 1975. "Modernization, Modernity and Perceptions of Aging: A Cross-cultural Study." *Journal of Gerontology* 30:688–95.

13   Bengtson, Vern L., and Joseph A. Kuypers. 1971. "Generational Differences and the Developmental Stake." *International Journal of Aging and Human Development* 2:249–60.

13   Bengtson, Vern, Carolyn Rosenthal, and Linda Burton. 1990. "Families and Aging: Diversity and Heterogeneity." In Robert H. Binstock and Linda K. George, eds. *Handbook of Aging and the Social Sciences.* San Diego: Academic Press.

8    Bennett, James, and T. Krasny. 1981. "Health Care in Canada." In D. Coburn, D. D'Arcy, P. New, and G. Torrance, eds. *Health and Canadian Society: Sociological Perspectives.* Toronto: Fitzhenry and Whiteside.

5    Bennett, Neil G., and Lea Keil Garson. 1986. "Extraordinary Longevity in the Soviet Union: Fact or Artifact?" *The Gerontologist* 26:358–61.

11   Berger, Earl, Richard Godin, and Alan C. Harvey. 1986. "Older Canadians: Housing Market Characteristics and Demand." In Gloria Gutman and Norman Blackie, eds. *Aging in Place: Housing Adaptations and Options for Remaining in the Community.* Burnaby, British Columbia: The Gerontology Research Centre, Simon Fraser University.

2    Berger, P.L., and T. Luckman. 1967. *The Social Construction of Reality.* Garden City, New York: Doubleday.

3    Berkner, Lutz. 1972. "The Stem Family and the Development Cycle of the Peasant Household: An Eighteenth-Century Austrian Example." *American Historical Review* 77:398–418.

2    Berman, L., and I. Sobkowska-Ashcroft. 1985. "Views of Sex in Old Age in the Great Literature of the Western World." Paper presented at the Canadian Association of Gerontology 14th Annual Scientific and Educational Meeting, Hamilton.

1,2  Berman, L., and I. Sobkowska-Ashcroft. 1986. "The Old in Language and Literature." *Language and Communication* 6:139–45.

1,2  Berman, Lorna, and Irina Sobkowska-Ashcroft. 1987. *Images and Impressions of Old Age in the Great Works of Western Literature (700 B.C.–1900 A.D.).* Lewiston, New York: The Edwin Mellen Press.

11   Bernardin-Haldemann, Verena. 1982. "Housing Satisfaction—Life Satisfaction." Paper presented at the Annual Scientific and Educational Meeting of the Canadian Association on Gerontology. Winnipeg.

1    Bernardin-Haldemann, Verena. 1988. "Research in Social Gerontology: Observe, Understand or Explain?" *Canadian Journal on Aging* 7:327–32.

10   Bertaux, D. ed. 1981. *Biography and Society: The Life History Approach in the Social Sciences.* Beverly Hills, California: Sage.

7    Bienvenue, R., and B. Havens. 1986. "Structural Inequalities, Informal Networks: A Comparison of Native and Non-Native Elderly." *Canadian Journal on Aging* 5:241–48.

3    Biesele, M., and N. Howell. 1981. "'The Old Give You Life': Aging Among Kung Hunter-gatherers." In P.T. Amoss and S. Harrell, eds. *Other Ways of Growing Old: Anthropological*

*Perspectives.* Stanford, California: Stanford University Press.

8    Biette, M. Gayle, Vince L. Matthews, and Cope W. Schwenger. 1983. "Public Health, Prevention and the Aged." *Canadian Journal of Public Health* 74:106–9.

15   Binstock, Robert H. 1972. "Interest-Group Liberalism and the Politics of Aging." *The Gerontologist* 12:265–80.

15   Binstock, Robert H. 1986. "Public Policy and the Elderly." *Journal of Geriatric Psychiatry* 19:115–43.

14   Binstock, Robert H., and Jeff Kahana. 1988. "An Essay on *Setting Limits: Medical Goals in an Aging Society.*" *The Gerontologist* 28:424–26.

2    Birren, James E. 1968. "Principles of Research on Aging." In Bernice L. Neugarten, ed. *Middle Age and Aging.* Chicago: University of Chicago Press.

5    Birren, J.E. 1974. "Translations in Gerontology—From Lab to Life: Psychophysiology and the Speed of Response." *American Psychologist* 29:808–15.

1    Birren, J.E., and V. Clayton. 1975. "History of Gerontology." In D.S. Woodruff and J.E. Birren, eds. *Aging: Scientific Perspectives and Social Issues.* New York: D. Van Nostrand.

2    Birren, James E., and V.L. Bengtson, eds. 1988. *Emergent Theories in Aging.* New York: Springer.

10   Bixby, Lenore E. 1976. "Retirement Patterns in the United States: Research and Policy Interaction." *Social Security Bulletin* 39:3–19.

13   Black, M. 1985. "Health and Social Support of Older Adults in the Community." *Canadian Journal on Aging* 4:213–26.

11   Blackie, Norman. 1985. "Shared Housing: Principles and Practices." In Gloria Gutman and Norman Blackie, eds. *Innovations in Housing and Living Arrangements for Seniors.* Burnaby, British Columbia: The Gerontology Research Centre, Simon Fraser University.

11   Blackie, Norman K. 1986. "The Option of 'Staying Put'." In Gloria Gutman and Norman Blackie, eds. *Aging in Place: Housing Adaptations and Options for Remaining in the Community.* Burnaby, British Columbia: The Gerontology Research Centre, Simon Fraser University.

7    Blandford, Audrey A., and Neena L. Chappell. 1990. "Subjective Well-being Among Native and Non-Native Elderly Persons: Do Differences Exist?" *Canadian Journal on Aging* 9:386–99.

11   Blandford, Audrey A., Neena L. Chappell, and Susan Marshall. 1989. "Tenant Resource Coor-dinators: An Experiment in Supportive Housing." *The Gerontologist* 29:826–29.

2    Blau, P.M. 1964. *Exchange and Power in Social Life.* New York: Wiley.

7,13 Blau, Zena Smith. 1973. *Old Age in a Changing Society.* New York: New Viewpoints.

10   Bolger, Joe. 1980. *Bill C-12 and the Debate Over Public Service Pension Indexing.* Unpublished master's essay. Ottawa: Carleton University.

14   Bolton, Anne M. 1989. "Who Can Let You Die?" *Canadian Journal on Aging* 8:238–43.

12   Bond, John B., Jr. 1982. "Volunteerism and Life Satisfaction Among Older Adults." *Canadian Counsellor* 16:168–72.

12   Bond, J.B., Jr., and C.D.H. Harvey. 1991. "Ethnicity and Intergenerational Perceptions of Family Solidarity." *International Journal of Aging and Human Development* 33:33–34.

13   Bond, J.B., Jr., M.R. Baril, S. Axelrod, and L. Crawford. 1990. "Support to Older Parents by Middle Aged Children." *Canadian Journal of Community Mental Health* 9:163–78.

12   Bond, J.B., Jr., C.D.H. Harvey, and E.A. Hildebrand. 1987. "Familial Support of the Elderly in a Rural Mennonite Community." *Canadian Journal on Aging* 6:7–17.

10   Bond, Sheryl L., and John B. Bond, Jr. 1980. "The Impact of a Preretirement Program." *Canadian Counsellor* 14:68–71.

8    Bosmann, Bruce H. 1984. "Pharmacology of Alcoholism and Aging." In J.T. Hartford and T. Samorajski, eds. *Alcoholism in the Elderly.* New York: Raven Press.

5    Boston Women's Health Collective. 1982. "Menopause." In Steven H. Zarit, ed. *Readings in Aging and Death: Contemporary Perspectives.* 2d ed. New York: Harper and Row.

2,5,6 Botwinick, J. 1984. *Aging and Behavior.* 3d ed. New York: Springer.

6    Botwinick, J., and I.C. Siegler. 1980. "Intellectual Ability Among the Elderly: Simultaneous Cross-Sectional and Longitudinal Comparisons." *Developmental Psychology* 16:49–53.

5    Botwinick, J., and L.W. Thompson. 1968. "A Research Note on Individual Differences in Reaction Time in Relation to Age." *Journal of Genetic Psychology* 112:73-75.

5    Botwinick, J., J.F. Brinley, and J.S. Robbin. 1958. "The Interaction Effects of Perceptual Difficulty and Stimulus Exposure Time on Age Differences in Speed and Accuracy of Response." *Gerontologia* 2:1–10.

5    Botwinick, J., J.R. Brinley, and J.S. Robbin. 1959. "Maintaining Set in Relation to Motiva-

tion and Age." *American Journal of Psychology* 72:585–88.

12    Bourdeau, Christiane. 1991. Personal correspondence.

6    Bowles, N.L., and L.W. Poon. 1982. "An Analysis of the Effect of Aging on Memory." *Journal of Gerontology* 37:212–19.

16    Boyce, M., and D. Morgan. 1982. "Educating a Government Bureaucracy in Gerontology: The Department of Veterans Affairs Experience." Paper presented at the 11th Annual Scientific and Educational Meetings of the Canadian Association on Gerontology, Winnipeg.

7    Boyd, R., and R.N. Koskela. 1970. "A Test of Erikson's Theory of Ego-Stage Development by Means of a Self-Report Instrument." *Journal of Experimental Education* 38:1–14.

3    Bradbury, Bettina. 1983. "The Family Economy and Work in an Industrializing City: Montreal in the 1970's." In W.P. Ward, comp. *The Social Development of Canada: Readings.* Richmond, British Columbia: Open Learning Institute.

5    Branch, L.G., and A.M. Jette. 1981. "Elders' Use of Informal Long-Term Care Assistance." Paper presented at the Annual Meeting of the Gerontological Society of America, Toronto.

3    Braudel, Fernand. 1981. *The Structure of Everyday Life: Civilization and Capitalism 15th–18th Century.* Vol. 1. Trans. Sian Reynolds. New York: Harper and Row.

7    Braun, Peter, and Robert Sweet. 1983-84. "Passages: Fact or Fiction?" *International Journal of Aging and Human Development* 18:161–76.

15    Braungart, Richard G., and Margaret M. Braungart. 1986. "Life-Course and Generational Politics." *Annual Review of Sociology* 12:205–31.

1    Brillon, Yves. 1986. "Les personnes agées face au crime." Rapport de Récherche. Centre International de Criminologie Comparée. Montreal: Université de Montréal.

1    Brillon, Yves. 1987. *Victimization and Fear of Crime Among the Elderly.* Trans. D.R. Crelinsten. Toronto: Butterworths.

11    Brink, Satya. 1985. "Housing Elderly People in Canada: Working Towards a Continuum of Housing Choices Appropriate to Their Needs." In Gloria Gutman and Norman Blackie, eds. *Innovations in Housing and Living Arrangements for Seniors.* Burnaby, British Columbia: The Gerontology Research Centre, Simon Fraser University.

13    Brody, Elaine M. 1981. " 'Women in the Middle' and Family Help to Older People." *The Gerontologist* 18:471-80.

13    Brody, Elaine M. 1983. "Women's Changing Roles and Help to Elderly Parents: Attitudes of Three Generations of Women." *Journal of Gerontology* 38:597–607.

13    Brody, Elaine M. 1990. *Women in the Middle: Their Parent-Care Years.* New York: Springer.

13    Brody, Elaine M., and Claire B. Schoonover. 1986. "Patterns of Parent-Care When Adult Daughters Work and When They Do Not." *The Gerontologist* 26:372–81.

3    Bronowski, Jacob. 1976. *The Ascent of Man.* London: BBC Publishing.

8    Brown, Mabel C. 1981. "Giving Seniors a Choice of Services and Facilities." *Ontario Medical Review* 48:45–48.

9,15    Bryden, Kenneth. 1974. *Old Age Pensions and Policy-Making in Canada.* Montreal, Quebec: McGill-Queen's University Press.

12    Buckingham, R.W., III, S.A. Lack, G.M. Mount, L.D. MacLean, and J.T. Collins. 1976. "Living with the Dying." *Canadian Medical Association Journal* 115:1211–15.

7    Bühler, C. 1951. "Maturation and Motivation." *Personality* 1:184–211.

1    Bultena, Gordon L., and Edward A. Powers. 1978. "Denial of Aging: Age Identification Reference Group Orientations." *Journal of Gerontology* 33:748–54.

10    Burbidge, John B., and A. Leslie Robb. 1980. "Pensions and Retirement Behaviour." *Canadian Journal of Economics* 13:421–37.

4    Burke, Mary Anne. 1991. "Implications of an Aging Society." *Canadian Social Trends* Spring:6–8.

2    Burwell, Elinor J. 1984. "Sexism in Social Science Research on Aging." In Jill McCalla Vickers, ed. *Taking Sex into Account: The Policy Consequences of Sexist Research.* Ottawa: Carleton University Press.

12    Butler, R.N. 1968. "The Life Review: An Interpretation of Reminiscence in the Aged." In Bernice L. Neugarten, ed. *Middle Age and Aging.* Chicago: University of Chicago Press.

1    Butler, R.N. 1969. "Age-ism: Another Form of Bigotry." *The Gerontologist* 9:243–46.

6    Butler, R.N. 1974. "The Creative Life and Old Age." In E. Pfeiffer, ed. *Successful Aging.* Durham, N.C.: Center for the Study of Aging and Human Development, Duke University.

6,7    Butler, R.N. 1975. *Why Survive? Being Old in America.* New York: Harper and Row.

1    Butler, R.N. 1989. "Dispelling Ageism: The Cross-cutting Intervention." *The Annals of the*

*American Academy of Political and Social Sciences* 503:138–47.

**11** Butler, R.N., and M.I. Lewis. 1976. *Sex After 60: A Guide for Men and Women for Their Later Years.* New York: Harper and Row.

**6** Butler, R.N., and M.I. Lewis. 1982. *Aging and Mental Health.* 3d ed. St. Louis, Missouri: Mosby.

**8** Buzzell, Mary. 1981. "So Very Vulnerable." *Journal of Gerontological Nursing* 7:286–87.

**11** Byerts, Thomas O. 1982. "The Congregate-Housing Model: Integrating Facilities and Services." In Robert D. Chellis, James F. Seagle, Jr., and Barbara Mackey Eagle, eds. *Congregate Housing for Older People: A Solution for the 1980s.* Lexington, Massachusetts: Lexington Books.

**7** Cain, L.D., Jr. 1964. "Life Course and Social Structure." In Robert E.L. Faris, ed. *Handbook of Modern Sociology.* Chicago: Rand McNally.

**10** Calasanti, Toni M. 1988. "Participation in a Dual Economy and Adjustment to Retirement." *International Journal of Aging and Human Development* 26:13–27.

**14** Callahan, Daniel. 1987. *Setting Limits: Medical Goals in an Aging Society.* New York: Simon and Schuster.

**13** Callahan, James J. 1986. "Guest Editor's Perspective." *Pride Institute Journal of Long-Term Home Health Care* 5:2–3.

**8** Caloren, Heather. 1980. "Problems of the Independent Elderly in Using the Telephone to Seek Health Care." In John Crawford, ed. *Canadian Gerontological Collection III: Selected Papers 1980: The Family of Later Life.* Winnipeg: Canadian Association on Gerontology.

**13** Campbell, Ruth, and Elaine Brody. 1985. "Women's Changing Roles and Help to the Elderly: Attitudes of Women in the United States and Japan." *The Gerontologist* 25:584–92.

**11** Canada Mortgage and Housing Corporation. 1978. *Housing the Elderly.* Ottawa: Minister of Supply and Services.

**11** Canada Mortgage and Housing Corporation. 1982. *HIFE Microdata File and Projections.* Ottawa: Canada Mortgage and Housing Corporation.

**11** Canada Mortgage and Housing Corporation. 1987. *Garden Suites: A New Housing Option for Elderly Canadians?* Ottawa: Minister of Supply and Services.

**11** Canada Mortgage and Housing Corporation. 1988. *Housing for Older Canadians: New Financial and Tenure Options.* Ottawa: Canada Mortgage and Housing Corporation.

**11** Canada Mortgage and Housing Corporation. No date. *Housing Choices for Older Canadians.* Ottawa: Minister of Supply and Services.

**13** Canadian Advisory Council on the Status of Women. 1990. *Women and Labour Market Poverty.* Ottawa: Canadian Advisory Council on the Status of Women.

**15** Canadian Association of Retired Persons. 1991. *C.A.R.P.* news release. Toronto: Canadian Association of Retired Persons.

**10** Canadian Association of University Teachers. 1991. "Mandatory Retirement." *CAUT Bulletin* 38:1–5.

**11** Canadian Broadcasting Corporation. 1986. Report on aging segment. "Midday," 4 December.

**1** Canadian Council on Social Development. 1973. *Beyond Shelter.* Ottawa: Canadian Council on Social Development.

**11** Canadian Council on Social Development. 1976a. *Housing the Elderly.* Ottawa: Canadian Council on Social Development.

**10** Canadian Council on Social Development. 1976b. *Statement on Retirement Policies.* Ottawa: Canadian Council on Social Development.

**4,8** Canadian Council on Social Development. 1990. *Canada's Social Programs Are in Trouble.* Ottawa: Canadian Council on Social Development.

**14,16** Canadian Medical Association. 1987. *Health Care for the Elderly: Today's Challenges, Tomorrow's Options.* Ottawa: Canadian Medical Association.

**5** Canadian National Institute for the Blind. 1988. *Statistical Information on the Client Population of the CNIB 1988.* Toronto: Canadian Institute for the Blind.

**7** Canadian Public Health Association. 1988. *Report of the National Workshop on Ethnicity and Aging.* Ottawa: Canadian Public Health Association.

**11,12** Canadian Red Cross Society. 1983. *Red Cross National Seniors' Services Needs Assessment.* Toronto: Canadian Red Cross Society.

**11** *Canadian Social Trends.* 1989. "1986 Census Highlights: Changes in Living Arrangements." *Canadian Social Trends.* Cat. No. 11-008E. Spring: 27–29.

**13** Cantor, M.H., and V. Little. 1985. "Aging and Social Care." In R.H. Binstock and E. Shanas, eds. *Handbook of Aging and the Social Sciences.* New York: Van Nostrand Reinhold.

**12** Cape, Elizabeth. 1983. "Activity and Independence: Issues in the Implementation of Activity

Programs for Institutionalized Elders." *Canadian Journal on Aging* 2:185–95.

4    Cape, Elizabeth. 1987. "Aging Women in Rural Settings." In Victor W. Marshall, ed. *Aging in Canada: Social Perspectives.* 2d. ed. Toronto: Fitzhenry and Whiteside.

5,8  Cape, Ronald D.T., and Philip J. Henschke. 1980. "Perspectives of Health in Old Age." *Journal of the American Geriatrics Society* 28:295–99.

8    Cape, Ronald D.T., C. Shorrock, R. Tree, R. Pablo, A. J. Campbell, and D.G. Seymour. 1977. "Square Pegs in Round Holes: A Study of Residents in Long-Term Institutions in London, Ontario. " *Canadian Medical Association Journal* 117:1284–87.

6    Cappliez, P. 1988. "Some Thoughts on the Prevalence and Etiology of Depressive Conditions in the Elderly." *Canadian Journal on Aging* 7:431–40.

6    Cattell, R.B. 1963. "Theory of Fluid and Crystallized Intelligence: An Initial Experiment." *Journal of Educational Psychology* 54:105–11.

6    Cavanaugh, J.C. 1983. "Comprehension and Retention of Television Programs by 20- and 60- Year Olds." *Journal of Gerontology* 38:190–96.

6    Cavanaugh, J.C., J.A. Grady, and M. Perlmutter. 1983. "Forgetting and Use of Memory Aids in 20 to 70 Year-Olds' Everyday Life." *International Journal of Aging and Human Development* 17:113–22.

5    Cerami, Anthony, Helen Vlassara, and Michael Brownlee. 1987. "Glucose and Aging." *Scientific American* 256:90–96.

6    Cerella, J. 1990. "Aging and Information-Processing Rate." In James E. Birren and K. Warner Schaie, eds. *Handbook of the Psychology of Aging.* 3d ed. San Diego: Academic Press.

5    Cerella, J., L.W. Poon, and D.H. Williams. 1980. "Age and Complexity Hypothesis." In L.W. Poon, ed. *Aging in the 80's.* Washington, D.C.: American Psychological Association.

15   Cernetig, Meiro. 1985. "Plans to De-Index Old Age Pensions Mean Poverty Jump Council Says." *Globe and Mail* 11 June.

8    Chambers, Larry W., Peter Tugwell, Charles H. Goldsmith, Patricia Caulfield, Murray Haight, Laura Pickard, and Mary Gibbon. 1990. "The Impact of Home Care on Recently Discharged Elderly Hospital Patients in an Ontario Community." *Canadian Journal on Aging* 9:327–47.

14   Chappell, Neena L. 1975. "Awareness of Death in Disengagement Theory: A Conceptualiza-

tion and an Empirical Investigation." *Omega* 6:325–43.

8,13 Chappell, Neena L. 1980. "Re-examining Conceptual Boundaries: Peer and Intergenerational Relationships." *Essence* 4:169–78

13   Chappell, Neena L. 1982a. "The Future Impact of the Changing Status of Women." In Gloria Gutman, ed. *Canada's Changing Age Structure: Selected Papers.* Burnaby, British Columbia: Simon Fraser University Publications.

2    Chappell, Neena L. 1982b. "The Value of Research to Practitioners in Work with the Elderly." *Canadian Journal on Aging* 1:62–5.

12,13 Chappell, Neena L. 1983a. "Informal Support Networks Among the Elderly." *Research on Aging* 5:77–99.

8    Chappell, Neena L. 1983b. "Who Benefits from Adult Day Care? Changes in Functional Ability and Mental Functioning During Attendance." *The Canadian Journal on Aging* 2:9–26.

9    Chappell, Neena L. 1987. "Canadian Income and Health-Care Policy: Implications for the Elderly." In Victor W. Marshall, ed. *Aging in Canada.* Toronto: Fitzhenry & Whiteside.

8    Chappell, Neena L. 1988. "Long-Term Care in Canada." In Eloise Rathbone-McCuan and Betty Havens, eds. *North American Elders: United States and Canadian Perspectives.* New York: Greenwood Press.

13   Chappell, Neena L. 1989a. "Health and Helping Among the Elderly: Gender Differences." *Journal of Aging and Health* 1:102–20.

11   Chappell, Neena L. 1989b. *Formal Programs for Informal Caregivers to Elders.* Paper prepared for the Aging Policy Section, Health Policy Division, Policy, Planning and Information Branch, Health and Welfare Canada. Ottawa: Health and Welfare Canada.

8,13 Chappell, Neena L. 1990. "Aging and Social Care." In Robert H. Binstock and Linda K. George, eds. *Handbook of Aging and the Social Sciences.* 3d ed. San Diego: Academic Press.

13   Chappell, Neena L. 1991. "Living Arrangements and Sources of Caregiving." *Journal of Gerontology: Social Sciences* 46:S1–S8.

13   Chappell, Neena L., and Mark Badger. 1989. "Social Isolation and Well-Being." *Journal of Gerontology: Social Sciences* 44:5169-76.

6    Chappell, Neena L., and G.E. Barnes. 1982. "The Practicing Pharmacist and the Elderly Client." *Contemporary Pharmacy Practice* 5:170–75.

8    Chappell, Neena L., and Audrey A. Blandford. 1983. *Adult Day Care: Its Impact on the Utilization of Other Health Care Services and on Quality of*

*Life*. Final report. Ottawa: NHRDP, Health and Welfare Canada.

8  Chappell, Neena L., and Audrey A. Blandford. 1987a. "Adult Day Care and Medical and Hospital Claims." *The Gerontologist* 27:773–79.

13  Chappell, Neena L., and Audrey A. Blandford. 1987b. "Health Service Utilization by Elderly Persons." *Canadian Journal of Sociology* 12:195–215.

5  Chappell, Neena L., and Betty Havens. 1980. "Old and Female: Testing the Double Jeopardy Hypothesis." *Sociological Quarterly* 21:157–71.

13  Chappell, Neena L., and Betty Havens. 1985. "Who Helps the Elderly Person: A Discussion of Informal and Formal Care." In Warren A. Peterson and Jill Quadagno, eds. *Social Bonds in Later Life: Aging and Interdependence*. Beverly Hills, California: Sage.

2  Chappell, Neena L., and Harold L. Ohrbach. 1986. "Socialization in Old Age: A Meadian Perspective." In Victor W. Marshall, ed. *Later Life: The Social Psychology of Aging*. Beverly Hills, California: Sage.

8,15  Chappell, Neena L., and Margaret Penning. 1979. "The Trend Away from Institutionalization: Humanism or Economic Efficiency?" *Research on Aging* 1:361–87.

13  Chappell, Neena L., and Alexander Segall. 1989. "Health, Helping Networks and Well-Being." *Journal of Aging Studies* 3:313–24.

7  Chappell, Neena L., and Laurel A. Strain. 1984. *Needs Assessment of Natives 50+ Living in Winnipeg*. Winnipeg: University of Manitoba Centre on Aging.

13  Chappell, Neena L., Alexander Segall, and Doris G. Lewis. 1990. "Gender and Helping Networks Among Day Hospital and Senior Centre Participants." *Canadian Journal on Aging* 9:220–33.

5,8  Chappell, Neena L., Laurel A. Strain, and Audrey A. Blandford. 1986. *Aging and Health Care: A Social Perspective*. Toronto: Holt, Rinehart and Winston of Canada.

6  Charness, Neil. 1981. "Aging and Skilled Problem Solving." *Journal of Experimental Psychology: General* 110:21–38.

6  Charness, Neil. 1982. "Problem Solving and Aging: Evidence from Semantically Rich Domains." *Canadian Journal on Aging* 1:21–28.

6  Charness, Neil. 1985. "Aging and Problem-solving Performance." In Neil Charness, ed. *Aging and Human Performance*. Chichester, England: John Wiley and Sons.

6  Charness, Neil. 1987. "Component Processes in Bridge Bidding and Novel Problem-solving Tasks." *Canadian Journal of Psychology* 41:223–43.

5  Charness, Neil, and Elizabeth A. Bosman. 1990. "Human Factors and Design for Older Adults." In James E. Birren and K. Warner Schaie, eds. *Handbook of the Psychology of Aging*. 3d ed. San Diego: Academic Press.

5  Charness, Neil, and Elizabeth Bosman. 1989. "The Role of Human Factors in Product Design for Older Adults." Paper presented at the 18th Annual Scientific and Educational Meeting of the Canadian Association on Gerontology, Ottawa.

6  Charness, Neil, and Jamie I.D. Campbell. 1988. "Acquiring Skill at Mental Calculation in Adulthood: A Task Decomposition." *Journal of Experimental Psychology: General* 117:115–29.

4  Chawla, Raj. 1991. "Dependency Ratios." *Canadian Social Trends*. Cat. No. 11-008E. Spring:3–5.

9,13  Cheal, David. 1983. "Intergenerational Family Transfers." *Journal of Marriage and the Family* 45:805–13.

9  Cheal, David. 1985a. *Moral Economy: Gift Giving in an Urban Society. Winnipeg Area Study Report No. 5*. Winnipeg: Institute for Social and Economic Research, University of Manitoba.

9,13  Cheal, David. 1985b. "The System of Transfers to and from Households in Canada." *Western Economic Review* 4:35–39.

13  Cheal, David. 1986. "The Social Dimensions of Gift Behaviour." *Journal of Social and Personal Relationships* 3:423–39.

13  Cheal, David J. 1989-90. "Theories of Serial Flow in Intergenerational Transfers." *International Journal of Aging and Human Development* 26:261–73.

4  Chen, Yung-Ping. 1987. "Making Assets Out of Tomorrow's Elderly." *The Gerontologist* 27:410–16.

13  Cherlin, Andrew, and Frank F. Furstenberg. 1985. "Styles and Strategies of Grandparenting." In Vern L. Bengtson and Joan F. Robertson, eds. *Grandparenthood*. Beverly Hills: Sage.

3  Cherry, Ralph, and Scott Magnuson-Martinson. 1981. "Modernization and the Status of the Aged in China: Decline or Equalization?" *The Sociological Quarterly* 22:253–61.

7  Chiriboga, David A. 1984. "Social Stressors as Antecedents of Change." *Journal of Gerontology* 39:468–77.

13  Chiriboga, David A., Philip G. Weiler, and Karen Nielsen. 1990. "The Stress of Caregiv-

ers." In David E. Biegel and Arthur Blum, eds. *Aging and Caregiving: Theory, Research, and Policy.* Newbury Park: Sage.

12    Christie, J. Lee. 1983. "Seniors Play Games Too." *Recreation Canada* February: 6–9.

7     Ciaccio, N.V. 1971. "A Test of Erikson's Theory of Ego Epigenesis." *Developmental Psychology* 4:306–11.

10    Ciffin, S., and J. Martin. 1977. *Retirement in Canada: Volume 1, When and Why People Retire.* Health and Welfare Canada, Policy Research and Long Range Planning (Welfare). Ottawa: Minister of Supply and Services.

8     Clarfield, A.M. 1983. "Home Care: Is It Cost Effective?" *Canadian Medical Association Journal* 129:1181–83.

12    Clarke, H.H. 1977. "Joint and Body Range of Motion." *Physical Fitness Research Digest* 7.

15    Clarke, Harold D., L. LeDuc, J. Jenson, and J. Pammett. 1980. *Political Choice in Canada.* Abridged ed. Toronto: McGraw-Hill Ryerson.

2,3   Cockerham, William C. 1991. *This Aging Society.* Englewood Cliffs, New Jersey: Prentice Hall.

6     Cohen, Gene D. 1990. "Psychopathology and Mental Health in the Mature and Elderly Adult." In James E. Birren and K. Warner Schaie, eds. *Handbook of the Psychology of Aging.* 3d ed. San Diego: Academic Press.

3     Cohn, R. 1982. "Economic Development and Status Change of the Aged." *American Journal of Sociology* 87:1150–61.

13    Colerick, E.J., and L.K. George. 1986. "Predictors of Institutionalization Among Caregivers of Patients with Alzheimer's Disease." *Journal of the American Geriatric Society* 34:493–98.

3     Colson, E., and T. Scudder. 1981. "Old Age in Gwembe District, Zambia." In P.T. Amoss and S. Harrell, eds. *Other Ways of Growing Old: Anthropological Perspectives.* Stanford, California: Stanford University Press.

5     Colvez, A., and M. Blanchet. 1981. "Disability Trends in the United States Population 1966–1976: Analysis of Reported Causes." *American Journal of Public Health* 71:464–71.

16    Connelly, J. Richard. 1981. "Education and the Future." In Gloria Gutman, ed. *Canada's Changing Age Structure: Implications for the Future.* Burnaby, British Columbia: Simon Fraser University.

9     Connelly, M. Patricia, and Martha MacDonald. 1990. *Women and the Labour Force.* Cat. No. 98-125. Ottawa: Minister of Supply and Services.

10    Connidis, Ingrid. 1982. "Women and Retirement: The Effect of Multiple Careers on Retirement Adjustment." *Canadian Journal on Aging* 1:17–27.

11    Connidis, Ingrid. 1983a. "Living Arrangement Choices of Older Residents: Assessing Quantitative Results with Qualitative Data." *Canadian Journal of Sociology* 8:359–75.

7     Connidis, Ingrid. 1983b. "The Pros, Cons and Worries of Aging." Paper presented at the Canadian Association on Gerontology 12th Annual Scientific and Educational Meeting, Moncton.

2,7,13 Connidis, Ingrid Arnet. 1989a. *Family Ties and Aging.* Toronto: Butterworths.

13    Connidis, Ingrid Arnet. 1989b. "Report on Seniors' Volunteer Work and Unpaid Help to Others." Paper commissioned by the National Advisory Council on Aging for the Symposium on Social Supports, Ottawa, March 28–29.

13    Connidis, Ingrid Arnet. 1989c. "Siblings as Friends in Later Life." *American Behavioral Scientist* 33:81–93.

13    Connidis, Ingrid Arnet, and Lorraine Davies. 1990. "Confidants and Companions in Later Life: The Place of Family and Friends." *Journal of Gerontology: Social Sciences* 45:S141–S149.

11    Connidis, Ingrid, and Judith Rempel. 1983. "The Living Arrangements of Older Residents: The Role of Gender, Marital Status, Age, and Family Size." *Canadian Journal on Aging* 2:91–105.

7     Constantinople, A. 1969. "An Eriksonian Measure of Personality Development in College Students." *Developmental Psychology* 1:357–72.

16    Continuing Education Division University of Manitoba. 1992. *Advanced Certificate in Gerontology Program Calendar.* Winnipeg: University of Manitoba.

13    Corby, Nan, and Judy Maes Zarit. 1983. "Old and Alone: The Unmarried in Later Life." In Ruth B. Weg, ed. *Sexuality in the Later Years: Roles and Behavior.* New York: Academic Press.

4     Corelli, Rae. 1986. "A Matter of Care." *Maclean's* 6 October.

13    Corin, Ellen. 1987. "The Relationship Between Formal and Informal Social Support Networks in Rural and Urban Contexts." In Victor W. Marshall, ed. *Aging in Canada: Social Perspectives.* 2d ed. Toronto: Fitzhenry and Whiteside.

11    Corke, Susan. 1986a. "Granny Flats as an Intensification Option for Housing the Elderly." In Susan Corke, Gregory S. Romanick, Michael Lazarowich, Joan Simon, eds. *Granny Flats: A Housing Option for the Elderly.* Report No. 13. Winnipeg: Institute of Urban Studies.

11 Corke, Susan. 1986b. "Provincial Housing and Shelter Support Programs for the Elderly: Ontario." In Gloria Gutman and Norman Blackie, eds. *Aging in Place: Housing Adaptations and Options for Remaining in the Community.* Burnaby, British Columbia: The Gerontology Research Centre, Simon Fraser University.

12 Covey, Herbert C. 1983. "Higher Education and Older People: Some Theoretical Considerations, Part II." *Educational Gerontology* 9:95–109.

3 Cowgill, Donald O. 1972. "A Theory of Aging in Cross-Cultural Perspective." In D. Cowgill and L. Holmes, eds. *Aging and Modernization.* New York: Appleton-Century-Crofts.

3,10 Cowgill, Donald O. 1974. "Aging and Modernization: A Revision of the Theory." In Jaber F. Gubrium, ed. *Late Life.* Springfield, Illinois: Charles C. Thomas.

3 Cowgill, Donald O. 1986. *Aging Around the World.* Belmont, California: Wadsworth.

3 Cowgill, Donald O., and Lowell D. Holmes, eds. 1972. *Aging and Modernization.* New York: Appleton-Century-Crofts.

10 Cox, Harold, and Albert Bhak. 1978–79. "Symbolic Interaction and Retirement Adjustment: An Empirical Assessment." *International Journal of Aging and Human Development* 9:279–86.

11 Cranz, Galen, and Thomas L. Schumacher. 1975. *The Impact of High-Rise Housing on Older Resident. Working Paper: 18.* Princeton, New Jersey: Research Centre for Urban and Environmental Planning, School of Architecture and Urban Planning.

8 Crichton, A. 1980. "Equality: A Concept in Canadian Health Care: From Intention to Reality of Provision." *Social Science and Medicine* 14C:243–57.

13 Crimmins, Eileen M., and Dominique G. Ingegneri. 1990. "Interaction and Living Arrangements of Older Parents and Their Children." *Research on Aging* 12:3–35.

3,4 Cross, D. Suzanne. 1983. "The Neglected Majority: The Changing Role of Women in Nineteenth-Century Montreal." In P.W. Ward, comp. *The Social Development of Canada: Readings.* Richmond, British Columbia: Open Learning Institute.

6 Crosson, C.W., and E.A. Robertson-Tchabo. 1983. "Age and Preference for Complexity Among Manifestly Creative Women." *Human Development* 26:149–55.

13 Crystal, S. 1986. "Social Policy and Elder Abuse." In K.A. Pillemer and R.S. Wolf, eds. *Elder Abuse: Conflict in the Family.* Dover, Mass.: Auburn House.

2,7 Cumming, E., and W.E. Henry. 1961. *Growing Old: The Process of Disengagement.* New York: Basic Books.

12 Cunningham, D.A., P.A. Rechnitzer, J.H. Howard, and A.P. Donner. 1987. "Exercise Training of Men at Retirement: A Clinical Trial." *Journal of Gerontology* 42:17–23.

15 Curtis, James E., and Ronald D. Lambert. 1976. "Voting, Election Interest, and Age: National Findings for English and French Canadians." *Canadian Journal of Political Science* 9:293–307.

12 Curtis, James E., and Barry D. McPherson. 1987. "Regional Differences in the Leisure Physical Activity of Canadians: Testing Some Alternative Interpretations." *Sociology of Sport Journal* 4:363–375.

3 Cutler, N.E., and R.A. Harootyan. 1975. "Demography of the Aged." In D.S. Woodruff and J.E. Birren, eds. *Aging: Scientific Perspectives and Social Issues.* New York: Van Nostrand.

12 Cutler, Stephen, and Jon Hendricks. 1990. "Leisure and Time Use Across the Life Course." In Robert H. Binstock and Linda K. George, eds. *Handbook of Aging and the Social Sciences.* 3d ed. San Diego: Academic Press.

12 Cyr, J., and M.M. Schnore. 1982. "Level of Education of the Future Elderly: Demographic Characteristics and Clinical Implications." *Essence* 5:153–67.

13 Damrosch, Shirley Petchel. 1984. "Graduate Nursing Students' Attitudes Toward Sexually Active Older Persons." *The Gerontologist* 24:299–302.

1 Davies, Leland J. 1977. "Attitudes Toward Old Age and Aging as Shown by Humor." *The Gerontologist* 17:220–26.

6 Dawson, Pam, and David W. Reid. 1987. "Behavioral Dimensions of Patients at Risk of Wandering." *The Gerontologist* 27:104–07.

2 de Beauvoir, Simone. 1978. *Old Age.* Harmondsworth, England: Penguin.

3 DeLehr, Esther Contreras. 1988. "Today's and Tomorrow's Aging in Latin America." In *Aging Around the World: A Report on the President's Symposium, 'Aging in Tomorrow's World: An International Perspective.'* The Gerontological Society of America.

12 Delisle, Marc-André. 1982. "Elderly People's Management of Time and Leisure." *Canada's Mental Health* 30:32.

7 Delisle, Marc-André. 1988. "What Does Soli-

tude Mean to the Aged?" *Canadian Journal on Aging* 7:358–71.

1 Demos, Vasilikie, and Ann Jache. 1981. "When You Care Enough: An Analysis of Attitudes Toward Aging in Humorous Birthday Cards." *The Gerontologist* 21:209–15.

6 Denney, N.W., and A.M. Palmer. 1981. "Adult Age Differences on Traditional and Practical Problem-Solving Measures." *Journal of Gerontology* 4:144–48.

6 Dennis, Wayne. 1968. "Creative Productivity Between the Ages of 20 and 80 Years." In Bernice L. Neugarten, ed. *Middle Age and Aging*. Chicago: University of Chicago Press.

4 Denton, Frank T., and Byron G. Spencer. 1980. "Canada's Population and Labour Force: Past, Present and Future." In Victor W. Marshall, ed. *Aging in Canada*. Toronto: Fitzhenry and Whiteside.

8 Denton, Frank T., and Byron G. Spencer. 1983. "Population Aging and Future Health Costs in Canada." *Canadian Public Policy* 9:155–63.

4 Denton, F.T., C.H. Feaver, and B. Spencer. 1986. "Prospective Aging of the Population and Its Implications for the Labour Force and Government Expenditures." *Canadian Journal on Aging* 5:75–98.

8 Denton, F.T., S.N. Li, and B.G. Spencer. 1987. "How Will Population Aging Affect the Future Costs of Maintaining Health-Care Standards?" In Victor W. Marshall, ed. *Aging in Canada*. 2d ed. Toronto: Fitzhenry and Whiteside.

12 Denton, F.T., P.C. Pineo, and B.G. Spencer. 1988. Participation in Adult Education by the Elderly: A Multivariate Analysis and Some Implications for the Future." *Canadian Journal on Aging* 7:4–16.

9 Department of Finance. 1988. *Saving for Retirement: A Guide to the Tax Legislation*. Ottawa: Minister of Supply and Services.

7 Department of Social and Family Services. 1969. *Cultural Differences Among the Aged in Ontario*. Toronto: Department of Social and Family Services.

6 de Santana, Hubert. 1980. "Portrait of the Artist as an Old Man." *Today Magazine*. 29 November.

12 Devereaux, M.S. 1985. *One in Every Five: A Survey of Adult Education in Canada*. Statistics Canada Cat. No. SZ-139/1984E. Ottawa: Minister of Supply and Services.

4 Devereaux, Mary Sue. 1987. "Aging of the Canadian Population." *Canadian Social Trends* Winter:37–38.

13 Devereaux, Mary Sue. 1988. "1986 Census Highlights: Marital Status." *Canadian Social Trends* Spring:24–27.

8 Devine, Barbara A. 1980. "Old Age Stereotyping: A Comparison of Nursing Staff Attitudes Toward the Elderly." *Journal of Gerontological Nursing* 6:25–32.

12 DeVries, Herbert A. 1975. "Physiology of Exercise and Aging." In Diana S. Woodruff and James E. Birren, eds. *Aging: Scientific Perspectives and Social Issues*. New York: D. Van Nostrand Co.

8 DeVries, Herbert A. 1980. "Physiology of Exercise and Aging." In Gari Lesnoff-Caravaglia, ed. *Health Care of the Elderly*. New York: Human Sciences Press.

2 de Vries, Patricia. 1987. "Every Old Person is Somebody: The Image of Aging in Canadian Children's Literature." *Canadian Children's Literature* 46:37-44.

14 Dickinson, G.E. 1976. "Death Education in U.S. Medical Schools." *Journal of Medical Education* 51:134–36.

14 Dickinson, G.E., and A.A. Pearson. 1980–81. "Death Education and Physicians' Attitudes Towards Dying Patients." *Omega* 11:167–74.

6 Dixon, R.A., and D.F. Hultsch. 1983. "Structure and Development of Metamemory in Adulthood." *Journal of Gerontology* 38:682–88.

6 Dobbs, Allen R., and Brendan Gail Rule. 1987. "Prospective Memory and Self-Reports of Memory Abilities in Older Adults." *Canadian Journal of Psychology* 41:209–22.

4 Dominion Bureau of Statistics. 1964. *Census of Canada* (1961 Census). Bulletin 7:1–4. Ottawa: The Queen's Printer.

1 Dooley, Stephen, and B. Gail Frankel. 1990. "Improving Attitudes Toward Elderly People: Evaluation of an Intervention Program for Adolescents." *Canadian Journal on Aging* 9:400–409.

11 Doolin, Joseph. 1986. "Planning for the Special Needs of the Homeless Elderly." *The Gerontologist* 26:229–31.

14 Doutre, D., D.M. Stillwell, and I. Ajemian. 1979. "Physiotherapy in Palliative Care." *Essence* 3:69–77.

2 Dowd, J.J. 1975. "Aging as Exchange: A Preface to Theory." *Journal of Gerontology* 30:584–94.

10 Dowd, J. J. 1980. *Stratification Among the Aged*. Monterey, California: Brooks/Cole.

13 Dranoff, L.S. 1984. "Ask a Lawyer: Do Adult Children Have a Legal Duty to Support Their Parents?" *Chatelaine* November.

2,4,7, Driedger, Leo, and Neena L. Chappell. 1987.
13 *Aging and Ethnicity: Toward an Interface*. Toronto: Butterworths.

8    Drummond, M.F. 1980. *Principles of Economic Appraisal in Health Care.* Oxford: Oxford University Press.

9,13    Dulude, Louise. 1987. "Getting Old: Men in Couples and Women Alone." In G.H. Neimiroff, ed. *Women and Men: Interdisciplinary Readings on Gender.* Toronto: Fitzhenry and Whiteside.

4    Dumas, Jean. 1990. *Current Demographic Analysis: Report on the Demographic Situation in Canada 1988.* Statistics Canada Cat. No. 91-209E. Ottawa: Minister of Supply and Services.

10    Dunlop, D.P. 1980. *Mandatory Retirement Policy: A Human Rights Dilemma?* Ottawa: Conference Board of Canada.

5    Dunn, Peter A. 1990. *Barriers Confronting Seniors with Disabilities in Canada. Special Topics Series: The Health and Activity Limitation Survey.* Statistics Canada Cat. No. 82-615. Ottawa: Minister of Supply and Services.

8    Dunn R.B., L. MacBeath, and D. Robertson. 1983. "Respite Admission and the Disabled Elderly." *Journal of the American Geriatric Society* 31:613–16.

8    Eagle, D. Joan, Gordon Guyatt, Christopher Patterson, and Irene Turpie. 1987. "Day Hospitals' Cost and Effectiveness: A Summary." *The Gerontologist* 27:735–740.

14    Eakes, G.G. 1985. "The Relationship Between Anxiety and Attitudes Toward the Elderly Among Nursing Staff." *Death Studies* 9:163–72.

8    Eakin, Joan M. 1987. "Care of the Unwanted: Stroke Patients in a Canadian Hospital." In D. Coburn, C. D'Arcy, G. Torrance, and P. New, eds. *Health and Canadian Society: Sociological Perspectives.* 2d ed. Toronto: Fitzhenry and Whiteside.

6,8    Eaton, Bill, M.J. Stones, and Ken Rockwood. 1986. "Poor Mental Status in Older Hospital Patients: Prevalence and Correlates." *Canadian Journal on Aging* 5:231–39.

14    Eaton, Joseph W. 1964. "The Art of Aging and Dying" *The Gerontologist* 4:94–112.

11    Eckert, J.K. 1980. *The Unseen Elderly.* San Diego, California: The Companile Press.

11    Economic Council of Canada. 1981. "Reverse Mortgages: A New Way to Help Pensioners." *Au Courant* 2:21.

8    Economic Council of Canada. 1987. *Aging with Limited Health Resources: Proceedings of a Colloquium on Health Care.* Ottawa: Minister of Supply and Services.

12    Edwards, Peggy. 1983. "New Frontier in Geriatric Science: Fitness in the 'Third Age'." *Canadian Journal of Public Health* 74:96–99.

11    Ehrlich, I., and P. Ehrlich. 1976. *The Invisible Elderly.* Washington, D.C.: National Council on the Aging.

3    Eisdorfer, Carl. 1981. "Foreword." In P.T. Amoss and S. Harrell, eds. *Other Ways of Growing Old: Anthropological Perspectives.* Stanford, California: Stanford University Press.

10    Ekerdt, David J., Raymond Bossé, and Sue Levkoff. 1985. "An Empirical Test for Phases of Retirement: Findings from the Normative Aging Study." *Journal of Gerontology* 40:95–101.

12    Elderhostel. 1981. *Annual Report.* Boston: Elderhostel.

12    Elderhostel Canada. 1987. *Welcome to Elderhostel Canada. May to October Issue.* Toronto, Ontario: Elderhostel Canada.

12    Elderhostel. 1991a. *Elderhostel Canada Summer 1991.* Toronto: Elderhostel Canada.

12    Elderhostel Canada. 1991b. *This Is Elderhostel Canada/1991.* Toronto: Elderhostel Canada.

8    Ellencweig, A.Y., N. Pagliccia, M. McCashin, A. Tourigny, and A.J. Stark. 1990. "Utilization Patterns of Clients Admitted or Assessed but not Admitted to a Long-Term Care Program—Characteristics and Differences." *Canadian Journal on Aging* 9:356–70.

6    Elo, A.E. 1965. "Age Changes in Master Chess Performance." *Journal of Gerontology* 20:289–99.

8    Epp, Jake. 1986. *Achieving Health for All: A Framework for Health Promotion.* Cat. No. H39-102/1986E. Ottawa: Minister of Supply and Services.

11    Epstein, Don. 1976. *Retirement Housing in Urban Neighbourhoods: Some Inner City Options.* Winnipeg: Institute of Urban Studies.

12    Ericsson, K. Anders. 1990. "Peak Performance and Age: An Examination of Peak Performance in Sports." In Paul B. Baltes and Margaret M. Baltes, eds. *Successful Aging: Perspectives from the Behavioral Sciences.* Cambridge: Cambridge University Press.

7    Erikson, Erik H. 1950. "Growth and Crises of the Health Personality." In M.J. Senn, ed. *Symposium on the Healthy Personality*, Supplement II: Problems of Infancy and Childhood. Transaction of Fourth Conference. New York: Josiah Macy, Jr., Foundation.

7    Erikson, Erik H. 1959. "Identity and the Life Cycle: Selected Issues." *Psychological Issues* 1:50–100, Appendix.

7,14    Erikson, Erik H. 1963. *Childhood and Society.* 2d ed. New York: W.W. Norton.

7    Erikson, Erik H. 1976. "Reflections on Dr.

Borg's Life Cycle." In Erik Erikson, ed. *Adulthood*. New York: W.W. Norton.

7  Erikson, Erik H. 1982. *The Life Cycle Completed*. New York: W.W. Norton.

2  Estes, C.L. 1979. *The Aging Enterprise*. San Francisco: Jossey-Bass.

2  Estes, C.L., S.P. Wallace, and E.A. Binney. 1989. "Health, Aging, and Medical Sociology." In H. Freeman and S. Levine, eds. *Handbook of Medical Sociology*. 4th ed. Englewood Cliffs, New Jersey: Prentice-Hall.

11  Evans, Aeron T., and G.J.M. Purdie. 1985. "Private Sector Financing for Elderly Housing." In Gloria Gutman and Norman Blackie, eds. *Innovations in Housing and Living Arrangements for Seniors*. Burnaby, British Columbia: The Gerontology Research Centre, Simon Fraser University.

11  Evans, Leonard. 1988. "Older Driver Involvement in Fatal and Severe Traffic Crashes." *Journal of Gerontology: Social Sciences* 43:S186–93.

8  Evans, R.G. 1976. "Does Canada Have Too Many Doctors? Why Nobody Loves an Immigrant Physician." *Canadian Public Policy* 2:147–60.

8  Evans, R.G. 1984. *Strained Mercy: The Economics of Canadian Health Care*. Toronto: Butterworths.

8,14  Federal/Provincial/Territorial Working Group on Home Care. 1990. *Report on Home Care*. Cat. No. H39-186/1990E. Ottawa: Minister of Supply and Services.

8  Fedorak, Sandra A., and Carole Griffin. 1986. "Developing a Self-Advocacy Program for Seniors: The Essential Component of Health Promotion." *Canadian Journal on Aging* 5:269–77.

14  Feigenberg, Loma. 1980. *Terminal Care: Friendship Contracts with Dying Cancer Patients*. New York: Brunner/Mazel.

8  Ferguson, Joyce Ann. 1990. "Patient Age as a Factor in Drug Prescribing Practices." *Canadian Journal on Aging* 9:278–95.

12  Ferraro, Kenneth F., and Catherine Cobb. 1987. "Participation in Multipurpose Senior Centers." *Journal of Applied Gerontology* 6:429–47.

10  Finlayson, Ann. 1985. "The Lure of Early Retirement." *Maclean's* 4 February.

2,3  Fischer, David Hackett. 1978. *Growing Old in America*. Expanded ed. New York: Oxford University Press.

12  Fisher, Andrew A. 1977. "The Effect of Aging and Physical Activity on the Stabile Component of Arterial Distensibility." In R.H. Harris and L.J. Frankel, eds. *Guide to Fitness After 50*. New York: Plenum Press.

14  Fisher, Rory H., and Ralph Shedletsky. 1979. "A Retrospective Study of Terminal Care of Hospitalized Elderly." *Essence* 3:91–100.

8  Fisher, Rory H., and M.L. Zorzitto. 1983. "Placement Problem: Diagnosis, Disease or Term of Denigration?" *Canadian Medical Association Journal* 129:331–33.

14  Fisher, Rory H., Grant W. Nadon, and Ralph Shedletsky. 1983. "Management of the Dying Elderly Patient." *Journal of the American Geriatric Society* 31:563–64.

12  Fitness and Amateur Sport. 1982. *Fitness and Aging: Canada Fitness Survey*. Ottawa: Minister of Supply and Services Canada.

13  Fitting, M., P. Rabins, M.J. Lucas, and J. Eastham. 1986. "Caregivers for Dementia Patients: A Comparison of Husbands and Wives." *The Gerontologist* 26:248–52.

10  Flanagan, Thomas. 1984. "The Future of Retirement in Canadian Universities." *The Canadian Journal of Higher Education* 14:10–34.

8  Flathman, D.P., and D.E. Larsen. 1976. "Evaluation of Three Geriatric Day Hospitals in Alberta." Unpublished report, Division of Community Health Services, Faculty of Medicine. Calgary: University of Calgary.

11  Fletcher, Susan, and Leroy O. Stone. 1980. "The Living Arrangements of Canada's Older Women." *Essence* 4:115–33.

8  Forbes, W.F., J.A. Jackson, and A.S. Kraus. 1987. *Institutionalization of the Elderly in Canada*. Toronto: Butterworths.

1  Forbes, W.F., B.D. McPherson, and M.A. Shadbolt-Forbes. 1989. "The Validation of Longitudinal Studies: The Case of the Ontario Longitudinal Study of Aging (LSA)." *Canadian Journal on Aging* 8:51–67.

2  Foundations Project. 1980. "Foundations for Gerontological Education." *The Gerontologist* 20:Pt. II.

5  Fozard, J.L. 1990. "Vision and Hearing." In James E. Birren and K. Warner Schaie, eds. *Handbook of the Psychology of Aging*. 3d ed. San Diego: Academic Press.

5  Fozard, J.L., and S.J. Popkin. 1978. "Optimizing Adult Development: Ends and Means of an Applied Psychology of Aging." *American Psychologist* 33:975–89.

8  Francoeur, Louise. 1990. "The Right Medicine: A Balancing Act." *Expression* 6:1–2.

11  Fraser, D. 1982. *Defining the Parameters of a Housing Policy for the Elderly*. Ottawa: Canada Mortgage and Housing Corporation.

1  Freeman, J.T. 1979. *Aging: Its History and Literature*. New York: Human Sciences Press.

13  Friend, Richard A. 1991. "Older Lesbian and Gay People: A Theory of Successful Aging." In John Alan Lee, ed. *Gay Midlife and Maturity* New York: Haworth.

5  Fries, James F. 1980. "Aging, Natural Death, and the Compression of Morbidity." *New England Journal of Medicine* 303:130–36.

5  Fries, James F. 1986. "The Elimination of Premature Disease." In Ken Dychtwald and Judy MacLean, eds. *Wellness and Health Promotion for the Elderly*. Rockville, Maryland: Aspen.

5  Fries, James F. 1990. "Medical Perspectives Upon Successful Aging." In Paul B. Baltes and Margaret M. Baltes, eds. *Successful Aging: Perspectives from the Behavioural Sciences*. Cambridge: Cambridge University Press.

8  Frisk, Allen. 1986. "The Pharmacist's Role in Health Promotion and Wellness for the Elderly." In Ken Dychtwald and Judy MacLean, eds. *Wellness and Health Promotion for the Elderly*. Rockville, Maryland: Aspen.

4  Gagan, D. 1983a. "Geographical and Social Mobility in Nineteenth-Century Ontario: A Microstudy." In P.W. Ward, comp. *The Social Development of Canada: Readings*. Richmond, British Columbia: Open Learning Institute.

3,4  Gagan, D. 1983b. "Land, Population, and Social Change: The 'Critical Years' in Rural Canada West." In P.W. Ward, comp. *The Social Development of Canada: Readings*. Richmond, British Columbia: Open Learning Institute.

1  Gallie, Karen A., and John F. Kozak. 1985. "Investigation Into a Possible Relationship Between Knowledge of Aging and Attitudes Toward Old People." Paper presented at the Canadian Association on Gerontology l4th Annual Scientific and Educational Meeting, Hamilton.

10  Gallup. 1984. "Les Canadiens Songent à la Préretraite." *Le Soleil* 2 February.

2  Garfinkel, Harold. 1967. *Studies in Ethnomethodology*. Englewood Cliffs, New Jersey: Prentice-Hall.

8  Garver, David L. 1984. "Age Effects on Alcohol Metabolism." In J.T. Hartford and T. Samorajski, eds. *Alcoholism in the Elderly*. New York: Raven Press.

13  Gatz, Margaret, Vern L. Bengtson, and Mindy J. Blum. 1990. "Caregiving Families." In James E. Birren and K. Warner Schaie, eds. *Handbook of the Psychology of Aging*. 3d ed. San Diego: Academic Press.

8  Gaudette, Leslie, and Georgia Roberts. 1988. "Trends in Cancer Since 1970." *Canadian Social Trends* Autumn:8–13.

1,10  Gauthier, Pierre. 1991. "Canada's Seniors." *Canadian Social Trends* Autumn:16–20.

6  Gauthier, Serge, Ian McDowell, and Gerry Hill. 1990. "Canadian Study of Health and Aging (CaSHA)." *Psychiatry Journal of the University of Ottawa* 1515:227–29.

14  Gee, Ellen M. 1985. "Historical Change in the Life Course of Canadian Women." Paper presented at the Canadian Association on Gerontology 14th Annual Scientific and Educational Meeting, Hamilton.

12  Gee, Ellen M. 1986. "The Life Course of Canadian Women: An Historical and Demographic Analysis." *Social Indicators Research* 18:263–83.

13  Gee, Ellen M. 1987. "Historical Change in the Family Life Course of Canadian Men and Women." In Victor W. Marshall, ed. *Aging in Canada: Social Perspectives*. 2d ed. Toronto: Fitzhenry and Whiteside.

13  Gee, Ellen M. 1988. "The Changing Demography of Intergenerational Relations in Canada." Paper presented at the 17th Annual Scientific and Educational Meeting of the Canadian Association on Gerontology, Halifax, October.

10,13  Gee, Ellen M., and Meredith M. Kimball. 1987. *Women and Aging*. Toronto: Butterworths.

13  George, Linda K. 1990. "Editorials: Caregiver Stress Studies—There Really Is More to Learn." *The Gerontologist* 30:580–81.

4,7  Gerber, Linda M. 1983. "Ethnicity Still Matters: Socio-Demographic Profiles of the Ethnic Elderly in Ontario." *Canadian Ethnic Studies* 15:60–80.

14  Gesser, Gina, Paul T.P. Wong, and Gary T. Reker. 1986. "Death Attitudes Across the Life-Span: The Development and Validation of the Death Attitude Profile (DAP)." Personal communication.

1  Gfellner, Barbara M. 1982. "Case Study Analysis: A Field Placement Program in the Study of Aging." Paper presented at the Canadian Association on Gerontology 11th Annual Scientific and Educational Meeting, Winnipeg.

10  Gherson, Giles. 1980. "Retirement 'A Moral, Not an Economic Issue'." *Financial Post* 8 March.

6  Gibson, R.W. 1970. "Medicare and the Psychiatric Patient." *Psychiatric Opinion* 7:17–22

7  Gibson, Rose C. 1988. "Minority Aging Research: Opportunity and Challenge." *The Gerontologist* 28:559–60.

15 Gifford, C.G. 1982. "Senior Power in Canada." Poster presentation at the Canadian Association on Gerontology 11th Annual Scientific and Educational Meeting, Winnipeg.

15 Gifford, C.G. 1983. "Senior Politics." *Policy Options* September: 12–15.

15 Gifford, C. 1985. "Grey Is Strong." *Policy Options* 6:16–18.

15 Gifford, C.G. 1987. Personal communication.

15 Gifford, C.G. 1990. *Canada's Fighting Seniors.* Toronto: James Lorimer & Co.

3 Gillin, C.T. 1986. "Aging in the Developing World." Paper presented at the Canadian Sociology and Anthropology Association 21st Annual Meeting, Winnipeg.

13 Gladstone, James W. 1987. "Factors Associated with Changes in Visiting Between Grandmothers and Grandchildren Following an Adult Child's Marriage Breakdown." *Canadian Journal on Aging* 6:117–27.

13 Gladstone, James W. 1988. "Perceived Changes in Grandmother-Grandchild Relations Following a Child's Separation or Divorce." *The Gerontologist* 28:66–72.

13 Gladstone, James W. 1989. "Grandmother-Grandchild Contact: The Mediating Influence of the Middle Generation Following Marriage Breakdown and Remarriage." *Canadian Journal on Aging* 8:355–65.

13 Gladstone, James W. 1991. "An Analysis of Changes in Grandparent-Grandchild Visitation Following an Adult Child's Remarriage." *Canadian Journal on Aging* 10:113–26.

3 Glascock, A.P., and S.L. Feinman. 1981. "Social Asset or Social Burden: Treatment of the Aged in Non-industrial Societies." In C.L. Fry, ed. *Dimensions: Aging, Culture, and Health.* New York: Praeger.

14 Glaser, Barney G., and Anselm L. Strauss. 1977. "The Ritual Drama of Mutual Pretense." In Steven H. Zarit, ed. *Readings in Aging and Death: Contemporary Perspectives.* Harper and Row: New York.

5 Glass, Robert H., and Nathan G. Kase. 1970. *Woman's Choice: A Guide to Contraception, Fertility, Abortion, and Menopause.* New York: Basic Books.

3 *Globe and Mail.* 1983. "Latin Americans Seek Refuge in Debtors' Club." 11 July.

15 *Globe and Mail.* 1985. "Seniors Urge Wilson to Drop De-Indexing Plan." 18 June.

8 Glor, Eleanor D. 1991. "An Effective Evaluation of a Small-Scale Seniors Health Promotion Centre: A Case Study." *Canadian Journal on Aging* 10:64–73.

13 Gnaedinger, Nancy. 1989. *Housing Alzheimer's Disease at Home.* Ottawa: Canada Mortgage and Housing Corporation.

12 Godin, G., R. Beamish, K. Wipper, R.J. Shephard, and A. Colantonio. 1988. "Who Intends to Participate in Health Promotion After Retirement?" *Canadian Journal of Public Health* 79:260–63.

5 Goggin, Noreen L., and George E. Stelmach. 1990. "Age-Related Differences in a Kinematic Analysis of Precued Movements." *Canadian Journal on Aging* 9:371–85.

7 Gold, Yhetta. 1980. "Ethnic and Cultural Aspects of Aging." Paper presented at the 9th Annual Scientific and Educational Meeting of the Canadian Association on Gerontology. Saskatoon.

5,12 Goldberg, Andrew P., and James M. Hagberg. 1990. "Physical Exercise and the Elderly." In Edward L. Schneider and John W. Rowe, eds. *Handbook of the Biology of Aging.* 3d ed. San Diego: Academic Press.

14 Goldberg, Helene S. 1981–82. "Funeral and Bereavement Rituals of Kota Indians and Orthodox Jews." *Omega* 12:117–28.

6 Goldmeier, John. 1986. "Pets or People: Another Research Note." *The Gerontologist* 26:203–06.

8 Gordon, Michael, and Harold Preiksaitis. 1988. "Drugs and the Aging Brain." *Geriatrics* 43:69–78.

5 Gordon, Paul, Bruce Ronsen, and Eric R. Brown. 1974. "Anti-Herpes Virus Action of Isoprinosine." *Antimicrobial Agents and Chemotherapy* 5:153–60.

7 Gordon, S. 1976. *Lonely in America.* New York: Simon and Schuster.

14 Gorer, Geoffrey. 1965. *Death, Grief and Mourning in Contemporary Britain.* London: Cresset.

14 Gorer, Geoffrey. 1967. *Death, Grief and Mourning.* New York: Anchor.

13 Gottlieb, Benjamin H. 1989. "A Contextual Perspective on Stress in Family Care of the Elderly." *Canadian Psychology* 30:596–606.

7 Gould, R.L. 1978. *Transformations: Growth and Change in Adult Life.* New York: Simon and Schuster.

9 Government of Canada. 1982a. *Better Pensions for Canadians* (Green Paper). Ottawa: Minister of Supply and Services.

9 Government of Canada. 1982b. *Better Pensions*

*for Canadians: Focus on Women.* Ottawa: Minister of Supply and Services.

11,15  Government of Canada. 1988. *Seniors' Guide to Federal Programs and Services.* Cat. No. H71-3/8-1988E. Ottawa: Minister of National Health and Welfare.

15  Government of Canada. 1989a. *Presenting the Minister of State for Seniors and Seniors Secretariat.* Cat. No. H88-3/6-1989. Ottawa: Minister of Supply and Services.

4  Government of Canada. 1989b. "Seniors— Aging in a Multicultural Canada." *Seniors Info Exchange* Fall:10.

1,2  Government of Manitoba. 1973. *Aging in Manitoba.* 10 vols. Winnipeg: Department of Health and Social Development.

8  Government of Manitoba. 1984. *Annual Report of the Provincial Office of Continuing Care.* Winnipeg: Government of Manitoba.

3  Graham, Ian D., and Paul M. Baker. 1989. "Status, Age, and Gender: Perceptions of Old and Young People." *Canadian Journal on Aging* 8:255–67.

11  Grant, Peter R. 1983. "Creating a Feasible Transportation System for Rural Areas: Reflections on a Symposium." *Canadian Journal on Aging* 2:30–35.

11  Grant, Peter R., and Bruce Rice. 1983. "Transportation Problems of the Rural Elderly: A Needs Assessment." *Canadian Journal on Aging* 2:107–24.

10  Grauer, H., and N.M. Campbell. 1983. "The Aging Physician and Retirement." *Canadian Journal of Psychiatry* 28:552–54.

3  Greene, J.P., ed. 1965. *Diary of Colonel Landon Carter of Sabine Hall, 1752–1778.* 2 vols. Charlottesville, Virginia.

1  Greenslade, V. 1986. "Evaluation of Postgraduate Gerontological Nursing Education." Unpublished manuscript.

14  Greer, D.S., V. Mor, H. Birnbaum, D. Kidder, S. Sherwood, and T.N. Morris. 1984. *Final Report of the National Hospice Study* (Draft). Providence, R.I.: Brown University.

11  Grescoe, Audrey. 1981. "Little Old Lady in a Hard Hat." *Today Magazine* 17 January.

12  Grescoe, Audrey. 1982. "Good Old." *Today Magazine* 9 January.

8  Gross, John, and Cope Schwenger. 1981. "Health Care Costs for the Elderly in Ontario: 1976–2026." Occasional Paper 11. Toronto: Ontario Economic Council.

11  Gross, L.P. 1985. "Federal Housing Programs." In Gloria Gutman and Norman Blackie, eds.

*Innovations in Housing and Living Arrangements for Seniors.* Burnaby, British Columbia: The Gerontology Research Centre, Simon Fraser University.

5  Grundy, E. 1984. "Mortality and Morbidity Among the Old." *British Medical Journal* 288:663–64.

2  Gubrium, Jaber F. 1986. *Oldtimers and Alzheimer's: The Descriptive Organization of Senility.* Greenwich, Connecticut: JAI Press.

3  Guemple, L. 1977. "The Dilemma of the Aging Eskimo." In Beattie, Christopher and Stewart Chrysdale, eds. *Sociology Canada: Readings.* 2d ed. Toronto: Butterworths.

3  Guemple, L. 1980. "Growing Old in Inuit Society." In Victor W. Marshall, ed. *Aging in Canada: Social Perspectives.* Toronto: Fitzhenry & Whiteside.

10  Guillemard, A.M. 1977. "The Call to Activity Amongst the Old: Rehabilitation or Regimentation." In Blossom T. Wigdor, ed. *Canadian Gerontological Collection I.* Winnipeg: Canadian Association on Gerontology.

2  Guillemard, A.M., ed. 1983. *Old Age in the Welfare State.* Beverly Hills, California: Sage.

10  Gunderson, Morley, and James E. Pesando. 1980. "Eliminating Mandatory Retirement: Economics and Human Rights." *Canadian Public Policy* 6:352–60.

10  Guppy, Neil. 1989. "The Magic of 65: Issues and Evidence in the Mandatory Retirement Debate." *Canadian Journal on Aging* 8:174–86.

6  Gurland, B.J. 1976. "The Comparative Frequency of Depression in Various Adult Age Groups." *Journal of Gerontology* 31:283–92.

6  Gurland, B.J., and J.A. Toner. 1983. "Depression in the Elderly: A Review of Recently Published Studies." *Annual Review of Gerontology and Geriatrics* 3:228–65.

6  Gurland, B.J., J. Copeland, J. Kuriansky, M. Kelleher, L. Sharpe, and L.L. Dean. 1983. *The Mind and Mood of Aging: Mental Health Problems of the Community Elderly in New York and London.* New York: Haworth Press.

16  Gutman, Gloria. 1977. "Survey of Educational Programs in Gerontology and Geriatrics Offered at Canadian Universities (mimeo)." Vancouver: President's Committee on Gerontology, University of British Columbia.

3,11  Gutman, Gloria. 1978. "Issues and Findings Relating to Multi-level Accommodation for Seniors." *Journal of Gerontology* 33:592–600.

11  Gutman, Gloria. 1983. *The Long Term Impact of Multi-Level, Multi-Service Accommodation for*

*Seniors.* Senior Citizen Housing Study Report No. 3. Ottawa: Canada Mortgage and Housing Corporation.

11    Gutman, Gloria. 1985. "The Long-Term Impact of Multi-Level, Multi-Service Accommodation for Seniors." Paper presented at the Symposium on Alternative Housing and Living Arrangement for Independent Living—Design Implications, Policy Development and Research held at the 13th International Congress of Gerontology, New York.

11    Gutman, Gloria, and Norman Blackie, eds. 1985. *Innovations in Housing and Living Arrangements for Seniors.* Burnaby, British Columbia: The Gerontology Research Centre, Simon Fraser University.

8    Gutman, Gloria, and Carol P. Herbert. 1976. "Mortality Rates Among Relocated Extended Care Patients." *Journal of Gerontology* 31:352–57.

12    Gutman, G., C.P. Herbert, and S.R. Brown. 1977. "Feldenkrais Versus Conventional Exercises for the Elderly." *Journal of Gerontology* 32:562–72.

8    Gutman, G., C. Jackson, A.J. Stark, and B. McCashin. 1986. "Mortality Rates Five Years after Admission to a Long-Term Care Program." *Canadian Journal on Aging* 5:9–17.

3,10    Haber, Carole. 1978. "Mandatory Retirement in Nineteenth-Century America: The Conceptual Basis for a New York Cycle." *Journal of Social History* 12:77–96.

5    Haber, Paul A.L. 1986. "Technology in Aging." *The Gerontologist* 26:350–57.

13    Hagestad, Gunhild O. 1985. "Continuity and Connectedness." In Vern L. Bengtson and Joan F. Robertson, eds. *Grandparenthood.* Beverly Hills: Sage.

13    Hagestad, Gunhild O. 1986. "The Aging Society As a Context for Family Life." *Daedalus* 115:119–39.

7    Hagestad, Gunhild O. 1990. "Social Perspectives on the LifeCourse." In Robert H. Binstock and Linda K. George, eds. *Handbook of Aging and the Social Sciences.* 3d ed. San Diego: Academic Press.

13    Hall, Barry L. 1989. "The Role of Adult Children in Helping Chronically Ill Hospitalized Parents." *Canadian Journal on Aging* 8:68–78.

1,16    Hancock, Gordon. 1984. *A Study of Gerontology Activities and of Centres of Gerontology on University Campuses in the United States and Canada.* Winnipeg: Centre on Aging, University of Manitoba.

8    Hansen, Signy, and Neena L. Chappell. 1985.

"Perspectives on Normal Aging and Health Promotion in Canada: A Strategic Analysis for Policy Development." Paper presented at the Meeting of the International Association of Gerontology, New York.

8    Hansen, Signy, and Gary Ledoux. 1985. "Developing a Health Promotion Resource for Older Adults." Paper presented at the Meeting of the International Association of Gerontology, New York.

8    Harbison, Joan, and Patricia M. Melanson. 1987. "Interdisciplinary Collaboration Between the Professional Social Worker and Nurse in Planning the Care of the Older Adult Living in a Long-term Care Facility." *Canadian Journal on Aging* 6:155–69.

1    Harding, Michele, and Sheila Neysmith. 1984. "Ageism and Health Costs: Reality and Implications." Paper presented at the Canadian Association on Gerontology 13th Annual Scientific and Educational Meeting, Vancouver.

5    Harley, Calvin B. 1988. "Biology and Evolution of Aging: Implications for Basic Gerontological Health Research. *Canadian Journal on Aging* 7:100–113.

11    Harper, I. 1984. "Housing Options for the Elderly in the Capital Region: Sheltered Housing and Other Alternatives." Victoria, British Columbia: Capital Regional Hospital District, Hospital and Health Planning Commission.

1    Harris, Louis, et al. 1975. *Myth and Reality of Aging in America.* Washington, D.C.: National Council on Aging.

14    Harrison, Albert A., and Neal E.A. Kroll. 1985–86. "Variations in Death Rates in the Proximity of Christmas: An Opponent Process Interpretation." *Omega* 16:181–92.

14    Harrison, Albert A., and M. Moore. 1982–83. "Birth Dates and Death Dates: A Closer Look." *Omega* 13:117–25.

8    Harshman, Frederick C. 1982. "Home Support for Elderly Persons: A Futuristic Example." *Canada's Mental Health* 3:4–6.

14    Harvard Medical School. 1968. "A Definition of Irreversible Coma: Report of the Ad Hoc Committee of the Harvard Medical School to Examine the Definition of Brain Death." *Journal of the American Medical Association* 205:337–40.

12    Harvey, A.S., and J.F. Singleton. 1989. "Canadian Activity Patterns Across the Life Span: A Time Budget Perspective." *Canadian Journal on Aging* 8:268–85.

12    Harvey, A.S., K. Marshall, and J.A. Frederick. 1991. *Where Does Time Go?* Cat. No. 11-612E,

no. 4. Ottawa: Ministry of Industry, Science and Technology.

13 Harvey, Carol H. 1984. "Decision-Making by Middle-Aged Widows in Winnipeg." Paper presented at the Beatrice Paolucci Symposium, Michigan State University, East Lansing, Michigan.

2,8,11 Havens, Betty. 1980. "Differentiation of Unmet Needs Using Analysis by Age/Sex Cohorts." In Victor W. Marshall, ed. *Aging in Canada*. Toronto: Fitzhenry and Whiteside.

7 Havens, Betty, and N.L. Chappell. 1983. "Triple Jeopardy: Age, Sex and Ethnicity." *Canadian Ethnic Studies* 15:119–32.

12 Hawkins, Terry. 1980. *Never Too Old: A Report to the Northumberland Newcastle Board of Education on the Educational Needs of Senior Adults Living in the Area Served by Its Schools*. Northumberland Newcastle, Ontario: Board of Education.

12 Hayashida, David. 1983. "Take A Closer Look at the National Parks." *Recreation Canada* February:16–18.

5 Hayflick, L. 1974. " The Strategy of Senescence." *The Gerontologist* 14:37–45.

5 Hayflick, L. 1970. "Aging Under Glass." *Experimental Gerontology* 5:291–303.

5 Hayflick, L., and P.S. Moorhead. 1961. "The Serial Cultivation of Human Diploid Cell Strains." *Experimental Cell Research* 25:585–621.

10 Haynes, Suzanne G., Anthony J. McMichael, and H.A. Tyroler. 1977. "The Relationship of Normal Involuntary Retirement to Early Mortality Among U.S. Rubber Workers." *Social Science and Medicine* 11:105–14.

16 Health and Welfare Canada. 1977a. *Medical Education in Geriatrics, Health Manpower Report No. 1/77*. Ottawa: Minister of Supply and Services.

10,11, Health and Welfare Canada. 1977b. *Social Secu-*
12 *rity Research Reports. Retirement in Canada: Summary Report, (Report No. 03)* Ottawa: Long Range Planning Directorate, Policy Research and Long Range Planning Branch (Welfare), National Health and Welfare.

7 Health and Welfare Canada. 1977c. *Who Commits Suicide in Old Age and Why?* Ottawa: Health and Welfare Canada.

1,10 Health and Welfare Canada. 1979. *Retirement Age*. Ottawa: Minister of Supply and Services.

9 Health and Welfare Canada. 1982a. *Better Pensions for Canadians: Highlights*. Ottawa: Minister of Supply and Services.

1,2,8, Health and Welfare Canada. 1982b. *Canadian*
10,11, *Governmental Report on Aging*. Ottawa: Minister
12 of Supply and Services.

12 Health and Welfare Canada. 1982c. *New Horizons: First Decade*. Ottawa: Minister of Supply and Services.

14 Health and Welfare Canada. 1982d. *Palliative Care in Canada*. Ottawa: Minister of Supply and Services.

4,5, Health and Welfare Canada. 1983. *Fact Book on*
8-13, *Aging in Canada*. Ottawa: Minister of Supply
15,16 and Services.

6 Health and Welfare Canada. 1984a. *Alzheimer's Disease: A Family Information Handbook*. Ottawa: Minister of Supply and Services.

8 Health and Welfare Canada. 1984b. *National Health Expenditures in Canada, 1970–1982*. Ottawa: Minister of Supply and Services.

16 Health and Welfare Canada, Health Information Division. 1985. *Canada Health Manpower Inventory 1985*. Ottawa: Minister of Supply and Services.

1,8 Health and Welfare Canada. 1988a. *Active Health Report: The Active Health Report on Seniors*. Cat No. H-39-124/1988E. Ottawa: Minister of Supply and Services.

8,9 Health and Welfare Canada. 1988b. *Canada's Health Promotion Survey: Technical Report*. Cat No. H39-119/1988E. Ottawa: Minister of Supply and Services.

8 Health and Welfare Canada. 1989. "Drug Use by the Elderly." *Issues* 20 September.

11 Health and Welfare Canada. 1989-90. "55 Alive: What Is It?" *Seniors Info Exchange*. Ottawa: Minister of Supply and Services.

5,6,8, Health and Welfare Canada and Statistics Can-
12 ada. 1981. *The Health of Canadians* (The Canada Health Survey). Cat. No.: 82-538E. Ottawa: Minister of Supply and Services.

8 *Health Care*. 1980. "Restrained in Canada— Free in Britain." *Health Care* 22:22.

15 Heclo, H. 1988. "Generational Politics." In J.L. Palmer, T. Smeeding, and B.B. Torrey, eds. *The Vulnerable*. Washington, D.C.: Urban Institute Press.

1 Hendrick, J.J., V.J. Knox, W.L. Gekoski, and K.J. Dyne. 1988. "Perceived Cognitive Ability of Young and Old Targets." *Canadian Journal on Aging* 7:192–203.

2,3 Hendricks, Jon. 1982. "The Elderly in Society: Beyond Modernization." *Social Science History* 6:321–45.

2 Hendricks, Jon, and C. Davis Hendricks. 1981. *Aging in Mass Society: Myths and Realities*. 2d ed. Cambridge, Mass.: Winthrop.

6,15 Hendricks, Jon, and C. Davis Hendricks. 1986.

*Aging in Mass Society: Myths and Realities.* 3d ed. Boston: Little, Brown and Company.

4   Henripin, J. 1972. *Trends and Factors of Fertility in Canada.* Ottawa: Statistics Canada (Dominion Bureau of Statistics).

4   Henripin, J., and Y. Peron. 1972. "The Demographic Transition of the Province of Quebec." In D. Glass and R. Revelle, eds. *Population and Social Change.* London: Edward Arnold.

14   Henteleff, Paul D. 1978. "Decisions in the Care of the Dying." *Essence* 2:15–17.

6   Herchak, Gail, and Brian Wilford. 1983. "The Therapy of Pets." *Alberta Report* 28 November.

13   Hess, Beth B., and Beth J. Soldo. 1985. "Husband and Wife Networks." In W.J. Sauer and R.T. Cowards, eds. *Social Support Networks and the Care of the Elderly.* New York: Springer.

13   Hess, R. 1982. "Self-help as a Service Delivery Strategy." *Prevention in Human Services* 1:1–2.

11   Heumann, L., and D. Boldy. 1982. *Housing for the Elderly.* New York: St. Martin's Press.

13   Hickey, Tom, and Richard L. Douglass. 1981. "Neglect and Abuse of Older Family Members: Professionals' Perspectives and Case Experiences." *The Gerontologist* 21:171–76.

8   Hirdes, John P., and William F. Forbes. 1989. "Estimates of the Relative Risk of Mortality Based on the Ontario Longitudinal Study of Aging." *Canadian Journal on Aging* 8:222–37.

1,8   Hirdes, J.P., K.S. Brown, W.F. Forbes, D. Vigoda, and L. Crawford. 1986. "The Association Between Self-reported Income and Perceived Health Based on the Ontario Longitudinal Study of Aging." *Canadian Journal on Aging* 6:189–204.

1   Hirdes, J., K.S. Brown, D.S. Vigoda, W.F. Forbes, and L. Crawford. 1987. "Health Effects of Cigarette Smoking: Data from the Ontario Longitudinal Study on Aging." *Canadian Journal of Public Health* 78:13–17.

12   Hobart, C. 1975. "Active Sports Participation Among the Young, the Middle-aged and the Elderly." *International Review of Sports Sociology* 10:27–40.

11   Hodge, Gerald. 1984a. *Shelter and Services for the Small Town Elderly: The Role of Assisted Housing.* Ottawa: Canada Mortgage and Housing Corporation.

12   Hodge, Gerald. 1984b. "Time and the Environment of the Small Town Elderly." Paper presented at the Canadian Association on Gerontology 13th Annual Scientific and Educational Meeting, Vancouver.

11   Hodge, Gerald. 1987. "Assisted Housing for Ontario's Rural Elderly: Shortfalls in Product and Location." *Canadian Journal on Aging* 6:141–54.

8   Hogan, David B. 1984. "Exercise in the Elderly." *Geriatric Medicine Today* 3:47–48.

7,13   Holmes, T.H., and R.H. Rahe. 1967. "The Social Readjustment Rating Scale." *Journal of Psychosomatic Research* 11:213–18.

17   Holzberg, Carol S. 1981. "Cultural Gerontology: Toward an Understanding of Ethnicity and Aging." *Culture* 1:110–22.

7   Holzberg, Carol S. 1982. "Ethnicity and Aging: Anthropological Perspectives on More than Just the Minority Elderly." *The Gerontologist* 22:249–57.

2   Homans, George C. 1961. *Social Behaviour: Its Elementary Forms.* New York: Harcourt Brace Jovanovich.

12   Homebound Learning Opportunities. 1989. "1988–1989 Program Statistics and Comments About HLO." Personal communication.

13   Hooyman, Nancy R. 1990. "Women as Caregivers of the Elderly: Implications for Social Welfare Policy and Practice." In David E. Biegel and Arthur Blum, eds. *Aging and Caregiving: Theory, Research, and Policy.* Newbury Park: Sage.

6   Horn, J.L. 1978. "Human Ability Systems." In P.B. Baltes, ed. *Life-Span Development and Behavior.* Vol. 1. New York: Academic Press.

6   Horn, J.L., and R.B. Cattel. 1966. "Age Differences in Primary Mental Ability Factors." *Journal of Gerontology* 21:210–20.

6   Horn, J.L., and R.B. Cattell. 1967. "Age Differences in Fluid and Crystallized Intelligence." *Acta Psychologica* 26:107–29.

13   Horowitz, Amy. 1985. "Sons and Daughters as Caregivers to Older Parents: Differences in Role Performance and Consequences." *The Gerontologist* 25:612–17.

13   Horowitz, Amy, and L.W. Shindelman. 1981. "Reciprocity and Affection: Past Influences on Current Caregiving." Paper presented at the 34th Annual Scientific Meeting of the Gerontological Society of America.

11   Hough, George S. 1981. *Tenant Receptiveness: Family and Senior Citizen Mixing in Public Housing.* Toronto: Policy and Program Development Secretariat, Ministry of Municipal Affairs and Housing.

9   House of Commons Canada. 1983. *Report of the Parliamentary Task Force on Pension Reform* (Frith Commission). Ottawa: Supply and Services Canada.

6   Howard, D.V., M.P. McAndrews, and M.I.

Lasagna. 1981. "Semantic Priming of Lexical Decisions in Young and Old Adults." *Journal of Gerontology* 36:707–14.

3 Howells, W.W. 1960. "Estimating Population Numbers Through Archaeological and Skeletal Remains." In R.F. Heizer, and C.F. Cook, eds. *The Application of Quantitative Methods to Archaeology.* Chicago: Quadrangle.

15 Hudson, R.B., and J. Strate. 1985. "Aging and Political Systems." In Robert Binstock and Ethel Shanas, eds. *Handbook of Aging and the Social Sciences.* 2d ed. New York: Van Nostrand Reinhold.

3 Hufton, O. 1975. *The Poor in Eighteenth-Century France.* Oxford: Oxford University Press.

7 Hughes, E.C., and H.M. Hughes. 1952. *Where Peoples Meet.* Glencoe, Illinois: Free Press.

2,6 Hultsch, David F., and Francine Deutsch. 1981. *Adult Development and Aging: A Life-Span Perspective.* New York: McGraw-Hill.

6 Hultsch, David F., and Roger A. Dixon. 1983. "The Role of Pre-Experimental Knowledge in Text Processing in Adulthood." *Experimental Aging Research* 9:7–22.

6 Hultsch, David F., and Roger A. Dixon. 1990. "Learning and Memory in Aging." In James E. Birren and K. Warner Schaie, eds. *Handbook of the Psychology of Aging*, 3d ed. San Diego: Academic Press.

6 Hultsch, D.F., C. Hertzog, and R.A. Dixon. 1987. "Age Differences in Metamemory: Resolving the Inconsistencies." *Canadian Journal of Psychology* 41:193–208.

3 *Human Behavior Magazine.* 1977. "Retirement to the Porch." In Steven H. Zarit, ed. *Readings in Aging and Death: Contemporary Perspectives.* New York: Harper and Row.

6 Iglauer, Edith. 1980. "The Unsinkable Hubert Evans." *Today Magazine* 20 December.

3 Ikels, C. 1981. "The Coming of Age in Chinese Society: Traditional Patterns and Contemporary Hong Kong." In C.L. Fry, ed. *Dimensions: Aging, Culture, and Health.* New York: Praeger.

2 Inter-Council Program Directorate. 1988. *Open Letter and Call for Proposal Submissions for Networks of Centres of Excellence.* Ottawa: Government of Canada.

8 Jackson, Marilyn F. 1983. "Day Care for Handicapped Elders: An Evaluation Study." *Canadian Journal of Public Health* 74:348–51.

15 Jacobs, Bruce. 1990. "Aging and Politics." In Robert H. Binstock and Linda K. George, eds. *Handbook of Aging and the Social Sciences.* 3d ed. San Diego: Academic Press.

15 Jacobs, Ruth Harriet, and Beth B. Hess. 1980.

"Panther Power: Symbol and Substance." In Jill S. Quadagno, ed. *Aging, the Individual and Society.* New York: St. Martin's Press.

6 Jacquish, G.A., and R.E. Ripple. 1981. "Cognitive Creative Abilities and Self-Esteem Across the Adult Life-Span." *Human Development* 24:110–9.

12 Jahn, Penelope. 1982. "Good Old." *Today Magazine* 9 January.

7 Jarvis, George K., and Menno Boldt. 1980. "Suicide in the Later Years." *Essence* 4:145–58.

13 Johnson, Colleen J. 1985. "Grandparenting Options in Divorcing Families: An Anthropological Perspective." In Vern L. Bengtson and Joan F. Robertson, eds. *Grandparenthood.* Beverly Hills: Sage.

10 Johnson, E.S., and J.B. Williamson. 1987. "Retirement in the United States." In K.S. Markides and C.L. Cooper, eds. *Retirement in Industrialized Societies.* New York: Wiley.

1 Johnson, Holly. 1990. "Violent Crime." In Craig McKie, ed. *Canadian Social Trends.* Toronto: Minister of Supply and Services and Thompson Educational Publishing.

5 Johnson, M.A., and D. Choy. 1987. "On the Definition of Age-Related Norms for Visual Function Testing." *Applied Optics* 26:1449–54.

6 Jones, H.E., and H.S. Conrad. 1933. "The Growth and Decline of Intelligence." *Genetic Psychology Monographs* 12:223–98.

11 Joseph, Alun E., and Anthony M. Fuller. 1991. "Towards an Integrative Perspective on the Housing, Services and Transportation Implications of Rural Aging." *Canadian Journal on Aging* 10:127–48.

7 Jung, C.G. 1976. "The Stages of Life." In Joseph Campbell, ed. *The Portable Jung.* Harmondsworth, England: Penguin.

13 Jutras, Sylvie. 1988. "Formal and Informal Caregivers: Towards a Partnership in Prevention." *Health Promotion* Fall:9–12.

13 Jutras, Sylvie, and France Veilleux. 1991. "Informal Caregiving: Correlates of Perceived Burden." *Canadian Journal on Aging* 10:40–55.

13 Kaden, Joan, and Susan A. McDaniel. 1990. "Caregiving and Care-Receiving: A Double Bind for Women in Canada's Aging Society." *Journal of Women and Aging* 2:3–26.

13 Kahana, B., and E. Kahana. 1970. "Grandparenthood from the Perspective of the Developing Grandchild." *Developmental Psychology* 3:98–105.

11 Kaill, Robert C. 1980. "Housing Canada's Aging." *Essence* 4:79–86.

4 Kalbach, Warren E., and Wayne M. McVey.

1979. *The Demographic Bases of Canadian Society.* 2d ed. Toronto: McGraw-Hill Ryerson.

14   Kalish, R.A. 1963. "An Approach to the Study of Death Attitudes." *American Behavioral Scientist* 6:68–70.

14   Kalish, R.A. 1981. *Death, Grief and Caring Relationships.* Monterey, California: Brooks/Cole.

8   Kane, R.L., and R.A. Kane. 1985. *A Will and a Way: What the United States Can Learn from Canada about Caring for the Elderly.* New York: Columbia University Press.

14   Kane, R.L., J. Wales, L. Bernstein, A. Leibowitz, and S. Kaplan. 1984. "A Randomized Controlled Trial of Hospice Care." *Lancet* 1:890–94.

10   Kaplan, M. 1979. *Leisure: Lifestyles and Lifespan.* Philadelphia: W.B. Saunders.

5   Kart, Cary S., Eileen S. Metress, and James F. Metress. 1978. *Aging and Health: Biologic and Social Perspectives.* Menlo Park, California: Addison-Wesley.

13   Kassel, Victor. 1983. "Long-Term Care Institutions." In Ruth B. Weg, ed. *Sexuality in the Later Years: Roles and Behavior.* New York: Academic Press.

3   Kastenbaum, R., and B. Ross. 1975. "Historical Perspectives on Care." In J.G. Howells, ed. *Modern Perspectives in the Psychiatry of Old Age.* New York: Brunner/Mazel.

3   Katz, Michael B. 1975. *The People of Hamilton, Canada West: Family and Class in a Mid-Nineteenth-Century City.* Cambridge, Massachusetts: Harvard University Press.

6   Kausler, D.H. 1982. *Experimental Psychology and Human Aging.* New York: Wiley.

10   Kaye, L.W., and A. Monk. 1984. "Sex Role Traditions and Retirement from Academe." *The Gerontologist* 24:420–26.

10   Keating, Norah C., and Priscilla Cole. 1980. "What Do I Do With Him 24 Hours a Day? Changes in the Housewife Role After Retirement." *The Gerontologist* 20:84–88.

10   Keating, Norah, and Barbara Jeffrey. 1983. "Work Careers of Ever Married and Never Married Retired Women." *The Gerontologist* 23:416–21.

13   Kehoe, Monika. 1989. *Lesbians Over 60 Speak for Themselves.* New York: Harrington Park Press.

13   Keith, Patricia M., Kathleen Hill, Willis J. Goudy, and Edward A. Powers. 1984. "Confidants and Well-Being: A Note on Male Friendship in Old Age." *The Gerontologist* 24:318–20.

8   Kelk, Doug. 1989. "CRD Quick-Response Team Keeps Woman, 89, Mobile." *Times-Colonist* (Victoria) 4 February.

14   Kelly, John L., G. Elphick, V. Mepham, and D.W. Molloy. 1989. *Let Me Decide.* Publisher and place of publication unknown.

12   Kelly, John R., M.W. Steinkamp, and J.R. Kelly. 1987. "Later-Life Satisfaction: Does Leisure Contribute?" *Leisure Sciences* 9:189–200.

12   Kelly, Paula. 1987. "Learning Begins at Home for Shut-In Seniors." *Seniors Today* December 30.

1   Kennedy, Leslie W., and Robert A. Silverman. 1984–85. "Significant Others and Fear of Crime Among the Elderly." *International Journal of Aging and Human Development* 20:241–56.

2   Kenyon, Gary M. 1988. "Basic Assumptions in Theories of Human Aging." In James E. Birren and Vern L. Bengtson, eds. *Emergent Theories of Aging.* New York: Springer.

15   Kernaghan, Kenneth. 1982. "Politics, Public Administration and Canada's Aging Population." *Canadian Public Policy* 8:69–79.

15   Kernaghan, Kenneth, and Olivia Kuper. 1983. *Coordination in Canadian Governments: A Case Study of Aging Policy.* Toronto: Institute of Public Administration of Canada.

12   Kidd, J.R. 1973. *How Adults Learn.* New York: Associated Press.

12   Kinsley, B., and F. Graves. 1983. *The Time of Our Lives.* Ottawa: Employment and Immigration Canada.

14   Klug, Leo F., and Earle H. Waugh. 1982. "Survey of Credit Courses in Thanatology Offered by Canadian Universities: 1971–80." *Essence* 5:227–33.

7   Kneem, Robert. 1963. "Sample Study of Estonian Old Age Population in Toronto." Unpublished paper.

1,3   Knox, V.J., and W.L. Gekoski. 1989. "The Effect of Judgement Context on Assessments of Age Groups." *Canadian Journal on Aging* 8:244–54.

1   Knox, V.J. and W.L. Gekoski, and E.A. Johnson. 1984. "The Relationship Between Contact with and Perceptions of the Elderly." Paper presented at the Canadian Association on Gerontology 13th Annual Scientific and Educational Meeting, Vancouver.

6   Koch, Kenneth. 1977. *I Never Told Anybody: Teaching Poetry Writing in a Nursing Home.* New York: Random House.

6   Koch, Kenneth. 1982. "Teaching Poetry Writing in a Nursing Home." In Steven H. Zarit, ed. *Readings in Aging and Death:*

*Contemporary Perspectives*. 2d ed. New York: Harper and Row.

5    Kosnik, W., L. Winslow, D. Kline, K. Rasinski, and R. Sekuler. 1988. "Visual Changes in Daily Life Throughout Adulthood." *Journal of Gerontology: Psychological Sciences* 43:63–70.

3    Koty, J. 1933. *Die Behandlung der Alten und Kranken bei den Naturvolkern*. Stuttgart.

10    Koyl, L.F. 1974. *Employing the Older Worker: Matching the Employee to the Job*. 2d ed. Washington: The National Council on the Aging, Inc.

7    Kozma, Albert, and M.J. Stones. 1978. "Some Research Issues and Findings in the Study of Psychological Well-being in the Aged." *Canadian Psychological Review* 19:241–49.

6    Kraus, Arthur S. 1984. "The Burden of Care for Families of Elderly Persons with Dementia." *Canadian Journal on Aging* 3:45–51.

5    Kraus, Arthur S. 1987. "The Increase in the Usual Life Span in North America." *Canadian Journal on Aging* 6:19–32.

5    Kraus, Arthur S. 1988. "Is a Compression of Morbidity in Late Life Occurring? Examination of Death Certificate Evidence." *Canadian Journal on Aging* 7:58–70.

6    Kraus, Arthur S., and C.P. McGeer. 1983. *Final Report on the Study: The Management of Elderly Persons with Dysfunctional Brain Syndrome (DBS)*. Kingston: Queen's University.

12    Kraus, H., and W. Raab. 1961. *Hypokinetic Disease*. Springfield, Illinois: Charles C. Thomas.

13    Krishnan, P. 1990. "Aging in Developed and Developing Countries." *University of Alberta Centre for Gerontology Newsletter* Fall.

11    Krivo, Lauren J., and Jan E. Mutchler. 1989. "Elderly Persons Living Alone: The Effect of Community Context on Living Arrangements." *Journal of Gerontology: Social Sciences* 44:S54–S62.

14    Kübler-Ross, Elisabeth. 1969. *On Death and Dying*. New York: Macmillan.

14    Kunz, Phillip, and Jeffrey Summers. 1979-80. "A Time to Die: A Study of the Relationship of Birthdays and Time of Death." *Omega* 10:281–89.

7    Kuypers, J.A., and V.L. Bengtson. 1973. "Social Breakdown and Competence: A Model of Normal Aging." *Human Development* 16:181–201.

10    Labour Canada. 1986. *Women in the Labour Force, 1985–1986*. Cat. No. L38-30/1986. Ottawa: Minister of Supply and Services.

9    *Labour Gazette*. 1924.

6    Labouvie-Vief, G. 1977. "Adult Cognitive Development: In Search of Alternative Interpretations." *Merrill Palmer Quarterly* 23:227–63.

6    Labouvie-Vief, G. 1985. "Intelligence and Cognition." In James E. Birren and K. Warner Schaie, eds. *Handbook of the Psychology of Aging*. 2d ed. New York: Van Nostrand Reinhold.

14    Labovitz, S. 1974. "Control Over Death: The Canadian Case." *Omega* 5:217–21.

5    LaBuda, Dennis R. 1990. "The Impact of Technology on Geriatric Rehabilitation." In Bryan Kemp, Kenneth Brummel-Smith, and Joseph W. Ramsdell, eds. *Geriatric Rehabilitation*. Boston: Little, Brown and Company.

4    Lachepelle, Réjean. 1988. "Changes in Fertility Among Canada's Linguistic Groups." *Canadian Social Trends* Autumn:2–8.

7    Lacy, William B., and Jon Hendricks. 1980. "Developmental Models of Adult Life: Myth or Reality." *International Journal of Aging and Human Development* 11:89–110.

5    Lai, Simon. 1990. *Living with Sensory Loss: Hearing*. Ottawa: National Advisory Council on Aging.

8    Lalonde, Marc. 1974. *A New Perspective on the Health of Canadians*. Ottawa: Minister of Supply and Services.

7    Lam, Leatrice. 1985. "The Implications of Multicultural Reality for Personal Care Home Development: A Chinese Canadian Case Study." A paper presented at the Canadian Asian Studies Association Meeting, Montreal.

5    Lane, N., D.A. Block, H.H. Jones, W.H. Marshall, P.D. Wood, and J.F. Fries. 1986. "Long-Distance Running, Bone Density, and Osteoarthritis." *Journal of the American Medical Association* 255:1147–51.

13    Laner, M.R. 1979. " Growing Older Female: Heterosexual and Homosexual." *Journal of Homosexuality* 4:267–75.

12    LaRocque P., and P.D. Campagna. 1983. "Physical Activity Through Rhythmic Exercise for Elderly Persons Living in a Senior Citizen Residence." *Activities, Adaptations and Aging* 4:77–81.

15    Laskin, Richard, and Richard Baird. 1970. "Factors in Voter Turnout and Party Preference in a Saskatchewan Town." *Canadian Journal of Political Science* 3:450–62.

3    Laslett, P. 1965. *The World We Have Lost*. New York: Charles Scribner's Sons.

3,4    Laslett, P. 1976. "Societal Development and Aging." In R.H. Binstock and E. Shanas, eds. *Handbook of Aging and the Social Sciences*. New York: Van Nostrand Reinhold.

14    Law Reform Commission of Canada. 1982. *Euthanasia, Aiding Suicide and Cessation of Treat-*

*ment.* Working Paper 28. Ottawa: Minister of Supply and Service.

**11** Lawton, M. Powell. 1976. "The Relative Impact of Enriched and Traditional Housing on Elderly Tenants." *The Gerontologist* 16:237–42.

**11** Lawton, M. Powell. 1980. *Environment and Aging.* Monterey, California: Brooks/Cole.

**11** Lawton, M. Powell. 1982. "Environmental Research: Issues and Methods." In Ronald Bayne and Blossom Wigdor, eds. *Research Issues in Aging: Report of a Conference, 1980.* Hamilton: Gerontology Research Council of Ontario.

**11** Lawton, M. Powell. 1985. "Housing and Living Environments of Older People." In Robert H. Binstock and Ethel Shanas, eds. *Handbook of Aging and the Social Sciences.* 2d ed. New York: Van Nostrand Reinhold.

**7,11** Lawton, M. Powell, and Lucille Nahemow. 1973. "Ecology and the Aging Process." In Carl Eisdorfer and M. Powell Lawton, eds. *The Psychology of Adult Development and Aging.* Washington, D.C.: American Psychological Association.

**13** Lawton, M.P., E.M. Brody, and A.R. Saperstein. 1989. "A Controlled Study of Respite Services for Caregivers of Alzheimer's Patients." *The Gerontologist* 29:8–16.

**11** Lazarowich, Michael. 1986. "The Perspective of the User in the Ontario Granny Flat Demonstration Project." In Susan Corke, Gregory S. Romanick, Michael Lazarowich, and Joan Simon, eds. *Granny Flats: A Housing Option for the Elderly.* Report No.13, Winnipeg: Institute of Urban Studies.

**11** Lazarowich, N. Michael. 1990. "A Review of the Victoria, Australia Granny Flat Program." *The Gerontologist* 30:171–77.

**11** Lazarowich, M., and B.W. Haley. 1982. *Granny Flats: Their Practicality and Implementation.* Ottawa: Canada Mortgage and Housing Corporation.

**4** Leacy, F., ed. 1983. *Historical Statistics of Canada.* 2d ed. Ottawa: Minister of Supply and Services.

**6** LeBlanc, Julia. 1985. "Combined Medical Psychiatric Day Centre." Paper presented at the Canadian Association on Gerontology 14th Annual Scientific and Educational Meeting, Hamilton.

**13** Lee, John Alan. 1987. "The Invisible Lives of Canada's Gray Gays." In Victor W. Marshall, ed. *Aging in Canada.* 2d ed. Toronto: Fitzhenry and Whiteside.

**4** Legare, J., and B. Desjardins. 1976. La Situation des Personnes Agées au Canada. *Canadian Review of Sociology and Anthropology* 13:321–36.

**6** Lehman, Harvey C. 1953. *Age and Achievement.* Princeton, New Jersey: Princeton University Press.

**6** Lehman, Harvey C. 1968. "The Creative Production Rates of Present versus Past Generations of Scientists." In Bernice L. Neugarten, ed. *Middle Age and Aging.* Chicago: The University of Chicago Press.

**7** Lemon, B., V. Bengtson, and J. Peterson. 1972. "Activity Types and Life Satisfaction in a Retirement Community." *Journal of Gerontology* 27:511–23.

**54** Leo, John, and Barbara Blonarz. 1981. "Fighting Off Old Age." *Time* 16 February.

**3** Lerner, M. 1970. "When, Why and Where People Die." In O.G. Brim, Jr., H.E. Freeman, S. Levine, and N.A. Scotch, eds. *The Dying Patient.* New York: Russell Sage Foundation.

**7** Levinson, D.J. 1978. *The Seasons of a Man's Life.* New York: Knopf.

**14** Levy, J.A. 1987. "A Life Course Perspective on Hospice and the Family." *Marriage and Family Review* 11:39–64.

**13** Lewis, J., and B. Meredith. 1988. "Daughters Caring for Mothers." *Ageing and Society* 8:1–21.

**8** Lexchin, Joel. 1990. "The Portrayal of the Elderly in Drug Advertisements: A Factor in Inappropriate Prescribing?" *Canadian Journal on Aging* 9:296–303.

**14** Ley, Dorothy C.H. 1985. "Palliative Care in Canada: The First Decade and Beyond." *Journal of Palliative Care* 1:32–34.

**8** Librach, Gershon, C. Davidson, and A. Peretz. 1972. "A Community Home Care Program," *Journal of the American Geriatrics Society* 20:500–04.

**7** Lieberman, M.A. 1975. "Adaptive Processes in Late Life." In N. Datan, and L.H. Ginsberg, eds. *Life-Span Developmental Psychology: Normative Life Crises.* New York: Academic Press.

**14** Lindemann, E. 1944. "Symptomatology and Management of Acute Grief." *American Journal of Psychiatry* 101:141–48.

**10** Lindsay, Colin. 1987. "The Decline in Employment Among Men Aged 55–64, 1975–1985." *Social Trends* Spring:12–15. Statistics Canada. Cat. No. 11-008E. Ottawa: Minister of Supply and Services.

**9** Lindsay, Colin, and Shelley Donald. 1988. "Income of Canada's Seniors." *Canadian Social Trends* Autumn: 20–25.

**7** Linton, Ralph. 1936. *The Study of Man.* New York: Appleton-Century-Crofts.

**13** Litwak, E. 1985. *Helping the Elderly: The Comple-*

*mentary Roles of Informal Networks and Formal Systems*. New York: The Guilford Press.

4    Litwak, Eugene, and Charles F. Longino, Jr. 1987. "Migration Patterns Among the Elderly: A Developmental Perspective." *The Gerontologist* 27:266–72.

4    Logan, Ronald. 1991. "Immigration During the 1980s." *Canadian Social Trends* Spring:10–13.

15   Long, Cathy, and Carol Shelton, researchers and compilers. 1982. *The Directory: Programs for Senior Citizens Across Canada*. Toronto: Canadian Pensioners Concerned, Ontario Division.

4    Longino, Charles F., Jr. 1988a. "The Gray Peril Mentality and the Impact of Retirement Migration." *The Journal of Applied Gerontology* 7:448–55.

4    Longino, Charles F., Jr. 1988b. "On the Nesting of Snowbirds: Canadian-Born Residents of the United States." In Larry C. Mullins and Richard D. Tucker, eds. *Snowbirds in the Sun Belt: Older Canadians in Florida*. Tampa, Florida: International Exchange Center on Gerontology.

7    Lopata, H.Z. 1969. "Loneliness: Forms and Components." *Social Problems* 17:248–61.

5    Lowe, Graham S. 1990. "Computer Literacy." *Canadian Social Trends* Winter:13–15.

7    Lowenthal, M.F. 1975. "Psychosocial Variations Across the Adult Life Course: Frontiers for Research and Policy." *The Gerontologist* 15:6–12.

13   Lowenthal, M.F., and C. Haven. 1968. "Interaction and Adaptation: Intimacy as a Critical Variable." In B.L. Neugarten, ed. *Middle Age and Aging*. Chicago: University of Chicago Press.

7    Lowenthal, M.F., M. Thurner, and D. Chiriboga. 1975. *Four Stages of Life*. San Francisco: Jossey-Bass.

10   MacBride, A. 1976. "Retirement as a Life Crisis: Myth or Reality?" *Canadian Psychiatric Association Journal* 21:547–56.

5    McCulloch, Robert G. 1990. "Calcium Intake and Bone Density: A Review." *Canadian Journal on Aging* 9:167–76.

2,4  McDaniel, Susan. 1986. *Canada's Aging Population*. Toronto: Butterworths.

2,10, McDaniel, Susan. 1989. "Women and Aging: A
13   Sociological Perspective." In Dianne J. Garner and Susan O. Mercer, eds. *Women As They Age: Challenge, Opportunity, and Triumph*. Binghamton, New York: Haworth Press.

2    McDaniel, Susan, and Ben Agger. 1982. *Social Problems Through Conflict and Order*. Don Mills, Ontario: Addison-Wesley.

11   MacDonald, Alison. 1989. *Transportation: Options for the Future*. National Advisory Council on Aging Cat. No. H71-2/1-5-1988E. Ottawa: Minister of Supply and Services.

8    McDonald, L., D. Badry, and C. Mueller. 1988. "The Elderly Physically and Developmentally Handicapped: An Analysis of Service Delivery." *Canadian Journal on Aging* 8:134–47.

10   McDonald, P. Lynn, and Richard A. Wanner. 1982. "Work Past Age 65 in Canada: A Socioeconomic Analysis." *Aging and Work* 5:169–80.

10   McDonald, P. Lynn, and Richard A. Wanner. 1984. "Socioeconomic Determinants of Early Retirement in Canada." *Canadian Journal on Aging* 3:105–16.

10   McDonald, P. Lynn, and Richard A. Wanner. 1987. "Retirement in a Dual Economy: The Canadian Case." In Victor W. Marshall, ed. *Aging in Canada: Social Perspectives*, 2d ed. Toronto: Fitzhenry and Whiteside.

1,2,10 McDonald, P. Lynn, and Richard A. Wanner. 1990. *Retirement in Canada*. Toronto: Butterworths.

6    Mace, Nancy L., and Peter V. Rabins. 1981. *The Thirty-Six-Hour Day*. Baltimore: Johns Hopkins University Press.

6    MacFadgen, S. Lynne. 1987. "The Care of Irreversible Dementia Sufferers in the Toronto and Peel Regions: Perceptions of Service Providers." *Canadian Journal on Aging* 6:271–89.

12   McGuire, Francis A., F.D. Dottavio, and J.T. O'Leary. 1987. "The Relationship of Early Life Experiences to Later Life Leisure Involvement." *Leisure Sciences* 9:251–57.

4    McInnis, R.M. 1977. "Childbearing and Land Availability: Some Evidence from Individual Household Data." In R. Lee, ed. *Population Patterns in the Past*. New York: Academic Press.

6    McIntyre, John S., and Fergus I.M. Craik. 1987. "Age Differences in Memory for Item and Source Information." *Canadian Journal of Psychology* 41:175–92.

5    McKie, Craig. 1987. "Lifestyle Risks: Smoking and Drinking in Canada." *Canadian Social Trends* Spring:20–26.

8    McKim, William A., and Brian L. Mishara. 1987. *Drugs and Aging*. Toronto: Butterworths.

8    McKim, W.A., M.J. Stones, and A. Kozma. 1990. "Factors Predicting Medicine Use in Institutionalized and Non-institutionalized Elderly." *Canadian Journal on Aging* 9:23–34.

8    Maclean, Mary Beth, and Jillian Oderkirk. 1991. "Surgery Among Elderly People." *Canadian Social Trends* Summer:11–13.

7    MacLean, Michael J. 1982. "Personal Major

Events and Individual Life Satisfaction in Old Age." *Essence* 5:119–266.

1    MacLean, M.J. 1983. "Differences Between Adjustment and Enjoyment of Retirement." *Canadian Journal on Aging* 2:3–8.

8    MacLean, M.J., and R. Bonar. 1983. "The Normalization Principle and the Institutionalization of the Elderly." *Canada's Mental Health* 31:16–18.

7    MacLean, M.S., N. Siew, D. Fowler, and I. Graham. 1987. "Institutional Racism in Old Age: Theoretical Perspectives and a Case Study About Access to Social Services." *Canadian Journal on Aging* 6:128–40.

8    MacLennan, Barbara A. 1983. "Some Possible Implications for Adapting the Milieu in Nursing Homes." *Activities, Adaptation and Aging* 4:33–38.

12    Macleod, Betty. 1985. "Education and Aging in Canada." *Convergence* 18:113–16.

12    McPherson, Barry D. 1983. *Aging as a Social Process*. Toronto: Butterworths.

12    McPherson, Barry D. 1985. "The Meaning and Use of Time Across the Life-Cycle: The Influence of Work, Family and Leisure." In Ellen M. Gee and Gloria M. Gutman, eds. *Canadian Gerontological Collection V: The Challenge of Time.* Winnipeg: Canadian Association on Gerontology.

10    McPherson, Barry D., and N. Guppy. 1979. "Preretirement Life-Style and Degree of Planning for Retirement." *Journal of Gerontology* 34:254–63.

12    McPherson, Barry D., and Carol Kozlik. 1980. "Canadian Leisure Patterns: Disengagement, Continuity or Ageism." In Victor W. Marshall, ed. *Aging in Canada*. Toronto: Fitzhenry and Whiteside.

12    McPherson, Barry D., and Carol Kozlik. 1987. "Age Patterns in Leisure Participation: The Canadian Case." In Victor W. Marshall, ed. *Aging in Canada*. 2d ed. Toronto: Fitzhenry and Whiteside.

3,4    McVey, Wayne. 1987. Personal communication.

7    Maddox, G.L. 1970. "Fact or Artifact: Evidence Bearing on Disengagement Theory." In Erdman Palmore, ed. *Normal Aging*. Durham, N.C.: Duke University Press.

3    Maddox, G.L. 1988. "Overview." In *Aging Around the World: A Report on the President's Symposium, 'Aging in Tomorrow's World: An International Perspective.'* The Gerontological Society of America.

14    Manitoba Law Reform Commission. 1990.

"Discussion Paper on Advance Directives and Durable Powers of Attorney for Health Care." Winnipeg: Manitoba Law Reform Commission.

14    Manitoba Health Organizations. No date. *Bulletin*. Winnipeg: Manitoba Health Organizations.

5    Manitoba Health Services Commission. 1980. *Planning Guide for Personal Care Homes In Manitoba*. Winnipeg: Manitoba Health Services Commission.

8    Manitoba Health Services Commission. 1985. "Manitoba Health Services Commission Study of Persons Age 65+ Presenting at the Emergency Departments of Three Winnipeg Hospitals." Winnipeg: Manitoba Health Services Commission.

2    Manning, Gerald F. 1989. "Fiction and Aging: 'Ripeness is All'." *Canadian Journal on Aging* 8:157–63.

5    Manton, Kenneth G. 1982. "Changing concepts of Mortality and Morbidity in the Elderly Population." *Milbank Memorial Fund Quarterly* 60:183–244.

5    Manton, Kenneth G. 1986. "Past and Future Life Expectancy Increases at Later Ages: Their Implications for the Linkage of Chronic Morbidity, Disability, and Mortality." *Journal of Gerontology* 41:672–81.

8    Manton, Kenneth G. 1989. "Life-Style Risk Factors." *The Annals of the American Academy of Political and Social Sciences* 503:72–88.

5    Manton, Kenneth G. 1990. "Mortality and Morbidity." In Robert H. Binstock and Linda K. George, eds. *Handbook of Aging and the Social Sciences*. 3d ed. San Diego: Academic Press.

7    Manton, K.G., D.G. Blazer, and M.A. Woodbury. 1987. "Suicide in Middle Age and Later Life: Sex and Race Specific Life Table and Cohort Analyses." *Journal of Gerontology* 42:219–27.

16    Marcus, Lotte. 1978. "Ageing and Education." In David Hobman, ed. *The Social Challenge of Aging*. London: Croom Helm.

16    Marcus, Lotte. 1980. "The Education of the Practitioner in Gerontology." Personal communication.

13    Marcus, Lotte, and Valerie Jaeger. 1984. "The Elderly as Family Caregivers." *Canadian Journal on Aging* 13:33–43.

13    Maris, R.W. 1969. *Social Forces in Urban Suicide*. Homewood, Illinois: Dorsey Press.

7    Markides, Kyriakos S., and Charles H. Mindel. 1987. *Aging and Ethnicity*. Newbury Park, California: Sage.

12    Marmel, Bernice, S. Sawyer, and D. Shell. 1983.

*A Study of the Needs of Tenants of Willow Centre Elderly Persons' Housing. Study #1.* Winnipeg: Nor'West Co-op Health and Social Services Centre, Inc.

14  Marshall, Victor W. 1974. "The Last Strand: Remnants of Engagement in the Later Years." *Omega* 5:25–35.

14  Marshall, Victor W. 1975. "Age and Awareness of Finitude in Developmental Gerontology." *Omega* 6:113–29.

1   Marshall, Victor W., ed. 1980a. *Aging in Canada.* Toronto: Fitzhenry and Whiteside.

14  Marshall, Victor W. 1980b. *Last Chapters: A Sociology of Aging and Dying.* Monterey, California: Brooks/Cole.

7   Marshall, Victor W. 1983. "Generations, Age Groups and Cohorts." *Canadian Journal on Aging* 2:51–61.

2   Marshall, Victor W. 1986. "A Sociological Perspective on Aging and Dying." In Victor W. Marshall, ed. *Later Life: The Social Psychology of Aging.* Beverly Hills, California: Sage.

13  Marshall, Victor W. 1987. "The Health of Very Old People as a Concern of Their Children." In Victor W. Marshall, ed. *Aging in Canada: Social Perspectives.* 2d ed. Toronto: Fitzhenry and Whiteside.

13  Marshall, Victor W. 1989. *Models for Community-Based Long Term Care.* Paper prepared for the Aging Policy Section, Health Policy Division, Policy, Planning and Information Branch, Health and Welfare Canada. Ottawa: Health and Welfare Canada.

14  Marshall, Victor W., and Judith A. Levy. 1990. "Aging and Dying." In Robert H. Binstock and Linda K. George, eds. *Handbook of Aging and the Social Sciences.* 3d ed. San Diego: Academic Press.

13  Marshall, Victor W., C.J. Rosenthal, and J. Synge. 1981. "The Family as a Health Service Organization for the Elderly." Paper presented at the Annual Meeting of Society for the Study of Social Problems, Toronto.

13  Marshall, V.W., C.J. Rosenthal, and J. Synge. 1983. "Concerns About Parental Health." In Elizabeth W. Markson, ed. *Older Women: Issues and Prospects.* Lexington, Massachusetts: D.C. Heath.

13  Masters, W., and V. Johnson. 1970. *Human Sexual Inadequacy.* Boston: Little, Brown.

13  Matthews, Anne Martin. 1982. "Review Essay—Canadian Research on Women as Widows: A Comparative Analysis of the State of the Art." *Resources for Feminist Research* 11:227–30.

13  Matthews, Anne Martin. 1985. "Support Systems of Widows in Canada." In Helena Z. Lopata, ed. *Widows: Other Countries/Other Places.* Forthcoming. Durham, North Carolina: Duke University Press.

13  Matthews, Anne Martin. 1987. "Widowhood as an Expectable Life Event." In Victor W. Marshall, ed. *Aging in Canada: Social Perspectives.* 2d ed. Toronto: Fitzhenry and Whiteside.

10  Matthews, Anne Martin, and Kathleen H. Brown. 1987. "Retirement as a Critical Life Event: The Differential Experience of Women and Men." *Research on Aging* 9:548–71.

10  Matthews, Anne Martin, and Joseph A. Tindale. 1987. "Retirement in Canada." In Kyriakos S. Markides and Cary L. Cooper, eds. *Retirement in Industrialized Societies: Social, Psychological and Health Factors.* Toronto: John Wiley & Sons.

1   Matthews, A.M., J.A. Tindale, and J.E. Norris. 1985. "The Facts on Aging Quiz: A Canadian Validation and Cross-Cultural Comparison." *Canadian Journal on Aging* 3:165–74.

9,   Matthews, Anne Martin, K.H. Brown, C.K.
10,13 Davis, and M.A. Denton. 1982. "A Crisis Assessment Technique for the Evaluation of Life Events: Transition to Retirement as an Example." *Canadian Journal on Aging* 1:28–39.

3   Matthews, C., and J.V. Thompson. 1985. "The Aged in Canadian Fiction: No Longer Tragic Figures." Paper presented at the Canadian Association on Gerontology 14th Annual Scientific and Educational Meeting, Hamilton.

1   Matthews, Sarah H. 1979. *The Social World of Old Women: The Management of Self-Identity.* Beverly Hills, California: Sage.

8   Maxwell, Robert J. 1981. *Health and Wealth.* Lexington, Massachusetts: Lexington Books.

3   Maxwell, Robert J,. and Philip Silverman. 1977. "Information and Esteem: Cultural Considerations in the Treatment of the Aged." In Wilbur H. Watson and Robert J. Maxwell, eds. *Human Aging and Dying: A Study in Sociocultural Gerontology.* New York: St. Martin's Press.

3   Mays, H.J. 1983. "A Place to Stand: Families, Land and Permanence in Toronto Gore Township, 1820–1890." In W.P. Ward, ed. *The Social Development of Canada: Readings.* Richmond, British Columbia: Open Learning Institute.

4   Mazess, Richard B., and Sylvia H. Forman. 1979. "Longevity and Age Exaggeration in Vilcabamba, Ecuador." *Journal of Gerontology* 34:94–98.

2   Mead, G.H. 1934. *Mind, Self and Society.* Chicago: University of Chicago Press.

1   Meadows, Rita E., and H. Thompson Fillmer. 1987. "Depictions of Aging in Basal Readers of the 1960s and 1980s." *Educational Gerontology* 13:85–100.

5   Medvedev, Z.A. 1974. "Caucasus and Altay Longevity: A Biological or Social Problem?" *The Gerontologist* 14:381–87.

10  Meier, E.L., and E.A. Kerr. 1976. "Capabilities of Middle-aged and Older Workers." *Industrial Gerontology* 3:147–156.

6   Mental Health Division, Health Services and Promotion Branch, Department of National Health and Welfare. 1988. *Guidelines for Comprehensive Services to Elderly Persons with Psychiatric Disorders.* Cat. No. H39-120/1988 E. Ottawa: Minister of Supply and Services.

10  Méthot, Suzanne. 1987. "Employment Patterns of Elderly Canadians." *Canadian Social Trends* Autumn:7–11.

14  Metzger, Anne M. 1979–80. "A Q-Methodological Study of the Kübler-Ross Stage Theory." *Omega* 10:291–301.

15  Milbrath, Lester W. 1965. *Political Participation: How and Why Do People Get Involved in Politics?* Chicago: Rand McNally.

6   Miles, C.C., and W.R. Miles. 1932. "The Correlation of Intelligence Scores and Chronological Age from Early to Late Maturity." *American Journal of Psychology* 44:44–78

7   Miller, Marv. 1979. *Suicide After Sixty: The Final Alternative.* New York: Springer.

12  Milton, B. 1975. *Social Status and Leisure Time Activities: National Survey Findings for Adult Canadians.* Monograph 3. Montreal: Canadian Sociology and Anthropology Association.

11  Minuk, M., and K. Davidson. 1981. *A Report on the Research Findings on the MHRC 1981 Shelter Allowance Program Review.* Winnipeg: Manitoba Housing and Renewal Corporation.

8   Mitchell-Pedersen, L., L. Edmund, E. Fingerote, and C. Powell. 1985. "Let's Untie the Elderly." *OAHA Quarterly* October:10–14.

12  Mittelman, K., S. Crawford, S. Holliday, G. Gutman, and G. Bhakthan. 1989. "The Older Cyclist: Anthropometric, Physiological, and Psychosocial Changes Observed During a Trans-Canada Cycle Tour." *Canadian Journal on Aging* 8:144–56.

13  Mohide, E.A., D.M. Pringle, D.L. Streiner, J.R. Gilbert, G. Muir, and M. Tew. 1990. "A Randomized Trial of Family Caregiver Support in the Home Management of Dementia." *Journal of the American Geriatrics Society* 38:446–54.

5   Molloy, D.W., D.A. Beerschoten, M.J.Borrie, R.G. Crilly, and R.D.T. Cape. 1988. "Acute Effects of Exercise on Neuropsychological Function in Elderly Subjects." *Journal of the American Geriatrics Society* 36:29–33.

8   Montgomery, P.R., A.J. Kirshen, and N.P. Roos. 1988. "Long-Term Care and Impending Mortality: Influence Upon Place of Death and Hospital Utilization." *The Gerontologist* 28:351–54.

15  Montgomery, Charlotte. 1985. "Tories Retreat on De-Indexing Pensions." *Globe and Mail* 28 June.

3   Moodie, S. 1853. *Life in the Clearings Versus the Bush.* New York: DeWitt and Davenport.

12  Moody, Harry R. 1988a. *Abundance of Life: Human Development Policies for an Aging Society.* New York: Columbia University Press.

2   Moody, Harry R. 1988b. "Toward a Critical Gerontology: The Contribution of the Humanities to Theories of Aging." In James E. Birren and Vern L. Bengtson, eds. *Emergent Theories of Aging.* New York: Springer.

12  Mori, G.A., and B. Burke. 1986. *Educational Attainment of Canadians.* Statistics Canada. Cat. No. 98-134. Ottawa: Minister of Supply and Services.

13  Morris, John N., and Sylvia Sherwood. 1983–84. "Informal Support Resources for Vulnerable Elderly Persons: Can They Be Counted on, Why Do They Work?" *International Journal of Aging and Human Development* 18:81–98.

10  Morrison, M. 1984. "Retirement and Human Resource Planning for the Aging Work Force." *Personnel Administrator* June:151–59.

14  Moss, Miriam S., and Sidney Z. Moss. 1984–85. "Some Aspects of the Elderly Widow(er)'s Persistent Tie with the Deceased Spouse." *Omega* 15:195–206.

7   Mossey, Jana M., B. Havens, N.P. Roos, and E. Shapiro. 1981. "The Manitoba Longitudinal Study on Aging: Description and Methods." *The Gerontologist* 21:551–58.

14  Mount, B.F., and J.F. Scott. 1983. "Whither Hospice Evaluation." *Journal of Chronic Diseases* 36:731–36.

14  Mount, R.M., A. Jones, and A. Patterson. 1974. "Death and Dying: Attitudes in a Teaching Hospital." *Urology* 4:741.

13  Mullens, Harry J. 1983. "Love, Sexuality, and Aging in Nursing Homes and Public Housing." Paper presented at the Canadian Association on Gerontology 12th Annual Scientific and Educational Meeting, Moncton.

4   Mullins, Larry C., R. Tucker, C.F. Longino, Jr., and V. Marshall. 1989. "An Examination of

Loneliness Among Elderly Canadian Seasonal Residents in Florida." *Journal of Gerontology: Social Sciences* 44:S80–S86.

2    Murphy, Barbara. 1982. *Corporate Capital and the Welfare State: Canadian Business and Public Pension Policy in Canada Since World War II*. Unpublished master's thesis. Ottawa: Carleton University.

8    Murray, D. 1974. *Multiple Drug Use Among the Elderly*. Unpublished. Winnipeg: Faculty of Medicine, University of Manitoba.

5    Murrell, F.H. 1970. "The Effect of Extensive Practice on Age Differences in Reaction Time." *Journal of Gerontology* 25:268–74.

6    Murrell, S.A., S. Himmelfarb, and K. Wright. 1983. "Prevalence of Depression and Its Correlates in Older Adults." *American Journal of Epidemiology* 117:173–85.

12   Myers, Anita M., and Gail Gonda. 1986. "Research on Physical Activity in the Elderly: Practical Implications for Program Planning." *Canadian Journal on Aging* 5:175–87.

12   Myers, Anita M., and N. Hamilton. 1985. "Evaluation of the Canadian Red Cross Society's Fun and Fitness Program for Seniors." *Canadian Journal on Aging* 4:201–12.

5    Myers, George C., and Kenneth G. Manton. 1984. "Compression of Mortality: Myth or Reality?" *The Gerontologist* 24:346–53.

9    Myles, John F. 1981a. "Income Inequality and Status Maintenance." *Research on Aging* 3:123–41.

9    Myles, John. 1981b. "The Trillion Dollar Misunderstanding." *Working Papers Magazine* July–August.

4,9  Myles, John. 1982. "Social Implications of a Changing Age Structure." In Gloria Gutman, ed. *Canada's Changing Age Structure: Implications for the Future*. Burnaby, British Columbia: SFU Publications.

2,9, 10,15   Myles, John. 1984. *Old Age in the Welfare State: The Political Economy of Public Pensions*. Boston: Little, Brown and Co.

9,15  Myles, John F. 1988. "Social Policy in Canada." In Eloise Rathbone-McEwan and Betty Havens, eds. *North American Elders: United States and Canadian Perspectives*. New York: Greenwood.

13   Myles, John. 1991. "Women, the Welfare State and Care-Giving." *Canadian Journal on Aging* 10:82–85.

4,8,12   Myles, John F., and Monica Boyd. 1982. "Population Aging and the Elderly." In Dennis Forcese and Stephen Richer, eds. *Social Issues:*

*Sociological Views of Canada*. Scarborough, Ontario: Prentice-Hall.

5    Naeyaert, Kathleen. 1990. *Living with Sensory Loss: Vision*. Ottawa: National Advisory Council on Aging.

4    Nagnur, Dhruva. 1986. *Longevity and Historical Life Tables 1921–1981 (Abridged) Canada and the Provinces*. Statistics Canada. Cat. No 89–506. Ottawa: Minister of Supply and Services.

13   Nagnur, Dhruva, and Owen Adams. 1987. "Tying the Knot: An Overview of Marriage Rates in Canada." *Canadian Social Trends* Autumn:2–6.

13   Nagnur, Dhruva, and Owen Adams. 1989. "Marrying and Divorcing: A Status Report for Canada." *Canadian Social Trends* Summer:24–27.

4,5  Nagnur, Dhruva, and Michael Nagrodski. 1988. "Cardiovascular Disease, Cancer and Life Expectancy." *Canadian Social Trends* Winter:25–27.

12   Nahmiash, Daphne. 1985. "Intergenerational Relationships." Paper presented at the Canadian Association on Gerontology 14th Annual Scientific and Educational Meeting, Hamilton.

3    Nason, J.D. 1981. "Respected Elder or Old Person: Aging in a Micronesian Community." In P. T. Amoss and S. Harrell, eds. *Other Ways of Growing Old: Anthropological Perspectives*. Stanford, California: Stanford University Press.

15   National Advisory Council on Aging. 1985a. *"Listen to Me!": The Technical Evaluation Report of The National Advisory Council on Aging's Consultation with Seniors*. News release. Ottawa: National Advisory Council on Aging.

15   National Advisory Council on Aging. 1985b. *Seniors and Decision-Making*. Ottawa: Minister of Supply and Services.

11   National Advisory Council on Aging. 1985c. *Expression* 2 (4). Ottawa: National Advisory Council on Aging.

11,13   National Advisory Council on Aging. 1986a. *Expression* 3 (1). Ottawa: National Advisory Council on Aging.

11   National Advisory Council on Aging. 1986b. *Expression* 3. Ottawa: National Advisory Council on Aging.

8    National Advisory Council on Aging. 1986c. "Toward a Community Support Policy for Canadians." Ottawa: National Advisory Council on Aging.

5    National Advisory Council on Aging. 1988. "NACA's Philosophy on Technology for an Aging Population." News release. Ottawa: Government of Canada.

15 National Advisory Council on Aging. 1989a. *1989 and Beyond: Challenges of an Aging Canadian Society.* Cat. No. H71-3/10-1989. Ottawa: Minister of Supply and Services.

12 National Advisory Council on Aging. 1989b. "Not All Learning Takes Place in Formal Classes." *Expression* 5:4.

8 National Advisory Council on Aging. 1989c. *Understanding Seniors' Independence Report No. 1: The Barriers and Suggestions for Action.* Cat. No. H71-3/11-1-1989E. Ottawa: Minister of Supply and Services.

11 National Advisory Council on Aging. 1989d. *Understanding Seniors' Independence: The Barriers and Suggestions for Action Summary Report.* Cat. No. H71-3/11-1-1989-1. Ottawa: Minister of Supply and Services.

13 National Advisory Council on Aging. 1990a. "Adult Children and Their Parents." *Expression* 6.

13 National Advisory Council on Aging. 1990b. "Grandparents' Rights." *Expression* 6.

8 National Advisory Council on Aging. 1990c. *The NACA Position on Community Services in Health Care for Seniors.* Cat. No. H71-2/2-8-1990. Ottawa: Minister of Supply and Services.

13 National Advisory Council on Aging. 1990d. *The NACA Position on Informal Caregiving: Support and Enhancement.* Cat. No. H71-2/2-9-1990. Ottawa: Minister of Supply and Services.

12 National Advisory Council on Aging. 1990e. *The NACA Position on Lifelong Learning.* Cat. No. H71-2/2-10-1990. Ottawa: Minister of Supply and Services.

9,11 National Advisory Council on Aging. 1991. *The Economic Situation of Canada's Seniors: A Fact Book.* Cat. No. H71-3/14-1991E. Ottawa: Minister of Supply and Services.

9 National Council of Welfare. 1979. *Women and Poverty.* Ottawa: Minister of Supply and Services.

9 National Council of Welfare. 1984a. *A Pension Primer.* Ottawa: Minister of Supply and Services.

4,9 National Council of Welfare. 1984b. *Sixty-five and Older.* Cat. No. H68-11/1984E. Ottawa: Minister of Supply and Services.

9 National Council of Welfare. 1985a. *Giving and Taking: The May 1985 Budget and the Poor.* Ottawa: Minister of Supply and Services.

9 National Council of Welfare. 1985b. *Poverty Profile.* Ottawa: Minister of Supply and Services.

9 National Council of Welfare. 1988. *Poverty Profile.* Cat. No. H67-1/4-1988E. Ottawa: Minister of Supply and Services.

9 National Council of Welfare. 1989a. *The 1989 Budget and Social Policy.* Cat. No. H68-22/1989E. Ottawa: Minister of Supply and Services.

9 National Council of Welfare. 1989b. *A Pension Primer.* Cat. No. H68-23/1989E. Ottawa: Minister of Supply and Services.

9, 11,13 National Council of Welfare. 1990a. *Women and Poverty Revisited.* Cat. No. H68-25/1990E. Ottawa: Minister of Supply and Services.

9 National Council of Welfare. 1990b. *Pension Reform.* Cat. No. H68-24/1990E. Ottawa: Minister of Supply and Services.

8 National Council of Welfare. 1991. *Funding Health and Higher Education: Danger Looming.* Cat. No. H68-30/1991E. Ottawa: Minister of Supply and Services.

9 National Health and Welfare. 1973. *Working Paper on Social Security in Canada.* 2d ed. Ottawa: Queen's Printer.

13 Neal, M.B., N.J. Chapman, B. Ingersoll-Dayton, A.C. Emlen, and L. Boise. 1990. "Absenteeism and Stress Among Employed Caregivers of the Elderly, Disabled Adults, and Children." In David E. Biegel and Arthur Blum, eds. *Aging and Caregiving: Theory, Research, and Policy.* Newbury Park: Sage.

5 Nessner, Katherine. 1990. "Profile of Canadians with Disabilities." *Canadian Social Trends* Autumn:2–5.

13 Nett, Emily M. 1988. *Canadian Families Past and Present.* Toronto: Butterworths.

7 Neugarten, B.L. 1964. *Personality in Middle and Late Life.* New York: Atherton Press.

7 Neugarten, B.L., ed. 1968. *Middle Age and Aging.* Chicago: University of Chicago Press.

7 Neugarten, B.L. 1969. "Continuities and Discontinuities of Psychological Issues into Adult Life." *Human Development* 12:121–30.

3,10 Neugarten, B.L. 1980. "Acting One's Age: New Rules for Old" (Interview with Elizabeth Hall). *Psychology Today* April.

13 Neugarten, B.L., and Karol K. Weinstein. 1964. "The Changing American Grandparent." *Journal of Marriage and the Family* 26:199–204.

3,15 Neugarten, B.L., and R.J. Havighurst. 1979. "Aging and the Future." In J. Hendricks and C.D. Hendricks, eds. *Dimensions of Aging: Readings.* Cambridge, Massachusetts: Winthrop.

7 Neugarten, B.L., and J.W. Moore. 1968. "The Changing Age-status System." In Bernice L. Neugarten, ed. *Middle Age and Aging.* Chicago: University of Chicago Press.

2,7 Neugarten, B.L., R.J. Havighurst, and S. Tobin. 1968. "Personality and Patterns of Aging." In

Bernice L. Neugarten, ed. *Middle Age and Aging*. Chicago: University of Chicago Press.

7    Neugarten, B.L., J.W. Moore, and J.C. Lowe. 1968. "Age Norms, Age Constraints, and Adult Socialization." In Bernice L. Neugarten, ed. *Middle Age and Aging*. Chicago: University of Chicago Press.

13    Neysmith, Sheila M. 1982. "The Social Contributions of Old People: A Description and Assessment." Revised version of a paper presented at the 11th Annual Scientific and Educational Meeting of the Canadian Association on Gerontology, Winnipeg.

9    Neysmith, Sheila M. 1984. "Poverty in Old Age: Can Pension Reform Meet the Needs of Women?" *Canadian Woman Studies* 5:17–21.

15    Neysmith, Sheila M. 1986. "Social Policy Implications of an Aging Society." In Victor W. Marshall, ed. *Aging in Canada: Social Perspectives*. 2d ed. Toronto: Fitzhenry and Whiteside.

15    Neysmith, Sheila M. 1987. "Organizing for Influence: The Relationship of Structure to Impact." *Canadian Journal on Aging* 6:105–16.

3    Neysmith, Sheila M., and Joey Edwardh. 1983. "Ideological Underpinnings of the World Assembly on Aging." *Canadian Journal on Aging* 2:125–36.

11    Nicklin, Robert L. 1985. "The Role of the Canada Mortgage and Housing Corporation in the Development Process." In Gloria Gutman and Norman Blackie, eds. *Innovations in Housing and Living Arrangements for Senior*. Burnaby, British Columbia: The Gerontology Research Centre, Simon Fraser University.

11    Niewind, A.C., M. Krondl, and D. Lau. 1988. "Relative Impact of Selected Factors on Food Choices of Elderly Individuals." *Canadian Journal on Aging* 8:32–47.

10    Nishio, Harry K., and Heather Lank. 1987. "Patterns of Labour Participation of Older Female Workers." In Victor W. Marshall, ed. *Aging in Canada: Social Perspectives*. 2d ed. Toronto: Fitzhenry and Whiteside.

13    Noelker, L.S., and S.W. Poulshock. 1982. *The Effects on Families of Caring for Impaired Elderly in Residence*. Washington, D.C.: U.S. Department of Health and Human Services, Administration on Aging.

13    Norris, J. 1980. "The Social Adjustment of Single and Widowed Older Women." *Essence* 4:134–44.

13    Norris, J.E., K.H. Rubin, J. Cohen, and L. Both. 1983. "Assessing Qualitative Dimensions of Adult Social Interaction: Examining Peer Relationships." Paper presented at the 12th Annual Scientific and Educational Meeting of the Canadian Association on Gerontology, Moncton.

1,7    Northcott, Herbert C. 1982. "The Best Years of Your Life." *Canadian Journal on Aging* 1:72–78.

4    Northcott, Herbert C. 1984. "The Interprovincial Migration of Canada's Elderly: 1956–61 and 1971–76." *Canadian Journal on Aging* 3:3–22.

4    Northcott, Herbert C. 1985. "The Geographic Mobility of Canada's Elderly." *Canadian Studies in Population* 12:183–202.

4    Northcott, Herbert C. 1988. *Changing Residence: The Geographic Mobility of Elderly Canadians*. Toronto: Butterworths.

2    Novak, Mark. 1983. "Discovering a Good Age." *International Journal of Aging and Human Development* 16:231–39.

7,14    Novak, Mark. 1985. *Successful Aging: The Myths, Realities and Future of Aging in Canada*. Markham, Ontario: Penguin.

7    Novak, Mark. 1985-86. "Biography After the End of Metaphysics." *International Journal of Aging and Human Development* 22:189–204.

12    Novak, Mark. 1987. "The Canadian New Horizons Program." *The Gerontologist* 27:353–55.

2    Novak, Mark. 1988. Review of *Oldtimers and Alzheimer's: The Descriptive Organization of Senility*, by Jaber F. Gubrium. *Canadian Journal on Aging* 7:71–77.

14    Novak, Mark, and Charles Axelrod. 1979. "Primitive Myth and Modern Medicine: *On Death and Dying*, by Elisabeth Kübler-Ross." *The Psychoanalytic Review* 66:443–50.

6    Novak, Mark, and Carol Guest. 1985. "Social Correlates of Caregiver Burden." Paper presented at the Canadian Association on Gerontology 14th Annual Scientific and Education Meeting, Hamilton.

13    Novak, Mark, and Carol Guest. 1989. "Application of a Multidimensional Caregiver Burden Inventory." *The Gerontologist* 29:798–803.

13    Novak, Mark, and Leroy O. Stone. 1985. "Changing Patterns of Aging." Paper presented at the annual meeting of the Canadian Sociology and Anthropology Association, Montreal.

6    Novak, M., N. Chappell, and C. Miles-Tapping. 1990. "Nursing Assistant Stress and the Cognitively Impaired Elderly." Paper presented at the 43rd Scientific Meeting of the Gerontological Society of America, Boston.

3    Nusberg, C. 1982. "World Assembly Seeks to Alert Developing Countries About Their Aging Populations." *Ageing International* 9:7–9.

13 O'Brien, J.E., and D.L. Wagner. 1980. "Help-seeking by the Frail Elderly: Problems in Network Analysis." *The Gerontologist* 20:78–83.

5,12 O'Brien, Sandra J., and Patricia A. Vertinsky. 1991. "Unfit Survivors: Exercise as a Resource for Aging Women." *The Gerontologist* 31:347–57.

12 O'Brien, Laird. 1989. "Beyond the Three R's." *The Review* Spring.

11 Okraku, Ishmael O. 1987. "Age and Attitudes Toward Multigenerational Residence, 1973 to 1983." *Journal of Gerontology* 42:280–87.

12 One Voice, The Canadian Seniors Network. 1989. *Illiteracy and Older Canadians: An Unrecognized Problem: A Literature Review.* Ottawa: One Voice, the Seniors Network (Canada).

12 One Voice, the Canadian Seniors Network. 1990a. *Learning–That's Life: Conference Report and Recommendations.* Ottawa: One Voice, the Seniors Network (Canada).

12 One Voice, the Canadian Seniors Network. 1990b. "Illiteracy a Major Threat to Seniors' Independence, Conference Reveals." Press release. Ottawa: One Voice, the Seniors Network (Canada).

11 Ontario Advisory Council on the Physically Handicapped and Ontario Advisory Council on Senior Citizens. 1987. *The Freedom to Move Is Life Itself: A Report on Transportation in Ontario.* Toronto.

11 Ontario Advisory Council on Senior Citizens. 1978. *Through the Eyes of Others.* Toronto: Ontario Advisory Council on Senior Citizens.

11 Ontario Advisory Council on Senior Citizens. 1980–81. *Seniors Tell All.* Toronto: Ontario Advisory Council on Senior Citizens.

8 Ontario Council of Health. 1978. "Health Care for the Aged: A Report of the Ontario Council of Health." Toronto: Ontario Council of Health.

11 Ontario Ministry of Municipal Affairs and Housing, Research and Special Projects Branch. 1983. *Towards Community Planning for an Aging Society.* Toronto: Queen's Printer for Ontario.

4 Ontario Ministry of Treasury and Economics. 1979. *Issues in Pension Policy: Demographic and Economic Aspects of Canada's Ageing Population.* Ontario Treasury Studies 16. Toronto: Ministry of Treasury and Economics, Taxation and Fiscal Policy Branch.

6 Ontario Public Health Association. 1983. "Creating a Healthy Ontario: Health Care in the 80's and Beyond." Toronto: Ontario Public Health Association.

3,10 O'Rand, Angela M. 1990. "Stratification and the Life Course." In Robert H. Binstock and Linda K. George, eds. *Handbook of Aging and the Social Sciences.* 3d ed. San Diego: Academic Press.

10 Orbach, Harold L. 1969. *Trends in Early Retirement.* Ann Arbor, Michigan: University of Michigan, Wayne State University Institute of Gerontology.

10 Orbach, Harold L. 1981. "Mandatory Retirement and the Development of Adequate Retirement Provisions for Older Persons." In George Gasek, ed. *Canadian Gerontological Collection II: Retirement Income Systems.* Winnipeg: Canadian Association on Gerontology.

8 Organization for Economic Co-operation and Development. 1985. *Measuring Health Care, 1960–1983.* Social Policy Studies No.2. Paris: Organization for Economic Co-operation and Development.

12 Ouellet, Pierre. 1986. "The Leisure Participation and Enjoyment Patterns of French and English-Speaking Members of Senior Citizens' Clubs in New Brunswick, Canada." *Canadian Journal on Aging* 5:257–68.

5 Paffenbarger, R.S., R.T. Hyde, A.L. Wing, and C. Hsieh. 1986. "Physical Activity, All-Cause Mortality, and Longevity of College Alumni." *The New England Journal of Medicine* 314:605–13.

7 Palmore, Erdman B. 1970. "The Effects of Aging on Activities and Attitudes." In Erdman Palmore, ed. *Normal Aging.* Durham, North Carolina: Duke University Press.

1 Palmore, Erdman B. 1971. "Attitudes Toward Aging as Shown in Humor." *The Gerontologist* 11:181–86.

1 Palmore, Erdman B. 1977. "Facts on Aging: A Short Quiz." *The Gerontologist* 17:315–20.

1 Palmore, Erdman B. 1979. "Advantages of Aging." *The Gerontologist* 19:220–23.

13 Palmore, Erdman B. 1981. *Social Patterns in Normal Aging: Findings from the Duke Longitudinal Study.* Durham, North Carolina: Duke University Press.

5 Palmore, Erdman B. 1984. "Longevity in Abkhazia: A Re-evaluation." *The Gerontologist* 24:95–96.

1 Palmore, Erdman B. 1988. *The Facts on Aging Quiz: A Handbook of Uses and Results.* New York: Springer.

3 Palmore, Erdman B., and K. Manton. 1974. "Modernization and the Status of the Aged: International Correlations." *Journal of Gerontology* 29:205–10.

3    Palmore, Erdman B., and F. Whittington. 1971. "Trends in the Relative Status of the Aged." *Social Forces* 50:84–91.

10   Palmore, E., B.M. Burchett, G.G. Fillenbaum, L.K. George, and L.M. Wallman. 1985. *Retirement: Causes and Consequences.* New York: Springer.

8    Parboosingh, Jean E., and Donald E. Larsen. 1987. "Factors Influencing Frequency and Appropriateness of Utilization of the Emergency Room by the Elderly." *Medical Care* 25:1139–47.

10   Paris, H. 1989. *The Corporate Response to Workers with Family Responsibilities.* Report 43–89. Ottawa: The Conference Board of Canada.

16   Parker, Brant. 1991. "Bridging the Generation Gap." Paper presented at the National Institute for Educational Innovation, Winnipeg, August.

12   Parks Canada. 1973. "Trends in Participation in Outdoor Recreational Activities." *CORD Technical Note No. 223.* Ottawa: National and Historic Parks Branch, Parks Canada.

4,5  Parliament, Jo-Anne. 1987. "Increased Life Expectancy, 1921–1986." *Canadian Social Trends* Summer:15–19.

4    Parliament, Jo-Anne. 1989. "The Decline in Cardio-Vascular Disease Mortality." *Canadian Social Trends* Autumn:28–29.

11   Parmelee, Patricia A., and M. Powell Lawton. 1990. "The Design of Special Environments for the Aged." In James E. Birren and K. Warner Schaie, eds. *Handbook of the Psychology of Aging.* 3d ed. San Diego: Academic Press.

2    Parsons, Talcott. 1937. *The Structure of Social Action.* New York: McGraw-Hill.

2    Parsons, Talcott. 1951. *The Social System.* New York: Free Press.

2    Passuth, Patricia M., and Vern L. Bengtson. 1988. In James E. Birren and Vern L. Bengtson, *Emergent Theories of Aging.* New York: Springer.

8    Paterson, Jody. 1989. "New Services Help Seniors Convalesce in Own Home." *Times-Colonist* (Victoria) 28 November.

7,14 Peck, Robert C. [1955] 1968. "Psychological Aspects of Aging." In John E. Anderson, ed. *Proceedings of a Conference on Planning Research*, Bethesda, Maryland, April 24–27, 1955; Washington, D.C.: American Psychological Association. Excerpted as "Psychological Developments in the Second Half of Life." In Bernice L. Neugarten, ed. *Middle Age and Aging.* Chicago: University of Chicago Press, 1968.

7    Penning, Margaret J. 1983. "Multiple Jeopardy: Age, Sex, and Ethnic Variations." *Canadian Ethnic Studies* 15:81–105.

13   Penning, Margaret J. 1990. "Receipt of Assistance by Elderly People: Hierarchical Selection and Task Specificity." *The Gerontologist* 30:220–27.

8    Penning, Margaret J., and Neena L. Chappell. 1980. "A Reformulation of Basic Assumptions About Institutionalization for the Elderly." In Victor Marshall, ed. *Aging in Canada.* Toronto: Fitzhenry and Whiteside.

8    Penning, Margaret J., and Neena L. Chappell. 1982. "Mental Health Status: A Comparison of Different Socio-Cultural Environments for the Elderly." *Essence* 5:169–82.

6    Peppard, N.R. 1985. *Special Nursing Home Units for Residents with Primary Degenerative Dementia: Alzheimer's Disease.* Rockville: Nancy R. Peppard and Associates.

7    Perlman, Daniel, A.C. Gerson, and B. Spinner. 1978. "Loneliness Among Senior Citizens: An Empirical Report." *Essence* 2:239–48.

6    Perlmutter, Marion. 1988. "Cognitive Potential Throughout Life." In James E. Birren and Vern L. Bengtson, eds. *Emergent Theories of Aging.* New York: Springer.

4    Perreault, J. 1990. *Population Projections for Canada, Provinces and Territories 1989–2011.* Cat. No. 91-520. Ottawa: Minister of Supply and Services.

12   Perri, Samuel, II, and Donald I. Templer. 1984–85. "The Effects of Aerobic Exercise Program on Psychological Variables in Older Adults." *International Journal of Aging and Human Development* 20:167–72.

10   Perry, Glenys. 1980. "The Need for Retirement Planning and Counselling." *Canadian Counsellor* 14:97–98.

10   Pesando, James. 1979. *The Elimination of Mandatory Retirement: An Economic Perspective.* Toronto: Ontario Economic Council.

10   Pesando James, and S. Rea. 1977. *Public and Private Pensions in Canadian Economic Analysis.* Toronto: University of Toronto Press.

13   Pfeiffer, E., A. Verwoerdt, and H.S. Wang. 1968. "Sexual Behavior in Aged Men and Women, I: Observations on 254 Community Volunteers," *Archives of General Psychiatry* 19:753–58.

5    Pfeiffer, S. 1990. "The Evolution of Human Longevity: Distinctive Mechanisms?" *Canadian Journal on Aging* 9:95–103.

6    Phifer, J.F., and S.A. Murrell. 1986. "Etiologic Factors in the Onset of Depressive Symptoms in

Older Adults." *Journal of Abnormal Psychology* 95:282–91.

14    Phillips, D.P., and K.A. Feldman. 1973. "A Dip in Deaths Before Ceremonial Occasions: Some New Relationships Between Social Integration and Mortality." *American Sociological Review* 38:678–96.

4     Philpot, H.J. 1871. *Guide Book to the Canadian Dominion Containing Full Information for the Emigrant, the Tourist, the Sportsman and the Small Capitalist.* London.

13    Pihlblad, C.T., D.L. Adams, and D.L. Rosencranz. 1972. "Socio-economic Adjustment to Widowhood." *Omega* 3:295–305.

13    Pillemer, Karl, and David Finkelhor. 1988. "The Prevalence of Elder Abuse: A Random Sample Survey." *The Gerontologist* 28:51–57.

5     Pitskhelauri, G.Z. 1982. *The Longliving of Soviet Georgia.* Trans. and ed. G. Lesnoff-Caravaglia. New York: Human Sciences.

10    Pitts, Gordon. 1983. "Getting Ready to Retire Can Be Full-Time Job." *The Financial Post* 21 May.

3     Plath, D.W. 1972. "Japan: The After Years." In D.O. Cowgill and L.D. Holmes, eds. *Aging and Modernization.* New York: Appleton-Century-Crofts.

1,13  Podnieks, E., K. Pillemer, J.P. Nicholson, T. Shillington, and A. Frizzell. 1989. *National Survey of Abuse of the Elderly in Canada: Preliminary Findings.* Toronto: Ryerson Office of Research and Innovation.

13    Podnieks, E., K. Pillemer, J.P. Nicholson, T. Shillington, and A. Frizzel. 1990. *National Survey on Abuse of the Elderly in Canada.* Toronto: Ryerson Polytechnical Institute.

6     Poon, Leonard W. 1985. "Differences in Human Memory with Aging: Nature, Causes, and Clinical Implications." In James E. Birren and K. Warner Schaie, eds. *Handbook of the Psychology of Aging.* 2d ed. New York: Van Nostrand Reinhold.

6     Poon, Leonard W., J.L. Fozard, D.R. Paulshock, and J.C. Thomas. 1979. "A Questionnaire Assessment of Age Differences in Retention of Recent and Remote Events." *Experimental Aging Research* 5:401–11.

3     Population Reference Bureau, Inc. 1980. *1980 World Population Data Sheet.* Washington, D.C.: Population Reference Bureau, Inc.

7     Porter, John. 1965. *The Vertical Mosaic: An Analysis of Social Class and Power in Canada.* Toronto: University of Toronto Press.

15    Powell, G.B. 1987. "Comparative Voting Behavior: Cleavages, Partisanship and Accountability." *Research in Micropolitics* 2:233–64.

13    Powers, Edward A., and Gordon L. Bultena. 1980. "Sex Differences in Intimate Friendships of Old Age." In Marie Marschall Fuller and Cora Ann Martin, eds. *The Older Woman: Lavender Rose or Gray Panther.* Springfield, Illinois: Charles C. Thomas.

15    Pratt, Henry J. 1979. "Politics of Aging." *Research on Aging* 1:155–86.

15    Pratt, Henry J. 1983. "National Interest Groups Among the Elderly: Consolidation and Constraint." In William P. Browne and Laura Katz Olson, eds. *Aging and Public Policy.* Westport, Connecticut: Greenwood Press.

15    Pratt, Henry J. 1984. "Aging in Canada: The Challenge to Political Science." *Canadian Journal on Aging* 3:55–61.

3     Press, I., and M. McKool. 1972. "Social Structure and Status of the Aged: Toward Some Valid Cross-Cultural Generalizations." *Aging and Human Development* 3:297–306.

6     Pressey, S.L., and Pressey, A.D. 1967. "Genius at 80; and Other Oldsters." *The Gerontologist* 7:183–87.

11    Priest, Gordon E. 1988. "Living Arrangements of Canada's 'Older Elderly' Population." *Canadian Social Trends* Cat. No. 11-008E. Autumn:26–30.

11    Pritchard, David C. 1983. "The Art of Matchmaking: A Case Study in Shared Housing." *The Gerontologist* 23:174–79.

1     Proby, Joscelyn. 1984. "Combat Skills Put to Use." *Winnipeg Free Press* 10 April.

12    Program Audit and Review Directorate. 1989. *Evaluation Study of the New Horizons Program: Executive Summary.* Ottawa: Health and Welfare Canada.

15    Pross, A. Paul. 1975. "Canadian Pressure Groups in the 1970's: Their Role and Their Relations with the Public Service." *Canadian Public Administration* 18:121–35.

13    Pruchno, Rachel A. 1990. "The Effects of Help Patterns on the Mental Health of Spouse Caregivers." *Research on Aging* 12:57–71.

8     Psychogeriatric Clinic. No date. "A Telephone Reassurance Service: An Evaluation." Ottawa: Ottawa General Hospital.

3     Quadagno, J. 1980. "The Modernization Controversy: A Socio-historical Analysis of Retirement in Nineteenth Century England." Paper presented at the meeting of the American Sociological Association, New York.

8     Quick Response Team. No date. *A Report on the*

*Capital Regional District Quick Response Team.* Victoria, British Columbia: Quick Response Team.

10    Quinn, Joseph F. 1981. "The Extent and Correlates of Partial Retirement." *The Gerontologist* 21:634–43.

10    Quinn, Joseph F., and Richard V. Burkhauser. 1990. "Work and Retirement." In Robert H. Binstock and Linda K. George, eds. *Handbook of Aging and the Social Sciences.* 3d ed. San Diego: Academic Press.

12    Radcliffe, David. 1982. "U3A: A French Model for the Later Years." A working paper prepared for the Annual Conference of the Comparative and International Education Society, New York.

1,11  Ram, Bali. 1990. *Current Demographic Analysis: Trends in the Family.* Statistics Canada. Cat. No. 91-535E. Ottawa: Minister of Supply and Services.

8     Rantucci, Melanie. 1989. "Health Professionals' Perceptions of Drug Use Problems of the Elderly." *Canadian Journal on Aging* 8:164–72.

11    Rapelje, Douglas H. 1985. "A Canadian Example: The Home Sharing Program for Older Adults in Regional Niagara." In Gloria Gutman and Norman Blackie, eds. *Innovations in Housing and Living Arrangements for Seniors.* Burnaby, British Columbia: The Gerontology Research Centre, Simon Fraser University.

12    Rapelje, Douglas H., B. Goodman, and P. Swick. 1986. "Volunteer Opportunities for Senior Citizens: Part of the Continuum of Care." Paper presented at the Canadian Association on Gerontology 15th Annual Scientific and Educational Meeting, Quebec City.

8     Rattenbury, C., and M.J. Stones. 1989. "A Controlled Evaluation of Reminiscence and Current Topics Discussion Groups in a Nursing Home Context." *The Gerontologist* 29:768–71.

8     Rechnitzer, Peter A. 1982. "Specific Benefits of Postcoronary Exercise Programs." *Geriatrics* 37:47–51.

15    Regenstreif, Peter. 1965. *The Diefenbaker Interlude: Parties and Voting in Canada.* Toronto: Longmans.

7     Reker, G.T., E.J. Peacock, and P.T.P. Wong. 1987. "Meaning and Purpose in Life and Well-Being: A Life-Span Perspective." *Journal of Gerontology* 42:44–49.

13    Rempel, Judith. 1985. "Childless Elderly: What Are They Missing?" *Journal of Marriage and the Family* 47:343–48.

1     Rempel, J.D. 1987. *Annotated Bibliography of Papers, Articles, and Other Documents Resulting*

from the Aging in Manitoba 1971, 1976, 1983 Cross-sectional and Panel Studies. Winnipeg: Government of Manitoba.

11    Renaud, François, and Martin Wexler. 1986. "Housing the Elderly in the Community: A Review of Existing Programs in Quebec." In Gloria Gutman and Norman Blackie, eds. *Aging in Place: Housing Adaptations and Options for Remaining in the Community.* Burnaby, British Columbia: The Gerontology Research Centre, Simon Fraser University.

8     Research and Planning Unit, Family and Community Support Services Division, Social Services Department. 1983. "A Profile of the Elderly in Calgary: A Demographic Profile and Needs Assessment." Calgary: City of Calgary.

13    Resnick, H., and J. Cantor. 1970. "Suicide and Aging." *Journal of the American Geriatric Society* 18:152–58.

6     Rhodes, Ann. 1983. "Five Women Who Defy the Stereotypes of Aging." *Chatelaine* February.

6     Riegel, Klaus F. 1975. "Adult Life Crises: A Dialectic Interpretation of Development." In Nancy Datan and Leon H. Ginsberg, eds. *Life-span Developmental Psychology: Normative Life Crisis.* New York: Academic Press.

7     Riegel, Klaus F. 1976. "The Dialectics of Human Development." *American Psychologist* 31:689–700.

2     Riley, Matilda White. 1971. "Social Gerontology and the Age Stratification of Society." *The Gerontologist* 11:79–87.

2     Riley, Matilda White. 1987. "On the Significance of Age in Sociology." *American Sociological Review* 52:1–14.

2     Riley, M.W., A. Foner, and J. Waring. 1988. "Sociology of Age." In N. Smelser, ed. *Handbook of Sociology.* Beverly Hills, California: Sage.

2,7,10 Riley, M.W., M.E. Johnson, and A. Foner, eds. 1972. *Aging and Society. Volume III: A Sociology of Age Stratification.* New York: Russell Sage Foundation.

10,12 Roadburg, Alan. 1985. *Aging: Retirement, Leisure and Work in Canada.* Toronto: Methuen.

8     Roberge, Roger, and René Beausejour. 1988. "Use of Restraints in Chronic Care Hospitals and Nursing Homes." *Canadian Journal on Aging* 8:377–81.

16    Robertson, Duncan. 1981. "Undergraduate Medical Education in Geriatric Medicine." *Annals Royal College of Physicians and Surgeons of Canada* 14:371–73.

6     Robertson, D., K. Rockwood, and P. Stolee. 1982. "Prevalence of Cognitive Impairment in

an Elderly Population." Paper presented at the Canadian Association on Gerontology 11th Annual Scientific and Education Meeting, Winnipeg.

6 Robertson, Ian. 1981. *Sociology.* 2d ed. New York: Worth.

13 Robertson, Joan F. 1977. "Grandmotherhood: A Study of Role Conceptions." *Journal of Marriage and the Family* 39:165–74.

10 Robinson, P.K., S. Coberly, and C.E. Paul. 1985. "Work and Retirement." In Robert H. Binstock and Ethel Shanas, eds. *Handbook of Aging and the Social Sciences.* 2d ed. New York: Van Nostrand Reinhold.

11 Romanick, Gregory S. 1986. "Municipal Mechanisms for the Implementation of Granny Flats." In Susan Corke, Gregory S. Romanick, Michael Lazarowich, and Joan Simon, eds. *Granny Flats: A Housing Option for the Elderly,* Report No.13. Winnipeg: Institute of Urban Studies.

4 Romaniuc, Anatole. 1984. *Current Demographic Analysis: Fertility in Canada: From Baby-Boom to Baby-Bust.* Statistics Canada Cat. No. 91-524E Occasional. Ottawa: Minister of Supply and Services Canada.

12 Romsa, G.H., and Ronald Johnson. 1983. "A Preliminary Analysis of Retirement Satisfaction and Leisure Patterns in Canada." In Thomas L. Burton and Jan Taylor, eds. *Proceedings of the Third Canadian Congress on Leisure Research.* Canadian Association for Leisure Studies.

5 Roos, Noralou P., and Betty Havens. 1991. "Predictors of Successful Aging: A Twelve-Year Study of Manitoba Elderly." *American Journal of Public Health* 81:63–68.

8 Roos, Noralou P., and Evelyn Shapiro. 1981. "The Manitoba Longitudinal Study on Aging." *Medical Care* 19:644–57.

7 Roos, N. P., E. Shapiro, and L.L. Roos, Jr. 1984. "Aging and the Demand for Health Services: Which Aged and Whose Demand?" *The Gerontologist* 24:31–36.

2 Rose, A.M. 1965. "The Subculture of Aging: A Framework for Research in Social Gerontology." In A.M. Rose and W.A. Peterson, eds. *Older People and Their Social World.* Philadelphia: F.A. Davis.

11 Rose, Albert, and J. Grant Macdonald. 1984. *Factors Influencing the Quality of Life of Community-Based Elderly, Part II: Housing Conditions of the Elderly in Ontario.* Research paper No. 152.

11 Rosenmayr, L., and E. Kockeis. 1963. "Propositions for a Sociological Theory of Aging and the Family." *International Social Science Journal* 15:410–26.

7 Rosenthal, Carolyn J. 1983. "The Anglo-Canadian Family: A Perspective on Ethnicity and Support to the Elderly." Paper presented at the 12th Annual Scientific and Educational Meeting of the Canadian Association on Gerontology, Moncton.

13 Rosenthal, Carolyn J. 1985. "Kinkeeping in the Familial Division of Labor." *Journal of Marriage and the Family* 47:965–74.

7 Rosenthal, Carolyn J. 1986a. "Family Supports in Later Life: Does Ethnicity Make a Difference?" *The Gerontologist* 26:19–24.

7 Rosenthal, Carolyn J. 1986b. *Intergenerational Solidarity in Later Life: Ethnic Contrasts in Jewish and Anglo Families.* Programme in Gerontology, University of Toronto Research Paper Series, Research paper No. 4.

13 Rosenthal, Carolyn J. 1987a. "Aging and Intergenerational Relations in Canada." In Victor W. Marshall, ed. *Aging in Canada: Social Perspectives.* 2d ed. Toronto: Fitzhenry and Whiteside.

13 Rosenthal, Carolyn J. 1987b. "The Comforter: Providing Personal Advice and Emotional Support to Generations in the Family." *Canadian Journal on Aging* 6:228–39.

13 Rosenthal, C.J., V.W. Marshall, and J. Synge. 1980. "The Succession of Lineage Roles as Families Age." *Essence* 4:179–93.

15 Rosenzweig, Robert M. 1991. "Generational Conflict Brewing, GSA Members Warned." *Gerontology News* January.

3 Rosow, Irving. 1965. "And Then We Were Old." *Transaction* 2:20–26.

7 Rosow, Irving. 1976. "Status and Role Change Through the Life Span." In R.H. Binstock and E. Shanas, eds. *Handbook of Aging and the Social Sciences.* New York: Van Nostrand Reinhold.

6 Ross, E. 1968. "Effects of Challenging and Supportive Instructions in Verbal Learning in Older Persons." *Journal of Educational Psychology* 59:261–66.

16 Ross, Elsie. 1990. "Computers Bridge Age Gap." *Calgary Herald* 30 April.

8 Ross, Val. 1983. "The Coming Old Age Crisis." *Maclean's* 17 January.

5 Rowe, John W., and Robert L. Kahn. 1991. "Human Aging: Usual and Successful." In Harold Cox, ed. *Aging, 7th ed.* Guilford, Connecticut: Dushkin. Originally published in *Science* 1987, 237:143–49.

8 Royal College of Physicians of London. 1984.

"Medication for the Elderly." Journal of the Royal College of Physicians of London 18:7–17.

9    Royal Commission on the Status of Pensions in Ontario. 1980. *Report. Vol. II. Design for Retirement.* Toronto: Government of Ontario.

13    Rushing, W.A. 1968. "Individual Behaviour and Suicide." In J. Gibbs, ed. *Suicide.* New York: Harper and Row.

11    Rutman, Deborah, and Jonathan L. Freedman. 1988. "Anticipating Relocation: Coping Strategies and the Meaning of Home for Older People." *Canadian Journal on Aging* 7:17–31.

1    Ryan, E.B., and R.K.B. Heaven. 1988. "The Impact of Situational Context on Age-based Attitudes." *Social Behaviour* 3:105–18.

6    Sainsbury, Robert S., and Marjorie Coristine. 1986. "Affective Discrimination in Moderately to Severely Demented Patients." *Canadian Journal on Aging* 5:99–104.

3    Salas, Rafael. 1982. "Aging: A Universal Phenomenon." *Populi* 9:3–7.

14    Salmon, C., and P. McGee. 1980. *Palliative Care.* Toronto: Institutional Planning Branch, Ontario Ministry of Health.

5    Salthouse, T.A. 1984. "Effects of Age and Skill in Typing." *Journal of Gerontology* 113:345–71.

5    Salthouse, T.A. 1985. "Speed of Behavior and Its Implications for Cognition." In J. Birren and K.W. Schaie, eds. *Handbook of the Psychology of Aging.* 2d ed. New York: Van Nostrand Reinhold Company.

10    Sammartino, F.J. 1987. "The Effect of Health on Retirement." *Social Security Bulletin* 50:31–47.

6    Sanders, R.E., and J.A. Sanders. 1978. "Long-Term Durability and Transfer of Enhanced Conceptual Performance in the Elderly." *Journal of Gerontology* 33:408–12.

6    Sanders, R.E., M.D. Murphy, F.A. Schmitt, and K.K. Walsh. 1980. "Age Differences in Free Recall Rehearsal Strategies." *Journal of Gerontology* 35:550–58.

11    Saskatchewan Housing Corporation. 1984. *Housing Need in Saskatchewan.* Regina: Saskatchewan Housing Corporation.

11    Saskatchewan Housing Corporation. No date. *Enriched Housing.* Regina: Saskatchewan Housing Corporation.

14    Saunders, Cicely. 1984. "St. Christopher's Hospice." In Edwin S. Shneidman, ed. *Death: Current Perspectives.* 3d ed. Palo Alto, California: Mayfield.

8    Schafer, A. 1985. "Restraints and the Elderly: When Safety and Autonomy Conflict." *Canadian Medical Association Journal* 132: 1257–60.

6    Schaie, K. Warner. 1959. "Cross-Sectional Methods in the Study of Psychological Aspects of Aging." *Journal of Gerontology* 14:208–15.

2,7    Schaie, K. Warner. 1968. "Age Changes and Age Differences." In Bernice L. Neugarten, ed. *Middle Age and Aging.* Chicago: University of Chicago Press.

6    Schaie, K. Warner. 1975. "Age Changes in Adult Intelligence." In Diana S. Woodruff and J.E. Birren, eds. *Aging: Scientific Perspectives and Social Issues.* New York: D. Van Nostrand.

6    Schaie, K. Warner. 1990a. "Intellectual Development in Adulthood." In James E. Birren and K. Warner Schaie, eds. *Handbook of the Psychology of Aging.* 3d ed. San Diego: Academic Press.

6    Schaie, K. Warner. 1990b. "The Optimization of Cognitive Functioning in Old Age: Predictions Based on Cohort-Sequential and Longitudinal Data." In Paul B. Baltes and Margaret M. Baltes, eds. *Successful Aging: Perspectives from the Behavioral Sciences.* Cambridge: Cambridge University Press.

2,6    Schaie, K. Warner, and G. Labouvie-Vief. 1974. "Generational Versus Ontogenetic Components of Change in Adult Cognitive Behavior: A Fourteen-Year Cross-Sequential Study." *Development Psychology* 10:305–20.

13    Schlesinger, Benjamin. 1983. "Institutional Life: The Canadian Experience." In Ruth B. Weg, ed. *Sexuality in the Later Years: Roles and Behavior.* New York: Academic Press.

5    Schneider, E.L., and J.A. Brody. 1983. "Aging, Natural Death and the Compression of Morbidity: Another View." *New England Journal of Medicine* 309:854–56.

5    Schneider, E.L., and J.D. Reed. 1985. "Modulations of Aging Processes." In Caleb E. Finch and Edward L. Schneider, eds. *Handbook of the Biology of Aging.* 2d ed. New York: Van Nostrand Reinhold.

1    Schonfield, David. 1982. "Who Is Stereotyping Whom and Why?" *The Gerontologist* 22:267–72.

6,11    Schooler, Carmi. 1990. "Psychosocial Factors and Effective Cognitive Functioning in Adulthood." In James E. Birren and K. Warner Schaie, eds. *Handbook of the Psychology of Aging.* 3d ed. San Diego: Academic Press.

13    Schorr, A. 1980. " ' .... thy father and thy mother .... ' A Second Look at Filial Responsibility and Social Policy." Social Security Administration Publication 13-11953. Washington, D.

C.: U.S. Department of Health and Human Services.

2    Schroots, Johannes J.F. 1988. "On Growing, Formative Change, and Aging." In James E. Birren and Vern L. Bengtson, eds. *Emergent Theories of Aging*. New York: Springer.

11   Schull, Christiane. 1981. "Bag Ladies." *Today Magazine* 15 April.

3,10  Schulz, James H. 1980. *The Economics of Aging*. 2d ed. Belmont, California: Wadsworth.

10   Schulz, James H. 1985. *The Economics of Aging*. 3d ed. Belmont, California: Wadsworth Publishing.

14   Schulz, Richard. 1978. *The Psychology of Death, Dying, and Bereavement*. Reading, Massachusetts: Addison-Wesley.

2    Schutz, Alfred. 1967. *The Phenomenology of the Social World*. Evanston, Illinois: Northwestern University Press.

13   Schwartz, A.N. 1979. "Psychological Dependency: An Emphasis on the Later Years." In P.K. Ragan, ed. *Aging Parents*. Los Angeles: University of Southern California.

6    Schwartzman, A.E., D. Gold, D. Andres, T.Y. Arbuckle, and J. Chaikelson. 1987. "Stability of Intelligence: A 40-Year Follow-Up." *Canadian Journal of Psychology* 41:244–56.

8    Schwenger, Cope, and M. Gross. 1980. "Institutional Care and Institutionalization of the Elderly in Canada." In Victor W. Marshall, ed. *Aging in Canada*. Toronto: Fitzhenry and Whiteside.

14   Scitovsky, A.A. 1984. "The High Cost of Dying: What Do the Data Show?" *Milbank Memorial Fund Quarterly* 62:591–608.

12   Searle, Mark S. 1987. *Leisure and Aging in Manitoba: A Report to Manitoba Culture, Heritage and Recreation*. Winnipeg: Faculty of Physical Education and Recreation Studies, University of Manitoba.

12   Searle, Mark S., and Michael J. Mahon. 1991. "Leisure Education in a Day Hospital: The Effects of Selected Social-Psychological Variables Among Older Adults." Paper presented at the 1990 National Recreation and Park Association Leisure Research Symposium.

5    Secretary of State of Canada. 1986. *Profile of Disabled Persons in Canada*. Ottawa: Minister of Supply and Services.

8    Segall, Alexander. 1987. "Age Differences in Lay Conceptions of Health and Self-Care Responses to Illness." *Canadian Journal on Aging* 6:47–65.

1    Senate of Canada. 1966. *Final Report of the Special Committee of the Senate on Aging*. Ottawa: Queen's Printer.

1,9  Senate of Canada. 1979. *Retirement Without*
10,15 *Tears: A Report of the Special Senate Committee on Retirement Age Policies* (Croll Commission). Ottawa: Minister of Supply and Services.

10   Senior Citizens' Job Bureau. 1986. *Report to the Board of Directors*. Winnipeg: Senior Citizens' Bureau.

11   Senior Citizens' Provincial Council. 1981. *Regina Social Support Survey*. Regina, Saskatchewan: Senior Citizens' Provincial Council.

11   Senior Citizens' Provincial Council. 1982. *A Survey of the Transportation Needs of the Rural Elderly*. Regina, Saskatchewan: Senior Citizens' Provincial Council.

8,13  Senior Citizens' Provincial Council. 1983. *Profile '83: The Senior Population in Saskatchewan. 3: Social Resources*. Regina: Senior Citizens' Provincial Council.

7    Senior Citizens' Provincial Council. 1988. *A Study of Unmet Needs of Off-Reserve Indian and Metis Elderly in Saskatchewan*. Regina: Senior Citizens' Provincial Council.

7    Sermat, Vello. 1978. "Sources of Loneliness." *Essence* 2:271–76.

13   Shanas, Ethel. 1967. "Family Help Patterns and Social Class in Three Societies." *Journal of Marriage and the Family* 29:257–66.

13   Shanas, Ethel. 1979. "The Family as a Social Support System in Old Age." *The Gerontologist* 19:169–74.

13   Shanas, E., P. Townsend, D. Wedderburn, H. Friis, P. Milhoj, and J. Stehouwer. 1968. *Older People in Three Industrial Societies*. New York: Atherton Press.

7,8,14 Shapiro, Evelyn. 1983. "Impending Death and the Use of Hospitals by the Elderly." *Journal of the American Geriatrics Society* 31:348–51.

8    Shapiro, Evelyn. 1988. "Hospital Use by Elderly Manitobans Resulting from an Injury." *Canadian Journal on Aging* 8:125–33.

8    Shapiro, Evelyn, and Leslie L. Roos. 1984. "Using Health Care: Rural/Urban Differences Among the Manitoba Elderly." *The Gerontologist* 24:270–74.

10   Shapiro, Evelyn, and Noralou P. Roos. 1982. "Retired and Employed Elderly Persons: Their Utilization of Health Care Services." *The Gerontologist* 22:187–93.

8    Shapiro, E., R.B. Tate, and N.P. Roos. 1987. "Do Nursing Homes Reduce Hospital Use?" *Medical Care* 25:1–8.

8    Shapiro, Evelyn, and Noralou P. Roos. 1986. "High Users of Hospital Days." *Canadian Journal on Aging* 5:165–74.

8    Shapiro, Evelyn, and N.P. Roos. 1987. "Predictors, Patterns and Consequences of Nursing-Home Use in One Canadian Province." In Victor W. Marshall, ed. *Aging in Canada: Social Perspectives.* 2d ed. Toronto: Fitzhenry and Whiteside.

8    Shapiro, Evelyn, and Robert B. Tate. 1985. "Predictors of Long Term Care Facility Use Among the Elderly." *Canadian Journal on Aging* 4:11–19.

8    Shapiro, Evelyn, and Robert Tate. 1988a. "Survival Patterns of Nursing Home Admissions and Their Policy Implications." *Canadian Journal of Public Health* 79:268–74.

8    Shapiro, Evelyn, and Robert Tate. 1988b. "Who Is Really at Risk of Institutionalization?" *The Gerontologist* 28:237–45.

8    Shapiro, Evelyn, and Linda M. Webster. 1984. "Nursing Home Utilization Patterns for All Manitoba Admissions, 1974-1981." *The Gerontologist* 24:610–15.

3    Sharp, H.S. 1981. "Old Age Among the Chipewyan." In P.T. Amoss and S. Harrell, eds. *Other Ways of Growing Old: Anthropological Perspectives.* Stanford, California: Stanford University Press.

14   Shedletsky, Ralph, and Rory Fisher. 1986. "Terminal Illness: Attitudes in Both an Acute and an Extended Care Teaching Hospital." *Journal of Palliative Care* 2:16–21.

13   Shedletsky, R., R. Fisher, and G. Nadon. 1982. "Assessment of Palliative Care for Dying Hospitalized Elderly." *Canadian Journal on Aging* 1:11–15.

12   Shell, Donna J. 1982. *Protection of the Elderly: A Study of Elder Abuse.* Winnipeg: Manitoba Council on Aging.

12   Shephard, Roy J. 1978. *Physical Activity and Aging.* London: Croom Helm.

12   Shephard, Roy J. 1986. "Physical Activity and Aging in a Post-Industrial Society." In Barry D. McPherson, ed. *Sport and Aging: The 1984 Olympic Scientific Congress Proceedings.* Vol. 5. Champaign, Illinois: Human Kinetics.

12   Shephard, Roy J. 1990. "Measuring Physical Activity in the Elderly: Some Implications for Nutrition." *Canadian Journal on Aging* 9:188–203.

14   Shneidman, Edwin S. 1984. "Malignancy: Dialogues with Life-Threatening Illnesses." In Edwin S. Shneidman, ed. *Death: Current Perspectives.* 3d ed. Palo Alto, California: Mayfield.

5    Shock, N.W. 1977. "Systems Integration." In C.E. Finch and L. Hayflick, eds. *Handbook of the Biology of Aging.* New York: Van Nostrand Reinhold.

12   Sidney, K.H., and Shephard, R.J. 1978. *Exercise and Aging: The Scientific Basis.* Hillsdale, N.J.: Enslow Publishers.

12   Sijpkes, P., M. MacLean, and D. Brown. 1983. "Hanging Around the Mall." *Recreation Canada* February.

3    Simmons, L.W. 1960. "Aging in Preindustrial Societies." In C. Tibbitts, ed. *Handbook of Social Gerontology: Societal Aspects of Aging.* Chicago: University of Chicago Press.

3    Simmons, L.W. 1970. *The Role of the Aged in Primitive Society.* New Haven, Connecticut: Yale University.

5    Simmons-Tropea, Daryl, and Richard Osborn. 1987. "Disease, Survival and Death: The Health Status of Canada's Elderly." In Victor W. Marshall, ed. *Aging in Canada.* 2d ed. Toronto: Fitzhenry and Whiteside.

6    Simonton, D.K. 1977. "Creative Productivity, Age, and Stress: A Biographical Time-Series Analysis of 10 Classical Composers." *Journal of Personality and Social Psychology* 35:791–804.

6    Simonton, Dean Keith. 1990. "Creativity and Wisdom in Aging." In James E. Birren and K. Warner Schaie, eds. *Handbook of the Psychology of Aging.* 3d ed. San Diego: Academic Press.

10   Simpson, I.H., K.W. Back, and J.C. McKinney. 1966. "Continuity of Work and Retirement Activities, and Self-Evaluation." In Ida H. Simpson and John C. McKinney, eds. *Social Aspects of Aging.* Durham, North Carolina: Duke University Press.

8    Sinclair, Douglas. 1984. "A New Approach to Geriatric Institutional Care." *Canadian Family Physician* 30:1373–76.

6    Ska, Bernadette, and Jean-Luc Nespoulous. 1988. "Encoding Strategies and Recall Performance of a Complex Figure by Normal Elderly Subjects." *Canadian Journal on Aging* 7:408–16.

14   Skelton, David. 1982. "The Hospice Movement: A Human Approach to Palliative Care." *Canadian Medical Association Journal* 126:556–58.

12   Smith, E.L. 1982. "Exercise for Prevention of Osteoporosis: A Review." *Physician and Sportsmedicine* 10:72–83.

5    Smith, E.L., W. Reddan, and P.E. Smith. 1981. "Physical Activity and Calcium Modalities for Bone Mineral Increase in Aged Women." *Medical Science Sports Exercise* 13:60–64.

11   Smith, Wendy. 1979. *Single Old Men on Main*

*Street: An Evaluation of Jack's Hotel.* Winnipeg: Canada Mortgage and Housing Corporation.

6    Smyer, M.A., S.H. Zarit, and S.H. Qualls. 1990. "Psychological Intervention with the Aging Individual." In James E. Birren and K. Warner Schaie, eds. *Handbook of the Psychology of Aging.* 3d ed. San Diego: Academic Press.

13   Snell, James G. 1990. "Filial Responsibility Laws in Canada: An Historical Study." *Canadian Journal on Aging* 9:268–77.

10   Snell, M. Leslie, and Kathleen Brown. 1987. "Financial Strategies of the Recently Retired." *Canadian Journal on Aging* 6:290–303.

13   Snider, Earle L. 1981. "The Role of Kin in Meeting Health Care Needs of the Elderly." *Canadian Journal of Sociology* 6:325–36.

3    Sokolovsky, Jay, ed. 1990. *The Cultural Context of Aging: Worldwide Perspectives.* New York: Bergin & Garvey.

11   Sokolovsky, J., and C. Cohen. 1981. "Measuring Social Interaction of the Urban Elderly: A Methodological Synthesis." *International Journal of Aging and Human Development* 12:233–44.

10   Solem, Per Erik. 1976. *Paid Work After Retirement Age, and Mortality in Retirement: Norwegian Experience.* Oslo: Norwegian Institute of Gerontology.

1    Solicitor General of Canada. 1983. *Canadian Urban Victimization Survey. Bulletin 1: Victims of Crime.* Ottawa: Minister of Supply and Services.

1    Solicitor General of Canada. 1985. *The Canadian Urban Victimization Survey. Bulletin 6: Criminal Victimization of Elderly Canadians.* Ottawa: Minister of Supply and Services Canada.

14   Somerville, M.S. 1989. "Legal Issues in Surgical Care of Elderly Persons." *Canadian Journal on Aging* 8:128–43.

14   Southall, H. 1982. *A Survey of Palliative Care Programs and Services in Canada.* Toronto: Palliative Care Foundation.

11   Spence, David. 1986. "Granny Flats: The Ontario Demonstration." In Gloria Gutman and Norman Blackie, eds. *Aging in Place: Housing Adaptations and Options for Remaining in the Community.* Burnaby, British Columbia: The Gerontology Research Centre, Simon Fraser University.

8    Spiers, Michael. 1988. "Empowerment in Long-Term Care: Platitude or Perturbation." Paper presented at the joint meeting of the CESCE/SAAC/CAMA/ACAM Annual Congress, Saskatoon, May.

5    Spirduso, W.W. 1980. "Physical Fitness, Aging, and Psychomotor Speed: A Review." *Journal of Gerontology* 35:850–65.

5    Spirduso, W.W. 1982. "Physical Fitness in Relation to Motor Aging." In J.A. Mortimer, F.J. Pirozzolo, and G.J. Maletta, eds. *The Aging Motor System.* New York: Praeger.

5    Spirduso, W.W., and P.G. MacRae. 1990. "Motor Performance and Aging." In James E. Birren and K. Warner Schaie, eds. *Handbook of the Psychology of Aging.* 3d ed. San Diego: Academic Press.

12   Spirduso, W.W., and P.G. MacRae. In Press. "Physical Activity and Quality of Life in the Frail Elderly." In J.E. Birren, D.E. Deutchman, J. Lubben, and J. Rowe, eds. *The Concept and Measurement of the Quality of Life in the Frail Elderly.* New York: Academic Press.

12   Stacey, C., A. Kozma, and M.J. Stones. 1985. "Simple Cognitive and Behavioral Changes Resulting from Improved Physical Fitness in Persons over 50 Years of Age." *Canadian Journal on Aging* 4:67–74.

13   Staff. 1985. "Volunteer Granny Becomes 'Friend' to All of the Family." *Winnipeg Sun* 22 December.

8    Staff. 1991. *Seniors Today* January 21:3.

10   Stagner, Ross. 1985. "Aging in Industry." In James E. Birren and K. Warner Schaie, eds. *Handbook of the Psychology of Aging.* 2d ed. New York: Van Nostrand Reinhold.

12   Starr, Bernard D., and Marcella Bakur Weiner. 1981. *The Starr-Weiner Report on Sex & Sexuality in the Mature Years.* New York: Stein and Day.

4    Statistics Canada. 1968. *1966 Census of Canada,* Vol. 1 (1–11). Ottawa: Queen's Printer.

10   Statistics Canada, Labour Division. 1972. *The Labour Force–January, 1972.* Cat. No. 71–001. Ottawa: Minister of Supply and Services.

4    Statistics Canada. 1973. *Census of Canada. Bulletin 1: 2–3.* (1971 Census). Ottawa: Minister of Supply and Services.

4    Statistics Canada. 1975. *Technical Report on Population Projections for Canada and the Provinces. 1976–2001.* Cat. No. 91–516. Occasional. Ottawa: Statistics Canada.

11   Statistics Canada. 1978a. *Family, Expenditure in Canada. Volume I. Preliminary Estimates: Eight Cities.* Cat. No. 62-549. Ottawa: Minister of Supply and Services.

4    Statistics Canada. 1978b. *1976 Census of Canada. Advanced Release.* Ottawa: Minister of Supply and Services.

4    Statistics Canada. 1978c. *Vital Statistics. Vol. I.*

*Births. 1975 and 1976.* Cat. No. 84–204. Ottawa: Statistics Canada.

14      Statistics Canada. 1978d. *Vital Statistics. Vol. III. Death. 1976.* Ottawa: Health Division, Vital Statistics and Diseases Registries Section, Minister of Supply and Services.

4,10    Statistics Canada. 1979a. *Canada's Elderly.* Cat. No. 98–800E. Ottawa: Minister of Supply and Services.

10      Statistics Canada, Labour Force Survey Division. 1979b. *The Labour Force–January. 1979.* Cat. No. 71–001. Ottawa: Minister of Supply and Services.

11      Statistics Canada. 1980a. *Expenditure Patterns and Income Adequacy for the Elderly. 1969-1976.* Cat. No. 13–575. Ottawa: Minister of Supply and Services.

13      Statistics Canada. 1980b. *Perspectives Canada III.* Cat. No. 11–511E. Ottawa: Minister of Supply and Services.

8       Statistics Canada. 1980c. *Surgical Procedures and Treatments 1976.* Cat. No. 82–208. Ottawa: Minister of Supply and Services Canada.

4       Statistics Canada. 1981a. *Canada Year Book 1980–81.* Ottawa: Minister of Supply and Services.

12      Statistics Canada. 1981b. *National Time Use Pilot Study.* Ottawa: Statistics Canada.

8       Statistics Canada. 1981c. *Surgical Procedures and Treatments 1977.* Cat. No. 82–208. Ottawa: Minister of Supply and Services.

7       Statistics Canada. 1984a. *Canada's Immigrants.* Cat. No. 99–936 Ottawa: Minister of Supply and Services.

4,7     Statistics Canada. 1984b. *The Elderly in Canada.* Cat. No. 99–932. Ottawa: Minister of Supply and Services.

11      Statistics Canada. 1984c. *Household Facilities by Income and Other Characteristics. 1983.* Cat. No. 13–567. Ottawa: Minister of Supply and Services.

13      Statistics Canada. 1984d. *Life Tables. Canada and Provinces. 1980-82.* Cat. No. 84–532. Ottawa: Minister of Supply and Services.

7       Statistics Canada. 1985a. *Language in Canada.* Cat. No. 99–935. Ottawa: Minister of Supply and Services.

13      Statistics Canada. 1985b. *Women in Canada: A Statistical Report.* Cat. No. 89–503E. Ottawa: Minister of Supply and Services.

4       Statistics Canada. 1986a. *Ethnic Diversity in Canada.* Cat. No. 98–132. Ottawa: Minister of Supply and Services.

10      Statistics Canada. 1986b. *The Labour Force–*

*August, 1986.* Cat. No. 71–001. Ottawa: Minister of Supply and Services.

4       Statistics Canada. 1987a. *Age, Sex and Marital Status: The Nation.* Cat. No. 93–101. Ottawa: Minister of Supply and Services.

2,4,5,  Statistics Canada. 1987b. *Health and Social Sup-*
8,12    *port, 1985: General Social Survey Analysis Series.* Cat. No. 11–612E, No. 1. Ottawa: Supply and Services.

4       Statistics Canada. 1987c. *Special Projections 1991–2031.* Unpublished data. September. Supplied to Statistics Canada, Health Division, Social Security Section. Ottawa: Minister of Supply and Services.

5       Statistics Canada. 1988. *Health and Activity Limitation Survey (HALS).* Ottawa: Minister of Supply and Services.

4,12    Statistics Canada. 1989a. *Canada Year Book 1990.* Cat. No. 11–402E/1990. Ottawa: Minister of Supply and Services.

12      Statistics Canada. 1989b. *Family Expenditure in Canada, 1986.* Cat. No. 62–555. Ottawa: Minister of Supply and Services.

12      Statistics Canada. 1989c. *Survey of Literacy Skills Used in Daily Activities.* Ottawa: Minister of Supply and Services.

8,15    Statistics Canada. 1990a. *Canada Year Book.* Ottawa: Minister of Supply and Services Canada.

5       Statistics Canada. 1990b. *Highlights: Disabled Persons in Canada.* Cat. No. 82–602. Ottawa: Minister of Supply and Services.

9       Statistics Canada. 1990c. *Income Distribution by Size in Canada 1989.* Cat. No. 13–207. Ottawa: Minister of Supply and Services.

9       Statistics Canada. 1990d. *Pension Plans in Canada 1988.* Cat. No. 74–401. Ottawa: Minister of Supply and Services.

1,2,4,  Statistics Canada. 1990e. *A Portrait of Seniors in*
6,8-13, *Canada.* Cat. No. 89–519. Ottawa: Minister of
15      Supply and Services.

4       Statistics Canada. 1991. "Life Tables, Canada and Provinces 1985–1987." Cat. No. 82–0038. *Health Reports, Supplement No. 13. Vol. 2. No. 4.* Ottawa: Minister of Supply and Services.

3       Stearns, Peter N. 1967. *European Society in Upheaval.* New York: Macmillan.

3       Stearns, Peter N. 1977. *Old Age in European Society: The Case of France.* London: Croom Helm.

13      Stearns, P. J. 1986. "Old Age Family Conflict: The Perspective of the Past." In K.A. Pillemer and R.S. Wolf, eds. *Elder Abuse: Conflict in the Family.* Dover, Mass.: Auburn House.

13       Stevenson, C. 1985. *Family Abuse of the Elderly in Alberta.* Unpublished manuscript prepared for the Senior Citizens Bureau, Alberta Social Services and Community Health.

11       Stewart, G. 1982. "Programme Principles." In Fitness and Amateur Sport, ed. *National Conference on Fitness in the Third Age: Workshop Discussion Papers.* Ottawa: Government of Canada.

12       Stirling, D.R., G. Miller, P. Barker, G. Rowden, S. Meehan, and M. Ralston. 1986. "Exercise: An Effective Strategy to Activate Seniors." In Barry D. McPherson, ed. *Sport and Aging: The 1984 Olympic Scientific Congress Proceedings, Vol. 5.* Champaign, Illinois: Human Kinetics.

8        Stockwell, H., and E. Vayda. 1979. "Variations in Surgery in Ontario." *Medical Care* 17:390–96.

13       Stolar, G.E., M.A. Hill, and A. Toblin. 1986. "Family Disengagement—Myth or Reality: A Follow-Up Study After Geriatric Assessment." *Canadian Journal on Aging* 5:113–23.

6        Stone, Leroy O. 1986. "On the Demography of Dementia." In M.R. Easterwood, chair. *Alzheimer's Disease and Other Dementias: The Magnitude and Management of the Problem.* Symposium presented at the Clarke Institute of Psychiatry, Toronto.

13       Stone, Leroy O. 1987. "Cohort Aging and Support Network Help Capacity." In George Maddox and E.W. Busse, eds. *Aging: The Universal Human Experience.* New York: Springer.

2,12,    Stone, Leroy O. 1988. *Family and Friendship Ties*
13       *Among Canada's Seniors.* Cat. No. 89–508. Ottawa: Minister of Supply and Services.

4        Stone, Leroy O., and Susan Fletcher. 1980. *A Profile of Canada's Older Population.* Montreal: Institute for Research on Public Policy.

5,8,     Stone, Leroy O., and Susan Fletcher. 1986. *The*
13,15    *Seniors Boom.* Statistics Canada. Cat. No. 89–515E. Ottawa: Minister of Supply and Services.

11       Stone, Leroy O., and Susan Fletcher. 1987. "The Hypothesis of Age Patterns in Living Arrangements Passages." In Victor W. Marshall, ed. *Aging in Canada.* 2d ed. Toronto: Fitzhenry and Whiteside.

1,4,     Stone, Leroy O., and Hubert Frenken. 1988.
8,11     *Canada's Seniors.* Cat. No. 98–121. Ottawa: Minister of Supply and Services.

9        Stone, Leroy O., and Michael MacLean. 1979. *Future Income Prospects for Canada's Senior Citizens.* Toronto: Butterworths.

12       Stones, M.J., and A. Kozma. 1980. "Adult Age Trends in Record Running Performances." *Experimental Aging Research* 6:407–16.

12       Stones, M.J., and A. Kozma. 1982. "Cross-Sectional, Longitudinal, and Secular Age Trends in Athletic Performance." *Experimental Aging Research* 8:185–88.

8        Stones, M.J., B. Dornan, and A. Kozma. 1989. "The Prediction of Mortality in Elderly Institution Residents." *Journal of Gerontology: Social Sciences* 44:P72–P79.

13       Strain, Laurel A., and Neena L. Chappell. 1982a. "Confidants: Do They Make a Difference in Quality of Life?" *Research on Aging* 4:479–502.

12       Strain, Laurel A., and Neena L. Chapell. 1982b. "Outdoor Recreation and the Rural Elderly: Participation, Problems and Needs." *Therapeutic Recreation Journal* 16:42–48.

7        Strain, Laurel A., and Neena L. Chappell. 1984. "Social Support Among Elderly Canadian Natives: A Comparison with Elderly Non-Natives." Paper presented at the Canadian Association on Gerontology 13th Annual Scientific and Educational Meetings, Vancouver.

5        Strehler, B. 1977. *Time, Cells and Aging.* 2d ed. New York: Academic Press.

2        Streib, Gordon F., and Robert H. Binstock. 1990. "Aging and the Social Sciences: Changes in the Field." In Robert H. Binstock and Linda K. George, eds. *Handbook of Aging and the Social Sciences.* 3d ed. San Diego: Academic Press.

2        Streib, Gordon F., and Carroll J. Bourg. 1984. "Age Stratification Theory, Inequality, and Social Change." *Comparative Social Research* 7:63–77.

1        Streib, Gordon, and Clement Schneider. 1971. *Retirement in American Society.* Ithaca, N.Y.: Cornell University Press.

11       Streib, Gordon F., N.E. Folts, and A.J. LaGreca. 1985. "Autonomy, Power, and Decision-Making in 36 Retirement Communities." *The Gerontologist* 25:403–09.

8        Strike, Carol. 1989. "Residential Care." *Canadian Social Trends* Autumn:25–26.

10       Stryckman, Judith. 1987. "Work Sharing and the Older Worker in a Unionized Setting." In Victor W. Marshall, ed. *Aging in Canada: Social Perspectives.* 2d ed. Toronto: Fitzhenry and Whiteside.

13       Stull, Donald E., and Annemarie Scarisbrick-Hauser. 1989. "Never-Married Elderly: A Reassessment with Implications for Long-Term Care Policy." *Research on Aging* 11:124–39.

8        Sturdy, Catherine, and Joseph A. Tindale. 1985. "The Social Organization of Health Care Provision to the Elderly in Ontario." Paper presented to the Conference of the Canadian Asso-

ciation on Gerontology 14th Annual Scientific and Educational Meetings, Hamilton.

**14** Subcommittee on Institutional Program Guidelines. 1989. *Palliative-Care Services.* Health and Welfare Canada. Cat. No. H39-32/1989E. Ottawa: Minister of Supply and Services.

**14** Sudnow, David. 1967. *Passing On.* Englewood Cliffs, New Jersey: Prentice-Hall.

**7** Sugiman, Pamela, and Harry Nishio. 1983. "Socialization and Cultural Duality Among Aging Japanese Canadians." *Canadian Ethnic Studies* 15:17–35.

**8** Sulman, Joanne, and Sue Wilkinson. 1989. "An Activity Group for Long-Stay Elderly Patients in an Acute Care Hospital: Program Evaluation." *Canadian Journal on Aging* 8:34–50.

**5** Surwillo, W. 1963. "The Relation of Simple Response Time to Brain-wave Frequency and the Effects of Age." *Electroencephalography and Clinical Neurophysiology* 15:105–14.

**3** Synge, Jane. 1980. "Work and Family Support Patterns of the Aged in the Early Twentieth Century." In Victor W. Marshall, ed. *Aging in Canada: Social Perspectives.* Toronto, Ontario: Fitzhenry & Whiteside.

**13** Synge, Jane. No date. "Women as Telephoners: On the Importance of Phoning and Writing in Maintaining Kin and Friendship Ties in Middle and Old Age." Personal communication.

**13** Synge, Jane, and M. Luxton. 1984. "Patterns of Sociability and Companionship Among the Middle Aged and the Aged with Special Reference to Elderly Women." Paper presented at the 13th Annual Meeting of the Canadian Sociology and Anthropology Association.

**13** Szasz, George. 1980. "The Sexual Consequences of Aging." In John Crawford, ed. *The Family in Later Life: Canadian Gerontological Collection III. Selected Papers 1980.* Winnipeg: Canadian Association on Gerontology.

**10** Szinovacz, M.E. 1982. "Introduction: Research on Women's Retirement." In M. Szinovacz, ed. *Women's Retirement.* Beverly Hills, California: Sage.

**10** Szinovacz, M.E. 1983. "Beyond the Hearth: Older Women and Retirement." In Elizabeth W. Markson, ed. *Older Women: Issues and Prospects.* Lexington, Massachusetts: D.C. Heath.

**6** Taub, H.A. 1979. "Comprehension and Memory of Prose Materials by Young and Old Adults." *Experimental Aging Research* 5:3–13.

**5** Tavris, Carol. 1991. "Old Age Is Not What It Used to Be." In Harold Cox, ed. *Aging: Annual Editions,* 7th ed. Guilford, Connecticut: Dushkin.

**12** Thacker, Charlene, and Mark Novak. 1991. "Middle-aged Re-entry Women and Student Role Supports: Application of a Life Event Model." *Canadian Journal of Higher Education* forthcoming.

**14** Thompson, Edward H. 1985–86. "Palliative and Curative Care: Nurses' Attitudes Toward Dying and Death in the Hospital Setting." *Omega* 16:233–42.

**1,13** Thompson, J. Victor. 1989. "The Elderly and Their Informal Social Networks." *Canadian Journal on Aging* 8:319–32.

**5** Thompson, L.W., and G.R. Marsh. 1973. "Psychophysiological Studies of Aging." In C. Eisdorfer and M.P. Lawton, eds. *The Psychology of Adult Development and Aging.* Washington, D.C.: American Psychological Association.

**5** Thompson, M.E. and W.F. Forbes. 1990. "The Various Definitions of Biological Aging." *Canadian Journal on Aging* 9:91–94.

**13** Thorman, George. 1980. *Family Violence.* Springfield, Illinois: Charles C. Thomas.

**8** Thornton, C., S.M. Dunstan, and P. Kemper. 1988. "The Evaluation of the National Long Term Care Demonstration. The Effect of Channeling on Health and Long-Term Care Costs." *Health Services Research* 23:129–42.

**8** Thurston, N.E., D.E. Larsen, A.W. Rademaker, and J.C. Kerr. 1982. "Health Status of the Rural Elderly: A Picture of Health." Paper presented at the 11th Annual Scientific and Educational Meetings of the Canadian Association on Gerontology, Winnipeg, Manitoba.

**5** *Time.* 1986a. "Extra Years for Extra Effort." 17 March.

**5** *Time.* 1986b. "Milestones: Died: Shigechiyo Izumi." 3 March.

**7** Tindale, J. 1980. "Identity Maintenance Processes of Old Poor Men." In Victor W. Marshall, ed. *Aging in Canada.* Toronto: Fitzhenry and Whiteside.

**4** Tindale, J., and V.W. Marshall. 1980. "A Generational Conflict Perspective for Gerontology." In Victor W. Marshall ed. *Aging in Canada.* Toronto: Fitzhenry and Whiteside.

**10** Tindale, J. 1991. *Older Workers in an Aging Work Force.* Cat. No. H71-2/1-10-1991E. Ottawa: Minister of Supply and Services.

**12** Tinsley, H.E.A., S.L. Colbs, J.D. Teaff, and N. Kaufman. 1987. "The Relationship of Age, Gender, Health and Economic Status to the Psychological Benefits Older Persons Report from Participation in Leisure Activities." *Leisure Sciences* 9:53–65.

4　Torrance, George M. 1981. "Introduction: Socio-Historical Overview: The Development of the Canadian Health System." In D. Coburn, C. D'Arcy, P. New, and G. Torrance, eds. *Health and Canadian Society: Sociological Perspectives.* Toronto: Fitzhenry and Whiteside.

8　Torrance, George M. 1987. "Socio-Historical Overview." In D. Coburn, C. D'Arcy, G. Torrance, and P. New, eds. *Health and Canadian Society: Sociological Perspectives.* 2d ed. Toronto: Fitzhenry and Whiteside.

5　Toufexis, Anastasia. 1986. "New Rub for the Skin Game." *Time* March 31.

8　Tourigny-Rivard, Marie-France, and Marilyn Drury. 1987. "The Effects of Monthly Psychiatric Consultation in a Nursing Home." *The Gerontologist* 27:363–66.

10　Tournier, Paul. 1972. *Learning to Grow Old.* London: SCM Press.

1　Towler, John C. 1983. "Ageism in Children's Popular Literature and Television." Paper presented at the Canadian Association on Gerontology 12th Annual Scientific and Educational Meeting, Moncton.

13　Treas, J. 1977. "Family Support Systems for the Aged, Some Social and Demographic Considerations." *The Gerontologist* 17:486–91.

4　Treasury Board Secretariat. 1977. *Changing Population and the Impact on Government Age-Specific Expenditures.* Ottawa: Planning Branch Effectiveness Evaluation Division, Treasury Board Secretariat.

15　Trela, James. 1976. "Status Inconsistency and Political Action in Old Age." In Jaber Gubrium, ed. *Time, Roles, and Self in Old Age.* New York: Human Sciences Press.

3　Trexler, Richard C. 1982. "A Widows' Asylum of the Renaissance: The Orbatello of Florence." In Peter N. Stearns, ed. *Old Age in Preindustrial Society.* New York: Holmes & Meier.

7　Trovato, Frank. 1988. "Suicide in Canada: A Further Look at the Effects of Age, Period and Cohort." *Canadian Journal of Public Health* 79:37–44.

4　Tucker, Richard D., and Victor Marshall. 1988. "Descriptive Overview of Older Anglophone Canadians in Florida." In Larry C. Mullins and Richard D. Tucker, eds. *Snowbirds in the Sun Belt: Older Canadians in Florida.* Tampa, Florida: International Exchange Center on Gerontology.

4　Tucker, Richard D., Victor W. Marshall, Charles F. Longino, Jr., and Larry C. Mullins. 1988. "Older Anglophone Canadian Snowbirds in Florida: A Descriptive Profile." *Canadian Journal on Aging* 7:218–32.

8　Tuominen, Jean D. 1988. "Prescription Drugs and the Elderly in B.C." *Canadian Journal on Aging* 8:174–82.

3　Turnbull, Colin. 1961. *The Forest People.* New York: Simon and Schuster.

13　Turner, Barbara F., and Catherine Adams. 1983. "The Sexuality of Older Women." In Elizabeth W. Markson, ed. *Older Women: Issues and Prospects.* Lexington, Massachusetts: D.C. Heath.

11　Turner, L., and E. Mangum. 1982. *Report on Housing Choice of Older Americans. Summary of Survey Findings and Recommendations for Practitioners.* Bryn Mawr, Pennsylvania: The Graduate School of Social Work and Social Research, Bryn Mawr College.

7　Ujimoto, V.K. 1983. "Introduction: Ethnicity and Aging in Canada." *Canadian Ethnic Studies* 15:iii-vii.

7　Ujimoto, Victor K. 1987. "The Ethnic Dimension of Aging in Canada." In Victor W. Marshall, ed. *Aging in Canada: Social Perspectives.* 2d. ed. Toronto: Fitzhenry and Whiteside.

4　United Nations. 1984. *Periodical on Aging.* 1(1): Tables 3,10,17,24,31,38. New York: Department of International Economic and Social Affairs.

11　United Senior Citizens of Ontario. 1985. "Elderly Residents in Ontario: Their Current Housing Situation and Their Interest in Various Housing Options." Ontario: Minister for Senior Citizen Affairs.

4　U.S. Census Bureau. 1987. *An Aging World.* Washington, D.C.: U.S. Government Printing Office.

13　Vachon, M.L.S. 1981. "The Importance of Social Relationships and Social Support in Widowhood." Paper presented to the Joint Meeting of the Canadian Association on Gerontology and the Gerontological Society of America, Toronto.

13　Vachon, M.L.S., A. Formo, K. Freedman, A. Lyall, J. Rogers, and S. Freeman. 1976. "Stress Reactions to Bereavement." *Essence* 1:23–33.

7　Vanderburgh, Rosamund M. 1988. "The Impact of Government Support for Indian Culture on Canada's Aged Indians." In Eloise Rathbone-McEwan and Betty Havens, eds. *North American Elders: United States and Canadian Perspectives.* New York: Greenwood.

5　Vandervoort, A.A., K.C. Hayes, and A.Y. Belanger. 1986. "Strength and Endurance of Skeletal Muscle in the Elderly." *Physiotherapy*

*Canada* 38:167–173.

8    Van Horne, Ron. 1986. *A New Agenda: Health and Social Service Strategies for Ontario's Seniors.* Toronto: Government of Ontario.

15   Van Loon, R. 1970. "Political Participation in Canada: The 1965 Election." *Canadian Journal of Political Science* 3:376–99.

3    Vatuk, Sylvia. 1982. "Old Age in India." In Peter N. Stearns, ed. *Old Age in Preindustrial Society.* New York: Holmes & Meier.

11   Veevers, Jean E. 1987. "The 'Real' Marriage Squeeze: Mate Selection, Mortality and the Mating Gradient." Paper presented at the Annual Meeting of the Pacific Sociological Association.

15   Verba, Sidney, and Norman H. Nie. 1972. *Participation in America: Political Democracy and Social Equality.* New York: Harper and Row.

15   Verba, Sidney, Norman H. Nie, and Jae-on Kim. 1971. *The Modes of Democratic Participation.* Beverly Hills: Sage.

12   Verduin, John R., and Douglas N. McEwen. 1984. *Adults and Their Leisure: The Need for Lifelong Learning.* Springfield, Illinois: Charles C. Thomas.

13   Verwoerdt, A., E. Pfeiffer, and H.S. Wang. 1969. "Sexual Behavior in Senescence—Changes in Sexual Activity and Interest of Aging Men and Women." Journal of Geriatric Psychiatry 2:163-80.

12   Vigoda, Debby, L. Crawford, and J. Hirdes. 1985. "The Continuity Theory: Empirical Support." In Norman K. Blackie, Sister Anne Robichaud, and Shawn MacDonald, eds. *Aging, Mirror of Humanity: Canadian Gerontological Collection IV.* Winnipeg: Canadian Association on Gerontology.

5    Walford, R.L. 1969. *The Immunologic Theory of Aging.* Copenhagen: Munksgaard.

13   Walker, Alan. 1991. "The Relationship Between the Family and the State in the Care of Older People." *Canadian Journal on Aging* 10:94–112.

8    Wall, R., S. Birch, and M. McQuillin. 1991. "Economic Evaluation of Alternative Programs of Reduced-Stay Senile Cataract Surgery." *Canadian Journal on Aging* 10:149–64.

8    Wallace, Marilyn M., and Wendy J.A. Thompson. 1985. "The Seniors' Well-Being Activation Team and Society: Annual Report." Vancouver: Seniors' Well-Being Activation Team.

14   Walton, Douglas N., and W.H. Fleming. 1980. "Responsibility for the Discontinuation of Treatment." *Essence* 4:57–61.

8    Wandless, I., and J.W. Davie. 1977. "Can Drug Compliance in the Elderly Be Improved?" *British Medical Journal* 1:359–61.

12   Wannell, T., and C. McKie. 1986a. "Expanding the Choices." *Canadian Social Trends.* Summer:13–18.

7,9  Wanner, Richard A., and P. Lynn McDonald. 1986. "The Vertical Mosaic in Later Life: Ethnicity and Retirement in Canada." *Journal of Gerontology* 41:662–71.

6    Watson, W.J., and H.S. Seiden. 1984. "Alzheimer's Disease: A Current Review." *Canadian Family Physician* 30:595–99.

6    Waugh, Nancy C., and Robin A. Barr. 1982. "Encoding Deficits in Aging." In F.I.M. Craik and Sandra Trehub, eds. *Aging and Cognitive Processes.* New York: Plenum Press.

2    Weber, M. 1978. *Economy and Society: An Outline of Interpretive Sociology.* 2 vols. G. Roth and C. Wittich, eds. Berkeley: University of California Press.

6    Wechsler, D. 1939. *A Measurement of Adult Intelligence.* Baltimore: Williams and Wilkins.

6    Wechsler, D. 1981. *WAIS-R Manual (Wechsler Adult Intelligence Scale Revised).* New York: Harcourt Brace Jovanovich.

13   Weg, Ruth B. 1983. "The Physiological Perspective." In Ruth B. Weg, ed. *Sexuality in the Later Years: Roles and Behavior.* New York: Academic Press.

13   Weinberg, Martin S. 1969. "The Aging Male Homosexual." *Medical Aspects of Human Sexuality* 3:66–72.

14   Weisman, Avery. 1972. *On Dying and Denying.* New York: Behavioral Press.

7    Weiss, R.S., ed. 1973. *Loneliness: The Experience of Emotional and Social Isolation.* Cambridge, Mass: MIT Press.

6    Welford, A.T. 1958. *Aging and Human Skill.* London: Oxford University Press.

5    Welford, A.T. 1977. "Motor Performance." In J.E. Birren and K.W. Schaie, eds. *Handbook of the Psychology of Aging.* New York: Van Nostrand Reinhold.

5    Welford, A.T. 1984. "Psychomotor Performance." In Carl Eisdorfer, ed. *Annual Review of Gerontology and Geriatrics.* New York: Springer.

4    Weller, Robert H., and Leon F. Bouvier. 1981. *Population: Demography and Policy.* New York: St. Martin's Press.

12   Werner, Lawrence. 1976. "Functional Analysis of Viewing for Older Adults." *Journal of Broadcasting* 20:77–87.

8    Wershow, H. 1976. "The Four Percent Fallacy:

Some Further Evidence and Policy Implications." *The Gerontologist* 16:52–55.

14  Wilcox, Sandra G., and Marilyn Sutton. 1985. *Understanding Death and Dying.* 3d ed. Palo Alto, California: Mayfield.

2   Wilson, T.P. 1970. "Normative and Interpretive Paradigms in Sociology." In J.D. Douglas, ed. *Understanding Everyday Life.* Chicago: Aldine.

13  Winnipeg Sun. 1985. "Volunteer Granny Becomes 'Friend' to All of the Family." *Winnipeg Sun* 22 December.

11  Wister, Andrew V. 1985. "Living Arrangement Choices Among the Elderly." *Canadian Journal on Aging* 4:127–44.

13  Wister, Andrew V. 1986. "Living Arrangements and Informal Social Support Among the Elderly." Personal communication.

13  Wister, Andrew V., and Laurel A. Strain. 1986. "Social Support and Well-Being: A Comparison of Older Widows and Widowers." Paper presented at the 21st Annual Meeting of the Canadian Sociology and Anthropology Association, Winnipeg.

7   Woehrer, C.E. 1978. "Cultural Pluralism in American Families: The Influence of Ethnicity on Social Aspects of Aging." *The Family Coordinator* October.

13  Wolf, R.S., and K.A. Pillemer. 1989. *Helping Elderly Victims: The Reality of Elder Abuse.* New York: Columbia University Press.

9,10 Women's Bureau, Labour Canada. 1990. *Women in the Labour Force, 1990-91 Edition.* Labour Canada Cat. No. L016-1728/90E Ottawa: Minister of Supply and Services Canada.

7   Wong, Paul T.P., and Gary T. Reker. 1985. "Stress, Coping, and Well–Being in Anglo and Chinese Elderly." *Canadian Journal on Aging* 4:29–38.

7   Wood, Linda A. 1978. "Loneliness, Social Identity and Social Structure." *Essence* 2:259–70.

7   Wood, Linda, and A. Guest. 1978. "Perspectives on Loneliness." *Essence* 2:199–201.

1   Woodruff, D.S. 1975. "Introduction: Multidisciplinary Perspectives of Aging." In D.S. Woodruff and J. E. Birren, eds. *Aging: Scientific Perspectives and Social Issues.* New York: D. Van Nostrand.

5   Woodruff, Diana S. 1982. "The Life Expectancy Test: Can You Live to Be 100?" In Steven H. Zarit, ed. *Readings in Aging and Death.* 2d ed. New York: Harper and Row.

8   Woods Gordon. 1984. *Investigating the Impact of Demographic Change in Canada.* Report for the Canadian Medical Association Task Force on Allocation of Health Care Resources.

8   World Health Organization. 1984. "Health Promotion: A World Health Organization Document on the Concept and Principles." *Canadian Public Health Association Digest* 8:101–2.

14  Wortman, Camille B., and Roxane Cohen Silver. 1990. "Successful Mastery of Bereavement and Widowhood: A Life-course Perspective." eds. Paul B. Baltes and Margaret M. Baltes. *Successful Aging.* Cambridge: Cambridge University Press.

13  Wylie, Betty Jane. 1981. "Coping with Survival: The Quiet Agony of the Widower." *Quest* Spring:34–38.

15  Yelaja, Shankar A. 1981. "Gray Power: A Study on Political Attitudes and Behaviour of Older People in a Canadian City." Paper presentation at the 12th International Congress of Gerontology, Hamburg.

15  Yelaja, Shankar A. 1989. "Gray Power: Agenda for Future Research." *Canadian Journal on Aging* 8:118–27.

11  Zamprelli, Jim. 1985. "Shelter Allowances for Older Adults: Programs in Search of a Policy." In Gloria Gutman and Norman Blackie, eds. *Innovations in Housing and Living Arrangements for Seniors.* Burnaby, British Columbia: The Gerontology Research Centre, Simon Fraser University.

11  Zamprelli, Jim. 1986. "Housing and Support Service Programs for Older Manitobans." In Gloria Gutman and Norman Blackie, eds. *Aging in Place: Housing Adaptations and Options for Remaining in the Community.* Burnaby, British Columbia: The Gerontology Research Centre, Simon Fraser University.

5   Zandri, Elaine, and Neil Charness. 1989. "Training Older and Younger Adults to Use Software." *Educational Gerontology* 15:615–31.

1   Zarit, Steven H. 1977. "Gerontology—Getting Better All the Time." In Steven H. Zarit, ed. *Readings in Aging and Death: Contemporary Perspectives.* New York: Harper and Row.

13  Zarit, S.H., K.E. Reever, and J. Bach-Peterson. 1980. "Relatives of the Impaired Elderly: Correlates of Feelings of Burden." *The Gerontologist* 20:649–55.

7   Zay, Nicholas. 1978. "Old Age and Aging in Canada's Ethnic Population." Paper presented at a National Symposium on Aging, Ottawa.

1   Zay, N., D. Carrier, A. Grandmaison, L. Lévesque, and C. Sicotte. 1984. "Profil de la Recherche en Gérontologie au Québec." *Le*

*Gérontophile* 6:1–23.

**14**   Zorza, Victor, and Rosemary Zorza. 1979. "Hospice—Death with Dignity? Or Giving Up on Life." *Texas Medicine* 75:35–37.

**8**   Zorzitto, M.L., D.P. Ryan, and R.H. Fisher. 1986. "The Practice of Respite Admissions on a Geriatric Assessment Unit: The Correlates of Successful Outcome." *Canadian Journal on Aging* 5:105–11.

**6**   Zuckerman, H. 1977. *Scientific Elite: Studies of Nobel Laureates in the United States.* New York: Free Press.

**12**   Zuzanek, Jiri, and Sheila J. Box. 1988. "Life Course and the Daily Lives of Older Adults in Canada." In Karen Altergott, ed. *Daily Life in Later Life: Comparative Perspectives.* Newbury Park, California: Sage.

# Index

Eaton, Joseph W., 380
Education
    in gerontology, 33
    for seniors, 324–31
        Elderhostel, 330–31
Ego development theory, 376–78
Elder abuse, 362–65
Elder Statesmen, 290
Encoding, 128
Environment. *See also* Housing; Transportation
    and coping with biological aging, 114, 115
    decoration, 115
    lighting, 115
    sound, 115
Environmental demand, 280
Epp, Jake, 215–17
Established Programs Financing (EPF), 193
Etal Islanders, 48
Ethnic groups
    defined, 170
    and pensions, 238
Ethnicity and aging, 81–85, 170–75, 178–81
    buffer theory of, 171–72
    levelling theory of, 171
    multiple jeopardy theory of, 172–73
Euthanasia, 392–97
    active, 395
    California Natural Death Act, 392, 393
    Criminal Code of Canada on, 396, 397
    and durable power of attorney, 394
    Law Reform Commission of Canada on, 392, 394,
        395, 396, 397
    and living wills, 392, 393
    Manitoba Law Reform Commission, 394
    and medical vitalist argument, 395
    and new definition of life, 395
Evans, Hubert, 140
Exchange theory of aging, 24–25
Exercise. *See also* Fitness
    and biological aging, 113, 118–19, 315, 316
Expanders, 312
Extended Health Care Services program, 207
Extrinsic aging, 103

"Facts on Aging" quiz, 10, 11
Fairley, Barker, 140
Fédération de l'Âge d'Or du Québec, 414
Feldenkrais, Moshe, 317
55 Alive, 303
Fitness. *See also* Exercise
    and aging, 316
    Canada Fitness Survey, 314–15, 318, 321
    Canada Health Survey, 314
    and physical health, 315–17

programs for seniors, 318–19
    and psychological well-being, 317–18
    Seniors' Games, 321
Flexible retirement, 261–62
Florida, migration of Canada's elderly to, 88
Franklin, Benjamin, 114
Free radical theory of biological aging, 104
Friends, as source of informal support, 354–55
Functional disability, defined, 112
Functional psychological disorders, 147–49

Garden suites. *See* Granny flats
General Social Survey, 37, 110, 117, 309, 314
Generation, defined, 168
Generational event theory, 168
Geriatric day hospitals, 206
Gerontological Society of America (GSA), 20
Gerontology
    in Canada, 15–19
    curriculum in, 21
    defined, 4
    goals of, 8
    history of, 13–15
    occupations and careers in, 432–33
    social, 21
    training for practitioners, 428, 431–32
    university courses in, 428–32
        University of Manitoba, 430–31
Glendon College, 329
Goethe, 141
Government agencies related to seniors, 421
Government policy on aging, 419–23
Government transfers, 193, 227–32
Grandma, Moses, 141
Grandparenting, 367–70
Grandparents for Equal Right to Access and Dignity
    (GRAND), 370
Granny flats, 299–300
Gray Panthers, 415
"Great Pension Debate," 225, 242
Grief, 400–401
Guaranteed Income Supplement (GIS), 81, 226–29,
    242–44
Gwembe Tonga, 48

Halley, Edmund, 13
Harvard Medical School, criteria for death, 392
Health and Welfare Canada, 37, 146, 148, 183, 201,
    214, 251, 258, 261, 262, 389, 421
Health care
    accessibility, 218–19
    availability, 218
    co-ordination, 219–20
    community. *See* Community health care